SOLIDWORKS 2015:
A Power Guide for Beginner and Intermediate Users

CADArtifex

The premium provider of learning products and solutions
www.cadartifex.com

SOLIDWORKS 2015: A Power Guide for Beginner and Intermediate Users

Published by
CADArtifex
www.cadartifex.com

ISBN-13: 978-1513605296

NOTICE TO THE READER
The publisher and the author make no representations or warranties with respect to the accuracy or completeness of the contents of this work/text and specifically disclaim all warranties, including without limitation warranties of fitness for a particular purpose. Publisher does not guarantee any of the products described in the text or perform any independent analysis in connection with any of the product information contained in the text. No warranty may be created or extended by sales or promotional materials. This work is sold with the understanding that the publisher is not engaged in rendering legal, accounting, or other professional services. Neither the publisher nor the author shall be liable for damages arising herefrom. Further, readers should be aware that Internet Web sites listed in this work may have changed or disappeared between when this work was written and when it is read.

Examination Copies
Textbooks received as examination copies in any form such as paperback and eBook are for review purposes only and may not be made available for student use. These files may not be transferred to any other party. Resale of examination copies is prohibited.

Electronic Files
The electronic file/eBook in any form of this textbook are licensed to the original user only and may not be transferred to any other party.

Disclaimer
The author has made sincere efforts to ensure the accuracy of the material described herein, however the author makes no warranty, expressed or implied, with respect to the quality, correctness, accuracy, or freedom from error of this document or the products it describes.

www.cadartifex.com

Dedication

First and foremost, I would like to thank my mom and dad for standing beside me throughout my carrier and writing this book.

Heartfelt thanks goes to my wife and my sisters for having the patience with me and supporting me taking this challenge which reduced the time I could spend with them

I would also like to acknowledge the efforts of the employees at CADArtifex for their dedication in editing the content of this textbook. It can be a difficult job making sure that a technical subject is treated properly.

Content at a Glance

Table of Contents

Chapter 3. Editing and Modifying Sketches .... 3.1 - 3.46

VIII

Preface

SOLIDWORKS, developed by Dassault Systèmes SOLIDWORKS Corp., one of the biggest technology provider to engineering which offers complete 3D software tools that let you create, simulate, publish, and manage your data. SOLIDWORKS products are easy to learn and use, and work together seamlessly to help you design better products, faster, and more cost-effectively. The SOLIDWORKS focus on ease-of-use allows more engineers, designers, and other technology professionals than ever before to take advantage of 3D in bringing their designs to life.

SOLIDWORKS delivers a rich set of integrated tools that are powerful and intuitive to use. It is a feature-based, parametric solid-modeling mechanical design, and automation software which allows you to create real-world 3D components and assemblies by using simple but highly effective tools. The 3D components and assemblies created in SOLIDWORKS can be converted into engineering 2D drawings with in few mouse clicks. You can also validate your designs by simulating their real-world conditions and assess the environmental impact of your products.

SOLIDWORKS 2015: A Power Guide for Beginner and Intermediate Users textbook is designed for instructor-led courses as well as for self-paced learning. This textbook is intended to help engineers and designers who are interested in learning SOLIDWORKS for creating 3D mechanical design. It will be a great starting point for new SOLIDWORKS users and a great teaching aid in classroom training. This textbook contains of 13 chapters covering major environments of SOLIDWORKS: Part, Assembly, and Drawing which teaches you how to use the SOLIDWORKS mechanical design software to build parametric models and assemblies, and how to make drawings of those parts and assemblies.

This textbook is not only focuses on the uses of tools/commands of SOLIDWORKS but also on the concept of design. Every chapter of this textbook contains tutorials which intend to help user to experience how things can be done in SOLIDWORKS step by step. Moreover, every chapter ends with hands-on test drives which allow users of this textbook to experience themselves the ease-of-use and powerful capabilities of SOLIDWORKS.

Who Should Read This Book

This book is written with a wide range of SOLIDWORKS users in mind, varying from beginner to advanced users and SOLIDWORKS instructors. Easy-to-follow chapters of this book allow you to easily understand different design techniques, SOLIDWORKS tools, and design principles.

What Is Covered in This Textbook

SOLIDWORKS 2015: A Power Guide for Beginner and Intermediate Users textbook will teach you everything you need to know to start using SOLIDWORKS 2015 with easy to understand explanation, step-by-step tutorials. This textbook covers:

Chapter 1, "Introduction to SOLIDWORKS," introduces SOLIDWORKS interface, different SOLIDWORKS environments, identifying SOLIDWORKS documents, various components of the initial screen of SOLIDWORKS, invoking and customizing shortcut menu, saving documents, and opening documents in SOLIDWORKS.

Chapter 2, "Drawing Sketches with SOLIDWORKS," introduces how to invoke Sketching environment, specify units system, grids and snaps settings. Also, introduces you various sketching tools such as Line, Arc, Circle, Rectangle, and Spline to draw sketches.

Chapter 3, "Editing and Modifying Sketches," introduces various editing and modifying operations such as trimming unwanted sketched entities, extending sketch entities, mirroring, patterning, moving, and rotating by using various editing/modifying tools available in the Sketching environment.

Chapter 4, "Applying Geometric Relations and Dimensions," introduces the concept of fully define sketches, creating fully define sketches by applying proper geometric relations and dimensions. Also, introduces different methods of applying geometric relations and various dimensions tools. You can modify the already applied dimensions and dimension properties such as dimension style, tolerance, and precision. This chapter also introduce you about different sketch states such as under define, fully defined, and over defined.

Chapter 5, "Creating First/Base Feature of a Solid Model," introduces how to create extruded and revolve base features by using the Extruded Boss/Base and Revolved Boss/Base tools. This chapter also introduces various navigating tools such as Zoom In/Out and Zoom To Fit. Also, this chapter introduces you how to manipulate the orientation of the model to the predefine standard views and custom views. Moreover, this chapter introduces you about changing the display style and view of the model.

Chapter 6, "Creating Reference Geometries," introduces that the three default planes: Front, Top, and Right may not be enough for creating models having multiple features therefore you need to create additional reference planes. In addition to creating additional reference planes, this chapter introduces you how to create reference axis, reference coordinate system and reference point by using their respective tools.

Chapter 7, "Advanced Modeling I," introduces advance options for creating extrude and revolve features. In addition to this, chapter introduces how to create cut features by using the Extruded Cut and Revolved Cut tools, how to work with different type of sketches such as close sketches, open sketches, and nested sketches. This chapter also introduces you about creating multiple features by using a single sketch having multiple contours/regions, projecting edges of the existing features on to the current sketching plane, editing individual feature of a model as per the design change. Moreover, this chapter introduces you how to measure distance and angle between lines, points, faces, planes, and so on by using the Measure tool, how to assign appearance/texture, and material properties to a model. You can also calculate mass properties of a model.

Chapter 8, "Advanced Modeling II," introduces how to create sweep features, sweep cut features, loft features, loft cut features, boundary features, boundary cut features, curves, split faces, and 3D Sketches.

Chapter 9, "Patterning and Mirroring," introduces various patterning and mirroring tools. After the successfully completion of this chapter, you can create different type of patterns such as linear pattern, circular pattern, Curve Driven Pattern, and Sketch Driven Pattern. Also, you can create mirror features, faces, or bodies about an mirroring plane.

Chapter 10, "Advanced Modeling III," introduces how to create standard and customized holes such as counterbore, countersink, straight tap, and tapered tap as per the standard specifications. You have learn that cosmetic threads can be used to represent the real threads on holes, fasteners, and cylindrical features to avoid increase in the complexity of the model and improve overall performance of the system. This chapter also introduces you how to add constant and variable radius fillets. Moreover, this chapter introduces you how to create chamfer on the edges of the model, rib features from open or closed sketch, and shell feature with uniform or variable wall thickness.

Chapter 11, "Working with Assemblies I," introduces how to create assemblies by using bottom-up assembly approach. You can apply Standard, Advanced, and Mechanical mates to assembly the components with respect to each other. This chapter also introduces you how to move and rotate individual component within the Assembly environment, detect collisions between components of the assembly, and working with SmartMates for applying Standard mates.

Chapter 12, "Working with Assemblies II," introduces how to create assemblies by using the Top-down Assembly approach. You can also edit the individual component of the assembly within the Assembly environment or by opening it in the Part modeling environment. This chapter also introduces you how to edit the existing mates applied between the components of an assembly and create different type of patterns such as Linear Component Pattern, Pattern Driven Component Pattern, and Chain Component Pattern in Assembly environment. Also how to mirror components in the Assembly environment. This chapter also introduces you about creating assembly features, suppressing or unsuppressing components of an assembly, and inserting components in the Assembly environment having multiple configurations. You can also create and dissolve sub-assemblies within the Assembly environment. In addition to this, this chapter introduce you about creating, editing, or collapsing the exploded view of an assembly. You can also animate the exploded/collapse view of an assembly and add exploded lines in an exploded view and create bill of material (BOM) of an assembly.

Chapter 13, "Working with Drawing," introduces how to create 2D drawings from parts and assemblies. This chapter also introduces the concept of angle of projections, defining angle of projection for a drawing, and edit sheet format. In addition to this, chapter introduces you about applying reference and driving dimensions, adding notes, surface finish symbol, weld symbols, hole callouts, center mark, and centerlines in drawing views. In this chapter, adding bill of material (BOM) and balloons are also be introduced.

Icons/Terms used in this Textbook

This icons used in this textbooks are:

Note

Note: Notes highlight information that requires special attention.

Tip

Tip: Tips provide additional advice that increases the efficiency of the users.

Flyout

A Flyout list is the one in which a set of tools are grouped together, see Figure 1.

Drop-down List

A drop-down list is the one in which a set of options/methods are grouped together to perform a task, see Figure 2.

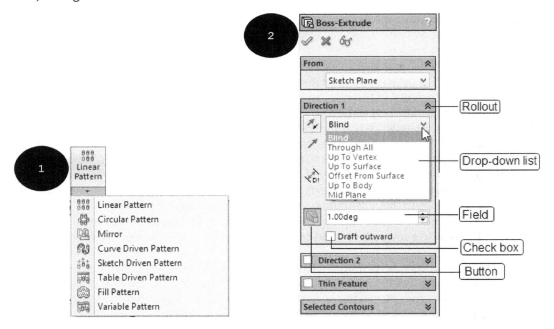

Rollout

A rollout is the one in which drop-down list, fields, buttons, check boxes may available to specify various parameters, see Figure 2. A rollout can be in expanded form or collapsed form. You can expand/collapse a rollout by clicking on the arrows available on the right of its title bar.

Field

A Field is the one which allows you to enter new values or modify existing/default values, as required, see Figure 2.

Check box

A Check box is the one which allows you to turn on or off the uses of particular option. Also, it appears as a check box to tick mark particular option to turned it on, see Figure 2.

Button

A Button is the one which appears as a 3D icon and is used to turn on or off the uses of particular option on activating it. You can activate and diactivate a button by clicking on it.

How to Contact the Author

We welcome your feedback concerning SOLIDWORKS 2015: A Power Guide for Beginner and Intermediate Users textbook. We want to hear what you liked, what you didn't, and what you think should be in the next edition. And if you find any mistake, please tell us so that we can fix it on our errata page and in reprints. Please email us at *cadartifex@gmail.com* or *info@cadartifex.com*. You can also login to our web site *www.cadartifex.com* and write your feedback about the textbook.

Thank you very much for purchasing SOLIDWORKS 2015: A Power Guide for Beginner and Intermediate Users textbook, we hope that the information and concepts introduced in this textbook will help you to accomplish your professional goals.

Introduction to SOLIDWORKS

In this chapter:

- Installing SOLIDWORKS
- Getting Started with SOLIDWORKS
- Invoking New SOLIDWORKS Document
- Identifying SOLIDWORKS Documents
- Invoking Part Modeling Environment
- Invoking Assembly Environment
- Invoking Drawing Environment
- Invoking Shortcut Menu
- Customizing Context toolbar of the Shortcut Menu
- Customizing CommandManager
- Saving Documents
- Opening Existing Documents

Welcome to the world of Computer Added Design (CAD) with SOLIDWORKS. SOLIDWORKS, the product of Dassault Systèmes SOLIDWORKS Corp., one of the biggest technology provider to engineering which offers complete 3D software tools that let you create, simulate, publish, and manage your data. By providing advanced solid modeling techniques, SOLIDWORKS help engineers to optimize performance while designing with capabilities, that cut down on costly prototypes, eliminate rework and delays, and save engineers time and development costs.

SOLIDWORKS delivers a rich set of integrated tools that are powerful and intuitive to use. It is a feature-based, parametric solid-modeling mechanical design and automation software which allows you to convert 2D sketches into solid models by using simple but highly effective modeling tools. SOLIDWORKS provide wide range of tools that allow you to create real-world components and assemblies. These real-world components and assemblies can then be converted into engineering 2D drawings for production, used to validate designs by simulating their real world conditions and assess the environmental impact of your products.

SOLIDWORKS is a solid modeler and utilizes a parametric feature-based approach to create models and assemblies. With SOLIDWORKS you can share your designs with your partners, subcontractors and colleagues in smart new ways, all so you can improve knowledge transfer and shorten the design cycle.

Installing SOLIDWORKS

If you do not have SOLIDWORKS installed in our system, you first need to get it install. However, before you start installing SOLIDWORKS, you need to first consult the system requirements and make sure that you have a system capable of running SOLIDWORKS adequately. Below are the system requirement for installing SOLIDWORKS 2015.

1. Operating Systems: Windows 8.1, 8, or 7 64-bit.
2. RAM: 8 GB or more recommended.
3. Disk Space: 5 GB or more.
4. Processor: Intel or AMD with SSE2 support, 64-bit operating system recommended.
5. Graphics Card: SOLIDWORKS certified graphics card drivers are recommended.

For more information about the system requirement for SOLIDWORKS, visit SOLIDWORKS website at *www.SOLIDWORKS.com/sw/support/systemrequirements.html*.

Once the system is ready, install SOLIDWORKS using the SOLIDWORKS DVD or by using the downloaded SOLIDWORKS data.

Getting Started with SOLIDWORKS

Once the SOLIDWORKS 2015 is installed on your system, start SOLIDWORKS 2015 by double clicking on the **SOLIDWORKS 2015** icon available in the desktop of your system. As soon as you double click on the SOLIDWORKS 2015 icon, the system prepares for starting SOLIDWORKS by loading all required files. Once all the required files have been loaded, the initial screen of SOLIDWORKS 2015 appears, see Figure 1.1. If you are starting SOLIDWORKS first time after installing the software, the **SOLIDWORKS License Agreement** window appears. Click on the **Accept** button of the **SOLIDWORKS License Agreement** window to accept the license agreement and start SOLIDWORKS 2015.

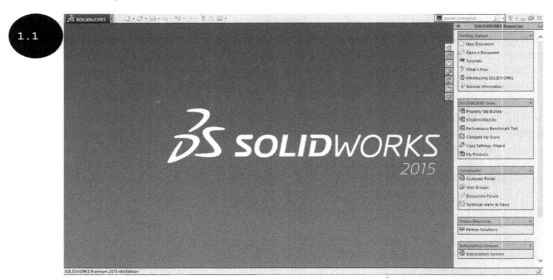

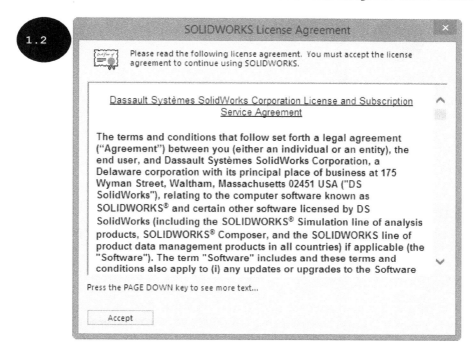

It is evident from the initial screen of SOLIDWORKS 2015 that SOLIDWORKS is very user friendly and easy to use. The components of the initial screen of SOLIDWORKS 2015 are discussed below.

Task Pane

The Task Pane is used to access SOLIDWORKS resources and documents, start new file, and so on. Its appear on the left side of the screen with various tabs for accessing various resources of SOLIDWORKS. By using the tools provided in various tabs of Task Pane, you can start new file, open an existing file, access to the tutorial help file, several applications, communities, library, and so on. Different tabs of the Task Pane are discussed later in this chapter.

Standard Toolbar

The **Standard** toolbar contains set of the most frequently used tools such as **New**, **Open**, and **Save**, see Figure 1.3.

SOLIDWORKS Menus

The SOLIDWORKS menus contain different menus such as **File**, **View**, and **Tools** for accessing different tools, see Figure 1.4. Note that the SOLIDWORKS menus appears when you move the cursor on the SOLIDWORKS logo that is available at the top left corner of the screen, see Figure 1.4. You can keep the SOLIDWORKS menus visible all time by clicking on the push-pin button 📌 that is available at the end of the SOLIDWORKS menus. The tools available in different menus of the SOLIDWORKS menus are depends upon the type of environment invoked.

SOLIDWORKS Search

The SOLIDWORKS Search is a search tool for searching command (tool), knowledge base (help topic), community forum, files and models, see Figure 2.5.

Invoking New SOLIDWORKS Document

The new SOLIDWORKS document such as Part and Assembly can be invoked by using the **New SOLIDWORKS Document** dialog box. This dialog box can be invoked by clicking on the **New** tool of the **Standard** toolbar or by clicking on the **New Document** tool of the **SOLIDWORKS Resources** task pane. You can also invoke this dialog box by choosing **File > New** from the SOLIDWORKS menus.

Click on the **New** tool of the **Standard** toolbar, the **New SOLIDWORKS Document** dialog box appears, see Figure 1-6. If you are invoking the **New SOLIDWORKS Document** dialog box first time after installing the software, the **Units and Dimension Standard** dialog box appears, see Figure 1.7. Specify the unit system as the default unit system for SOLIDWORKS by using this dialog box. After specifying the unit system, click on the **OK** button of the dialog box to invoke the **New SOLIDWORKS Document** dialog box. This dialog box have three buttons and are discussed next.

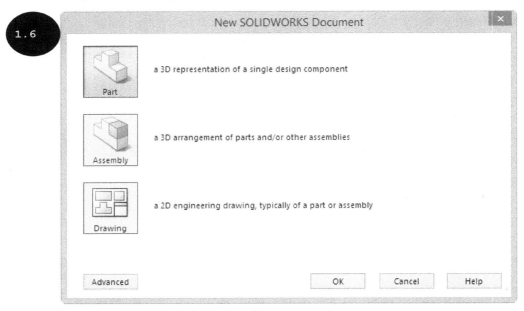

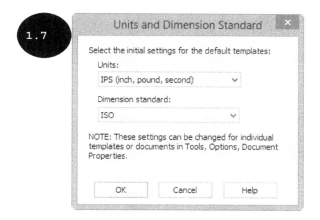

Note: In this textbook, the metric unit system and ANSI standard has been used. Therefore, select the **MMGS (millimeter, gram, second)** option from the **Units** drop-down list and **ANSI** option from the **Dimension standard** drop-down list of the **Units and Dimension Standard** dialog box.

Part

The **Part** button is activated by default in the **New SOLIDWORKS Document** dialog box. As a result, clicking on the **OK** button from this dialog box, the Part modeling environment appears, see Figure 1.8. The Part environment is used to create solid, surface, and sheet metal models.

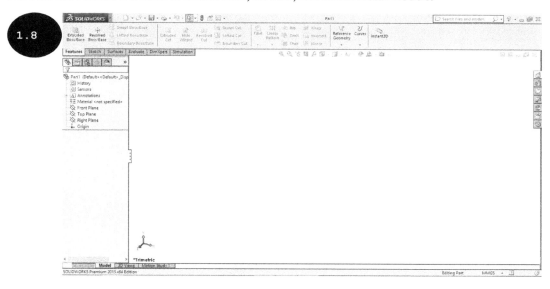

Assembly

The **Assembly** button of the **New SOLIDWORKS Document** dialog box is used to invoke the Assembly environment. In this environment, you can assemble parts/components created in the Part environment and create assemblies, see Figure 1.9.

Drawing

The **Drawing** button of the **New SOLIDWORKS Document** dialog box is used to invoke the Drawing environment. In this environment, you can create 2D drawings for production by using the parts and assemblies created in their respective environments, see Figure 1.10.

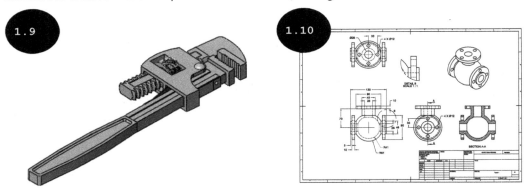

Identifying SOLIDWORKS Documents

The documents created in different environments (Part, Assembly, and Drawing) of SOLIDWORKS have different file extension, see Table below.

Environments	File Extension
Part Modeling Environment	.sldprt
Assembly Modeling Environment	.sldasm
Drawing Modeling Environment	.slddrw

Invoking Part Modeling Environment

Click on the **New** tool of the **Standard** toolbar to invoke the **New SOLIDWORKS Document** dialog box. Next, make sure that the **Part** button is activated in this dialog box and then click on the OK button, the initial screen of the Part modeling environment appears, see Figure 1.11.

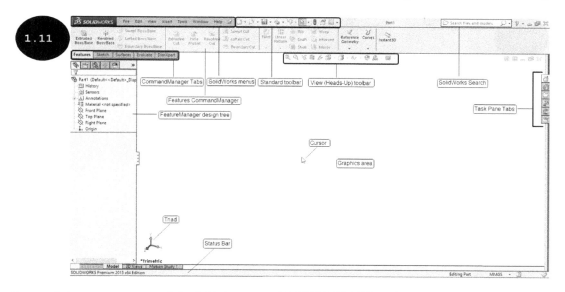

Some of the components of the initial screen of SOLIDWORKS such as SOLIDWORKS menus, Standard toolbar, and SOLIDWORKS Search has already been discussed earlier. The remaining components of the initial screen of the Part modeling environment are discussed next.

Command Manager

CommandManager is available at the top of the graphics area and provides access to different SOLIDWORKS tools. There are various CommandManagers such as **Features CommandManager**, **Sketch CommandManager, Evaluate CommandManager,** and so on are available in the Part modeling environment. When the **Features** tab is activated in the **CommandManager** tabs, the **Features CommandManager** invokes and provide access to different tools for creating solid 3D models. On clicking on the **Sketch** tab, the **Sketch CommandManager** invokes and provides access to different tools for creating sketches.

Note: The different environments (Part, Assembly, and Drawing) of SOLIDWORKS are provided with different set of Command Managers.

Some of the CommandManagers of the Part modeling environment are discussed next.

Features CommandManager

The **Features CommandManager** is provided with different set of tools that are used for creating solid 3D models. See Figure 1.12 for **Features CommandManager** and Figure 1.13 for a solid 3D model. To invoke the **Features CommandManager**, click on the **Features** tab of the **CommandManager**. Note that initially most of the tools of the **Features CommandManager** are not activated. These tools become activated as soon as you create a base/first solid feature of a solid 3D component.

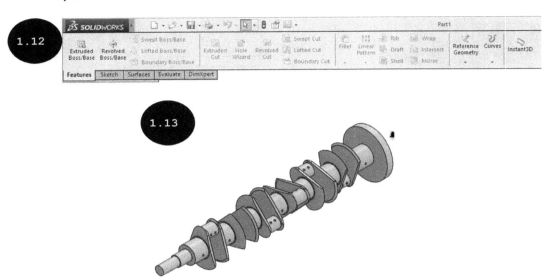

Sketch CommandManager

The **Sketch CommandManager** is provided with different set of tools that are used for creating 2D and 3D sketches. See Figure 1.14 for **Sketch CommandManager** and Figure 1.15 for a 2D sketch. To invoke the **Sketch CommandManager**, click on the **Sketch** tab of the **CommandManager**.

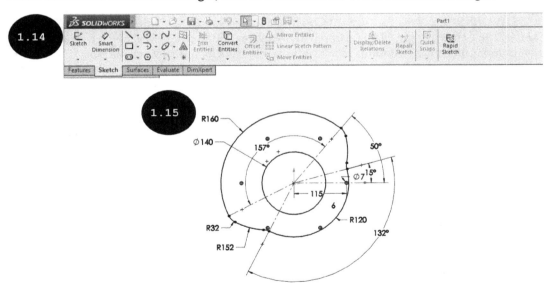

Evaluate CommandManager

The tools available in the **Evaluate CommandManager** are used to evaluate your model by measuring entities, calculating mass properties of solid model, checking the tangent or curvature continuity, draft analysis, calculating section properties, geometry analysis, and so on, see Figure 2.16. To invoke the **Evaluate CommandManager**, click on the **Evaluate** tab of the **CommandManager**.

1.16

Note: The Surface modeling environment and Sheet Metal environment of SOLIDWORKS can be invoked within the Part modeling environment by using their respective CommandManagers.

Surfaces CommandManager

The **Surfaces CommandManager** is provided with different set of tools that are used for creating surface models. See Figure 1.17 for **Surfaces CommandManager** and Figure 1.18 for a surface model. To invoke the **Surfaces CommandManager**, click on the **Surfaces** tab of the **CommandManager**. Note that initially most of the tools of the **Surfaces CommandManager** are not activated. These tools become activated as soon as you create a base/first surface feature of a surface model.

1.17

1.18

Note: In addition to the default CommandManager tabs, you can also add additional CommandManager tabs that are not available by default. To add additional CommandManager tabs, right click on any of the available CommandManager tab to display a shortcut menu, see Figure 1.16. This shortcut menu displays a list of available CommandManagers. Note that a tick mark at the front of CommandManager indicates that the respective CommandManager is already added. Click on the required CommandManager to be added.

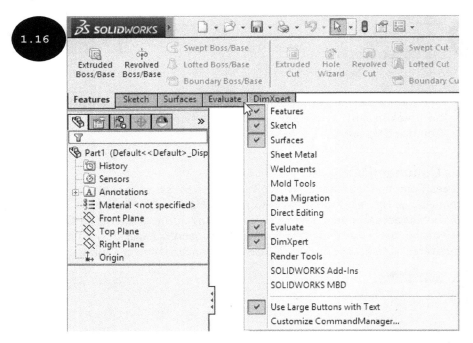

Sheet Metal CommandManager

The **Sheet Metal CommandManager** is provided with different set of tools for creating sheet metal components. See Figure 1.19 for the **Sheet Metal CommandManager** and Figure 1.20 for a sheet metal component.

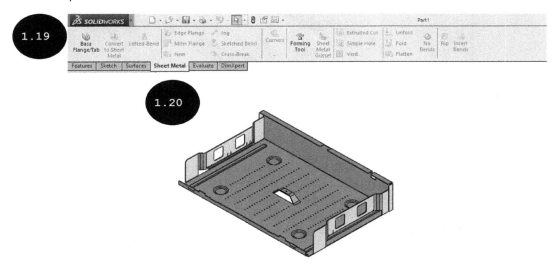

Weldments CommandManager

The **Weldments CommandManager** is provided with different set of tools for creating weldments structure components. See Figure 1.21 for the **Weldments CommandManager** and Figure 1.22 for a weldments component.

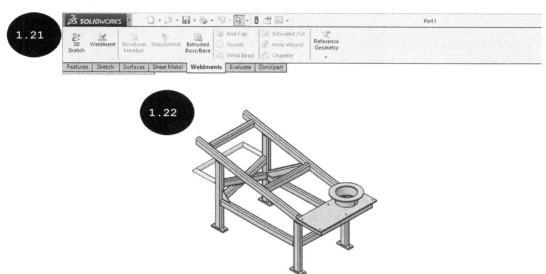

FeatureManager Design Tree

FeatureManager design tree appears at the left side of the graphics area and keeps record of all operations/features used for creating a model, see Figure 1.23. Note that the first created feature appears at the top and then the next created features appears one after another in an order in the FeatureManager design tree. Every time on invoking a new Part modeling environment, three default planes and an origin appears in the FeatureManager design tree, by default.

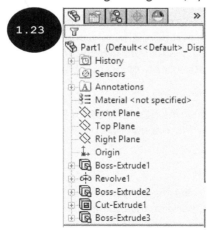

> **Tip:** A feature is an logical operation that performed for creating an component. In other words, a component can be designed by creating number of features such as extrude, sweep, hole, fillet, draft, and so on.

View (Heads-Up) toolbar

View (Heads-Up) toolbar is available at the top center of the graphics area, see Figure 1.24. This toolbar is provided with different set of tools that are used to manipulating the view or display of an model available in the graphics area.

Status Bar

Status Bar is available at the bottom of the graphics area and is used to provides the information about the action to be taken based on the current active tool. It also displays the current state of sketch being created, coordinate system, and so on.

Task Pane

As discussed earlier, the Task Pane is used to access SOLIDWORKS resources and documents, start new file, and so on. Its appear on the left side of the screen with various tabs (**SOLIDWORKS Resources, Design Library, File Explorer, View Palette, Appearances, Scenes, and Decals,** and **Custom Properties**) for accessing various resources of SOLIDWORKS, see Figure 1.25. Some of the tabs of this Task Pane are discussed next.

SOLIDWORKS Resources

The **SOLIDWORKS Resources** Task Pane is provided with tools to get started with SOLIDWORKS, and links to access SOLIDWORKS Community and Online Resources. To display the **SOLIDWORKS Resources** Task Pane, click on the **SOLIDWORKS Resources** tab of the Task Pane, refer to Figure 1.25. This task pane is provided with various rollouts: **Getting Started, SOLIDWORKS Tools, Community, Online Resources,** and **Subscription Services**. Some of these rollouts are discussed next.

Getting Started

The **Getting Started** rollout of the **SOLIDWORKS Resources** task pane is provided will tools that are used to start a new file, open an existing file, a file covering the new features of this release, tutorials, and so on.

SOLIDWORKS Tools

The **SOLIDWORKS Tools** rollout is used to access several applications such as **Property Tab Builder, SOLIDWORKS Rx, Performance Benchmark Test,** and so on.

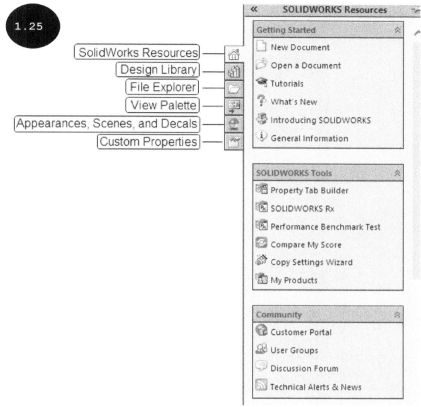

1.25

SolidWorks Resources
Design Library
File Explorer
View Palette
Appearances, Scenes, and Decals
Custom Properties

Community
The **Community** rollout is used to access SOLIDWORKS customer portals, various SOLIDWORKS user groups, discussion forum, and updates about technical alerts and news.

Design Library
The **Design Library** Task Pane is used to access SOLIDWORKS design library, toolbox components, 3D Content Central, and SOLIDWORKS Content. You can access this Task Pane by clicking on the **Design Library** tab.

Appearances, Scenes, and Decals
The **Appearances, Scenes, and Decals** Task Pane is used to change or modify the appearance of the model and the graphics display area.

Invoking Assembly Environment
Click on the **New** tool of the **Standard** toolbar to invoke the **New SOLIDWORKS Document** dialog box. Next, click on the **Assembly** button and then click on the **OK** button, the initial screen of the Assembly environment appears with the display of the **Begin Assembly PropertyManager**, see Figure 1.26. The **Begin Assembly PropertyManager** is used to insert components in the assembly environment for assemble them together to create an assembly. You will learn more about creating assembly in the later chapters.

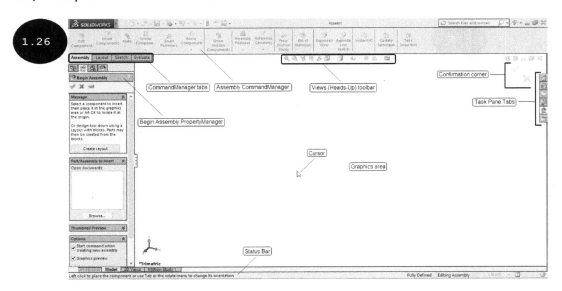

Most of the components of the initial screen of the Assembly environment are same as of the Part modeling environment. The **Assembly CommandManager** of the Assembly environment are discussed next.

Assembly CommandManager

The **Assembly CommandManager** is provided with different set of tools that are used to insert components in the assembly environment, apply relations/mates between the inserted components, exploded view, pattern, and so on. See Figure 1.27 for the **Assembly CommandManager** and Figure 1.28 for an assembly. By default, the tools of this CommandManager are not activated. These tools become activated as soon as you exit from the **Begin Assembly PropertyManager**.

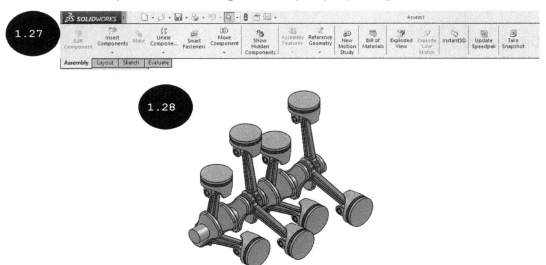

Invoking Drawing Environment

Click on the **New** tool of the **Standard** toolbar to invoke the **New SOLIDWORKS Document** dialog box. Next, click on the **Drawing** button and then click on the **OK** button, the **Sheet Format/Size** dialog box appears, see Figure 1.29. This dialog box allows you to define the sheet size and format for creating drawings. Once you are done with defining sheet size and format, click on the **OK** button, the initial screen of the Drawing environment appears with the display of the **Model View PropertyManager**, see Figure 1.30. The **Model View PropertyManager** is used to select a component or assembly for creating its different drawing views. You will learn more about creating drawing views of components and assembly in the later chapters.

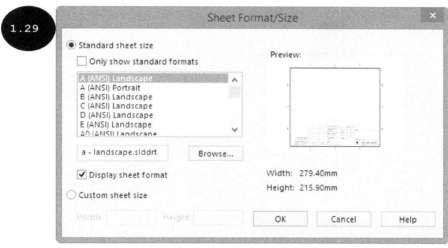

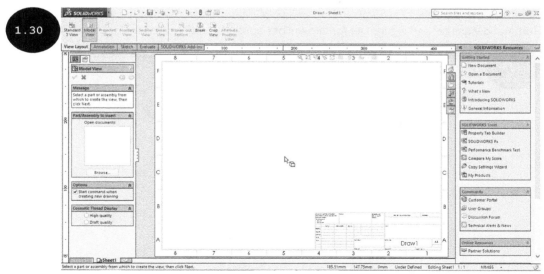

Most of the components of the initial screen of the Drawing environment are same as of the Part modeling environment. The **View Layout CommandManager** and **Annotation CommandManager** of the Drawing environment are discussed next.

View Layout CommandManager

The **View Layout CommandManager** is provided with different set of tools that are used to create different drawing views such as orthogonal views, section views, and detail view of a component or an assembly. See Figure 1.31 for the **View Layout CommandManager** and Figure 1.32 for different drawing views. By default, the tools of this CommandManager are not activated. These tools become activated as soon as you exit from the **Model View PropertyManager**.

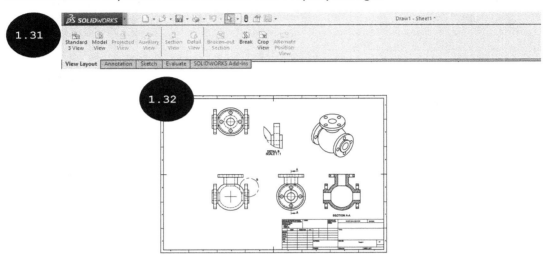

Annotation CommandManager

The **Annotation CommandManager** is provided with different set of tools that are used to apply dimensions, note, surface/welding symbols, create BOM, and so on. See Figure 1.33 for the **Annotation CommandManager** and Figure 1.34 for dimensions applied on different drawing views.

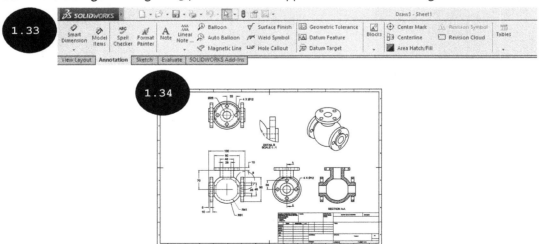

Invoking Shortcut Menu

A shortcut menu invokes when you right click in the graphics area. It provides quick access to the most frequently used tools such as **Zoom to Fit, Zoom In/Out**, and **Pan**, see Figure 1.35. Note that a shortcut menu also includes a context toolbar, see Figure 1.35.

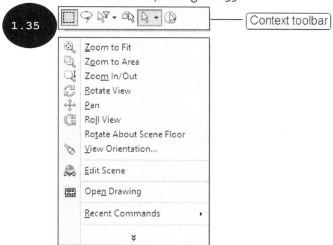

Note that if you select any item from the graphics area or FeatureManager design tree and then invoke a shortcut menu, the shortcut menu displays with the **Context** toolbar which is provided with different set of tools depending upon the item selected. Figure 1.36 shows a shortcut menu appears on selecting a line from the graphics area and Figure 1.37 shows a shortcut menu which appears on selecting a feature from the FeatureManager design tree.

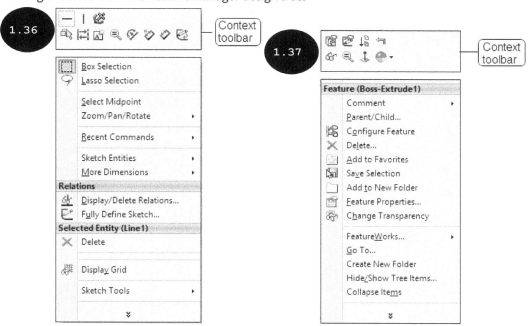

Customizing Context toolbar of the Shortcut Menu

As discussed, the **Context** toolbar of a shortcut menu is provided with different set of tools depending upon the item selected to invoke it. In addition to the display of default tools in the **Context** toolbar, you can also customize it to add frequently used tools. To customize the **Context** toolbar, move the cursor over the **Context** toolbar of a shortcut menu and then right click, the **Customize** option appears, see Figure 1.38. Click on the **Customize** option, the **Customize** dialog box with the **Graphics Area** toolbar appear, see Figure 1.39.

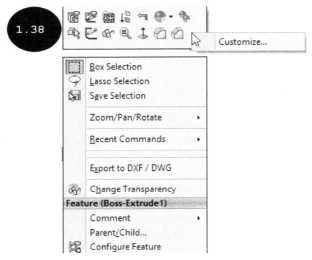

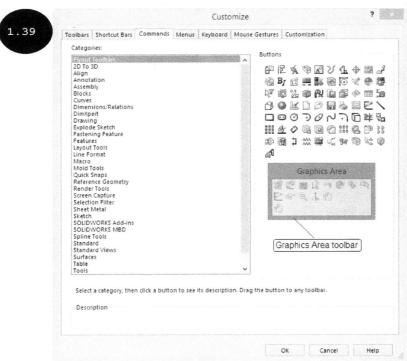

Once the **Customize** dialog box and the **Graphics Area** toolbar appears, select the required category of tools from the **Categories** area of the dialog box. As soon as you select the category, the tools available in the selected category appears on the right side of the dialog box in the **Buttons** area. You can drag and drop tools from the **Buttons** area of the dialog box to the **Graphics Area** toolbar. Note that the tools added in the **Graphics Area** toolbar also appears in the **Context** toolbar of the shortcut menu.

Customizing CommandManager

In addition to the default set of tools available in a **CommandManager**, you can customize to added more tools as required. To customize a **CommandManager**, right click on a tool of the **CommandManager** to display a shortcut menu. Next, click on the down arrow which is available at the bottom of the shortcut menu to display the **Customize** tool of the shortcut menu. Click on the **Customize** tool of the shortcut menu, the **Customize** dialog box appears. Click on the **Commands** tab of the **Customize** dialog box, see Figure 1.40.

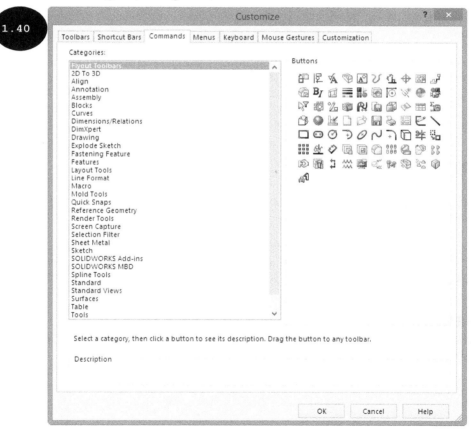

Next, select the required category of tools from the **Categories** area of the dialog box. As soon as you select the category, the tools available in the selected category appears on the right side of the dialog box in the **Buttons** area. You can drag and drop tools from the **Buttons** area of the dialog box to the **CommandManager**. You can also drag and drop tools back to the **Buttons** area from the **CommandManager**.

Saving Documents

To save an document created in any of the environment of SOLIDWORKS, click on the **Save** button of the **Standard** toolbar or click on the **File** > **Save** from the SOLIDWORKS menus, the **Save As** dialog box appears. Enter name of the document in the **File name** field of the dialog box and then browse to the location where you want to save the document. Next, click on the **Save** button to save the document.

Opening Existing Documents

To open an existing SOLIDWORKS Document, click on the **Open** button of the **Standard** toolbar or click on the **File** > **Open** from the SOLIDWORKS menus, the **Open** dialog box appears. To open an existing SOLIDWORKS document, select the **SOLIDWORKS Files (*.sldprt; *.sldasm; *.slddrw)** file extension from the **File Type** drop-down list of this dialog box. You can select the file extension from this drop-down list depending upon the document to be opened. After selecting the required file extension, browse to the location where the SOLIDWORKS document is saved and then click to select the document. Next, click on the **Open** button, the selected document is opened in SOLIDWORKS.

Similar to opening existing SOLIDWORKS documents, you can also open/import documents created in other CAD applications. SOLIDWORKS allows you to open documents created in CATIA V5, ProE/Creo, Unigraphics/NX, Inventor, Solid Edge, CADKEY, Rhino, DWG, and so on by selecting their respective file type from the **File Type** drop-down list of the **Open** dialog box. In addition to this, you can also open documents saved in universal CAD formats such as IGES, STEP, SLT, and Parasolid.

Summary

In this chapter, you have learn that for installing SOLIDWORKS you need to first consult the system requirements and make sure that you have a system capable of running SOLIDWORKS adequately.

You have also learn about how to invoke different SOLIDWORKS environments, identifying SOLIDWORKS documents, various components of the initial screen of SOLIDWORKS, invoking and customizing shortcut menu, saving documents, and opening documents in SOLIDWORKS.

Questions

- The surface modeling environment and the Sheet Metal environment of SOLIDWORKS can be invoked within the _____ modeling environment.

- The file extension of the documents created in the Part modeling environment is _____, the Assembly environment is _____, and the Drawing environment is _____.

- In SOLIDWORKS, a component can be designed by creating all its _____ one by one.

- The FeatureManager design tree is used to keep record of all operations/features in an order.

Drawing Sketches with SOLIDWORKS

In this chapter:

- Invoking the Part Modeling Environment
- Invoking the Sketching Environment
- Understanding the Concept of Selecting Planes
- Specifying Units
- Specifying Grids and Snaps Settings
- Drawing Line Entities
- Drawing Arc by using the Line tool
- Drawing the Centerline
- Drawing Rectangles
- Drawing Circles
- Drawing Arcs
- Drawing Polygons
- Drawing Slots
- Drawing Ellipses
- Drawing Elliptical Arcs
- Drawing Parabola
- Drawing Conic Curve
- Drawing Splines
- Editing Spline

Before you start creating solid 3D components in SOLIDWORKS, it is very important to understand that SOLIDWORKS is a feature-based, parametric solid-modeling mechanical design and automation software. Therefore to design a component in SOLIDWORKS, you need to create all its features one by one. Note that features are divided into two main categories: Sketched based features and Placed features. A feature which is created by drawing a sketch is know as Sketch based feature. A Placed feature is a feature which can be created by specifying placement on an existing feature and sketch is not required. Out of these two categories, the Sketched base feature is the first feature of any real world component to be design. That is why drawing sketches become important to learn first.

Figure 2.1 shows a components consist of base feature, cut feature, loft feature, fillet, and chamfer. Out of all these features base, cut, and loft are created by drawing a sketch. Therefore these features are known as Sketch based features. On the other hand the fillet and chamfer are known as Placed features because for creating these features sketch is not used. Note that as discussed, the first/base feature of any real world component is always be a Sketch Based feature. Figure 2.2 show a base/first feature created and Figure 2.3 shows the sketched used for creating it.

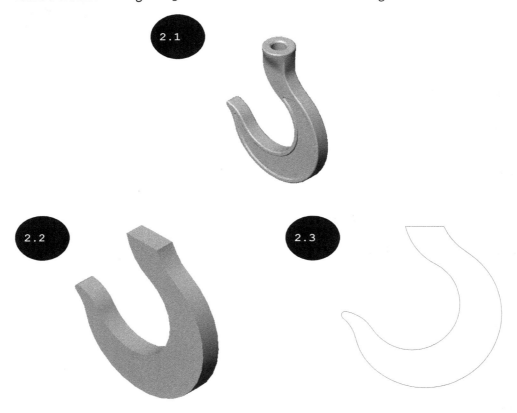

As base/first feature of any component is a Sketch Based Feature, you need to first learn how to create sketches in the Sketching environment of SOLIDWORKS.

Note that in SOLIDWORKS, the Sketching environment can be invoke within the Part modeling environment.

Invoking the Part Modeling Environment

Start SOLIDWORKS by double clicking on the **SOLIDWORKS 2015** icon available in your desktop. Once the new session of SOLIDWORKS has been invoked, click on the **New** tool available in the **Standard** toolbar or click on the **New Document** tool of the **SOLIDWORKS Resources** Task Pane, the **New SOLIDWORKS Document** dialog box appears, see Figure 2.4.

Note: If you are invoking the **New SOLIDWORKS Document** dialog box first time after installing the software, the **Units and Dimension Standard** dialog box appears. You can specify the unit system as the default unit system for SOLIDWORKS by using this dialog box.

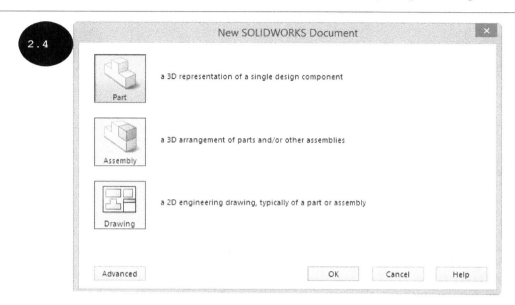

Click on the **Part** button of the **New SOLIDWORKS Document** dialog box and then click on the **OK** button, the initial screen of the Part modeling environment of SOLIDWORKS appears, see Figure 2.5.

Once the Part modeling environment is invoked, you can invoke the Sketching environment for drawing sketches. The various components of the Part modeling environment has been discussed in Chapter 1.

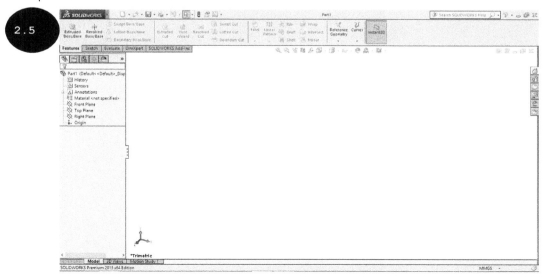

Invoking the Sketching Environment

Once the Part modeling environment is invoked, you need to start with creating design by first drawing the sketch of the base feature in the Sketching environment. To invoke the Sketching environment, click on the **Sketch** tab available in the **Command Manager**, the **Sketch CommandManager** appears, see Figure 2.6.

It is evident from the **Sketch CommandManager** that it is provided with number of tools for creating sketches. Click on the **Sketch** tool to invoke the Sketching environment, three default planes: Front, Top, and Right planes appears in the graphics area, see Figure 2.7. Also, the **Edit Sketch PropertyManager** appears at the left side of the graphics area. You can select any of the three default planes for drawing sketch as per your requirement by moving the cursor over the plane to be selected and then clicking the left mouse button on it. As soon as you select a plane, the Sketching environment is invoked with a Confirmation corner at its top right corner, see Figure 2.8. Also, the selected plane becomes the sketching plane for drawing the sketch and it is oriented normal to your viewing direction so that you can easily create sketch. Note that the Confirmation corner appears at the top right corner of the graphics area has two icon: **Exit Sketch** and **Cancel Sketch**. The **Exit Sketch** icon in the Confirmation corner is used to confirm the creation of sketch successfully and to exit from the Sketching environment. However, the **Cancel Sketch** icon is used discard the sketch created.

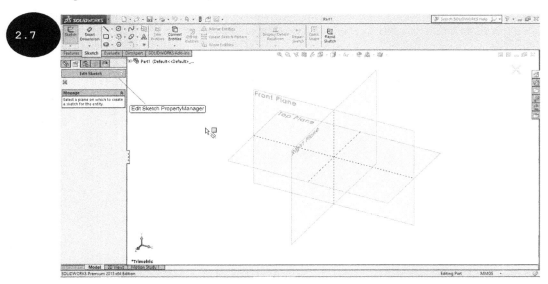

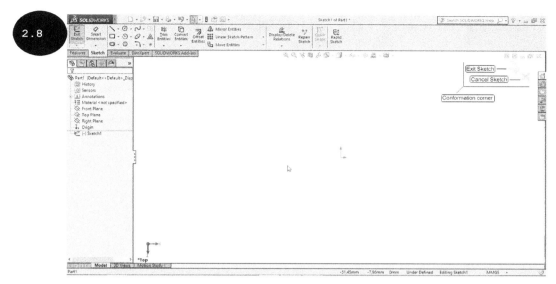

The Sketching environment also displays a red color point with two perpendicular arrows at the center of the graphics area. This point represents the origin of the Sketching environment and the perpendicular arrows represents the X and Y axis directions of the sketching plane. Note that the coordinates of origin are 0,0. If the red color point does not appears by default in the graphics area, you turn on the appearance of the origin by clicking on the **Hide/Show Items > View Origins** from the **View (Heads-Up)** toolbar, see Figure 2.9. The **View Origins** tool of the **View (Heads-Up)** toolbar is a toggle button.

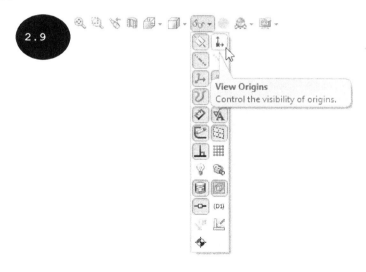

Understanding the Concept of Selecting Planes

As discussed earlier, for invoking the Sketching environment, you need to select a sketching plane for drawing the sketch, the selection of right sketching planes is very important in order to define the right orientation of the model. Figure 2.10 show the isometric view of a feature having length is 200 mm, width is 100 mm, and height is 40 mm. To create this feature with same isometric view, if you select the Top plane as the sketching plane then you need to draw a rectangular sketch of 200X100. However, if you select the Front plane for creating the same feature, you need to draw the rectangular sketch of 200X40. At the same time on selecting the Right plane as the sketching plane, you need to draw a rectangular sketch of 100X40.

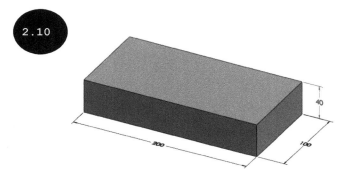

2.10

Once the Sketching environment is invoked, you can start drawing the sketch by using different sketching tools that are available in the **Sketch CommandManager**. However, before you start with drawing sketch, it is important to understand the procedure for setting units of measurements and grid settings.

Specifying Units

When you invoke the SOLIDWORKS software first time after installing it, the **Units and Dimension Standard** dialog box appears which allows you to specify units and measuring standard as the default settings. Note that the units and measuring standard settings specified in this dialog box becomes the default settings for all the new documents open there after. However, SOLIDWORKS allows you to modify the default unit settings at any point of your design for any particular document.

To modify default unit settings, click on the **Options** tool 🔲 of the **Standard** toolbar, the **System Options** dialog box appears, see Figure 2.11.

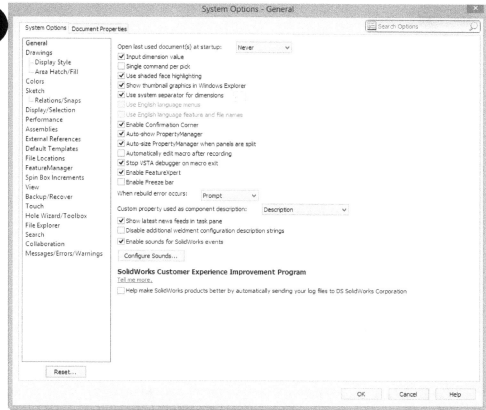

This dialog box contains two tabs: **System Options** and **Document Properties**. By default, the **System Options** tab is activated. Click on the **Document Properties** tab, the name of the dialog box changes to **Document Properties**. Also, all options related to the document properties appears in the dialog box. In this dialog box, click on the **Units** options available at the left panel of the dialog box, the options related to setting the units appears on the right panel of the dialog box, see Figure 2.12.

Note that the **Unit system** area of the dialog box displays the list of predefine standard unit systems. You can select the required predefined unit system for the current opened document by clicking on their respective radio button from this area of the dialog box. For example, clicking on the radio button available in the front of **MMGS (millimeter, gram, second)** unit system, the metric unit system becomes the unit system for the current opened document. In the metric unit system, length measures in millimeters, mass calculates in grams, and time represents in seconds.

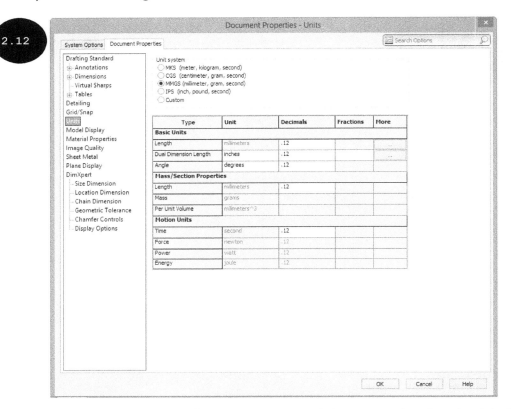

You can also specify the units system for the current opened document other than the default predefined standard unit systems by clicking on the **Custom** radio button. On clicking the **Custom** radio button, the options available in the table appears at the bottom of the dialog box gets activated. Now, you can change the units for length measurement, angle measurement, units for mass calculation, and time as per your requirement other than the standard combination. For example, changing the unit for the length measurement, click on the field corresponding to the **Unit** column and **Length** row in the table, a down arrow appears. Next, click on this down arrow, a flyout appears with the list of different units for length measurement. You can select the required unit from this flyout. Similarly, you can change the units for other measurement in this table. You can also specify the decimal places of the measurement as per your requirement from this table. Once you have set all the units of the measurement for the current opened document as per your requirement, click on the OK button to accept the changes made in the dialog box.

Specifying Grids and Snaps Settings

Grids are used to guide you for specifying points in the drawing area and act as reference lines. By default, the display of grids are turned off. You can turn on the display of grids in the drawing area by using the **Document Properties - Grid/Snap** dialog box. In this dialog box, you can also specify the snap settings. By specifying the snap settings, you can restricts the movement of cursor to specified intervals.

To invoke the **Document Properties - Grid/Snap** dialog box for specifying the grid and snaps settings, click on the **Options** tool in the **Standard** toolbar, the **System Options - General** dialog box appears. Click on the **Document Properties** tab, the options related to the document properties appears. Also, the name of the dialog box changes to **Document Properties - Drafting Standard**. Next, select the **Grid/Snap** option from the left panel of the dialog box, the options related to grid and snaps settings appears on the right panel of the dialog box. Also, the name of the dialog box changes to **Document Properties - Grid/Snap**, see Figure 2.13.

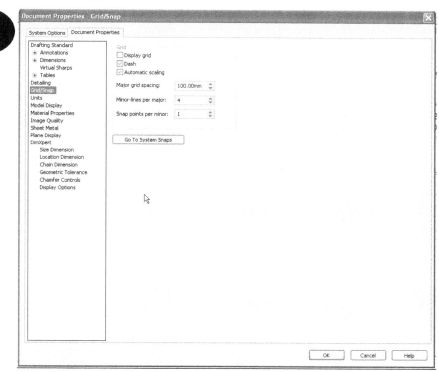

In the **Major grid spacing** field of the **Grid** area, specify the distance between two major grid lines. In the **Minor -lines per major** field of the dialog box, specify the number of minor lines between two **major grid lines**. Note that the value entered in the **Minor - lines per major** field defines the number of division between two major grid lines. For example, if the value entered in the **Minor-lines per major** field is 5 then two major grid lines divided into 5 small area horizontally or vertically. In the **Snap points per minor** field, you can specify the number of snap point for cursor between two minor grid lines.

To turn on the display of grid in the drawing area, select the **Display grid** check box of the **Grid** area in the dialog box. Similarly, you can turn on the snap mode on for snapping cursor to the specified snap settings by selecting the **Grid** check box. To select **Grid** check box, click on the **Go To System Snaps** button of the dialog box, the name of the dialog box changes to **System Options - Relations/Snaps**. In this dialog box, you can select the **Grid** check box for turning the snap mode on. If you also select the **Snap only when grid appears** check box of this dialog box, the cursor snaps only when the display of grids is turned on. Note that snapping cursor to a specific interval is very useful in order to defines the exist points in the drawing area for drawing sketches.

Drawing Line Entities

A line is define as a shortest distance between two points. To draw a line, click on the **Line** tool of the **Sketch CommandManager**, the **Insert Line PropertyManager** appears with three rollouts: **Message**, **Orientation**, and **Options** in the left of the drawing area, refer to Figure 2.14. Also, the appearance of cursor changes to line cursor ✎ . The line cursor appears as a pencil with symbol of line at its bottom options available in the rollouts of the **Insert Line PropertyManager** are as follows.

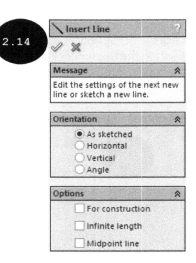

Message

The **Message** rollout of the PropertyManager is used to guide you by displaying appropriate informations about the required action to be taken next.

Orientation

The **Orientation** rollout of the PropertyManager is used to control the orientation of the line to be drawn. The options available in the **Orientation** rollout are as follows.

As sketched

By default, the **As sketched** radio button is activated in the **Orientation** rollout. As a result, you can draw a line of any orientation by clicking the left mouse button in the drawing area. In this case, the orientation of the line depends upon the points you specify in the drawing area by clicking the left mouse button.

Horizontal

On selecting the **Horizontal** radio button in the **Orientation** rollout, you can draw a horizontal line or a line of horizontal orientation only. Notice that when you select this radio button, the **Parameters** rollout appears below the **Options** rollout in the PropertyManager, see Figure 2.15. In the **Parameters** rollout, the **Length** field is activated, by default. You can specify the required length of the horizontal line to be drawn in this filed. By default, value **0** is entered in this filed. As a result, you can draw a horizontal line of any length by specifying the two points in the drawing area. However, on entering length value, the creation of line locked to the specified length.

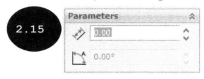

Tip: You can specify points in the drawing area by clicking the left mouse button. Note that the coordinates of the current location of the cursor appears in the **Status Bar**. Notice that as you move the cursor in the drawing area, the coordinates value appears in the **Status Bar** dynamically modified. You can refer to the coordinates value in the **Status Bar** while specifying point in the drawing area.

Vertical

Similar to drawing horizontal line by selecting the **Horizontal** radio button, you can draw vertical lines by selecting the **Vertical** radio button in the **Orientation** rollout of the PropertyManager. Notice that on selecting the **Vertical** radio button, you can only draw vertical lines.

Angle

On selecting the **Angle** radio button in the **Orientation** rollout, you can draw a line at an angle. As soon as, you select this radio button, the **Parameters** rollout appears below the **Options** rollout with the **Length** and **Angle** fields enabled. You can specify the required length and angle of the line to be drawn in their fields, respectively. By default, value **0** is entered in both these fields. As a result, you can draw a line of any length and angle by specifying the points in the drawing area. However, on entering length and angle value, the creation of line locked to the specified angle and length values.

> **Note:** The angle values of the line entered in the **Angle** field of the **Parameters** rollout in the PropertyManager, measures from the X axis of the plane.

Options

The options available in the **Options** rollout of the **PropertyManager** are as follows.

For construction

The **For construction** check box of the **Options** rollout in the **PropertyManager** is used to draw a construction or reference line. On checking the **For construction** check box, the construction line drawn by specifying the points in the drawing area.

Infinite length

The **Infinite length** check box is used to draw a line of infinite length. On checking the **Infinite length** check box, the line of infinite length drawn by specifying two points in the drawing area.

Midpoint line

The **Midpoint line** check box is used to draw a symmetric line about the mid point of the line. On checking the **Midpoint line** check box, you can specify the mid point of the line and then specifying the end point of the line.

Procedure to Draw Line

1. Click on the **Line** tool in the **Sketch CommandManager**, the **Line** tool activates and the **Insert Line PropertyManager** appears at the left side of the drawing area. Also, the appearance of cursor changes to line cursor ✎ . The line cursor appears as a pencil with symbol of line at its bottom.
2. Select the required option from the **Orientation** rollout of the PropertyManager, else accept the default selected option.
3. Move the cursor towards the origin and when it snaps to the origin, click to specify the start point of the line.

Tip: As discussed earlier, you can specify the start point of the line in any location by clicking the left mouse button. For specifying the location of the point in the drawing area, refer to **Status Bar**. The **Status Bar** is available at the bottom of the drawing area which displays the coordinate values of the current location of the cursor. As you move the cursor in the drawing area, the coordinates value will also modified in the **Status Bar** accordingly.

4. Move the line cursor away from the start point specified, a rubber band line appears whose one end is fixed at the start point and second end is attached with the line cursor. Notice that as you move the cursor, the length of the rubber band line changes, accordingly and displays above the cursor, see Figure 2.16.

98.77

Note: If you move the cursor in horizontal or vertical direction after specifying the start point of the line, the symbol of horizontal − or vertical ❙ relation displays near the cursor. These symbol of relations indicates that if you click the left mouse button now to specify the second point of the line, the corresponding relation will be applied. You will learn more about relations later in this chapter.

5. Click the left mouse button to specify the second point of the line when the length of the line displays above the cursor, closer to the required one. As soon as you specify the second point of the line, a line between the specified points is drawn. Also, notice that a rubber band line is still appears whose one end is fix with the last specified point and other end is attached with the cursor tip. It indicates that you can draw chain of continue lines by clicking the left mouse button in the drawing area.

Tip: As SOLIDWORKS is parametric 3D solid modeling software, you can first draw a sketch in which measurements of the entities may not be exact. Once the sketch without dimensions has been drawn, you need to apply dimensions by using the **Smart Dimension** tool. You will learn more about dimensioning sketch entities later in this chapter.

6. Once all the line entities has been drawn, press the **ESC** key to exit from the **Line** tool. You can also right click in the drawing area and select the **Select** option from the shortcut menu appears to terminate the creation of line.

Example 1

Draw the sketch of the model shown in Figure 2.17. Dimensions and model shown in the figure are for your reference.

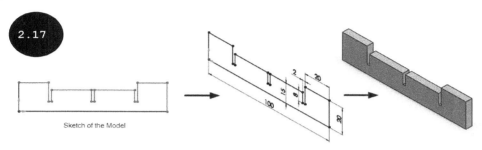

Sketch of the Model

Section 1: Starting SOLIDWORKS

1. Start SOLIDWORKS by clicking on the **SOLIDWORKS** icon on your desktop.

Section 2: Invoking Part Modeling Environment

1. Click on the **New** tool of the **Standard** toolbar, the **New SOLIDWORKS Document** dialog box appears.

2. Click on the **Part** button, if not activated and then click on the **OK** button in the dialog box, the Part modeling environment is invoked, see Figure 2.18.

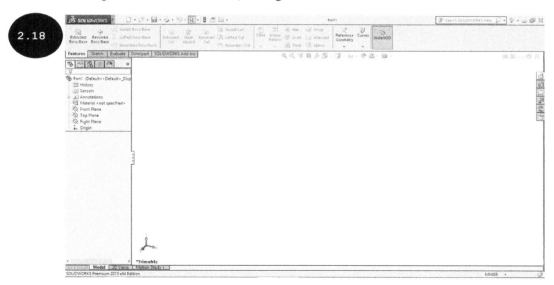

Section 3: Invoking Sketching Environment

1. Click on the **Sketch** tab in the **Command Manager**, the **Sketch CommandManager** appears which provides all the tools required to draw sketches.

2. Click on the **Sketch** button of the **Sketch CommandManager**, three default planes mutually perpendicular to each other appears in the graphic area.

3. Move the cursor over the Front plane and click to select it as the sketching plane when the boundary of the plane highlighted, the **Sketching** environment is invoked. Also, the Front plane orientated normal to the viewing direction and the Confirmation corner appears at the upper right corner of the drawing area, see Figure 2.19.

Note: In this example, the display of grids and snaps setting are turned off.

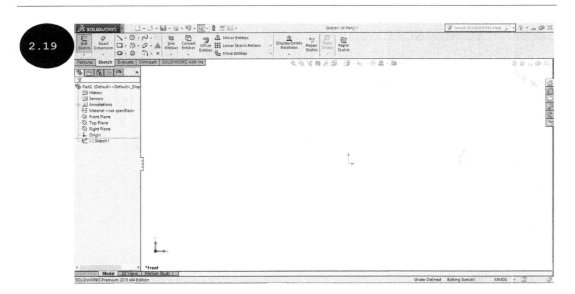

2.19

Section 4: Drawing Sketch

1. Click on the **Line** tool in the **Sketch CommandManager**, the **Line** tool activates and the **Insert Line PropertyManager** appears in left side of the drawing area. Also, the appearance of cursor changes to line cursor .

2. Move the cursor towards the origin and click to specify the start point of the line when cursor snaps to origin.

3. Move the cursor horizontal towards the right and click to specify the second line of the line when the length of the line displays above the cursor closer to 100 mm, see Figure 2.20.

4. Move the cursor vertically upwards and click to specify the next point when the length of the line displays above the cursor closer to 20mm, see Figure 2.21.

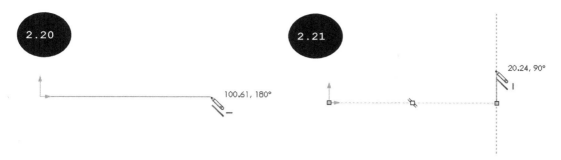

5. Move the cursor horizontally towards the right and click to specify the next point when the length of the line displays above the cursor closer to 20 mm.

6. Move the cursor vertically downwards and click to specify the next point when the length of the line displays above the cursor closer to 13mm, see Figure 2.22.

7. Scroll the middle mouse button to Zoom in the drawing display area.

8. Move the cursor horizontal towards the left and click to specify the next point when the length of the line displays above the cursor closer to 2 mm.

9. Move the cursor vertically upwards and click to specify the next point when the length of the line displays above the cursor closer to 8 mm, see Figure 2.23.

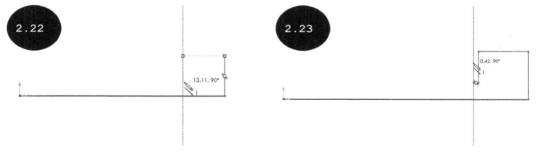

10. Move the cursor horizontally towards the left and click to specify the next point when the length of the line displays above the cursor closer to 27 mm, see Figure 2.24.

11. Move the cursor vertically downwards and click to specify the next point when interfacing lines originating from the line being drawn and the left horizontal line of 2mm drawn intersect each other, see Figure 2.25.

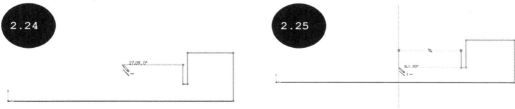

12. Similarly, draw the remaining sketch entities. The Figure 2.26 shows the sketch after completing all the sketch entities. Next, press the **ESC** key to terminate the creation of line.

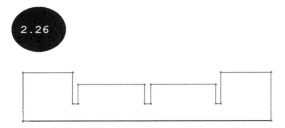

Tip: In the example, the display of automatic applied relations such as horizontal and vertical is turned off. To turned off or on the display of relations in the drawing area, click on the **Hide/ Show Items > View Sketch Relations** from the **View (Heads-Up)** toolbar. The **View Sketch Relations** button is toggle button.

Hands-on Test Drive 1

Draw the sketch of the model shown in Figure 2.27. Dimensions and model shown in the figure are for your reference.

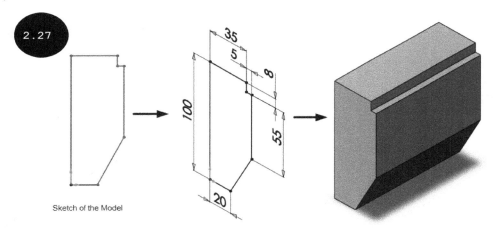

Sketch of the Model

Drawing Arc by Using the Line tool

SOLIDWORKS is provided with different set of tools for drawing arcs: **Centerpoint Arc, 3 Point Arc,** and **Tangent Arc** which are discussed later in this chapter. However, in addition to these tools, you can also draw an tangent arc by using the **Line** tool. Note that to draw an tangent arc by using the **Line** tool at least one line or arc entity has to be drawn in the drawing area.

Procedure to Draw Arc by Using the Line tool

1. Invoke the **Line** tool and then draw a line by specifying two points in the drawing area. The procedure to draw a line is discussed earlier. Once a line has been drawn by specifying two points, do not exit from the **Line** tool.

2. Move the line cursor away from the last specified point and than move it back to the last specified point, a dot filled with orange color appears in the drawing area, see Figure 2.28.

3. Move the cursor away from the point, the arc mode is activated and the preview of a tangent arc appears in the drawing area, see Figure 2.29.

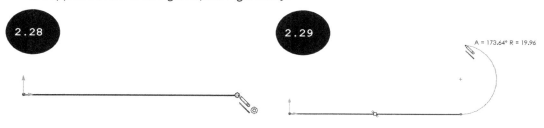

Note: The creation will depends upon how you move the cursor from the last specified point in the drawing area. Figure 2.30 shows the possible movement directions of the cursor and the respective arc creation in that particular direction.

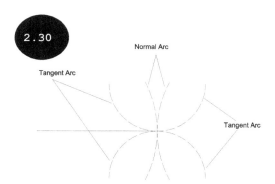

Tip: If a line or arc entity already exist in the drawing area, you can directly invoke the arc mode after invoking the **Line** tool. To do so, after invoking the **Line** tool, click on a end point of the already existing entity. Next, move cursor away from the specify point and then move back to the specified point and when the dot filled with orange color appears, move the cursor to the required direction to invoke the arc mode.

4. Click the left mouse button to specify the end point of the arc when the angle and radius value displays above the cursor closer to the required one. As soon as you specify the end point of the arc, the tangent arc is drawn. Also, the line mode is activated again. You can continue with

the creation of line entities or move the cursor back to the last specified point to invoke the arc mode for drawing arc again. In this way you can draw continues chain of lines and arcs.

5. Once you are done, press the ESC key to exit from the tool.

Example 2

Draw the sketch of the model shown in Figure 2.31 by using the **Line** tool. Dimensions and model shown in the figure are for your reference only. You will draw all the entities of the sketch by using the **Line** tool. Also, as all the dimensions are multiple of 5 mm, you can set snap settings such that cursor snap to the incremental of 5 mm.

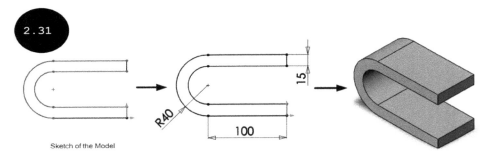

Sketch of the Model

Section 1: Starting SOLIDWORKS

1. Start SOLIDWORKS by clicking on the SOLIDWORKS icon on your desktop, if not started already.

Section 2: Invoking the Part Modeling Environment

1. Click on the **New** tool in the **Standard** toolbar, the **New SOLIDWORKS Document** dialog box appears.

2. Click on the **Part** button, if not activated and then click on the **OK** button, the Part modeling environment is invoked.

Section 3: Invoking the Sketching Environment

1. Click on the Sketch tab in the Command Manager, if not activated, the Sketch CommandManager appears.

2. Click on the **Sketch** button of the **Sketch CommandManager**, three default planes mutually perpendicular to each other appears in the graphic area.

3. Move the cursor over the Front plane and click to select it as the sketching plane when the boundary of the plane highlighted, the Sketching environment is invoked. Also, the Front plane orientated normal to the viewing direction and the Confirmation corner appears at the upper right corner of the drawing area, see Figure 2.32.

It is evident from the Figure 2.31 that all the sketch entities are multiple of 5 mm. Therefore, you can set snap settings such that cursor snap to the increment of 5 mm only. It helps you to specify points in the drawing area while drawing the sketch. Also, in this example, you need to specify metric unit system for measurement.

Section 4: Setting Grid and Snap Settings

1. Click on the **Options** tool in the **Standard** toolbar, the **System Options - General** dialog box displays.

2. In the **System Options - General** dialog box, click on the **Document Properties** tab, the name of the dialog box changes to **Document Properties - Drafting Standard**.

3. Select the **Units** option available in the left panel of the dialog box, the options related to specifying the unit system displays on the right side panel of the dialog box.

4. Select the **MMGS (millimeter, gram, second)** radio button from the **Unit system** area of the dialog box, if not selected by default. Once the unit system is specified do not exit from the dialog box.

    Now, you need to specify the grid and snap settings such that the cursor snaps the increment of 5 mm.

5. Select the **Grid/Snap** option available in the left side panel of the dialog box, the options related to the grid and snap settings displays on the right side panel of the dialog box. Also, the name of the dialog box changes to **Document Properties - Grid/Snap** dialog box.

6. Enter **20** in the **Major grid spacing**, **4** in the **Minor -lines per major**, and **1** in the **Snap points per minor** fields of the **Grid** area in the dialog box.

Tip: The value entered in the **Major grid spacing** field defines the distance between two major grid lines in the drawing area and the value entered in the **Minor -lines per major** field defines the number of divisions between two major gird lines. The value entered in the **Snap points per minor** fields defines the number of snap point in each divisions. As per the step 12, the distance between two major grid lines will be 20 mm and number of division between two major lines will be 4. It means that the division will be of 5 mm each (20/4 = 5). Therefore, the number of snap points in each division will be 1, so that cursor snaps to the distance of 5 mm only.

---

7. Select the **Display grid** check box of the **Grid** area in the dialog box to turn on the display of grids in the drawing area as per the grid settings specified in the above step.

8. Click on the **Go To System Snaps** button of the **Document Properties - Grid/Snap** dialog box, the name of the dialog box changes to **System Options - Relations/Snaps**.

9. Select the **Grid** check box in the **Sketch snaps** area of the **System Options - Relations/Snaps** dialog box, if not selected by default to turn on the snap mode.

10. Click on the **OK** button of the dialog box, the grid and snap settings has been specified and the dialog box is closed. Also, the drawing area displays similar to one shown in Figure 2.33.

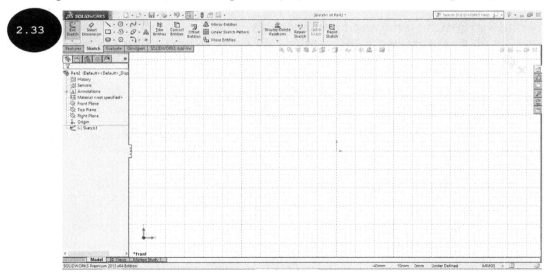

Once the units, grid, and snap settings has been specified, you can start drawing the sketch by using the **Line** tool.

Section 5: Drawing Sketch

1. Click on the **Line** tool in the **Sketch CommandManager**, the **Line** tool activates and the **Insert Line PropertyManager** appears in left side of the drawing area. Also, the appearance of cursor changes to line cursor ✎ .

2. Move the cursor towards the origin and click to specify the start point of the line when cursor snaps to origin.

3. Move the cursor horizontal towards the left and click to specify the second point of the line when the length of the line displays above the cursor is 100 mm, see Figure 2.34. Notice that the cursor is only snapping to the distance of 5 mm increment.

4. Move the line cursor away to a small distance and than move it back to the last specified point, a dot filled with orange color appears in the drawing area, see Figure 2.35.

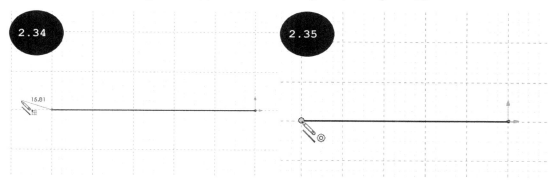

5. Move the cursor horizontal towards the left to a small distance and then move it vertical upwards to a small distance, the arc mode is activated and the preview of a tangent arc appears in the drawing area, see Figure 2.36.

6. Click to specify the end point of the tangent arc when the angle and radius values of the arc displays above the cursor are 180 and 40, respectively. As soon as you specify the end point of the arc, the tangent arc is created and the preview of a line is attached with the cursor.

7. Move the cursor horizontal towards the right and click to specify the end point of the line when the length of the line displays above the cursor is 100, see Figure 2.37.

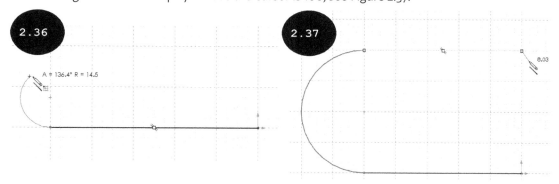

8. Move the cursor vertical downward and click to specify the left mouse button when the length of the line displays above the cursor is 15.

9.   Move the cursor horizontal towards the left and click to specify the next point when the length of the line displays above the cursor is 100.

10. Move the cursor away from the last specified point and than move it back to the last specified point, a dot filled with orange color appears in the drawing area, see Figure 2.38.

11. Move the cursor horizontal towards the left to a small distance and then move it vertical downwards to a small distance, the arc mode is activated and the preview of a tangent arc appears in the drawing area, see Figure 2.39.

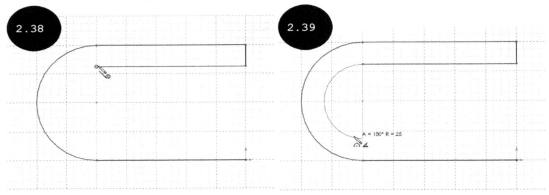

12. Click to specify the end point of the tangent arc when the angle and radius values of the arc displays above the cursor are 180 and 25, respectively. As soon as you specify the end point of the arc, the tangent arc is created and the line mode is attached.

13. Move the cursor horizontally towards the right and click to specify the next point when the length of the line displays above the cursor 100.

14. Move the cursor vertically downwards and click to specify the last point of the line when the cursor snap to the start point of the sketch line.

15. Next, press the ESC key to terminate the creation of line and click any where in the drawing area. The final sketch is drawn, see Figure 2.40.

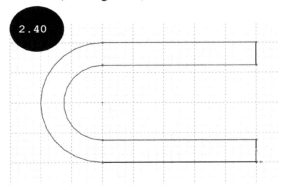

Hands-on Test Drive 2

Draw the sketch of the model shown in Figure 2.41. Dimensions and model shown in the figure are for your reference. You will draw all the entities of the sketch by using the **Line** tool. Also, as all the dimensions are multiple of 5mm, you can set snap setting such that cursor snap to an increment of 5 mm.

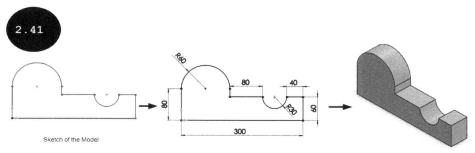

Sketch of the Model

Drawing Centerline

The centerlines are define as reference or construction lines and are drawn for the aid of sketches. In SOLIDWORKS, you can draw centerline by using the **Centerline** tool which is available in the **Line** flyout. To invoke the **Line** flyout, click on the down arrow available next to the **Line** tool in the **Sketch CommandManager**, see Figure 2.42. Next, click on the **Centerline** tool from this flyout, the **Centerline** tool is invoked. Also, the **Insert Line PropertyManager** appears at the left of the drawing area, see Figure 2.43. The options available in this PropertyManager are same as discussed earlier while drawing line entities.

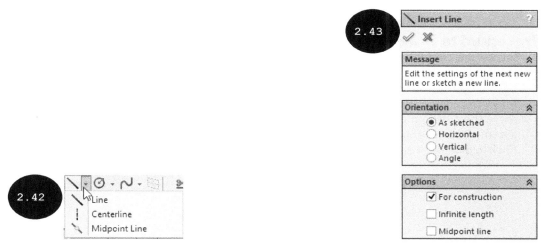

Notice that when you invoke the **Insert Line PropertyManager** by clicking on the **Centerline** tool, the **For construction** check box in the **Options** rollout is selected, by default. The procedure of drawing centerlines is same as of drawing continuous lines. Figure 2.44 shows a horizontal centerline drawn by specifying two points in the drawing area.

Tip: You can also draw a centerline from the **Line** tool and vise versa by clearing or selecting the **For construction** check box of the respective **Insert Line PropertyManager**.

Drawing Midpoint Line

A midpoint line is a line created symmetrically about its mid point. In SOLIDWORKS, you can draw midpoint lines by using the **Midpoint Line** tool which is available in the **Line** flyout. To invoke the **Line** flyout, click on the down arrow available next to the **Line** tool in the **Sketch CommandManager**, see Figure 2.42. Next, click on the **Midpoint Line** tool from this flyout, the **Midpoint Line** tool is invoked. Also, the **Insert Line PropertyManager** appears with **Midpoint line** check box is selected, see Figure 2.45. The options available in this PropertyManager are same as discussed earlier.

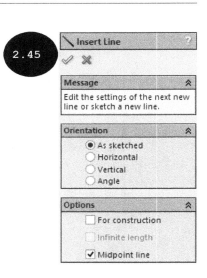

Procedure to Draw Midpoint Line
1. Invoke the **Line** flyout and then click on the **Midpoint Line** tool.
2. Click to specify the midpoint of the line in the drawing area, see Figure 2.46.
3. Move to cursor to the required location to define the end point of the line. Note that as you move the cursor, the preview of the symmetric line about the midpoint of the line appears, automatically, see Figure 2.46.
4. Click to define the end point of the line, the symmetric line about the mid point is created.

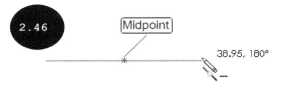

Drawing Rectangle

In SOLIDWORKS, you can draw rectangle by different methods. The tools for drawing rectangle by different methods are group together into the **Rectangle** flyout. To invoke the **Rectangle** flyout, click on the down arrow available next to the activated **rectangle** tool in the **Sketch CommandManager**, see Figure 2.47 The different tools used for drawing rectangle are as follows.

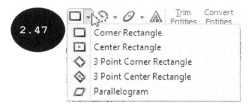

Corner Rectangle

The **Corner Rectangle** tool of the **Rectangle** flyout is used to draw a rectangle by specify its two diagonally opposite corner. The first specified corner defines the position of the first corner of the rectangle and the second specified corner defines the length and width of the rectangle, see Figure 2.48.

To create rectangle by using the **Corner Rectangle** tool, click on the down arrow available next to activated **Rectangle** tool in the **Sketch CommandManager**, the **Rectangle** flyout appears, see Figure 2.47. Next, click on the **Corner Rectangle** tool available first in the list of flyout appears, the **Corner Rectangle** tool is activated and the **Rectangle PropertyManager** appears at the left of the drawing area, see Figure 2.49. The options available in the rollouts of the **Rectangle PropertyManager** are as follows.

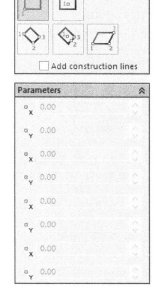

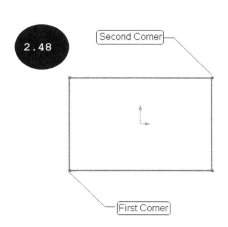

Rectangle Type

The buttons available in the **Rectangle Type** rollout of the PropertyManager allows you to switch different method of drawing rectangle even after invoking the **Rectangle PropertyManager**. By default, depending upon the tool chosen from the **Rectangle** flyout to invoke the PropertyManager, the respective button become activated in this rollout. For example, if the **Rectangle PropertyManager** is invoked by clicking on the **Corner Rectangle** tool then the **Corner Rectangle** button become activated in the **Rectangle Type** rollout of the PropertyManager.

The **Add construction lines** check box of this rollout is used to add construction lines in the rectangle. On selecting this check box, the **From Corners** and **From Midpoints** radio buttons become enabled, see Figure 2.50. When the **From Corners** radio button is selected, you can add corner to corner connecting construction lines in the rectangle, see Figure 2.51. On selecting the **From Midpoints** radio button, you can add construction lines in the rectangle from the midpoint of the line segments, see Figure 2.52.

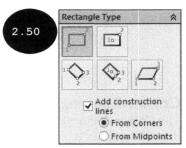

2.50

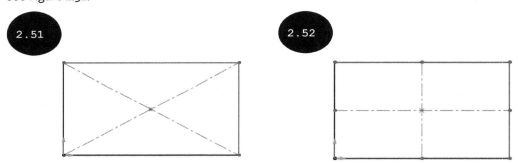

2.51   2.52

Parameters

The options available in the **Parameters** rollout of the PropertyManager are used to display or control the parameters of the rectangle being drawn. However, all the options of this rollout is activated once the rectangle has been drawn and it is selected in the drawing area.

Procedure to Draw Rectangle by Specifying Two Corner

1. Invoke the **Rectangle** flyout, see Figure 2.47. Next, click on the **Corner Rectangle** tool, the **Rectangle PropertyManager** appears at the left of the drawing area.
2. Move the cursor in the drawing area and click to specify first corner of the rectangle.
3. After specifying the first corner of the rectangle, move the cursor to specify the diagonally opposite corner of the rectangle.
4. Click to specify the second corner of the rectangle when the length and width values of the rectangle shows above the cursor closer to the required one, see Figure 2.53.

Note: The length of the rectangle measure in X axis direction of the plane and width measures in Y axis direction.

Center Rectangle

The **Center Rectangle** tool of the **Rectangle** flyout is used to draw the rectangle by specify its center point and a corner, see Figure 2.54.

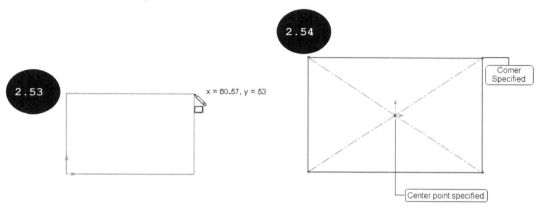

Procedure to Draw Rectangle by Specifying Centerpoint and a Corner

1. Invoke the **Rectangle** flyout and then click on the **Center Rectangle** tool.
2. Move the cursor in the drawing area and then click to specify the center point of the rectangle.
3. Move the cursor away from the center point, a preview of the rectangle whose one corner attached with the cursor tip appears.
4. Click to specify the corner point of the rectangle when the length and width values of the rectangle shows above the cursor closer to the required one, see Figure 2.55.

Note: The length of the rectangle measure in X axis direction of the plane and width measures in Y axis direction

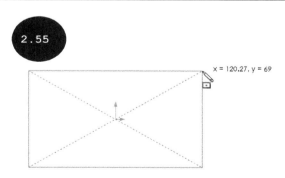

3 Point Corner Rectangle

The **3 Point Corner Rectangle** tool of the **Rectangle** flyout is used to draw a rectangle by specify its 3 corners. The first two corners defines the width and orientation of the rectangle and the third corner defines the length of the rectangle, see Figure 2.56.

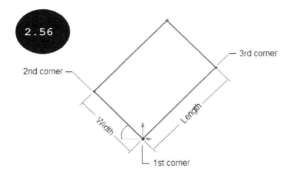

Procedure to Draw Rectangle by Specifying 3 Corners

1. Invoke the **Rectangle** flyout and then click on the **3 Point Corner Rectangle** tool.
2. Move the cursor in the drawing area and then click to specify the first corner of the rectangle.
3. After specify the first corner of rectangle, move the cursor away from the specified point, a interfacing line appears attached with the cursor, see Figure 2.57.
4. Click to specify the second corner of the rectangle when the distance and angle values of the width of rectangle shows above the cursor closer to the required one.
5. Move the cursor away from the specified point, the preview of the rectangle appears whose other end is attached with the cursor tip, see Figure 2.58.
6. Click to specify the third corner point of the rectangle when the value of the length shows above the cursor closer to the required one.

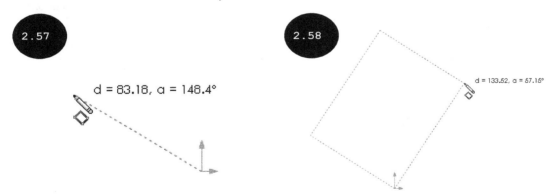

3 Point Center Rectangle

The **3 Point Center Rectangle** tool of the **Rectangle** flyout is used to draw a rectangle at an angle by specify three points. The first point define the center of the rectangle, second point defines the width and orientation of the rectangle, and the third point defines the length of the rectangle, see Figure 2.59.

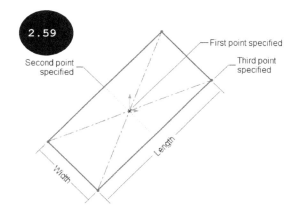

2.59

First point specified

Second point specified

Third point specified

Length

Width

Procedure to Draw Rectangle by Specifying Centerpoint, a Point, and a Corner

1. Invoke the **Rectangle** flyout and then click on the **3 Point Center Rectangle** tool.
2. Move the cursor in the drawing area and then click to specify the center of the rectangle.
3. After specify the center point of rectangle, move the cursor away from the specified point, a interfacing line appears attached with the cursor, see Figure 2.60. Note that the displacement of interfacing lines depends upon the moving direction of the cursor.
4. Click to specify the second point when the distance value shows above the cursor closer to the half of the required total width of the rectangle.
5. Move the cursor away from the second specified point, the preview of the rectangle appears in the drawing area with one corner attached in the cursor tip, see Figure 2.61.
6. Click to specify the third point of the rectangle when the length shows above the cursor closer to the required one, see Figure 2.61.

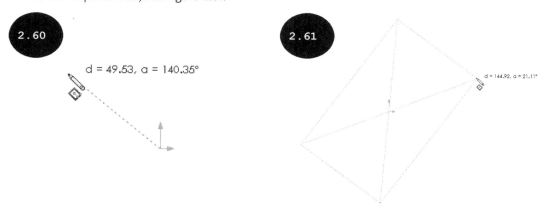

2.60

d = 49.53, a = 140.35°

2.61

d = 144.92, a = 21.11°

Parallelogram

The **Parallelogram** tool of the **Rectangle** flyout is used to draw a parallelogram whose sides are not perpendicular to each other. You can draw a parallelogram by specifying its three corner points after invoking the **Parallelogram** tool. First two specified corners defines the length and orientation of the parallelogram and the third corner defines the width and the angle between the parallelogram sides, see Figure 2.62.

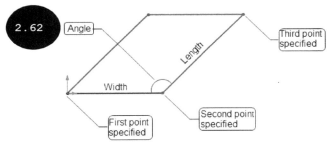

Procedure to Draw Parallelogram

1. Invoke the **Rectangle** flyout and then click on the **Parallelogram** tool.
2. Move the cursor in the drawing area and then click the left mouse button to specify the first corner of the parallelogram.
3. After specify the first corner of the parallelogram, move the cursor away from the specified point, a interfacing line displays attached with the cursor, see Figure 2.63. Note that the orientation of interfacing line depends upon the moving direction of the cursor.
4. Click to specify the second corner of the parallelogram when the distance and angle value shows above the cursor closer to the required width and angle.
5. Move the cursor away from the second specified corner, the preview of the parallelogram appears in the drawing area with one corner attached to the cursor tip, see Figure 2.64.
6. Click to specify the third corner of the parallelogram when the distance and angle value shows above the cursor closer to the required length and angle between its sides.

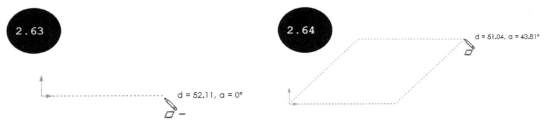

Drawing Circles

In SOLIDWORKS, you can draw circles by different methods. The tools for drawing circles by different methods are group together into the **Circle** flyout. To invoke the **Circle** flyout, click on the down arrow available next to the activated circle tool in the **Sketch CommandManager**, see Figure 2.65. The different tools used for drawing circle are as follows.

2.65

Circle

The **Circle** tool of the **Circle** flyout is used to draw a circle by specify its center and a point on the circumference, see Figure 2.66.

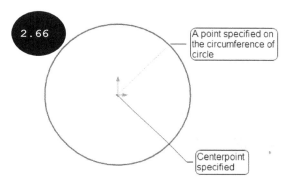

2.66

A point specified on the circumference of circle

Centerpoint specified

To create a circle by using the **Circle** tool, click on the down arrow available next the active circle tool in the **Sketch CommandManager**, the **Circle** flyout appears, see Figure 2.65. Next, click on the **Circle** tool, the **Circle PropertyManager** appears at the left of the drawing area, see Figure 2.67. The options available in the rollouts of this PropertyManager are as follows.

2.67

Circle Type

The buttons available in the **Circle Type** rollout of the PropertyManager allows you to switch to other method of drawing circle even after invoking the **Circle PropertyManager**. By default, depending upon the tool chosen from the **Circle** flyout to invoke the PropertyManager, the respective button become activated in this rollout. For example, if the **Circle PropertyManager** is invoked by clicking on the **Circle** tool from the **Circle** flyout, the **Circle** button become activated in the **Circle Type** rollout of the PropertyManager.

Parameters

The options available in the **Parameters** rollout of the PropertyManager are used to display or control the parameters of the circle being drawn. However, all the options of this rollout is activated once the circle has been drawn and it is selected in the drawing area.

Procedure to Draw Circle by Specifying Centerpoint

1. Invoke the **Circle** flyout.
2. Click on the **Circle** tool of the **Circle** flyout, the **Circle PropertyManager** appears.
3. Move the cursor in the drawing area and click to specify the center point of the circle at the location whose coordinates value are closer to the required one.
4. After specifying the center point of the circle, move the cursor to a distance for specifying a point on the circumference of the circle. As you move the cursor, the preview of the circle appears attached with the cursor.
5. Click to specify the point in the drawing area when the radius of the circle shows above the cursor closer to the required one, see Figure 2.68.

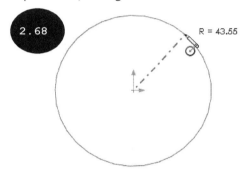

Perimeter Circle

The **Perimeter Circle** tool of the **Circle** flyout is used to draw a circle by specify the three point on the circumference of the circle.

Procedure to Draw Circle by Specifying 3 Points

1. Invoke the **Circle** flyout and then click on the **Perimeter Circle** tool, the **Circle PropertyManager** appears with the **Perimeter Circle** button activated by default in the **Circle Type** rollout.
2. Move the cursor in the drawing area and then click to specify the first point on the circumference of the circle, see Figure 2.69.
3. Move the cursor to a distance, the preview of the circle attached to the cursor.
4. Click to specify the second point on the circumference of the circle, see Figure 2.69.
5. Move the cursor and then click to specify the third point on the circumference of the circle, the circle is drawn defined by three point of its circumference, see Figure 2.70.

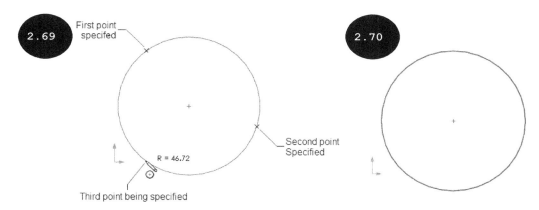

Tip: You can also convert created continuous circle into the construction circle. To do so, select the circle drawn in the drawing area and then select the **For construction** check available in the **Options** rollout of the **Circle PropertyManager** which appears on selecting the circle. Alternatively, select the circle from the drawing area and do not move the cursor, a Pop-up toolbar appears. Next, click on the **Construction Geometry** button from the Pop-up toolbar, the selected circle is converted into construction circle. Similarly, you can convert any selected sketch entity into construction entity.

Drawing Arcs

In SOLIDWORKS, you can draw arcs by different methods. The tools for drawing arcs are group together into the **Arc** flyout. To invoke the **Arc** flyout, click on the down arrow available next to the activated **Arc** tool in the **Sketch CommandManager**, see Figure 2.71. The different tools used for drawing arc are as follows.

Centerpoint Arc

The **Centerpoint Arc** tool of the **Arc** flyout is used to draw an arc by defining its centerpoint, start point, and end point, see Figure 2.72.

To create an arc by using the **Centerpoint Arc** tool, click on the down arrow available next the active arc tool in the **Sketch CommandManager**, the **Arc** flyout appears, see Figure 2.71. Next, click on the **Centerpoint Arc** tool of flyout, the **Arc PropertyManager** appears at the left of the drawing area, see Figure 2.73. The options available in the rollouts of this PropertyManager are as follows.

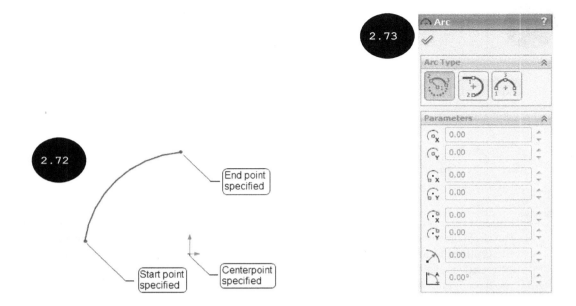

Arc Type

The buttons available in the **Arc Type** rollout of the PropertyManager allows you to switch different method of drawing arc ever after invoking the **Arc PropertyManager**. By default, depending upon the tool chosen from the **Arc** flyout to invoke the PropertyManager, the respective button is activated in this rollout. For example, if you click on the **Centerpoint Arc** tool of **Arc** flyout, the **Centerpoint Arc** button become activated in the **Arc Type** rollout of the PropertyManager.

Parameters

The options available in the **Parameters** rollout of the PropertyManager are used to display or control the parameters of the arc being drawn. However, all the options of this rollout is activated once the arc has been drawn and it is selected in the drawing area.

Procedure to Draw Arc by Specifying Center, Start, and End Points

1. Invoke the **Arc** flyout.
2. Click on the **Centerpoint Arc** tool in the **Arc** flyout.
3. Move the cursor in the drawing area and then click to specify the centerpoint of the arc at the required location.
4. Move the cursor to a distance from the specified centerpoint, a construction circle appears attached with the cursor.
5. Click in the drawing area to define the start point of the arc.
6. Move the cursor clockwise or anti-clockwise and then click to specify the end point of the arc in the drawing area when the angle appears above the cursor closer to the required angle value.

3 Point Arc

The **3 Point Arc** tool of the **Arc** flyout is used to draw an arc by defining three point on the arc length, see Figure 2.74.

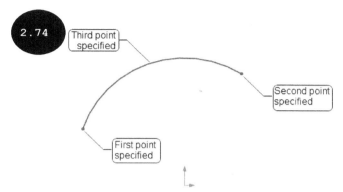

2.74

Third point specified

Second point specified

First point specified

Procedure to Draw Arc by Specifying 3 Points

1. Invoke the **Arc** flyout and click on the **3 Point Arc** tool, the **Arc PropertyManager** appears.
2. Move the cursor in the drawing area and click to specify the start point or first point of the arc.
3. Move the cursor to the location where you want to specify the endpoint or second point of the arc. Next, click to specify the endpoint of the arc in the drawing area.
4. Move the cursor to a distance and then click to specify a point on the arc length when the value of arc angle and radius appears above the cursor closer to the required one, see Figure 2.75.

Tangent Arc

The **Tangent Arc** tool of the **Arc** flyout is used to draw an arc tangent to an existing entity, see Figure 2.76. To draw an tangent arc by using the **Tangent Arc** tool, at least a line, arc, or spline entity need to be exist in the drawing area.

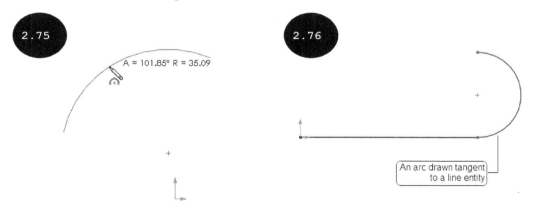

2.75

A = 101.85° R = 35.09

2.76

An arc drawn tangent to a line entity

Procedure to Draw Tangent Arc

1. Invoke the **Arc** flyout and then click on the **Tangent Arc** tool.
2. Move the cursor towards the existing entity in the drawing area to which you want to draw an tangent arc and then click to specify the start point of the tangle arc when the cursor snaps to the point of the existing entity.
3. Move the cursor to a distance away from the specified point, the preview of tangent arc appears and its one endpoint is attached with the cursor.

Note: The tangency of the arc will depends upon how you move the cursor from the specified point in the drawing area. To change the tangent direction, you need to move the cursor back to the start of the arc specified and then you can move towards the direction you want to draw an tangent arc. Figure 2.77 shows the possible movement direction of cursor and the respective arc creation in that particular direction.

---

4. Click to specify the endpoint of the tangent arc in the drawing area when the value of arc angle and radius appears above the cursor closer to the required one, see Figure 2.78. After specifying the endpoint of the tangent arc, tangent arc is drawn and still the **Tangent Arc** tool is activated. Also, a preview of the another tangent arc appears in the drawing area. It indicated that you can continue drawing the tangent arcs one after another by click the left mouse button.

5. Once you are done, press the **ESC** key to exit from the **Tangent Arc** tool.

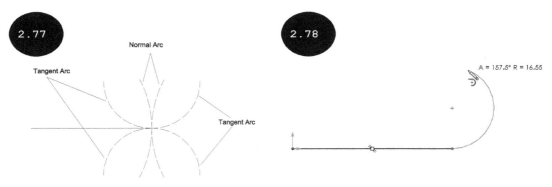

Drawing Polygons

SOLIDWORKS allow you to draw polygons of sides in the range between 3 to 40. A polygon is multisided geometry have equal length of all the sides as well as equal angle between the sides, see Figure 2.79.

To draw polygon, click on the **Polygon** tool available in the **Sketch CommandManager**, the **Polygon PropertyManager** appears, see Figure 2.80. The options available in the different rollouts of the **Polygon PropertyManager** are as follows.

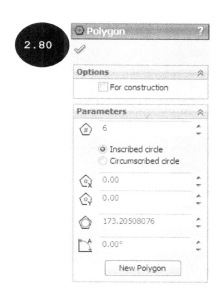

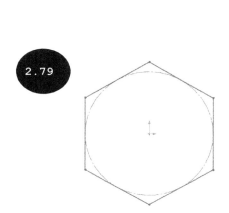

Options

By default, the **For construction** check box available in the **Options** rollout is cleared. As a result, the polygon drawn have continuous or solid sketch entities, see Figure 2.81. If you select the **For construction** check box, the polygon drawn have construction sketch entities, see Figure 2.82.

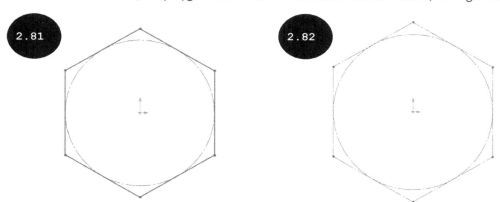

Parameters

The options available in the **Parameters** rollout of the PropertyManager is used to specify the parameters of the polygon to be drawn and are as follows.

Number of Sides

The **Number of Sides** field of the **Parameters** rollout of the PropertyManager is used to specify the number of sides of the polygon to be drawn. You can specify number of side in the range between 3 to 40.

Inscribed circle

The **Inscribed circle** radio button of the **Parameters** rollout is used to draw the polygon by drawing a imaginary construction circle inside the polygon. In this case, the mid point of all the sides of the polygon toughs the imaginary construction circle drawn inside, see Figure 2.83.

Circumscribed circle

The **Circumscribed circle** radio button of the **Parameters** rollout is used to draw the polygon by drawing an imaginary construction circle outside the polygon. In this case, all the vertices of the polygon toughs the imaginary construction circle drawn outside, see Figure 2.84.

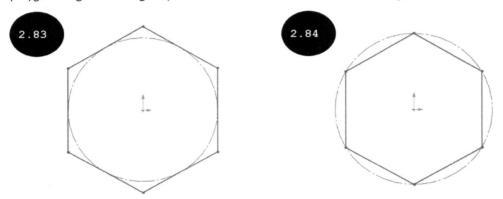

Center X Coordinate

The **Center X Coordinate** filed of the **Parameters** rollout is used to display or control the X coordinate value of the center of the polygon.

Center Y Coordinate

The **Center Y Coordinate** filed of the **Parameters** rollout is used to display or control the Y coordinate value of the center of the polygon.

Center Diameter

The **Center Diameter** filed of the **Parameters** rollout is used to display or control the diameter of the inscribe or circumscribed imaginary construction circle of the polygon.

Angle

The **Angle** filed of the **Parameters** rollout is used to display or control the angle value of the sides of the polygon with respect to the X axis of the plane.

New Polygon

The **New Polygon** button of the **Parameters** rollout is used to start the process of drawing new polygon.

Procedure to Draw Polygon

1. Click on the **Polygon** tool available in the **Sketch CommandManager**.
2. Enter the number of sides for the polygon to be drawn in the **Number of Sides** field.
3. Select the **Inscribed circle** or **Circumscribed circle** radio button, as required.
4. Move the cursor in the drawing area and click to specify the center point of the polygon. You can also enter X and Y coordinate values in their respective fields of the PropertyManager.
5. Move the cursor to a distance, the preview of the polygon appears in the drawing area with a imaginary construction circle.
6. Click to specify a point in the drawing area to define the diameter of the imaginary circle, the polygon is drawn. Alternatively, enter the diameter of the imaginary circle in the **Center Diameter** filed of the PropertyManager.

Tip: As soon as you define the diameter of the imaginary circle by clicking point, the polygon will be drawn and selected in the drawing area. Also, notice that still the **Polygon PropertyManager** is invoked and displays the current parameter of the polygon drawn. You can further control the parameters of the polygon drawn by using the fields available in the **Parameters** rollout of the PropertyManager.

---

7. Once your are done, click on the **OK** button from the PropertyManager.

Drawing Slots

In SOLIDWORKS, you can draw straight and arc slots by different methods. The tools for drawing straight and arc slots are group together into the **Slot** flyout. To invoke the **Slot** flyout, click on the down arrow available next to the activated slot tool in the **Sketch CommandManager**, see Figure 2.85. The different tools used for drawing slots are as follows.

Straight Slot

The **Straight Slot** tool of the **Slot** flyout is used to draw a straight slot by defining start and end center points of the slot. To draw straight slot, click on the **Straight Slot** tool available in the **Slot** flyout, the **Slot PropertyManager** appears at the left of the drawing area, see Figure 2.86. The options available in the rollouts of the **Slot PropertyManager** are as follows.

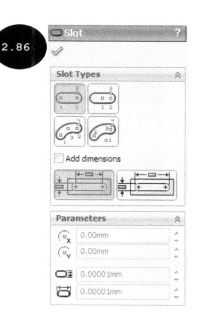

Slot Types

The **Slot Type** rollout allows you to switch to other methods of drawing slot ever after invoking the **Slot PropertyManager**. By default, depending upon the tool chosen from the **Slot** flyout to invoke the PropertyManager, the respective button is activated in this rollout.

By default, the **Add dimensions** check box is cleared in this rollout. As a result, the dimension values is not applied to the straight slot drawn, see Figure 2.87. If this check box is selected, the dimension value to the straight slot drawn is applied automatically and appears in the drawing area, see Figures 2.88.

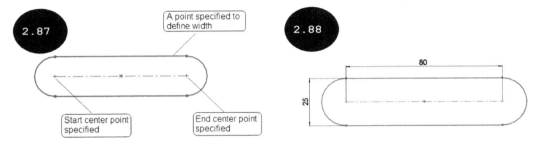

The **Center to Center** button of the **Slot Type** rollout is activated by default. As a result, the straight slot drawn measures the length from center to center and displays in the **Slot Length** field of the **Parameters** rollout of the PropertyManager. On choosing the **Overall Length** button, the straight slot drawn measures the overall length of the slot.

Parameters
The options available in the **Parameters** rollout of the PropertyManager are used to display or control the parameters of the slot drawn. Note that the options available in this rollout activates once the slot has been drawn and selected in the drawing area. You can modify the X and Y coordinate values of the center point of the slot, width of the slot, and length of the slot by using their respective field available in this rollout.

Procedure to Draw Straight Slot by Specifying Start and End Points
1.   Invoke the **Slot** flyout by clicking on the down arrow available next to an active slot tool.
2.   Click on the **Straight Slot** tool in the **Slot** flyout, the **Slot PropertyManager** appears.
3.   Move the cursor in the drawing area and click to specify the start center point of the slot, see Figure 2.87.
4.   Move the cursor to a distance from the specified point, a straight rubber band construction line appears whose one end is attached with the cursor.
5.   Click the left mouse button in the drawing area to define the end center point of the slot when the length between the center to center of the slot, displays above the cursor closer to the required one.
6.   Move the cursor to a distance to define the width of the slot, the preview of the slot appears.
7.   Click to specify a point in the drawing to define the width of the slot, the slot is drawn, see Figure 2.87.

Center Point Straight Slot

The **Center Point Straight Slot** tool of the **Slot** flyout is used to draw a straight slot by defining its center point and end point, see Figure 2.89.

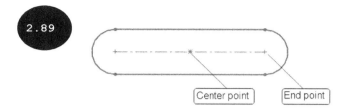

Procedure to Draw Straight Slot by Specifying Centerpoint

1. Invoke the **Slot** flyout and then click on the **Center Point Straight Slot** tool.
2. Move the cursor in the drawing area and then click to specify the center point of the slot, see Figure 2.90.
3. Move the cursor to a distance from the specified point, a straight construction line appears whose one end is attached with the cursor.
4. Click the left mouse button in the drawing area to define the end point of the slot.
5. Move the cursor to a distance to define the width of the slot, the preview of the slot appears.
6. Click to specify a point in the drawing to define the width of the slot, see Figure 2.90.

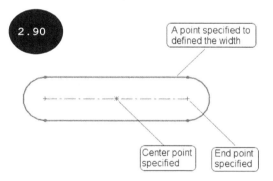

3 Point Arc Slot

The **3 Point Arc Slot** tool is used to draw an arc slot by defining three points, see Figure 2.91.

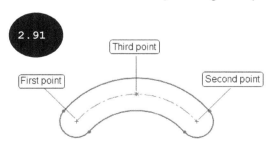

Procedure to Draw Arc Slot by Specifying 3 Points

1. Invoke the **Slot** flyout and then click on the **3 Point Arc Slot** tool, the **Slot PropertyManager** appears.
2. Move the cursor in the drawing area and click to specify the first point of the arc slot, see Figure 2.92.
3. Move the cursor to a distance from the specified point, a construction arc appears whose one end is attached with the cursor.
4. Click the left mouse button to define the second point of the arc slot, see Figure 2.92.
5. Move the cursor to a distance and specify the third point in the arc length, see Figure 2.92.
6. Move the cursor to a distance to define the width of the slot.
7. Click to specify a point in the drawing to define the width of the slot, see Figure 2.92.

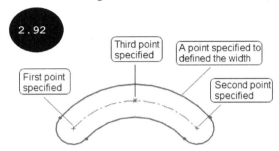

Centerpoint Arc Slot

The **Centerpoint Arc Slot** tool of the **Slot** flyout is used to draw an arc slot by defining center, start, and end points, see Figure 2.93.

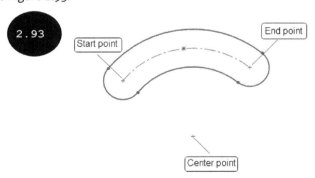

Procedure to Draw Arc Slot by Specifying Centerpoint

1. Invoke the **Slot** flyout and then click on the **Centerpoint Arc Slot** tool, the **Slot PropertyManager** appears.
2. Move the cursor in the drawing area and click to specify the center point of the arc slot, see Figure 2.94.
3. Move the cursor to a distance from the specified point, a rubber band construction circle appears.
4. Click the left mouse button in the drawing area to specify the start point of the arc slot, see Figure 2.94.

5. Move the cursor, clockwise or counterclockwise direction, a construction arc appears. Next, specify the endpoint of the arc slot, see Figure 2.94
6. Move the cursor to a distance to define the width of the slot, the preview of the slot appears.
7. Click to specify a point in the drawing to define the width of the arc slot, see Figure 2.94.

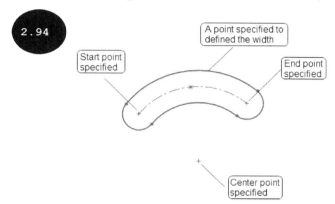

Drawing Ellipses

A ellipse is drawn by defining its major axis and minor axis, see Figure 2.95. You can draw ellipses by using the **Ellipse** tool available in the **Sketch CommandManager**.

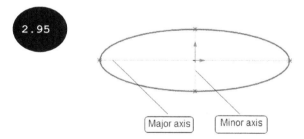

Procedure to Draw Ellipse

1. Click on the **Ellipse** tool available in the **Sketch CommandManager**, the **Ellipse** tool is activated.
2. Move the cursor in the drawing area and click to specify the center point of the ellipse, see Figure 2.96.
3. Move the cursor to a distance from the specified center point, a construction circle appears. Also, the **Ellipse PropertyManager** appears on the left of the drawing area. However, the options available in this PropertyManager are not activated at this moment. These options become activated once the ellipse has been drawn.
4. Click the left mouse button in the drawing area to define the major axis of the ellipse, see Figure 2.96.
5. Move the cursor, the preview of the ellipse appears and then click to specify the minor axis of the ellipse, the ellipse is drawn and selected in the drawing area, see Figure 2.96.
6. Press the **ESC** tool to exit from the tool.

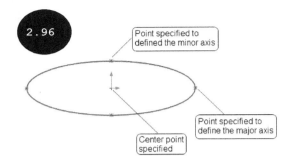

Drawing Elliptical Arcs

You can draw elliptical arcs by using the **Partial Ellipse** tool available in the **Ellipse** flyout. Figure 2.97 shows the **Ellipse** flyout invoked by clicking on the down arrow available on the right of the **Ellipse** tool in the **Sketch CommandManager**. Figure 2.98 shows an elliptical arc.

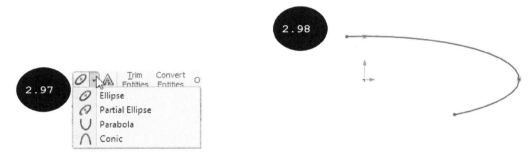

Procedure to Draw Elliptical Arc

1. Click on the down arrow available next to the **Ellipse** tool in the **Sketch CommandManager**, the **Ellipse** flyout appears.
2. Click on the **Partial Ellipse** tool in the flyout, the **Partial Ellipse** tool become activated.
3. Move the cursor in the drawing area and click to specify the center point of the elliptical arc.
4. Move the cursor to a distance in the drawing area, a construction circle appears. Also, the **Ellipse PropertyManager** appears at the left of the drawing area.
5. Click the left mouse button in the drawing area to define the major axis of the elliptical arc and then move the cursor in the drawing area, the preview of the imaginary ellipse appears, see Figure 2.99.
6. Click to specify the start point of the elliptical arc, see Figure 2.99.
7. Move the cursor, the preview of the elliptical arc appears in the drawing area depending upon the movement of the cursor, see Figure 2.100.
8. Click to specify the end point of the elliptical arc, the elliptical arc is created, see Figure 101.
9. Press the ESC key to exit the tool.

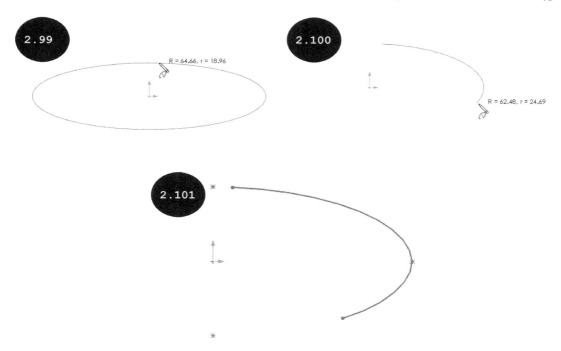

Drawing Parabola

Parabola is a symmetrical plane curve which is formed by the intersection of a cone with a plane parallel to its side. You can draw a parabola by defining its focus point, apex point, and then two points on the parabolic curve, see Figure 2.102. In SOLIDWORKS, you can draw parabola by using the **Parabola** tool which is available in the **Ellipse** flyout, see Figure 2.97.

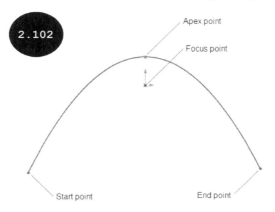

Procedure to Draw Parabola

1. Click on the down arrow available next to the **Ellipse** tool in the **Sketch CommandManager**, the **Ellipse** flyout appears.
2. Click on the **Parabola** tool of the flyout, the **Parabola** tool is activated and cursor is changed to parabola cursor ⋎.
3. Move the cursor in the drawing area and click to specify the focus point of the parabola, see Figure 2.103.
4. Move the cursor to a distance, a construction parabola appears and the cursor is attached at its apex, see Figure 2.103. Also, the **Parabola PropertyManager** appears.
5. Click the left mouse button in the drawing area to define the apex of the parabola, the preview of the imaginary parabola appears in the drawing area.
6. Move the cursor over the imaginary parabola and then click to specify the start point for the parabola, see Figure 2.104.
7. Move the cursor in clockwise or counterclockwise direction, the preview of the parabolic arc appears in the drawing area depending upon the movement of cursor.
8. Click to specify the end point of the parabola, the parabola is drawn, see Figure 2.104.
9. Press the **ESC** key to exit the tool.

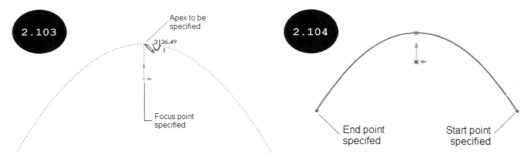

Drawing Conic Curve

SOLIDWORKS allows you to draw conic curves by specifying its start point, end point, and rho value, see Figure 2.105. You can draw conic curve by using the **Conic** tool available in the **Ellipse** flyout.

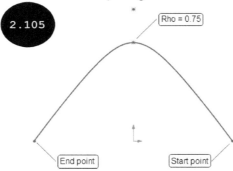

Procedure to Draw Conic Curves

1. Invoke the **Ellipse** flyout and then click on the **Conic** tool, the **Conic** tool is activated. Also, the cursor is changed to conic cursor.
2. Move the cursor in the drawing area and click to specify the start point of the curve, see Figure 2.106.
3. Move the cursor to a distance in the drawing area, a construction line appears. Also, the **Conic PropertyManager** appears at the left of the drawing area.
4. Click the left mouse button in the drawing area to define the end point of a conic curve, see Figure 2.106.
5. Move the cursor, the preview of a conic curve appears in the drawing area with cursor is attached with its top vertex, see Figure 2.106. Next, click to specify the top vertex of the conic curve.
6. Move the cursor up or down with respect to the top vertex specified, the preview of the conic curve appears in the drawing area. Also, the current rho value of the curve appears above the cursor, see Figure 2.107.

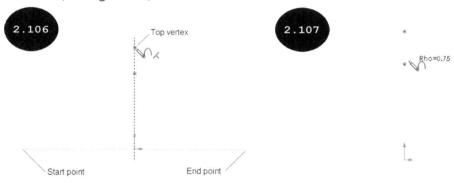

7. Move the cursor at the location where the rho value displays above the cursor, closer to the required one and then click to specify the apex of the conic curve, see Figure 2.108.

Note: The rho value of the conic curve defines the type of curve, if rho value is less than 0.5 then the conic is an ellipse, if the rho value is equal to 0.5 then the conic is an parabola, and if the rho value is grater than 0.5 then the conic is an hyperbola.

8. Press the **ESC** key to exit the tool.

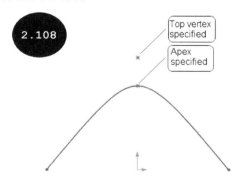

Drawing Splines

Spline is define as a curve having high degree of smoothness and used to create free form features. You can draw spline by specifying two or more than two points in the drawing area. In SOLIDWORKS, you can also draw a spline by defining mathematical equation. The tools used for drawing spline by different methods are discussed.

Spline

The **Spline** tool is used to create a spline by defining two or more than two points in the drawing area, see Figure 2.109.

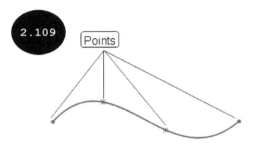

Procedure to Draw Spline by Specifying Points

1. Click on the **Spline** tool available in the **Sketch CommandManager**, the cursor changes to spline cursor and displays as pencil with spline image at its bottom ✎.
2. Move the cursor in the drawing area and click to specify the first point of the spline.
3. Move the cursor to a distance, a reference curve appears in the drawing area whose one end is fix at the specified point and other is attached with the cursor. Also, the **spline PropertyManager** appears at the left of the drawing area.
4. Click to specify the second point and then move the cursor to a distance from the specified point, the preview of the spline curve passing through the two specified points appears in the drawing area, see Figure 2.110.
5. Click to specify the third point of the spline, the preview of the curve passing through three points specified appears in the drawing area. Similarly, you can keep on specifying the points for drawing the spline.
6. Once all the point has been specified for drawing the spline, press the ESC key to exit from the creation of spline and the **Spline** tool. You can also right-click and select the **Select** option from the shortcut menu to exit from the tool. Figure 2.111 shows a spline drawn by defining five points in the drawing area.

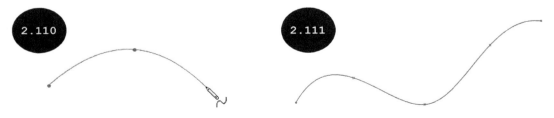

Equation Driven Curve

The **Equation Driven Curve** tool is used to create a spline driven by mathematical equations. To draw equation driven spline curve, click on the down arrow available next to the **Spline** tool in the **Sketch CommandManager**, a **Spline** flyout appears, see Figure 2.112. Next, click on the **Equation Driven Curve** tool in the **Spline** flyout, the **Equation Driven Curve PropertyManager** appears in the left side of the drawing area, see Figure 2.113. The options available in this PropertyManager are as follows.

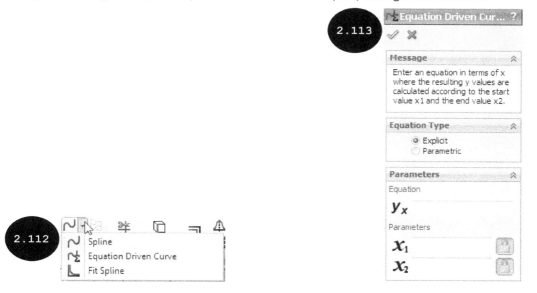

Message

The **Message** rollout of the PropertyManager is used to guide you by displaying appropriation informations about the required action to be taken next.

Equation Type

The **Equation Type** rollout of the PropertyManager is used to select the type of equation to be used for drawing curve. The options available in this rollout are as follows.

Explicit

The **Explicit** radio button is selected by default and is used to define the equation for calculating the value of y as the function of x. The resulting y values is calculated as per the start and end values of the function x and the equation.

Parametric

The **Parametric** radio button is used to define the two equations for calculating the values of x and y as the function of t. The resulting x and y values is calculated as per the start and end values of the function t and their respective equation.

Parameters

The **Parameters** rollout of the PropertyManager is used to specify the driving equation and the start and end values of their function. The options available in this rollout depends upon the type of equation selected in the **Parametric** rollout of the PropertyManager. Figures 2.114 and 2.115 shows the **Parameters** rollout when the respective **Explicit** and **Parametric** radio buttons are selected in the **Equation Type** rollout.

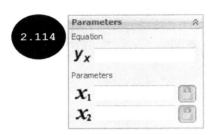

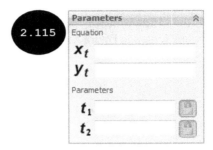

When the **Explicit** radio button is selected, you can define the equation for Y as the function of x in the **Yx** field of the **Equation** area in the **Parameters** rollout. Also, in the **X1** and **X2** fields of the **Parameters** rollout, you can define the start and end values for the function x.

When the **Parametric** radio button is selected, you can define the equations for X and Y as the function of t in the **Xt** and **Yt** fields of the **Parameters** rollout. Also, in the **t1** and **t2** fields of the **Parameters** rollout, you can define the start and end values for the function t. The procedures to draw equation driven spline using the explicit and parameters equation types are as follows.

Procedure to Draw Spline Using the Explicit Equation Type

1. Invoke the **Equation Driven Curve PropertyManager** by clicking on the **Equation Driven Curve** tool in the **Spline** flyout.
2. Make sure that the **Explicit** radio button is selected in the **Equation Type** rollout of the **Equation Driven Curve PropertyManager**.
3. Enter the equation for Y as the function of x in the **Yx** field of the **Parameters** rollout. For example, enter the equation $2* \sin(x)^{\wedge}12$ in the **Yx** field.
4. Enter the start and end value of the function x in the **x1** and **x2** fields of the **Parameters** rollout. For example, enter **0** in the **x1** field and **38** in the **x2** field as the start and end values of the function x.
5. Press **ENTER**, the preview of the equation driven cover appears in the drawing area. Next, click on **OK** to accept the creation of curve and to exit from the PropertyManager. Figure 2.116 shows a explicit equation type spline drawn.

Procedure to Draw Spline Using the Parametric Equation Type

1. Invoke the **Equation Driven Curve PropertyManager** by clicking on the **Equation Driven Curve** tool of the **Spline** flyout.
2. Select the **Parametric** radio button in the **Equation Type** rollout.
3. Enter the equations for X and Y as the function of t in the **Xt** and **Yt** fields of the **Parameters** rollout, respectively. For example, enter **(t + sin(t)^2)** in the **Xt** field and **2* sin(t)** in the **Yt** field.
4. Enter the start and end values of the function t in the **t1** and **t2** fields of the **Parameters** area. For example, enter **0** in the **t1** field and **38** in the **t2** field as the start and end values of the function t.
5. Press **ENTER**, the preview of the equation derived spline appears in the drawing area. Next, click on **OK** to accept the creation of spline and to exit from the PropertyManager. Figure 2.117 shows a parametric equation type cover drawn.

2.117

Fit Spline

By using the **Fit Spline** tool, you can convert multiple existing sketch entities into a single spline curve. To convert the existing sketch entities into a spline, invoke the **Spline** flyout and then click on the **Fit Spline** tool, the **Fit Spline PropertyManager** appears, see Figure 2.118. The options available in the **Fit Spline PropertyManager** are as follows.

Parameters

The options available in the **Parameters** rollout of the PropertyManager is used to specify different parameters for converting existing sketch entities into a single spline curve and are as follows.

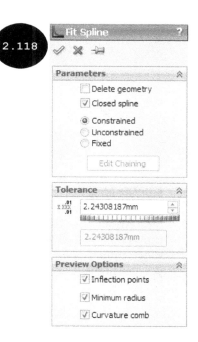

2.118

Delete geometry

On selecting the **Delete geometry** check box, the original entities selected for converting into a spline curve is deleted from the drawing area and the resultant curve is created.

Constrained
By default, the **Constrained** radio button is selected. As a result, the relations or parametrically links is applied between the original geometry and the curve created. Therefore, any change made in the original geometry will also be reflected on the curve created and vice-versa.

Unconstrained
On selecting the **Unconstrained** radio button, the spline curve created and the original geometry have no relation with each other. Therefore, any change made in the original geometry will not be reflected on the curve created and vice-versa.

Fixed
On selecting the **Fixed** radio button, the fix relation applies to the spline curve created. As a result, you cannot make any change related to changing position, dimensions, and so on to the curve created. However, the original geometry become free to change that is unconstrained with curve created.

Closed spline
By default, the **Closed spline** check box is selected. As a result, the resultant curve created by selecting open entities become closed. Figure 2.119 shows the preview of the resultant curve when the **Closed spline** check box is cleared. Figure 2.120 shows the preview of the resultant curve when the **Closed spline** check is selected.

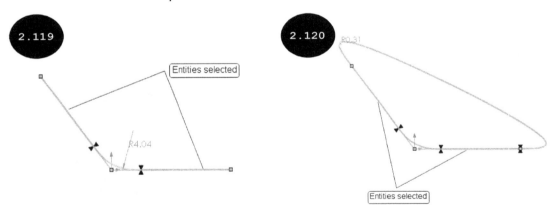

Edit Chaining
The **Edit Chaining** button is used to alter the chain of contiguous splines creation. Note that this button is activated only on selecting the contiguous entities for creating fit spline curve. Figure 2.121 shows non contiguous entities (entities that are not in contact with each other). Figure 2.122 shows the preview of the default resultant contiguous spline appears and Figure 2.123 shows the preview of the resultant contiguous spline appears on clicking the **Edit Chaining** button.

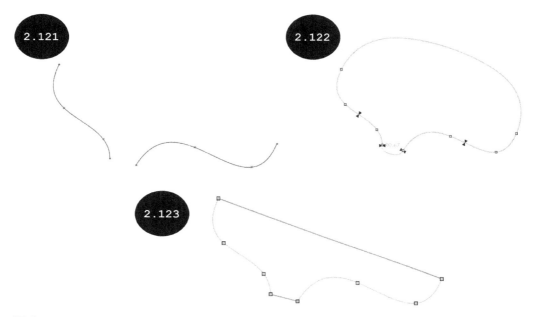

Tolerance

The **Tolerance** rollout of the PropertyManager is used to specify the maximum deviation allowed from the original sketch geometry. You can enter the tolerance value in the **Tolerance** field of this rollout. You can also drag the thumbwheel available at the bottom of **Tolerance** filed to set the tolerance value.

Preview Options

The options available in this rollout are used to control the preview of the resultant fit spline curve and are as follows.

Inflection points

By default, the **Inflection points** check box is selected. As a result, the preview of spline display along with all the points where the concavity of the fit spline changes. You can click on the inflection point appears in the drawing area and check for alternative solution.

Minimum radius

By default, the **Minimum radius** check box is selected. As a result, the preview of the spline displays along with the minimum radius measurement on the spline.

Curvature comb

By default, the **Curvature comb** check box is selected. As a result, the visual enhancement of the slope and curvature appears in the drawing area.

Procedure to Draw Fit Spline

1. Invoke the **Fit Spline PropertyManager** by clicking on the **Fit Spline** tool of the **Spline** flyout.
2. Select the entities to be converted into a single spline curve, see Figure 2.124. As soon as you select the entities, the preview of the fit spline curve appears in the drawing area.
3. Specify the parameters to create the fit spline curve, as required, by using the options available in the **Fit Spline PropertyManager**.
4. After specifying the parameters, click on the **OK** button in the PropertyManager, the fit spline curve is created from the selected entities. Figure 2.125 shows a open fit spline curve created and its original sketched entities has been deleted.

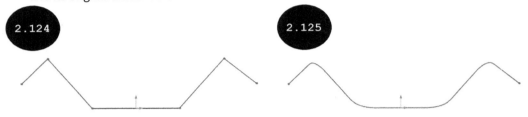

Editing Spline

Editing spline is very important to a required curve having high degree of smoothness and curvature. You can edit the spline by using its control points and spline handle. The control points are the points specified in the drawing area for drawing spline. To modify or edit the spline by using the control points, click on the control point of the spline to be modified, the selected control point is highlighted and appears with spline handles in the drawing area, see Figure 2.126. Also, the **Point PropertyManager** appears at the left of the drawing area. You can drag the selected control point to change its location in the drawing area. Alternatively, enter the new X and Y coordinate values of the selected point in their respective fields of the **Parameters** rollout of the **Point PropertyManager**.

You can also used the spline handle to edit the curvature of the spline. Figure 2.127 shows the spline handle components and are as follows.

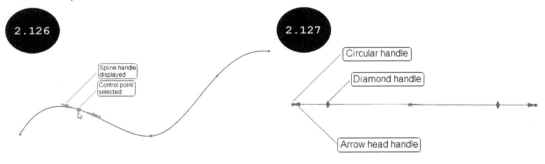

Circular handle

The circular handle of a spline handle is used to control the tangency, curvature, and angle of inclination of the spline, asymmetrically, about the control point by dragging it. Note that if you drag the circular handle by pressing the ALT key, the tangency, curvature, and angle of inclination of the spline is controlled, symmetrically, about the control point.

Arrow head handle

The arrow head handle of a spline handle is used to control the tangency of the spline, asymmetrically, about the control point by dragging it. Note that if you drag the arrow head handle by pressing the ALT key, the tangency is controlled, symmetrically, about the control point.

Diamond handle

The diamond handle of a spline handle is used to control the tangent vector or tangency angle of the spline about the control point by dragging it.

Tutorial 1

Draw the sketch shown in Figure 2.128. Dimensions and model shown in the figure are for your reference. You will draw all the entities of the sketch by using the **Line** tool. Also, as all the dimensions are multiple of 5 mm, you can set snap setting such that cursor snap to an incremental of 5 mm.

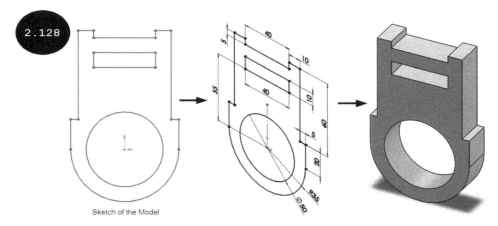

Sketch of the Model

Section 1: Starting SOLIDWORKS

1. Start SOLIDWORKS by clicking on the **SOLIDWORKS icon** on your desktop.

Section 2: Invoking Sketching Environment

1. Click on the **New** tool in the **Standard** toolbar, the **New SOLIDWORKS Document** dialog box appears.

2. Make sure that the **Part** button is activated and then click on the **OK** button, the Part modeling environment is invoked.

3. Click on the **Sketch** tab in the **Command Manager**, the **Sketch CommandManager** appears.

4. Click on the **Sketch** button of the **Sketch CommandManager**, three default planes mutually perpendicular to each other appears in the graphic area.

6. Move the cursor over the Front plane and click to select it as the sketching plane, the Sketching environment is invoked. Also, the Front plane orientated normal to the viewing direction and the confirmation corner appears at the upper right corner of the drawing area.

   As all the sketch entities are multiple of 5 mm, set snap settings such that cursor snap to the increment of 5 mm only. Also, specify metric unit system for measurement.

Section 3: Specifying Snap and Unit Settings

1. Click on the **Options** tool in the **Standard** toolbar, the **System Options - General** dialog box appears.

2. In the **System Options - General** dialog box, click on the **Document Properties** tab, the name of the dialog box changes to **Document Properties - Drafting Standard**.

3. Select the **Units** option available in the left panel of the dialog box, the options related to specifying the unit system displays on the right side panel of the dialog box.

4. Select the **MMGS (millimeter, gram, second)** radio button from the **Unit system** area of the dialog box, if not selected by default. Once the unit system is specified do not exit from the dialog box.

   Now, you need to specify the grid and snap settings such that the cursor snaps the increment of 5 mm.

5. Select the **Grid/Snap** option available in the left side panel of the dialog box, the options related to the grid and snap settings displays on the right side panel of the dialog box. Also, the name of the dialog box changes to **Document Properties - Grid/Snap** dialog box.

6. Enter **20** in the **Major grid spacing, 4** in the **Minor -lines per major**, and **1** in the **Snap points per minor** fields of the **Grid** area in the dialog box.

7. Select the **Display grid** check box of the **Grid** area in the dialog box to turn on the display of grids in the drawing area as per the grid settings specified in the above step.

8. Click on the **Go To System Snaps** button of the **Document Properties - Grid/Snap** dialog box, the name of the dialog box changes to **System Options - Relations/Snaps**.

9. Select the **Grid** check box in the **Sketch snaps** area of the **System Options - Relations/Snaps** dialog box, if not selected by default to turn on the snap mode.

10. Click on the **OK** button of the dialog box, the grid and snap settings has been specified and the dialog box is closed. Also, the drawing area displays similar to one shown in Figure 2.129.

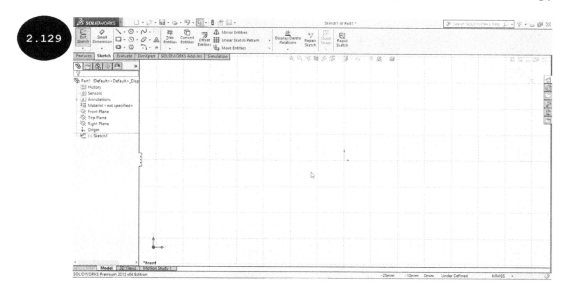

2.129

Section 4: Drawing Sketch

Once the units, grid, and snap settings has been specified, you can start drawing the sketch.

1. Click on the **Circle** tool in the **Sketch CommandManager**, the **Circle** tool activates and the **Circle PropertyManager** appears in left side of the drawing area. Also, the appearance of cursor changes to circle cursor ⊘ .

2. Move the cursor towards the origin and click to specify the center point of the circle when cursor snaps to origin.

3. Move the cursor horizontal towards the left and click to specify a point when the radius of the circle displays above the cursor is 25, see Figure 2.130, a circle of diameter 50 is drawn. Next, press the **ESC** key to exit from the **Circle** tool.

4. Invoke the **Arc** flyout by clicking on the down arrow available next to the active **Arc** tool in the **Sketch CommandManager**, refer to Figure 2.131.

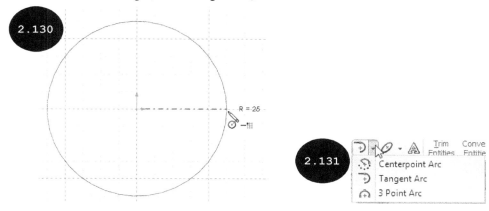

2.130

R = 25

2.131

Centerpoint Arc

Tangent Arc

3 Point Arc

5. Click on the **Centerpoint Arc** tool in the **Arc** flyout, the **Centerpoint Arc** tool activates and the **Arc PropertyManager** appears in left side of the drawing area. Also, the appearance of cursor changes to arc cursor .

6. Move the cursor towards the origin and click to specify the center point of the arc when cursor snaps to origin.

7. Move the cursor horizontal towards the right, the preview of the imaginary circle appears in the drawing area, see Figure 2.132. Next, click to specify the start point of the arc when the radius of the imaginary circle displays above the cursor is 35, see Figure 2.132.

8. Move the cursor in clockwise direction, the preview of a arc is displays in the drawing area. Next, click to specify the end point of the arc when angle value displays above the curse is 180 degree, see Figure 2.133, an arc is drawn. Press the **ESC** key to exit from the tool.

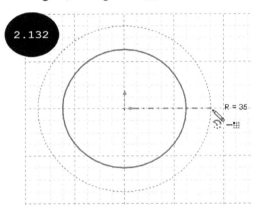

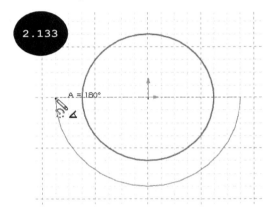

9. Click on the **Line** tool in the **Sketch CommandManager**, the **Line** tool activates and the **Insert Line PropertyManager** appears in left side of the drawing area. Also, the appearance of cursor changes to line cursor .

10. Move the cursor towards the start point of the arc drawn and click to specify the start point of the line when cursor snaps to start point of the arc.

11. Move the cursor vertical upwards and click to specify the end point of the line when the length of the line displays above the cursor is 20, see Figure 2.134, a line of length 20 mm is drawn.

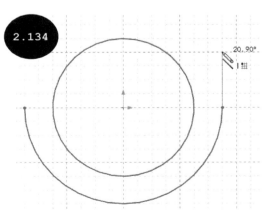

12. Move the cursor horizontal towards the left and click to specify the end point of the line when the length of the line displays above the cursor is 5.

13. Move the cursor vertical upwards and click to specify the end point when the length of the line displays above the cursor is 60.

14. Move the cursor horizontal towards the left and click to specify the end point of the line when the length of the line displays above the cursor is 10, a line of length 10 mm is drawn.

15. Move the cursor vertical downwards and click to specify the end point of the line when the length of the line displays above the cursor is 5, a line of length 5 mm is drawn.

16. Move the cursor horizontal towards the left and click to specify the end point of the line when the length of the line displays above the cursor is 40, a line of length 40 mm is drawn.

17. Move the cursor vertical upwards and click to specify the end point of the line when the length of the line displays above the cursor is 5, a line of length 5 mm is drawn.

18. Move the cursor horizontal towards the left and click to specify the end point of the line when the length of the line displays above the cursor is 10, a line of length 10 mm is drawn.

19. Move the cursor vertical downwards and click to specify the end point of the line when the length of the line displays above the cursor is 60, a line of length 60 mm is drawn.

20. Move the cursor horizontal towards the left and click to specify the end point of the line when the length of the line displays above the cursor is 5, a line of length 5 mm is drawn.

21. Move the cursor vertical downwards and click to specify the end point of the line when the cursor snaps to the end point of the arc drawn earlier. The sketch drawn displays similar to one shown in Figure 2.135. Next, press the **ESC** key to exit from the **Line** tool.

22. Invoke the **Rectangle** flyout, see Figure 2.136 and then click on the **Corner Rectangle** tool, the **Line** tool activates and the **Rectangle PropertyManager** appears in left side of the drawing area. Also, the appearance of cursor changes to rectangle cursor ⬚ .

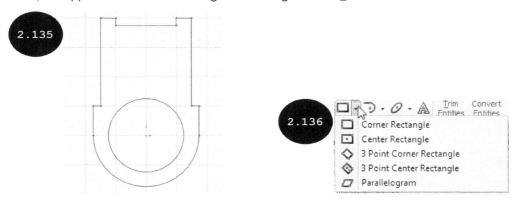

23. Move the cursor in the drawing area and click to specify the first corner point of the rectangle when x, y, and z coordinates displays in the **Status Bar** are 20, 65, and 0, respectively.

24. Move the cursor in the drawing area and click to specify the second corner point of the rectangle when x and y coordinates displays above the cursor are 40, and 10, respectively, see Figure 2.137. Next, press the **ESC** key to exit from the tool. Figure 2.138 shows the final sketch of Tutorial 1.

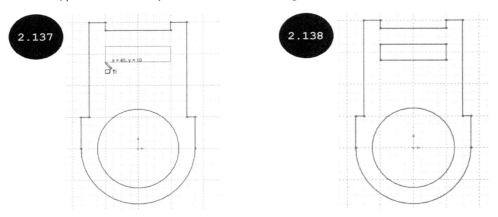

Tutorial 2

Draw the sketch shown in Figure 2.139. Dimensions and model shown in the figure are for your reference. As all the dimensions are multiple of 5, you can set snap setting such that cursor snap to an incremental of 5 mm.

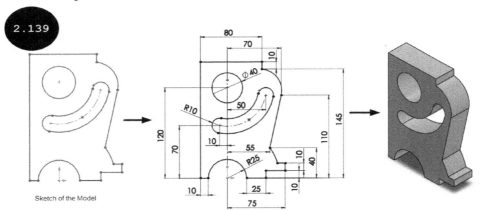

Sketch of the Model

Section 1: Starting SOLIDWORKS

1. Start SOLIDWORKS by clicking on the **SOLIDWORKS** icon on your desktop, if not started already.

Section 2: Invoking Sketching Environment

In SOLIDWORKS, the Sketching environment invokes within the Part modeling environment therefore first you first need to invoke the Part modeling environment.

1. Click on the **New** tool in the **Standard** toolbar, the **New SOLIDWORKS Document** dialog box appears.

2. Click on the **Part** button, if not activated and then click on the **OK** button, the Part modeling environment is invoked.

3. Click on the **Sketch** tab in the **Command Manager**, if   not   activated, the **Sketch CommandManager** appears.

4. Click on the **Sketch** button of the **Sketch CommandManager**, three default planes mutually perpendicular to each other appears in the graphic area.

5. Move the cursor over the Front plane and click to select it as the sketching plane when the boundary of the plane highlighted, the Sketching environment is invoked. Also, the Front plane orientated normal to the viewing direction and the confirmation corner appears at the upper right corner of the drawing area.

   As all the sketch entities are multiple of 5 mm, set snap settings such that cursor snap to the increment of 5 mm only. Also, specify metric unit system for measurement.

Section 3: Specifying Snap and Unit Settings

1. Click on the **Options** tool in the **Standard** toolbar, the **System Options** - General dialog box appears.

2. In the **System Options** - General dialog box, click on the **Document Properties** tab, the name of the dialog box changes to **Document Properties** - Drafting Standard.

3. Select the **Units** option available in the left panel of the dialog box, the options related to specifying the unit system displays on the right side panel of the dialog box.

4. Select the **MMGS (millimeter, gram, second)** radio button from the **Unit system** area of the dialog box, if not selected by default. Once the unit system is specified do not exit from the dialog box.

   Now, you need to specify the grid and snap settings.

5. Select the **Grid/Snap** option available in the left side panel of the dialog box, the options related to the grid and snap settings displays on the right side panel of the dialog box. Also, the name of the dialog box changes to **Document Properties** - Grid/Snap dialog box.

6. Enter **20** in the **Major grid spacing**, **4** in the **Minor -lines per major**, and **1** in the **Snap points per minor** fields of the **Grid** area in the dialog box.

7. Select the **Display grid** check box of the **Grid** area in the dialog box to turn on the display of grids in the drawing area as per the grid settings specified in the above step.

8. Click on the **Go To System Snaps** button of the **Document Properties** - Grid/Snap dialog box, the name of the dialog box changes to **System Options** - Relations/Snaps.

9. Select the **Grid** check box in the **Sketch snaps** area of the **System Options - Relations/Snaps** dialog box, if not selected by default to turn on the snap mode.

10. Click on the **OK** button of the dialog box, the grid and snap settings has been specified and the dialog box is closed. Also, the drawing area appears similar to one shown in Figure 2.140.

    Once the units, grid, and snap settings has been specified, you can start drawing the sketch. First you need to draw the outer closed loop of the sketch and then inner slop and circle.

Section 4: Drawing Outer Loop of the Sketch

1. Invoke the **Arc** flyout by clicking on the down arrow available next to the active arc tool in the **Sketch CommandManager**, refer to Figure 2.141.

2. Click on the **Centerpoint Arc** tool in the **Arc** flyout, the **Centerpoint Arc** tool activates and the **Arc PropertyManager** appears.

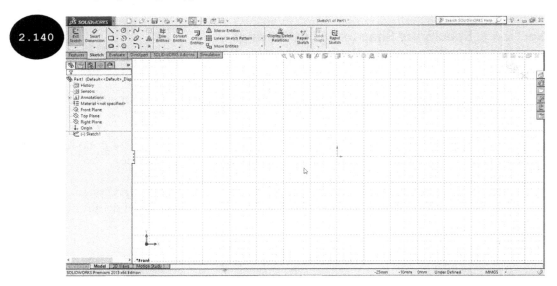

3. Move the cursor towards the origin and click to specify the center point of the arc when cursor snaps to origin.

4. Move the cursor horizontal towards the right, the preview of the imaginary circle appears in the drawing area. Next, click to specify the start point of the arc when the radius of the imaginary circle displays above the cursor is 25.

5. Move the cursor in anti-clockwise direction, the preview of an arc is displays in the drawing area. Next, click to specify the end point of the arc when angle value displays above the curse is 180 degree, see Figure 2.142, an arc is drawn. Press the ESC key to exit from the tool.

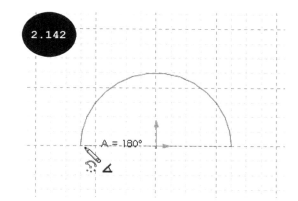

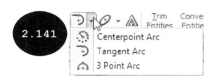

6. Click on the **Line** tool in the **Sketch CommandManager**, the **Line** tool activates and the **Insert Line PropertyManager** appears in left side of the drawing area. Also, the appearance of cursor changes to line cursor ✎ .

7. Move the cursor towards the start point of the arc drawn and click to specify the start point of the line when cursor snaps to start point of the arc.

8. Move the cursor horizontal towards the right and click to specify the end point of the line when the length of the line displays above the cursor is 25, see Figure 2.143, a line of length 25 mm is drawn.

9. Move the cursor vertical upwards and click to specify the end point of the line when the length of the line displays above the cursor is 10.

10. Move the cursor horizontal towards the right and click to specify the end point of the line when the length of the line displays above the cursor is 25, a line of length 25 mm is drawn.

11. Move the cursor vertical upwards and click to specify the end point of the line when the length of the line displays above the cursor is 10.

12. Move the cursor horizontal towards the left and click to specify the end point of the line when the length of the line displays above the cursor is 10, a line of length 10 mm is drawn, see Figure 2.144. Press the **ESC** key to exit from the **Line** tool.

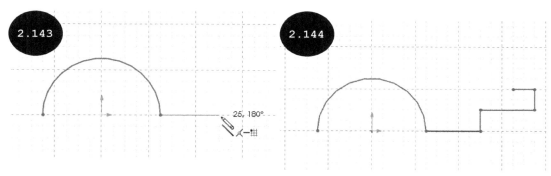

13. Invoke the **Arc** flyout by clicking on the down arrow available next to the active arc tool in the **Sketch CommandManager**.

14. Click on the **Centerpoint Arc** tool in the **Arc** flyout, the **Centerpoint Arc** tool activates and the **Arc PropertyManager** appears in left side of the drawing area.

15. Move the cursor towards the origin and click to specify the center point of the arc when cursor snaps to origin.

16. Move the cursor towards the end point of the last drawn line of length 10 and click to specify the start point of the arc when cursor snaps to it.

17. Move the cursor in anti-clockwise direction, the preview of an arc is displays in the drawing area. Next, click to specify the end point of the arc when the x, y, and z coordinates displays in the Status Bar are 55, 40, and 0, see Figure 2.145. Next, press the **ESC** key to exit from the tool.

18. Click on the **Line** tool in the **Sketch CommandManager**, the **Line** tool activates.

19. Move the cursor towards the end point of the last drawn arc and then click to specify the start point of the line when cursor snaps to it.

20. Move the cursor to the location where the x, y, and z coordinates displays in the Status Bar are 70, 110, and 0, see Figure 2.146.

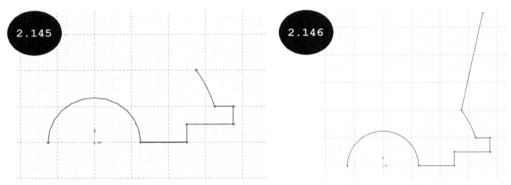

21. Invoke the **Arc** flyout by clicking on the down arrow available next to the active **Arc** tool in the **Sketch CommandManager**.

22. Click on the **Tangent Arc** tool in the **Arc** flyout, the **Tangent Arc** tool activates and the **Arc PropertyManager** appears in left side of the drawing area.

23. Move the cursor towards the end point of the last drawn line in the drawing area and click to specify the start point of the tangle arc when cursor snaps to it.

24. Move the cursor in anti-clockwise direction, the preview of an tangent arc is displays in the drawing area. Next, click to specify the end point of the arc when the x, y, and z coordinates

displays in the Status Bar are 45, 145, and 0. Next, press the **ESC** key to exit from the tool. Figure 2.147 shows the sketch similar to the one displays in the drawing area.

25. Click on the **Line** tool in the **Sketch CommandManager**, the **Line** tool activates.

26. Move the cursor towards the end point of the last drawn tangent arc and then click to specify the start point of the line when cursor snaps to it.

27. Move the cursor vertical upwards and click to specify the end point when the length of the line displays above the cursor is 10.

28. Move the cursor horizontal towards the left and click to specify the end point of the line when the length of the line displays above the cursor is 80, a line of length 80 mm is drawn, see Figure 2.148.

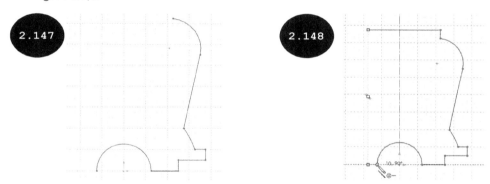

29. Move the cursor vertical downwards and click to specify the end point of the line when the length of the line displays above the cursor is 115, a line of length 115 mm is drawn.

30. Move the cursor horizontal towards the right and click to specify the end point of the line when the cursor snaps to the end point of the first drawn arc, see Figure 2.149. Next, press the **ESC** key to exit from the **Line** tool.

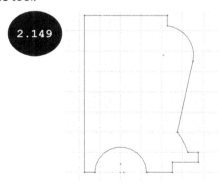

Section 5: Drawing Inner Slot and Circle of the Sketch

1. Invoke the **Slot** flyout and then click on the **3 point arc slot** tool, the **3 Point Arc Slot** tool activates. Also, the **Slot PropertyManager** appears in left side of the drawing area.

2. Move the cursor in the drawing area and then click to specify the center point of the slot when the X, Y, and Z coordinates displays in the Status Bar are 0, 120, and 0, see Figure 2.150.

3. Move the cursor towards the right and click to specify the start point of the slot arc when the coordinate value displays in the Status Bar is 50, 110, 0.

4. Move the cursor in clockwise direction and click to specify the end point of the slot arc when the coordinate value displays in the Status Bar is -10, 70, 0, see Figure 2.151.

5. Move the cursor downward to a small distance and click to specify a point to define the width of the slop when the width value displays closer to 20 mm in the **Slot Width** field of the **Slot PropertyManager**.

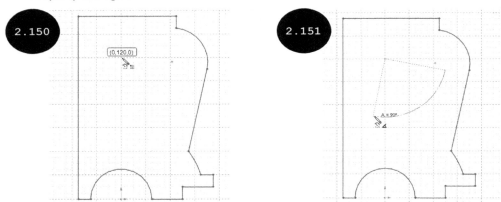

As soon as you specifying the point in the drawing area to define the width of the slot, the slot is drawn and is selected in the drawing area, see Figure 2.152. Also, the fields available in the **Parameters** rollout of the **Slot PropertyManager** are enabled, see Figure 2.153.

6. Enter the value 20 in the **Slot Width** field of the **Parameters** rollout of the PropertyManager. Next, press ENTER, the slot width is modified to 20 mm.

7. Click on the **OK** button of the PropertyManager, the PropertyManager is closed. Next, click anywhere in the drawing area.

8. Draw a circle of diameter 40 mm by using the **Circle** tool. Figure 2.154, shows the final sketch after drawing all the entities of the sketch.

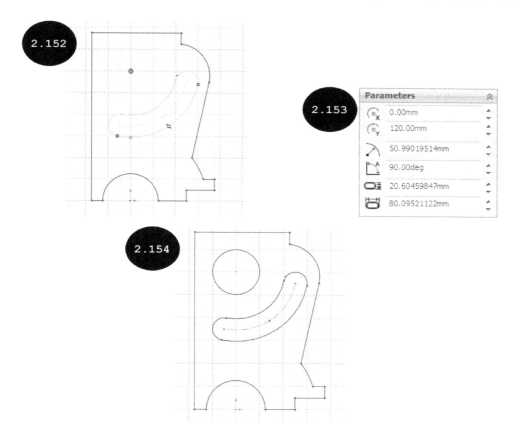

Parameters

x	0.00mm
y	120.00mm
	50.99019514mm
	90.00deg
	20.60459847mm
	80.09521122mm

Hands-on Test Drive 3

Draw the sketch of the model shown in Figure 2.155. Dimensions and model shown in the figure are for your reference.

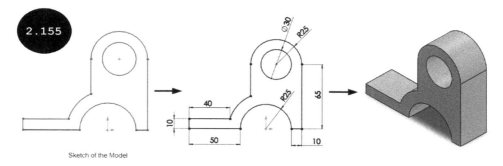

Sketch of the Model

Summary

In this chapter, you have learnt that the Sketching environment can be invoked within the Part modeling environment. To invoke Sketching environment, you need to specify a sketching plane. Once the Sketching environment is invoked, you can specify the units system as per your requirement by using the **Document Properties - Units** dialog box and specify grids and snaps settings. After understanding about all the required settings of the Sketching environment, you have learnt about drawing sketches by using the different sketching tools such as **Line, Arc, Circle, Rectangle**, and **Spline**.

Questions

- Features are divided into two main categories: _____ and _____ .

- The _____ feature of any real world component is Sketch Based feature.

- A polygon has number of side in the range between _____ to _____.

- To draw an ellipse, you need to define its _____ axis and _____ axis.

- If the rho value of conic curve is less than 0.5 then the conic is an _____.

- A parabola is a symmetrical plane curve which is formed by the intersection of a cone with a plane parallel to its side (True/False).

- Can you draw an tangent arc by using the **Line** tool (True/False).

- A fillet feature is known as Placed features (True/False).

Editing and Modifying Sketches

In this chapter:

- Trimming Sketch Entities
- Extending Sketch Entities
- Offsetting Sketch Entities
- Mirroring Sketch Entities
- Patterning Sketch Entities
- Moving Sketch Entities
- Coping Sketch Entities
- Rotating Sketch Entities
- Scaling Sketch Entities
- Stretching Sketch Entities

Performing editing and modifying operations in an sketch is very important in order to achieve the desire shape of the sketch. In SOLIDWORKS, you can perform various editing operations such as trimming unwanted sketched entities, extending sketch entities, mirroring, patterning, moving, and rotating by using the editing/modifying tools available in the Sketching environment. These tools are discussed next.

Trimming Sketch Entities

You can trim the unwanted entities of a sketch by using the **Trim Entities** tool which is available in the **Sketch CommandManager**. In addition to trimming the unwanted sketch entities by using the **Trim Entities** tool, you can also extend the sketch entities up to the next intersection. Although, in SOLIDWORKS, for extending sketch entities there is a separate tool available named as **Extend Entities** and is discussed later in this chapter.

To trim the sketch entities by using the **Trim Entities** tool, click on the **Trim Entities** tool in the **Sketch CommandManager**, the **Trim PropertyManager** appears, see Figure 3.1. The options available in the **Trim PropertyManager** are as follows.

Message

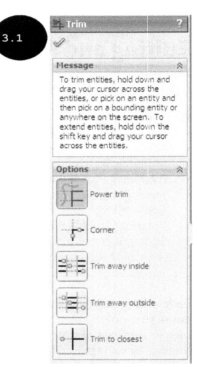

The **Message** rollout of the PropertyManager is used to guide you by displaying appropriation informations about the required action to be taken next. The information provided in the **Message** rollout depends upon the options selected in the **Options** rollout of the PropertyManager.

Options

The **Options** rollout allow you to select the required method for trimming the sketch entities and are as follows.

Power trim

The **Power trim** button of the **Options** rollout is used to trim the multiple adjacent sketch entities by holding and dragging the cursor across the entities to be trim. Notice that when you hold the left mouse button and drag the cursor after activating this button in the drawing area, a light color tracing line following the cursor is displaying in the drawing area and the sketch entities coming across this tracing line are getting trimmed from their nearest intersection. Figure 3.2 shows a sketch before trimming the sketch entities and Figure 3.3 shows the same sketch after trimming the entities that come across the tracing line.

Similar to trimming sketch entities by using the **Power trim** button, you can also extend the sketch entities up to their nearest intersection. To extend the sketch entities by using this tool, activate the **Power trim** button, and then press and hold the **SHIFT** key and the left mouse button then drag the cursor, a light color tracing line follows the cursor is appears and the entities come across this tracing line gets extended up to their next intersection. Figure 3.4 shows a sketch before extending a sketch entity and Figure 3.5 shows the same sketch after extending the entity that come across the tracing line.

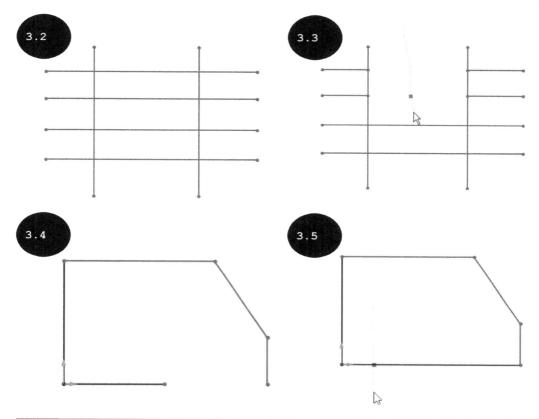

You can also extend a sketch entity up to a particular distance when the **Power trim** button is activated. To extend an entity up to a distance, click on the entity to be extend in the drawing area and then move the cursor in the required direction, the preview of the extended sketch entity appears. Next, click the left mouse button in the drawing area, the selected entity is extended to the point specified.

Corner

The **Corner** button is used to create corner between two selected entities by trimming or extending the entities. To create a corner between the entities, click on the **Corner** button and then select two sketch entities one by one. As soon as you select two entities, the corner is created between them either by trimming or extending the entities, see Figures 3.6 and 3.7.

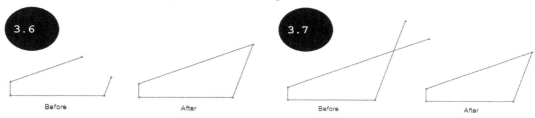

Trim away inside

The **Trim away inside** button is used to trim the entities that lies inside the defined boundary. To trim always inside the defined boundary, click on the **Trim away inside** button and then select two entities as the boundary entities one by one. Next, select the entities to be trimmed, the portion of the entities that lies inside the boundary get trimmed. Figure 3.8 shows the boundary entities and the entities to be trimmed and Figures 3.9 shows the resultant sketch after trimming the portion of the entity that lies inside the boundary.

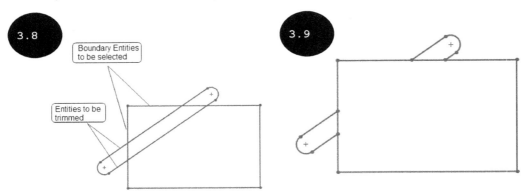

Trim away outside

The **Trim away outside** button of the **Options** rollout is used to trim the entities that lies outside the defined boundary. To trim always outside the defined boundary, click on the **Trim away outside** button and then select two entities as the boundary entities one by one. Next, select the entities to be trimmed, the portion of the entities that lies outside the boundary gets trimmed. Figure 3.10 shows the boundary selected and the entities to be trimmed and Figures 3.11 shows the resultant sketch after trimming the portion of the entity that lies outside the boundary.

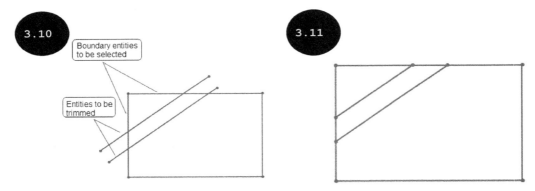

Trim to closest

The **Trim to closest** button is used to trim the sketch entities from their nearest intersection by clicking the left mouse button. To trim the sketch entities by using this option, click on the **Trim to closest** button and then click on the entity to be trimmed, the selected entity is trimmed from their nearest intersection, see Figures 3.12 and 3.13.

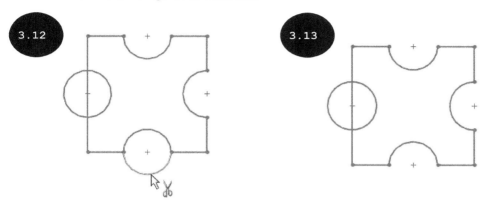

Procedure to Trim Entities Using the Trim Entities tool

Trim Entities

1. Click on the **Trim Entities** tool, the **Trim PropertyManager** appears.
2. Select the required method of trimming by clicking on the required button available in the **Options** rollout of the PropertyManager.
3. Depending upon the button selected from the **Options** rollout for trimming, you can trim the sketched entities. Refer to the above description for trimming the sketch entities by using different trimming methods.

Tip: As discussed, you can also extend the sketch entities by using the **Trim Entities** tool. For extending the sketch entities, activate the **Power trim** button. Next, press and hold the **SHIFT** key and the left mouse button and then drag the cursor, a light color tracing line follows the cursor and the entities come across this tracing line gets extended up to their next intersection.

Alternately, click on the entity to be extend in the drawing area and then move the cursor in the required direction, the preview of the extended sketch entity appears. Next, click the left mouse button in the drawing area, the selected entity is extended to the point specified.

Extending Sketch Entities

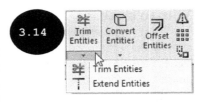

You can extend the sketch entities of a sketch up to their nearest intersection by using the **Extend Entities** tool. The entities that can be extended by using this tool are line, centerline, ellipse, spline, arc, and so on. This tool is available in the **Trim** flyout of the **Sketch CommandManager**, see Figure 3.14. Figure 3.15 shows a sketch and its entity to be extended and Figure 3.16 shows the resultant sketch after extending the entity upto their nearest intersection.

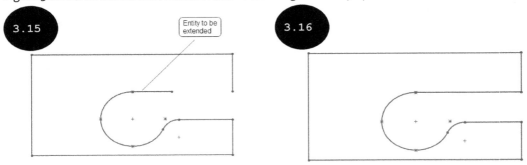

Procedure to Extend Sketch Entities Using the Extend Entities tool

1. Click on the down arrow available below the **Trim Entities** tool in the **Sketch CommandManager**, the **Trim** flyout appears, see Figure 3.14. Next, click on the **Extend Entities** tool, the cursor changes to extend cursor ⊧T.

2. Move the cursor over the entity to be extended, the preview of the extended line upto the next intersection displays in the drawing area, see Figure 3.17.

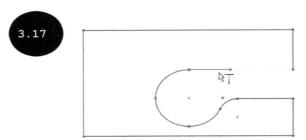

3. Click the left mouse button when the preview of the extended line appears, the selected entity has been extended upto their next intersection.

4. Similarly, you can extend the other sketch entities. Once you are done with extending the sketch entities, press the **ESC** key to exit from the tool.

Note: The direction of extension depends upon the position of the cursor over the entity to be extended. The end point which is closer to the cursor position is extended.

Tip: To change the direction of extension, move the cursor to the other half side of the sketch entity to be extended.

Offsetting Sketch Entities

The **Offset Entities** tool is used to offset sketch entities or edges of the existing feature at an specified offset distance. When you invoke the **Offset Entities** tool for offsetting sketch entities, the **Offset PropertyManager** appears, see Figure 3.18. Select entities to be offset from the drawing area, the preview of the offset entities appears in the drawing area depending upon the parameters specified in the PropertyManager. You can select sketch entities, edges, faces to offset. The options of the PropertyManager are as follows.

3.18

Parameters

The options available in the **Parameters** rollout of the PropertyManager are used to specify parameters for offsetting the selected sketch entities. The options of this rollout are as follows.

Offset Distance

The **Offset Distance** field of the **Parameters** rollout of the PropertyManager is used to specify the offset distance.

Tip: In addition to controlling the offset distance by using the **Offset Distance** field, you can also dynamically control the offset distance. To do so, press and hold the left mouse button in the drawing area and then drag the cursor. Note that as you drag the cursor, the offset distance is modified dynamically. Once the required distance has been achieved, released the left mouse button, the offset entity is created.

Add dimensions

On selecting the **Add dimensions** check box, the offset distance value specified is applied in the resultant offset sketch and if this check box is cleared, the offset distance value will not applied in the resultant offset sketch, see Figure 3.19.

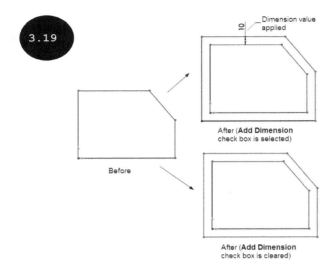

Reverse

The **Reverse** check box is used to reverse the offset direction of the entities.

Select chain

When the **Select chain** check box is selected, on selecting a sketch entity, all its contiguous entities is selected.

Bi-directional

When the **Bi-directional** check box is selected, entities is offset in bi-directional with respect to the selected parent entities (in both directions of the parent entities), see Figure 3.20.

Make base construction

On selecting the **Make base construction** check box, the original or parent sketch entities converts into construction entities and offset entities is created, see Figure 3.21.

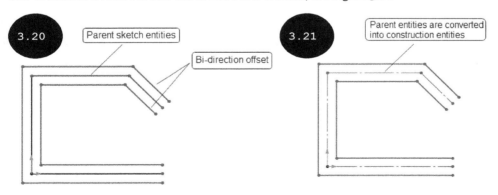

Cap ends

The **Cap ends** check box is used to cap the open ends of the offset entities by using lines or arcs entities, see Figures 3.22 and 3.23. This check box enables only if the **Bi-directional** check box is selected.

On selecting the **Cap ends** check box, the **Arcs** and **Lines** radio buttons enables its below in the PropertyManager. On selecting **Arcs** radio button, the offset entities is capped with arcs entities, see Figure 3.22. If you select the **Lines** radio button, the offset entities is capped with lines, see Figure 3.23.

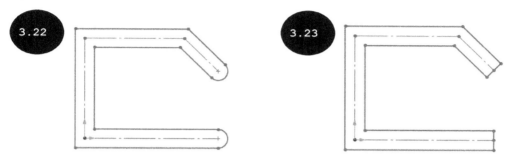

Procedure to Offset entities

1.   Invoke the **Offset PropertyManager** by clicking on the **Offset Entities** tool.
2.   Select the sketch entities to be offset from the drawing area, the preview of the offset entities displays in the drawing area.
3.   Enter the required offset distance in the **Offset distance** field of the PropertyManager.
4.   Select the **Reverse** check box to reverse the direction of offset, if required.
5.   Specify the other parameters for offsetting the sketch entities in the PropertyManager, as required.
6.   After specifying all the parameters, click on the green tick mark button of the PropertyManager, the offset entities is created.

Mirroring Entities

In SOLIDWORKS, you can create a mirror image of the sketch entities about a mirroring line by using **Mirror Entities** and **Dynamic Mirror** tools. Both these tools are as follows.

Mirroring Entities Using Mirror Entities tool

The **Mirror Entities** tool is used to create mirror image of the selected entities about a mirroring line. You can select a line, centerline, or a linear edge of existing features as a mirroring line about which you want to create mirror image of the selected sketch entities. To create mirror image, click on the **Mirror Entities** tool, the **Mirror PropertyManager** appears, see Figure 3.24. The options available in this PropertyManager are as follows.

Tip: The **Message** rollout of the PropertyManager is used to guide you by displaying appropriate information about the required action to be taken next.

Entities to mirror

The **Entities to mirror** selection field of the **Options** rollout of the PropertyManager is used to select sketch entities to be mirrored. By default, this selection field is activated. As a result, you can select the sketch entities by clicking the left mouse button or by using the window selection method. Note that the name of the selected entities appears in this selection field. You can also select the sketch entities to be mirrored before invoking the PropertyManager. If you do so than on invoking the PropertyManager, the name of the selected entities appears in this selection field.

Copy

By default, the **Copy** check box is selected. As a result, the original sketch entities will retain and a mirror image is created in the resultant sketch after mirroring. However, on clearing this check box, the original sketch entities will removed and a mirrored image is created in the resultant sketch.

Mirror about

The **Mirror about** selection field is used to select the mirroring line about which the selected entities has to be mirrored. Click on the **Mirror about** selection field to activate it. Once this field got activated, you can select the mirroring line from the drawing area. You can select a line, centerline, or an linear edge of existing features as the mirroring line.

As soon as you select the mirroring line, the preview of the mirror images of the selected entities appears in the drawing area. Now, you can click on the green tick mark ✓ button of the PropertyManager to create the mirror image of the selected entities. Figure 3.25 shows sketch entities to be mirrored and the mirroring line. Figure 3.26 shows the resultant sketch after mirroring the sketch entities about the mirroring line.

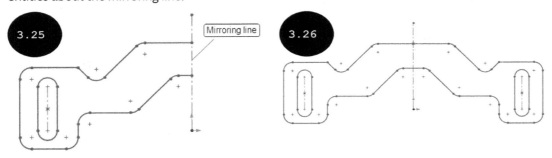

Note: When you mirror the sketch entities, the symmetric relation is applied between the original entities and the mirror image with respect to the mirroring line. As a result, on modifying the original sketch entities, the mirror image will automatically be modified, dynamically and vice-versa. You will learn more about relations in later chapters.

Procedure to Mirror Entities Using Mirror Entities tool

1. Click on the **Mirror Entities** tool, the **Mirror PropertyManager** appears.

2. Select the sketch entities to be mirrored from the drawing area, if not selected before invoking the PropertyManager.
3. Make sure that the **Copy** check box is selected in the PropertyManager to retain the original sketch entities in the resultant sketch.
4. Click on the **Mirror about** selection field to activate it and then select the mirroring line, the preview of the mirror image appears in the drawing area.
5. Click on the green tick mark ✓ button of the PropertyManager, the mirror image of the selected entities is created.

Mirroring Sketch Entities Using Dynamic Mirror tool

The **Dynamic Mirror** tool is also used to mirror sketch entities about an mirroring line similar to mirroring entities by using the **Mirror Entities** tool with the only different that this tool dynamically mirror the sketch entities while drawing them.

Procedure to Mirror Sketch Entities Using Dynamic Mirror tool

1. Invoke the **Dynamic Mirror** tool by clicking on the **Tools > Sketch Tools > Dynamic Mirror** from the SOLIDWORKS menus. On invoking this tool, the **Mirror PropertyManager** appears.
2. Select the mirroring line, the symbol of dynamic mirror appears on both ends of the selected mirroring line, see Figure 3.27. This symbol indicates that now if you draw any sketch entity either side of the mirroring line, the respective mirroring image will automatically be created on the other side of the mirroring line.
3. Draw the sketch entities on one side to the mirroring line by using the sketch tools, their respective mirror image is created dynamically on other side of the mirroring line, see Figure 3.28.
4. Once you are done with creating the sketch, click the **Tools > Sketch Tools > Dynamic Mirror** from the SOLIDWORKS menus again to exit from the tool.

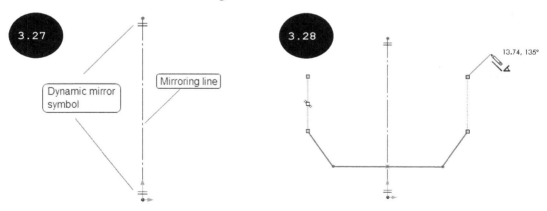

Patterning Sketch Entities

In SOLIDWORKS, you can create linear or circular patterns of the sketch entities by using the **Linear Sketch Pattern** or **Circular Sketch Pattern** tool, respectively. Both these patters are as follows.

Linear Sketch Pattern

Creating multiple instances of a sketch entity linearly along the X and Y directions by using the **Linear Sketch Pattern** tool is known as linear sketch pattern. To create linear sketch pattern, click on the **Linear Sketch Pattern** tool of the **Sketch CommandManager**, the **Linear Pattern PropertyManager** appears, refer to Figure 3.29.

Once the PropertyManager invoked, select the sketch entity or entities to be pattern, the preview of the linear pattern with the default parameters appears in the drawing area. Also, the name of the selected sketch entities appears in the selection field of the **Entities to Pattern** rollout of the PropertyManager. You can select the sketch entity to be patterned before or after invoking the PropertyManager. The options available in the **Linear Pattern PropertyManager** are used for defining the parameters for creating linear sketch pattern and are as follows.

Direction 1

The options available in the **Direction 1** rollout of the PropertyManager are used to specify the parameters for patterning sketch entities in direction 1 that is x axis direction. These options are as follows.

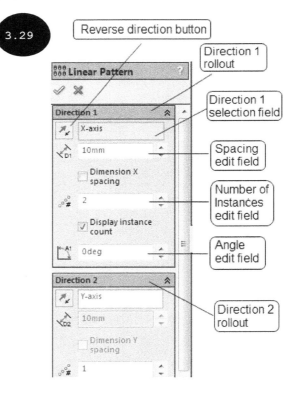

Direction 1

By default, the X-axis is selected in the **Direction 1** selection field in the **Direction 1** rollout. As a result, the patterning direction is along the x axis. You can also select any linear edge of the model or linear entity of the existing sketch as the direction of pattern.

Reverse direction

The **Reverse direction** button available in front of **Direction 1** selection field is used to reverse the pattern direction. You can reverse the pattern direction by clicking on this button. Its a toggle button.

Spacing

The **Spacing** field is used to specify the distance/spacing between the two pattern instances.

Number of Instances

The **Number of Instances** field is used to specify the number of pattern instances in direction 1.

The number of pattern instances specified in the **Number of Instances** field is counted including parent or original instance. For example, if the value 6 is specified in the **Number of Instances** field, the number of pattern instances created is 6 including parent instance.

Angle

The **Angle** field is used to specify the angle for the direction 1 with respective to the horizontal X axis. By default, the 0 degree angle is specified in this field. As a result, the linear pattern is created along the X axis direction at 0 degree angle, see Figure 3.30. Figure 3.31 shows the preview of the linear pattern along the X axis direction at 15 degree angle.

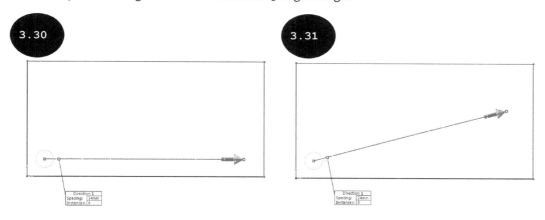

In the preview of the linear pattern, a arrow appears with a dot at its tip, see Figure 3.30. You can also drag the dot in the drawing area to change the orientation or angle of pattern direction. For dragging, press and hold the left mouse button over the dot appears at the tip of the arrow and than drag the cursor.

Dimension X spacing

On selecting the **Dimension X spacing** check box, the distance/spacing specified between two pattern instances appears in the resultant pattern sketch, see Figure 3.32.

Display Instance count

On selecting the **Display instance count** check box, the number of pattern instances specified in direction 1 appears in the resultant pattern sketch, see Figure 3.32.

Direction 2

The options available in the **Direction 2** rollout of the PropertyManager are same as of the **Direction 1** rollout with the only different that these options are used to specify the parameters for the linear pattern in the second direction that is Y-axis, by default, see Figure 3.33.

Note: By default, all the options available in the **Direction 2** are not enabled except the **Number of Instances** field. This is because number of pattern instances specify in the **Number of Instances** field is 1. On specifying the number of pattern instances two or more than two in this field, the other options of the **Direction 2** rollout is enabled.

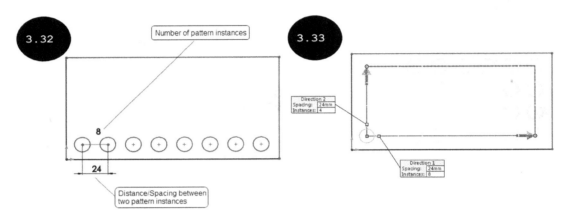

Entities to Pattern

The selection field of the **Entities to Pattern** rollout display the list of entities selected for patterning. You can select entities to be pattern before or after invoking the PropertyManager and the entities selected is listed or appears in this selection field.

Instances to Skip

The **Instances to Skip** rollout of the PropertyManager is used to skip or remove the unwanted instances of the pattern. To skip the instances of the pattern, click on the title bar of the **Instances to Skip** rollout to expand it. As soon as rollout is expanded, it become activated and pink dots appears in all the instances of the pattern in the drawing area, see Figure 3.34, if not, click on its selection field to activate it. Move the cursor over the pink dot of the instance to be skipped and click the left mouse button, the preview of the selected instance is disabled and will not be the part of resultant pattern, see Figure 3.35. Also, the pink dot turned to orange dot and the number of skipped instance appears in the selection field of the **Instances to Skip** rollout. Similarly, you can skip multiple instances of the pattern.

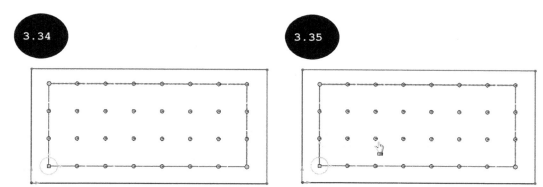

Note: To recall the skipped instances in the pattern, you can click on the orange dots of the respective skipped instances which appears in the preview of the pattern. Also, you can select its respective number, listed in the selection filed of the **Entities to Pattern** rollout and then right click to display a shortcut menu. Next, click on the **Delete** option to remove the respective instance from the list of skipped instance.

After defining the required parameters for patterning the sketch entities, linearly, in the **Linear Pattern PropertyManager**, click on the green tick mark ✅ button of the PropertyManager, the linear pattern is created.

Procedure to Create Linear pattern
1. Click on the **Linear Sketch Pattern** tool, the **Linear Pattern PropertyManager** ⊞ Linear Sketch Pattern appears.
2. Select the entities to be patterned from the drawing area, the preview of the linear pattern along the X-axis appears, with the default settings. Also, the name of the selected entities appears in the selection field of the **Entities to Pattern** rollout of the PropertyManager.
3. Reverse the direction, if required, by clicking on the **Reverse direction** button.
4. Specify the distance between the pattern instances in the **Spacing** field of the **Direction 1** rollout.
5. Specify the number of pattern instances to be created in the direction 1 in the **Number of Instances** field of the **Direction 1** rollout.
6. Specify the number of pattern instances to be created in the direction 2 in the **Number of Instances** field of the **Direction 2** rollout.
7. Specify the other parameters such as distance between instances and number of instances for direction 2 pattern in their respective fields.
8. After specifying all the parameters for direction 1 and direction 2 pattern, click on the green tick mark ✅ button of the PropertyManager, the linear pattern is created.

Circular Sketch Pattern

Creating multiple instances of a sketch entity circularly about an center point by using the **Circular Sketch Pattern** tool is known is circular sketch pattern. To create circular sketch pattern, invoke the **Pattern** flyout by clicking on the down arrow available next to the **Linear Sketch Pattern** tool in the **Sketch CommandManager**, see Figure 3.36. Next, click on the **Circular Sketch Pattern** tool from this flyout, the **Circular Pattern PropertyManager** appears, refer to Figure 3.37.

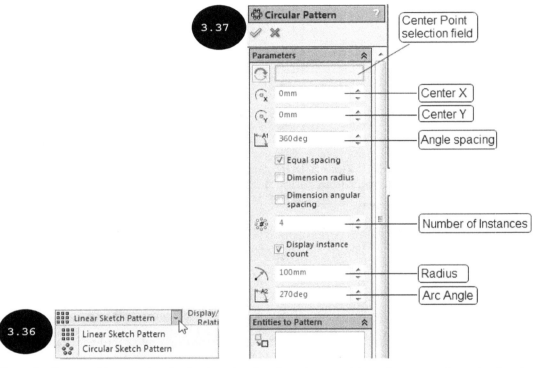

Once the PropertyManager invoked, select the sketch entity or entities to be pattern from the drawing area, the preview of the circular pattern with the default parameters appears in the drawing area, see Figure 3.38. Also, the name of the selected sketch entities appears in the selection field of the **Entities to Pattern** rollout of the PropertyManager. You can select the sketch entity to be patterned before or after invoking the PropertyManager. The options available in the **Circular Pattern PropertyManager** are used for defining the parameters for creating circular sketch pattern and are as follows.

Parameters

The options available in the **Parameters** rollout are used to specify the parameters for patterning sketch entities in circular manner. These options are as follows.

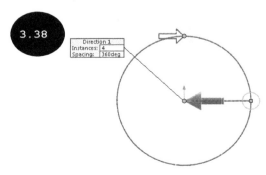

Center Point

The **Center Point** selection field is used to specify the center point for the pattern instances. By default, when you select sketch entities to be patterned, the origin point (0,0) is selected as the center point for patterning, see Figure 3.38. You can specify any other sketch point as the center point for patterning by using the **Center X** and **Center Y** fields of the PropertyManager.

Center X

The **Center X** field is used to specify the X coordinate of the center point.

Center Y

The **Center Y** field is used to specify the Y coordinate of the center point.

Note: Instead of specifying X and Y coordinates for defining the center point of the pattern being created in their respective fields, you can also change the location or position of the pattern center point by dragging the dot appears at the tip of the arrow which appears in the preview of the circular pattern, see Figure 3.38. For doing so, press and hold the left mouse button over the dot appears at the tip of the arrow and than drag the cursor. As you change the location of center point by dragging, the coordinates of the center point changes accordingly in the **Center X** and **Center Y** fields, dynamically. Next, drop to the required location. In addition to this, you can also select a sketch point as the center point for patterning.

Angle spacing

The **Angle spacing** field is used to specify the total angle value for pattern. By default, the value entered in this field is 360 degrees. As a results, the circular pattern creates such that its covers 360 degrees in the pattern and number of pattern instances adjusted within the total 360 degrees, equally. This is because the **Equal spacing** check box is selected, by default in this rollout.

Equal spacing

By default the **Equal spacing** check box is selected. As a result, the angle between the pattern instances is set equally with respective to the total angle specified in the **Angle spacing** field. However, on clearing this check box, the angle entered in the **Angle spacing** field is the angle between two instances of the pattern.

Dimension radius

On selecting the **Dimension radius** check box, the pattern radius with respective to the center point appears in the resultant pattern, see Figure 3.39.

Dimension angular spacing

On selecting the **Dimension angular spacing** check box, the angular distance between two instances appears in the resultant pattern, see Figure 3.39.

Number of Instances

The **Number of Instances** field is used to specify the total number of instances in the pattern. Note that number of instances specified in this field including the parent instance.

Display instance count
On selecting the **Display instance count** check box, the pattern instances count appears in the resultant pattern, see Figure 3.39.

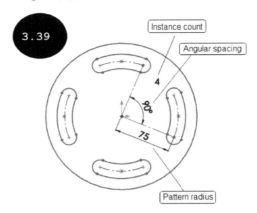

3.39

Instance count
Angular spacing
Pattern radius

Radius
The **Radius** field is used to specify the pattern radius. By default, as origin is defined as the center point for patterning, the **Radius** field displays the pattern radius by keeping the origin as the center point for measurement. You can change the default radius value by entering the new radius value in this field.

Arc Angle
The **Arc Angle** field is used to specify the angle measurement from the center of the selected entities to the center point of the pattern.

Instances to Skip
Similar to skipping the pattern instances while creating linear pattern, you can also skip pattern instances of the circular pattern by using the **Instances to Skip** rollout of the PropertyManager. To skip the instances of the pattern, click on the title bar of this rollout to expand it. As soon as this rollout expands, it become activated and a pink dot appears in all the instances of the pattern in the drawing area, if not, click on its selection field, see Figure 3.40. Next, move the cursor over the pink dot of the instance to be skipped and then click the left mouse button, the preview of the selected instance is disabled and will not be the part of resultant pattern, see Figure 3.41. Also, the pink dot turns to orange dot and the respective instance number displays in the selection field of the **Instances to Skip** rollout.

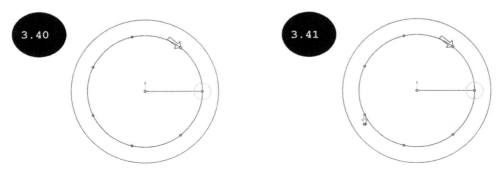

3.40

3.41

After defining the required parameters for patterning the sketch entities, circularly, in the **Circular Pattern PropertyManager,** click on the green tick mark ✓ button of the PropertyManager, the circular pattern is created.

Procedure to Create Circular Pattern

1. Click on the **Circular Sketch Pattern** tool in the **Pattern** flyout, see Figure 3.36, the **Circular Pattern PropertyManager** appears.
2. Select the entities to be patterned, the preview of the circular pattern about the origin appears. You can select the entities to be pattern before or after invoking the PropertyManager.
3. If needed, reverse the pattern direction by clicking the **Reverse Direction** button.
4. If needed, change the center point of the pattern by dragging the dot available at the arrow tip in the preview or by specifying the coordinates of center point in the **Center X** and **Center Y** field of the PropertyManager.
5. Specify the total pattern angle or the angle between two instances in the **Angle spacing** field.

Tip: If the Equal spacing check is selected, the angle specified in the **Angle spacing** field measures the total angle between which all the pattern instances arrange equally.

---

6. Specify the number of pattern instances to create in the **Number of Instances** field.
7. After specifying all the parameters, click on the green tick mark ✓ button of the PropertyManager, the circular pattern is created.

Moving Sketch Entities

You can move sketch entities from one position to another in the drawing area by using the **Move Entities** tool. To move the sketch entities, click on the **Move Entities** tool, the **Move PropertyManager** appears, see Figure 3.42. The options available in this PropertyManager are as follows.

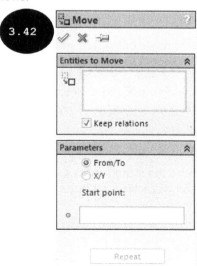

Entities to Move
The options available in the **Entities to Move** rollout are as follows.

Sketch items and annotations
The **Sketch items and annotations** selection field of the **Entities to Move** rollout is used to select the entities to be moved. By default, this field is activated. As a result, select the entities to be moved from the drawing area. The name of the selected entities displays in this selection field. You can select the sketch entities before or after invoking the PropertyManager.

Keep relations
The **Keep relations** check box is used to maintain relations between the sketch entities being moved. If the **Keep relations** check box is selected then the existing relations between sketch entities being moved and the other entities of the sketch remain maintained. However, on clearing this check box, the relation between the sketch entities selected for moving and the other entities of the sketch is broken.

Parameters
The options of the **Parameters** rollout are used to specify the parameters of moving the entities and are as follows.

From/To
By default, the **From/To** radio button is selected. As a result, you can move the selected sketch entities with respect to a base point upto a specific location. To move entities when this radio button is selected, click on the **Start point** selection field to activate it. Next, specify a point in the drawing area as the base point for moving the selected entities. As soon as you specify the base point, the preview of the selected entities is attached with the cursor and as you move the cursor, the preview of the selected entities move dynamically in the drawing area with respect to the specified base point. Now, specify the new position for the selected entities in the drawing area by clicking the left mouse button.

X/Y
The X/Y radio button allows you to move the sketch entities by specifying the translation distance along the X and Y directions with respect to the original location of the sketch entities. When you select the X/Y radio button, the $\triangle$X and $\triangle$Y fields enabled in the rollout. In this fields, you can specify the translation distance along the X and Y directions, respectively. Note that the distance specified in the $\triangle$X and $\triangle$Y fields measures from the center point of the original location of the sketch entities.

Repeat
The **Repeat** button is used to move the sketch entities with the incremental distance specified in the $\triangle$X and $\triangle$Y fields every time on clicking this button.

Procedure to Move Sketch Entities

1. Click on the **Move Entities** tool, the **Move PropertyManager** appears.
2. Select the sketch entities to be moved. You can select the sketch entities before or after invoking the PropertyManager.
3. Select the **From/To** or **X/Y** radio button for moving the sketch entities, as required. By default, the **From/To** radio button is selected.
4. Depending upon the radio button selected in the Step 3, specify the new position for the sketch entities being moved.

Coping Sketch Entities

You can create a copy of a set of sketch entities by using the **Copy Entities** tool. To copy sketch entities, click on the down arrow available next to the **Move Entities** tool, a flyout appears, see Figure 3.43. Next, click on the **Copy Entities** tool, the **Copy PropertyManager** appears, see Figure 3.44. The options available in this PropertyManager are same as of the **Move PropertyManager** with the only difference that it creates copy of the original sketch entities in the specified location.

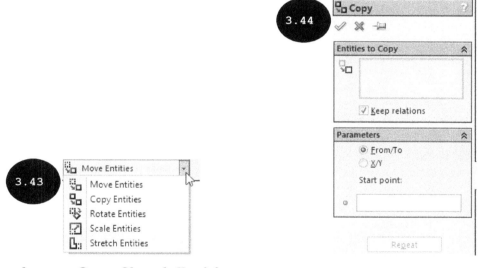

Procedure to Copy Sketch Entities

1. Invoke the **Copy PropertyManager** and then select the sketch entities to be copied. Note that you can select the sketch entities to be copied before or after invoking the PropertyManager.
2. Select the **From/To** or **X/Y** radio button from the **Parameters** rollout for coping the sketch entities, as required. By default, the **From/To** radio button is selected.
3. Depending upon the radio button selected in the Step 3, specify the position for the sketch entities, the copy of the select entities is created on the specified location.

Rotating Entities

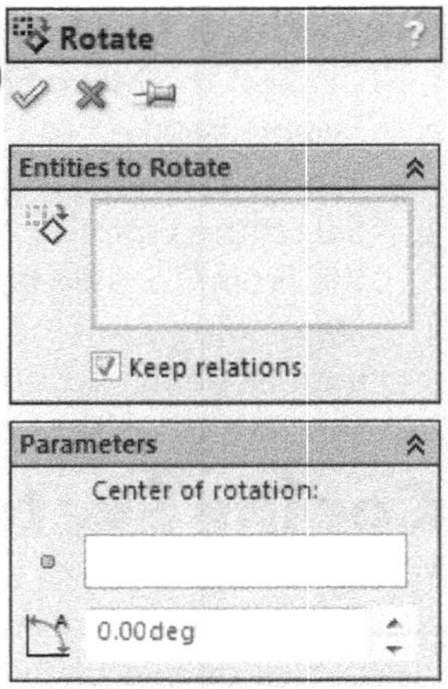

You can rotate sketch entities at an angle by using the **Rotate Entities** tool. To rotate the sketch entities, click on the down arrow available next to the **Move Entities** tool, a flyout appears, see Figure 3.43. Next, click on the **Rotate Entities** tool of this flyout, the **Rotate PropertyManager** appears, see Figure 3.45. The options available in this **PropertyManager** are as follows.

Entities to Rotate

The options available in the **Entities to Rotate** rollout are as follows.

Sketch items and annotations

The **Sketch items and annotations** selection field of this rollout is used to select the entities to be rotated. Select the entities to be rotated from the drawing area, the name of the selected entities appears or listed in this selection field. You can also select the entities before invoking this PropertyManager.

Keep relations

The **Keep relations** check box is used to maintain existing relations between the sketch entities. If this check box is selected then the existing relations between sketch entities selected for rotating and the other entities of the sketch remain maintained. However, on clearing this check box, the relation between the sketch entities is broken.

Parameters

The **Parameters** rollout of the PropertyManager is used to specify the parameters for rotating the entities. The options available in this rollout are as follows.

Center of rotation

The **Center of rotation** selection field is used to specify the base point or the center point for rotation. To specify the base point for rotating the sketch entity, click on the **Center of rotation** selection field to activate it and specify the point in the drawing area by clicking the left mouse button. As soon as you specify the center point, a triad appears in the drawing area, see Figure 3.46 . Also, the **Angle** field enabled below this selection field in the PropertyManager. Now, you can specify the angle of rotation in the **Angle** field with respect to the center point. Note that as you modify the angle value in this field, the preview of the selected entities rotate accordingly in the drawing area. Figure 3.46 shows a sketch before or after rotating the slot at an angle of 30 with respect to its center point.

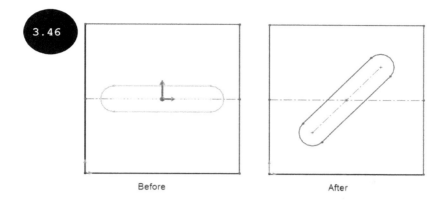

Before   After

On specifying the positive angle value, the rotation direction is in the anti-clockwise direction. At the same time, on specifying the negative angle value, the rotation direction is in the clockwise direction.

Procedure to Rotate Sketch Entities

1. Invoke the **Rotate PropertyManager** by clicking on the **Rotate Entities** tool, see Figure 3.43.
2. Select the sketch entities to be rotated.
3. Activate the **Center of rotation** selection field and then specify the center point for rotation.
4. Specify the angle for rotation in the **Angle** field.
5. Click on the green tick mark ✅ button of the PropertyManager, the selected entities got rotated.

Scaling Sketch Entities

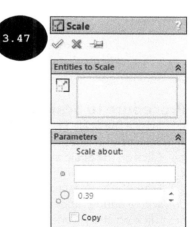

You can increase or decrease the scale of the sketch entities by using the **Scale Entities** tool. To scale the sketch entities, click on the down arrow available next to the **Move Entities** tool, a flyout appears, see Figure 3.43. Next, click on the **Scale Entities** tool, the **Scale PropertyManager** appears, see Figure 3.47. The options available in this PropertyManager are as follows.

Entities to Scale

The selection field of the **Entities to Scale** rollout is used to select the entities to be scaled. Select the entities to be scaled from the drawing area, the name of the entities appears in this selection field.

Parameters

The options of the **Parameters** rollout is used to specify the parameters for scaling the selected sketched entities. These options are as follows.

Scale about and Scale Factor

The **Scale about** field is used to specify the base point or the center point for scaling the selected sketch entities. To specify the base point, click on the **Scale about** selection field to activate it. Next, specify a point in the drawing area as the base point for scaling by clicking the left mouse button. As soon as you specify the base point, a dot filled with color appears in the drawing area, see Figure 3.48. Also, the preview of the scaled sketched appear with the default scale factor in the drawing area, see Figure 3.48. Next, click on the green tick mark ✅ button of the PropertyManager, the selected entities got scaled.

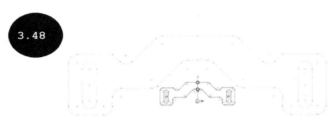

Copy

By default, the **Copy** check box is cleared. As a result, the original sketch entities selected is scaled to the new scaled factor without retaining a copy of the original sketch. However, if you select the **Copy** check box, you can create multiple copies of the scaled sketch entities. As soon as, you select the **Copy** check box, the **Number of Copies** field is available in the rollout. You can specify the number of copies of the scaled sketch entities to be created in the **Number of Copies** field.

> **Note:** The number of copies specified in the **Number of Copies** field, excluding the set of original sketch entities. For example, if you specify the value 2 in this field then two set of copies of the scaled entities in addition to the original sketch entities is created. Also, note that, every scaled copy created is of incremental scale factor.

Procedure to Scale Sketch Entities

1. Invoke the **Scale PropertyManager** by clicking on the **Scale Entities** tool.
2. Select the entities to be scaled.
3. Click on the **Scale about** selection field to activate it.
4. Select a base point for scaling the sketch entities.
5. Enter the scale factor for scaling the sketch entities in the **Scale Factor** field, the preview of the scaled entities appears with respect to the specified base point.
6. Click on the green tick mark ✅ button of the PropertyManager, the selected entities got scaled.

Stretching Entities

You can stretch sketch entities of a sketch by using the **Stretch Entities** tool. To stretch sketch entities, click on the down arrow available next to the **Move Entities** tool to invoke a flyout, see Figure 3.43. Next, click on the **Stretch Entities** tool, the **Stretch PropertyManager** appears, see Figure 3.49. The options available in this PropertyManager are as follows.

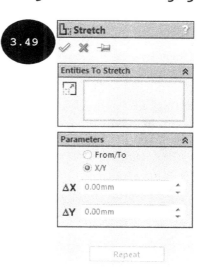

Entities to Stretch

The selection field of the **Entities to Stretch** rollout is used to select the entities to be stretched. By default, this field is activated. Select sketch entities from the drawing area to be stretched, the name of the entities displays in this selection field.

Parameters

The options available in the **Parameters** rollout are used to specify the parameters for stretching the entities. These options are as follows.

From/To

The **From/To** radio button is used to stretch the sketch entities with respect of a base point. On selecting this radio button, the **Stretch about** selection field is enabled in the **Parameters** rollout. Click on this selection field to activate it and then select the base point for stretching the sketch entities. After specifying the base point, move the cursor, the preview of the selected entities appears attached with the cursor in the drawing area with respect to the specified base point. Next, specify the new position for the stretched entities by clicking the left mouse button in the drawing area.

X/Y

The X/Y radio button allows you to stretch the sketch entities by specifying the translation distance along the X and Y directions with respect to the original location of the sketch entities. When you select the X/Y radio button, the $\triangle$X and $\triangle$Y fields are enabled in the **Parameters** rollout. In this fields, you can specify the translation distance along the X and Y directions, respectively.

Repeat

The **Repeat** button is used to stretch the sketch entities with the incremental distance specified in the $\triangle$X and $\triangle$Y fields.

Procedure to Stretch Sketch Entities

1. Invoke the **Stretch PropertyManager** by clicking on the **Stretch Entities** tool.
2. Select the sketch entities to be stretched.
3. Select the **From/To** or X/Y radio button from the **Parameters** rollout.
4. Depending upon the radio button selected in the Step 3, specify the new position for the stretched entities.

Tutorial 1

Draw the sketch shown in Figure 3.50. Dimensions and model shown in the figure are for your reference.

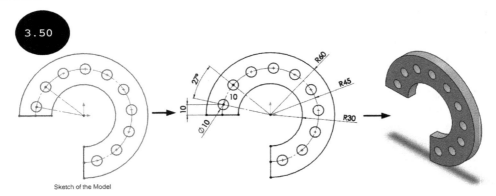

Sketch of the Model

Section 1: Starting SOLIDWORKS

First you need to start the SOLIDWORKS software.

1. Clicking on the **SOLIDWORKS** icon on your desktop to start SOLIDWORKS, if not started already.

Section 2: Invoking Sketching Environment

Now invoke the Sketching environment by selecting the Front plane as the sketching plane.

1. Click on the **New** tool in the **Standard** tool, the **New SOLIDWORKS Document** dialog box appears.

2. In this dialog box, the **Part** button is activated by default. As a result, click on the **OK** button to invoke the Part modeling environment.

   Once the Part modeling environment is invoked, you can invoke the sketching environment and create the sketch of this tutorial.

3. Click on the **Sketch** tab in the **Command Manager**, the **Sketch CommandManager** appears.

4. Click on the **Sketch** button of the **Sketch CommandManager**, three default planes mutually perpendicular to each other appears in the graphics area.

5. Move the cursor over the Front plane and click to select it as the sketching plane when the boundary of the plane highlighted, the Sketching environment is invoked. Also, the Front plane orientated normal to the viewing direction and the confirmation corner appears at the upper right corner of the drawing area.

Section 3: Specifying Snap and Unit Settings

Once the Sketching environment is invoked, set the snap settings such that cursor snap to the increment of 5 mm. Also, specify metric unit system for measurement.

1. Click on the **Options** tool in the **Standard** toolbar, the **System Options - General** dialog box appears.

2. In this dialog box, click on the **Document Properties** tab, the name of the dialog box changes to **Document Properties - Drafting Standard**.

3. Select the **Units** option available in the left panel of the dialog box, the options related to specifying the unit system displays on the right side of the dialog box.

4. Select the **MMGS (millimeter, gram, second)** radio button from the **Unit system** area of the dialog box, if not selected by default. Once the unit system is specified do not exit from the dialog box.

   Now, you need to specify the snap settings such that the cursor snaps the increment of 5 mm.

5. Select the **Grid/Snap** option available in the left side panel of the dialog box, the options related to the grid and snap settings displays on the right side panel of the dialog box. Also, the name of the dialog box changes to **Document Properties - Grid/Snap** dialog box.

6. Enter **20** in the **Major grid spacing** field, **4** in the **Minor -lines per major** field, and **1** in the **Snap points per minor** field of the **Grid** area in the dialog box.

7. Clear the **Display grid** check box of the **Grid** area in the dialog box to turned Off the display of grids in the drawing area.

8. Click on the **Go To System Snaps** button, the name of the dialog box changes to **System Options - Relations/Snaps**.

9. Select the **Grid** check box in the **Sketch snaps** area of the dialog box to turn on the snap mode, if not selected by default. Also, make sure that the **Snap only when grid appears** check box available below the **Grid** check box is cleared.

10. Clear the **Snap only when grid appears** check box available below the **Grid** check box.

11. Click on the **OK** button of the dialog box, the snap settings has been specified and the dialog box is closed.

Section 4: Drawing Sketch Entities

Once the units and snap settings has been specified, you can start drawing the sketch.

1. Click on the **Circle** tool in the **Sketch CommandManager**, the **Circle** tool activates and the **Circle PropertyManager** appears on left side of the drawing area. Also, the appearance of cursor changes to circle cursor ⟋ .

2. Move the cursor towards the origin and click to specify the center point of the circle when the cursor snaps to the origin.

3. Move the cursor horizontally towards the right to a distance, the preview of the circle appears and attached with the cursor tip. Also, the radius to the circle displays near to the cursor. Notice that as you move the cursor, the preview of the circle and its radius modified dynamically.

4. Move the cursor to the location where the radius of the circle appears above the cursor 60, see Figure 3.51 and then click at this location, the circle of radius 60 is created.

Tip: After creating a circle, the **Circle** tool is still activated. As a result, you can continue with creating the remaining circles. Once you are done with creating all the circles of the drawing, you can terminate the creation of circle or deactivating the **Circle** tool by pressing the ESC key.

---

5. As the **Circle** tool is still activated, move the cursor towards the origin and click to specify the center point of the second circle when cursor snaps to the origin.

6. Move the cursor horizontally towards the right and click when the radius of the second circle displays 30 radius above the cursor, see Figure 3.52.

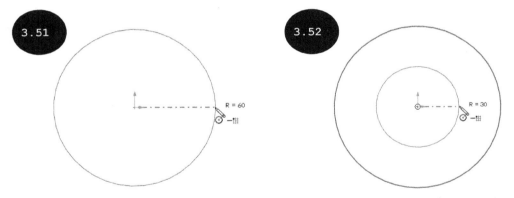

After creating circles of radius 60 and 30, now you need to create a reference/construction circle of radius 45 that defines the PCD for holes, see Figure 3.50.

7. Create a circle of radius 45 whose center point is at the origin, see Figure 3.53. Next, terminate the creation of circle by exiting from the **Circle** tool.

    Once you are done with creating the circle of radius 45, you need to convert it to a reference/construction circle.

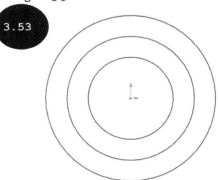

8. Select the circle of radius 45 from the drawing area, if not already selected, the **Circle PropertyManager** appears on the left of the drawing area. Also, a Pop-up toolbar appears near the cursor in the drawing area, see Figure 3.54.

9. Select the **For construction** check box from the **Options** rollout of the PropertyManager, the selected circle of radius 45 converted into the construction circle, see Figure 3.55. You could have also select the **Construction Geometry** button from the Pop-up toolbar.

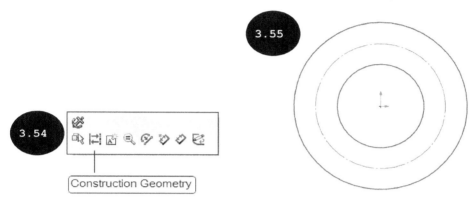

10. Click on the **Line** tool, the **Insert Line PropertyManager** appears.

11. Specify the start point of the line at the origin and then move the cursor horizontally towards the left.

12. Click to specify the end point of the line when the length of the line displays 60 above the cursor, see Figure 3.56.

13. Right click in the drawing area and select the **End chain (double-click)** option from the shortcut menu to terminate the creation of continuous chain of lines. However, the **Line** tool is still activated.

Tip: To exit from the **Line** tool, select the **Select** option from the shortcut menu which appears on right clicking in the drawing area. On selecting the **End chain (double-click)** option from the shortcut menu, only the creation of continuous chain of lines is terminated and the **Line** tool remains activated.

14. As the **Line** tool is still activated, move the cursor towards the origin and click to specify the start point of the line when cursor snaps to the origin.

15. Move the cursor vertically downwards and click to specify the end point of the line when the length displays 60 above the cursor, see Figure 3.57.

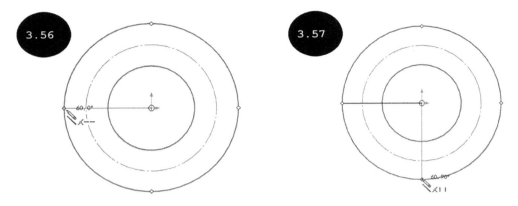

16. Right click in the drawing area and then select the **Select** option from the shortcut menu to exit from the **Line** tool.

   Now, you need to create a circle of diameter 10. It is evident from the Figure 3.50 that the circles of diameter 10 are 10 in counts. As the diameter of all the circles are same and are on the same PCD (Pitch Circle Diameter), you can create one circle and then pattern it circularly to create its other instances or remaining circles.

17. Click on the **Circle** tool, the **Circle PropertyManager** appears. Make sure that the **Circle** button is activated in this PropertyManager.

18. Move the cursor at the location when the coordinates displays -45, 10, 0 in the Status Bar and the construction circle highlighted in the drawing area, see Figure 3.58. For coordinates refer to the Status Bar available at the bottom of the drawing area, see Figure 3.59.

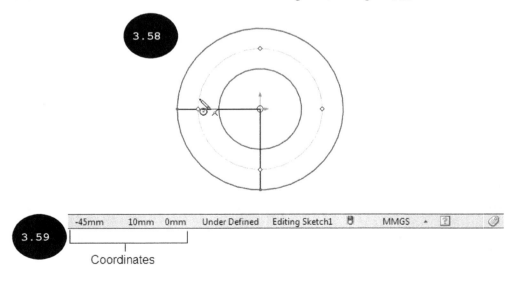

19. Click the left mouse button to specify the center point of the circle when coordinates displays -45, 10, 0 and construction circle highlights.

20. Move the cursor horizontal towards the right and click when the radius of the circle displays close to 5, see Figure 3.60. As soon as you click the left mouse button, the circle of radius close to 5 is created and is currently selected in the drawing area. Also, the options of the **Circle PropertyManager** enabled to control the parameters of the selected circle.

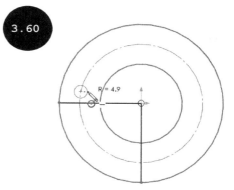

21. Enter 5 in the **Radius** field of the **Parameters** rollout of the PropertyManager as the radius value for the selected circle and then press ENTER, the radius of the circle modified to 5.

22. Right click in the drawing area and then select the **Select** option from the shortcut menu to exit from the **Circle** tool.

Section 5: Trimming Sketch Entities

Now, you will trim the unwanted sketch entities of the sketch drawn.

1. Click on the **Trim Entities** tool of the **Sketch CommandManager**, the **Trim PropertyManager** appears at the left of the drawing area.

2. Activate the **Trim to closest** button in the **Options** rollout of the PropertyManager by clicking on it, if not activated by default, the cursor appears changes to trim cursor ⟶.

3. Move the cursor over the portion of the entity to be trimmed, see Figure 3.61 and then click when it highlighted in the drawing area, the selected portion of the entity is trimmed, see Figure 3.62.

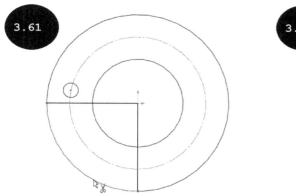

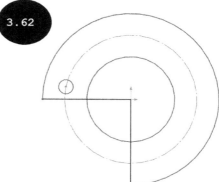

4. Similarly, trim the other unwanted portion of the entities of the sketch. Figure 3.63 shows the entities to be trimmed and Figure 3.64 shows the sketch after trimming all the unwanted entities.

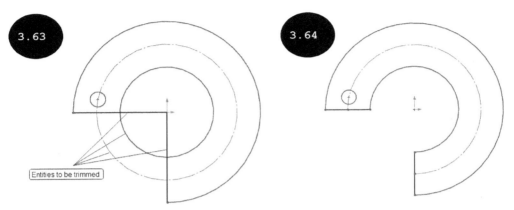

3.63   Entities to be trimmed

3.64

5. Once you are down with the trimming operation, click on the green tick mark ✅ of the PropertyManager to exit from the tool.

Section 6: Creating Circular Pattern

Now, you will create circular pattern of the circle having diameter 10 to create its remaining instances.

1. Select the circle of diameter 10 to be patterned from the drawing area.

2. Click on the down arrow available next to the **Linear Sketch Pattern** tool, the **Pattern** flyout appears, see Figure 3.65.

3. Click on the **Circular Sketch Pattern** tool from the flyout, the preview of the circular pattern of the selected circle appears in the drawing area. Also, the **Circular Pattern PropertyManager** appear at the left of the drawing area.

4. Clear the **Equal spacing** check box of the **Parameters** rollout of the PropertyManager.

5. Enter **27** in the **Angle** field of the **Parameter** rollout as the angle between two instances.

6. Enter **10** in the **Number of Instances** field as the number of pattern instances to be created.

7. Click on the green tick mark ✅ of the PropertyManager, the circle pattern is created, see Figure 3.66.

Note: The circular pattern shown in Figure 3.66 has been created when the **Dimension angular spacing** and **Display instance count** check boxes are selected in the **Parameter** rollout of the **Circular PropertyManager**.

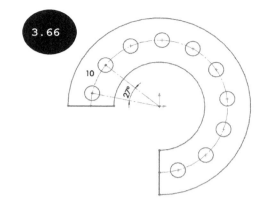

Tutorial 2

Draw the sketch shown in Figure 3.67. Dimensions and model shown in the figure are for your reference.

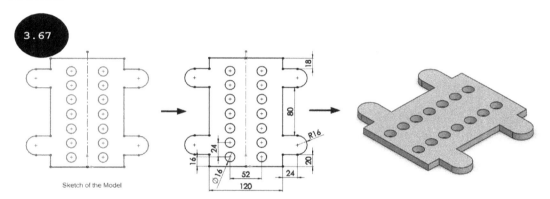

Sketch of the Model

Section 1: Starting SOLIDWORKS

First you need to start the SOLIDWORKS software.

1. Double click on the **SOLIDWORKS** icon on your desktop to start SOLIDWORKS, if not started already.

Section 2: Invoking Sketching Environment

Now, first invoke the Part modeling environment and then invoke the Sketching environment by selecting the Top plane as the sketching plane.

1. Click on the **New** tool in the **Standard** toolbar, the **New SOLIDWORKS Document** dialog box appears.

2. In this dialog box, the **Part** button is activated by default. Click on the **OK** button to invoke the Part modeling environment.

Once the Part modeling environment is invoked, you can now invoke the Sketching environment and create the sketch of this tutorial.

3. Click on the **Sketch** tab in the **Command Manager**, the **Sketch CommandManager** appears.

4. Click on the **Sketch** button of the **Sketch CommandManager**, three default planes which are mutually perpendicular to each other appears in the graphics area.

5. Move the cursor over the Top plane and click to select it as the sketching plane when the boundary of the plane highlighted, the Sketching environment is invoked. Also, the Top plane orientated normal to the viewing direction and the confirmation corner appears at the upper right corner of the drawing area.

Section 3: Specifying Snap and Unit Settings

Once the Sketching environment is invoked, set the snap settings such that cursor snap to the increment of 2mm. This is because the dimensions of all the sketch entities are multiple of 2 mm. Also, specify metric unit system for measurement.

1. Click on the **Options** tool in the **Standard** toolbar, the **System Options - General** dialog box appears.

2. In this dialog box, click on the **Document Properties** tab, the name of the dialog box changes to **Document Properties - Drafting Standard**.

3. Select the **Units** option available in the left panel of the dialog box, the options related to specifying the unit system displays on the right side of the dialog box.

4. Select the **MMGS (millimeter, gram, second)** radio button from the **Unit system** area if not selected by default. Once the unit system is specified do not exit from the dialog box.

Now, you need to specify the snap settings such that the cursor snaps the increment of 2 mm.

5. Select the **Grid/Snap** option available in the left side panel of the dialog box, the options related to the grid and snap settings displays on the right side panel of the dialog box. Also, the name of the dialog box changes to **Document Properties - Grid/Snap** dialog box.

6. Enter **10** in the **Major grid spacing** field, **5** in the **Minor -lines per major** field, and **1** in the **Snap points per minor** field of the **Grid** area in the dialog box.

7. Clear the **Display grid** check box of the **Grid** area in the dialog box to turned Off the display of grids in the drawing area, if not cleared by default.

8. Click on the **Go To System Snaps** button, the name of the dialog box changes to **System Options - Relations/Snaps**.

9. Select the **Grid** check box in the **Sketch snaps** area of the dialog box, if not selected by default to turn on the snap mode. Also, make sure that the **Snap only when grid appears** check box available below the **Grid** check box is cleared.

10. Click on the **OK** button of the dialog box, the snap settings has been specified and the dialog box is closed.

Section 4: Drawing Right Half of the Sketch

It is evident from the Figure 3.67 that the sketch is symmetric about its center line therefore you can draw right half of the outer loop of the sketch and then mirror it about the center line to create its left half of the outer loop by using the **Mirror** tool.

1. Click on the **Line** tool in the **Sketch CommandManager**, the **Line** tool invoked and the **Insert Line PropertyManager** appears on left side of the drawing area. Also, the appearance of cursor changes to the line cursor ✎ .

2. Move the cursor towards the origin and click to specify the start point of the line when the cursor snaps to the origin.

3. Move the cursor horizontal towards the right and click to specify the end point of the first line when the length of the line displays 60 above the cursor, see Figure 3.68.

4. Move the cursor vertically upwards and click to specify the end point of second line entity when the length of the line displays 20, see Figure 3.69.

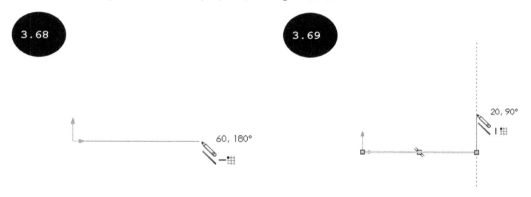

5. Move the cursor horizontal towards the right and click to specify the end point of the next line when the length of the line displays 24, see Figure 3.70.

   Now, you need to create an arc of radius 16. To create arcs, you can use arc tools. However, in this tutorial, you will create the arcs by using the **Line** tool.

6. Move the cursor to a small distance from the last specified end point and then move the cursor back to the end point, a orange color dot appears, see Figure 3.71.

7. Move the cursor horizontally toward the right to a small distance and then vertically upwards, the arc mode is invoked and the preview of the arc appears in the drawing area, see Figure 3.72.

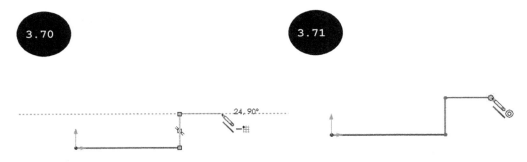

3.70   3.71

24, 90°

8. Click to specify the end point of the arc when the radius and angle of the arc being created displays 16 and 180, respectively, above the cursor, see Figure 3.72. As soon as you specify the end point of the arc, the line mode invoked again. As a result, you can continue with the creation of line entities.

9. Move the cursor horizontal towards the left and click when the length appears 24 above the cursor, see Figure 3.73.

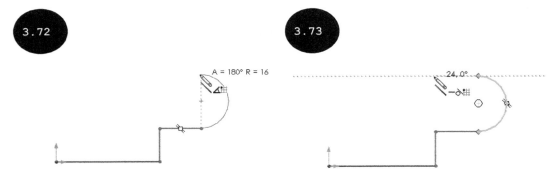

3.72   3.73

A = 180° R = 16   24, 0°

10. Move the cursor vertically upwards and click when the length of the line appears 80 above the cursor.

11. Move the cursor horizontal towards the right and click when the length of the line appears 24 above the cursor.

    Now you need to create an arc of radius 16.

12. Move the cursor to a small distance and then move the cursor back to the last specified end point, a orange color dot appears, see Figure 3.74.

13. Move the cursor horizontally toward the right to a small distance and then vertically upwards, the arc mode is invoked and the preview of the arc appears in the drawing area, see Figure 3.75.

14. Click to specify the end point of the arc when the radius and angle of the arc being created displays 16 and 180, respectively, above the cursor, see Figure 3.75. As soon as you specify the end point of the arc, the line mode invoked again.

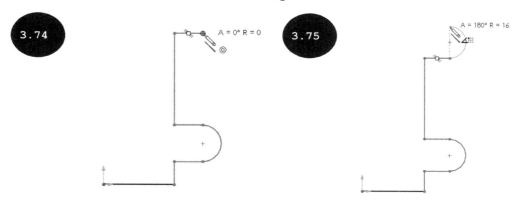

3.74

A = 0° R = 0

3.75

A = 180° R = 16

15. Move the cursor horizontal towards the left and click when the length appears 24 above the cursor.

16. Move the cursor vertically upwards and click when the length appears 18 above the cursor.

17. Move the cursor horizontal towards the left and click when the length appears 60 above the cursor, the right half of the sketch is created, see Figure 3.76. Next, press the ESC key to exit from the **Line** tool.

Section 5: Drawing Centerline

After creating the right half of the outer loop of the sketch, you can mirror it about the centerline to create its left half of the outer loop by using the **Mirror** tool.

1. Click on the down arrow available next to the **Line** tool, the **Line** flyout appears, see Figure 3.77.

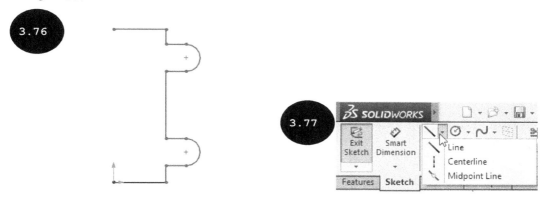

3.76

3.77

2. Click on the **Centerline** tool from the **Line** flyout, the **Insert Line PropertyManager** appears with the **For construction** check box selected in it.

3. Move the cursor towards the origin and click to specify the start point of the centerline when cursor snaps to the origin.

4. Move the cursor vertically upwards and click to create a vertical centerline of any length, see Figure 3.78. Next, right click and click on the **Select** option from the shortcut menu to exit from the **Centerline** tool.

Section 6: Mirroring Sketch Entities

After creating the centerline, you can mirror the right half of the outer loop of the sketch about the centerline by using the **Mirror Entities** tool.

1. Click on the **Mirror Entities** tool, the **Mirror PropertyManager** appears.

2. Select all the sketch entities except the centerline, the name of all the selected entities appears in the **Entities to mirror** field of the PropertyManager.

3. Click on the **Mirror about** field of the PropertyManager to activate it.

4. Select the centerline as the mirroring line, the preview of the mirror image appears in the drawing area.

5. Make sure that the **Copy** check box is selected in the PropertyManager.

6. Click on the green tick mark ✅ of the PropertyManager, the mirror image of the selected sketch entities has been created, see Figure 3.79.

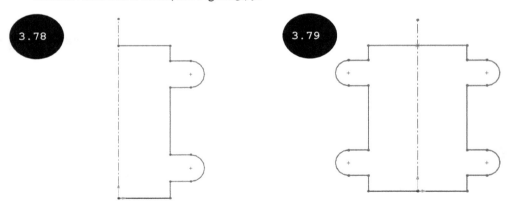

Section 7: Creating a Circle

Now, you need to create a circle of diameter 16 at the coordinate -25, 15, 0, and then later you will pattern it linearly along the X and Y axis directions to create other instances of the circle.

1. Click on the **Circle** tool, the **Circle PropertyManager** appears.

2. Move the cursor at the location whose coordinates are -26, 16, 0. For coordinates, refer to the Status Bar available at the bottom of the drawing area, see Figure 3.80.

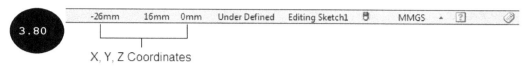

3.80

-26mm   16mm   0mm   Under Defined   Editing Sketch1   MMGS

X, Y, Z Coordinates

3. Once the coordinates -26, 16, 0 displays in the Status Bar, click to specify the center point of the circle.

4. Move the cursor horizontal towards the right and click when the radius of the circle being created displays 8, see Figure 3.81, the circle of diameter 16 is created.

5. Press the ESC key to exit from the **Circle** tool.

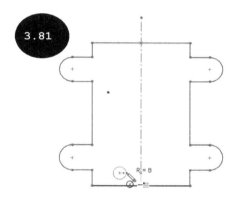

3.81

R = 8

Section 8: Creating Linear Pattern

Now, you will create linear pattern of the circle having diameter 16 to create its remaining instances.

1. Make sure that the circle of diameter 16 is selected in the drawing area. If not selected, you need to select it by clicking the left mouse button on it.

2. Click on the **Linear Sketch Pattern** tool, the **Linear Pattern PropertyManager** appears. Also, the preview of the linear pattern in X direction with default parameters appears in the drawing area.

3. Make sure that **2** is entered in the **Number of Instances** field of the **Direction 1** rollout in the PropertyManager.

4. Enter **52** in the **Spacing** field of the **Direction 1** rollout as the distance between two instances in the X direction.

5. In the **Direction 2** rollout of the PropertyManager, enter **7** in the **Number of Instances** field as the number of instances to be created in the Y direction. Next, click anywhere, the preview of the linear pattern in Y direction appears. Also, the other fields such as **Spacing** and **Angle** of the **Direction 2** rollout enabled.

6. Enter **24** in the **Spacing** field of the **Direction 2** rollout as the distance between two instances in the Y direction.

7. Click on the green tick mark ✅ of the PropertyManager, the pattern is created, see Figure 3.82.

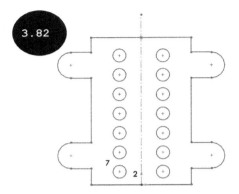

Note: The linear pattern shown in Figure 3.82 has been created when the **Display instance count** check boxes are selected in the **Direction 1** and **Direction 2** rollouts of the PropertyManager.

Tutorial 3

Draw the sketch shown in Figure 3.83. Dimensions and model shown in the figure are for your reference.

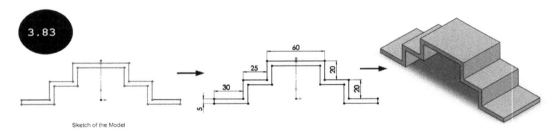

Sketch of the Model

Section 1: Starting SOLIDWORKS

First you need to start the SOLIDWORKS software.

1. Clicking on the **SOLIDWORKS** icon on your desktop to start SOLIDWORKS, if not started already.

Section 2: Invoking Sketching Environment

First invoke the Part modeling environment and then invoke the Sketching environment by selecting the Front plane as the sketching plane.

1. Click on the **New** tool in the **Standard** toolbar, the **New SOLIDWORKS Document** dialog box appears.

2. In this dialog box, the **Part** button is activated by default. Click on the **OK** button to invoke the Part modeling environment.

   Once the Part modeling environment is invoked, you can now invoke the Sketching environment and create the sketch of this tutorial.

3. Click on the **Sketch** tab in the **Command Manager**, the **Sketch CommandManager** appears.

4. Click on the **Sketch** button of the **Sketch CommandManager**, three default planes which are mutually perpendicular to each other appears in the graphics area.

5. Select the Front plane as the sketching plane, the Front plane orientated normal to the viewing direction.

Section 3: Specifying Unit and Snap Settings

Once the Sketching environment is invoked, set the snap settings such that cursor snap to the increment of 5 mm. This is because the dimensions of all the sketch entities are multiple of 5 mm. Also, specify metric unit system for measurement.

1. Click on the **Options** tool in the **Standard** toolbar, the **System Options - General** dialog box appears.

2. In this dialog box, click on the **Document Properties** tab, the name of the dialog box changes to **Document Properties - Drafting Standard**.

3. Select the **Units** option which is available in the left panel of the dialog box, the options related to specifying the unit system displays on the right panel of the dialog box.

4. Select the **MMGS (millimeter, gram, second)** radio button from the **Unit system** area if not selected by default. Once the unit system is specified do not exit from the dialog box.

   Now, you need to specify the snap settings such that the cursor snaps the increment of 5 mm.

5. Select the **Grid/Snap** option available in the left side panel of the dialog box, the options related to the grid and snap settings displays on the right side panel of the dialog box.

6. Enter **50** in the **Major grid spacing** field, **10** in the **Minor -lines per major** field, and **1** in the **Snap points per minor** field of the **Grid** area in the dialog box.

7. Clear the **Display grid** check box of the **Grid** area in the dialog box to turned Off the display of grids in the drawing area, if not cleared by default.

8. Click on the **Go To System Snaps** button, the name of the dialog box changes to **System Options - Relations/Snaps**.

9.   Select the **Grid** check box in the **Sketch snaps** area of the dialog box, if not selected by default to turn on the snap mode. Also, make sure that the **Snap only when grid appears** check box available below the **Grid** check box is cleared.

10. Click on the **OK** button of the dialog box, the snap settings has been specified and the dialog box is closed.

It is evident from the Figure 3.83 that the sketch has two loops: upper and lower. Therefore, you will first create the upper loop and then offset it to create the lower loop. Once both the loops has been created, you will join them using the line entities.

Tip: Alternatively, you can create all the entities of the sketch by using the **Line** tool or you can create one half of the sketch and then mirror it to create its other half by using the **Mirror Entities** tool.

Section 4: Drawing Upper Loop of the Sketch

As the sketch of this tutorial is symmetric about its center line, you will create left half of the upper loop of the sketch and mirror it dynamically about the center line to create the right half of the loop by using the **Dynamic Mirror** tool.

1.   Click on the down arrow available next to the **Line** tool, the **Line** flyout appears, see Figure 3.84.

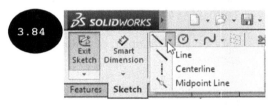

2.   Click on the **Centerline** tool from the flyout, the **Insert Line PropertyManager** appears with the **For construction** check box selected.

3.   Move the cursor towards the origin and click to specify the start point of the centerline when the cursor snaps to the origin.

4.   Move the vertical upwards and click to create a vertical centerline of length close to 50, see Figure 3.85.

After creating the centerline now you need to invoke the **Dynamic Mirror** tool so that on creating the sketch entities on one side of the centerline their respective mirror images creates dynamically on the other side of the centerline.

5.   Click on the **Tools > Sketch Tools > Dynamic Mirror** from the SOLIDWORKS menus, the **Mirror PropertyManager** appears.

6.   Move the cursor over the centerline in the drawing area and click to select it, the symbol of dynamic mirror represented by two small horizontal line appears on both side of the centerline, see Figure 3.85.

7. Click on the **Line** tool to invoke it.

8. Move the cursor at the location whose coordinates are -85, 0, 0 in the drawing area. For coordinates refer to the Status Bar available at the bottom of the drawing area.

9. Once the coordinates -85, 0, 0 displays in the Status Bar, click to specify the start point of the line.

10. Move the cursor horizontally towards the right and click to specify the end point of the first line entity when the length of the line displays 30 above the cursor, the line of length 30 is created. Also, its mirror image is created on the other side of the centerline, automatically, see Figure 3.86.

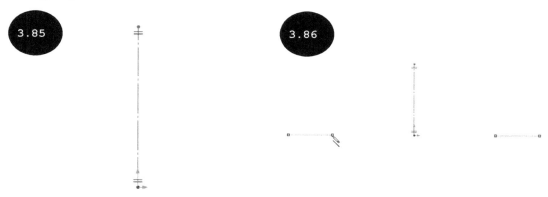

11. Move the cursor vertically upwards and click to create a line of length 20, the line of length 20 is created on both side of the centerline, see Figure 3.87. Note that as you are creating entities on the left side of the centerline their respective mirror image is being created on the right side of the centerline. This is because the **Dynamic Mirror** tool is invoked.

12. Move the cursor horizontally towards the right and click to create a line of length 25.

13. Move the cursor vertically upwards and click to create a line of length 20.

14. Move the cursor horizontally towards the right and click when the cursor snaps to the centerline. As soon as you click, the upper loop of the sketch has been created, see Figure 3.88.

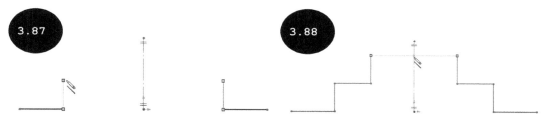

15. Right click and then click to select the **Select** option from the shortcut menu to exit from the **Line** tool.

Note that still the symbol of dynamic mirror appears on both side of the centerline. Therefore, you need to now exit from the **Dynamic Mirror** tool.

16. Click on the **Tools > Sketch Tools > Dynamic Mirror** from the SOLIDWORKS menus again to exit from the **Dynamic Mirror** tool.

Section 5: Offsetting Sketch Entities

After creating the upper loop of the sketch, you can create the lower loop by offsetting its entities to a distance of 5 mm using the **Offset Entities** tool.

1. Click on the **Offset Entities** tool, the **Offset Entities PropertyManager** appears.

2. Make sure that the **Select chain** check box is selected in this PropertyManager.

3. Select an entity of the upper loop, the preview of all the entities at an default offset distance appears in the drawing area, see Figure 3.89.

4. Make sure that the direction of offset entities being created is towards the lower side of the sketch, see Figure 3.89. If not, select the **Reverse** check box to reverse the direction of offset entities being created.

5. Enter **5** in the **Offset Distance** field of the PropertyManager and then click on the green tick mark button of the PropertyManager, the lower loop is created, see Figure 3.90.

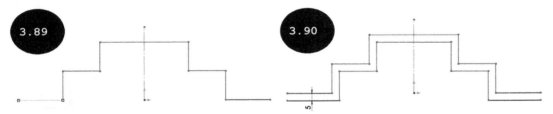

Section 6: Joining the Upper and Lower Loops

Now you need to join the upper and lower loops together by using the line entities in order to create a close sketch.

1. Invoke the **Line** tool and then move the cursor over the start point of the upper loop, see Figure 3.91 and then click to specify the start point of the line when cursor snaps, see Figure 3.91.

2. Move the cursor vertically downwards and click to specify the end point of the line when it snaps to the start point of the lower loop of the sketch, left side of the sketch is joined with the line drawn.

3. Similarly, create a line on the other open side of the sketch and then exit from the tool. Figure 3.92 shows the final sketch of this Tutorial.

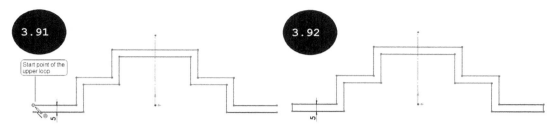

Hands-on Test Drive 1

Draw the sketch shown in Figure 3.93. Dimensions and model shown in the figure are for your reference.

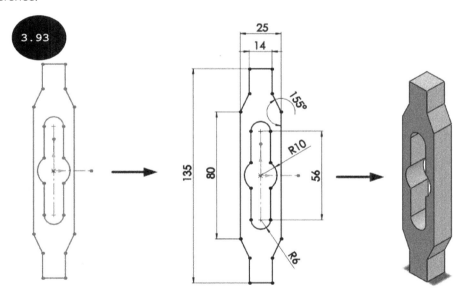

Summary

So far in this chapter, you have learnt about editing and modifying sketch entities by using various editing tools such as **Trim Entities, Extend Entities, Offset Entities, Mirror Entities**, and **Linear Sketch Pattern**. Pattern tools discussed in this chapter allows you to create linear and circular pattern. Also, the mirroring tools allows you to create mirror image of the selected entities about an mirroring line. You can also dynamically mirror the sketch entities while drawing them by using the **Dynamic Mirror** tool. Moreover, you have learnt about moving sketch entities from one position to another, coping sketch entities, rotating sketch entities, scaling, and stretching sketch entities by using their respective tools.

Questions

- The _____ tool is used to offset sketch entities or edges of the existing feature at an specified offset distance.

- You can rotate sketch entities at an angle by using the _____ tool.

- You can stretch sketch entities of a sketch by using the _____ tool.

- To rotate the sketch entities in the anti-clockwise direction, you need to define the _____ angle value.

- While offsetting sketch entities, if you select the _____ check box, all the contiguous entities of the selected sketch entity will be selected.

- The number of pattern instances specified in the **Number of Instances** field includes the parent or original instance selected to pattern (True/False).

- You can not recall the skipped pattern instances (True/False).

- In addition to trimming the sketch entities, you can extend the sketch entities by using the **Trim Entities** tool (True/False).

CHAPTER

4

Applying Geometric Relations and Dimensions

In this chapter:

- Understanding Geometric Relations
- Applying Geometric Relations
- Controlling Display of Geometric Relations
- Applying Dimensions
- Modifying Applied Dimensions
- Modifying Dimension Properties
- Different Sketch States

Once you are done with creating sketch by using the sketching tools, it is very important to make your sketch fully defined by applying proper geometric relations and dimensions. A Fully defined sketch is a sketch whose all degree of freedoms are fixed and can not move or change its shape and positions by simply dragging their entities. You will learn more about fully defined sketches later in this chapter. Before that you need to understand about geometric relations and dimensions.

Understanding Geometric Relations

Geometric relations are used to restrict some degree of freedom of the sketch. You can apply geometric relation to a sketch entity, between sketch entities, and between sketch entities and planes, axes, edges, or vertices. Some of the geometric relations such as horizontal, vertical, and coincident are applied automatically while drawing sketch entities. For example, while drawing line entity, when you move the cursor horizontally after specifying its start point, a symbol of horizontal relation appears near the cursor, see Figure 4.1. This indicates that if you click the left mouse button now to specify the end point of the line, the horizontal relation is applied to the line. Similarly, on moving the cursor vertically after specifying the start point, the symbol of vertical relation appears and applied automatically as soon as you specify the end point of the line. The various geometric relations are as follows.

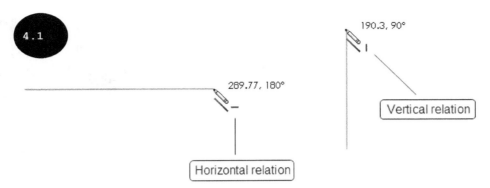

Horizontal Relation

The horizontal relation is used to change the orientation of a entity to horizontal and then force it to remain horizontal. You can apply horizontal relation to a line, centerline, and between two points or vertices.

Vertical Relation

The Vertical relation is used to change the orientation of a entity to vertical and then force it to remain vertical. You can apply vertical relation to a line, centerline, and between two points or vertices.

Coincident

The Coincident relation is used to lies/coincident a sketch point on to a line, arc, or elliptical entity and then force them to remain coincident. You can apply the Coincident relation between a point and a line, arc, or ellipse. You can also make coincident relation between a point and the origin or vertex.

Collinear

The Collinear relation is used to make two or more than two lines collinear with each other and then force them to remain collinear. You can also make line entities collinear to a planar edge or a reference plane.

Perpendicular

The Perpendicular relation is used to make two line entities perpendicular to each other and then force them to remain perpendicular. You can also make a line perpendicular to a planar edge or a plane.

Parallel

The Parallel relation is used to make two or more than two line entities parallel to each other and then force them to remain parallel. You can also make line entities parallel to a planar edge or a plane.

Tangent

The Tangent relation is used to make two sketch entities such as a circle and a line tangent to each other. You can also make two circles, arcs, ellipses, splines, and a entity: circle, arc, ellipse, spline and a line tangent to each other. Additionally, you can also make sketch entities tangent to a planar or cylindrical edge of the model.

Concentric

The Concentric geometric relation is used to make two or more than two arcs or circles, a point and an arc, and a point and a circle concentric to each other. Means, the selected entities will share the same centerpoint. You can also make sketch entities such as arcs or circles concentric to a vertex or cylindrical edge of the model.

Coradial

The Coradial relation is used to make two or more than two arcs or circles coradial to each other. Means, the selected entities share the same centerpoint as well as radius. You can also make sketch entities such as arcs or circles coradial to an cylindrical edge of the model.

Equal

The Equal relation is used to make two or more than two arcs, circle, or lines equal to each other. Means, the length of the line entities and radii of the arc entities become equal.

Midpoint

The Midpoint relation is used to make a point coincident at the middle of the line entity. You can apply midpoint relations between a sketch point and a line, a vertex and a line, or a sketch point and an planar edge.

Symmetric

The Symmetric relation is used to make two points, lines, arcs, circles, or ellipses equidistant/symmetric about a centerline.

Merge

The Merge relation is used to merge two points together to share a single point. You can merge end points of two lines.

Pierce

The Pierce relation is used to coincident a sketch point to an axis, edge, or curve of the other sketch.

Fix

The Fix relation is used to fix the current position and size of a sketch entity. However, in case of fixed line, arc, circle, and ellipse sketch entity, the end points are free to move without disturbing the position.

Applying Geometric Relations

In SOLIDWORKS, you can apply geometric relations either by using the **Add Relation** tool and **Pop-up** toolbar. Both the methods of applying geometric relations are as follows.

Applying Geometric Relation by using Add Relation tool

To apply geometric relation by using the **Add Relation** tool, click on the arrow available at the lower side of the **Display/Delete Relations** tool in the **Sketch CommandManager**, a flyout appears, see Figure. 4.2. Next, click on the **Add Relation** tool from the flyout, the **Add Relations PropertyManager** appears, see Figure 4.3. Notice that at this moment, in the **Add Relations PropertyManager** their is only **Selected Entities** rollout is available. This rollout is used to displays the list of entities, selected for applying relation.

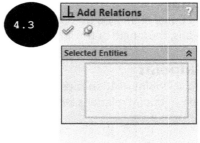

As soon as, you select entities from the drawing area for applying relation, the **Add Relations PropertyManager** modified and the name of selected entities appear in the field of the **Selected Entities** rollout. Figure 4.4 shows the modified PropertyManager after selecting two circles. The different rollouts available in the modified PropertyManager are as follows.

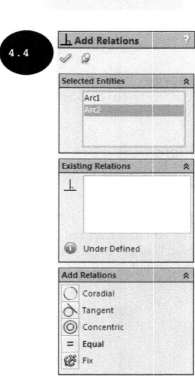

Selected Entities

The selection field of the **Selected Entities** rollout displays the list of entities selected for applying relations. You can select the entities from the drawing area.

You can also remove an entity from the list appears in the selection field of the **Selected Entities** rollout. For removing the entity, select it and then right click, a shortcut menu appears. Select the **Delete** option from the shortcut menu, the selected entity removed from the list. If you select the **Clear Selections** option from the shortcut menu, all the entities listed is removed from selection.

Existing Relations

The selection field of the **Existing Relations** rollout is used to displays the list of already applied relations between the selected entities.

> **Tip:** You can delete the already applied relations between the selected entities. To delete the existing relations, selected the relation to be deleted from the **Existing Relations** selection field and then right click, a shortcut menu appears. Select the **Delete** option from the shortcut menu, the selected relation is deleted and also removed from the list. If you select the **Delete All** option from the shortcut menu, all the existing applied relations between the selected entities is deleted.

Add Relations

The **Add Relations** rollout displays the list of all possible relations that can be applied between the selected entities. Also, the most suitable relation is highlighted, by default, see Figure 4.4. You can select the required relation to be applied between the selected entities.

Procedure to Apply Relations by using Add Relation tool

1. Click on the arrow available at the lower side of the **Display/Delete Relations** tool in the **Sketch CommandManager**, a flyout appears, see Figure 4.2.
2. Click on the **Add Relation** tool in the flyout, the **Add Relations PropertyManager** appears.
3. Select sketch entities from the drawing area to apply relation.
4. Click on the required relation to be applied between the selected entities from the selection field of the **Add Relations** rollout, the selected relation is applied.
5. Click on the green tick mark ✅ button of the PropertyManager.

Applying Geometric Relation by using Pop-up toolbar

In addition to applying geometric relations by using the **Add Relations PropertyManager**, you can also apply them by using the Pop-up toolbar. Applying geometric relations using the Pop-up toolbar is the time saving method. To apply geometric relation by using the Pop-up toolbar, directly select entities from the drawing area by pressing the CTRL key without invoking any tool. Next, release the CTRL key and do not move the cursor, a Pop-up toolbar appears near the cursor tip, see Figure 4.5. Select the required relation to be applied from the Pop-up toolbar. As soon as, you select the relation, the selected relation is applied between the entities.

> **Note:** The list of relations appears in the Pop-up toolbar depends upon the type of entities selected for applying relation. Figure 4.5 shows a Pop-up toolbar appears on selecting two circle entities.

Procedure to Apply Relations by using Pop-up toolbar

1. Select sketch entities from the drawing area by pressing the CTRL key.
2. Release the CTRL key and do not move the cursor, a Pop-up toolbar appears.
3. Select the required relation from the Pop-up toolbar.

Controlling Display of Geometric Relations

You can control the display or visibility of the applied geometric relations to sketch entities of a sketch by using the **View Sketch Relations** tool available in the **View (Heads-Up)** toolbar. To turn on or off the display of geometric relations, click on the **Hide/Show Items** button of the **View (Heads-Up)** toolbar, a flyout appears, see Figure 4.6. Next, click on the **View Sketch Relations** tool, see Figure 4.6. The display of all the geometric relations applied in the sketch entities are turn on or off. Note that this is a toggle tool.

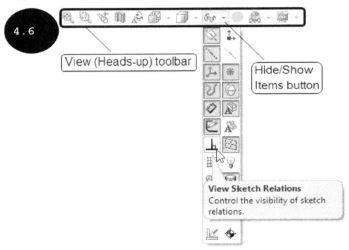

Applying Dimensions

Once the sketch has been drawn and the required geometric relations has been applied, you need to apply dimensions by using the dimension tools. As SOLIDWORKS is parametric software, the parameters of the sketch entities such as length and angle are controlled or driven by dimensions values. On modifying the dimension value, the respective sketch entity will also be modified accordingly. The tools used for applying dimensions are group together into the **Dimensions** flyout of the **Sketch CommandManager**. To invoke this flyout, click on the down arrow available at the bottom of the **Smart Dimensions** tool in the **Sketch CommandManager**, see Figure 4.7. All the dimension tools are as follows.

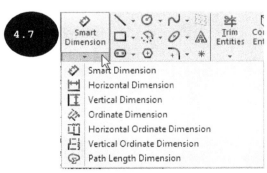

Smart Dimension tool

The **Smart Dimension** tool is used to apply dimension depending upon the type of entity selected. For example, if you select a circle, the diameter dimension is applied and if you select a line entity, the linear dimension is applied. To apply dimensions by using the **Smart Dimension** tool, click on the **Smart Dimension** tool in the **Sketch CommandManager**, the cursor changes to dimension cursor and you are prompted to selected sketch entity to be dimensioned. Select the entity to be dimensioned from the drawing area, the depending upon the type of entity selected, the respective dimension with the current dimension value is attached to the cursor tip, see Figure 4.8. Notice that as you move the cursor in the drawing area, the dimension attached will also move accordingly. Move the cursor to the location where you want to place the attached dimension in the drawing. Next, click the left mouse button for specifying the placement point in the drawing area. As soon as you click the left mouse button, the **Modify** dialog box appears, see Figure 4.9. By default, the **Modify** dialog box displays the current dimension value of the sketch entity in its **Dimension** field. Enter the required dimension value in the field of the **Modify** dialog box and then click on its green tick mark, the dimension is applied to the selected entity. Figure 4.9 shows various components of the **Modify** dialog box and are as follows.

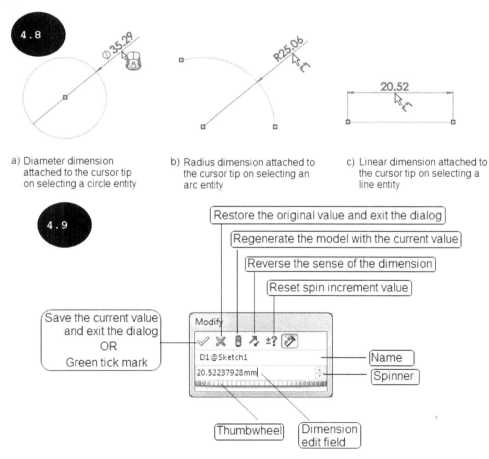

4.8

a) Diameter dimension attached to the cursor tip on selecting a circle entity

b) Radius dimension attached to the cursor tip on selecting an arc entity

c) Linear dimension attached to the cursor tip on selecting a line entity

4.9

Restore the original value and exit the dialog

Regenerate the model with the current value

Reverse the sense of the dimension

Reset spin increment value

Save the current value and exit the dialog OR Green tick mark

Modify

D1@Sketch1

20.52237928mm

Name

Spinner

Thumbwheel

Dimension edit field

The various components of the **Modify** dialog box are as follows.

Name Field

The **Name** filed of the **Modify** dialog box displays the name of the dimension. By default, the name for the dimensions assigned as D1, D2, D3 ...., and Dn. You can specify name other than default as per your convenient. For doing so, click on the **Name** field and then enter the new name, as required.

Dimension field

The **Dimension** field of the dialog box is used to specify the dimension value for the sketched entity. By default, it displays the current dimension value of the sketch entity. You can enter the new dimension value, as required, in this field.

Spinner

You can also set or control the dimension value by using the **Spinner**, see Figure 4.9. On clicking the up arrow of the **Spinner**, the dimension value is increased or add with a predefined default spin increment value. Similarly, on clicking down arrow of the spinner, the dimension value is decreased or subtract. Note the increase or decrease in dimension value is based on the default predefined spin increment value set. You can control the predefined spin increment by using the **Reset spin increment value** button of the dialog box which is discussed next.

Reset spin increment value

The **Reset spin increment value** button is used to reset the spin increment value for the dimension. To set the spin increment value using this button, click on the **Reset spin increment value** button, see Figure 4.9, the **Increment** window appears with the default spin increment value. Enter the new spin increment value as required in the field of this window and then Press the **ENTER** key, the newly entered value is set as the current spin increment value for the dimensions.

Note: On selecting the **Make Default** check box in the **Increment** window, the specified spin increment value is set as the default value for other dimensions as well.

You can also set the spin incremental value by using the **System Options - Spin Box Increments** dialog box. To invoke the **System Options - Spin Box Increments** dialog box, click on the **Options** tool of the **Standard** toolbar, the **System Options - General** dialog box appears. Select the **Spin Box Increments** option from the left panel of the dialog box, the name of the dialog box changes to **System Options - Spin Box Increments** and the options related to setting the spin increments are appear on the right panel of the dialog box.

In this dialog box, the **English units** and **Metric units** fields of the **Length increments** area are used to specify spin increment value of dimension for the English and metric unit documents, respectively.

You can specify the spin increment value for angle and time measurements by using the **Angle increments** and **Time increments** fields of the dialog box, respectively.

Thumbwheel

You can also set or control the dimension value by sliding the thumwheel, see Figure 4.9.

Regenerate the model with the current value

The Regenerate the model with the current value button is used to regenerate or refresh the drawing with the current dimension value entered in the Dimension field. This button is used when you enter the dimension value in the Dimension field of the dialog box and change in the dimension value is not reflected in the drawing area.

Reverse the sense of the dimension

The Reverse the sense of the dimension button is used to flip or reverse the dimension value from positive dimension value to negative dimension value and vice versa. Note that this button enables only when the selected dimension or dimension being applied is linear dimension.

Save the current value and exit the dialog

The Save the current value and exit the dialog button or green tick mark of the dialog box is used to accept the change in the dimension value entered in the Dimension field and to exit from the dialog box.

Restore the original value and exit the dialog

The Restore the original value and exit the dialog button or red cross mark is used to discard the change made in the dimension value. On clicking on this button, the original dimension value is restored and the Modify dialog box is closed.

Applying Dimensions using Smart Dimension tool

As discussed earlier, the Smart Dimension tool is used to apply dimensions depending upon the type of sketch entity or entities selected. You can apply horizontal, vertical, aligned, angular, diameter, radius, and linear diameter dimensions by using this tool. The method of applying different dimensions using the Smart Dimension tool are as follows.

Applying Horizontal Dimension using Smart Dimension tool

To apply horizontal dimension by using the Smart Dimension tool, click on the Smart Dimension tool to activate it. Now, you can select the sketch entity or entities to apply horizontal dimension. To apply horizontal dimension, you can select an horizontal sketch entity, an aligned sketch entity, two points, or two vertical sketch entities.

Applying Horizontal Dimension on Horizontal Entity

Once the Smart Dimension tool is activated, on selecting a horizontal sketch entity, the horizontal dimension attached with the cursor with the current dimension value, automatically. You can move the cursor vertically up or down and then click the left mouse button in the drawing to specify the placement point for the horizontal dimension. Next, enter the required dimension value in the Dimension field of the Modify dialog box and then click on the green tick mark, the horizontal dimension applied to the horizontal entity, see Figure 4.10.

Applying Horizontal Dimension on Aligned Entity

Once the **Smart Dimension** tool is activated, on selecting an aligned sketch entity, the current dimension value attached with the cursor. Move the cursor vertically downwards or upwards and click to specify the placement point for the horizontal dimension. As soon as, you specify the placement point, the **Modify** dialog box displays. In this dialog box, enter the required dimension value and then click on the green tick mark button of the dialog box, the horizontal dimension is applied to an aligned entity, see Figure 4.10.

Tip: If you move the cursor in the direction other than the vertical after selecting the aligned entity, the vertical or aligned dimension attached with the cursor.

Applying Horizontal Dimension between two Points

Once the **Smart Dimension** tool is activated, on selecting two points of the sketch entities, the current distance value between the selected points attached with the cursor. Move the cursor vertically downwards or upwards and click to specify the placement point for the horizontal dimension. As soon as, you specify the placement point, the **Modify** dialog box appears. In this dialog box, enter the required dimension value and then click on the green tick mark of the dialog box, the horizontal dimension applied between two points, see Figure 4.10.

Applying Horizontal Dimension between two Vertical Entities

Once the **Smart Dimension** tool is activated, on selecting two vertical sketch entities, the horizontal dimension value attached with the cursor. Move the cursor vertically downwards or upwards and click to specify the placement point for the horizontal dimension. Next, enter the required dimension value in the field of the **Modify** dialog box and then click on the green tick mark button, the horizontal dimension applied between two vertical entities, see Figure 4.10.

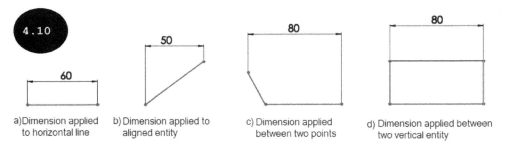

a) Dimension applied to horizontal line   b) Dimension applied to aligned entity   c) Dimension applied between two points   d) Dimension applied between two vertical entity

Applying Vertical Dimension using Smart Dimension tool

Similar to applying horizontal dimension by using the **Smart Dimension** tool, you can also apply vertical dimension to an vertical sketch entity, aligned sketch entity, between two points, and between two horizontal sketch entities, see Figure 4.11.

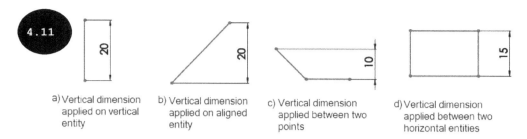

a) Vertical dimension applied on vertical entity

b) Vertical dimension applied on aligned entity

c) Vertical dimension applied between two points

d) Vertical dimension applied between two horizontal entities

Applying Aligned Dimension using Smart Dimension tool

Similar to applying horizontal and vertical dimension by using the **Smart Dimension** tool, you can also apply aligned dimension to an aligned sketch entity or between two points, see Figure 4.12. It is generally used to measure the aligned length of an inclined line or line at an angle. Note that after selecting an entity or entities, you need to move the cursor perpendicular to the entity selected for specifying the placement point.

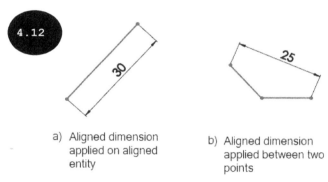

a) Aligned dimension applied on aligned entity

b) Aligned dimension applied between two points

Applying Angular Dimension using Smart Dimension tool

By using the **Smart Dimension** tool you can apply angular dimension between two line entities or three points. Both are as follows.

Applying Angular Dimension between two Lines

Once the **Smart Dimension** tool is activated, select two lines, see Figure 4.13, and then move the cursor to a small distance, the angular dimension between the selected entities is attached with the cursor. Move the cursor to the location where you want to place the dimension and then click to specify the placement point. As soon as you specify the placement point, the **Modify** dialog box appears. Enter the required angular value in this dialog box and then press **ENTER**, the angular dimension applied between two line entities. Note the angular dimension appears attached with the cursor depends upon the movement of cursor after selecting the entities, see Figure 4.13.

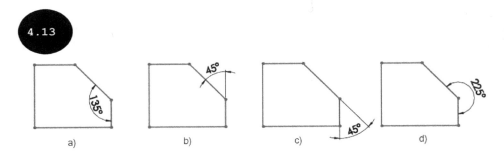

4.13

a)   b)   c)   d)

Applying Angular Dimension between three Points

On selecting three points, when you move the cursor to a small distance, the angular dimension between the selected points is attached with the cursor. Move the cursor to the location where you want to place the dimension attached and then click to specify the placement point at that location. As soon as you click the left mouse button, the modify dialog box appears, specify the angular value in this dialog box and then press **ENTER**. Note the angular dimension appears attached with the cursor depends upon the movement of cursor after selecting the entities to be dimensioned, see Figure 4.14.

Applying Diameter Dimension using Smart Dimension tool

The diameter dimension can be applied to a circle by using the **Smart Dimension** tool. To apply diameter dimension, click on the **Smart Dimension** tool and then select a circle, the diameter dimension is attached with the cursor. Move the cursor to the required location and click to specify the placement point, the **Modify** dialog box appears. Enter the diameter value in this dialog box and then press **ENTER**, the diameter dimension is applied, see Figure 4.15.

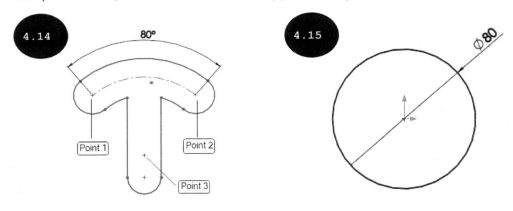

4.14

4.15

Note: By default, you can apply diameter dimension to a circle by using the **Smart Dimension** tool. However, you can also apply radius dimension to the circle. For doing so, after applying the diameter dimension to a circle, select the applied diameter dimension and right click to display a shortcut menu. Next, select **Display Options > Display As Radius** from the shortcut menu. If the **Display Options** is not visible in the shortcut menu, you need to expand the shortcut menu by clicking on the two down arrows available at the lower side of the shortcut menu. Also, note that, if the **Smart Dimension** tool is activated then you can directly select the **Display As Radius** option from the shortcut menu.

Applying Radius Dimension using Smart Dimension tool

The radius dimension can be applied to an arc by using the **Smart Dimension** tool. To apply radius dimension, click on the **Smart Dimension** tool and then select an arc, the radius dimension is attached with the cursor. Move the cursor to the required location and click to specify the placement point, the **Modify** dialog box appears. Enter the radius value in this dialog box and then press **ENTER**, the radius dimension is applied, see Figure 4.16.

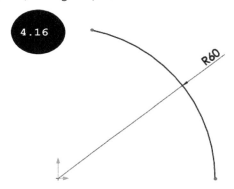

Note: By default, you can apply radius dimension to an arc by using the **Smart Dimension** tool. However, you can also apply diameter dimension to an arc. For doing so, after applying the radius dimension to an arc, select the applied radius dimension and right click to display a shortcut menu. Next, select the **Display Options > Display As Diameter** from the shortcut menu. If the **Display Options** option is not visible in the shortcut menu, you need to expand it by clicking on the two down arrows available at the lower side of the shortcut menu. Also, note that, if the **Smart Dimension** tool is activated then you can directly select the **Display As Diameter** option from the shortcut menu.

Applying Linear Diameter Dimension using Smart Dimension tool

The linear diameter dimension is used to apply linear diameter dimension to a sketch that represent revolve features, see Figure 4.17. To apply linear diameter dimension by using the **Smart Dimension** tool, click on the **Smart Dimension** tool. Next, select a linear sketch entity of a revolve sketch, a linear dimension is attached with the cursor. Next, select the centerline or revolving axis of the sketch, the linear dimension between the sketch line and centerline is attached with the cursor. Move the cursor to the other side of the centerline, the linear diameter dimension is attached with the cursor. Next, click to specify the placement point, the **Modify** dialog box appears. Enter the linear diameter value in the dialog box and then press **ENTER**, the linear diameter dimension is applied.

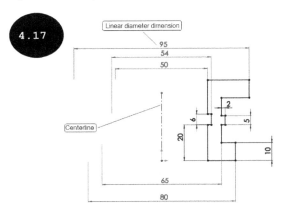

Horizontal Dimension and Vertical Dimension tools

In additional to applying horizontal and vertical dimensions by using the **Smart Dimension** tool, you can also apply these dimensions by using the **Horizontal Dimension** and **Vertical Dimension** tools available in the **Dimension** flyout, see Figure 4.18. To apply horizontal dimension by using the **Horizontal Dimension** tool, click on the down arrow available below the **Smart Dimension** tool, the **Dimension** flyout appears, see Figure 4.18.

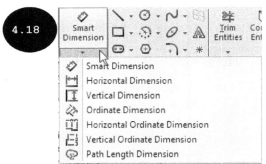

Click on the **Horizontal Dimension** tool in the flyout, cursor changes to horizontal dimension cursor. Next, move the cursor over the sketch entity to be horizontal dimensioned and when the entity highlights, click to select it. As soon as you select the entity, the horizontal dimension is attached with the cursor. Move the cursor to the location where you want to place the dimension and then click to specify the placement point in the drawing area, the **Modify** dialog box appears. Enter the required dimension value in the **Modify** dialog box and then press **ENTER**, the horizontal dimension is applied.

Similar to applying horizontal dimension by using the **Horizontal Dimension** tool, you can apply vertical dimension by using the **Vertical Dimension** tool of the **Dimension** flyout.

Ordinate Dimension tool

The **Ordinate Dimension** tool is used to apply ordinate dimensions. Ordinate dimensions are the dimensions that measures from a base entity. The base entity defines as the start measuring entity from where all other sketch entities measures, see Figure 4.19. The ordinate dimensions are generally used for the components created using CNC machines. Figure 4.20 shown a model and Figure 4.21 shows the sketch used to created this model. Notice that in the Figure 4.21 the horizontal dimensions applied to the sketch having symmetric tolerance value of 0.1. It means that the maximum accepted length of the entities measures 100, 30, and 40 are 100.1, 30.1, and 40.1, respectively. Now, when you sum the maximum accepted dimension of the entities (2, 4, and 6) measuring 30, 40, and 30, you will get that the maximum accepted horizontal length of the model which is 100.3 (30.1+40.1+30.1). At the same time when you look at the entity (8) of the sketch, the maximum accepted horizontal length of the model is 100.1. Since one side the maximum accepted horizontal length of the model measured as 100.3 and other side it measured as 100.1 which is not correct, you need to apply ordinate dimensions. Applying ordinate dimensions to components machined using CNC machine is the recommended method to overcome with problems like this. Figure 4.19 show the sketch with ordinate dimensions applied where the maximum accepted horizontal length measured as 100.1 only.

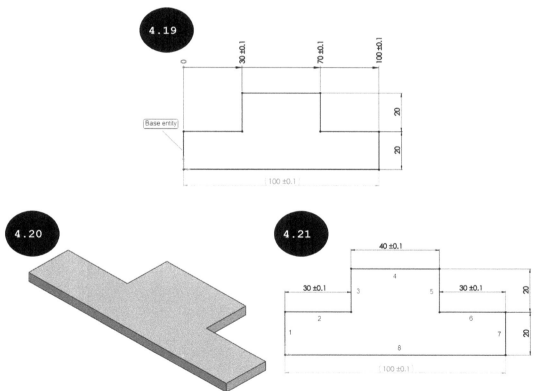

You can apply horizontal and vertical ordinate dimensions by using the **Ordinate Dimension** tool and are as follows.

Applying Horizontal Ordinate Dimensions

To apply horizontal ordinate dimension, click on the down arrow available below the **Smart Dimension** tool, the **Dimension** flyout appears, see Figure 4.18. Click on the **Ordinate Dimension** tool in the flyout, cursor changes to ordinate dimension cursor and you is prompted to select an entity as the base entity for measuring dimensions. Select an vertical entity as the base entity, the zero dimension value is attached with the cursor. Move the cursor to the required location and click to specify the placement point. Next, select the second vertical entity for measuring the horizontal distance from the zero base dimension value. As soon as you select the second entity, the horizontal distance from the zero dimension value to the second entity is applied and appears in the drawing area. Similarly, select the other vertical entities for measuring the horizontal dimensions from the zero dimension value, see figure 4.22.

Applying Vertical Ordinate Dimensions

Similar to applying horizontal ordinate dimension, you can apply vertical ordinate dimensions by using the **Ordinate Dimension** tool. To apply vertical ordinate dimension, after invoking the **Ordinate Dimension** tool and select an horizontal entity as the base entity, the zero dimension value is attached with the cursor. Move the cursor to the required location and then click to specify the placement point, see Figure 4.23. Next, select the second horizontal entity for measuring the vertical distance from the zero dimension. As soon as you select the second entity, the vertical distance from the zero value to the second entity is applied and appears in the drawing area. Similarly, select the other entities for measuring the vertical dimensions from the zero dimension, see Figure 4.23.

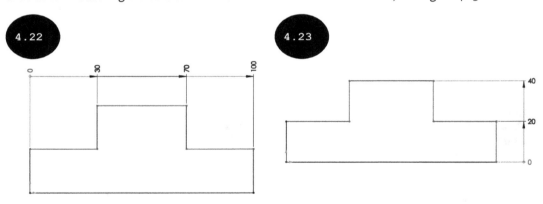

Tip: Similar to applying horizontal and vertical ordinate dimensions by using the **Ordinate Dimension** tool, you can also apply horizontal ordinate dimension by using the **Horizontal Ordinate Dimension** tool and vertical ordinate dimension by using the **Vertical Ordinate Dimension** tool available in the **Dimension** flyout.

Modifying Applied Dimensions

After applying dimensions, you may need to modify them due to the change in design, revisions in design, and so on. To modified already applied dimensions, double click on the dimension to be modified, the **Modify** dialog box appears. Enter the new modified dimension value in the **Dimension** field of the dialog box. You can also set the new dimension value by using the **Spinner** and **Thumbwheel** available in the **Modify** dialog box. Once the new dimension value has been specified, click on the green tick mark button of the **Modify** dialog box.

Modifying Dimension Properties

In SOLIDWORKS, when you apply dimension, the dimension applies with default parameters. You can modify the default parameters such as dimension style, tolerance, and precision by using the **Dimension PropertyManager**. To invoke the **Dimension PropertyManager**, select the dimension whose parameters has to be modified. As soon as, you select dimension, the **Dimension PropertyManager** appears at the left of the drawing area, see Figure 4.24. The options available in this PropertyManager are as follows.

Value Tab

By default, the **Value** tab of the **Dimension PropertyManager** is activated and the options available in this tab are used to modify parameters related to the dimension value. These options are as follows.

Style

The **Style** rollout of the **Value** tab is used to restore default attributes such as dimension height, fonts, and arrow type to default style, add new style, update existing style, delete added style, save style, and load existing style in the current document. The options available in this rollout are as follows.

Apply the default attributes to selected dimensions

The **Apply the default attributes to selected dimensions** button of the **Style** rollout is used to restore the dimension attributes such as dimension height, fonts, arrow type to the as per the default style. If you have modified any dimension attributes of the default style then on click this button, the modified dimension attributes or style restores to the default dimension attributes.

Add or Update a Style

The **Add or Update a Style** is used to add new dimension style or update existing dimension style. To add new dimension style, click on the **Add or Update a Style** button, the **Add or Update a Style** dialog box appears, see Figure 4.25. Enter the name of the style to be added in the **Enter a new name or choose an existing name** field of this dialog box. Next, choose the **OK** button from the dialog box, the new style is added in the current document and set as the current style for the document. Also, its name appears in the **Set a current Style** drop-down list of the **Style** rollout. Now you can specify different attributes for this newly added style such as dimension height, fonts, arrow type. You will learn more about specifying dimension attributes later.

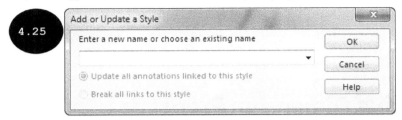

To update the existing dimension style attributes, click on the **Add or Update a Style** button of the **Style** rollout to display the **Add or Update a Style** dialog box. In this dialog box, click on the down arrow available on the right of the **Enter a new name or choose an existing name** field, a drop-down appears. Select the dimension style to be updated. As soon as you select the dimension style, the **Update all annotations linked to this style** and **Break all links to this style** radio buttons are enabled in this dialog box. By default, the **Update all annotations linked to this style** radio button is selected. As a result, any modification made in the attributes of the selected style for a selected dimension, will also be reflected to the other dimensions of the same style after choosing the **OK** button from this dialog box.

Note: If the modification is not reflected in the other dimensions of the same style after choosing the **OK** button from the **Add or Update a Style** dialog box, click on the dimensions in the drawing area to update them.

On selecting the **Break all links to this style** radio button and then the link between the other dimensions assigned to this selected style is braked on choosing the **OK** button of the dialog box. In other words, the other dimensions associated to the selected dimension style will no longer be associated with the same dimension style.

Delete a Style

The **Delete a Style** button of the **Style** rollout is used to delete existing style that is no longer required. To delete a style, select the style from the **Set a current Style** drop-down list of the **Style** rollout and then click on the **Delete a Style** button, the selected style is deleted from the current document.

Save a Style

The **Save a Style** button of the **Style** rollout is used to save the style as an external file so that you can load the same style to the other documents as well. To save the style, select the style in the **Set a current Style** drop-down list of the **Style** rollout and then click on the **Save a Style** button, the **Save As** window appears. Browse to the location where you want to save the style and then click on the **Save** button. The selected style is saved in the specified location in the file *.sldstl* extension.

Load Styles

The **Load Style** button of the **Style** rollout is used to load the existing saved style to the current document. To load the style, click on the **Load Style** button, the **Open** window appears. Browse to the location where the style has been saved and then select the style. After selecting the style to be loaded, click on the **Open** button, the selected style is loaded in the current document and set as the activated style. Also, its name is selected in the **Set a current Style** drop-down list of the **Style** rollout.

Set a current Style

The **Set a current Style** drop-down list displays the list of all the added styles in the current document. By default, the **None** option is selected in this drop-down list. As a result, the default dimension style is used, by default.

Tolerance/Precision

The options in the **Tolerance/Precision** rollout is used to specify the tolerance and precision values for the selected dimension style. By default, the **None** style is selected in the **Set a current Style** drop-down list of the **Style** rollout. You can selected a style whose parameters has to be modified or specified, as required from this drop-down list. The options of this rollout are as follows.

Tolerance Type

The **Tolerance Type** drop-down list is used to select the type of tolerance to be applied for the selected dimension or dimensions. By default, the **None** option is selected in this drop-down list. As a result, no tolerance is applied to the dimensions. Depending upon the type of tolerance selected in this drop-down list, their respective field is available below this drop-down list in the **Tolerance/Precision** rollout for specifying tolerance values.

Unit Precision

The **Unit Precision** drop-down list is used to select the unit of precision or number of digits after decimal point in a dimension value.

Primary Value

The **Primary Value** rollout is used to display or control the information of the primary dimension value. The primary dimension value is the original dimension value of the entities and which drives the entities when any modification made in it. The options in this rollout are as follows.

Name

The **Name** field of the **Primary Value** rollout is used to display the name of the dimension selected. By default, a default name is assigned to dimensions. You enter new name for the selected dimension in this field. Note that the name you entered in this field will automatically be followed by *@Sketch1* (Sketch1 is the name of the sketch). In your case, it can be different sketch name may be Sketch2, Sketch3, ... or Sketch'n'.

Dimension value

The **Dimension Value** field of the **Primary Value** rollout is used to display the current dimension value of the selected dimension. You enter the new dimension value in this field for the selected dimension. The value entered in this field drives the sketch entity of the selected dimension.

Dimension Text

The **Dimension Text** rollout is used to add text and geometric symbols to the selected dimension. The options available in this rollout are as follows.

Add Parentheses

The **Add Parentheses** button of the **Dimension Text** rollout is used to display dimension value or text as a driven or reference dimension with parentheses, see Figure 4.26.

Inspection Dimension

The **Inspection Dimension** button is used to display dimension value or text with inspection, see Figure 4.26.

Center Dimension

The **Center Dimension** button is used to display dimension value or text between the dimension extension line. Note that when you drag the dimension text, the text snaps to the center of the extension line, see Figure 4.26.

Offset Text

The **Offset Text** button is used to display dimension value or text at an offset distance from the dimension line by using a leader, see Figure 4.26.

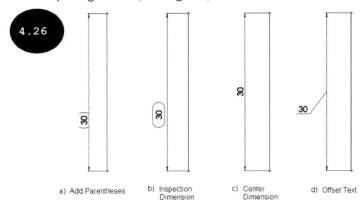

4.26

a) Add Parentheses   b) Inspection Dimension   c) Center Dimension   d) Offset Text

Text Field

The **Text** field displays <DIM>, where the DIM represents the dimension value. You can add text, prefixes, and suffixes before or after <DIM> in the field. Figure 4.27 shows a dimension value after adding L- in front of <DIM> in the **Text** field.

Note: If you delete <DIM> from the **Text** field, the dimension value will also be deleted or removed from the drawing area. Also, the **Add Value** button ⬚ is enabled in the **Dimension Text** rollout. On choosing this **Add Value** button, the dimension value is restored in the drawing area. Also the <DIM> displays in the **Text** field.

Left Justify/Center Justify/Right Justify

The **Left Justify**, **Center Justify**, and **Right Justify** buttons are used to left, center, and right justify the dimension value and text entered in the **Text** field of the **Dimension Text** rollout, respectively.

Symbols

The **Symbols** area of the rollout is used to add different types of symbols in the selected dimensions, see Figure 4.28. To add a symbol, click to place the cursor where you want to insert or add the symbol in the **Text** field and then click on the required symbol button to be added, the selected symbol is added in the field as well as displays in the drawing area. On clicking on the **More** button of this area, the **Symbol Library** dialog box appears, see Figure 4.29.

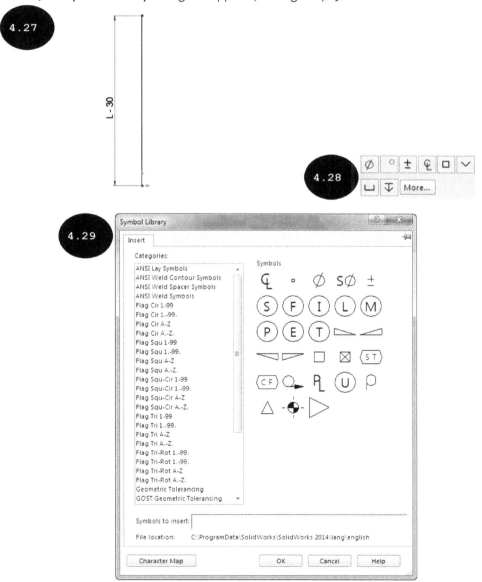

Dual Dimension

The **Dual Dimension** rollout is used to display dual or alternative dimension measurement for sketch entities. By default, this rollout is collapse. As a result, the dimension values displays for sketch entities in the drawing area are only in the document's unit system. To display dimensions in dual dimension unit, expand the **Dual Dimension** rollout by selecting the check box available in front of the **Dual Dimension** rollout. As soon as, the **Dual Dimension** rollout expanded, the dimension displays in the drawing area in the default dual dimension unit along with the current document unit, see Figure 4.30. Also, the expanded **Dual Dimension** rollout displays the **Unit Precision** and **Tolerance Precision** drop-down lists. By using these drop-down lists you can specify precision values for dual dimension and tolerance.

4.30

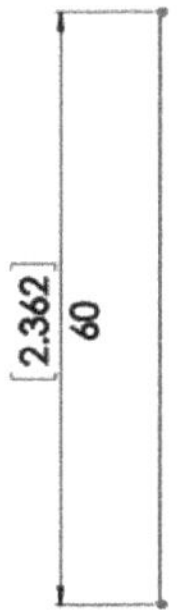

Note: You can specify unit system for dual dimensions by using the **Document Properties - Units** dialog box. To invoke this dialog box, click on the **Options** tool in the **Standard** toolbar to display the **System Options - General** dialog box. Next, click on the **Document Properties** tab in the dialog box and then select the **Units** option from its left panel, the name of the dialog box changes to **Document Properties - Units**. Next, specify the dual dimension unit for dimension in the field respective to the **Unit** column and the **Dual Dimension Length** field.

Leaders Tab

The options available in the **Leaders** tab of the **Dimension PropertyManager** are used to control the properties of the dimension leader. Figure 4.31 shows the PropertyManager with **Leader** tab is activated. The options available in this tab are as follows.

Withness/Leader Display

The **Withness/Leader Display** rollout is used to specify the parameters for dimension arrows. The options available in this rollout are as follows.

Outside

The **Outside** button of this rollout is used to place dimension arrows outside the dimension extension lines, see Figure 4.32.

Inside

The **Inside** button of this rollout is used to place dimension arrows inside the dimension extension lines, see Figure 4.32.

Smart

By default, the **Smart** button is activated. As a result, the placement of arrows either inside or outside the extension lines of the dimensions depends upon the availability of space between the extension lines of the dimension. For example, if the space available between the extension lines of the dimension is not enough to place arrows inside then automatically the arrows is placed outside the extension lines.

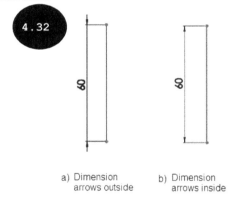

a) Dimension arrows outside b) Dimension arrows inside

Directed Leader

The **Directed Leader** button is used to orient the leader at an angle with respect to the surface on which it is applied, see Figure 4.33. The leaders that can be oriented by using this button are applied by using the tools available in the **DimXpert CommandManager**. Also, note that this button is enabled in the **Withness/Leader Display** rollout only when the selected leader applied on the cylindrical surface.

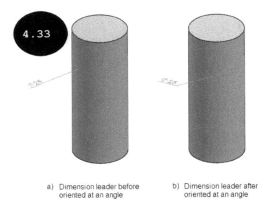

a) Dimension leader before oriented at an angle

b) Dimension leader after oriented at an angle

Style Drop-down List

The **Style** drop-down list of the rollout is used to select type of arrow style to be used for the selected dimension. You can define different arrow styles for different dimensions in a sketch.

Radius

The **Radius** button is used to apply radius dimension even if the selected dimension is a diameter dimension of a circle. Note that this button enabled only if the selected dimension is either a diameter or radius dimension. On selecting the **Radius** button, the selected diameter dimension becomes radius dimension. Also, three buttons: **Foreshortened**, **Solid Leader**, and **Open Leader** enabled bellow this button in the rollout, see Figure 34. By using these buttons, you can specify the leader type for radius dimension, see Figures 4.35.

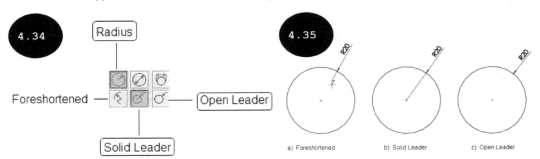

a) Foreshortened

b) Solid Leader

c) Open Leader

Diameter

The **Diameter** button is used to apply diameter dimension even if the selected dimension is a radius dimension of an arc. Note that this button enabled only if the selected dimension is either a diameter or radius dimension. On selecting the **Diameter** button, the selected dimension becomes diameter dimension. Also, four buttons: **Two Arrows / Solid Leader**, **Two Arrows / Open Leader**, **One Arrow / Solid Leader**, and **One Arrow / Open Leader** displays bellow the **Diameter** button in the rollout, see Figure 4.36. These buttons are used to specify the type of leader, see Figures 4.37. Note that the **Two Arrows / Solid Leader** and **Two Arrows / Open Leader** buttons is enabled when the **Use document second arrow** check box is cleared in the rollout.

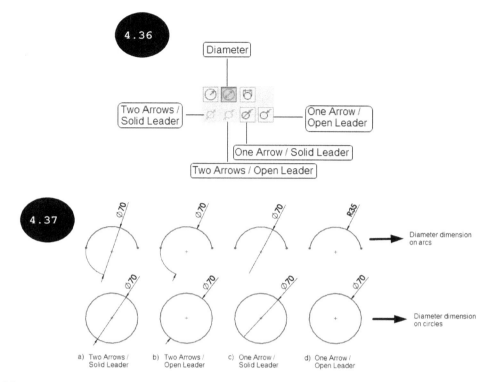

Linear

The **Linear** button is used to display diameter dimension linearly. On selecting the **Linear** button, the selected diameter dimension displays linearly in the drawing area. Also, the two buttons: **Perpendicular To Axis** and **Parallel To Axis** enabled. By default, the **Perpendicular To Axis** button is activated.

Use document second arrow

The **Use document second arrow** check is used to specify second arrow for diameter dimension as per the document default setting. If this check box is selected, the diameter dimension second arrow is specified as per the document default setting. If you clear this check box, the **Two Arrows / Solid Leader**, **Two Arrows / Open Leader** buttons is enabled for specifying the type of second arrow for diameter dimension. Note that this check box available when the **Diameter** button is activated in the **Witness/Leader Display** rollout.

Note: To specify the document default setting for the second arrow, invoke the **Document Properties - Diameter** dialog box. To invoke this dialog box, click on the **Options** tool in the **Standard** toolbar, the **System Options - General** dialog box appears. In this dialog box, click on the **Document Properties** tab and then expand the **Dimensions** node by clicking on the plus (+) sign available on its front. Next, select the **Diameter** option, the name of the dialog box changed to **Document Properties - Diameter**. In this dialog box, you can specify the default document setting for the display of second arrow for diameter dimensions by selecting the **Display second outside arrow** check box available at the lower side of the dialog box. Also, on selecting the **Display with solid leader** check box available below the **Display second outside arrow** check box in the dialog box, the display of second arrow for diameter dimension with solid leader is specified as the default document setting.

Use document bend length

The **Use document bend length** check box is used to specify the leader length after bend. If this check box is selected, the default bend leader length specified in the **Document Properties - Dimensions** dialog box is used. However, if you clear this check box, you can specify the bend length for the selected leader in the field available below this check box.

Note: To specify the default bend setting for leaders, invoke the **Document Properties - Dimensions** dialog box. To invoke this dialog box, click on the **Options** tool in the **Standard** toolbar, the **System Options - General** dialog box appears. In this dialog box, click on the **Document Properties** tab and then select **Dimensions** node, the options related to the dimension styles are appear on the right side of the dialog box. Also, the name of the dialog box changes to the **Document Properties - Dimensions** dialog box. In this dialog box, specify the bend length for dimension leaders in the **Leader length** field of the **Bent leaders** area as the default leader bend length.

Leader/Dimension Line Style

The options available in the **Leader/Dimension Line Style** rollout are used to specify the leader style and thickness properties for the leader. By default, the **Use document display** check box is selected in this rollout. As as result, the default properties of the leader specified in the **Document Properties** dialog box is used. On clearing this check box, the **Leader Style** and **Leader Thickness** drop-down lists is enabled in this rollout. By using these drop-down lists, you can specify the leader style and leader thickness for the selected dimension leader.

You can specify the default leader style and thickness for angle dimensions, arc length, chamfer, hole, linear, ordinate, and radius dimensions. To specify the default leader style and thickness for angle dimension, invoke the **Document Properties - Angle** dialog box. To invoke this dialog box, click on the **Options** tool in the **Standard** toolbar, the **System Options - General** dialog box appears. In this dialog box, click on the **Document Properties** tab and then expand the **Dimensions** node by clicking on the plus (+) sign available on its front. Next, select the **Angle** option from the expanded **Dimensions** node, the dialog box appear as **Document Properties - Angle** dialog box. In this dialog box, you can specify the default leader style and thickness for angle dimensions by using the **Leader Style** and **Leader Thickness** drop-down lists of the **Leader Style** area. Similarly, you can specify the default leader style and thickness for arc length, chamfer, hole, linear, ordinate, and radius dimensions by invoking their respective dialog boxes.

Custom Text Position

The options of the **Custom Text Position** rollout is used to custom the position of dimension text with respect to the dimension leader. By default, this rollout is collapse. As a result, the dimension text and leader is placed as per the default settings. Expand the **Custom Text Position** rollout by selecting the check box available in the front of the title bar of this rollout. When you click on the **Solid Leader, Aligned Text** button, the selected dimension appears in the drawing area having the solid dimension leader with aligned dimension text. On clicking the **Broken Leader, Horizontal Text** button, the selected dimension appears in the drawing area having the broken dimension leader with horizontal dimension text. On the other hand, clicking on the **Broken Leader, Aligned Text** button, the selected dimension appears in the drawing area having the broken dimension leader with aligned dimension text, see Figure 4.38.

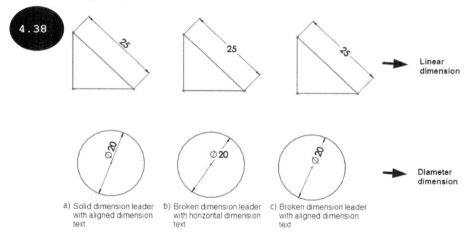

a) Solid dimension leader with aligned dimension text   b) Broken dimension leader with horizontal dimension text   c) Broken dimension leader with aligned dimension text

Other Tab

The options available in the **Other** tab of the **Dimension PropertyManager** are as follows.

Override Units

The **Override Units** rollout is used to override the default unit specified in the **Document Properties – Units** dialog box for all the dimensions. You can override the default units of the selected dimension by using this rollout. For doing so, expand the **Override Units** rollout by selecting the check box available in the front of its title bar, see Figure 4.39. Once the **Override Units** rollout is expanded, select the unit type from the **Length Units** drop-down list of the rollout as the override unit for the selected dimension.

Note: The other options available in the **Override Units** rollout are depends upon the type of unit selected in the **Length Units** drop-down list of the rollout. For example, if **Inches** is selected in the **Length Units** drop-down list, the **Decimal** and **Fractions** radio buttons is available in the **Override Units** rollout of the PropertyManager. You can select the required radio button to display the override unit in either decimal or fractions.

Tip: The method of specifying the default units for measurement by using the **Document Properties - Units** dialog box as discussed in earlier chapters.

Text Fonts

The **Text Fonts** rollout is used to specify the font for the selected dimension. By default, the **Use document font** check box is selected. As a result, the default dimension font specified in the **Document Properties - Dimensions** dialog box is used for all the dimensions. However, if you clear the **Use document font** check box, the **Fonts** button is enabled bellow this check box. Click on the **Fonts** button, the **Choose Font** dialog box appears, see Figure 4.40. By using this dialog box, you can specify required font, font style, and dimension text height.

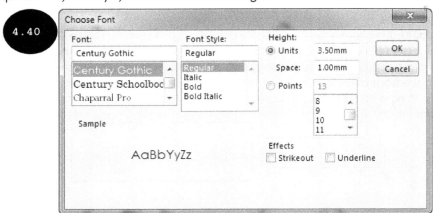

To specify the default dimension font for dimensions, invoke the **Document Properties - Dimension** dialog box. To invoke this dialog box, click on the **Options** tool in the **Standard** toolbar, the **System Options - General** dialog box appears. In this dialog box, click on the **Document Properties** tab and then select **Dimensions**, the options related to dimension styles are appears on the right side of the dialog box. Also, the name of the dialog box changes to the **Document Properties - Dimensions**. In this dialog box, click on the **Font** button available in the **Text** area of the dialog box, the **Choose Font** dialog box appears. By using this **dialog** box, you can specify the default font, font style, text height for dimensions.

Options

The **Options** rollout is provided with **Read only** and **Driven** check boxes. By default, both the check boxes are cleared. On selecting the **Read only** check box, the selected dimension becomes read only dimension and can not be or modified. If you select the **Driven** check box, the selected become driven or reference dimension which can not drive the sketch entity.

Different Sketch States

In SOLIDWORKS, a sketch can be either **Under defined**, **Fully defined**, or **Over defined**. These are the different states of sketches that appears at the right side of the Status Bar in the Sketching environment. All these states of sketches are as follows.

Under defined Sketch

A under defined sketch is a sketch whose all the degree of freedoms of the sketch entities are not fixed. Means, the entities can change its shape, size, and position by dragging them. Figure 4.41 shows a rectangular sketch in which length of the rectangle is defined as 100 mm. However, the width and position with respect to the origin of the rectangle is not define. It means that width and position of rectangle can be changed by dragging the respective entities of the rectangle. The current status of sketch appears in the right side of the Status Bar available at the lower side of the drawing area. Note that the entities of a under defined sketch are displays in blue color.

Fully defined Sketch

A fully defined sketch is a sketch whose all the degree of freedoms are fixed. Means, the entities of the sketch can not change its shape, size, and position by dragging them. Figure 4.42 shows a rectangular sketch in which its length, width, and position with respect to the origin is defined. Note that the entities of a fully defined sketch are appears in black color.

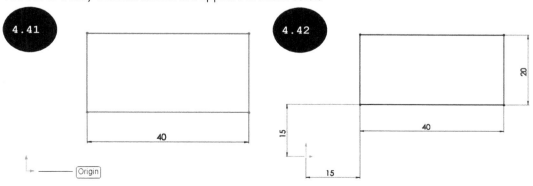

> **Tip:** The sketch shown in Figure 4.42 is fully defined as all its entities are dimensioned and the required geometrical relations have been applied. The required geometrical relations applied in this sketch are horizontal to the horizontal entity and vertical to the vertical entity. The relation such as horizontal and vertical applies automatically to the sketch entities while drawing them.

Over defined Sketch

A over defined sketch is a sketch which is over defined by dimensions or geometric relations. Figure 4.43 shows a over defined rectangular sketch. As the length of both sides of the rectangle is same therefore applying dimension to both the side of the rectangle makes it over define. Note that the entities of a over defined sketch are appears in yellow color. Also, when you apply over define dimension to an entity, the **Make Dimension Driven?** dialog box appears, see Figure 4.44. In this dialog box, if you select the **Make this dimension driven** and click **OK** button, the newly applied dimension becomes the driven dimension and act as a reference dimension only. As a result, the sketch will not become an over defined sketch. However, if you select the **Leave this dimension driving** radio button and click **OK** button of the dialog box then the newly applied dimension applied as driving dimension. As a result, the sketch becomes the over defined dimension.

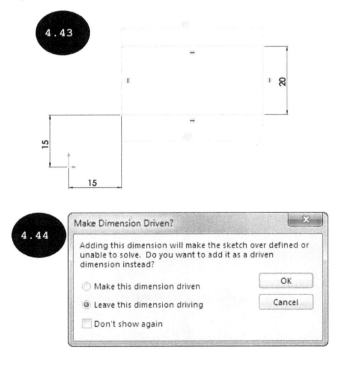

Tutorial 1

Draw the sketch shown in Figure 4.45 and make it fully defined by applying all the dimensions and relations. The model shown in the figure is for your reference only. You will learn about creating model from the sketch in later chapters.

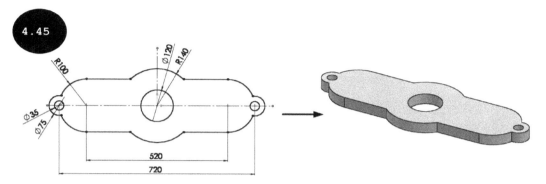

4.45

Section 1: Starting SOLIDWORKS

First you need to start the SOLIDWORKS software.

1. Double click on the **SOLIDWORKS** icon on your desktop to start SOLIDWORKS, if not started already.

Section 2: Invoking Sketching Environment

Now, first invoke the Part modeling environment and then invoke the Sketching environment by selecting the Top plane as the sketching plane.

1. Click on the **New** tool in the **Standard** toolbar, the **New SOLIDWORKS Document** dialog box appears.

2. In this dialog box, the **Part** button is activated by default. Click on the **OK** button to invoke the Part modeling environment.

   Once the Part modeling environment is invoked, you can now invoke the Sketching environment and create the sketch of this tutorial.

3. Click on the **Sketch** tab in the **Command Manager**, the **Sketch CommandManager** appears, see Figure 4.46.

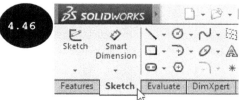

4.46

4. Click on the **Sketch** button of the **Sketch CommandManager**, three default planes which are mutually perpendicular to each other appears in the graphics area.

5. Move the cursor over the Top plane and click to select it as the sketching plane when the boundary of the plane highlighted, the Sketching environment is invoked. Also, the Top plane orientated normal to the viewing direction and the confirmation corner appears at the upper right corner of the drawing area.

Section 3: Specifying Unit Settings

Once the Sketching environment is invoked, specify metric unit system for measurement.

1. Click on the **Options** tool in the **Standard** toolbar, the **System Options - General** dialog box appears.

2. In this dialog box, click on the **Document Properties** tab, the name of the dialog box changes to **Document Properties - Drafting Standard**.

3. Select the **Units** option available in the left panel of the dialog box, the options related to specifying the unit system appears on the right side of the dialog box.

4. Select the **MMGS (millimeter, gram, second)** radio button from the **Unit system** area if not selected by default.

    Now, you need to make sure that the snap setting is turned off.

5. Select the **Grid/Snap** option available in the left side panel of the dialog box, the options related to the grid and snap settings appears.

6. Make sure that the **Display grid** check box of the **Grid** area is cleared.

7. Click on the **Go To System Snaps** button, the name of the dialog box changes to **System Options - Relations/Snaps**.

8. Make sure that the **Grid** check box in the **Sketch snaps** area of the dialog box is cleared.

9. Click on the **OK** button of the dialog box to accept the change and close the dialog box.

Section 4: Drawing Sketch Entities

Now you need to create sketch by using the sketching tools.

1. Click on the **Circle** tool in the **Sketch CommandManager**, the **Circle** tool invoked and the **Circle PropertyManager** appears. Also, the appearance of cursor changes to the circle cursor ⌀ .

2. Move the cursor towards the origin and click to specify the center point of the circle when the cursor snaps to the origin.

3. Move the cursor horizontal towards the right and click when the radius of the circle appears close to 60 above the cursor, see Figure 4.47, a circle of radius 60 is created. Also, the **Circle** tool is still activated.

4. Move the cursor towards the origin and click to specify the center point of another circle when the cursor snaps to the origin.

5. Move the cursor horizontal towards the right and click when the radius of the circle appears close to 140 above the cursor, see Figure 4.48, a circle of radius 140 is created. Also, the **Circle** tool is still activated.

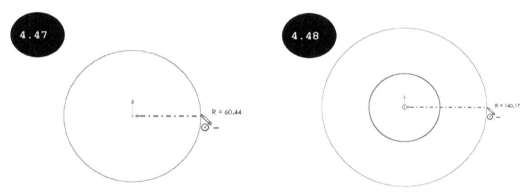

6. Press the ESC key to exit from the **Circle** tool.

7. Invoke the Slot flyout, see Figure 4.49. Next, click on the **Centerpoint Straight Slot** tool.

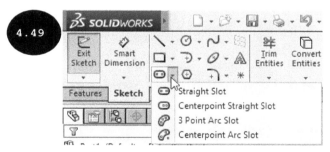

8. Move the cursor towards the origin and click to specify the center point of the slot when the cursor snaps to the origin.

Note: You can scroll the middle mouse button to zoom in and zoom out the drawing display area.

9. Move the cursor horizontal towards the right and click when the length of the slot appears close to 260 (520/2 = 260) above the cursor, see Figure 4.50, the preview of the slot appears.

10. Click the left mouse button when the width of the slot appears close to 200 in the **Parameters** rollout of the **Slot PropertyManager**, see Figure 4.51, a slot is created, see Figure 4.52.

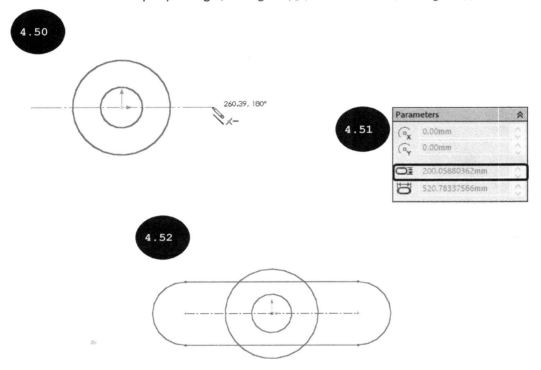

11. Click on the **Zoom to Fit** tool available in the **View (Heads-Up)** toolbar to fit the sketch completely in the screen.

12. Click on the **Circle** tool and then move the cursor towards the right end of the slot length, see Figure 4.53.

13. Click to specify the center point of the circle when the circle snaps as shown in Figure 4.53.

14. Move the cursor horizontal towards the right and click when the radius of the circle appears close to 17.5 above the cursor, see Figure 4.54, a circle of radius 17.5 is created. Also, the **Circle** tool is still activated.

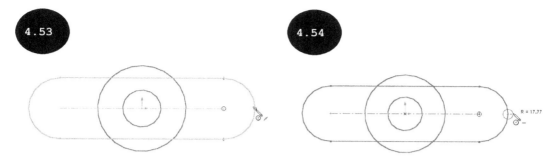

15. Move the cursor towards the center point of the previously created circle of radius close to 17.5 and click to specify the center point when the cursor snaps to it.

16. Move the cursor horizontal towards the right and click when the radius of the circle appears close to 37.5 above the cursor, see Figure 4.55, a circle is created.

17. Similarly, create two circles on the left side of the slot length, see Figure 4.56.

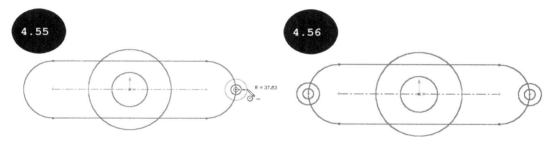

18. Click on the down arrow available next to the **Line** tool, a flyout appears, see Figure 4.57.

19. Click on the **Centerline** tool of the flyout. Next, create a vertical centerline starting from origin, see Figure 4.58.

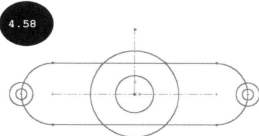

Section 5: Trimming Sketch Entities

Now, you will trim the unwanted sketch entities of the sketch drawn.

1. Click on the **Trim Entities** tool of the **Sketch CommandManager**, the **Trim PropertyManager** appears at the left of the drawing area.

2. Activate the **Trim to closest** button available in the **Options** rollout of the PropertyManager by clicking on it, the cursor appears changes to trim cursor ⌖.

3. Move the cursor over a portion of an entity to trim, see Figure 4.59 and then click when it highlighted in the drawing area, the **SOLIDWORKS** window appears informing you that the trim operation will destroy the slot entity.

4. Click on the **OK** button of the window, the selected portion of the entity is trimmed, see Figure 4.60.

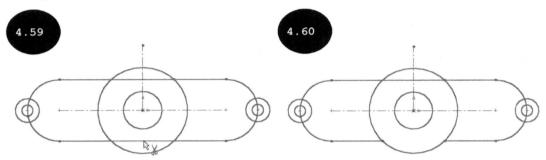

5. Similarly, trim the other unwanted portion of the sketch entities. Figure 4.61 shows the sketch after trimming all the unwanted entities.

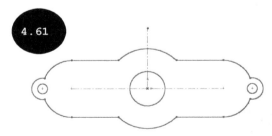

6. Once you are down with the trimming operation, press the ESC key to exit from the tool.

Section 6: Applying Relations

After creating the sketch you need to make it fully defined by applying proper relations and dimensions to the sketch entities.

1. Select two smaller circles of diameter 35 by pressing the CTRL key to apply equal relation between them, see Figure 4.62. Next, release the CTRL key, the Pop-up toolbar appears, see Figure 4.63.

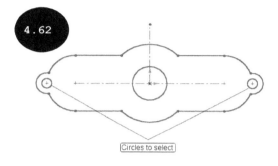

Circles to select

2. Click on the **Make Equal** button = of the Pop-up toolbar, the equal relation is applied between the selected circles. You can also select the required relation button from the **Add Relations** rollout of the PropertyManager appears on the left of the drawing area.

3. Similarly, select arcs of radius 37.5 by pressing the CTRL key and apply equal relation between them, see Figure 4.64.

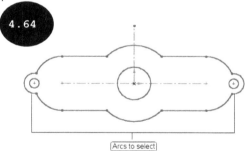

Arcs to select

4. Select center points of the slot and the vertical centerline by pressing the CTRL key, see Figure 4.65. Next, release the CTRL key to display the Pop-up toolbar.

5. Click on the **Make Symmetric** button ▫ of the Pop-up toolbar, the symmetric relation is applied.

6. Similarly, select center points of two circles and the vertical centerline, see Figure 4.66, and apply symmetric relation between them.

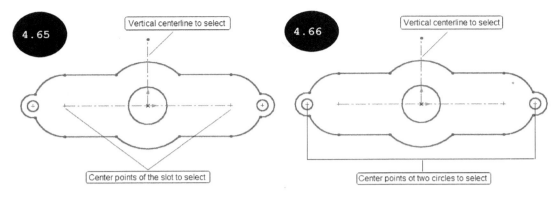

7. Apply tangent relations ⟳ between the set of horizontal line and arc, see Figure 4.67.

8. Select the horizontal centerline and the origin by pressing the CTRL key, see Figure 4.68 to apply coincident relation between them. Next, click on the **Make Coincident** button ⟨ from the Pop-up toolbar.

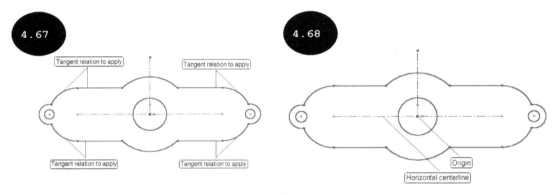

9. Select a horizontal line of the sketch and apply horizontal relation to it by selecting the **Make Horizontal** button — from the Pop-up toolbar.

10. Similarly, apply the horizontal relation to all the remaining horizontal lines of the sketch.

11. Select the center points of two circles and the origin, see Figure 4.69 by pressing the CTRL key and then apply horizontal relation — between them.

Note: You can turn on or off the display of applied relations in the drawing area by clicking on the **View Sketch Relations** button of the **Hide/Show Items** flyout available in the **View (Heads-Up)** toolbar, see Figure 4.70.

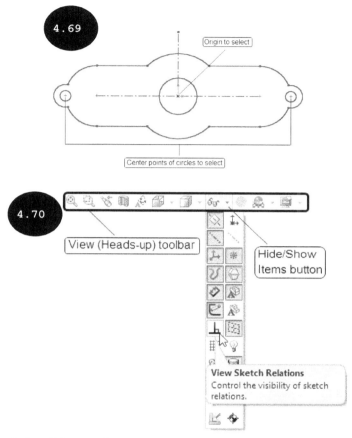

Section 7: Applying Dimensions

After applying the required relations, you need to apply dimensions to make the sketch fully defined.

1. Click on the **Smart Dimension** tool of the **Sketch CommandManager**.

2. Select the circle whose center point is at the origin, the diameter dimension is attached with the cursor.

3. Move to the cursor to the location where you want to place the dimension in the drawing area, see Figure 4.71, and then click to specify its placement point, the **Modify** dialog box appears, see Figure 4.72.

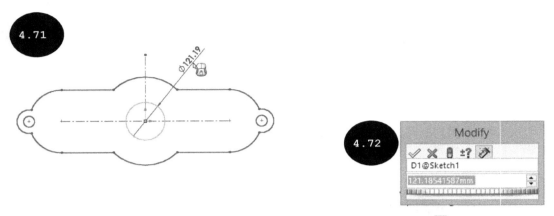

4. Enter 120 in the **Modify** dialog box and then click on the green tick mark ✓ of the dialog box, the diameter of circle is modified to 120 and diameter dimension is applied, see Figure 4.73.

5. Similarly apply the remaining dimension of the sketch. Figure 4.74 shows the sketch fully defined sketch after applying all the dimensions.

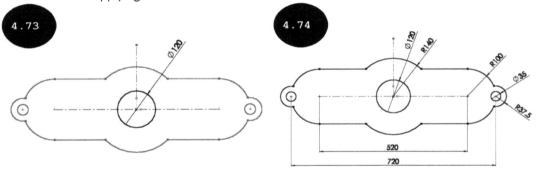

Section 8: Saving the Sketch

After creating the sketch, you need to save it.

1. Click on the **Save** tool of the **Standard** toolbar, the **Save As** window appears.

2. Browse to the *SOLIDWORKS* folder and then create a *Chapter 4* folder inside the *SOLIDWORKS* folder. Next, save the sketch with the name Tutorial 1 in the *Chapter 4* folder.

Tutorial 2

Draw the sketch shown in Figure 4.75 and make it fully defined by applying all the dimensions and relations. You will learn about creating model from the sketch in later chapters.

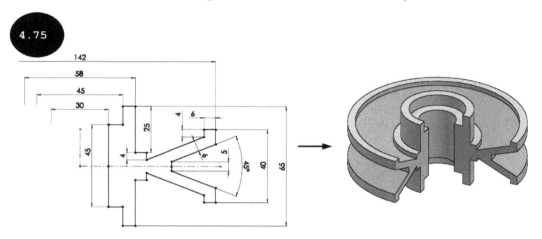

4.75

Section 1: Starting SOLIDWORKS

First you need to start the SOLIDWORKS software.

1. Double click on the **SOLIDWORKS** icon on your desktop to start SOLIDWORKS, if not started already.

Section 2: Invoking Sketching Environment

Now, first invoke the Part modeling environment and then invoke the Sketching environment by selecting the Top plane as the sketching plane.

1. Click on the **New** tool in the **Standard** toolbar, the **New SOLIDWORKS Document** dialog box appears.

2. In this dialog box, the **Part** button is activated by default. Click on the **OK** button to invoke the Part modeling environment.

    Once the Part modeling environment is invoked, you can now invoke the Sketching environment and create the sketch of this tutorial.

3. Click on the **Sketch** tab in the **Command Manager**, the **Sketch CommandManager** appears, see Figure 4.76.

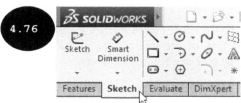

4.76

4. Click on the **Sketch** button of the **Sketch CommandManager**, three default planes which are mutually perpendicular to each other appears in the graphics area.

5. Move the cursor over the Front plane and click to select it as the sketching plane when the boundary of the plane highlighted, the Sketching environment is invoked. Also, the Front plane orientated normal to the viewing direction and the confirmation corner appears at the upper right corner of the drawing area.

Section 3: Specifying Unit Settings

Once the Sketching environment is invoked, specify the metric unit system for measurement.

1. Click on the **Options** tool in the **Standard** toolbar, the **System Options - General** dialog box appears.

2. In this dialog box, click on the **Document Properties** tab.

3. Select the **Units** option available in the left panel of the dialog box.

4. Select the **MMGS (millimeter, gram, second)** radio button from the **Unit system** area.

   Now, you need to make sure that the snap setting is turned off.

5. Select the **Grid/Snap** option available in the left side panel of the dialog box. Next, make sure that the **Display grid** check box of the **Grid** area is cleared.

6. Click on the **Go To System Snaps** button, Next, make sure that the **Grid** check box in the **Sketch snaps** area of the dialog box is cleared.

7. Click on the **OK** button of the dialog box to accept the change and close the dialog box.

Section 4: Drawing Upper Half of the Sketch Entities

Now you need to create sketch by using the sketching tools. In this section you will draw upper half of the sketch and the lower half of the sketch is created by mirroring it in the next section of this Tutorial.

1. Click on the down arrow available next to the Line tool, a flyout appears, see Figure 4.77.

2. Click on the **Centerline** tool of the flyout. Next, create vertical and horizontal centerlines starting from origin one by one, see Figure 4.78 and then exit from the tool by pressing the ESC key.

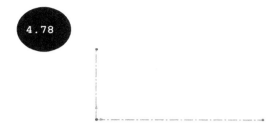

3. Click on the **Line** tool and then move the cursor over the horizontal centerline, see Figure 4.79. Next, click to specify the start point of the line when the coordinates appears close to 15, 0, 0 in the Status Bar, see Figures 4.79.

4. Move the cursor vertical upwards and click to specify the end point of the line when the length of the line appears close to 22.5 above the cursor, see Figure 4.80.

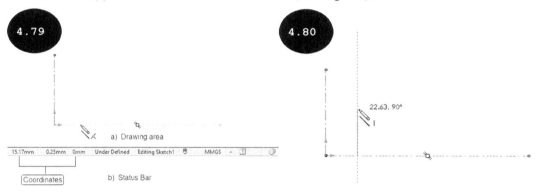

5. Move the cursor horizontally towards the right and click to specify the end point of the second line entity when the length of the line appears close to 7.5 above the cursor.

6. Move the cursor vertically upwards and click to specify the end point of the third line entity when the length of the line appears close to 10 above the cursor.

7. Move the cursor horizontally towards the right and click to specify the end point of the line when the length of the line appears close to 6.5 above the cursor.

8. Move the cursor vertically downwards and click to specify the end point of the line when the length of the line appears close to 25 above the cursor.

9. Move the cursor horizontally towards the right and click to specify the end point of the line when the length of the line appears close to 6 above the cursor.

10. Move the cursor vertically downwards and click to specify the end point of the line when the length of the line appears close to 4 above the cursor.

11. Move the cursor horizontal towards the right and then vertically upwards to a small distance. Next, click to specify the end point of the inclined line when the line appears similar to one shown in Figure 4.81.

12. Move the cursor vertically upward and click to specify the end point of the line when the length of the line appears close to 4 above the cursor, see Figure 4.82.

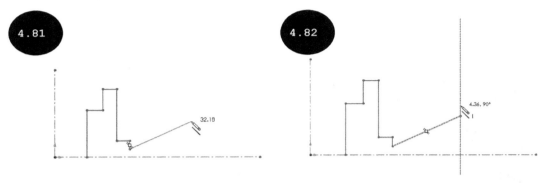

13. Move the cursor horizontally towards the right and click to specify the end point of the line when the length of the line appears close to 5 above the cursor.

14. Move the cursor vertically downwards and click to specify the end point of the line when the length of the line appears close to 8 above the cursor.

15. Move the cursor vertically downwards and then horizontal towards the left to a small distance and then click to specify the end point of the inclined line when the line appears similar to one shown in Figure 4.83.

16. Move the cursor vertically downwards and click to specify the end point of the line when the cursor snaps to the horizontal centerline. Next, press the ESC key to exit from the **Line** tool. Figure 4.84 shows the sketch after creating the upper half of the sketch.

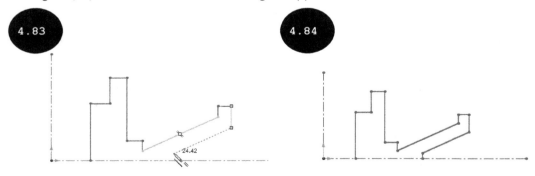

Section 5: Creating Lower Half of the Sketch

After creating the upper half of the sketch, you need to mirror it to create the lower half of the sketch.

1. Click on the **Mirror Entities** tool of the **Sketch CommandManager**, the **Mirror PropertyManager** appears in the left of the drawing area.

2. Select all the sketch entities of the upper half of the sketch as the entities to mirror except the centerlines.

3. Click on the **Mirror about** field of the PropertyManager to activate it and then select the horizontal centerline of the sketch as the mirroring the line, the preview of the lower half of the sketch appears.

4. Make sure that the **Copy** check box is selected in the PropertyManager. Next, click on the green tick mark of the PropertyManager, the lower half of the sketch is created, see Figure 4.85.

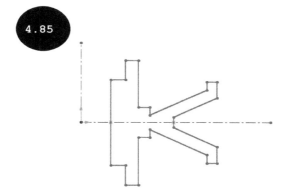

Section 6: Applying Dimensions

After applying the required relations, you need to apply dimensions to make the sketch fully defined.

1. Click on the **Smart Dimension** tool of the **Sketch CommandManager**.

2. Select the left most vertical line of the sketch, the linear dimension is attached with the cursor.

3. Move to the cursor towards the left to a small distance, see Figure 4.86, and then click to specify its placement point, the **Modify** dialog box appears, see Figure 4.87.

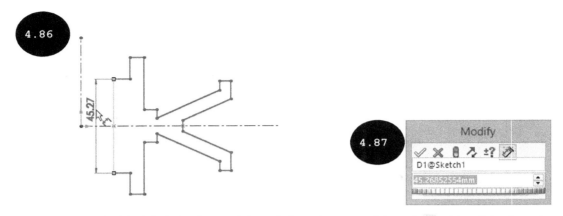

4. Enter 45 in the **Modify** dialog box and then click on the green tick mark ✓ of the dialog box, the length of the line is modified to 45 and the linear dimension is applied, see Figure 4.88.

5. Similarly apply the remaining linear dimensions, see Figure 4.89.

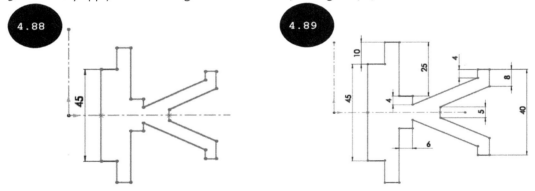

After applying the linear dimensions to the sketch, you need to apply the linear diameter dimensions to the sketch.

6. Make sure that the **Smart Dimension** tool is activated and then select the left most vertical line of length 45, the linear dimension is attached with the cursor. Next, select the vertical centerline and move the cursor to the left side of the vertical centerline, the linear diameter dimension attached with the cursor, see Figure 4.90.

7. Click the left mouse button to specify the placement point for the linear diameter dimension, the **Modify** dialog box appears.

8. Enter 30 in the **Modify** dialog box and then click on the green tick mark ✓ of the dialog box, the linear diameter dimension is applied, see Figure 4.91.

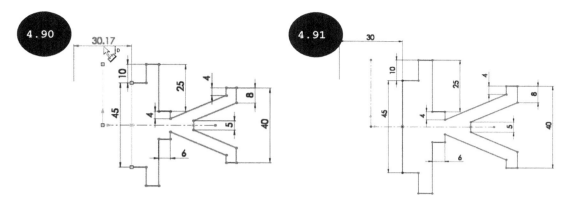

9. Select the second vertical line of length 10, the linear diameter dimension attached with the cursor, see Figure 4.92.

10. Click to specify the placement point for the linear diameter dimension, the **Modify** dialog box appears.

11. Enter 45 in the **Modify** dialog box and then click on the green tick mark ✓ of the dialog box, the linear diameter dimension is applied, see Figure 4.93.

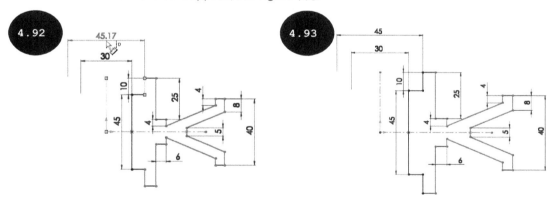

12. Similarly, apply the remaining linear diameter dimensions to the sketch, see Figure 4.94.

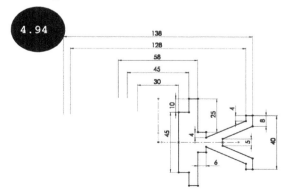

13. Press the ESC key to exit from the **Smart Dimensions** tool. Figure 4.94 shows the fully defined sketch.

Section 7: Saving the Sketch

After creating the sketch, you need to save it.

1. Click on the **Save** tool of the **Standard** toolbar, the **Save As** window appears.

2. Browse to the *Chapter 4* folder and then save the sketch with the name Tutorial 2. If the folder is not created, create the *Chapter 4* folder inside the *SOLIDWORKS* folder.

Tutorial 3

Draw the sketch shown in Figure 4.95 and make it fully defined by applying all the dimensions and relations. The model shown in the figure is for your reference. You will learn about creating model in later chapters.

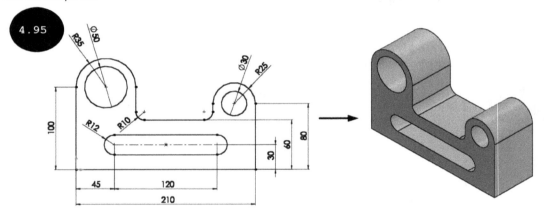

Section 1: Starting SOLIDWORKS

First you need to start the SOLIDWORKS software.

1. Double click on the **SOLIDWORKS** icon on your desktop to start SOLIDWORKS, if not started already.

Section 2: Invoking Sketching Environment

Now, first invoke the Part modeling environment and then invoke the Sketching environment by selecting the Top plane as the sketching plane.

1. Click on the **New** tool in the **Standard** toolbar, the **New SOLIDWORKS Document** dialog box appears.

2. In this dialog box, the **Part** button is activated by default. Click on the **OK** button to invoke the Part modeling environment.

Once the Part modeling environment is invoked, you can now invoke the Sketching environment and create the sketch of this tutorial.

3. Click on the **Sketch** tab in the **Command Manager**, the **Sketch CommandManager** appears, see Figure 4.96.

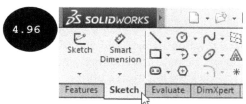

4. Click on the **Sketch** button of the **Sketch CommandManager**, three default planes which are mutually perpendicular to each other appears in the graphics area.

5. Move the cursor over the Front plane and click to select it as the sketching plane, the Sketching environment is invoked. Also, the Front plane orientated normal to the viewing direction.

Section 3: Specifying Unit Settings

Once the Sketching environment is invoked, specify the metric unit system for measurement.

1. Click on the **Options** tool in the **Standard** toolbar, the **System Options – General** dialog box appears.

2. In this dialog box, click on the **Document Properties** tab.

3. Select the **Units** option available in the left panel of the dialog box.

4. Select the **MMGS (millimeter, gram, second)** radio button from the **Unit system** area.

   Now, you need to make sure that the snap setting is turned off.

5. Select the **Grid/Snap** option available in the left side panel of the dialog box. Next, make sure that the **Display grid** check box of the **Grid** area is cleared.

6. Click on the **Go To System Snaps** button, Next, make sure that the **Grid** check box in the **Sketch snaps** area of the dialog box is cleared.

7. Click on the **OK** button of the dialog box to accept the change and close the dialog box.

Section 4: Drawing Sketch Entities

Now, you need to create sketch by using the sketching tools.

1. Click on the **Line** tool of the **Sketch CommandManager**.

2. Move the cursor towards the origin and click to specify the start point of the line when cursor snaps to the origin and the coincident symbol appears, see Figure 4.97.

Note: If you click the left mouse button when a relation symbol such as coincident, horizontal, and vertical appears while drawing an sketch entity, the respective relation is applied between the entities. In Figure 4.97, the coincident relation is applied between the start point of the line and the origin as soon as you click the left mouse button.

---

3. Move the cursor horizontal towards the right and click to specify the end point of the line when the length of the line appears close to 210 and the symbol of horizontal relation appears, see Figure 4.98. As soon as you click the left mouse button, a horizontal line of length close to 210 is created. Also, the horizontal relation is applied to the line.

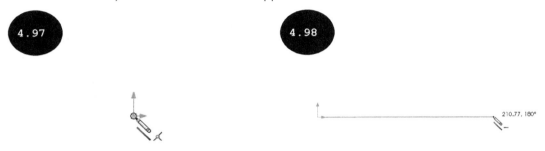

Tip: While drawing sketch entities you may need to increase or decrease the drawing display area. You can increase or decrease the drawing display area by Zoom In or Zoom Out. You can Zoom In or Zoom Out the drawing display area by scrolling the middle mouse button.

---

4. Move the cursor vertically upwards and create a vertical line of length close to 80.

   Now you need to create an tangent arc. In addition to creating tangent arc by using the **Tangent Arc** tool, you can also create it by using the **Line** tool.

5. Move the line cursor away to a small distance and than move it back to the last specified point, a dot filled with orange color appears, see Figure 4.99.

6. Move the cursor vertically upwards to a small distance and then move it horizontally towards the left to a small distance, the arc mode is activated and the preview of a tangent arc appears, see Figure 4.100.

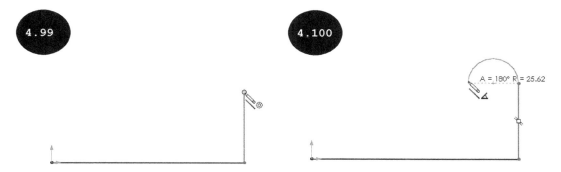

7. Click to specify the end point of the tangent arc when the angle and radius values of the arc appears 180 and 25, respectively above the cursor, see Figure 4.100. As soon as you specify the end point of the arc, the tangent arc is created and the line mode activated again.

8. Move the cursor vertically downwards and create a vertical line of length close to 20.

9. Move the cursor horizontally towards the left and create a horizontal line of length close to 90.

10. Move the cursor vertically upwards and create a vertical line of length close to 40.

11. Create an tangent arc of radius 35, see Figure 4.101.

12. Move the cursor vertically downwards and specify the end point of the line when the cursor snaps to the start point of the first created line of the sketch, see Figure 4.102.

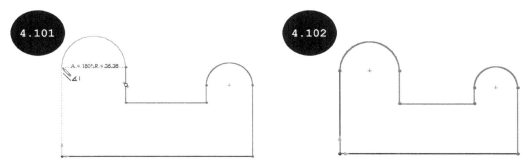

13. Press the ESC key to exit from the **Line** tool.

Now you need to create circles.

14. Click on the **Circle** tool and then create two circles, see Figure 4.103. Next, exit from the **Circle** tool by pressing the ESC key.

Tip: You need to create circles such that the center point of circles and the arcs of the sketch share a same center point, respectively.

---

15. Invoke the **Slot** flyout, see Figure 4.104, and then click on the **Straight Slot** tool from the flyout.

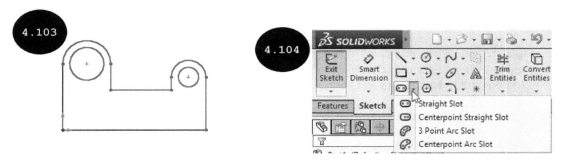

16. Create a straight slot similar to one shown in Figure 4.105 and then exit from the tool.

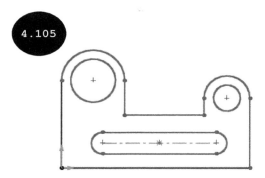

Now, you need to create fillets in the sketch.

17. Click on the **Sketch Fillet** tool, the **Sketch Fillet PropertyManager** appears.

18. Enter 10 in the **Fillet Radius** field of the **Fillet Parameters** rollout in the PropertyManager.

19. Move the cursor towards a vertex of the sketch to create the fillet of radius 10, the preview of the fillet appears, see Figure 4.106. Next, click the left mouse button to accept the fillet preview.

20. Move the cursor towards the another vertex of the sketch to create the fillet of radius 10, the preview of the fillet appears, see Figure 4.107. Next, click the left mouse button to accept the fillet preview.

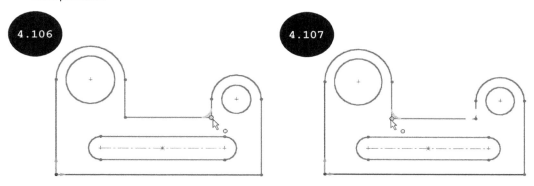

21. After selecting the vertex to create fillets, click on the green tick mark of the PropertyManager, the fillets of radius 10 is created, see Figure 4.108. Also, the radius dimension is applied.

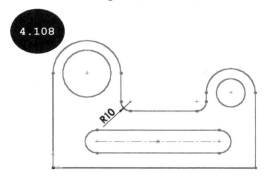

Section 5: Applying Dimensions

After creating the sketch, you need to apply required relations and dimensions to make it fully defined. In this sketch all the required relations has been applied automatically while creating the sketch entities. Therefore you only need to apply dimensions.

1. Click on the **Smart Dimension** tool of the **Sketch CommandManager**.

2. Select the lower horizontal line of the sketch and then move the cursor downwards, the linear dimension is attached with the cursor, see Figure 4.109.

3. Click to specify the placement point for the attached linear dimension, the **Modify** dialog box appears, see Figure 4.110.

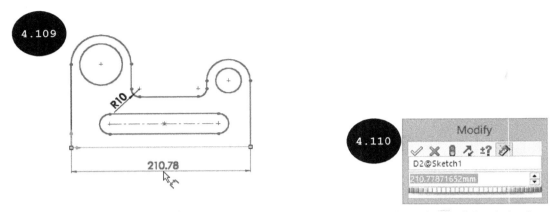

4. Enter 210 in the **Modify** dialog box and then click on the green tick mark ✓ of the dialog box, the length of the line is modified to 210 and the linear dimension is applied, see Figure 4.111.

5. Similarly apply the remaining dimensions by selecting the required sketch entity or entities to apply dimensions, see Figure 4.112.

Tip: The **Smart Dimensions** tool applies dimensions depending upon the type of entity or entities selected to apply dimension. For example, on selecting a line entity, a linear dimension applies, on selecting a circle, a diameter dimension applies, and on selecting an arc, a radius dimension applies to the selected entity.

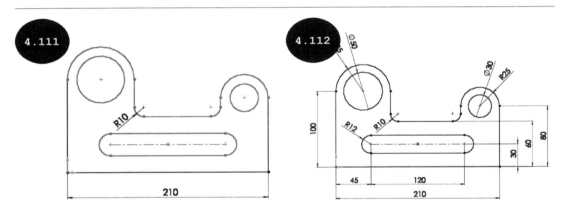

6. Press the ESC key to exit from the **Smart Dimensions** tool. Figure 4.112 shows the fully defined sketch after applying all the dimensions.

Section 6: Saving the Sketch

1. Click on the **Save** tool of the **Standard** toolbar, the **Save As** window appears.

2. Browse to the *Chapter 4* folder and then save the sketch as Tutorial 3.

Hands-on Test Drive 1

Draw the sketch shown in Figure 4.113 and apply dimensions to make it fully defined sketch. The model shown in the figure is for your reference, you will learn about creating models in later chapters.

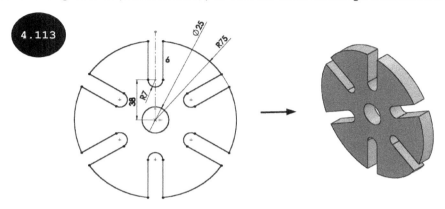

Hands-on Test Drive 2

Draw the sketch shown in Figure 4.114 and apply dimensions to make it fully defined sketch. The model shown in the figure is for your reference, you will learn about creating models in later chapters.

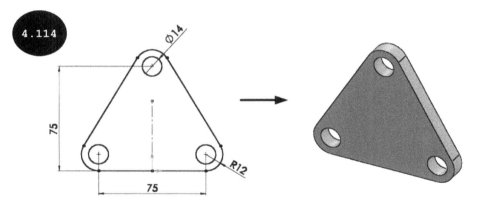

Summary

In this chapter, you have learnt about creating fully defined sketches by applying proper geometric relations and dimensions. You can apply geometric relations by using the **Add Relation** tool and the Pop-up toolbar. Once the sketch has been drawn and the required geometric relations has been applied, you need to apply dimensions by using the various dimension tools. You can also modify the already applied dimensions and dimension properties such as dimension style, tolerance, and precision. At last in this chapter, you have learnt about different sketch states such as under define, fully defined, and over defined.

Questions

- The _____ relation is used to lies/coincident a sketch point on to a line, arc, or elliptical entity.

- You can control the display or visibility of the applied geometric relations by using the _____ tool.

- The _____ dimension is used to apply to a sketch that represent revolve features.

- The _____ are the dimensions that measures from a base entity.

- A _____ sketch is a sketch whose all the degree of freedoms are fixed.

- The list of suggested relations appears in the Pop-up toolbar depends upon the type of entities selected for applying relation. (True/False).

- Once the dimensions have been applied, you can not modify them. (True/False).

- You can not delete the already applied relations between the selected entities. (True/False).

- Geometric relations are used to restrict some degree of freedom of the sketch (True/False).

Creating First/Base Feature of a Solid Model

In this chapter:

- Creating Extruded Base Feature
- Creating Revolved Base Feature
- Navigating 3D Model in Graphics Area
- Manipulating the Orientation of the Model
- Changing Display Style of the Model
- Changing View of the Model

Once the sketch has been creating and fully defined by using the different sketching tools, you can convert sketch into a solid feature by using feature modeling tools. All the feature modeling tools are available in the **Features** tab of the **CommandManager** in the Part modeling environment, see Figure 5.1. Note that in the **Features CommandManager**, most of the tools are not activated initially. These tools become activated after creating the base feature of the model. The base feature of the model is also known as the first feature or the parent feature of the model. In SOLIDWORKS, you can create base feature of a model by using the **Extruded Boss/Base**, **Revolved Boss/Base**, **Swept Boss/Base**, **Lofted Boss/Base**, or **Boundary Boss/Base** tool. The name of these tools are ends with Boss/Base. It suggest that these tools are the base and boss tools for the feature modeling. However, out of all the base tools, the **Swept Boss/Base**, **Lofted Boss/Base**, and **Boundary Boss/Base** tools are not activated in the **Features CommandManager**, initially. These tools become activated only after creating the respective profiles or sketches required by these tools. You will learn more about these tools in the later chapters of this textbook. In this chapter, you will learn about creating base feature using **Extruded Boss/Base** and **Revolved Boss/Base** tools.

Creating Extruded Base Feature

The **Extruded Boss/Base** tool is used to create extruded feature by adding material to the sketch, normal to the sketching plane. Note that the sketch defines the geometry of the material added. Figures 5.2 shows different sketches and features created from their respective sketch.

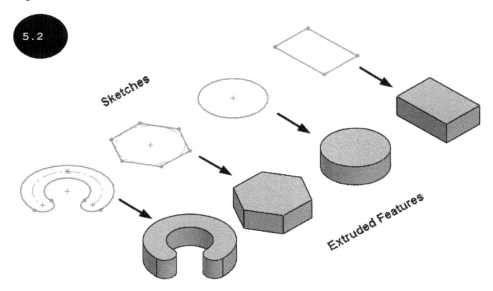

Note: In addition to adding material normal to the sketching plane, you can also add material other than the normal direction of the sketching plane by using this tool. By default, material is added normal to the sketching plane. You will learn more about adding material normal and at angle to the sketching plane in this topic of creating extruded base feature.

After drawing the sketch by using the sketching tools in the Sketching environment, do not exit from the Sketching environment. Next, click on the **Features** tab in the **CommandManager**, the **Features CommandManager** appears, see Figure 5.1. Next, click on the **Extruded Boss/Base** tool in the **Features CommandManager**, the preview of the extruded feature (extruded by adding material normal to the sketching plane) appears in the graphics area with the default extrusion parameters. Also, the **Boss - Extrude PropertyManager** appears at the left side of the graphics area, see Figure 5.3. Figure 5.4 shows a rectangular sketch created on the Top Plane and Figure 5.5 shows the preview of the resultant extruded feature.

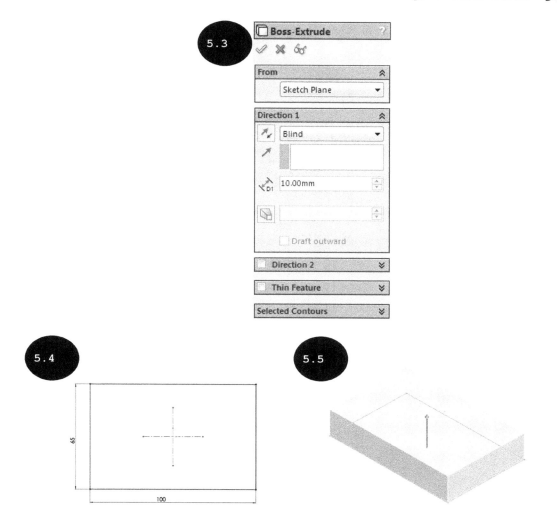

Note: If you exit from the Sketching environment after creating the sketch and sketch is not selected in the graphics area then on invoking the **Extruded Boss/Base** tool, the **Extrude PropertyManager** appears, see Figure 5.6. Also, you are prompted to select the sketch from the graphics area to be extruded and if the sketch is created, select the sketching plane to create the sketch. On selecting the sketch to be extruded, the preview of the extruded feature appears in the graphics area as well as the **Boss - Extrude PropertyManager** appears, see Figure 5.3. On selecting the sketching plane, the Sketching environment invokes for creating the sketch.

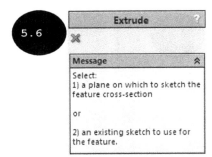

The options available in the **Boss-Extrude PropertyManager** are used to specify parameters for extrude feature being created. Some of this options are as follows.

From

The options available in the **From** rollout of the **Boss-Extrude PropertyManager** are used to define the starting condition of the extrude feature. These options are available in the **From** drop-down list of this rollout, see Figure 5.7. Some of the options of this drop-down list are used while creating second and further extruded features and are discussed later in this chapter. The options that can be used for creating base features are as follows.

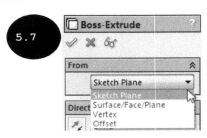

Sketch Plane

By default, the **Sketch Plane** option is selected in the **From** drop-down list. As a result, the extrusion starts exactly from the sketching plane of the sketch. Figure 5.8 shows the preview of the extruded feature from its front view when the **Sketch Plane** option is selected.

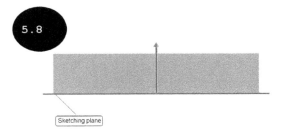

Sketching plane

Offset

The **Offset** option is used to start the creating of an extrude feature at an offset distance from the sketching plane. On selecting this option, the **Enter Offset Value** field and **Reverse Direction** button appears in the **From** rollout, see Figure 5.9. By default, the value entered in the Enter **Offset Value** field is 0 (zero). You can enter the required offset value in this field to define the start condition of the extrusion. Figure 5.10 shows the preview of the extruded feature from its front view after specifying a offset distance as the starting condition for extrusion. You can also use the spinner available right of this field to set the offset value by clicking on the up and down arrows of the spinner. To reverse the offset direction of starting condition, click on the **Reverse Direction** button available in front of the **From** drop-down list in the PropertyManager.

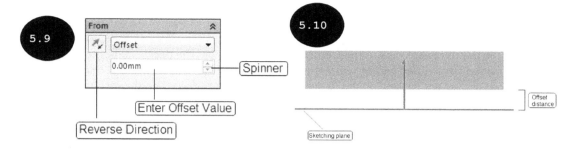

Note: The **Surface/Face/Plane** and **Vertex** options are discussed later in this chapter.

Direction 1

The options available in the **Direction 1** rollout of the PropertyManager are used to define the end condition for extruded feature in one direction. These options are as follows.

End Condition

The **End Condition** drop-down list of the **Direction 1** rollout allows you to select a methods from defining the end condition of the extraction. Figure 5.11 shows the **End Condition** drop-down list of the **Direction 1** rollout. Some of the options of this drop-down list are used while creating second and further extruded features and are discussed later in this chapter. The options that can be used for creating base features are as follows.

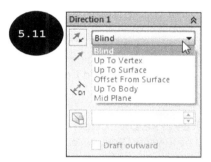

Blind

The **Blind** option of the **End Condition** drop-down list is used to define the end condition or termination of the extrusion by specifying the depth value. By default, this option is selected in this drop-down list. As a result, the **Depth** field is available in the **Direction 1** rollout, see Figure 5.12. In this **Depth** field, you can enter the depth value of the extrusion.

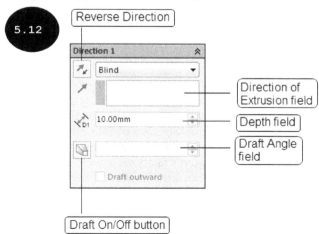

Mid Plane

The **Mid Plane** option of the **End Condition** drop-down list allows you to extrude the feature symmetrically about the sketching plane, see Figure 5.13. After selecting this option, you can enter the depth of extrusion in the **Depth** field of the rollout. The depth value specified in this field divided equally and create symmetrical extrusion in both side of the sketching plane. For example, if the depth value 100 mm is specified in the **Depth** field then the resultant extruded feature is created by adding material 50 mm in one side and 50 mm in other side of the sketching plane.

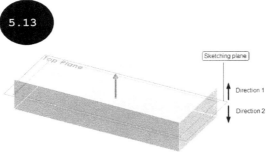

Note: The remaining options such as **Up To Vertex**, **Up To Surface**, and **Offset From Surface** of the **End Condition** drop-down list are discussed in later chapters.

Reverse Direction

The **Reverse Direction** button of the **Direction 1** rollout is used to reverse/flip the direction of extrusion from one side of the sketching plane to the other side.

Depth

The **Depth** field of the **Direction 1** rollout is used to specify the depth of extrusion. You can enter the depth value of the extrusion in this field. You can also used the spinner arrows available in the right of this field to set the depth value. Note that clicking on the down arrow of the spinner, the value is decreased and clicking on the up arrow of the spinner, the value is increased. Also, note that the **Depth** field available only when the **Blind** or **Mid Plane** option is selected in the **End Condition** drop-down list.

Direction of Extrusion

The **Direction of Extrusion** field is used to define the direction of extrusion other than the direction normal to the sketching plane. Note that as discussed earlier, by default, the direction of extrusion is normal to the sketching plane. To specify the direction of extrusion other than the default normal direction to the sketching plane, click on the **Direction of Extrusion** filed to activate it. Next, select the direction reference to define the direction of extrusion. The direction reference can be a linear sketch entity, a linear edge, or an axis. Figure 5.14 shows a sketch to be extruded and a direction reference (a sketch line). The Figure 5.15 shows the preview of the resultant feature.

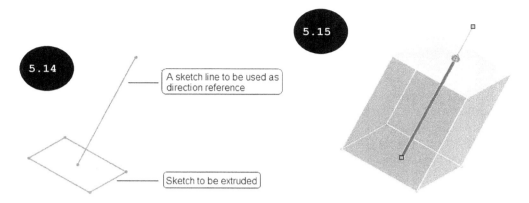

A sketch line to be used as direction reference

Sketch to be extruded

Tip: In Figure 5.14, the sketch to be extruded is created on the Top plane and the sketch to be used as direction reference is created on the Front plane at an angle 65 degrees from the X axis.

Draft On/Off

The **Draft On/Off** button is used to add tapering in the extrude feature being created. By default, the **Draft On/Off** button is not activated. As a result, the resultant feature does not have tapering, and the start and end sections of the resultant feature remain same. To add tapering to the extrude feature being created, click on the **Draft On/Off** button, the preview of the feature with tapering as per the default draft angle appears in the graphics area. Also, the **Draft Angle** field and **Draft outward** check box are enabled in the rollout of the PropertyManager.

You can enter the taper or draft angle in the **Draft Angle** field, see Figure 5.13. By default, the **Draft outward** check box is cleared in the rollout. As a result, the tapering added is in the inwards direction of the sketch, see Figure 5.16. On selecting this check box, tapering adds outwards to the sketch, see Figure 5.17.

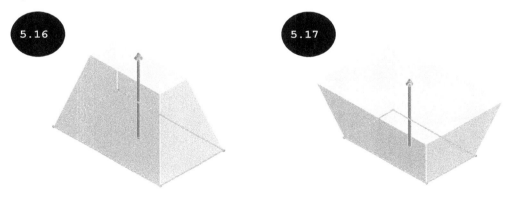

Direction 2

The options available in the **Direction 2** rollout are same as of the options available in the **Direction 1** rollout of the PropertyManager with the only difference that these options are used to specify the end condition in the second direction of the sketching plane. Note that by default this rollout is in collapsed form. As a result, the extrusion take place in one direction of the sketching plane only. To add material in the second direction of the sketching plane, expand this rollout by selecting the check box available in the title bar of this rollout, see Figure 5.18. Figure 5.19 show the preview of an extruded feature being extruded in both side of the sketching plane with different extrusion depth. Note that the **Direction 2** rollout will not be available if the **Mid Plane** option is selected in the **End Condition** drop-down list of the **Direction 1** rollout.

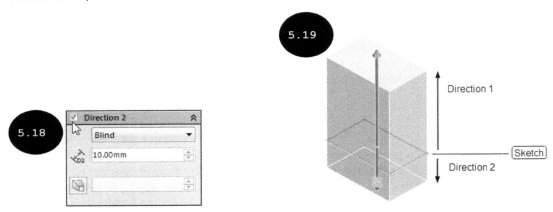

Thin Feature

The options available in the **Thin Feature** rollout are used to create a thin solid feature of specified wall thickness, see Figure 5.20. By default, this rollout is collapsed. To expand the **Thin Feature** rollout, select the check box available on the title bar of this rollout, see Figure 5.21. As soon as this rollout expands, the preview of the thin feature appears in the graphics area with the default wall thickness. The options available in this rollout are as follows.

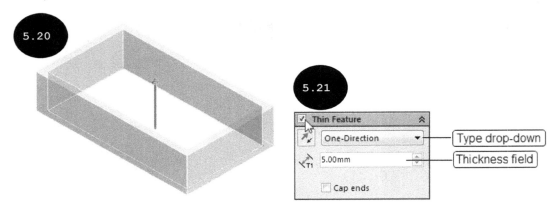

Type

The options available in the **Type** drop-down list of the **Thin Feature** rollout are used to select method to add material thickness and are as follows.

One-Direction

By default, the **One-Direction** option is selected in the **Type** drop-down list. As a result, the thickness is added in one direction of the sketch. You can enter the thickness value for the thin feature being created in the **Thickness** field of this rollout. Figures 5.22 and 5-23 shows the preview of a thin feature with material added in outward and inward directions of the sketch. To reverse the direction of extrusion in either side of the sketch, click on the **Reverse Direction** button of this rollout.

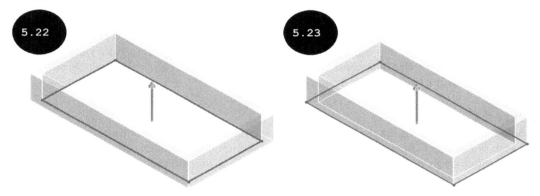

Mid-Plane

The **Mid-Plane** option of the **Type** drop-down list is used to add thickness symmetrically in both the side of the sketch. You can enter the thickness value of the thin feature being created in the **Thickness** field of the rollout. Note that the thickness entered in the **Thickness** field divided equally in both the side of the sketch and create a thin feature.

Two-Direction

The **Two-Direction** option is used to add asymmetric/different thickness in both the direction of sketch. As soon as, you select this option, the **Direction 1 Thickness** and **Direction 2 Thickness** fields are available in the rollout. You can enter different thickness value in direction 1 and direction 2 of the sketch in their respective fields.

Note: You can create a thin feature from an closed and open sketch. Figures 5.22 and 5.23 show a thin feature created by using a closed sketch. Figure 5.24 shows a thin feature created by using a open sketch.

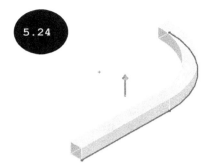

5.24

Cap ends

The **Cap ends** check box is used to close the thin feature by adding caps or covers at its both opened ends and created a hollow feature. On selecting this check box, the opened ends of the thin feature capped and create a hollow thin feature. You can also specify required thickness for cap ends of the hollow thin feature in the **Cap Thickness** field. Note that the **Cap ends** check box available only when you create thin feature by using the closed sketch.

Selected Contours

The **Selected Contours** rollout of the PropertyManager is used to select contour or closed region of a sketch to extrude. Figure 5.25 show a sketch with multiple contours/closed regions (4 contours/regions). Note that, by default, when you extrude a sketch having multiple contours/regions/areas, the outer most contour/region of the sketch is extruded, see Figure 5.26. In this figure, the contour/region 1 of the sketch shown in Figure 5.25 has been extruded, by default, and the remaining contours are left unextruded.

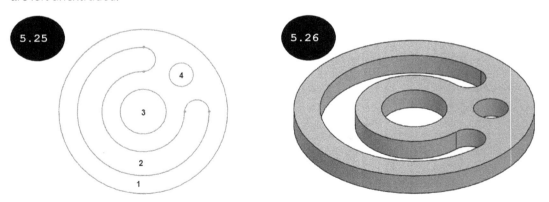

5.25

5.26

In additional to adding material to the outer most closed region of a multi-contour sketch (this is the default procedure), SOLIDWORKS allows you to select required contour/region a sketch to be extruded by using the **Selected Contours** rollout. To extrude the required contour of a multi-contour sketch, expand the **Selected Contours** rollout of the PropertyManager and then move the cursor over the closed region/contour of the sketch to be extruded in the graphics area and then click to select it when the closed region/contour highlights, see Figure 5.27, the preview of the extruded feature appears such that material is added to the selected closed region. You can select multiple contours/regions of a sketch to be extruded at the same time.

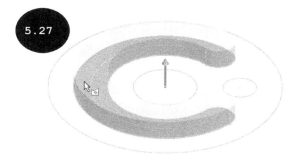

After specifying the required parameters for extruding the sketch, click on the green tick ✓ mark of the **Boss-Extrude PropertyManager** to accept the parameters define, the extruded feature created.

Creating Revolved Base Feature

A revolve feature is a feature created such that material is added by revolving a sketch around a centerline or the axis of revolution. You can create revolve feature by using the **Revolved Boss/Base** tool. Figures 5.28 shows sketches with axes of revolution and the resultant revolved features created by revolving sketch around their respective axis of revolution.

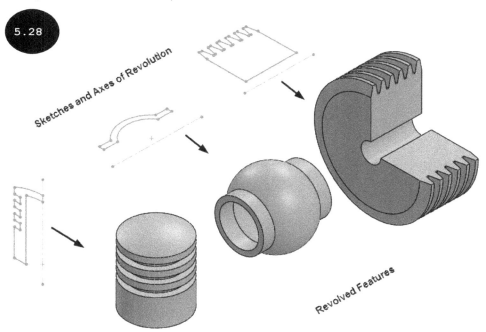

After drawing the sketch of the revolve feature and a centerline as the axis of revolution by using the sketching tools in the Sketching environment, do not exit from the Sketching environment. Next, click on the **Features** tab in the **CommandManager** and then click on the **Revolved Boss/Base** tool, the preview of the revolve feature (revolved by adding material around to the centerline) appears in the graphics area with the default parameters. Also, the **Revolve PropertyManager** appears at the left side of the graphics area, see Figure 5.29. If the preview does not appears, select the centerline as the axis of revolution. Figure 5.30 shows a sketch with a centerline created on the Front plane and Figure 5.31 shows the preview of the resultant revolved feature.

Note: If the sketch to be revolved has only one centerline then the drawn centerline will automatically be selected as the axis of revolution and preview of resultant revolve feature appears in the graphics area. However, if the sketch does not have any centerline drawn, or two or more than two centerline are drawn then on invoking the **Revolved Boss/Base** tool, the preview of the revolve feature will not be appears and you is prompted to select centerline as the axis of revolution. As soon as you select the centerline, the preview of the revolve feature appears in the graphics area. You can select linear entity of a sketch, centerline, axis, and an edge as the axis of revolution.

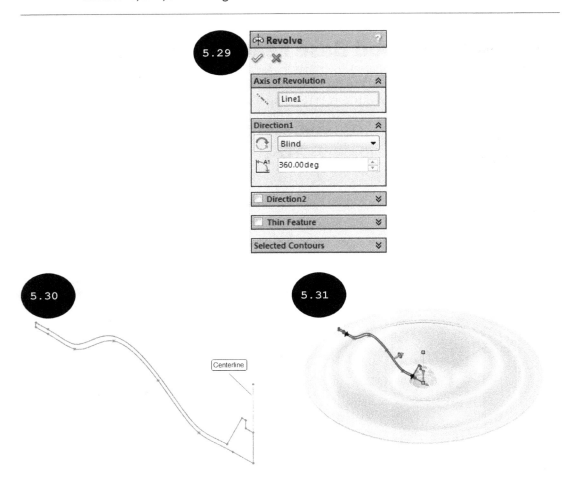

Note: If you exit from the Sketching environment after creating the sketch of the revolve feature and sketch is not selected in the graphics area then on invoking the **Revolved Boss/Base** tool, the **Revolve PropertyManager** appears, see Figure 5.32. Also, you are prompted to either select the sketch from the graphics area to be revolved or if the sketch is not created, select the sketching plane to create the sketch. On selecting the sketch to be revolved, the preview of the revolve feature appears in the graphics area. Also, the **Revolve PropertyManager** modified and appears as shown in Figure 5.29.

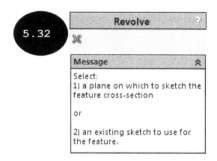

The options available in the **Revolve PropertyManager**, see Figure 5.29, are used to specify parameters for revolve feature being created. Some of this options are as follows.

Axis of Revolution

The **Axis of Revolution** field of the **Axis of Revolution** rollout in the PropertyManager is used to select the axis of revolution for the sketch. You can select a linear sketch entity, centerline, axis, or linear edge as the axis of revolution. Note that if the sketch to be revolve contain a centerline than automatically the centerline is selected as the axis of revolution on invoking the **Revolve PropertyManager.** However, if the sketch contains two or more than two centerlines than you is prompted to select the axis of revolution on invoking the **Revolve PropertyManager.**

Direction 1

The options available in the **Direction 1** rollout of the PropertyManager are used to define the end condition of the revolve feature in one direction. These options are as follows.

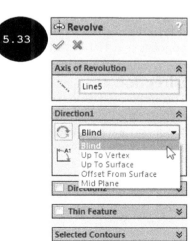

Revolve Type

The **Revolve Type** drop-down list of the **Direction 1** rollout allows you to select different methods for revolving a sketch. Figure 5.33 shows the options of this drop-down list. The options of this drop-down list that can be used for creating base revolve feature are as follows and the remaining options are discussed in later chapters.

Blind

The **Blind** option of the **Revolve Type** drop-down list is used to define the end condition or termination of the revolve feature by specifying the angle of revolution. By default, this option is selected in this drop-down list. As a result, the **Direction 1 Angle** field is available in the **Direction 1** rollout. You can enter the required angle revolution in this field.

Mid Plane

The **Mid Plane** option allows you to revolve a sketch about the centerline symmetrically in both side of the sketching plane, see Figure 5.34. After selecting this option, you can enter the angle of revolution in the **Direction 1 Angle** field of the rollout. Depending upon the angle entered in this field, material added symmetrically in both side of the sketching plane by revolving the sketch about the centerline.

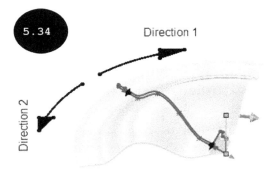

> **Note:** The options such as **Up To Vertex**, **Up To Surface**, and **Offset From Surface** of the **Revolve Type** drop-down list of the **Direction 1** rollout are discussed in later chapters.

Reverse Direction

The **Reverse Direction** button of the rollout is used to reverse the direction of revolution from one side of the sketching plane to the other side. This option will not be enabled when the **Mid Plane** option is selected in the **Revolve Type** drop-down list of the PropertyManager.

Direction 2

The options available in the **Direction 2** rollout are same as of the options available in the **Direction 1** rollout of the PropertyManager with the only difference that these options are used to specify the end condition for the revolve feature in the second direction of the sketching plane. Note that the **Direction 2** rollout is not available when the **Mid Plane** option is selected in the **Revolve Type** drop-down list of the **Direction 1** rollout. To expand the **Direction 2** rollout, select the check box available in the title bar of the **Direction 2** rollout, see Figure 5.35. Figure 5.36 show the preview of a revolved feature being created at revolving angle of 120 degree in direction 1 and 45 degree in direction 2.

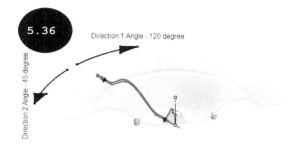

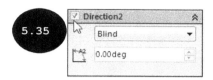

Thin Feature

The options available in the **Thin Feature** rollout are used to create a thin revolve feature with uniform wall thickness, see Figure 5.37. By default, the options available in this rollout are not activated. To activate the **Thin Feature** rollout, expand it by selecting the check box available left to the title bar of the rollout. As soon as the **Thin Feature** rollout expands, the preview of the thin feature appears in the graphics area with the default parameters. The options available in this rollout are same as discussed earlier while create the extrude feature.

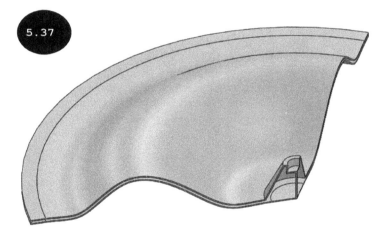

Selected Contours

The **Selected Contours** rollout is used to select contours or closed regions of a multi-contour sketch to be revolved. To revolve a required contour of a multi-contour sketch, expand the **Selected Contours** rollout of the PropertyManager and then move the cursor over the closed region/contour of the sketch to be revolved in the graphics area and then click to select it when the closed region/contour highlights, the preview of the revolved feature appears such that material is added by revolving the closed region about the centerline.

Navigating 3D Model in Graphics Area

In SOLIDWORKS, you can navigate the model by using mouse buttons and navigating tools. You can access the navigating tools from the **View (Heads-Up)** toolbar (this toolbar is available at the top of screen, see Figure 5.38), the **View > Modify** from the SOLIDWORKS menus, and shortcut menu appears on right clicking in the graphics area. The different navigating tools are as follows.

5.38

Zoom In/Out

You can zoom in or out in the graphics area, dynamically by using the **Zoom In/Out** tool. In other words, you can dynamically enlarge or reduce the view of the model by using the **Zoom In/Out** tool. To zoom in or out in the graphics area, dynamically, invoke the **Zoom In/Out** tool either from the SOLIDWORKS menus or from the shortcut menu. You can also use middle mouse button to zoom in or out the graphics area.

To invoke the **Zoom In/Out** tool from the SOLIDWORKS menus, click on the **View** menu of the SOLIDWORKS menu and then move the cursor over the **Modify** option, a cascading menu appears, see Figure 5.39. Next, click on the **Zoom In/Out** tool, the tool is invoked and the cursor is change to **Zoom In/Out** cursor. Once the **Zoom In/Out** tool has been invoked, move the cursor in the graphics area and then press and hold the left mouse button. Next, drag the cursor upward or downward in the graphics area. On dragging the cursor upwards, the view is enlarged and on dragging the cursor downwards, the view is reduced. Note that in the process of zooming in or out the view, the scale of the model will remain the same. However, the viewing distance will modify in order to enlarge or reduce the view.

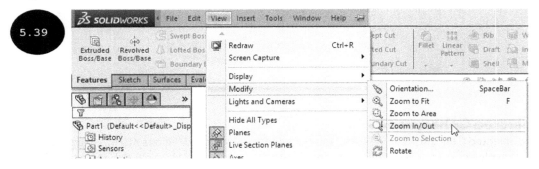

5.39

To invoke the **Zoom In/Out** tool from the shortcut menu, right click in the graphics area, a shortcut menu appears, see Figure 5.40. In the shortcut menu, click on the **Zoom In/Out** tool. Once the tool is invoked, the procedure to zoom in or out in the graphics area is same as discussed earlier.

You can also zoom in or zoom out the graphics area by scrolling the middle mouse button. Alternatively, by pressing and holding the **SHIFT** key and then dragging the cursor by pressing the middle mouse button in the graphics area up or down.

Zoom To Fit

The **Zoom To Fit** tool is used to fit the model completely inside the graphics area. To fit the model in the graphics area, invoke the **Zoom To Fit** tool either from the SOLIDWORKS menus, shortcut menu, or **View (Heads-Up)** toolbar. You can also press **F** key to fit the model completely inside the graphics area.

To fit the model completely inside the graphics area, click on the **Zoom To Fit** tool available in the **View (Heads-Up)** toolbar. Alternative, click on the **View > Modify > Zoom to Fit** from the SOLIDWORKS menu. You can also invoke this tool from the shortcut menu displays on right clicking in the graphics area.

Zoom to Area

The **Zoom to Area** tool is used to zoom a particular portion or area of a model by defining a boundary box. To zoom a particular area of a model, invoke the **Zoom to Area** tool either from the **View (Heads-Up)** toolbar, SOLIDWORKS menus, or from the shortcut menu which appears on right clicking in the graphics area.

Once the **Zoom To Area** tool is invoked, define a boundary box by dragging the cursor, the area inside the boundary box is enlarged.

Zoom to Selection

The **Zoom to Selection** tool is used to fit the selected object or geometry completely inside in the graphics area. To fit the selection (selected object or geometry) inside the graphics area, invoke the **Zoom to Selection** tool by clicking the **View > Modify > Zoom to Selection** from the SOLIDWORKS menu, the selected object or geometry is fitted completed inside the graphics area. Note that this tool is enabled only if the object to be fit is selected in the graphics area.

Pan

The **Pan** tool is used to pan/move the model in the graphics area. You can invoke this tool from the SOLIDWORKS menus and the shortcut menu. Once the **Pan** tool is invoked, you can pan the model in the graphics area by pressing and hold the left mouse button and then drag the cursor. In addition to this, you can also pan the model by pressing the **CTRL** key and middle mouse button to pan the model in the graphics area.

Rotate

The **Rotate** tool is used to rotate model freely in the graphics area. To rotate the model, invoke the **Rotate** tool by clicking on the **View > Modify > Rotate** from the SOLIDWORKS menus. You can also invoke this tool from the shortcut menu that appears on right clicking the graphics area. After invoking the **Rotate** tool, press and hold the left mouse button and then drag the cursor to rotate the model freely in the graphics area.

Manipulating the Orientation of the Model

The modifying view orientation of a 3D model is very important in order to review it from different views and angle. In SOLIDWORKS, you can change the orientation of a 3D model to predefine standard views such as front, top, right, side, bottom, and isometric by using the **View Orientation** flyout, **Orientation** dialog box, **Reference Triad**, and **View Selector Cube**, see Figure 5.41. In addition to the predefine standard views, you can create custom views as required. The various methods of manipulating the orientation of a model are as follows.

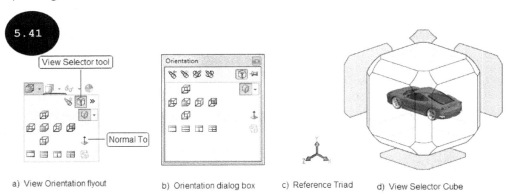

a) View Orientation flyout   b) Orientation dialog box   c) Reference Triad   d) View Selector Cube

Manipulating Orientation using View Orientation flyout

To manipulate the orientation of a model by using the **View Orientation** flyout, click on the down arrow available in the **View Orientation** tool of the **View (Heads-Up)** toolbar, the **View Orientation** flyout appears, see Figure 5.41. By using the tools of this flyout, you can manipulating the orientation of the model and are as follows.

Top/Front/Right/Left/Bottom/Back/Isometric

The **Top, Front, Right, Left, Bottom, Back,** and **Isometric** tools of the **View Orientation** flyout are used to display predefine standard views such as front, top, right, and isometric, respectively, of the model in the graphics area.

Normal To

The **Normal To** tool of the **View Orientation** flyout is used to display selected face of a 3D model normal to the viewing direction. If you are in the Sketching environment then this tool is used to make the current sketching plane normal to the viewing direction.

> **Tip:** If you choose the **Normal To** tool without selecting any face of the model, the nearest face of the model towards the normal direction is come normal to the viewing direction.

View Drop-Down list

The tools available in the **View** drop-down list of the **View Orientation** flyout are used to display the isometric, dimetric, or trimetric view of the model. Figure 5.42 shows the **View** drop-down list of the **View Orientation** flyout. By default, the **Trimetric** tool is activated in this drop-down list. As a result, on invoking the **View Orientation** flyout, the trimetric view of the model displays in the graphics area. You can activate the required tool to display the respective view of the model.

View Selector tool

The **View Selector** tool of the **View Orientation** flyout is used to display the **View Selector Cube** around the 3D model available in the graphics area, see Figure 5.41. By default, this tool is activated. As a result, on invoking the **View Orientation** flyout, the **View Selector Cube** appears in the graphics area. Note that the orientation of the model inside the **View Selector Cube** depends upon the tool activated in the **View** drop-down list of the flyout.

You can use the faces of the **View Selector Cube** to manipulate the orientation of the model. You will learn more about manipulating the orientation of the model by using the **View Selector Cube** later in this chapter.

New View

The **New View** tool is used to create custom/user defined view of the model. To create custom view, first set the orientation of the model, as required, by using different navigating tools. Once the orientation of the model set as required in the graphics area, click on the **New View** tool, the **Named View** dialog box appears, see Figure 5.43. In the **View name** field of this dialog box, enter the name of the custom view being created and then click on the **OK** button, the view is created and the name of the view created is added in the **View Orientation** flyout. You can display the model as per the custom view created any time by clicking on its name in the flyout. You can create multiple custom views of a model.

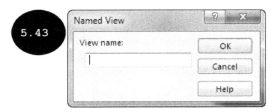

Manipulating Orientation using Orientation dialog box

To manipulate the orientation of a model by using the **Orientation** dialog box, press the SPACE key from your keyboard. As soon as you press the SPACE key, the **Orientation** dialog box appears in the graphics area with the **View Selector** tool activated by default in it. As a result, the **View Selector Cube** appears around the 3D model available in the graphics area, see Figure 5.41. The most of the tools available in the **Orientation** dialog box are same as discussed earlier in the **View Orientation** flyout and the remaining tools are as follows.

Pin/Unpin the dialog

By default, as soon as you invoke a view such as Front, Top, or Right of a model by clicking on their respective tool of the **Orientation** dialog box, the dialog box disappears. If you do not want to exit from the dialog box, click to active the **Pin/Unpin the dialog** tool of the dialog box. This tool is used pin the dialog box in the graphics area. Note that this is a toggle button.

Previous View

The **Previous View** tool is used to orient the model to its previously appears orientation. Note that by using this tool you can undo the last 10 view changes.

Update Standard Views

The **Update Standard Views** tool is used to update/change predefine standard views such as top, front, and right of the model, as required. To update/change a standard view, first orient the 3D model, as required, in the graphics area and then choose the **Update Standard Views** tool. Next, select a required standard tool such as Top and Front from the **Orientation** dialog box, the SOLIDWORKS message window appears. It informs you that changing this standard view will change the orientation of the standard orthogonal view of this model. Click the **Yes** button to make this change. As soon as you click on the **Yes** button, the selected standard view is updated/changed to the current display of the model in the graphics area.

Reset Standard Views

The **Reset Standard Views** tool is used to reset all the standard views back to the default settings. If you have updated any of the standard view, as per your requirement, then on clicking this tool, you can back to the default standard view orientation. When you click on the **Reset Standard Views** tool, the SOLIDWORKS message window appears. This window ask you whether you want to reset all the standard views to default settings. Click on the **Yes** button to reset all the views to the default settings.

Manipulating Orientation using View Selector Cube

Manipulating view orientation by using the **View Selector Cube** is one of the easiest way to achieve different views such as right, left, front, back, top, and isometric views of a 3D model. By default, on invoking the **View Orientation** flyout and **Orientation** dialog box, the **View Selector Cube** appears around the 3D model present in the graphics area. This is because, by default, the **View Selection** tool is activated in the **View Orientation** flyout as well as in the **Orientation** dialog box.

Note: The default orientation of the model inside the **View Selector Cube** depends upon the tool activated in the **View** drop-down list of the **View Orientation** flyout and the **Orientation** dialog box.

To manipulate the view orientation of a 3D model by using the **View Selector Cube**, move the cursor to a face of the **View Selector Cube** and click to select it when the face highlighted in the graphics area, see Figure 5.44. Note that depending upon the face of the **View Selector Cube** selected, the model is orientated accordingly, see Figure 5.45.

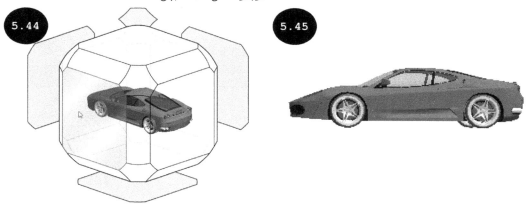

Manipulating the View Orientation using the Triad

A triad appears at the lower left corner of the graphics area and is used to guide you while orient the model in different views. You can also use the triad to manipulate the view orientation of the model normal to the screen, 180 degrees, and 90 degrees about an axis.

To orient the model normal to the screen, click on the axis of the triad, the model oriented normal to the screen with respect to the selected axis. Note that the direction of axis selected will also become normal to the screen. To orient the modal 180 degrees, click on the axis that is normal to the screen. To rotate the model, 90 degrees about an axis, press the **SHIFT** key and then click on the axis as the axis of rotation.

You can also rotate the model at an predefined angle that is specified in the **System Options - View** dialog box. To invoke this dialog box, click on the **Options** tool in the **Standard** toolbar, the **System Options - General** dialog box appears. Next, select the **View** option from the left panel of the dialog box to display the **System Options - View** dialog box. In the **Arrow keys** field of this dialog box, you can specify the predefined angle for rotation by using the triad. For rotating the model at an predefined angle, press the **ALT** key and then click on the axis of triad.

Changing Display Style of the Model

You can change the display style of the 3D model to wireframe, hidden lines visible, hidden lines removed, shaded, edges in shaded mode, and shadows in shaded mode display styles. The tools used to change the display style of the model are available in the **Display Style** flyout of the **View (Heads-Up)** toolbar, see Figure 5.46. All these tools are as follows.

Shaded With Edges

The **Shaded With Edges** tool is used to display the model in shaded with edges display style. In this style, the model displays in shaded mode with the display of outer edges turned On, see Figure 5.47. This tool is activated, by default. As a result, the model displays in shaded with edges display style, by default.

Shaded

The **Shaded** tool is used to display the model in shaded display style. In this style, the model displays in shaded mode with the display of outer edges turned Off, see Figure 5.48.

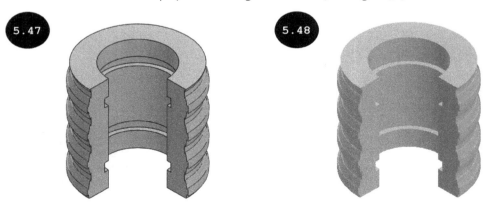

Hidden Lines Removed

The **Hidden Lines Removed** tool is used to display the model in hidden lines removed display style. In this style, the hidden lines of the model removed from the display of the model, see Figure 5.49.

Hidden Lines Visible

The **Hidden Lines Visible** tool is used to display the model in hidden lines visible display style. In this style, the visibility of the hidden lines of the model are turned On and appears in dotted lines, see Figure 5.50.

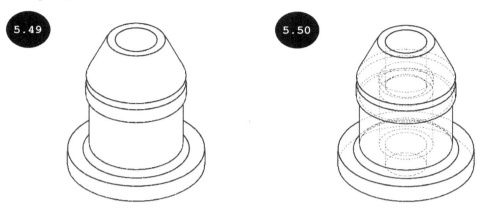

Wireframe

The **Wireframe** tool is used to display the model in wireframe display style. In this style, the hidden lines of the model display in continuous solid lines , see Figure 5.51.

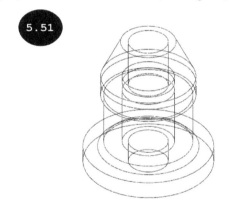

Changing View of the Model

In SOLIDWORKS, you can change the view of the model to perspective, shadows, and ambient occlusion by using the tools available in the **View Settings** flyout of the **View (Heads-Up)** toolbar, see Figure 5.52. These tools are as follows.

Shadows In Shaded Mode

The **Shadows In Shaded Mode** tool is used to displays the model with its shadow, see Figure 5.53. In this view of the model, the light appears from the top and due to which shadow appears at the bottom of the model. Note that on rotating the model, the shadow of the model rotates accordingly.

Perspective

The **Perspective** tool is used to displays the perspective view of the model, see Figure 5.54. A perspective view is the view which appears as it viewed normally from the eyes. Note that the perspective view depends upon the size of the model being viewed and the distance between the model and the viewer.

Ambient Occlusion

The **Ambient Occlusion** tool is used to display the ambient view of the model. The ambient view is the view of the model which displays due to the attenuation of the ambient light.

Tutorial 1

Open the sketch created in Tutorial 1 of Chapter 4, see Figure 5.55, and then create the model by extruding it to the depth of 40 mm, see Figure 5.56.

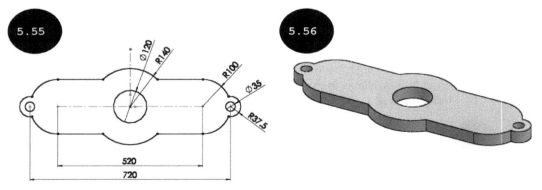

Section 1: Starting **SOLIDWORKS**

Start SOLIDWORKS software.

1. Double click on the **SOLIDWORKS** icon on your desktop to start SOLIDWORKS, if not started already.

Section 2: **Opening Sketch of Tutorial 1, Chapter 4**

Now, you need to open the sketch of Tutorial 1 created in Chapter 4.

1. Click on the **Open** tool in the **Standard** toolbar, the **Open** dialog box appears.

2. Browse to the *Tutorial* folder of Chapter 4 and then click to select the **Tutorial 1**.

3. Click on the **Open** button of the dialog box, the sketch of Tutorial 1 created in Chapter 4 is opened in the current session of SOLIDWORKS, see Figure 5.57.

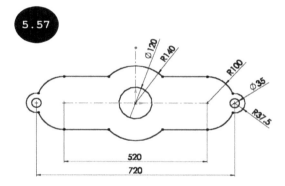

Section 3: **Saving Sketch**

Now, you need to save the sketch as the Tutorial 1 of Chapter 5.

1. Click on the **File > Save As** from the SOLIDWORKS menus, the **Save As** dialog box appears.

2. Browse to the *SOLIDWORKS* folder and then create a folder named as *Chapter 5* in it. Next, create another folder named as *Tutorial* inside the *Chapter 5* folder.

3. Click on the **Save** button to save the sketch inside the *Tutorial* folder of Chapter 5.

> **Note:** It is important to save the sketch in different location or different name before you make any modification so that the original file will not be modified.

Section 4: Extruding Sketch

Now, you can extrude the sketch and convert it into a feature.

1. Click on the **Features** tab of the **CommandManager** to displays the tools of the **Features CommandManager**, see Figure 5.58.

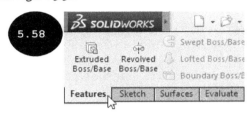

2. Click on the **Extruded Boss/Base** tool of the **Features Command Manager**, the **Boss-Extrude PropertyManager** and the preview of the extruded feature appears in the graphics area, see Figure 5.59. Also, the orientation of the model changes to **Trimetric**.

> **Note:**   On invoking the **Extruded Boss/Base** tool without exiting from the Sketching environment, the preview of the features appears in the graphics area, automatically. If you invoke the **Extruded Boss/Base** tool after exiting from the Sketching environment then you need to select the sketch to extrude before or after invoking the tool.

3. Enter 40 in the **Depth** field of the **Direction 1** rollout and then press ENTER key, the depth of the extruded feature chances to 40 mm.

4. Click on the green tick mark ✅ of the PropertyManager, the extruded feature is created, see Figure 5.60.

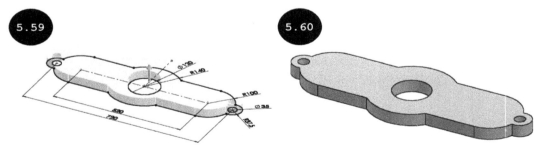

Section 5: Saving Model

Now, you need to save the model.

1. Click on the **Save** button of the **Standard** toolbar, the model is saved as *Tutorial 1* in the *Tutorial* folder of Chapter 5.

Tutorial 2

Open the sketch created in Tutorial 2 of Chapter 4, see Figure 5.61, and then revolve it around the vertical centerline to the angle of 270 degree, see Figure 5.62. Also, you need to change the display style of the model to Hidden Lines Removed style.

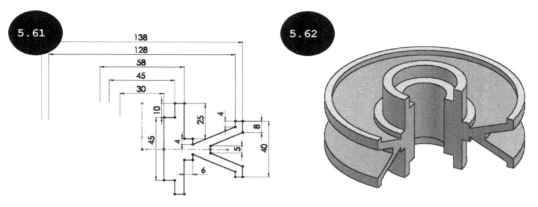

Section 1: Starting SOLIDWORKS

Start SOLIDWORKS software.

1. Double click on the **SOLIDWORKS** icon available on your desktop to start **SOLIDWORKS**, if not started already.

Section 2: Opening Sketch of Tutorial 2, Chapter 4

Now, you need to open the sketch of Tutorial 2 created in Chapter 4.

1. Click on the **Open** tool in the **Standard** toolbar, the **Open** dialog box appears.

2. Browse to the *Tutorial* folder of Chapter 4 and then click to select the **Tutorial 2**.

3. Click on the **Open** button of the dialog box, the sketch of Tutorial 2 created in Chapter 4 is opened in the current session of SOLIDWORKS, see Figure 5.63.

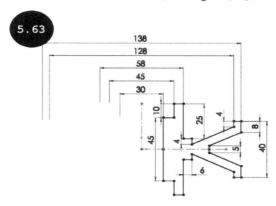

Section 3: Saving Sketch

Now, you need to save the sketch as the Tutorial 2 of Chapter 5.

1. Click on the **File > Save As** from the SOLIDWORKS menus, the **Save As** dialog box appears.

2. Browse to the *Tutorial* folder of Chapter 5 and then save the sketch in it.

Section 4: Revolving Sketch

1. Click on the **Features** tab of the **CommandManager** to displays the tools of the **Features CommandManager**, see Figure 5.64.

2. Click on the **Revolved Boss/Base** tool of the **Features Command Manager**, the **Revolve PropertyManager** appears. Also, the orientation of the sketch changes to **Trimetric** orientation.

Note: You can change the orientation of the model/sketch by using the **View Orientation** flyout of the **View (Heads-Up)** toolbar, see Figure 5.65.

3. Select the vertical centerline as the axis of revolution, the preview of the revolve feature appears in the graphics area, see Figure 5.66.

4. Enter 270 degree in the **Direction 1 Angle** field of the **Direction 1** rollout of the PropertyManager and then press ENTER key, the angle of revolution of the feature chances to 270 degree.

5. Click on the green tick mark ✅ of the PropertyManager, the revolved feature is created, see Figure 5.67.

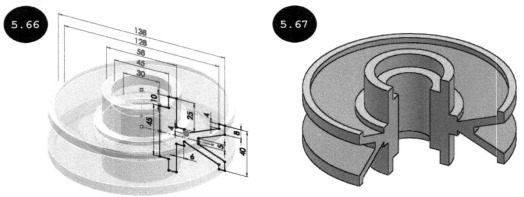

Section 5: Changing Display Style

Now, you need to change the display style of the model.

1. Invoke the **Display Style** flyout of the **View (Heads-Up)** toolbar, see Figure 5.68.

2. Click on the **Hidden Lines Removed** tool of the **Display Style** flyout, the display style of the model is changed to hidden lines removed display style, see Figure 5.69.

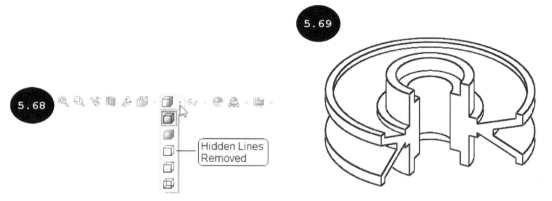

Section 6: Saving Model

Now, you need to save the model.

1. Click on the **Save** button of the **Standard** toolbar, the model is saved as *Tutorial 2* in the *Tutorial* folder of Chapter 5.

Tutorial 3

Open the sketch created in Tutorial 3 of Chapter 4, see Figure 5.70, and then extrude it to the depth of 60 mm symmetrically about the sketching plane, see Figure 5.71. Also, you need to change the view orientation of the model to isometric and navigate the model in the graphics area.

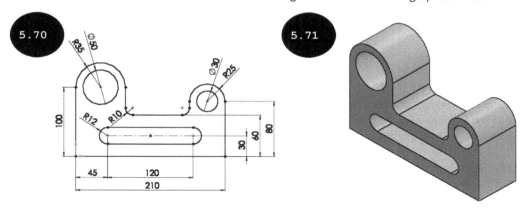

Section 1: Starting SOLIDWORKS

Start SOLIDWORKS software.

1. Double click on the **SOLIDWORKS** icon available on your desktop to start **SOLIDWORKS**, if not started already.

Section 2: Opening Sketch of Tutorial 3, Chapter 4

Now, you need to open the sketch of Tutorial 3 created in Chapter 4.

1. Click on the **Open** tool in the **Standard** toolbar, the **Open** dialog box appears.

2. Browse to the *Tutorial* folder of Chapter 4 and then open the **Tutorial 3**, see Figure 5.72.

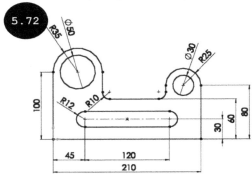

Section 3: Saving Sketch

Now, you need to save the sketch as the Tutorial 3 of Chapter 5.

1. Click on the **File > Save As** from the SOLIDWORKS menus, the **Save As** dialog box appears.

2. Browse to the *Tutorial* folder of Chapter 5 and then save the sketch in it.

Section 4: Extruding Sketch

Now, you can extrude the sketch and convert it into a extrude feature.

1. Click on the **Features** tab of the **CommandManager** to displays the tools of the **Features CommandManager**.

2. Click on the **Extruded Boss/Base** tool of the **Features Command Manager**, the **Boss-Extrude PropertyManager** and the preview of the extruded feature appears in the graphics area, see Figure 5.73. Also, the orientation of the model changes to **Trimetric**.

3. Enter 60 in the **Depth** field of the **Direction 1** rollout and then press ENTER key, the depth of the extruded feature chances to 60 mm.

4. Invoke the **End Condition** flyout of the **Direction 1** rollout, see Figure 5.74.

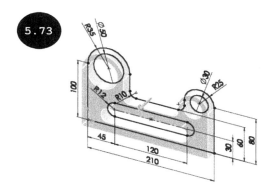

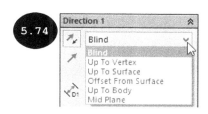

5. Click on the **Mid Plane** option from the **End Condition** flyout, the depth of the extrusion chances such that it added symmetrically on both side of the sketching plane, see Figure 5.75.

6. Click on the green tick mark ✅ of the PropertyManager, the extruded feature is created symmetrically about the Sketching plane, see Figure 5.76.

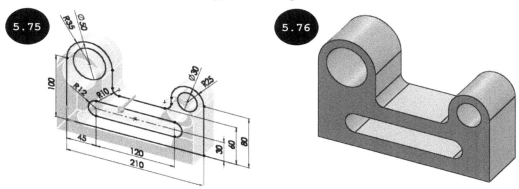

Section 5: Changing View Orientation to Isometric

1. Invoke the **View Orientation** flyout of the **View (Heads-Up)** toolbar, see Figure 5.77. As soon as you invoke the **View Orientation** flyout, the **View Selector Cube** appears around the model in the graphics area, see Figure 5.78.

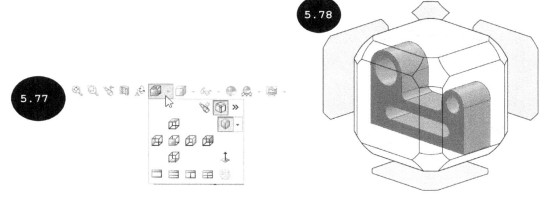

Tip: You can change the orientation of the model by using the tools of the **View Orientation** flyout or by using the faces of the **View Selector Cube**.

2. Invoke the **View** drop-down list of the **View Orientation** flyout, see Figure 5.79. Next, click on the **Isometric** option of this drop-down list, the view orientation of the model changed to isometric.

Section 6: Navigating the Model

Now, you can to navigate the model.

1. Right click in the graphics area, a shortcut menu appears, see Figure 5.80.

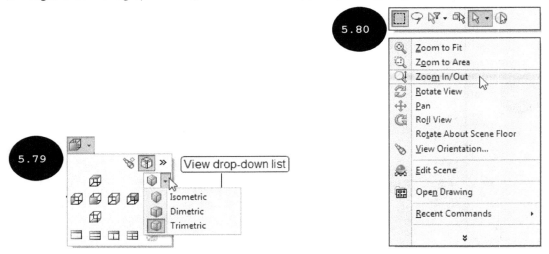

2. Click on the **Zoom In/Out** tool from the shortcut menu, the **Zoom In/Out** tool invoked and cursor changes to zoom cursor.

3. Press and hold the left mouse button and then drag the cursor upward or downward in the graphics area. On dragging the cursor upwards, the view is enlarged and on dragging the cursor downwards, the view is reduced. Once you are done, press the ESC key.

4. Once you are done, right click and then click on the Select tool from the shortcut menu to exit from the tool.

5. Similarly, you can invoke the remaining navigating tools such as Rotate View and Pan to navigate the model.

Section 7: Saving Model

Now, you need to save the model.

1. Click on the **Save** button of the **Standard** toolbar, the model is saved as *Tutorial 3* in the *Tutorial* folder of Chapter 5.

Hands-on Test Drive 1

Create the revolve model as shown in Figure 5.81.

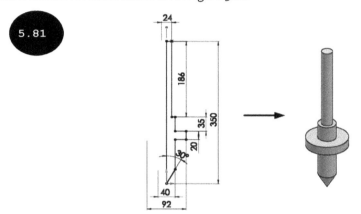

5.81

Hands-on Test Drive 2

Create the extrude model as shown in Figure 5.82.

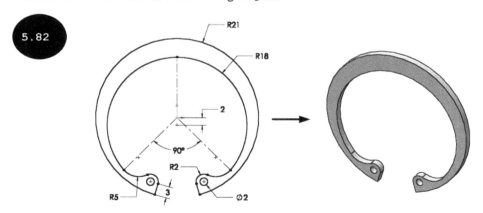

5.82

Summary

In this chapter, you have learnt about creating extruded and revolved base features by using the **Extruded Boss/Base** and **Revolved Boss/Base** tools. An extruded feature is created by adding material normal or at an angle to the sketching plane. A revolve feature is created by adding material by revolving a sketch around an centerline or the axis of revolution. You can create solid and thin extruded/revolved features. You have also learnt about how to navigate the model by using mouse buttons and navigating tools such as **Zoom In/Out** and **Zoom To Fit**. You can also manipulate the orientation of the model to the predefine standard views such as front, top, right, side, and custom views. At last in this chapter, you have learnt about changing display style and view of the model.

Questions

- The _____ tool is used to create feature by adding material normal to the sketching plane.

- The _____ tool is used to create feature by adding material by revolving a sketch around an centerline or the axis of revolution.

- The _____ tool is used to fit the model completely inside the graphics area.

- The _____ tool of the **View Orientation** flyout is used to display the **View Selector Cube** around the 3D model available in the graphics area.

- The _____ button of the **Boss-Extrude PropertyManager** is used to taper the extrude feature being created.

- The _____ option is used to extrude/revolve the feature symmetrically about the sketching plane.

- You can only create a thin feature from an open sketch. (True/False).

- In SOLIDWORKS, manipulating view orientation of a model by using the **View Selector Cube** is one of the easiest way to achieve different views such as right, left, and isometric. (True/False).

- In SOLIDWORKS, you can not navigate the model by using mouse buttons. (True/False).

- While creating a revolve feature, if the sketch to be revolved has only one centerline then the drawn centerline will automatically be selected as the axis of revolution (True/False).

Creating Reference Geometries

In this chapter:

- Creating Reference Planes
- Creating Reference Axis
- Creating Reference Coordinate System
- Creating Reference Point

By default, in SOLIDWORKS, three default reference planes: Front, Top, and Right are available for creating features. These reference planes may be good enough for create base features of a model by extruding and revolving the sketch, as discussed in earlier chapters. However, to create a real world model with multiple features, you may required addition reference planes. In other words, the three default reference planes may not enough for creating all the features of a real world components and for that you need to create additional reference planes. By keeping this in mind, SOLIDWORKS allows you to create additional reference plane as many as required for creating any complex real world model. You can create additional reference planes by using the **Plane** tool available in the **Reference Geometry** flyout, see Figure 6.1. Figure 6.2 shows a multiple featured model for your reference which is created by creating all its feature one by one.

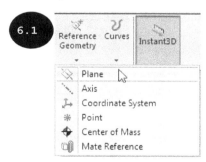

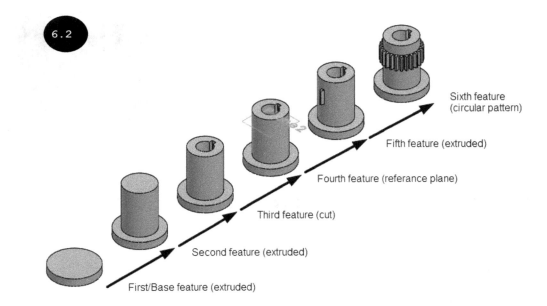

6.2

Sixth feature
(circular pattern)

Fifth feature (extruded)

Fourth feature (referance plane)

Third feature (cut)

Second feature (extruded)

First/Base feature (extruded)

The model shown in Figure 6.2 having six features. Its first feature is a extruded feature created on the Top plane, second feature is a extruded feature created on the top planar face of the first feature, third feature is a cut feature created on the top planar face of the second feature, fourth feature is a user defined reference plane created by using the **Plane** tool of the **Reference Geometry** flyout, fifth feature is a extruded feature created on the user defined reference plane, and sixth feature is a circular pattern of the fifth feature.

Note: From the above explanation it is cleared that you may need to create additional reference planes for creating features of a model. Also, you can select any of the planar face of an existing features as the sketching plane for creating features of the model.

Creating Reference Planes

In SOLIDWORKS, in addition to the three default planes: Top, Front, and Right, you can create reference planes at an offset distance from an existing plane/planar face, parallel to an existing plane/planar face, at an angle to the existing plane/planar face, passing through points/vertices, normal to an curve, and at the middle of two faces/planes. All these type of planes can be created by using the **Plane** tool which is available in the **Reference Geometry** flyout, see Figure 6.1.

To invoke the **Reference Geometry** flyout, click on the down arrow available on the **Reference Geometry** button of the **Features CommandManager**. Once this flyout invoked, click on the **Plane** tool, the **Plane PropertyManager** appears, see Figure 6.3. The options available in this PropertyManager are used to create different type of reference planes and are as follows.

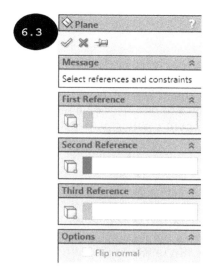

Message

The **Message** rollout is used to prompt you for creating reference planes and also displays the current status of the plane being created. Note that when the current status of the plane being created displays as Fully defined, it means that all the required references for creating the plane has been defined and the plane is created. Also, the background color of this rollout changes to green when the plane being created become fully defined.

First Reference

For creating any type of reference plane maximum three reference are required to make it fully defined. The **First Reference** rollout is used to defined the first reference for the plane being created. You can select any existing planar face, plane, vertex, point, edge, or curve as the first reference for creating plane. Note that selection of reference depend upon type of plane to be created. You will learn more about selection of reference planes depending upon type of plane to be creation later in this chapter. As soon as you select the first reference, the rollout expands with the additional options and the most suitable option is selected or activated by default in it, see Figure 6.4. Note that the additional available options and the default selection depends upon the type of first reference selected. For example, on selecting an existing planar face or plane as the first reference, the **Offset distance** button is activated, by default. You can select any option/button other than the one selected by default, as required. These options are as follows.

Coincident

The **Coincident** button is used to apply coincident relation between the selected planar/point reference and the reference plane being created.

Parallel

The **Parallel** button is used to apply parallel relation between the selected planar reference and the reference plane being created. As a result, the plane being created will be parallel to the selected reference. Note that for creating parallel plane, you also need to define second reference. You will learn more about creating parallel plane later in this chapter.

Perpendicular

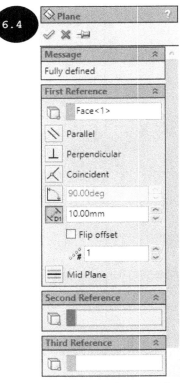

The **Perpendicular** button is used to apply perpendicular relation between the selected planar reference and the reference plane being created. On applying this relation, the plane being created will be perpendicular to the selected reference. Note that for creating perpendicular plane, you also need to define second reference. You will learn more about creating perpendicular plane later in this chapter.

Tangent

The **Tangent** button is used to create a plane tangent to an cylindrical face and passing through an edge, axis, or sketch line. Note that the **Tangent** button enabled in the PropertyManager on selecting the cylindrical face as the first reference. After selecting a cylindrical face as the first reference, you also need to define an edge, axis, or sketch line as the second reference. You will learn more about creating tangent plane later in this chapter.

At angle

The **At angle** button is used to create a plane at an angle to a planar or cylindrical face and passing through an edge, axis, or sketch line. To create plane at an angle, you can select a planar or cylindrical face as the first reference and an edge, axis, or sketch line as the second reference. You will learn more about creating plane at an angle later in this chapter.

Mid Plane

The **Mid Plane** button is used to create a plane at the middle of two selected planar faces.

Project

The **Project** button is used to create a plane onto a non-planar surface passing through a projected point. The projected point is created by projecting a point, vertex, origin, or coordinates system onto the non-planar surface.

Offset distance

The **Offset distance** button is used to create a plane at an offset distance from the selected reference.

Parallel to screen

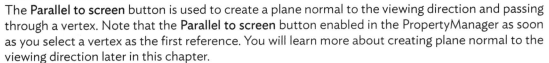

The **Parallel to screen** button is used to create a plane normal to the viewing direction and passing through a vertex. Note that the **Parallel to screen** button enabled in the PropertyManager as soon as you select a vertex as the first reference. You will learn more about creating plane normal to the viewing direction later in this chapter.

Number of planes to create

The **Number of planes to create** field is used to specify the number of planes to be created. By default, the value entered in this field is 1. As a result, the only one reference plane will be created with the specified parameters. Note that this field will be available only when the **At angle** or **Offset distance** button is activated.

Second Reference

The **Second Reference** rollout is used to defined the second reference for creating the reference plane. The options available in this rollout are same as discussed above. You need to define the second reference while creating planes such as plane at an angle, plane tangent to an cylindrical face, and plane perpendicular to an planar face. You will learn more about creating different types of plane by specifying second references later in this chapter.

Third Reference

The **Third Reference** rollout is used to defined the third reference for creating a reference plane. The options available in this rollout are same as discussed above. You need to define the third reference while creating planes such as plane passing through three points or vertices.

In SOLIDWORKS, you no need to much worry about options available in the **Plane PropertyManager** while creating reference planes. It allows you to more focus on creating reference planes rather than selecting suitable options for creating it. This is because, on selecting the required reference geometry for creating plane, the most suitable option will automatically be selected in the PropertyManager and the preview of the respective reference plane appears in the graphics area. Below are the procedures for creating different type of reference planes.

Creating Plane at an Offset Distance

1. Invoke the **Reference Geometry** flyout from the **Features CommandManager** and then click on the **Plane** tool (see Figure 6.1), the **Plane PropertyManager** appears, see Figure 6.3.
2. Select a planar face or an existing plane from the graphics area as the first reference, the preview of the offset plane appears, see Figure 6.5.
3. Enter the required offset value in the **Distance** field available in front of the **Offset distance** button.
4. To flip the direction of plane creation, select the **Flip** check box, see Figure 6.6.
5. Click on the green tick mark ✅ of the PropertyManager, the reference plane at an specified offset distance is created.

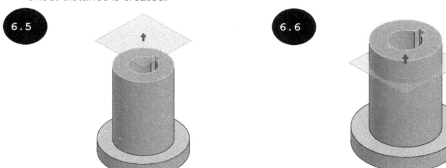

Tip: To create a reference plane at an offset distance to an existing plane or planar face of the model, you only need to select first reference.

Creating Parallel Plane

1. Invoke the **Reference Geometry** flyout and then click on the **Plane** tool.
2. Select a planar face or an existing plane from the graphics area as the first reference.

Note: As soon as you select a planar face or an plane, the preview of the offset plane appears in the graphics area with the default offset value. Also, the **Offset distance** button is activated automatically in the **First Reference** rollout of the PropertyManager.

3. Select a point or a vertex from the graphics area as the second reference, the preview of the reference plane, parallel to the selected face and coincident to the vertex/point appears in the graphics area.
4. Click on the green tick mark ✅ of the PropertyManager, the parallel plane is created, see Figure 6.7.

Tip: To create a reference plane parallel to a planar face of the model, you only need to select two references: first reference will be the planar face and second reference can be a point, vertex, or an edge. On selecting an edge as the second reference, you need to activate the **Parallel** button, manually.

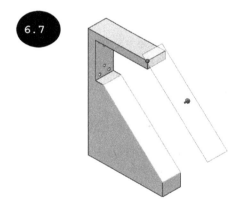

6.7

Creating Plane at an Angle

1. Invoke the **Plane PropertyManager**.
2. Select a planar face or an existing plane from the graphics area as the first reference. Next, click on the **At angle** button to activate it in the **First Reference** rollout of the PropertyManager.
3. Enter the required angle value in the **Angle** field available in front of the **At angle** button.
4. Select an edge, axis, or a sketch line as the second reference, the preview of the reference plane, see Figure 6.8.
5. To flip the direction of angle, select the **Flip** check box available below the **At angle** button.
6. Click on the green tick mark ✅ of the PropertyManager, the reference plane is created.

Tip: To create a reference plane at an angle to an planar face/plane, you only need to select two references: first reference will be the planar face/plane and second reference can be an edge, axis, or a sketch line.

Creating Plane Passing through three Points/Vertices

1. Invoke the **Plane PropertyManager**.
2. Select a point or vertex from the graphics area as the first reference.
3. Select another point or vertex as the second reference.
4. Select the third point or vertex as the third reference, the preview of the reference plane passing through three points/verities appears in the graphics area, see Figure 6.9.
5. Click on the green tick mark ✓ of the PropertyManager, the reference plane passing through three specified points/verities is created.

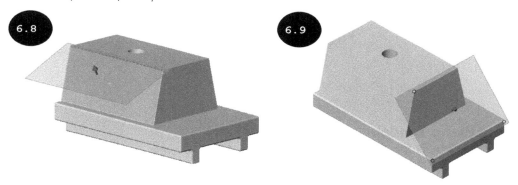

Creating Plane Normal to a Curve

1. Invoke the **Plane PropertyManager**.
2. Select a curve from the graphics area as the first reference, see Figure 6.10.
3. Select a point of the curve as the second reference, see Figure 6.10, the preview of the reference plane normal to the curve and passing through the selected point appears, see Figure 6.11.
4. Click on the green tick mark ✓ of the PropertyManager, the reference plane normal to the curve and passing through the point is created.

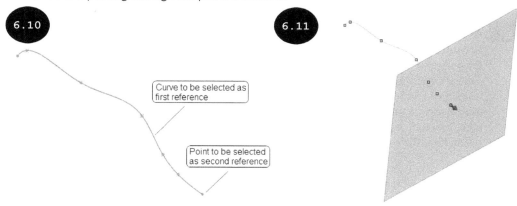

Creating Plane at the middle of two Faces/Planes

1. Invoke the **Plane PropertyManager**.
2. Select a face of the model in the graphics area as the first reference, see Figure 6.12.
3. Select the second face of the model as the second reference, see Figure 6.12, the preview of the plane passing at the middle of two selected faces appears in the graphics area, see Figure 6.12.
4. Click on the green tick mark ✅ of the PropertyManager, the reference plane at the middle of two selected faces is created.

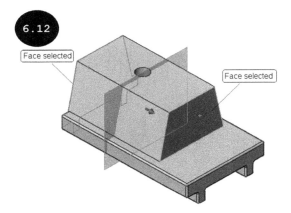

Creating Plane Tangent to a Cylindrical Face

1. Invoke the **Plane PropertyManager**.
2. Select a cylindrical face of the model as the first reference, see Figure 6.13, a preview of the plane tangent to the selected cylindrical face appears in the graphics area.

Tip: After specifying the first reference that is a cylindrical face, you also need to specify second reference that can be a planar face or a plane in order to create plane tangent to a cylindrical face and perpendicular or parallel to the second reference (a planar face/plane).

3. Select a planar face or a plane as the second reference, see Figure 6.13, the preview of the plane tangent to the cylindrical surface and perpendicular to the selected planar face appears in the graphics area, see Figure 6.14.

Note: As soon as you specify the second reference (a planar face), the **Perpendicular** button activated automatically (by default) in the **Second Reference** rollout of the PropertyManager. As a result, the preview of the reference plane appears tangent to the cylindrical surface and perpendicular to the selected planar face. If you click on the **Parallel** button of the **Second Reference** rollout to activate it, the preview of the tangent plane modified and appears as tangent to the cylindrical face and parallel to the selected planar face. You can also flip the direction of creation of plane by selecting the **Flip** check box of the **First Reference** rollout.

4. Click on the green tick mark ✅ of the PropertyManager, the reference plane tangent to the selected cylindrical face and perpendicular/parallel to the planar face/plane is created.

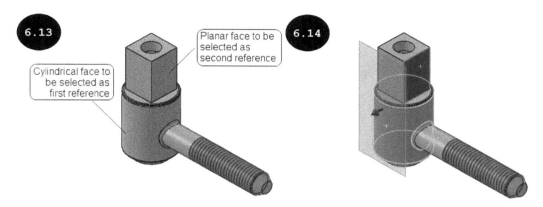

Creating Plane Parallel to the Screen

1. Invoke the **Plane PropertyManager**.
2. Select a vertex as the first reference, see Figure 6.15.
3. Click to activate the **Parallel to screen** button 🔲 of the **First Reference** rollout, the preview of a plane normal to the viewing direction and passing through the vertex appears, see Figure 6.16.
4. If needed, enter the offset distance in the **Offset distance** field of the PropertyManager.

Note: If the value in the **Offset distance** field is entered 0 then the plane will be created normal to the viewing direction and passing through the vertex. To create a plane at an offset distance to the vertex and normal to the viewing direction, you need to enter the offset distance in the **Offset distance** field of the PropertyManager.

5. Click on the green tick mark ✅ of the PropertyManager, the reference plane normal to the viewing direction (parallel to the screen) and passing through the vertex is created.

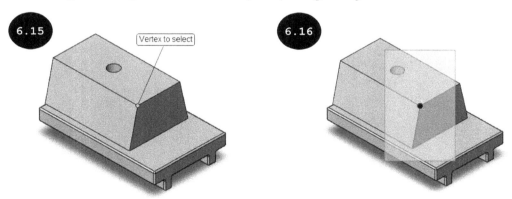

Creating Plane Projected to Non-Planar Face

1. Invoke the **Plane PropertyManager**.
2. Select a point to be projected onto a non planar face as the first reference, see Figure 6.17.
3. Select the non planar face of the model to create a projected plane, see Figure 6.17, the preview of the projected plane appears in the graphics area, see Figure 6.18.

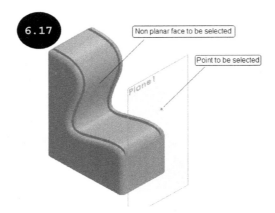

Non planar face to be selected

Point to be selected

Note: Note that by default, the preview of the projected plane appears such that the selected point projected on to the nearest location on the non planar face, see Figure 6.18. This is because the **Nearest location on surface** radio button is selected by default in the **First Reference** rollout. On selecting the **Along sketch normal** radio button, the preview of the plane appears such that the selected point projected normal to the non planar face, see Figure 6.19. You can also flip the project direction of the plane by selecting the **Flip** button. Note that the **Flip** button will be enabled only when the **Along sketch normal** radio button is selected.

4. Select the required radio button from the **First Reference** rollout (**Nearest location on surface** or **Along sketch normal**), the preview of the projected plane appears accordingly.
5. Click on the green tick mark ✅ of the PropertyManager, the reference plane tangent to the selected cylindrical face and perpendicular/parallel to the planar face/plane is created.

Creating Reference Axis

Similar to creating reference planes, in SOLIDWORKS, you can create reference axis by using the **Axis** tool available in the **Reference Geometry** flyout, see Figure 6.20. The reference axis can be used for creating features such as revolve feature, and circular pattern. In revolve feature and circular pattern, you can use reference axis as the axis of revolution.

You can create reference axis along an existing line/edge/axis, at the intersection of two planes/surfaces, passing through two points/vertices, along the axis of cylindrical/conical face, and passing through a point/vertices and normal to a surface/plane. All these type of reference axes can be created by using the options available in the **Axis PropertyManager**. To invoke this PropertyManager, click on the **Axis** tool available in the **Reference Geometry** flyout. Figure 6.21 shows the **Axis PropertyManager** appears on clicking the **Axis** tool. The options available in the PropertyManager are as follows.

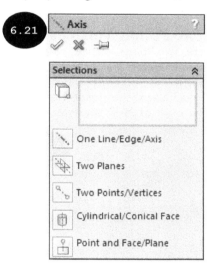

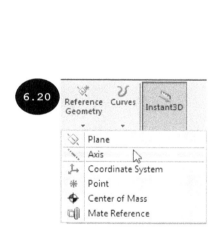

One Line/Edge/Axis

The **One Line/Edge/Axis** option is used to create an axis along an existing line, edge, or axis. To create an axis along an existing line, edge, or axis, activate the **One Line/Edge/Axis** button. Next, select an existing line, edge, or axis, the preview of the axis along the selected entity appears in the graphics area. Next, click on the green tick mark ✓ of the PropertyManager to create the reference axis. Figure 6.22 shows an reference axis created along an existing edge of the model.

Two Planes

The **Two Planes** option is used to create an axis at the intersection of two planar surfaces or planes. To create an axis at the intersection of two surfaces or planes, activate the **Two Planes** button and then select two planar surfaces or planes, the preview of the axis at the intersection the selections appears in the graphics area. Next, click on the green tick mark ✓ of the PropertyManager to create the reference axis. Note that the planes or surfaces to be selected need to be non-parallel to each other. Figure 6.23 shows an reference axis created at the intersection of two surfaces.

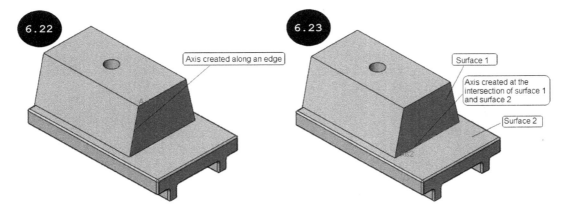

Two Points/Vertices

The **Two Points/Vertices** option is used to create an axis passing through two points or vertices. To create reference axis passing through two points/vertices, activate the **Two Points/Vertices** button and then select two points or vertices, the preview of the resultant axis appears in the graphics area. Figure 6.24 shows the preview of the axis passing through two vertices. Next, click on the green tick mark ✓ of the PropertyManager to create the reference axis.

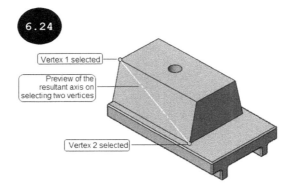

Cylindrical/Conical Face

The **Cylindrical/Conical Face** option is used to create an axis along the axis of cylindrical/conical face. To create reference axis along the axis of cylindrical/conical face, activate the **Cylindrical/Conical Face** button and then select a cylindrical or conical surface, the preview of the resultant axis appears in the graphics area, see Figures 8.25 and 8.26. Next, click on the green tick mark ✓ of the PropertyManager to create the reference axis.

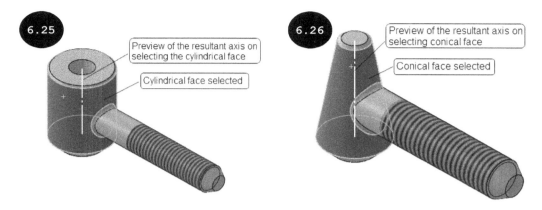

Point and Face/Plane

The **Point and Face/Plane** option is used to create an axis normal to the selected face/plane and passing through a point/vertex. To create reference axis normal to a surface/plane and passing through a point/vertex, activate the **Point and Face/Plane** button and then select a planar face and a point/vertex, see Figure 6.27, the preview of the axis normal to the selected face and passing through the point appears in the graphics area, see Figure 6.28. Next, click on the green tick mark ✅ of the PropertyManager to create the reference axis.

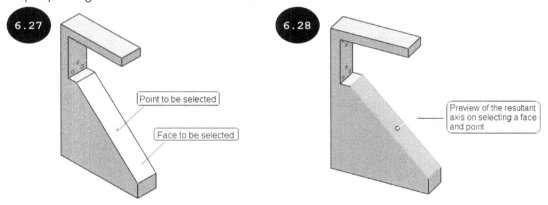

Creating Reference Coordinate System

In addition to reference plane and axis, you can also create reference coordinate systems by using the **Coordinate System** tool of the **Reference Geometry** flyout, see figure 6.29. It is mainly used for machining or analyzing the model by positioning the origin of the model relative to its features, as required. You can also use coordinate system for applying relations, calculating mass properties, measurement, and so on.

Procedure to Reference Coordinate System

1. Invoke the **Reference Geometry** flyout and then click on the **Coordinate System** tool, see Figure 6.29, the **Coordinate System PropertyManager** appears, see Figure 6.30. Also, the preview of coordinate system appears at the origin in the graphics area.

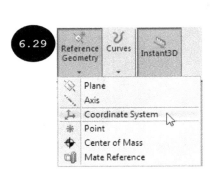

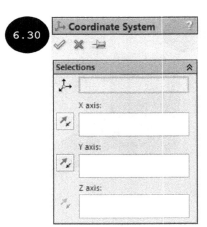

2. Select a point or vertex to specify the origin location of the coordinate system. After specifying the origin location of the coordinate system, you need to define the direction of its axis.

3. Click on the **X Axis Direction Reference** field of the PropertyManager to activate it, if not activated. Next, select a linear edge of the model to define the X axis direction of the coordinate system, the X axis of the coordinate system aligned along with the selected direction. You can also reverse the direction of axis by clicking on the **Reverse X Axis Direction** button available in the left of the **X Axis Direction Reference** field.

4. Similarly, you can specify the Y axis direction of the coordinate system. You can also define the Z axis, if needed. Once the origin, and axes directions of coordinate system has been defined, click on the green tick mark ✅ of the PropertyManager to create the resultant coordinate system. Figure 6.31 shows a coordinate system created by defining origin, X axis, and Y axis.

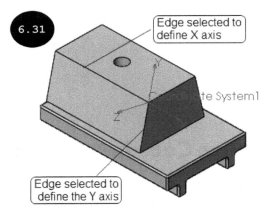

Creating Reference Point

The reference point is a point that can be created any where on a 3D model or space and can be used as a reference for measuring distance, creating planes, and so on. To created reference point, invoke the **Reference Geometry** flyout and then click on the **Point** tool, the **Point PropertyManager** appears, see Figure 6.32. The options available in this PropertyManager are as follows.

Reference Entities

The **Reference Entities** field is used to select entities as the reference entities for creating points.

Arc Center

The **Arc Center** button is used to create a point at the center of a circular or semi-circular edge, see Figure 6.33. Note that as soon as you select a circular or semi-circular edge, the preview of reference point at its center appears and the **Arc Center** button activates automatically in the PropertyManager.

Center of Face

The **Center of Face** button is used to create a point at the center of selected planar or non-planar face, see Figure 6.34. Note that as soon as you select a planar or non-planar face, the preview of reference point at the center of selected face appears and the **Center of Face** button activates, automatically in the PropertyManager.

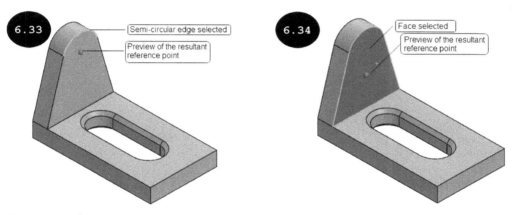

Intersection

The **Intersection** button is used to create a point at the intersection of two entities. You can select edges, curves, and sketch segments. Note that as soon as you select two entities, the preview of reference point at their intersection appears in the graphics area and the **Intersection** button activates, automatically in the PropertyManager. Figure 6.35 show the preview of a reference point at the intersection of two edges.

Projection

The **Projection** button is used to create a point by projecting one entity onto another entity. You can select sketch points, endpoints of curves, or vertices as the entities to be projected and a planar or non planar face as the entity onto which you wanted to project. Figure 6.36 shows the preview of a reference point by projecting a vertex onto a planar face.

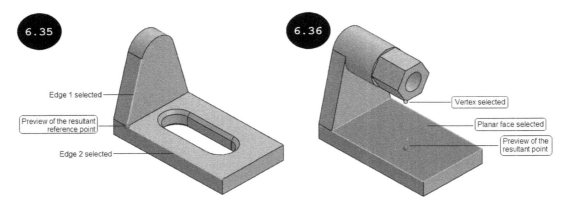

On point

The **One point** button is used to create a reference point on to a sketch point or on the end points of a sketch entity. As soon as you select a sketch point or a point of the sketch, the **On point** button gets activated, automatically in the PropertyManager and preview of the resultant reference point appears in the graphics area, see Figure 6.37 and 6.38.

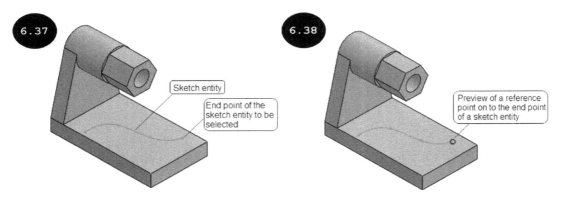

Along curve distance or multiple reference point

The **Along curve distance** or **multiple reference point** button is used to create reference points on an edge, curve, or sketch entity. Note that as soon as you select an edge, curve, or sketch entity, this button activates, automatically, and the preview of reference point displays in the graphic area with default settings, see Figure 6.39. Also, three radio buttons: **Distance**, **Percentage**, and **Evenly Distribute** appears in the PropertyManager, see Figure 6.40. These radio buttons are as follows.

Distance Radio button

This radio button is used to specify position of the reference point being created by specifying distance value in the **Distance/Percentage** field of the PropertyManager.

Percentage

This radio button is used to specify position of the reference point being created by specifying percentage value in the **Distance/Percentage** field. Note that the percentage value is calculated in terms of the total length of the selected entity.

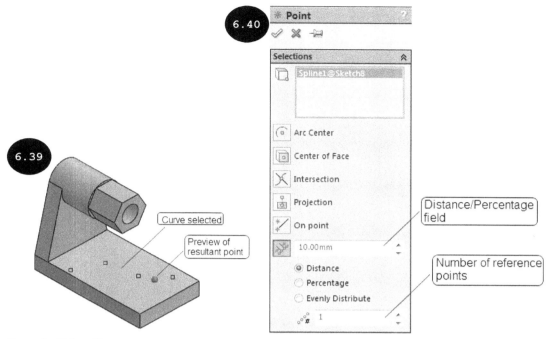

Evenly Distribute

This radio button is used to evenly distributes the number of reference points on the selected entity.

Number of reference points

The **Number of reference points** field is used to specify number of reference points to be created on the selected entity. By default, 1 is entered in this field. As a result, only one reference point creates on the selected entity. You can create multiple reference points on to an selected entity by specifying the required number in this field.

Once the preview of the reference points appears in the graphics area, click on the green tick mark ✓ of the PropertyManager, the respective reference point is created.

Tutorial 1

Create the multi-featured model shown in Figure 6.41. You need to create the model by creating its all features one by one.

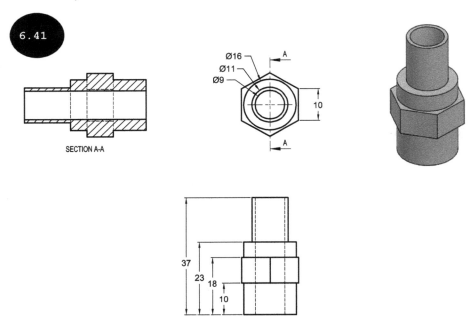

Section 1: Starting SOLIDWORKS

1.   Double click on the **SOLIDWORKS** icon on your desktop to start SOLIDWORKS.

Section 2: Invoking Part Modeling Environment

1.   Click on the **New** tool in the **Standard** toolbar, the **New SOLIDWORKS Document** dialog box appears.

2.   In this dialog box, the **Part** button is activated by default. Click on the **OK** button.

Once the Part modeling environment is invoked, you can set the unit system and create the base/first feature of the model.

Section 3: Specifying Unit Settings

1.   Move the cursor towards the lower right corner of the screen over the Status Bar and then click on the **Unit System** area of the Status Bar, the **Unit System** flyout appears, see Figure 6.42.

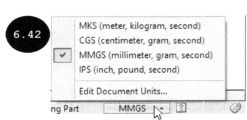

2. Make sure that the **MMGS (millimeter, gram, second)** option is ticked marked in this flyout, see Figure 6.42. If not, click to select it.

Tip: A tick mark in front of any unit system indicated that it is selected as the unit system for the current document of SOLIDWORKS. You can also open the **Document Properties - Units** dialog box to specify a unit system for the current document by selecting the **Edit Document Units** option of this flyout.

Section 4: Creating Base/First Feature

1. Invoke the Sketching environment by selecting the Top Plane as the sketching plane and then create the sketch of the base feature, see Figure 6.43.

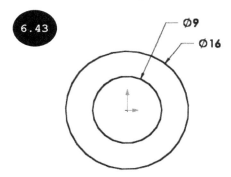

2. Click on the **Feature** tab in the **Command Manager**, see Figure 6.44.

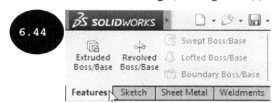

3. Click on the **Extruded Boss/Base** tool of the **Features Command Manager**, the **Boss-Extrude PropertyManager** and the preview of the extruded feature appears in the graphics area, see Figure 6.45.

4. Enter 10 in the **Depth** field of the **Direction 1** rollout and then press ENTER key, the depth of the extruded feature chances to 10 mm.

5. Click on the green tick mark ✓ of the PropertyManager, the base/first extruded feature of depth 10 mm is created, see Figure 6.46.

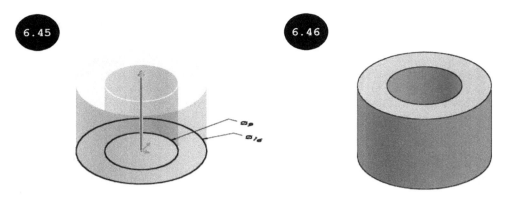

6.45 **6.46**

Section 5: Creating Second Feature

1. Invoke the **Sketch CommandManager** by clicking on the **Sketch** tab, see Figure 6.47, and then click on the **Sketch** tool.

2. Click to select the top planar face of the base/first feature as the sketching plane, see Figure 6.48, the sketching environment is invoked.

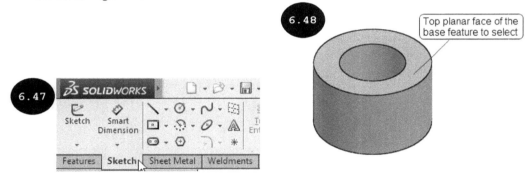

6.48 Top planar face of the base feature to select

6.47

3. Invoke the **View Orientation** flyout by using the **View (Heads-Up)** toolbar, see Figure 6.49. Next, click on the **Normal To** tool of this flyout to change the orientation of the model normal to the viewing direction.

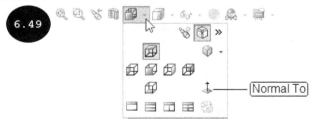

6.49 Normal To

4. Create the sketch of the second feature by using the **Polygon** and **Circle** tools, see Figure 6.50.

Tip: To make the sketch fully defined, you need to apply vertical relation to a vertical line of the polygon and the linear dimension to a side of the polygon.

---

5. Click on the **Features** tab of the **CommandManager** to displays the tools of the **Features CommandManager**.

6. Click on the **Extruded Boss/Base** tool of the **Features Command Manager**, the **Boss-Extrude PropertyManager** and the preview of the extruded feature appears in the graphics area. Next, change the orientation of the model to isometric by using the **View Orientation** flyout of the **View (Heads-Up)** toolbar, see Figure 6.51.

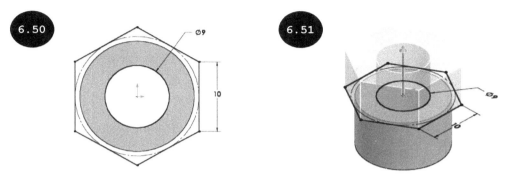

7. Enter 8 in the **Depth** field of the **Direction 1** rollout and then press ENTER key.

8. Click on the green tick mark ✓ of the PropertyManager, the extruded feature is created, see Figure 6.52.

Section 6: Creating Third Feature

1. Invoke the Sketching environment by selecting the top planar face of the second feature as the sketching plane, the sketching environment is invoked.

2. Invoke the **View Orientation** flyout by using the **View (Heads-Up)** toolbar and then click on the **Normal To** tool to change the orientation of the model normal to the viewing direction, see Figure 6.53.

3. Create the sketch of the third feature by creating two circles of diameter 9 and 16 using the **Circle** tool and apply dimensions, see Figure 6.54.

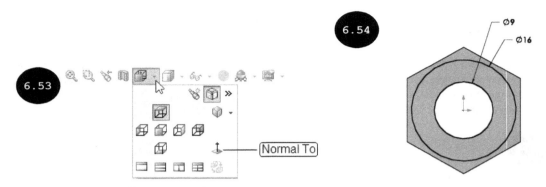

4. Click on the **Features** tab of the **CommandManager** to displays the tools of the **Features** CommandManager.

5. Click on the **Extruded Boss/Base** tool of the **Features Command Manager**, the **Boss-Extrude PropertyManager** and the preview of the extruded feature appears in the graphics area. Next, change the orientation of the model to isometric by using the **View Orientation** flyout of the **View (Heads-Up)** toolbar, see Figure 6.55.

6. Enter **5** in the **Depth** field of the **Direction 1** rollout and then press ENTER key.

7. Click on the green tick mark ✅ of the PropertyManager, the extruded feature is created, see Figure 6.56.

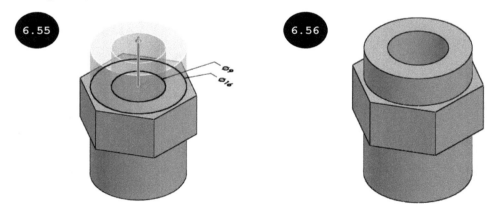

Section 7: Creating Forth Feature

1. Invoke the Sketching environment by selecting the top planar face of the third feature as the sketching plane, see Figure 6.57, the sketching environment is invoked.

2. Invoke the **View Orientation** flyout by using the **View (Heads-Up)** toolbar and then click on the **Normal To** tool to change the orientation of the model normal to the viewing direction, see Figure 6.58.

3. Create the sketch of the forth feature by creating two circles of diameter 9 and 11 using the **Circle** tool and apply dimensions, see Figure 6.59.

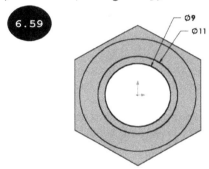

4. Click on the **Features** tab of the **CommandManager** to displays the tools of the **Features CommandManager**.

5. Click on the **Extruded Boss/Base** tool of the **Features Command Manager**, the **Boss-Extrude PropertyManager** and the preview of the extruded feature appears in the graphics area. Next, change the orientation of the model to isometric by using the **View Orientation** flyout of the **View (Heads-Up)** toolbar, see Figure 6.60.

6. Enter **14** in the **Depth** field of the **Direction 1** rollout and then press ENTER key.

7. Click on the green tick mark ✅ of the PropertyManager, the extruded feature is created and Figure 6.61 shows the model after creating all the features.

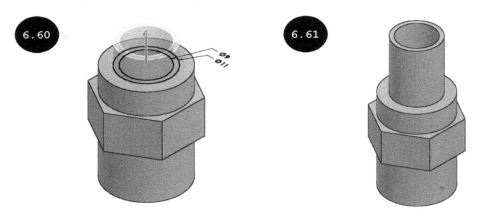

Section 8: Saving the Sketch

After creating the sketch, you need to save it.

1.   Click on the **Save** tool of the **Standard** toolbar, the **Save As** window appears.

2.   Browse to the *SOLIDWORKS* folder and then create a folder named as *Chapter 6*. Next, create another folder named as *Tutorial* inside the *Chapter 6* folder.

3.   Enter **Tutorial 1** in the **File name** field of the dialog box as the name of the file to save and then click on the **Save** button, the model is saved as Tutorial 1 in the *Tutorial* folder of *Chapter 6*.

Tutorial 2

Create the multi-featured model shown in Figure 6.62.

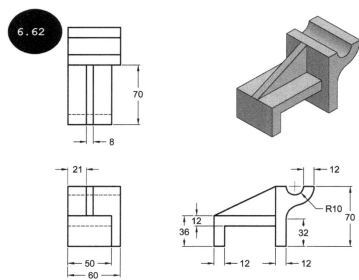

Section 1: Starting **SOLIDWORKS**

1.	Double click on the **SOLIDWORKS** icon on your desktop to start SOLIDWORKS.

Section 2: Invoking **Part Modeling Environment**

1.	Click on the **New** tool in the **Standard** toolbar, the **New SOLIDWORKS Document** dialog box appears.

2.	In this dialog box, the **Part** button is activated by default. Click on the **OK** button.

Section 3: Specifying **Unit Settings**

1.	Move the cursor towards the lower right corner of the screen over the Status Bar and then click on the **Unit System** area of the Status Bar, the **Unit System** flyout appears, see Figure 6.63.

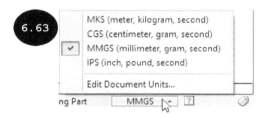

2.	Make sure that the **MMGS (millimeter, gram, second)** option is ticked marked in this flyout, see Figure 6.63. If not, click to select it.

Section 4: Creating **Base/First Feature**

1.	Invoke the Sketching environment by selecting the Right Plane as the sketching plane.

2.	Create the sketch of the base feature and then apply required relations and dimensions, see Figure 6.64.

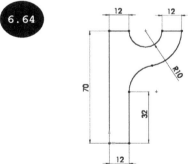

Tip:	To make the sketch of the base feature fully defined, you need to apply the tangent relation between line and arc entities of the sketch and the concentric relation between the arcs of radius 10 and 22. The relations such as horizontal and vertical applies automatically while drawing the horizontal and vertical line entities.

---

3. Click on the **Feature** tab in the **Command Manager** and then click on the **Extruded Boss/Base** tool, the **Boss-Extrude PropertyManager** and the preview of the extruded feature appears in the graphics area, see Figure 6.65.

4. Invoke the **End Condition** flyout of the **Direction 1** rollout, see Figure 6.66.

5. Click on the **Mid Plane** option from the **End Condition** flyout.

6. Enter 60 in the **Depth** field of the **Direction 1** rollout and then press ENTER key, the depth of the extrusion added symmetrically on both side of the sketching plane, see Figure 6.67.

7. Click on the green tick mark ✅ of the PropertyManager, the extruded feature is created symmetrically about the Sketching plane, see Figure 6.68.

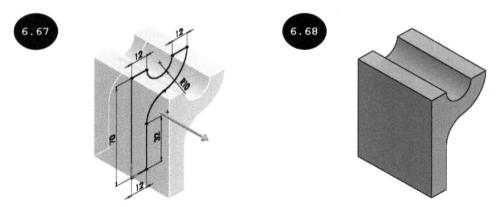

Section 5: Creating Second Feature

To create the second feature of the model, you will first create a reference plane at an office distance of 10 mm from the right planar face of the base feature.

1. Invoke the **Reference Geometry** flyout of the **Features CommandManager**, see Figure 6.69.

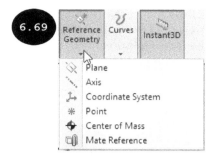

2. Click on the **Plane** tool of this flyout, the **Plane PropertyManager** appears.

3. Select the right planar face of the base feature as the first reference, the preview of an office reference plane appears in the graphics area, see Figure 6.70.

4. Enter **10** in the **Distance** field of the **First Reference** rollout of the PropertyManager and then select the **Flip** check box to flip the direction of plane being creation.

5. Click on the green tick mark ✅ of the PropertyManager, the offset reference plane is created, see Figure 6.71.

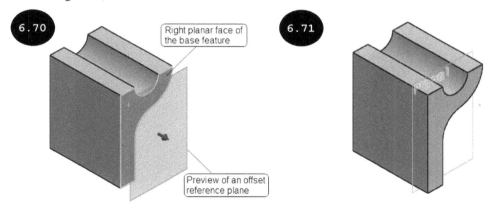

After creating the reference plane, you can create the second feature of the model.

6. Invoke the Sketching environment by selecting the newly created reference plane as the sketching plane.

7. Change the orientation of the model normal to the viewing direction by using the **Normal To** tool of the **View Orientation** flyout.

8. Create the sketch of the second feature and apply dimensions, see Figure 6.72.

9. Click on the **Features** tab of the **CommandManager** to displays the tools of the **Features CommandManager**.

10. Click on the **Extruded Boss/Base** tool of the **Features CommandManager**, the **Boss-Extrude PropertyManager** and the preview of the extruded feature appears in the graphics area. Next, change the orientation of the model to isometric by using the **View Orientation** flyout of the **View (Heads-Up)** toolbar.

11. Click on the **Reverse Direction** button of the **Direction 1** rollout to reverse the direction of extrusion similar to one shown in Figure 6.73.

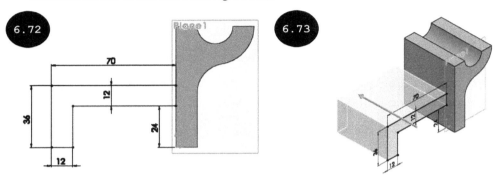

12. Enter 50 in the **Depth** field of the **Direction 1** rollout and then press ENTER key.

13. Click on the green tick mark ✓ of the PropertyManager, the extruded feature is created, see Figure 6.74.

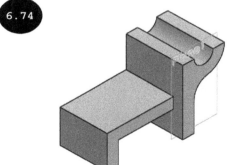

Section 6: Creating Third Feature

To create the third feature of the model, you will create a reference plane passing at the middle of the second feature.

1. Invoke the **Reference Geometry** flyout of the **Features CommandManager**, see Figure 6.75.

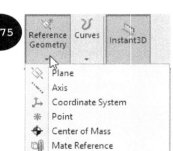

2. Click on the **Plane** tool of this flyout, the **Plane PropertyManager** appears.

3. Select the right planar face of the second feature as the first reference, the preview of an office reference plane appears in the graphics area, see Figure 6.76.

4. Rotate the model by dragging the cursor after pressing and holding the middle mouse button such that you can view the left planar face of the second feature, see Figure 6.77.

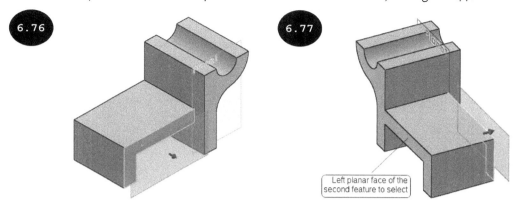

6.76

6.77

Left planar face of the second feature to select

5. Click to select the left planar face of the second feature as the second reference for creating the plane, the preview of a reference plane at the middle of two selected planar faces appears in the graphics area, see Figure 6.78.

6. Change the view orientation of the model to isometric.

7. Click on the green tick mark ✓ of the PropertyManager, the middle reference plane is created.

   After creating the reference plane, you can create the third feature of the model.

8. Invoke the Sketching environment by selecting the newly created reference plane as the sketching plane.

9. Change the orientation of the model normal to the viewing direction by using the **Normal To** tool of the **View Orientation** flyout.

10. Create the closed sketch of the third feature, see Figure 6.79.

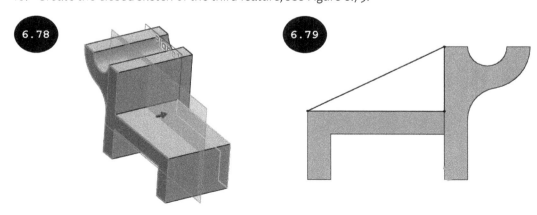

6.78

6.79

11. Click on the **Features** tab of the **CommandManager** to displays the tools of the **Features CommandManager**.

12. Click on the **Extruded Boss/Base** tool of the **Features CommandManager**, the **Boss-Extrude PropertyManager** and the preview of the extruded feature appears in the graphics area. Next, change the orientation of the model to isometric by using the **View Orientation** flyout of the **View (Heads-Up)** toolbar.

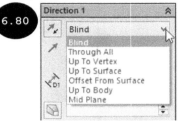

13. Invoke the **End Condition** flyout of the **Direction 1** rollout, see Figure 6.80.

14. Click on the **Mid Plane** option from the **End Condition** flyout.

15. Enter 8 in the **Depth** field of the **Direction 1** rollout and then press ENTER key, the depth of the extrusion added symmetrically on both side of the sketching plane, see Figure 6.81.

16. Click on the green tick mark ✓ of the PropertyManager, the extruded feature is created symmetrically about the Sketching plane. Figure 6.82 shows the model after creating all the features.

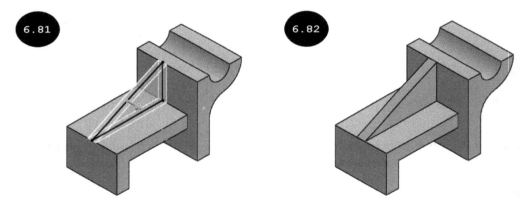

Section 7: Saving the Sketch

After creating the sketch, you need to save it.

1. Click on the **Save** tool of the **Standard** toolbar, the **Save As** window appears.

2. Browse to the *Tutorial* folder of the *Chapter 6* and then save the model as Tutorial 2.

Tutorial 3

Create the model shown in Figure 6.83.

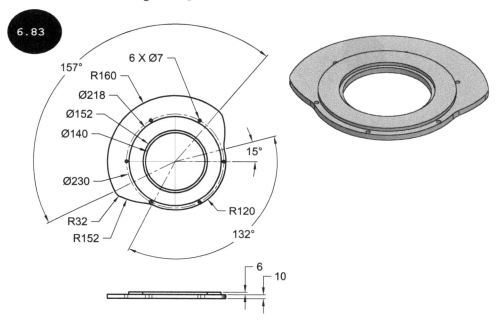

Figure 6.83

Section 1: Starting SOLIDWORKS

1. Double click on the **SOLIDWORKS** icon on your desktop to start SOLIDWORKS, if not started already.

Section 2: Invoking Part Modeling Environment

1. Click on the **New** tool in the **Standard** toolbar, the **New SOLIDWORKS Document** dialog box appears.

2. In this dialog box, the **Part** button is activated by default. Click on the **OK** button.

Section 3: Specifying Unit Settings

1. Move the cursor towards the lower right corner of the screen over the Status Bar and then click on the **Unit System** area of the Status Bar, the **Unit System** flyout appears, see Figure 6.84.

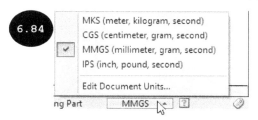

Figure 6.84

2. Make sure that the **MMGS (millimeter, gram, second)** option is ticked marked in this flyout, see Figure 6.84. If not, click to select it.

Section 4: Creating Base/First Feature

1. Invoke the Sketching environment by selecting the Top Plane as the sketching plane.

2. Create the sketch of the base feature and then apply required relations and dimensions, see Figure 6.85.

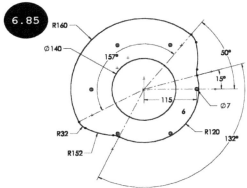

Tip: To make the sketch of the base feature fully defined, you need to apply the tangent relation between all connecting arcs of the sketch. Also, you need to apply equal relation between the arcs whose radius value is equal. To create all circles of diameter 7 of the sketch, you can create a circle and then create the circular pattern to create the remaining circles of the sketch. After creating the sketch and applying the required relations, you can apply the dimensions as shown in Figure 6.85.

3. Click on the **Feature** tab in the **Command Manager** and then click on the **Extruded Boss/Base** tool, the **Boss-Extrude PropertyManager** and the preview of the extruded feature appears in the graphics area, see Figure 6.86.

4. Enter 10 in the **Depth** field of the **Direction 1** rollout and then press ENTER key.

5. Click on the green tick mark ✅ of the PropertyManager, the extruded feature is created, see Figure 6.87.

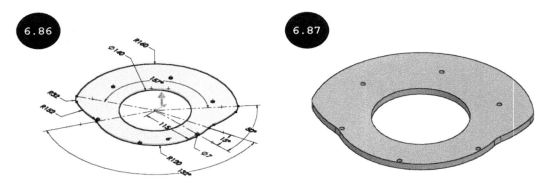

Section 5: Creating Second Feature

1. Invoke the Sketching environment by selecting the top planar face of the base feature as the sketching plane.

2. Change the orientation of the model normal to the viewing direction by using the **Normal To** tool of the **View Orientation** flyout.

3. Create the sketch of the second feature and apply dimensions, see Figure 6.88.

4. Click on the **Features** tab of the **CommandManager** to displays the tools of the **Features CommandManager**.

5. Click on the **Extruded Boss/Base** tool of the **Features CommandManager**, the **Boss-Extrude PropertyManager** and the preview of the extruded feature appears in the graphics area. Next, change the orientation of the model to isometric by using the **View Orientation** flyout of the **View (Heads-Up)** toolbar.

6. Enter 6 in the **Depth** field of the **Direction 1** rollout and then press ENTER key.

7. Click on the green tick mark ✅ of the PropertyManager, the extruded feature is created, see Figure 6.89.

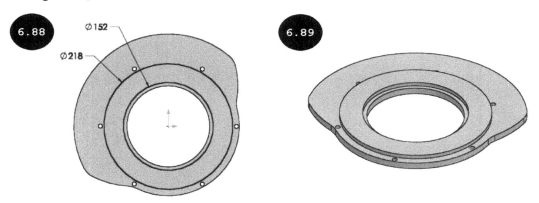

Section 6: Saving the Sketch

After creating the sketch, you need to save it.

1. Click on the **Save** tool of the **Standard** toolbar, the **Save As** window appears.

2. Browse to the *Tutorial* folder of the *Chapter 6* and then save the model as Tutorial 3.

Hands-on Test Drive 1

Create the model shown in Figure 6.90.

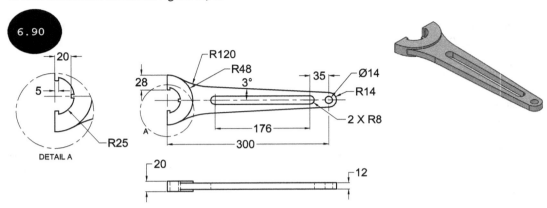

Summary

In this chapter, you have learnt that the three default planes: Front, Top, and Right may not be enough for creating models having multiple features therefore you need to create additional reference planes. In addition to creating additional reference planes, you have also learnt about creating reference axis, reference coordinate system and reference point by using their respective tools.

Questions

*   In addition to the three default planes: Top, Front, and Right you can create reference planes by using the _____ tool.

*   To create a reference plane parallel to an planar face of the model, you only need to select two references: first reference can be a planar face and second reference can be a _____, _____, or _____ .

*   To create a reference plane at an angle to an planar face/plane, you only need to select two references: first reference can be a planar face/plane and second reference can be a _____, _____, or _____ .

*   On selecting two planar faces as the first and second references for creating a reference plane, the preview of the plane passing through the _____ of selected faces appears.

*   The _____ tool is used to create reference axis.

*   In SOLIDWORKS, you can create a reference point at the intersection of two entities. (True/False).

*   You can not select a planar face of existing features as the sketching plane for creating a feature. (True/False).

Advanced Modeling I

In this chapter:

- Advance Options of Extruded Boss/Base tool
- Creating Cut Features
- Working with Different Type of Sketches
- Working with Contours/Regions of a Sketch
- Projecting Edges on to the Sketching Plane
- Editing Features
- Measuring Distance between Entities/Faces
- Assigning Appearance/Texture
- Applying Material
- Calculating Mass Properties

In the previous chapters you have learnt how to create base features by using the **Extruded Boss/Base** and **Revolved Boss/Base** tools. In this chapter, you will learn the advanced options of the **Extruded Boss/Base** and **Revolved Boss/Base** tools. In addition to these tools, you will also learn about creating cut features by using the **Extruded Cut** and **Revolved Cut** tools, different type of sketches, measuring model geometry, changing appearance, assigning customizing appearance, applying material properties, and calculating mass properties.

Advance Options of Extruded Boss/Base tool

As discussed earlier, while extruding a sketch by using the **Extruded Boss/Base** tool, the **Boss-Extrude PropertyManager** appears at the left of the graphics area, see Figure 7.1. Some of the options of this PropertyManager have been discussed earlier while creating base features and the remaining options are as follows.

From Drop-down List

The options available in the **From** drop-down list of the **From** rollout are used to define the start condition of the extrusion. The options: **Sketch Plane** and **offset** of this drop-down list have been discussed earlier while creating base features and the remaining options are as follows. Figure 7.2 shows the **From** drop-down list.

Surface/Face/Plane

The **Surface/Face/Plane** option of the **From** drop-down list allows you to select a surface, face, or plane as the start condition (from where extrusion starts). On selecting this option, the **Select a Surface/Face/Plane** field displays below the **From** drop-down list and is activated by default. As a result, you can select a surface, face, or plane as the start condition for the extrusion, see Figure 7.3 and 7.4. Figure 7.3 shows a sketch to be extruded (which is created at the top planar face of the model) and a face of the model to be selected as the start condition for the extrusion. Figure 7.4 shows the preview of the resultant extruded feature after selecting the face as the start condition.

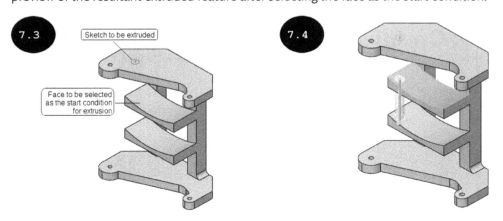

Vertex

The **Vertex** option allows you to select a vertex as the start condition (from where extrusion starts). On selecting this option, the **Select A Vertex** field displays below the **From** drop-down list and is activated by default. As a result, you can select a vertex as the start condition for the extrusion, see Figure 7.5.

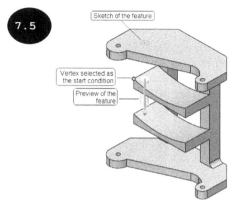

7.5

Sketch of the feature

Vertex selected as the start condition

Preview of the feature

End Condition Drop-down List

The **End Condition** drop-down list of the **Direction 1** rollout allows you to select different options from defining the end condition of the extrusion. The options: **Blind** and **Mid Plane** of this drop-down list have been discussed earlier while creating base features and the remaining options are as follows. Figure 7.6 shows the options of the **End Condition** drop-down list.

Up To Vertex

The **Up To Vertex** option of the **End Condition** drop-down list allows you to define the end condition or termination of the extrusion by selecting a vertex. On selecting this option, the **Vertex** field become available in the rollout and is activated by default. As a result, you can select a vertex of the model up to which you want to extrude the feature. The Figure 7.7 shows a preview of a feature being created such that it end condition is defined by selecting a vertex.

7.6

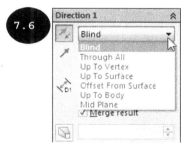

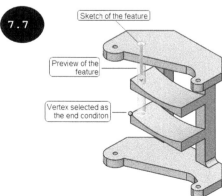

7.7

Sketch of the feature

Preview of the feature

Vertex selected as the end conditon

> **Note:** On selecting a vertex as the end condition for extrusion, the resultant feature will have start and end sections parallel to each other.

Up To Surface

The **Up To Surface** option allows you to define the end condition or termination of the extrusion up to a selected surface. When you select the **Up To Surface** option, the **Face/Plane** field become available in the **Direction 1** rollout and is activated by default. As a result, you can select a surface, face, or a plane up to which you want to extrude the feature. The Figure 7.8 shows a preview of a feature being created such that it end condition is defined by selecting a face of the model.

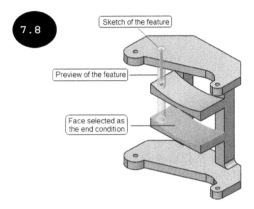

7.8

Sketch of the feature

Preview of the feature

Face selected as the end condition

> **Note:** On selecting a face/surface as the end condition for extrusion, the end section of the resultant feature merge with face/surface selected as the end condition.

Offset From Surface

The **Offset From Surface** option allows you to define the end condition or termination of the extrusion at an offset distance from a selected surface, see Figure 7.10. When you select the **Offset From Surface** option, the **Face/Plane** and **Offset Distance** fields become available in the **Direction 1** rollout. You can select an existing surface, face, or a plane from the graphic area and then enter the offset distance in the **Offset Distance** field. The resultant feature terminated at an offset distance from the selected surface. The Figure 7.9 shows a preview of a feature being created such that it end condition is defined by entering offset distance from a surface.

Up To Body

The **Up To Body** option allows you to define the end condition or termination of the extrusion up to a selected body. When you select this option, the **Solid/Surface Body** field become available in the **Direction 1** rollout and is activated by default. As a result, you can select a solid or surface body up to which you want to extrude the feature. Note that this option can be used when multiple bodies are available in the graphics area. You will learn more about creating multiple bodies in the graphics area later in this chapter.

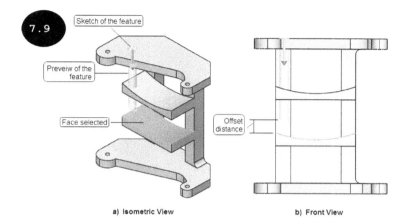

7.9

Sketch of the feature

Preveiw of the feature

Face selected

Offset distance

a) Isometric View   b) Front View

Merge result

The **Merge result** check box of the **Direction 1** rollout is used to merge the feature being created with the existing features of the model. By default, this check box is selected. As a result, the feature of the model being created merged with the existing features of the model. If you clear this check box, the feature being created will not merge with the existing feature and a separate body is created. Note that this check box is not available while creating base/first extruded feature.

Note: Similar to the options of the **Direction 1** rollout of the **Boss-Extrude PropertyManager**, the options available in the **Direction 2** rollout are same with the only difference that these options are used to specify the end condition for the extrusion in the second direction of the sketching plane.

Also, similar to defining the start and end condition for extrude features, you can define the start and end condition for revolve features by using the options available in the **Revolve PropertyManager**.

Creating Cut Features

Similar to adding material by extruding and revolving a sketch, you can remove material by using the **Extruded Cut** and **Revolved Cut** tools. By using these tools you can create extruded cut and revolved cut features, respectively. Both these tools of creating cut features are as follows.

Creating Extruded Cut Features

You can create extruded cut features by using the **Extruded Cut** tool. A extruded cut feature is a feature created by removing material normal to the sketching plane. Note that the geometry of the material removed is defined by the sketch. Figures 7.10 show a sketch created on the top planar face of the model and the resultant extruded cut features.

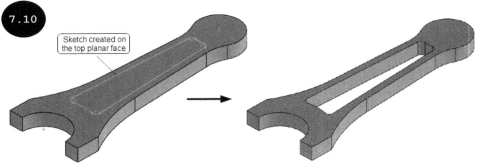

7.10

Sketch created on the top planar face

To create extrude cut feature, click on the **Extruded Cut** tool available in the **Features CommandManager**, the **Extrude PropertyManager** appears. Next, select the sketch, the preview of the extruded cut feature appears in the graphics area with the default parameters. Also, the **Cut-Extrude PropertyManager** appears, see Figure 7.11. The options available in this PropertyManager are used to define the parameters for the extruded cut feature that is being created. These options are same as discussed earlier while created extruded feature with the only difference that these options are used to remove material. You can also flip the side of the material to remove from the model by selecting or clearing the **Flip side to cut** check box of the PropertyManager, see Figure 7.12. After specifying the parameters for creating the extruded cut feature, click on the green tick mark ✓ of the PropertyManager, the extruded cut feature is created.

7.11

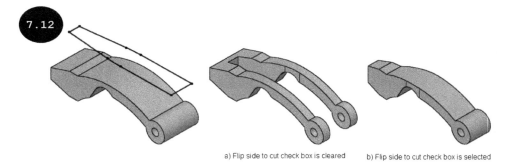

7.12

a) Flip side to cut check box is cleared   b) Flip side to cut check box is selected

Note: You can also select the sketch to be extruded before invoking the **Extruded Cut** tool. If you do so, the preview of the extruded cut appears as soon as you invoke the tool. Also the **Cut-Extrude PropertyManager** appears at the left side of the graphics area.

Procedure to Extruded Cut Feature Using Extruded Cut tool

1. Create a sketch that defines the geometry of the material to be removed by using the sketching tools. After creating the sketch do not exit from the Sketching environment.
2. Click on the **Features** tab of the **CommandManager** and then click on the **Extruded Cut** tool, the preview of the cut features appears in the graphics area. Also, the **Cut-Extrude PropertyManager** appears.
3. Specify the required parameters for removing the material in the PropertyManager.
4. Click on the green tick mark ✓ of the PropertyManager, the extruded cut feature is created.

Tip: If you exit from the Sketching environment after creating the sketch and sketch is not selected in the graphics area then on clicking the **Extruded Cut** tool, the **Extrude PropertyManager** appears. Also, you are prompted to select the sketch to be extruded (cut feature) or a sketching plane to create sketch for the extruded cut feature. As soon as you select the sketch, the preview of the extruded cut feature appears in the graphics area. Also, the **Cut-Extrude PropertyManager** appears.

Creating Revolve Cut Features

You can create revolve cut features by using the **Revolved Cut** tool. A revolve cut feature is a feature created by removing material by revolving a sketch around a centerline or an axis. Note that sketch to be revolve should be on either side of the centerline. Figures 7.13 and 7.14 show sketches to be revolved cut and their respective resultant revolved cut features created.

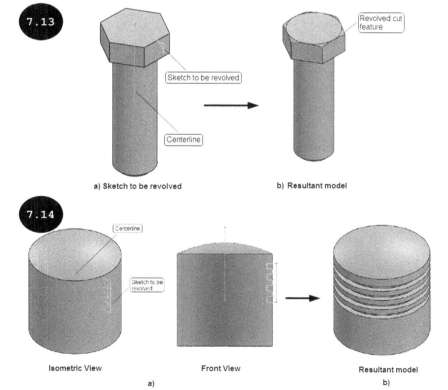

7.13

Sketch to be revolved

Revolved cut feature

Centerline

a) Sketch to be revolved

b) Resultant model

7.14

Centerline

Sketch to be revolved

Isometric View

Front View

Resultant model

a)

b)

To create revolved cut feature, click on the **Revolved Cut** tool available in the **Features CommandManager**, the **Revolve PropertyManager** appears. Next, select the centerline of the sketch as the axis of revolution, the preview of the revolved cut feature appears in the graphics area with the default parameters. Also, the **Cut-Revolve PropertyManager** appears, see Figure 7.15. The options available in this PropertyManager are used to define the parameters for the revolved cut feature that is being created. These options are same as discussed earlier while created revolved feature with the only difference that these options are used to remove material. After specifying the parameters for creating the revolved cut feature, click on the green tick mark ✅ of the PropertyManager, the revolved cut feature is created.

7.15

Procedure to Revolved Cut Feature Using Revolved Cut tool

1. Create a sketch that defines the geometry of the material to be removed with a centerline. After creating the sketch do not exit from the Sketching environment.
2. Click on the **Features** tab of the **CommandManager** and then click on the **Revolved Cut** tool, the preview of the revolved cut features appears in the graphics area. Also, the **Cut-Revolve PropertyManager** appears.

> **Note:** If the sketch has two or more than two centerline then on invoking the **Revolved Cut** tool, you are prompted to select the centerline as the axis of revolution. As soon as you select the centerline, the preview of the revolve cut feature appears in the graphics area.

3. Specify the required parameters for removing the material in the PropertyManager.
4. Click on the green tick mark ✅ of the PropertyManager, the revolved cut feature is created.

> **Tip:** If you exit from the Sketching environment after creating the sketch and sketch is not selected in the graphics area then on clicking the **Revolved Cut** tool, the **Revolve PropertyManager** appears. Also, you are prompted to select the sketch to be revolved or a sketching plane to create sketch for the revolved cut feature. As soon as you select the sketch, the preview of the revolved cut feature appears in the graphics area. Also, the **Cut-Revolve PropertyManager** appears at the left of the graphics area.

Working with Different Type of Sketches

It is important to understand different type of sketches and their performance. Some of the important type of sketches are Closed sketches, Open sketches, Nested sketches, and Intersecting sketch. All these sketches are as follows.

Close Sketches

The Closed sketches are those having all the entities end to end connected with each other without any gap. Note that on extruding a closed sketch, a solid extruded feature is created. Figure 7.16 shows a close sketch having one closed region/area and their resultant extruded feature.

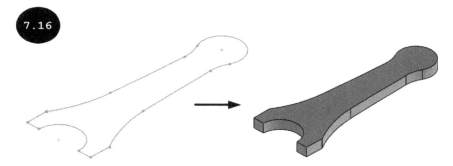

7.16

Open Sketches

The Open Sketches are those sketches that are open from one or more ends. Note that on extruding a open sketches, a thin feature is created. Figure 7.17 shows a open sketch and their resultant thin extruded feature.

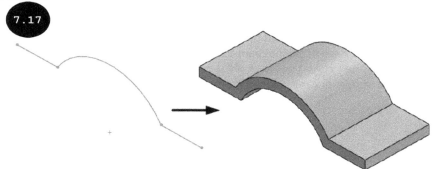

7.17

Nested Sketches

The Nested sketches are similar to Close sketches with the only difference that Nested sketches have more that one closed loop, one inside the other and form a multiple close regions/contours. Note that on extruding a nested sketch having multiple close regions/contours, by default a solid feature is created by extruding its outer most closed region. Figure 7.18 shows a nested sketch having two closed regions/contours and their resultant extruded feature. Figure 7.19 shows a nested sketch having three closed regions/contours and their resultant extruded feature.

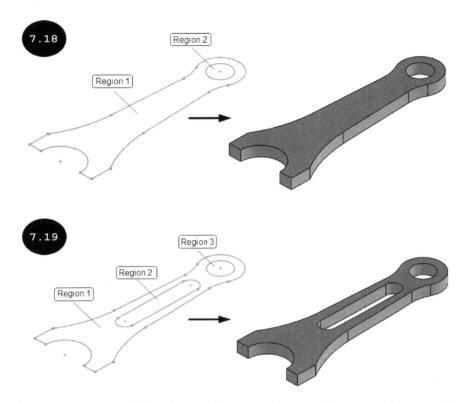

However, on extruding nested sketches similar to one shown in Figure 7.20 having multiple close regions, the automatic selection of a close region/contour to be extruded is not possible. As a result, in such cases, you are prompted to define a region/contour to be extruded. You can select a required region/contour to be extruded by using the **Selected Contours** rollout of the respective PropertyManager, as discussed in earlier chapters. Figure 7.21 shows preview of an extruded feature being created by selecting a region/contour of the multi-nested sketch. You will learn more about extruding different contours or close regions of a multi-nested sketch later in this chapter.

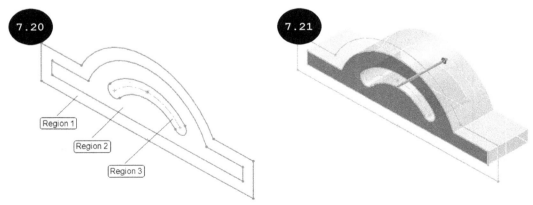

Intersecting Sketch

The Intersecting sketches are those sketches have self intersection between their entities, see Figure 7.22. By default, on extruding a intersecting sketch, the automatic selection of a close region/contour to be extruded is not possible. As a result, you are prompted to select a close region/contour of the intersecting sketch to be extruded. You can select a required region/contour to be extruded by using the **Selected Contours** rollout of the respective PropertyManager, as discussed in earlier chapters. Figure 7.21 shows a intersection sketch and Figure 7.22 shows a preview of the extruded feature being created by extruding a close region of the intersection sketch. You will learn more about extruding close regions/contours later in this chapter.

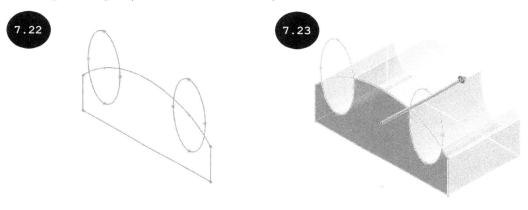

Note: Working with different type of sketches: Closed, Open, Nested, and Intersecting are same for all tools such as **Extruded Base/Boss** and **Revolved Base/Boss**.

Working with Contours/Regions of a Sketch

In SOLIDWORKS, you can create multiple features by using a single sketch having multiple contours/regions. Figure 7.24 shows a sketch having multiple contours and Figure 7.25 shows a multi-feature component.

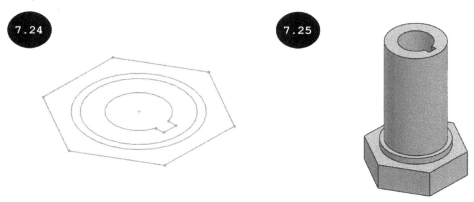

To extrude contours/regions of a sketch for creating features, you can use the **Selected Contours** rollout of the PropertyManager or the **Contour Select Tool**. The procedure to create a feature from a contour of a sketch using the **Selected Contours** rollout has already been discussed in earlier chapters while creating base features. In this session, you will learn procedures to create multiple features from contours of a sketch by using the **Selected Contours** rollout and the **Contour Select Tool**.

Procedure to Create Features using Selected Contour Rollout

1. After creating a sketch having multiple contours, exit from the Sketching environment.
2. Select the sketch from the FeatureManager design tree.
3. Invoke the tool such as **Extruded Boss/Base** and **Revolved Boss/Base**, as required from the **Features CommandManager**, depending upon tool invoked their respective PropertyManager appears with the expanded **Selected Contours** rollout. Also, the cursor is changed to contour cursor ⤭.
4. Move the cursor ⤭ over the contour to be selected and click to select it when it highlights in the graphics area, the preview of the respective feature appears, see Figure 7.26.
5. Specify the parameters for creating the feature in the PropertyManager.
6. Click on the green tick mark ✔ of the PropertyManager, the respective feature is created and its name is added in the FeatureManager design tree. Also, the sketch is disappear from the graphics area.
7. In the FeatureManager design tree, expand the node of the created feature by clicking on the +sign available in front of its name, see Figure 7.27.

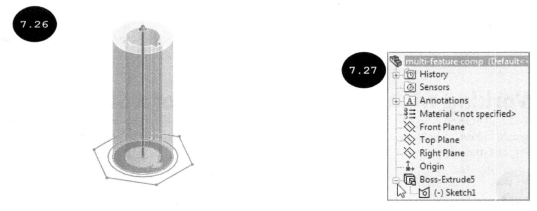

8. Select the sketch, a Pop-up toolbar appears, see Figure 7.28 and then select the **Show** tool, see Figure 7.28.

9. Repeat the step 2 through 8 for creating the remaining features by using another contours of the same sketch. Figure 7.29 shows a model created by using multi-contours of a sketch.

> **Note:** In Figure 7.29, the sketch has been hidden. To hide the sketch, select the sketch, a Pop-up toolbar appears. Next, click on the **Hide** tool.

Procedure to Create Features using Contour Select Tool

1. After creating a sketch having multiple contours, exit from the Sketching environment.
2. Right click in the graphics area to display a shortcut menu.
3. Expand the shortcut menu by clicking on the down arrows available at its bottom, see Figure 7.30.
4. Click on **Contour Select Tool** from the expanded shortcut menu, see Figure 7.31, the cursor is changed to contour cursor. Also, you are prompted to select a sketch whose contour is to be used.

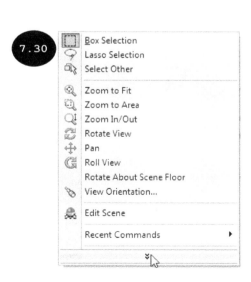

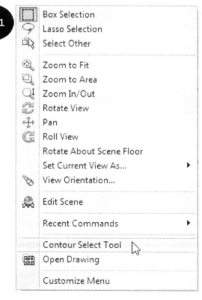

5. Move the contour cursor ⬚ towards the sketch and select it by clicking on any of its entity.
6. Move the cursor over the required contour of the sketch to be selected and then click to select it when it is highlighted in the graphics area, see Figure 7.32.

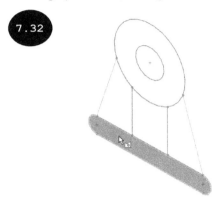

7.32

7. Invoke the tool such as **Extruded Boss/Base** and **Revolved Boss/Base** from the **Features CommandManager** to be used for the selected contour, a preview of the respective feature appears in the graphics area, see Figure 7.33. Also, depending upon tool invoked their respective PropertyManager appears at the left side of the graphics area.
8. Specify the parameters for creating the feature in the PropertyManager.
9. Click on the green tick mark ✔ of the PropertyManager, the respective feature is created and its name is added in the FeatureManager design tree. Also, the sketch is disappear from the graphics area.
10. Expand the node of the created feature by clicking on the +sign available in front of its name in the FeatureManager design tree, see Figure 7.34.

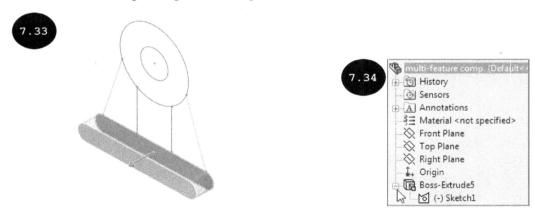

7.33

7.34

11. Select the sketch, a Pop-up toolbar appears, see Figure 7.35 and then select the **Show** tool, see Figure 7.35.

7.35

12. Repeat the step 2 through 9 for creating the remaining features by using another contours of the same sketch. Figure 7.36 shows a model created by using multi-contours of a sketch.

7.36

Note: In Figure 7.36, the sketch has been hidden. To hide the sketch, select the sketch, a Pop-up toolbar appears. Next, click on the **Hide** tool .

Projecting Edges on to the Sketching Plane

In SOLIDWORKS, while sketching, you can project edges of the existing features as the sketch entities on to the current sketching plane by using the **Convert Entities** tool. Figure 7.37 shows a model in which edges of the existing feature has been projected as sketch entities on to a sketching plane (planar face of the cylinder).

Convert Entities

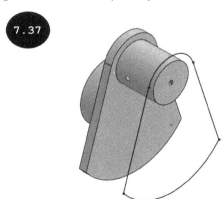

7.37

Procedure to Project Edges on to the Sketching Plane

1. Invoke the Sketching environment by selecting a plane or planar face as the sketching plane.
2. Select the existing edges of the model to be projected as sketch entities.

Note: In addition to selecting edges to be projected, you can also select a planar face of the model. In this case, all the edges of the selected face are projected on to the current sketching plane.

3. Click on the **Convert Entities** tool available in the **Sketch CommandManager**, all the selected edges are projected as sketch entities on to the current sketching plane, see Figure 7.37.

Tip: You can also select edges to be projected as sketch entities after invoking the **Convert Entities** tool. In this case, the **Convert Entities PropertyManager** appears which allow you to select edges/faces to be projected. Once you are done with the selection, click on the green tick mark ✅ of the PropertyManager.

---

4. Once the edges has been projected as the sketch entities on to the current sketching planes, you can convert the sketch into a feature, see Figure 7.38.

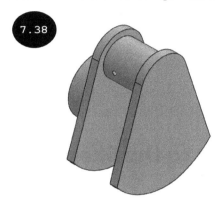

7.38

Editing Features

Keeping design change and revisions in mind, SOLIDWORKS allows you to edit features as per the design change. As mentioned earlier, the FeatureManager design tree displays the list of all the features created for an model, see Figure 7.39. In SOLIDWORKS, you can edit individual features and their sketches of an model listed in the FeatureManager design tree. Procedure to edit feature and their sketch is given next.

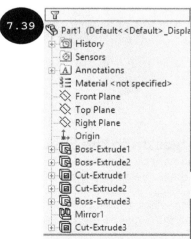

7.39

Procedure to Edit Feature

1. Click to select the feature to edit from the FeatureManager design tree, a Pop-up toolbar appears, see Figure 7.40.
2. Click to select the **Edit Feature** button of the Pop-up toolbar, see Figure 7.41, the respective PropertyManager of the feature to edit appears.
3. Change the parameters as required by entering the modified value in the PropertyManager.
4. Once you are done with editing, click on the green tick mark ✅ of the PropertyManager.

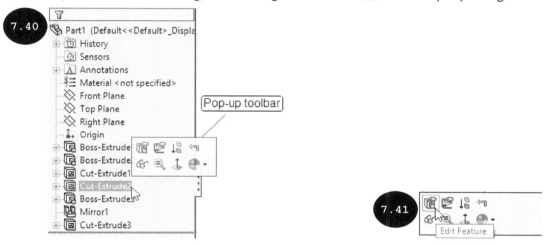

Procedure to Edit Sketch of the Feature

1. Click to select the feature to edit from the FeatureManager design tree, a Pop-up toolbar appears, see Figure 7.40.
2. Click to select the **Edit Sketch** button of the Pop-up toolbar, see Figure 7.42, the Sketching environment of the respective sketch of the feature invoked.

3. By using sketching tools of the Sketching environment, you can modify the sketch of the feature as required.
4. Once you are done with editing, exit from the Sketching environment.

Measuring Distance between Entities/Faces

In SOLIDWORKS, you can measure distance and angle between lines, points, faces, planes, and so on by using the **Measure** tool available in the **Evaluate CommandManager**, see Figure 7.43. In Addition to this, you can also measure radius and other parameters of different geometrical entities.

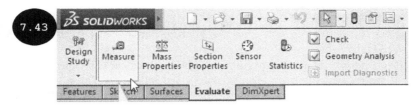

7.43

To measure the distance between entities, click on the **Evaluate** tab of the **CommandManager** and then click on the **Measure** tool (see Figure 7.43), the **Measure** window appears, see Figure 7.44. Also, the cursor is changed to measure cursor. You can expand the **Measure** window, if not expanded by default on clicking the down arrows available at the right of the window. Figure 7.45 shows the expanded **Measure** window. Some of the options available in this window are as follows.

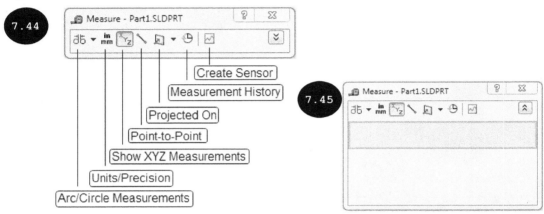

7.44

7.45

Create Sensor
Measurement History
Projected On
Point-to-Point
Show XYZ Measurements
Units/Precision
Arc/Circle Measurements

Arc/Circle Measurements flyout

The options available in this flyout are used to specify the method for measuring arcs and circles, see Figure 7.46. To invoke this flyout, click on the down arrow available next to **Arc/Circle Measurements** button. The options of this flyout are as follows.

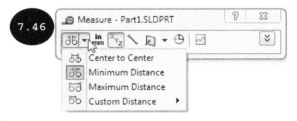

7.46

Center to Center
Minimum Distance
Maximum Distance
Custom Distance

Center to Center

When the **Center to Center** option is selected, on selecting two arcs/circular entities or faces, their center to center distance is measured and appears in the graphics area as well as in the display field of the expanded **Measure** window, see Figure 7.47.

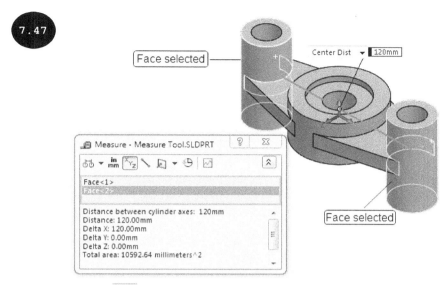

Minimum Distance

On selecting the **Minimum Distance** option, the minimum distance between two selected arcs or circular entities/faces is measured and appears in the graphics area, see Figure 7.48.

Maximum Distance

On selecting the **Maximum Distance** option, the maximum distance between two selected arcs or circular entities/faces is measured and appears in the graphics area, see Figure 7.49.

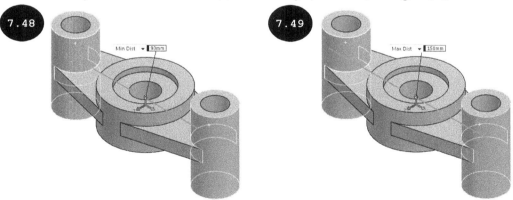

Custom Distance

The **Custom Distance** option allow you to measure customized distance between the entities/faces. When you move the cursor over the **Custom Distance** option of the flyout, a cascading menu appears, see Figure 7.50. By using this cascading menu, you can specify start and end measurement conditions. Depending upon the custom start and end condition specified, on selecting the entities/faces, their respective distance is measured and appears in the graphics area.

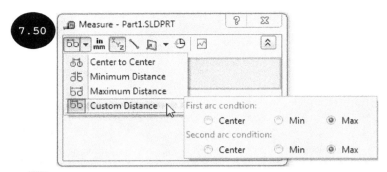

Units/Precision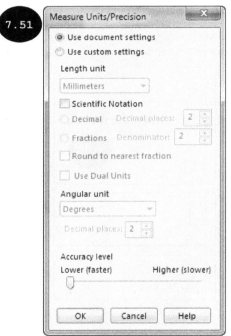

The **Units/Precision** button is used to specify the units and precision for measurement. When you click on this button, the **Measure Units/Precision** dialog box appears, see Figure 7.51. By default, the **Use document settings** radio button is selected in this dialog box. As a result, the units and precision values specified in the current document of SOLIDWORKS is used for the measurement. If you select the **Use custom settings** radio button then you can customized the units and precision values for the measurement.

Show XYZ Measurements

On activating the **Show XYZ Measurements** button by clicking on it, the dX, dY, and dZ measurements between the selected entities appears in the graphics area, see Figure 7.52.

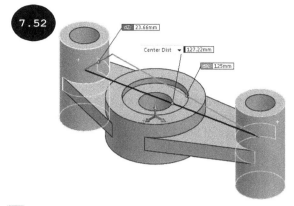

Point-to-Point

On activating this button, the point-to-point mode of measurement activates and is used to measure the distance between any two points/vertices.

Measurement History

The **Measurement History** button is used to display the history of all measurements made in the current session of SOLIDWORKS. When you click on this button, the **Measurement History** dialog box appears with the details of measurement made so far in the current session, see Figure 7.53.

Procedure to Measuring Distance between Entities/Faces

1. Click on the **Measure** tool of the **Evaluate CommandManager**, the **Measure** window appears.
2. Specify the required option for measurement in the **Measure** window.
3. Select the entities/faces to measure from the graphics area, the distance between the selected entities/faces appears.
4. After viewing the measurement, click anywhere in the graphics area to exit from the current measurement.
5. Similarly, you can continue measure the distance between other entities/faces.
6. Once you are done with measurement, press the ESC to exit from the tool.

Assigning Appearance/Texture

In SOLIDWORKS, you can change the default appearance/texture of the model by assigning predefined or customized appearance to the model, features, and faces. The procedures of assigning predefined and customized appearance/texture are as follows.

Assigning Predefined Appearance/Texture

You can assign predefined appearance/texture to a model by using the **Appearances, Scenes, and Decals** task pane available at the right of the graphics area, see Figure 7.54.

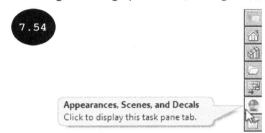

Procedure to Assign Predefined Appearance/ Texture

1. Click on the **Appearances, Scenes, and Decals** tab of the **Task Pane** which is available at right of the graphics area (see Figure 7.54), the **Appearances, Scenes, and Decals** task pane appears, see Figure 7.55.
2. Expand the **Appearance(color)** node by clicking on the +sign, the predefine appearance categories appears.
3. Expand the required category, the sub-categories available in it appears, see Figure 7.56.
4. Select the required sub-category, the thumbnails of the predefined appearance available in the selected sub-category appears at the lower half of the task pane, see Figure 7.56.
5. Drag and drop the required predefined appearance (thumbnail) from the lower half of the task pane over an face of the model, a Pop-up toolbar appears, see Figure 7.57.

Note: The options available in this Pop-up toolbar allow to choose the required target for assigning the appearance. You can assign appearance to a face, feature, body, or part by clicking on the required tool of this Pop-up toolbar.

6. Click on the required tool of the Pop-up toolbar, the respectively appearance is assigned, accordingly.

Note: If you drag and drop the appearance thumbnail in the empty area of the graphics area, the appearance assigns to the entire part and the Pop-up toolbar will not appear.

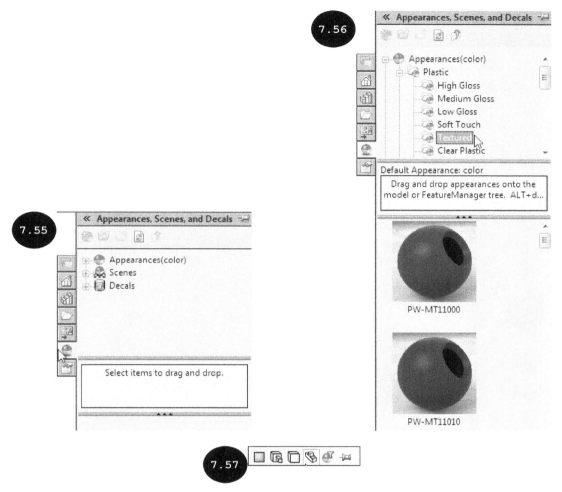

Assigning Customizing Appearance

In addition to assigning predefined appearance to faces/features/body, you can customize the appearance properties, as required and then assign it. To assign the customized appearance, click on the **Edit Appearance** tool in the **View (Heads-up)** toolbar, see Figure 7.58, the **color PropertyManager** appears at the left side of the graphics area, see Figure 7.59. Also, the **Appearances, Scenes, and Decals** task pane invoked on the right side of the graphics area. The options available in the **color PropertyManager** allows you to assign colors, material appearances, and transparency to faces/features/body. These options are as follows.

You can also invoke the **color PropertyManager** by clicking **Edit > Appearance > Appearance** from the SOLIDWORKS menus. Alternatively, select a face of the model, a Pop-up toolbar appears, see Figure 7.60. In this Pop-up toolbar, click on the down arrow available next to the **Appearances** button, a flyout appears, see Figure 7.60. Next, in this flyout, click on the field next to the *face name, feature name, body name,* or *Part name* to display the **color PropertyManager.**

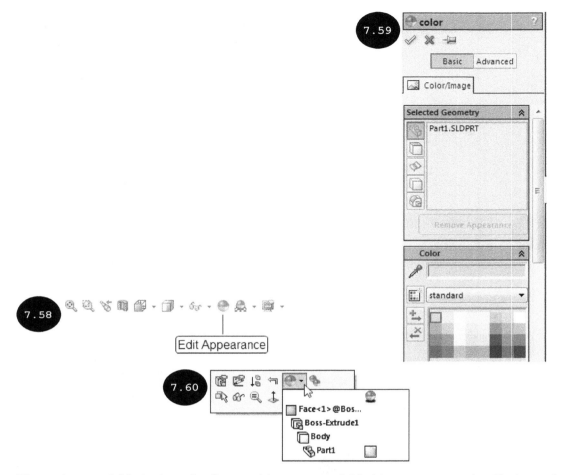

The options available in the **color PropertyManager** are divided into two categories (Basics and Advanced). By default, on invoking this PropertyManager, the **Basic** tab is activated. As a result, the PropertyManager displays basics options for customizing the appearance. To access advanced options, you need to activate the **Advance** tab. Some of the options of both these tabs are as follows.

Basic Tab
The **Basic** tab of the PropertyManager displays the basic and important options for assigning appearance to faces/features/body, see Figure 7.59. Some of these options are as follows.

Selected Geometry
The **Selected Geometry** rollout allows you to select the geometry for applying the appearance. You can select faces, features, bodies, or a part by clicking on their respective button (**Select Part, Select Faces, Select Surfaces, Select Bodies,** or **Select Features**) available at the left of this rollout, see Figure 7.61. For example, if you want to assign color on a face of the model, click on the **Select Faces** button and then select the face of the model from the graphics area. The name of the selected geometries appears in the display field of this rollout.

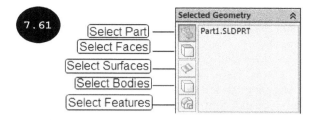

7.61

Note: To clear the existing selected geometries, selected for applying appearance/color, right click on the display field of the **Selected Geometry** rollout and then select the **Clear Selection** option from the shortcut menu, all the selection set has been cleared. You can also clear individual selected geometry. For doing so, select the geometry name from the display field of the rollout and then right click, a shortcut menu appears. Select the **Delete** option to remove the selected geometry from the selection set.

Color

The **Color** rollout allows you to select the required color to be assigned to the selected geometry or geometries.

Advanced Tab

The **Advanced** tab of the **color PropertyManager** displays the additional and advanced options for assigning appearance to faces/features/body, see Figure 7.62. Some of the options of the **Advanced** tab are as follows.

Color/Image

By default the **Color/Image** button of the Advance tab is activated. As the result, additional and advanced options for assigning appearance are available in the PropertyManager, see Figure 7.62. Some of these options are same as discussed earlier and the remaining are as follows.

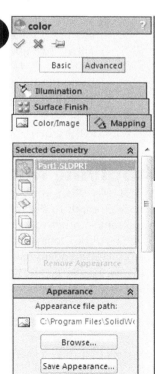

7.62

Appearance: The **Appearance** rollout allows you specify the appearance/image file. By default, the **color.p2m** file is specified. You can select any other appearance/image file such as JPG and TIFF as the image to be assigned. For doing so, click on the **Browse** button of this rollout, the **Open** dialog box appears. Browse to the location where the image file is saved and then select it. Next, click on the **Open** button of the dialog box, the **Save As** dialog box appears. Click on the **Save** button to save the file as *.p2m* for future use, the selected image file has been assigned to the model. You can also save the current customized appearance file for future use by using the **Save Appearance** button of the rollout.

Illumination

The options appears in the **Illumination** tab are used to specify the lighting properties for the specified appearance.

Mapping

The options of the **Mapping** tab are used to map the specified image (texture/appearance). By using these options, you can control size, orientation, and location of specified image. Note that the options of this tab are available only when the texture (using image file or predefine appearance) is applied to the geometry.

Surface Finish

The options of the **Surface Finish** tab are used to specify the type surface finishing of the appearance such as knurled, dimpled, or sandblasted.

Procedure to Assign Customizing Appearance/ Texture

1. Invoke the **color PropertyManager** (see Figure 7.59) by click on the **Edit Appearance** tool of the **View (Heads-up)** toolbar. Alternatively, select a face of the model, a Pop-up toolbar appears. In this Pop-up toolbar, click on the down arrow available next to the **Appearances** button, a flyout appears (see Figure 7.60). In this flyout, click on the field next to the *face name, feature name, body name,* or *Part name* to display the **color PropertyManager.**

2. Select the required geometries (faces/features/surface/bodies/part) by using their respective button available in the **Selected Geometry** rollout.

3. Select the required color by using the **Color** rollout, the preview appears in the graphics area.

Note: To assign image/texture, click on the **Advance** tab and then click on the **Browse** button of the Appearance rollout. Next, select the required file extension such as **JPEG Image Files** (*.jpg;*.jpg) and **TIFF Files** (*.tif;*.tiff) from the **File Type** drop-down list of the **Open** dialog box. Next, select the required image file to be assigned and click on the **Open** button, the image is assigned and the **Save As** dialog box appears. Click on the **Save** button to save the file as *.p2m* file extension for future use.

---

4. Click on the green tick mark ✅ of the PropertyManager.

Applying Material

In SOLIDWORKS, you can assign the standard material properties such as density, elastic modulus, tensile strength to the model. Note that assigning standard material properties to the model is important in order to calculate its mass properties and to perform static and dynamic analysis. SOLIDWORKS contains almost all the standard materials in its material library. You can directly apply the required standard material from the material library to the model. In addition to apply standard material, you can also customize material properties and apply to the model. The procedure to apply standard material and custom material are as follows.

Applying Standard Material

1. Select the **Material <not specified>** option from the FeatureManager design tree and then right click to display a shortcut menu, see Figure 7.63.

2. Select the **Edit Material** option from the shortcut menu, the **Material** dialog box appears, see Figure 7.64.

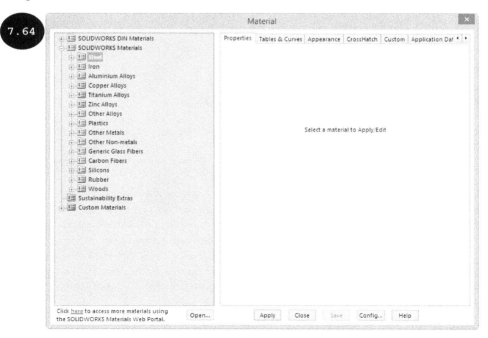

3. Expand the **SOLIDWORKS Materials** node (if not expanded by default), the different category of material available in it appears, see Figure 7.64.
4. Expand the required material category such as steel, Iron, and Aluminium Alloys, the materials available in the expanded material category appears. Figure 7.65 shows expanded **Steel** category.
5. Select the required material from the list of available materials, the material properties of the selected material appears at the right half of the dialog box. Figure 7.65 shows the Alloy Steel (SS) material is selected and its material properties appears on the right half of the dialog box.
6. Click on the **Apply** button of the dialog box to apply the material properties of the selected material.
7. Click on the **Close** button to exit from the dialog box.

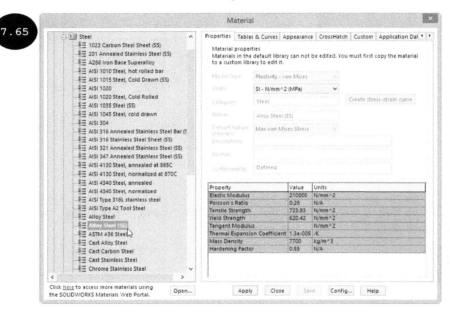

Applying Customize Material Properties

1. Invoke the **Material** dialog box.
2. Select the **Custom Material** node and then right click to display a shortcut menu.
3. Select the **New Category** option (see Figure 7.66) from the shortcut menu, a new category is added under the **Custom Material** node. Also, its default name *New Category* appears in the field.
4. Assign a new name to the category added and then click anywhere in the graphics area.
5. Select the newly added category and then right click to display a shortcut menu.
6. Select the **New Material** option from the shortcut menu, a new material is added under the selected category. Also, its default name *Default* appears in a edit box.
7. Assign a new name to the new added material and then click anywhere in the graphics area.
8. Select the newly added material, all the default properties of the selected material appears at the right half of the dialog box, see Figure 7.67. Figure 7.67 shows the **Material** dialog box with **SW CAD** material category and **SW 1001** material is added.
9. Specify the new material properties such as Poission's ratio, Density, and Yield Strength as per

the requirement in their respective field of the dialog box. Next, click on the **Save** button to save the properties specified.

10. Click on the **Apply** button to apply the custom material to the model.
11. Click on the **Close** button to exit from the dialog box.

Note: You can also copy the material properties of a standard material and then customize it. For doing so, select the standard material and then right click to display a shortcut menu. Next, select the **Copy** option. After coping the standard material, select the custom material category and then right click to display a shortcut menu. Next, select the **Paste** option, the selected standard material is added in the selected custom material category. Select the newly added material, its material properties appears on the right half of the dialog box. Now, you can customize the material properties of the standard material, as required and then apply it.

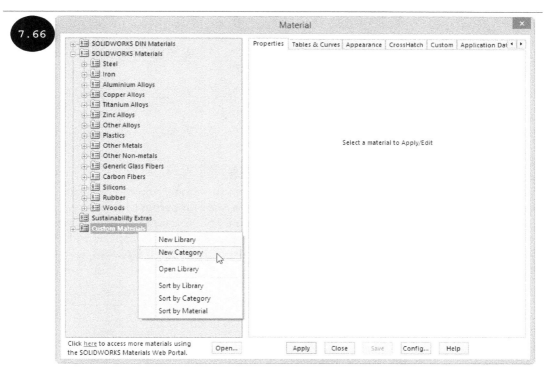

7.66

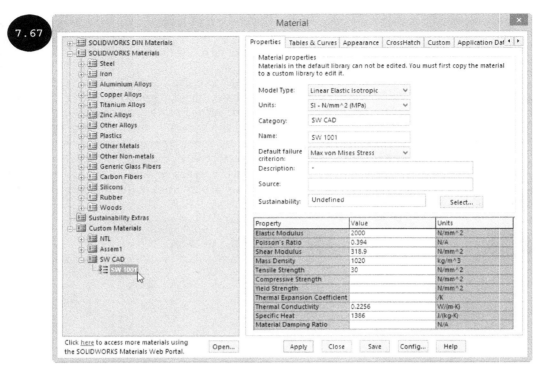

7.67

Calculating Mass Properties

In SOLIDWORKS, after assigning the material properties to a model, you can calculate its mass properties such as mass and volume by using the **Mass Properties** tool. This tool is available in the **Evaluate CommandManager**, see Figure 7.68. To calculate the mass properties of a model, click on the **Mass Properties** tool, the **Mass Properties** dialog box appears and displays the mass properties of the model opened in the current document of SOLIDWORKS, see Figure 7.69. The options available in this dialog box are as follows.

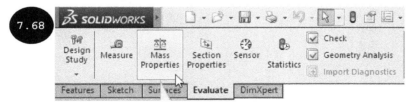

7.68

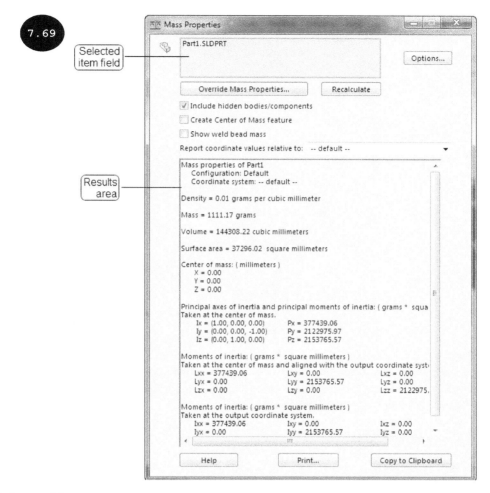

7.69

Selected item field

Results area

Selected items

The **Selected items** field of the dialog box allows you to select the model for calculating its mass properties. By default, the name of the current available model in the graphics area appears in this filed, see Figure 7.69. As a result, the properties such as mass, volume, and center of mass of the current available model appears in the **Results** area of the dialog box, see Figure 7.69.

Options

The **Options** button of the dialog box is used to specify the unit settings for measurement. When you click on the **Options** button, the **Mass/Section Property Options** dialog box appears, see Figure 7.70. By default, the **Use document settings** radio button is selected in this dialog box. As a result, the units and precision values specified in the current document of SOLIDWORKS is used for the measurement. If you select the **Use custom settings** radio button then you can customized the units and precision for the measurement, as required. After customize the units and precision values, click on the **OK** button.

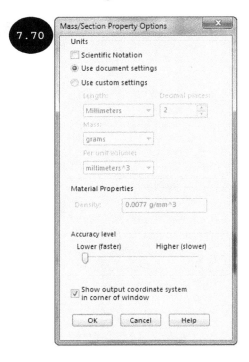

Recalculate

The **Recalculate** button of the **Mass Properties** dialog box is used to recalculate the mass properties of the selected model when you have made any change in the model, added any new item in the selection, or deleted any item from the selection.

Override Mass Properties

The **Override Mass Properties** button is used to override the calculated mass properties of the model, as required. On clicking this button, the **Override Mass Properties** dialog box appears, see Figure 7.71. This dialog box allow you to override the default calculated properties such as mass and center of mass. Note that by default, the edit boxes of this dialog box are not enabled. To enabled these edit boxes, you need to select the check boxes available in front of the edit boxes. After defining the override mass properties, click on the **OK** button.

Note: The override properties are not the actual properties of the model.

Include hidden bodies/components

By default, the **Include hidden bodies/components** check box is selected in the dialog box. As a result, all the hidden bodies or components of the selected model is included while calculating the mass properties. However, if you clear this check box, the hidden bodies/components will not be included in the calculation.

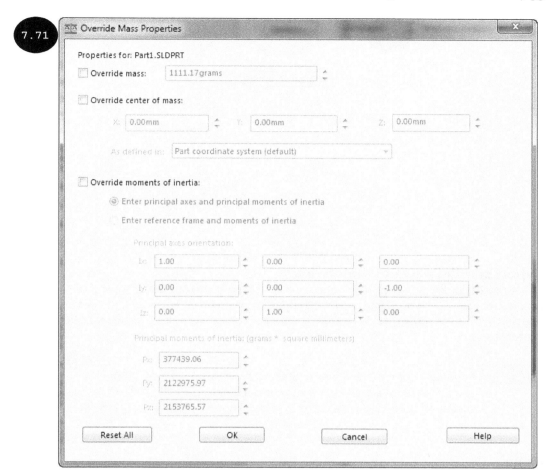

7.71

Create Center of Mass feature

On selecting this check box, the Center of Mass appears in the graphics area and its symbol is added in the FeatureManager design tree when you exit from the **Mass Properties** dialog box.

Note: The Center of Mass of a model appears in the graphics area either when its added symbol is selected in the FeatureManager design tree or its visibility is turn on. To turn on the visibility of the Center of Mass, click on the **Hide/Show Items** button of the **View (Heads-Up)** toolbar to display a flyout, see Figure 7.72. Next, click on the **View Center of Mass** button.

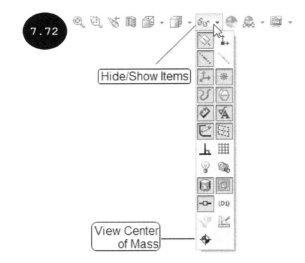

Report coordinate values relative to

The **Report coordinate values relative to** drop-down list is used to select the coordinate system with respect to which you want to calculate the mass properties. By default, the default option is selected in this drop-down list. As a result, the default coordinate system is used for calculating the mass properties.

Note: The **Report coordinate values relative to** drop-down list displays the list of coordinate system which are added in the current document of SOLIDWORKS. If you have not added any coordinate system then this drop-down list displays only the **default** option.

Result

The Result display area of the dialog box is used to display all the calculated results.

Print

The **Print** option is used to print the calculated results.

Copy to Clipboard

The **Copy to Clipboard** button is used to copy the results to the clipboard.

Procedure to Calculate Mass Properties

1. After specifying the material properties to the model, click on the **Mass Properties** tool of the **Evaluate CommandManager**, the **Mass Properties** dialog box appears with the mass properties results.
2. Review the mass properties results and then exit from the dialog box.

Tutorial 1

Create the model shown in Figure 7.73. You need to create the model by creating its all features one by one.

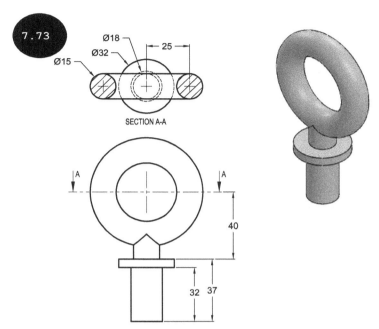

Section 1: Starting SOLIDWORKS

1. Double click on the **SOLIDWORKS** icon on your desktop to start SOLIDWORKS.

Section 2: Invoking Part Modeling Environment

1. Click on the **New** tool in the **Standard** toolbar, the **New SOLIDWORKS Document** dialog box appears.

2. In this dialog box, the **Part** button is activated by default. Click on the **OK** button.

    Once the Part modeling environment is invoked, you can set the unit system and create the base/first feature of the model.

Section 3: Specifying Unit Settings

1. Move the cursor towards the lower right corner of the screen over the Status Bar and then click on the **Unit System** area of the Status Bar, the **Unit System** flyout appears, see Figure 7.74.

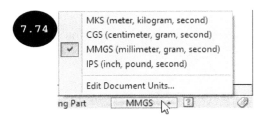

2. Make sure that the **MMGS (millimeter, gram, second)** option is ticked marked in this flyout, see Figure 7.74. If not, click to select it.

Tip: A tick mark in front of any unit system indicated that it is selected as the unit system for the current document of SOLIDWORKS. You can also open the **Document Properties - Units** dialog box to specify a unit system for the current document by selecting the **Edit Document Units** option of this flyout.

Section 4: Creating Base/First Feature - Revolve Feature

1. Invoke the Sketching environment by selecting the Top Plane as the sketching plane and then create the sketch of the base feature, see Figure 7.75. The base feature of the model is a revolved feature.

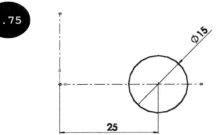

Tip: To make the sketch of the base feature fully defined, you need to make sure that the center point of the circle has coincident relation with the horizontal centerline. The vertical centerline is used as the axis of revolution to create revolve feature (base feature).

---

2. Click on the **Feature** tab in the **Command Manager**, see Figure 7.76.

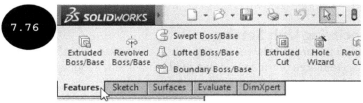

3. Click on the **Revolved Boss/Base** tool of the **Features Command Manager**, the **Revolve PropertyManager** appears. Also, the orientation of the sketch changes to Trimetric orientation, see Figure 7.77.

Note: If the sketch to revolve has only one centerline than on invoking the **Revolved Boss/Base** tool, the available centerline will automatically be selected as the axis of revolution and the preview of the revolve feature appears in the graphics area.

4. Click to select the vertical centerline of the sketch as the axis of revolution, the preview of the revolve feature appears in the graphics area, see Figure 7.78.

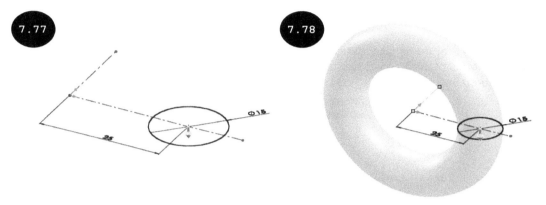

5. Make sure that the 360 degree angle is specified in the **Direction 1 Angle** field of the PropertyManager.

6. Click on the green tick mark ✓ of the PropertyManager, the base/first revolved feature is created, see Figure 7.79.

Section 5: Creating Second Feature - Extrude Feature

To create the second feature of the model, you will first create a reference plane at an offset distance of 40 mm from the Top Plane.

1. Invoke the **Reference Geometry** flyout of the **Features CommandManager**, see Figure 7.80.

2. Click on the **Plane** tool of this flyout, the **Plane PropertyManager** appears.

3. Expand the FeatureManager design tree available on the top left corner of the graphics area by clicking on its +sign, see Figure 7.81.

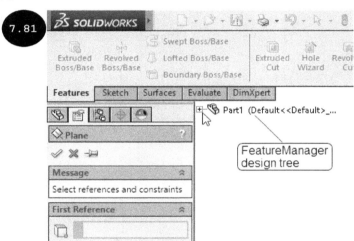

Note: As soon as a PropertyManager invoked, the location of the FeatureManager design tree shifts to the top left corner of the graphics area, see Figure 7.81.

---

4. Click to select the Top Plane of the FeatureManager design tree as the first reference, the preview of an offset reference plane appears in the graphics area, see Figure 7.82.

5. Select the **Flip** check box of the **First Reference** rollout to flip the direction of plane creation.

6. Enter **40** in the **Distance** field of the **First Reference** rollout of the **Plane PropertyManager**.

7. Click on the green tick mark ✅ of the PropertyManager, the offset reference plane is created, see Figure 7.83.

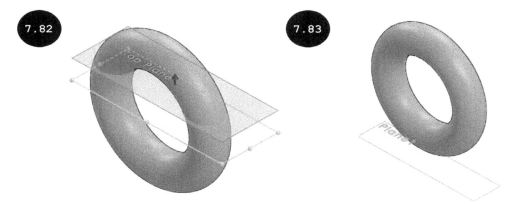

After creating the reference plane, you can create the second feature of the model.

8. Invoke the Sketching environment by selecting the newly created reference plane as the sketching plane.

9. Change the orientation of the model normal to the viewing direction by using the **Normal To** tool of the **View Orientation** flyout, see Figure 7.84.

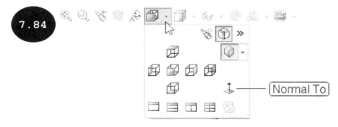

10. Create the sketch of the second feature and apply dimensions, see Figure 7.85.

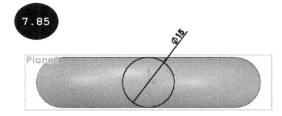

11. Click on the **Features** tab of the **CommandManager** to displays the tools of the **Features CommandManager**.

12. Click on the **Extruded Boss/Base** tool of the **Features CommandManager**, the **Boss-Extrude PropertyManager** and the preview of the extruded feature appears in the graphics area. Next, change the orientation of the model to isometric by using the **View Orientation** flyout, see Figure 7.86.

13. Invoke the **End Condition** flyout of the **Direction 1** rollout, see Figure 7.87.

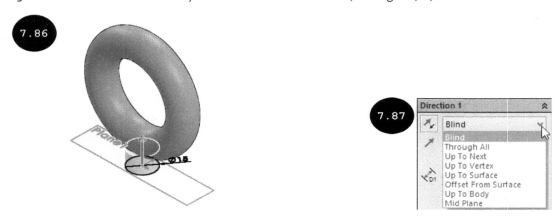

14. Click to select the **Up To Next** option of the **End Condition** flyout, the preview of the feature appears in the graphics area such that it terminated at its next intersection, see Figure 7.88.

15. Click on the green tick mark ✅ of the PropertyManager, the extruded feature is created, see Figure 7.89.

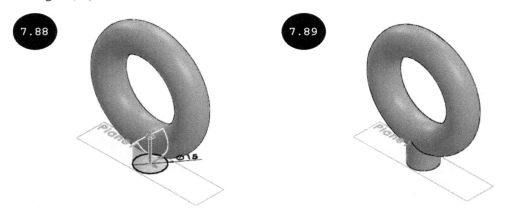

Section 6: Hiding Reference Plane

1. Click to select the reference plane from the graphics area, a Pop-up toolbar appears, see Figure 7.90.

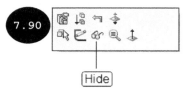

2. Click on the **Hide** tool of the Pop-up toolbar, the selected reference plane is no longer shown the graphics area.

Section 7: Creating Third Feature - Extrude Feature

1. Rotate the model by dragging the cursor after pressing and holding the middle mouse button such that you can view the bottom planar face of the second feature, see Figure 7.91.

2. Invoke the Sketching environment by selecting the bottom planar face of the second feature.

3. Change the orientation of the model normal to the viewing direction by using the **Normal To** tool of the **View Orientation** flyout.

4. Create the sketch of the third feature, see Figure 7.92.

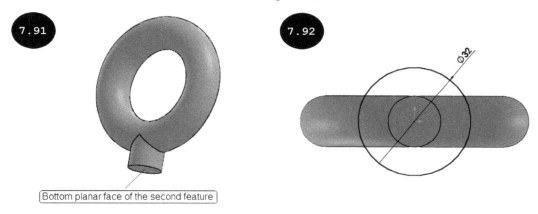

Bottom planar face of the second feature

5. Click on the **Features** tab of the **CommandManager** to displays the tools of the **Features CommandManager**.

6. Click on the **Extruded Boss/Base** tool, the **Boss-Extrude PropertyManager** and the preview of the extruded feature appears. Next, change the orientation of the model to isometric by using the **View Orientation** flyout of the **View (Heads-Up)** toolbar, see Figure 7.93.

7. Enter 5 in the **Depth** field of the **Direction 1** rollout and then press ENTER key.

8. Click on the green tick mark ✔ of the PropertyManager, the extruded feature is created, see Figure 7.94.

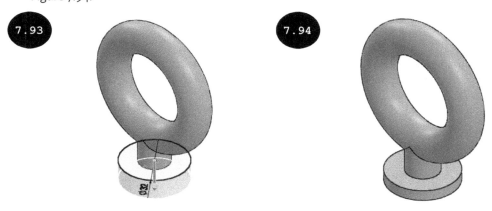

Section 8: Creating Forth Feature - Extrude Feature

1. Rotate the model such that you can view the bottom planar face of the third feature and then invoke the Sketching environment by selecting the bottom planar face of the third feature as the sketching plane.

2. Change the orientation of the model normal to the viewing direction by using the **Normal To** tool of the **View Orientation** flyout.

3. Create the sketch of the forth feature, see Figure 7.95.

4. Click on the **Extruded Boss/Base** tool of the **Features CommandManager**, the **Boss-Extrude PropertyManager** and the preview of the extruded feature appears. Next, change the orientation of the model to isometric.

5. Enter 32 in the **Depth** field of the **Direction 1** rollout and then press ENTER key.

6. Click on the green tick mark ✅ of the PropertyManager, the extruded feature is created, see Figure 7.96.

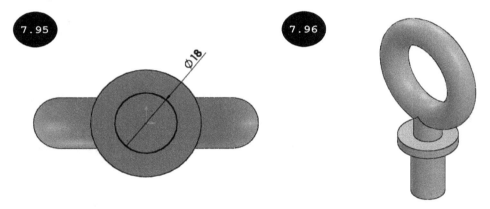

Section 9: Saving the Model

1. Click on the **Save** tool of the **Standard** toolbar, the **Save As** window appears.

2. Browse to the *SOLIDWORKS* folder and then create a folder named as *Chapter 7*. Next, create another folder named as *Tutorial* inside the *Chapter 7* folder.

3. Type **Tutorial 1** in the **File name** field of the dialog box as the name of the file and then click on the **Save** button, the model is saved as Tutorial 1 in the *Tutorial* folder of *Chapter 7*.

Tutorial 2

Create the model shown in Figure 7.97. You need to create the model by creating its all features one by one. After creating the model, assign the Alloy Steel material and calculate the mass properties of the model.

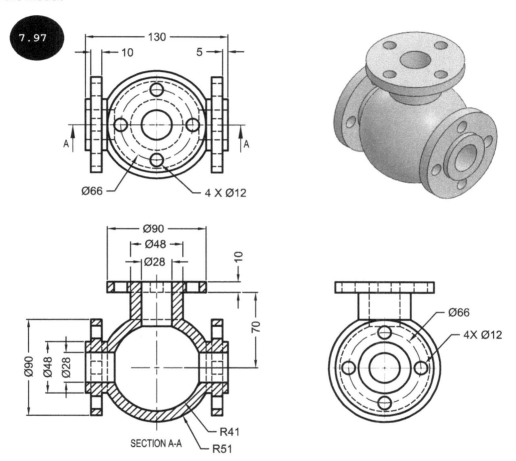

Section 1: Starting SOLIDWORKS

1.   Double click on the **SOLIDWORKS** icon on your desktop to start SOLIDWORKS.

Section 2: Invoking Part Modeling Environment

1.   Click on the **New** tool in the **Standard** toolbar, the **New SOLIDWORKS Document** dialog box appears.

2.   In this dialog box, the **Part** button is activated by default. Click on the **OK** button.

      Once the Part modeling environment is invoked, you can set the unit system and create the base/first feature of the model.

Section 3: Specifying Unit Settings

1. Move the cursor towards the lower right corner of the screen over the Status Bar and then click on the **Unit System** area of the Status Bar, the **Unit System** flyout appears, see Figure 7.98.

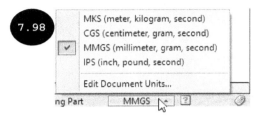

2. Make sure that the **MMGS (millimeter, gram, second)** option is ticked marked in this flyout, see Figure 7.98.

Section 4: Creating Base/First Feature - Revolve Feature

1. Invoke the Sketching environment by selecting the Front Plane as the sketching plane and then create the sketch of the base feature, see Figure 7.99. The base feature of the model is a revolved feature.

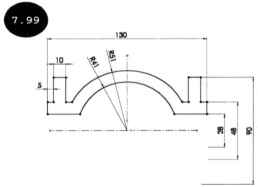

> **Tip:** The sketch created in Figure 7.99 is symmetric about the vertical centerline. As a result, the line entities on the left side of the centerline are equal in length to the right side of the centerline, respectively. You can create line entities of the left side and then mirror them about the vertical centerline to create the line entities of the other side of the sketch.

2. Click on the **Feature** tab in the **Command Manager** and then click on the **Revolved Boss/Base** tool, the **Revolve PropertyManager** appears. Also, the orientation of the sketch changes to Trimetric orientation, see Figure 7.100.

> **Note:** If the sketch to revolve has only one centerline than on invoking the **Revolved Boss/Base** tool, the available centerline will automatically be selected as the axis of revolution and the preview of the revolve feature appears in the graphics area.

3. Click to select the horizontal centerline of the sketch as the axis of revolution, the preview of the revolve feature appears in the graphics area, see Figure 7.101.

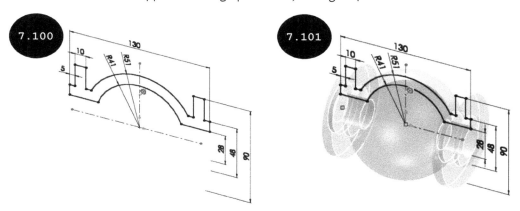

4. Make sure that the 360 degree angle is specified in the **Direction 1 Angle** field of the PropertyManager.

5. Click on the green tick mark ✅ of the PropertyManager, the base/first revolved feature is created, see Figure 7.102.

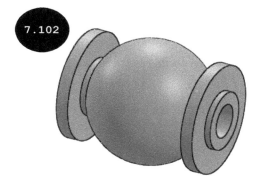

Section 5: Creating Second Feature - Extrude Feature

To create the second feature of the model, you will first create a reference plane at an office distance of 70 mm from the Top Plane.

1. Invoke the **Reference Geometry** flyout of the **Features CommandManager**, see Figure 7.103.

2. Click on the **Plane** tool of this flyout, the **Plane PropertyManager** appears.

3. Expand the FeatureManager design tree available on the top left corner of the graphics area by clicking on its +sign.

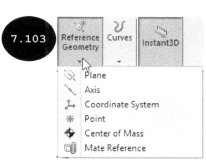

4. Click to select the Top Plane of the FeatureManager design tree as the first reference, the preview of an offset reference plane appears in the graphics area.

5. Enter *70* in the **Distance** field of the **First Reference** rollout of the **Plane PropertyManager**.

6. Click on the green tick mark ✅ of the PropertyManager, the offset reference plane is created, see Figure 7.104.

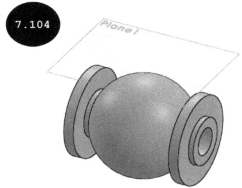

After creating the reference plane, you can create the second feature of the model.

7. Invoke the Sketching environment by selecting the newly created reference plane as the sketching plane.

8. Change the orientation of the model normal to the viewing direction by using the **Normal To** tool of the **View Orientation** flyout.

9. Create the sketch of the second feature, see Figure 7.105.

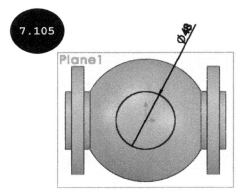

10. Click on the **Features** tab of the **CommandManager** to displays the tools of the **Features CommandManager**.

11. Click on the **Extruded Boss/Base** tool of the **Features CommandManager**, the **Boss-Extrude PropertyManager** and the preview of the extruded feature appears in the graphics area. Next, change the orientation of the model to isometric by using the **View Orientation** flyout, see Figure 7.106.

12. Click on the **Reverse Direction** button of the **Direction 1** rollout to reverse the direction of extrusion to downwards.

13. Invoke the **End Condition** flyout of the **Direction 1** rollout, see Figure 7.107.

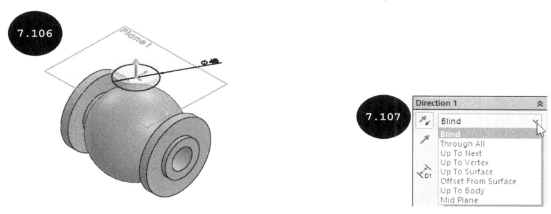

14. Click to select the **Up To Next** option of the **End Condition** flyout, the preview of the feature appears in the graphics area such that it terminated at its next intersection.

15. Click on the green tick mark ✅ of the PropertyManager, the extruded feature is created, see Figure 7.108.

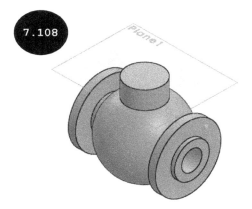

Section 6: Hiding Reference Plane

1. Click to select the reference plane from the graphics area, a Pop-up toolbar appears, see Figure 7.109.

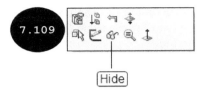

2. Click on the **Hide** tool of the Pop-up toolbar, the selected reference plane is no longer shown in the graphics area.

Section 7: Creating Third Feature - Extrude Feature

1. Invoke the Sketching environment by selecting the top planar face of the second feature as the sketching plane.

2. Change the orientation of the model normal to the viewing direction by using the **Normal To** tool of the **View Orientation** flyout.

3. Create a circle of diameter 90 mm, see Figure 7.110.

4. Click on the **Features** tab of the **CommandManager** to displays the tools of the **Features CommandManager**.

5. Click on the **Extruded Boss/Base** tool, the **Boss-Extrude PropertyManager** and the preview of the extruded feature appears. Change the orientation of the model to isometric by using the **View Orientation** flyout of the **View (Heads-Up)** toolbar.

6. Enter *10* in the **Depth** field of the **Direction 1** rollout and then press ENTER key.

7. Click on the green tick mark ✅ of the PropertyManager, the extruded feature is created, see Figure 7.111.

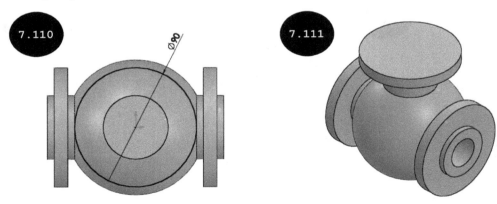

Section 8: Creating Forth Feature - Extrude Cut Feature

1. Invoke the Sketching environment by selecting the top planar face of the third feature as the sketching plane.

2. Change the orientation of the model normal to the viewing direction by using the **Normal To** tool of the **View Orientation** flyout.

3. Create a circle of diameter 28 mm, see Figure 7.112.

4. Click on the **Extruded Cut** tool of the **Features CommandManager**, the **Cut-Extrude PropertyManager** and the preview of the extruded cut feature appears. Change the orientation of the model to isometric.

5. Invoke the **End Condition** flyout of the **Direction 1** rollout, see Figure 7.113.

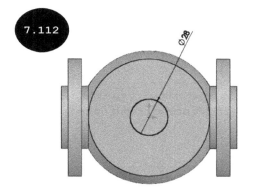

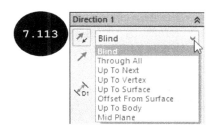

6. Click to select the **Up To Surface** option of the **End Condition** flyout, the **Face/Plane** field become available in the **Direction 1** rollout and is activated by default.

7. Rotate the model by dragging the cursor after pressing and holding the middle mouse button such that you can view the inner circular face of the base feature of the model, see Figure 7.114.

8. Click to select the inner circular face of the base feature as the surface up to which you want to extrude cut feature, the preview of the extrude cut feature appears in the graphics area.

9. Click on the green tick mark ✅ of the PropertyManager, the extruded cut feature is created, see Figure 7.115.

Note: In Figure 7.115, the display style of the model has been changed to Hidden Lines Visible display style by using the **Display Style** flyout of the **View (Heads-Up)** toolbar. Also, the orientation of the model has been changed to **Front** view orientation by using the **View Orientation** flyout for better understand of the cut feature.

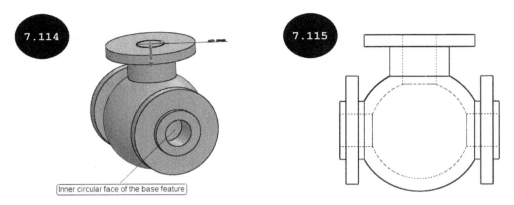

Inner circular face of the base feature

Section 9: Creating Fifth Feature - Extrude Cut Feature

1. Invoke the Sketching environment by selecting the right planar face of the model as the sketching plane, see Figure 7.116.

2. Change the orientation of the model normal to the viewing direction by using the **Normal To** tool of the **View Orientation** flyout.

3. Create a circle of diameter 12 mm, see Figure 7.117. Next, create circular pattern of it to create remaining circles of same diameter and PCD by using the **Circular Sketch Pattern** tool, see Figure 7.118.

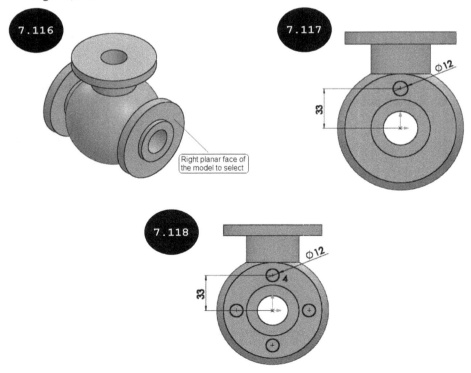

Right planar face of the model to select

Make sure that the center point of the circular pattern created is coincident with the origin.

Similar to pattern sketch entity and create its multiple instances, you can also pattern a feature and create its multiple instances. Creating pattern of features is discussed in later chapters.

4. Click on the **Extruded Cut** tool of the **Features CommandManager**, the **Cut-Extrude PropertyManager** and the preview of the extruded cut feature appears. Change the orientation of the model to isometric, see Figure 7.119.

5. Invoke the **End Condition** flyout of the **Direction 1** rollout and click to select the **Up To Next** option.

6. Click on the green tick mark ✅ of the PropertyManager, the extruded cut feature is created, see Figure 7.120.

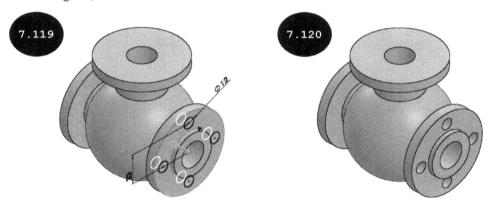

Section 10: Creating Sixth Feature - Extrude Cut Feature
1. Similarly to creating cut feature on the right planar face of the model, also create on the left planar face of the model, see Figure 7.121.

Instead of creating the feature on the left planar face of the model, you can mirror the feature created on the right planar face to the left planar face about the Right Plane. Mirroring features is discussed in later chapters.

Section 11: Creating Seventh Feature - Extrude Cut Feature
1. Similarly to creating cut feature on the right and left planar faces of the model, also create on the top planar face of the model, see Figure 7.122.

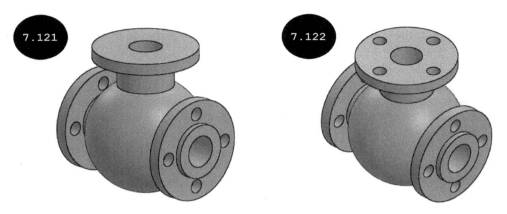

Section 12: Assigning Material

1. Click to select the **Material <not specified>** from the FeatureManager design tree and then right click to display the shortcut menu, see Figure 7.123.

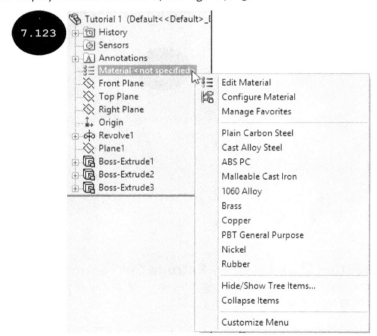

2. Click on the **Edit Material** option from the shortcut menu, the **Material** dialog box appears, see Figure 7.124.

3. Expand the **SOLIDWORKS Materials** node (if not expanded by default), the different category of material available in it appears, see Figure 7.124.

4. Expand the **Steel** category, the materials available in the **Steel** category appears.

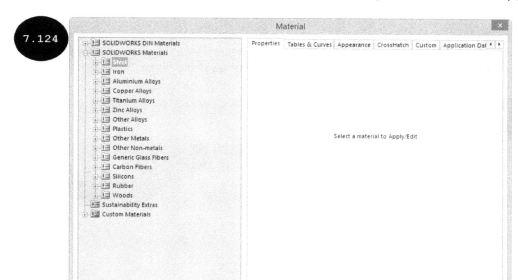

5.   Select the **Alloy Steel** material from the list of available materials, the material properties of the **Alloy Steel** appears at the right half of the dialog box.

6.   Click on the **Apply** button of the dialog box to apply the material.

7.   Click on the **Close** button to exit from the dialog box.

Section 13: Calculating Mass Properties

1.   Click on the **Evaluate** tab of the **CommandManager** to invoke the **Evaluate CommandManager**, see Figure 7.125.

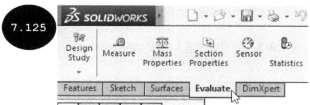

2.   Click on the **Mass Properties** tool of the **Evaluate CommandManager**, the **Mass Properties** dialog box appears displays the mass properties of the model.

Section 14: Saving the Model

1.   Click on the **Save** tool of the **Standard** toolbar, the **Save As** window appears.

2.   Browse to the *Tutorial* folder of *Chapter 7* and then save the file as Tutorial 2.

Tutorial 3

Create the model shown in Figure 7.126. You need to create the model by creating its all features one by one. After creating the model, assign the AISI 316 Stainless Steel Sheet (SS) material and calculate the mass properties of the model.

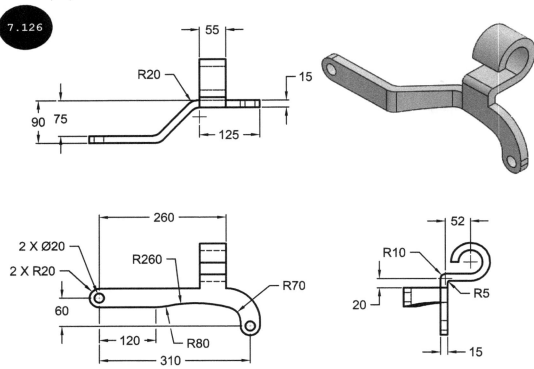

7.126

Section 1: Starting SOLIDWORKS
1. Double click on the **SOLIDWORKS** icon on your desktop to start SOLIDWORKS.

Section 2: Invoking Part Modeling Environment
1. Click on the **New** tool in the **Standard** toolbar, the **New SOLIDWORKS Document** dialog box appears.

2. In this dialog box, the **Part** button is activated by default. Click on the **OK** button.

Section 3: Specifying Unit Settings
1. Move the cursor towards the lower right corner of the screen over the Status Bar and then click on the **Unit System** area of the Status Bar, the **Unit System** flyout appears, see Figure 7.127.

2. Make sure that the **MMGS (millimeter, gram, second)** option is ticked marked in this flyout, see Figure 7.127.

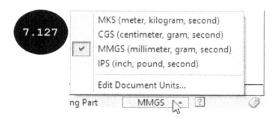

Section 4: Creating Base/First Feature - Extrude Feature

1. Invoke the Sketching environment by selecting the Front Plane as the sketching plane and then create the sketch of the base feature, see Figure 7.128.

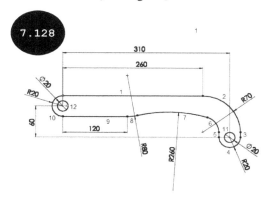

Tip: To make the sketch fully define, you need to apply tangent relation between connecting line and arc of the sketch. Also, concentric relation is applied between circle (11) and arc (4), circle (12) and arc (10), and arc (2) and arc (6), respectively. The entities of the sketch shown in Figure 7.114 have been numbered for your reference.

2. Click on the **Feature** tab in the **Command Manager** and then click on the **Extruded Boss/Base** tool, the **Boss-Extrude PropertyManager** and preview of the extrude feature appears. Also, the orientation of the model changes to Trimetric orientation, see Figure 7.129.

3. Invoke the **End Condition** flyout of the **Direction 1** rollout, see Figure 7.130.

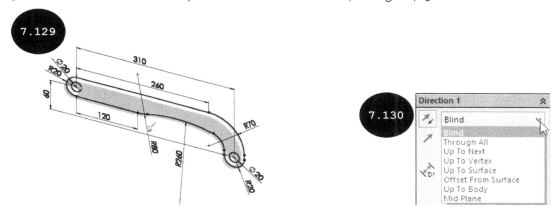

4.   Click to select the **Mid Plane** option of the **End Condition** flyout, the preview of the feature appears in the graphics area symmetric about the sketching plane.

5.   Enter **90** in the **Depth** field of the **Direction 1** rollout of the PropertyManager.

6.   Click on the green tick mark ✅ of the PropertyManager, the extruded feature is created, see Figure 7.131.

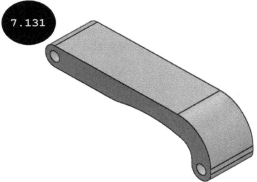

Section 5: Creating Second Feature - Extrude Cut Feature

1.   Invoke the Sketching environment by selecting the top planar face of the base feature as the sketching plane.

2.   Change the orientation of the model normal to the viewing direction by using the **Normal To** tool of the **View Orientation** flyout.

3.   Create a sketch of the second feature and apply dimensions, see Figure 7.132.

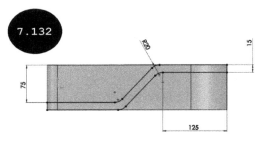

Tip: The arc entities of the sketch shown in Figure 7.132 are of equal radius therefore equal relation is applied between them.

---

4. Click on the **Extruded Cut** tool of the **Features CommandManager**, the **Cut-Extrude PropertyManager** and the preview of the extruded cut feature appears. Change the orientation of the model to isometric, see Figure 7.133.

5. Invoke the **End Condition** flyout of the **Direction 1** rollout, see Figure 7.134.

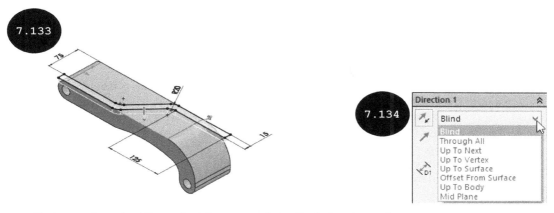

6. Click to select the **Through All** option of the **End Condition** flyout to cut through all the model.

7. Click to select the **Flip side to cut** check box of the Direction 1 rollout, the side of material to remove is flipped.

8. Click on the green tick mark ✅ of the PropertyManager, the extruded cut feature is created, see Figure 7.135.

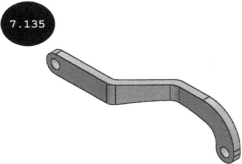

Section 6: Creating Third Feature - Extrude Feature

To create the third feature of the model, you will first create a reference plane parallel to Right Plane and passing through a vertex.

1. Invoke the **Reference Geometry** flyout of the **Features CommandManager**, see Figure 7.136.

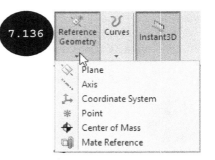

2. Click on the **Plane** tool of this flyout, the **Plane PropertyManager** appears.

3. Expand the FeatureManager design tree available on the top left corner of the graphics area by clicking on its +sign.

4. Click to select the Right Plane as the first reference, the preview of an offset reference plane appears in the graphics area.

5. Move the cursor in the graphics area to select a vertex as the second reference for creating a plane, see Figure 7.137. Next, click to select the vertex as the second reference, see Figure 7.137, the preview of the reference plane parallel to Right plane and passing through a vertex appears in the graphics area, see Figure 7.138.

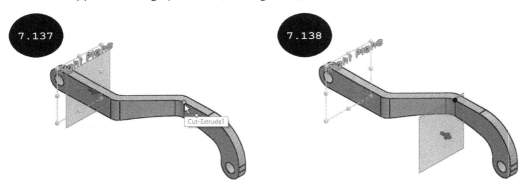

6. Click on the green tick mark ✅ of the PropertyManager, the reference plane is created.

    After creating the reference plane, you can create the third feature of the model.

7. Invoke the Sketching environment by selecting the newly created reference plane as the sketching plane.

8. Change the orientation of the model normal to the viewing direction by using the **Normal To** tool of the **View Orientation** flyout.

9. Create the sketch of the third feature, see Figure 7.139.

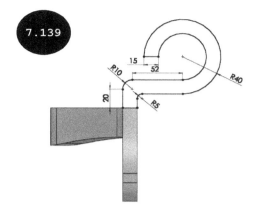

7.139

10. Click on the **Features** tab of the **CommandManager** to displays the tools of the **Features CommandManager**.

11. Click on the **Extruded Boss/Base** tool of the **Features CommandManager**, the **Boss-Extrude PropertyManager** and the preview of the extruded feature appears in the graphics area. Next, change the orientation of the model to isometric by using the **View Orientation** flyout, see Figure 7.140.

12. Invoke the **End Condition** flyout of the **Direction 1** rollout of the PropertyManager.

13. Click to select the **Up To Vertex option** of the **End Condition** flyout, the **Vertex** field become available in the **Direction 1** rollout and is activated by default.

14. Move the cursor in the graphics area and click to select a vertex, see Figure 7.141, the preview of the extruded feature appears in the graphics area up to the selected vertex, see Figure 7.142.

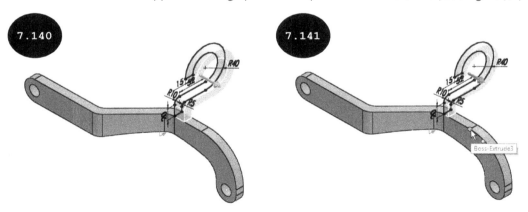

7.140

7.141

15. Click on the green tick mark ✅ of the PropertyManager, the extruded feature is created, see Figure 7.143.

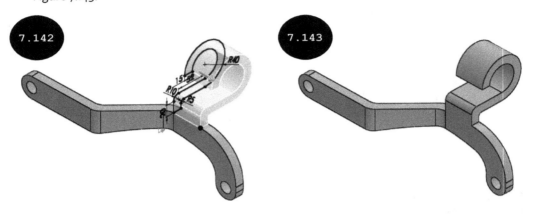

7.142

7.143

Note: The reference plane has been hidden.

Section 7: Assigning Material

1. Click to select the **Material <not specified>** from the FeatureManager design tree and then right click to display the shortcut menu, see Figure 7.144.

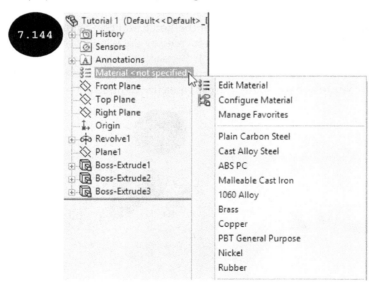

7.144

Tutorial 1 (Default<<Default>_[
⊕ 🕐 History
   ⊘ Sensors
⊕ 🅰 Annotations
   ≋ Material <not specified>
   ◇ Front Plane
   ◇ Top Plane
   ◇ Right Plane
   ⌞ Origin
⊕ 🔄 Revolve1
   ◇ Plane1
⊕ 📦 Boss-Extrude1
⊕ 📦 Boss-Extrude2
⊕ 📦 Boss-Extrude3

Edit Material
Configure Material
Manage Favorites

Plain Carbon Steel
Cast Alloy Steel
ABS PC
Malleable Cast Iron
1060 Alloy
Brass
Copper
PBT General Purpose
Nickel
Rubber

2. Click on the **Edit Material** option from the shortcut menu, the **Material** dialog box appears.

3. Expand the **SOLIDWORKS Materials** node (if not expanded by default) to display different material categories available in it.

4. Expand the **Steel** category, the materials available in the **Steel** category appears, see Figure 7.145.

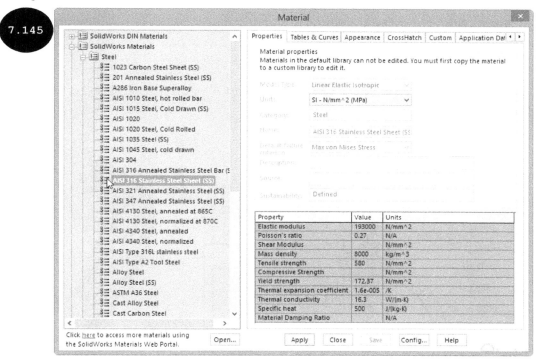

5. Select the **AISI 316 Stainless Steel Sheet (SS)** material from the list of available materials, the material properties of the **AISI 316 Stainless Steel Sheet (SS)** appears at the right half of the dialog box, see Figure 7.145.

6. Click on the **Apply** button of the dialog box to apply the material.

7. Click on the **Close** button to exit from the dialog box.

Section 8: Calculating Mass Properties

1. Click on the **Evaluate** tab of the **CommandManager** to invoke the **Evaluate CommandManager**, see Figure 7.146.

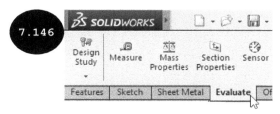

2. Click on the **Mass Properties** tool of the **Evaluate CommandManager**, the **Mass Properties** dialog box appears displays the mass properties of the model.

Section 9: Saving the Model

1.   Click on the **Save** tool of the **Standard** toolbar, the **Save As** window appears.

2.   Browse to the *Tutorial* folder of *Chapter 7* and then save the model as Tutorial 3.

Hands-on Test Drive 1

Create the model shown in Figure 7.147, apply the Cast Alloy Steel material, and calculate mass properties of the model.

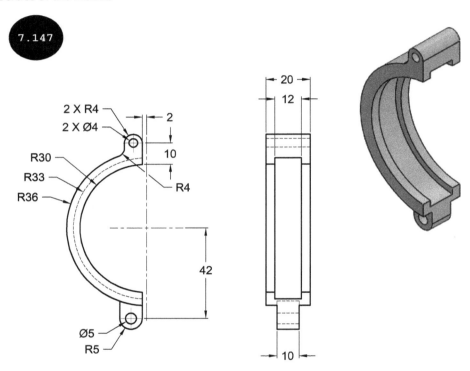

Hands-on Test Drive 2

Create the model shown in Figure 7.148, apply the Alloy Steel (SS), and calculate mass properties of the model.

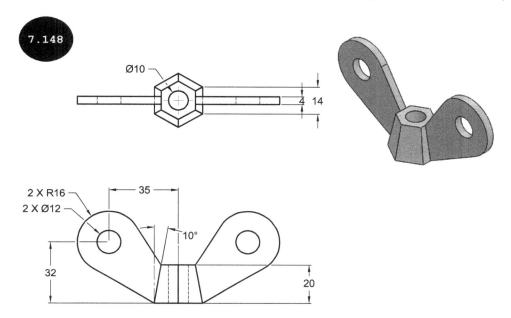

7.148

Ø10

4 14

2 X R16
2 X Ø12

35

10°

32

20

Summary

In this chapter, you have learnt advanced options for creating extrude/revolve features. In addition to this, you have learnt how to create cut features by using the **Extruded Cut** and **Revolved Cut** tools, how to work with different type of sketches such as close sketches, open sketches, and nested sketches. Also, how to create multiple features by using a single sketch having multiple contours/ regions. After reading this chapter, you can project edges of the existing features on to the current sketching plane by using the **Convert Entities** tool. Also, you can edit individual feature and their sketch of a model as per the design change.

You have also learnt how to measure distance and angle between lines, points, faces, planes, and so on by using the **Measure** tool and how to assign appearance/texture to a model, features, and faces. In addition to this, you have learnt about how to assign material properties and calculate mass properties of a model.

Questions

• The options available in the _____ drop-down list are used to define the start condition of the extrusion.

• The _____ option allows you to select a surface, face, or plane as the start condition of the extrusion.

• The _____ option allows you to define the end condition or termination of the extrusion by selecting a vertex.

- You can create extruded cut features by using the _____ tool.

- The _____ sketches are those having all the entities are end to end connected with each other without any gap.

- You can project edges of the existing features as the sketch entities on to the current sketching plane by using the _____ tool.

- The _____ tool is used to calculate the mass properties such as mass and volume of the model.

- A revolve cut feature is a feature created by removing material by revolving a sketch around a centerline or an axis (True/False).

- You can edit individual features and their sketches of an model as required. (True/False).

- In SOLIDWORKS, you can not customize material properties. (True/False).

_____

Advanced Modeling II

In this chapter:

- Creating Sweep Feature
- Creating Sweep Cut Feature
- Creating Loft feature
- Creating Loft Cut Feature
- Creating Boundary features
- Creating Boundary Cut Feature
- Creating Curve Feature
- Splitting Faces of a Model
- Creating 3D Sketches

In the earlier chapters, you learnt about primary modeling tools that are used to create 3D parametric components. Also, you learnt the basic workflow of creating components that is first create the base feature of the component and then build the entire component by creating its remaining features one after another. In this chapter, you will explore some of the advance tools such as **Swept Boss/Base** and **Lofted Boss/Base**. Also, you will learn about creating different types of 3D curves.

Creating Sweep Feature

A sweep feature is a feature which is created by adding material by sweeping a profile along a path. Figure 8.1 shows a profile and a path. Figure 8.2 shows the resultant sweep feature created by sweeping the profile along the path.

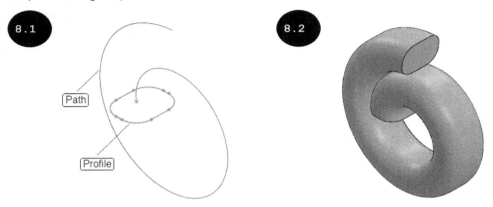

It is evident from the above figures that for creating sweep feature, you first need to create a path and profile where profile follows the path and creates a swept feature. To create a profile, you need to identify the cross-section of the feature to be created and to create a path, you need to identify the route taken by the profile for creating the feature. In SOLIDWORKS, you can create sweep feature by using the **Swept Boss/Base** tool of the **Features CommandManager**. Note that to creating a sweep feature, you also need to take care of the following points:

1. The profile must be a closed sketch.
2. The path can be a open or closed sketch which can be made-up of set of end to end connected sketched entities, a curve, or a set of model edges.
3. The start point of the path must be laying on the plane of the profile created.
4. The profile and path as well as resultant sweep feature should not have self-intersection.

After creating the path and profile, click on the **Swept Boss/Base** tool available in the **Features CommandManager**, the **Sweep PropertyManager** appears, see Figure 8.3. The options available in this PropertyManager are as follows.

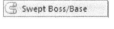

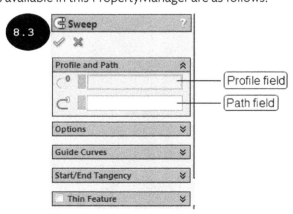

Profile and Path

The **Profile** and **Path** rollout of the PropertyManager is provided with two fields: **Profile** and **Path**. Both are as follows.

Profile

The **Profile** field is used to select a profile of the sweep feature. By default, this field is activated. As a result, on invoking the **Sweep PropertyManager**, you are prompted to select a profile of the feature. Refer to Figure 8.4 for profile.

Path

The **Path** field is used to select a path of the sweep feature. By default, this field is not activated. However, as soon as you select the profile, the **Path** field activates automatically and you are prompted to select a path. You can also click on the field to activate its selection mode. Refer to Figure 8.4 for path.

Note that as soon as you are done with the selection of profile and path, the preview of the resultant sweep feature appears in the graphics area, see Figure 8.5.

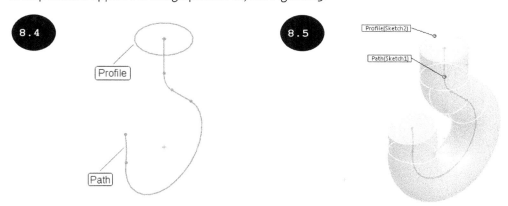

If the preview of the sweep feature is the same as required, you can click on the green tick mark of the PropertyManager, the sweep features is created. However, you can further control the sweep feature by using the options available in the other rollouts of the **Sweep PropertyManager**. These options are as follows.

Options

By default, the **Options** rollout of the PropertyManager is in collapsed formed. To expand this rollout, click on its title bar. Figure 8.6 shows the expanded **Options** rollout. The options available in this rollout are as follows.

Orientation/twist type drop-down list

The options available in the **Orientation/twist type** drop-down list are used to control the orientation of the profile along the path, see Figure 8.7. All these options are as follows.

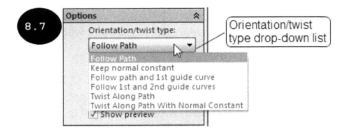

Follow Path

By default, the **Follow Path** option is selected in the drop-down list. As a result, the profile follows the path. Also, the profile maintain the same angle of orientation with respect to the path from start to end, see Figures 8.8 and 8.9.

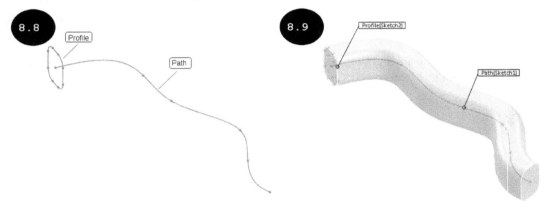

Note that when the **Follow Path** option is selected, the **Path alignment type** drop-down list become available in the rollout with the options used to control the alignment of profile with the path, see Figure 8.10. The options available in this drop-down list are as follows.

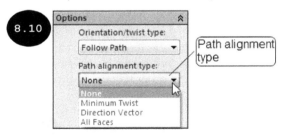

None: By default, the **None** option is selected in the **Path alignment type** drop-down list. As a result, the profile follows the path such that it maintain normal alignment with path, see Figure 8.9. Also, refer to Figures 8.11 and 8.12 for another profile and path, and their resultant preview with the **None** option is selected.

Tip: The path shown in Figure 8.11 is a 3D path. You will learn more about creating 3D path and 3D sketches later in this chapter.

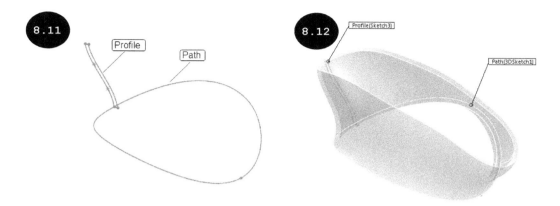

Minimum Twist: On selecting the **Minimum Twist** option, the minimum twist is allowed to profile while follows the path in order to avoid self-intersection. Note that this option works better with 3D path. You will more learn about creating 3D paths later in this chapter. Refer Figure 8.11 for profile and a 3D path, and Figure 8.13 for the preview of the resultant sweep feature with the **Minimum Twist** option selected.

Direction Vector: On selecting the **Direction Vector** option, the **Direction Vector** field appears below the **Path alignment type** drop-down list which allows you to select a direction vector for aligning the profile in the direction of vector selected. Figure 8.14 shows the preview of the sweep feature when the Top Plane is selected as the direction vector. You can select a plane, planar face, line, and linear edge as the direction vector.

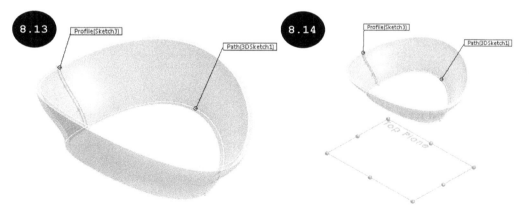

All Faces: If the path has adjacent face then on selecting the **All Faces** option, the profile maintain the tangency with the adjacent face of the path, see Figures 8.15 and 8.16.

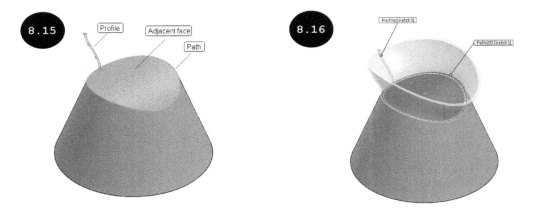

Keep normal constant

On selecting the **Keep normal constant** option, the profile follows the path such that the cross-sections of the resultant sweep feature remain parallel throughout the path. In other words, the start and end sections of the sweep feature being created become parallel to each other. Figure 8.17 (a) shows the preview of a sweep feature when the **Follow Path** option is selected and Figure 8.17 (b) shows the preview of the sweep feature when the **Keep normal constant** option is selected.

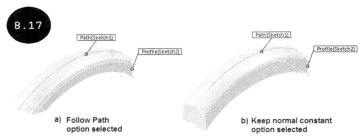

a) Follow Path option selected

b) Keep normal constant option selected

Follow path and 1st guide curve

On selecting the **Follow path and 1st guide curve** option, the profile follows the path as well as the 1st guide curve. A guide curve is used to guide the profile (section) of the sweep feature. Note that as soon as you select this option, the **Guide Curves** rollout of the PropertyManager expands and the selection field available in this rollout become activated which allows you to select guide curves. Make sure that the guide curve must be coincident with the profile. Figure 8.18 shows a path, profile, and a guide curve. Figure 8.19 shows the preview of the resultant sweep feature.

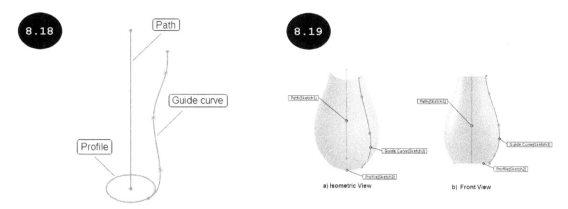

a) Isometric View   b) Front View

Note: In Figure 8.18, the path and guide curve are created on the Front plane an individual sketches, and profile is created on the Top plane.

Tip: To create a sweep feature with guide curves, it is recommended that you first create a path and then guide curve. After creating path and guide curve, create profile coincident to guide curve and path. Creating profile at the last helps you in making profile coincident with the guide curves easily.

Follow 1st and 2nd guide curves

On selecting the **Follow 1st and 2nd guide** curves option, the profile follows the path as well as the two guide curves. You can guide the profile (section) of the sweep feature by using two guide curves. Note that on selecting this option, the **Guide Curves** rollout of the PropertyManager expands for selecting guide curves. Figure 8.20 shows a path, profile, and guide curves. Figure 8.21 shows the preview of resultant sweep feature.

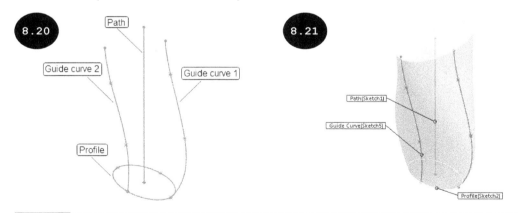

Note: In Figure 8.20, the path and guide curve 1 are created on the Front plane an individual sketches, and guide curve 2 is created on the Right plane. Also, the profile is created on the Top plane.

Tip: If the profile fail to follow both the guide curves, make sure that sweep feature being created should not have any self intersection. Also, the profile (section) should not be constrain with dimensions as the section of the resultant feature has to varies with respect to the guide curves.

Twist Along Path

On selecting the **Twist Along Path** option, you can twist a profile along a path. Figure 8.22 shows a path and profile, and Figure 8.23 shows the preview of the resultant twist sweep feature. Also, refer to Figures 8.25 and 8.26. On selecting this option, the **Define by** drop-down list available in the **Options** rollout, see Figure 8.24. The options available in this drop-down list are used to define the method for twisting the profile along the path and are as follows.

Note: In Figure 8.22, the path and profile are created on the Front plane as an individual sketches.

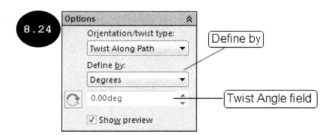

Degrees: By default, the **Degree** option is selected in the **Define by** drop-down list. As a result, the **Twist Angle** field is available which allows you to specify the twist angle in degrees. Figure 8.25 shows a profile and a path. Figure 8.26 shows the preview of the sweep feature being created on twisting the profile (540 degrees) along the path.

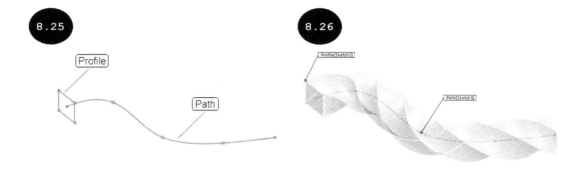

Radians: On selecting the **Radians** option, you can specify the twist angle in radians.

Turn: On selecting the **Turn** option, the **Angle defined in number of turns** field become available, which allows you to specify the number of twisting turns for profile along the path. Figures 8.27 and 8.28 shows the preview of sweep features being created by defining 3 number of turns for the profile to twist along the path.

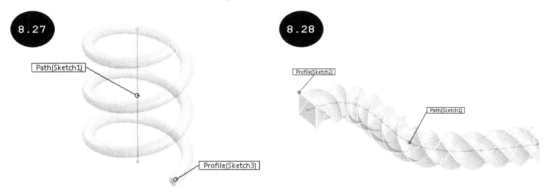

Twist Along Path With Normal Constant

On selecting the **Twist Along Path With Normal Constant** option, you can twist a profile along a path by keeping the start and end section (profile) of the sweep feature parallel to each other while twisting, see Figure 8.29. You can define the twisting for the sweep feature by selecting the **Degree, Radians,** or **Turn** options, as discussed earlier.

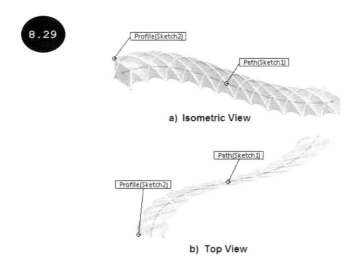

a) Isometric View

b) Top View

Merge tangent faces

On selecting the **Merge tangent faces** check box of the **Options** rollout, the tangent faces of the resultant feature merged and form a single face. Figure 8.30 shows a sweep feature created by selecting the **Merge tangent faces** check box. Figure 8.31 shows a sweep feature created by clearing the **Merge tangent faces** check box.

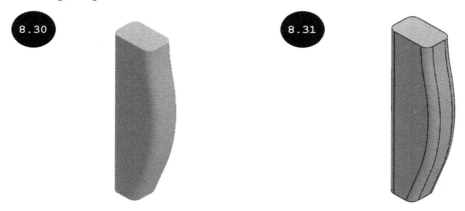

Merge result

By default the **Merge result** check box is selected in the **Options** rollout. As a result, the feature being created merges with the existing features of the model and form a single body. If you clear this check box, the feature being created will not merge with the existing features and forms a separate body. Note that this check box is not available while creating the base/first feature.

Align with end faces

On selecting the **Align with end faces** check box, the end section of the sweep feature being created will aligned with the end face of an existing feature which is encountered by the path.

Figure 8.32 shows the preview of the sweep feature when the **Align with end faces** check box is selected and Figure 8.33 shows the preview of the sweep feature when the **Align with end faces** check box is cleared.

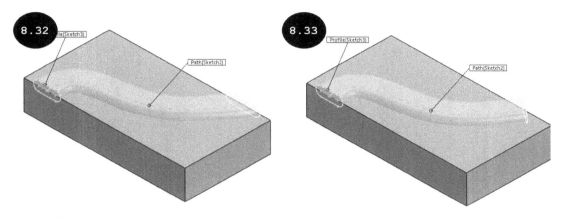

Note: The **Merge result** and **Align with end faces** check boxes are not available if the sweep feature being created is the base/first feature of the model.

Show preview
By default, the **Show preview** check box is selected. As a result, while creating a sweep feature, its preview appears in the graphics area.

Guide Curves
The options available in the **Guide Curves** rollout of the PropertyManager are as follows. Figure 8.34 shows the expanded **Guide Curves** rollout.

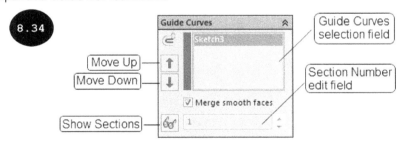

Guide Curves Selection field
The **Guide Curves** selection field is used to select guide curves from the graphics area for guiding the profile while following the path. As you select guide curves their names listed in this selection field, in the sequence they are selected. Note that the guide curves need to be coincident with the profile.

Move Up and Move Down
The **Move Up** and **Move Down** buttons are used to change the order/sequence of the guide curves that are listed in the **Guide Curves** selection field. These buttons are available on the left of the **Guide Curves** selection field.

Merge smooth faces

By default, the **Merge smooth faces** check box is selected. As a result, the smooth segments of the sweep feature being created by using the guide curve having tangent entities will be merged together. Figure 8.35 shows a sweep feature created by selecting the **Merge smooth faces** check box. Figure 8.36 shows a sweep feature created by clearing the **Merge smooth faces** check box.

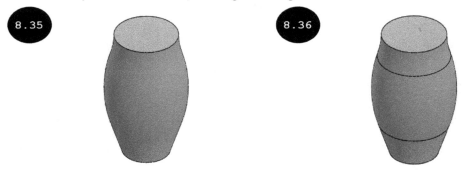

Show Sections

The **Show Sections** button of the rollout is used to view the intermediate sections of the sweep feature being created by using the guide curves. By default, this button is not activated, see Figure 8.34. Click on the **Show Sections** button of the rollout to activate it. As soon as this button is activated, the **Section Number** edit field is enabled. On entering the section number in this field, the preview of the respective section displays in the graphics area, see Figure 8.37.

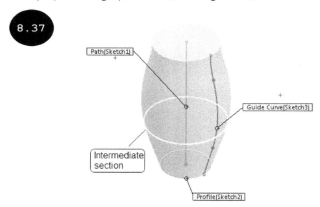

Start/End Tangency

The options available in the **Start/End Tangency** rollout are used to specify the start and end tangency type for the sweep feature being created. This rollout has two drop-down lists, see Figure 8.38 and are as follows.

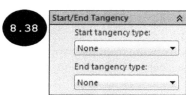

Start tangency type:

The options available in this drop-down list are used to specify the start tangency type for the sweep feature to be created. By default, the **None** option is selected in this drop-down list. As a result, tangency will not be maintained at the starting of the sweep feature being created. On selecting the **Path Tangent** option, sweep feature being created maintain tangency with the path at its start. Figure 8.39 shows the preview of the sweep feature on selecting the **None** option and Figure 8.40 shows the preview of the sweep feature on selecting the **Path Tangent** option as the start tangency type.

End tangency type:

The options available in this drop-down list are used to specify the end tangency type for the sweep feature. By default, the **None** option is selected in this drop-down list. As a result, the tangency will not be maintained at the end of the sweep feature being created. On selecting the **Path Tangent** option, sweep feature being created maintain tangency with the path at its start. Figure 8.39 shows the preview of the sweep feature on selecting the **None** option and Figure 8.40 shows the preview of the sweep feature on selecting the **Path Tangent** option as the end tangency type.

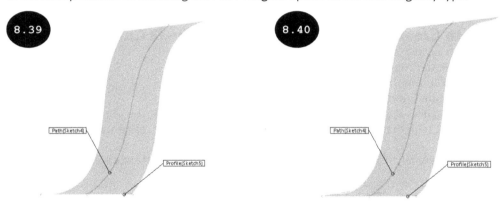

Thin Feature

The **Thin Feature** rollout is used to create thin sweep feature, see Figure 8.41. To create thin sweep feature, expand this rollout by selecting the check box available on the title bar of this rollout. The options for creating the thin sweep feature are same as discussed earlier while creating thin extruded & thin revolved features.

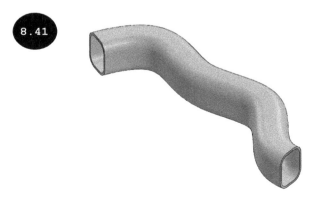

Procedure to Create Sweep Feature

1. Create a path and profile as a individual sketches.
2. Click on the **Swept Boss/Base** tool, the **Sweep PropertyManager** appears.
3. Select the Profile from the graphics area.
4. Select the path from the graphics area, the preview of the sweep feature appears.
5. Click on the green tick mark ✅ of the PropertyManager, the sweep feature is created.

Procedure to Create Sweep Feature with one Guide Curve

1. Create a path, profile, and a guide curve as individual sketches.
2. Click on the **Swept Boss/Base** tool, the **Sweep PropertyManager** appears.
3. Select the profile from the graphics area.
4. Select the path from the graphics area, the preview of the sweep feature appears.
5. Expand the **Guide Curves** rollout of the PropertyManager.
6. Select the guide curve from the graphics area, the preview of the sweep feature appears such that profile follows the path as well as its outer shape maintained by guide curves.
7. Click on the green tick mark ✅ of the PropertyManager, the sweep feature is created.

Procedure to Create Sweep Feature with two Guide Curves

1. Create a path, profile, and two guide curves as individual sketches.
2. Invoke the **Sweep PropertyManager**.
3. Select the Profile and then select the path from the graphics area.
4. Expand the **Guide Curves** rollout of the PropertyManager.
5. Select the first guide curve and then select the second guide curve, the preview of the sweep feature appears such that profile follows the path as well as its outer shape maintained by guide curves.
6. Click on the green tick mark ✅ of the PropertyManager, the sweep feature is created.

Procedure to Create Twist Sweep Feature

1. Create a path and profile as individual sketches.
2. Invoked the **Sweep PropertyManager**.
3. Select the profile and then select the path from the graphics area.
4. Expand the **Options** rollout of the PropertyManager.
5. Select the **Twist Along Path** option from the **Orientation/twist type** drop-down list of the **Option** rollout of the PropertyManager.
6. Select either **Turns**, **Degrees**, or **Radians** option from the **Define by** drop-down list.
7. Specify the number of turns in the **Angle defined in number of turns** field of the rollout, preview of the sweep feature appears.
8. Click on the green tick mark ✅ of the PropertyManager, the twisted sweep feature is created.

Creating Sweep Cut Feature

Creating sweep cut features are same as of creating sweep features with the only difference that the sweep cut features are created by removing material. You can create sweep cut features by using the **Swept Cut** tool available in the **Features CommandManager**. Figure 8.42 shows a profile and a path. Figure 8.43 shows the resultant sweep cut feature created by sweeping the profile along the path and material has been removed accordingly.

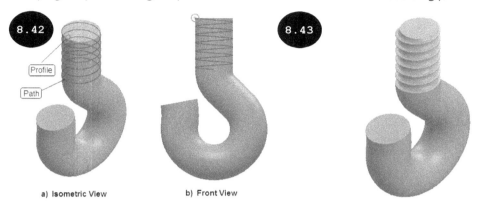

| 8.42 | Profile / Path | 8.43 |

a) Isometric View   b) Front View

Note: In Figure 8.42, a helical curve is created as path and a circle is created as profile. You will learn more about creating helical curves later in this chapters.

Also, see Figures 8.44 and 8.45, for a path and profile, and their resultant sweep cut feature.

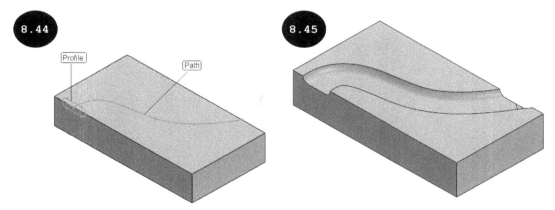

| 8.44 | Profile | Path | 8.45 |

After creating the path and profile, to create sweep cut feature, click on the **Swept Cut** tool available in the **Features CommandManager**, the **Cut-Sweep PropertyManager** appears, see Figure 8.46. In this PropertyManager, by default, the **Profile sweep** radio button is selected. As a result, the **Profile** field appears in the PropertyManager which allows you to select profile that follows the path in order to create sweep cut feature, see figures 8.42 through 8.45. However, on selecting the **Solid sweep** radio button of the PropertyManager, the **Tool body** field appears, see Figure 8.47, which allows you to select tool body that follows the path in order to create sweep cut feature. Figures 8.48 shows a tool body and a helical path, and Figure 8.49 shows the resultant sweep cut feature created by sweeping tool body along the path. Also, see Figures 8.50 and 8.51. Note the options for the creating sweep cut features are same as explained while creating sweep feature.

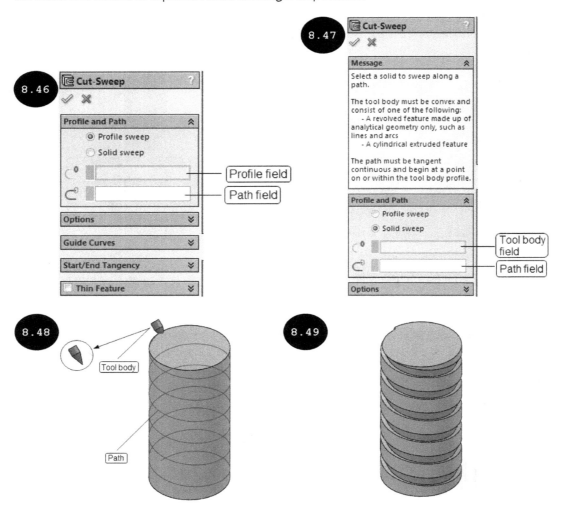

Note: In Figure 8.48, a solid body is used as tool body. The tool body should be created as a separate body. To create a separate body, you need to cleared the **Merge result** check box of the PropertyManager while creating a feature. On clearing the **Merge result** check box, the resultant feature treated as a separate body.

Also in this figure, a helical curve is used as path. You will learn more about creating helical curve later in this chapter.

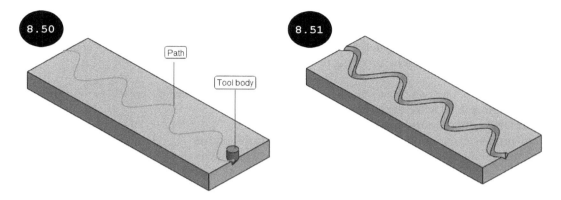

Procedure to Sweep Cut Feature using Profile and Path

1.   Create a path and profile as a individual sketches.
2.   Click on the **Swept Cut** tool, the **Cut-Sweep PropertyManager** appears.
3.   Be sure that the **Profile sweep** radio button is selected
4.   Select the profile from the graphics area.
5.   Select the path from the graphics area, the preview of the sweep cut feature appears.
6.   Click on the green tick mark ✅ of the PropertyManager, the sweep cut feature is created.

Procedure to Sweep Cut Feature using Tool Body and Path

1.   Create a path and tool body (solid body).
2.   Click on the **Swept Cut** tool, the **Cut-Sweep PropertyManager** appears.
3.   Select the **Solid sweep** radio button.
4.   Select the tool body from the graphics area.
5.   Select the path from the graphics area, the preview of the sweep cut feature appears.
6.   Click on the green tick mark ✅ of the PropertyManager, the sweep cut feature is created.

Creating Loft feature

A loft feature is a feature created by lofting two or more than two profiles (sections) such that its cross-sectional shape transitions from one profile to another. Figure 8.52 shows two dissimilar profiles/ sections created on different planes having offset distance between each other. Figure 8.53 shows the resultant lofted feature created.

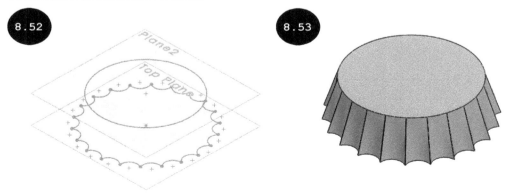

It is evident from the above figures that for creating loft feature, you first need to create all its sections that basically defines the shape of the loft feature. In SOLIDWORKS, you can create loft feature by using the **Lofted Boss/Base** tool of the **Features CommandManager**. Note that to creating a loft feature, you also need to take care of the following points:

1. Two or more than two profiles/sections (similar or dissimilar) must be available in the graphics area before you invoke the **Lofted Boss/Base** tool.
2. Profiles/sections must be a closed sketches.
3. All profiles/sections must be created as an individual sketches.
4. The sections as well as resultant loft feature should not have self-intersection.

To create loft feature, click on the **Lofted Boss/Base** tool, the **Loft** PropertyManager appears, see Figure 8.54. The options available in this PropertyManager are as follows.

Profiles

The **Profiles** rollout of the PropertyManager is used to select the sections/profiles for the loft feature being created. Note that as soon as you select the sections/profiles, the preview of the loft feature displays in the graphic area with connectors connecting the sections, refer to Figure 8.55. Also, the name of the selected sections displays in the **Profile selection** field of the rollout in an order in which they are selected. You can change the order of selection by using the **Move Up** and **Move Down** buttons available on the left of the **Profile selection** field of the rollout, see Figure 8.54.

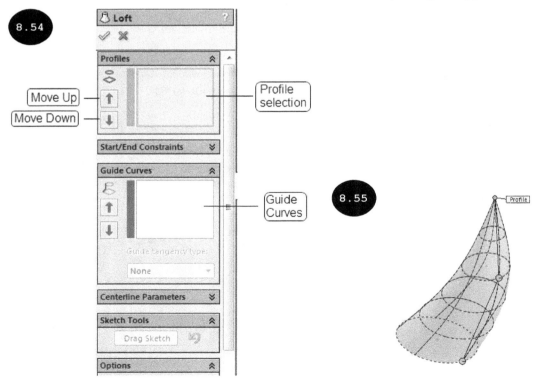

Note: You can drag the connectors appears in the preview of a loft feature in order to create twist in the loft feature. By default, only one handle with its connectors appears in the graphics area. You can turn on the display of all the handles in the graphics area. To turn on all the handles, right-click in the graphics area and then select the **Show All Connectors** option from the shortcut menu appears.

Start/End Constraints

The **Start/End Constraints** rollout is used to define the normal, tangency, or curvature continuity as the start and end constraints for the loft feature being created. See Figure 8.56 for the expanded **Start/End Constraints** rollout. The options available in this rollout are as follows.

Start constraint

The options of the **Start constraint** drop-down list are used to define the start constraint for the loft feature, see Figure 8.57. The options of this drop-down list are as follows.

None

By default, the **None** option is selected in this drop-down list. As a result, no constraint is applied and cross-sectional shape transitions from one profile to another, linearly, see Figure 8.58.

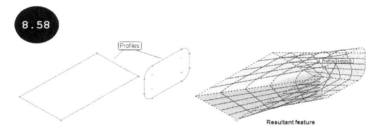

Direction Vector

On selecting the **Direction Vector** option, the **Direction Vector**, **Draft angle**, and **Start Tangent Length** fields become available below the **Start constraint** drop-down list, see Figure 8.59.

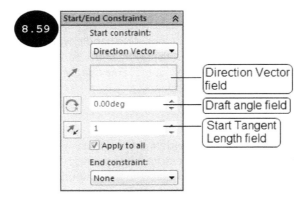

The **Direction Vector** field allows you to select direction vector for defining the start constraint for the loft feature. You can select a plane, linear edge, linear sketch entity, or an axis as the direction vector. Note that based on the selected direction vector, the start constraint applies to the loft feature with respect to the direction vector selected. Figure 8.60 shows a preview of the loft feature when the Top plane is selected as the direction vector.

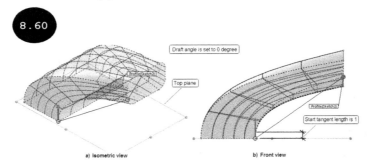

The **Draft angle** field allows you to define the draft angle for the start constraint. By default, the draft angle is set to 0 degree, see Figure 8.60. Figure 8.61 shows the preview of the loft feature having 10 degree draft angle set.

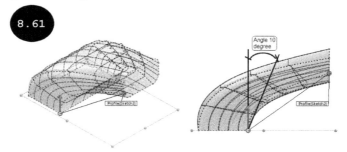

The **Start Tangent Length** field allows you to define the start tangent length for the start constraint. By default, the start tangent length is specified as 1, refer to Figure 8.60. The Figure 8.62 shows the preview of the loft feature having draft angle set to 0 degree and the start tangent length set to 2.

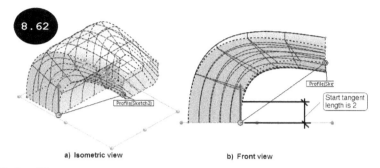

a) Isometric view   b) Front view

Normal To Profile

On selecting the **Normal To Profile** option, the tangency constraint applies normal to the start section/profile of the loft feature. Also, the **Draft angle** and **Start Tangent Length** fields become available on selecting this option. The methods of specifying draft angle and start tangent length are same as explained earlier.

Tangency To Face

On selecting the **Tangency To Face** option, the start section/profile of the loft feature maintain tangency with adjacent faces of the existing geometry, see Figure 8.63. You can also define the start tangent length for the feature by using the **Start Tangent Length** field.

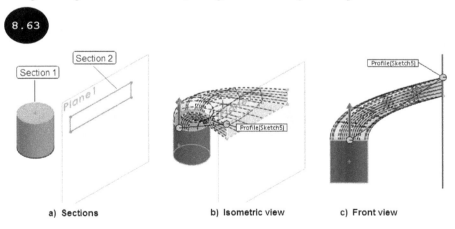

a) Sections   b) Isometric view   c) Front view

Note: The **Tangency To Face** option available only when an existing feature is available in the graphics area. If the loft feature being created is the **base/first** feature than this option will not be available in the drop-down list.

Curvature To Face

On selecting the **Curvature To Face** option, the start section/profile of the loft feature maintain the curvature continuity with adjacent faces of the existing geometry, see Figure 8.64.

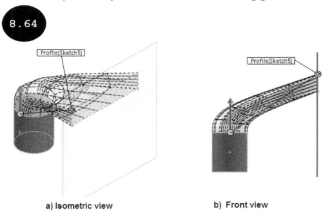

8.64

a) Isometric view   b) Front view

Note: The **Curvature To Face** option available only when an existing feature is available in the graphics area. If the loft feature being created is the base/first feature than this option will not be available in the drop-down list.

Reverse Direction and Reverse Tangent Direction Buttons

The **Reverse Direction** and **Reverse Tangent Direction** buttons of the **Start/End Constraint** rollout are used to reverse the direction of applied constraints, see Figure 8.65. Note that the **Reverse Direction** button is available in the rollout when the **Direction Vector** or **Normal To Profile** option is selected. On the other hand, the **Reverse Tangent Direction** button available in the rollout when the **Direction Vector**, **Normal To Profile**, **Tangency To Face**, or **Curvature To Face** option is selected in the **start constraint** drop-down list.

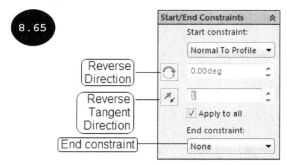

8.65

Apply to all

By default, the **Apply to all** check box is selected. As a result, in the preview of an loft feature, only one handle appears which is used to controls the constraints of the entire profile. However, if you clear this check box, multiple handles appears in the preview of the loft feature and allows you to control the constraints of the individual segments for the profile. Figure 8.66 show a preview of the loft feature with the **Apply to all** check box is selected and Figure 8.67 shows the preview when the **Apply to all** check box is cleared. Note that you can also modify the constraints of a loft feature by dragging the handles appears in the preview of an loft feature.

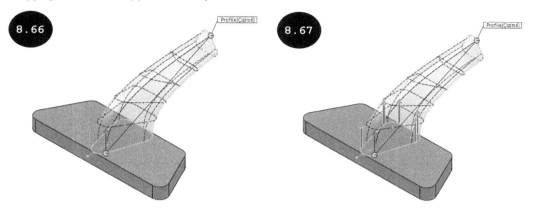

End constraint

The **End constraint** drop-down list is used to define the end constraint for the loft feature. The options available in this drop-down list are same as discussed earlier with the only difference these options are used to define the end constraint. Figure 8.68 shows a preview of loft feature with no start and end constraint defined whereas Figure 8.69 shows the preview with end constraint defined as normal to profile.

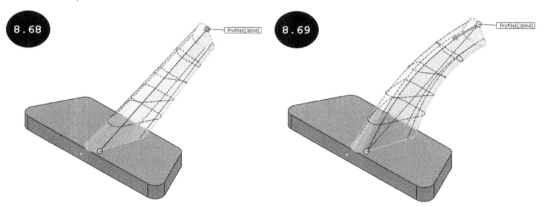

Guide Curves

In addition to controlling cross-sectional shape of loft feature by transiting one profiles to another, you can also control its shape by using guide curves. You can create multiple guide curves as an individual sketches for controlling the shape of an loft feature. The **Guide Curves** rollout of the PropertyManager allows you to select guide curves. Figure 8.70 shows two profiles and guide curves, and Figure 8.71 shows the resultant loft feature. Note that the guide curves must have pierce/coincident relation with the profiles of the feature.

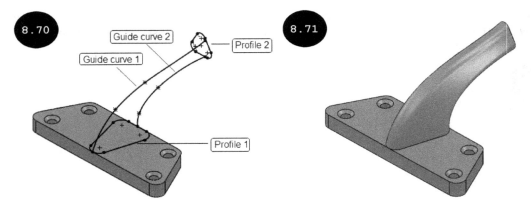

To select guide curves, activate the **Guide Curves** field of the **Guide Curves** rollout by clicking on it and then select the guide curves from the graphics area. As soon as you select the guide curve, the preview of the loft feature appears such that its cross-sectional shape is controlled by the selected guide curve. Also, the **Guide curves influence type** drop-down list appears in the **Guide Curves** rollout, see Figure 8.72. The options available in this drop-down list allow you to further control the influence of guide curves. These options are as follows.

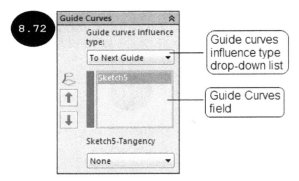

To Next Guide

The **To Next Guide** option of the **Guide curves influence type** drop-down list is used to extend the guide curve influence up to the next guide curve only. Figure 8.73 shows two profiles and a guide curve. Figure 8.74 shows the preview of the resultant loft feature when the **To Next Guide** option is selected.

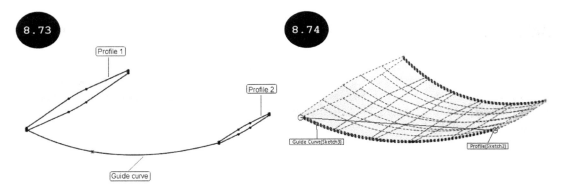

To Next Sharp

The **To Next Sharp** option is used to extend the guide curve influence up to the next sharp only. A sharp is a hard corner of the profile.

To Next Edge

The **To Next Sharp** option is used to extend the guide curve influence to the next edge only, see Figure 8.75.

Global

The **Global** option is used to extend the guide curve influence to the entire loft feature, see Figure 8.76.

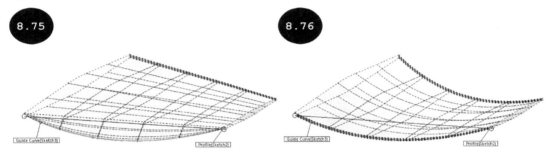

Centerline Parameters

The **Centerline Parameters** rollout of the PropertyManager allows you to select centerline for creating loft feature. The centerline is used to maintain the neutral axis of the loft feature being created. To select a centerline, expand the **Centerline Parameters** rollout (after selecting all the profiles) and then select the centerline from the graphics area, preview of the resultant loft feature appears in the graphics area. Note that in case of selecting centerline, intermediate sections of the resultant loft feature are normal to the centerline. Figure 8.77 shows different profiles and a centerline, and Figure 8.78 shows the preview of the resultant loft feature after selecting the centerline.

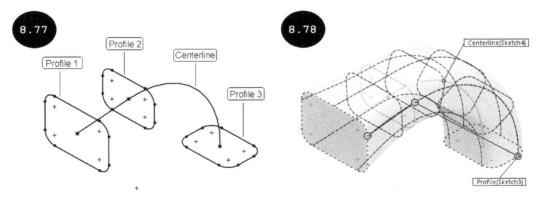

The **Show Sections** button of this rollout is used to show different sections in the graphics area. On activating this button, the display of different sections turned on. Also, the **Section Number** field is enabled. This field allow you to enter section number to be displayed in the graphics area.

Sketch Tools

The **Sketch Tools** rollout is used to edit the 3D sections/profiles of the loft feature. You can edit the 3D sketch sections/profiles of the loft feature by dragging their sketch entities in the graphics area by using the **Drag Sketch** button of this rollout. Note that the **Drag Sketch** button enabled only when you edit a loft feature. Also, the sections of the loft feature to be edited are drawn as a 3D sketch. You will learn more about drawing 3D sketches later in this chapter.

Options

The options available in the **Options** rollout of the PropertyManager are as follows.

Merge tangent faces

On selecting the **Merge tangent faces** check box, the tangent edges of the feature merges with each other. Figure 8.79 shows a loft feature with the **Merge tangent faces** check box is selected and Figure 8.80 shows the loft feature with the **Merge tangent faces** check box is cleared.

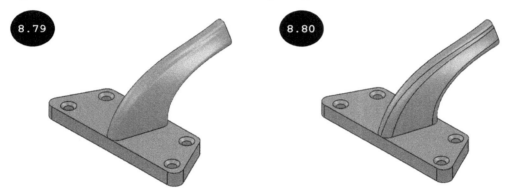

Close Loft

The **Close loft** check box is used to create a closed loft feature where start and end sections/profiles of the loft feature connects automatically with each other and form a closed loft feature. Figure 8.81 shows a preview of an open loft feature when the **Close loft** check box is cleared and Figure 8.82 shows the closed loft feature created by selecting the **Close loft** check box.

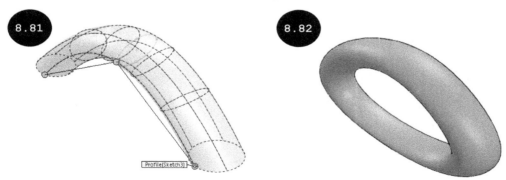

Note: To create close loft feature, minimum three sections are required. Also, the total measuring angle between the start and end sections should be more than 120 degree.

Show preview

The **Show preview** check box is used to show the preview of the loft feature being created in the graphics area. By default, this check box is selected. As a result, the preview of the loft feature appears in the graphics area.

Thin Feature

The **Thin Feature** rollout is used to create a thin lofted feature, see Figure 8.83. The options available in this rollout are same as discussed earlier.

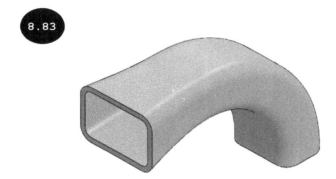

Procedure to Create Loft Feature using Profiles

1. Create all profiles of the loft feature as an individual sketches.
2. Click on the **Lofted Boss/Base** tool, the **Loft PropertyManager** appears.
3. Select all the profiles one by one from the graphics area, the preview of the loft feature with connectors appears in the graphics area.
4. Make sure that the connectors are in one direction to avoid twisting. To achieve twisting in the loft feature being created, you can change the position of the connectors by dragging them.
5. Click on the green tick mark ✅ of the PropertyManager, the loft feature is created.

Procedure to Create Loft Feature using Profiles and Guide Curves

1. Create all profiles and guide curves of the loft feature as an individual sketches.
2. Click on the **Lofted Boss/Base** tool, the **Loft PropertyManager** appears.
3. Select all the profiles one by one from the graphics area, the preview of the loft feature with connectors appears in the graphics area.
4. Make sure that the connectors are in one direction to avoid twisting. To achieve twisting in the loft feature being created, you can change the position of the connectors by dragging them.
5. Expand the **Guide Curves** rollout of the PropertyManager and then activate its **Guide Curves** field, if not activated.

6.   Select a guide curve from the graphics area, the preview of the feature modified such that its shape is controlled by the guide curve selected. You can also select two or more than two guide curves.
7.   Click on the green tick mark ✅ of the PropertyManager, the loft feature is created.

Procedure to Create Loft Feature with Centerline

1.   Create all profiles and a centerline of the loft feature to be created.
2.   Invoke the **Loft PropertyManager**.
3.   Select all the sections/profiles one by one from the graphics area.
4.   Expand the **Centerline Parameters** rollout and then select the centerline from the graphics area, the preview of the loft feature appears with respect to the centerline selected.
5.   Click on the green tick mark ✅ of the PropertyManager, the loft feature is created.

Creating Loft Cut Feature

Creating loft cut features are same as of creating loft features with the only difference   🟦 Lofted Cut
that the loft cut features are created by removing material. You can create loft cut features by using the **Lofted Cut** tool available in the **Features CommandManager**. Figure 8.84 shows profiles to be used for creating a loft cut feature, Figure 8.85 shows a preview of the resultant loft cut feature, and Figure 8.86 shows the resultant loft cut feature created.

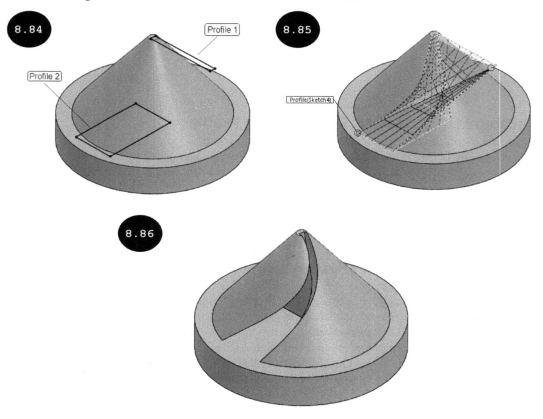

Creating Boundary features

The boundary features are high quality, complex shaped and accurate features. At some extend boundary features are same as of loft features having different sections. However, boundary features are used for maintaining high curvature continuity and for complex shape features. You can create boundary features by using the **Boundary Boss/Base** tool which is one of the powerful tool in the Part modeling environment. To create boundary feature, you need to create all its sections as direction 1 guides and curves as direction 2 guides. Figure 8.87 shows sections (direction 1 guides) and curves (direction 2 guides). Figure 8.88 shows the resultant boundary features.

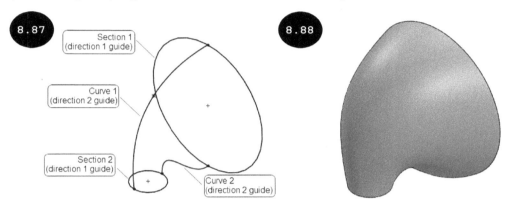

Also see Figures 8.89 and 8.90. Figure 8.89 shows one section as direction 1 guide and three curves as direction 2 guides.

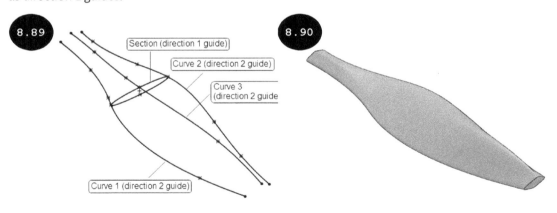

To create boundary feature, after creating its sections and curves as directions 1 and 2 guides, click on the **Boundary Boss/Base** tool of the **Features CommandManager**, the **Boundary PropertyManager** appears, see Figure 8.91. The options available in this propertyManager are as follows.

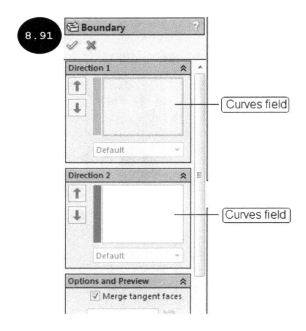

Direction 1

The **Curves** field of the **Direction 1** rollout is used to select sections created as direction 1 guides. By default, this field is activated. As a result, you are prompted to select sections/profiles. Select the sections from the graphics area one by one, the preview of the boundary feature appears in the graphics area, see Figures 8.92 and 8.93. Also, the **Tangent Type** drop-down list and the **Draft angle** field enabled in the **Direction 1** rollout. You can select multiple sections as well as single section as direction one guides/guide. The options available in this drop-down list and field are same as explained earlier while creating loft feature.

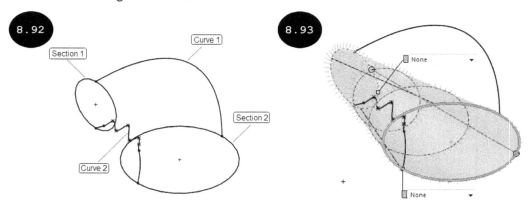

Tip: You can drag the position of connectors connecting the sections with each other, as required.

Direction 2

The **Curves** field of the **Direction 2** rollout is used to select curves as direction 2 guides. By default this selection field is not activated. Click on this field to activate it and then select curves from the graphics area. As soon as you select the curves, the preview of the boundary feature modified with respect to the curves selected, see Figure 8.94. You can select multiple curves to control the shape of the boundary feature in 2 direction. You can specify the type of tangent continuity by using the options available in the **Tangent Type** drop-down list. Also, control the influence of curves by using the options available in the **Guide curves influence** type drop-down list of this rollout.

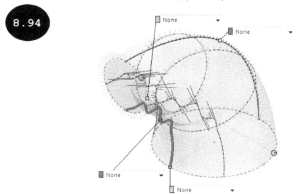

8.94

Tip: You can also flip the connectors connecting each other (sections and curves) in order to achieve the required shape. To flip the direction of connectors, select the curve/section whose connector connection is to be flip from the **Curves** field of the **Direction 1/Direction 2** rollout and then right click, a shortcut menu appears, select the **Flip Connectors** option.

Options and Preview

All the options of the **Options and Preview** rollout are same as explained earlier while creating loft feature except the **Trim by direction 1** check box and is discussed next.

Trim by direction 1

The **Trim by direction 1** check box is used to trim the extended portion of the feature beyond the direction 1 guides (sections). By default, this check box is cleared. To trim the extended portion of the feature by direction 1 curves, select this check box. Figure 8.95 shows sections (direction 1 guides) and a curve (direction 2 guide). Figure 8.96 shows the preview of the resultant boundary feature when the **Trim by direction 1** check box is cleared and Figure 8.97 shows the preview of the resultant feature when the **Trim by direction 1** check box is selected.

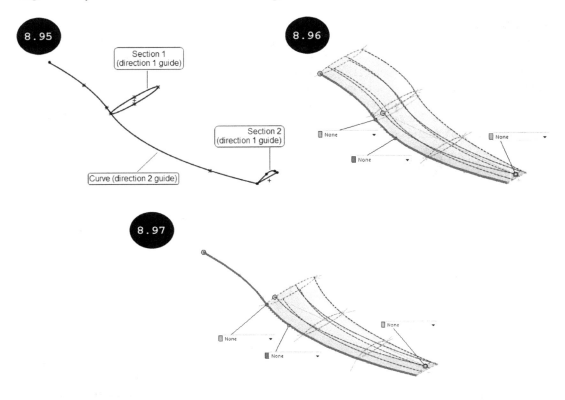

Thin Feature

The **Thin Feature** rollout is used to create a thin boundary feature, see Figure 8.98. The options available in this rollout are same as explained earlier.

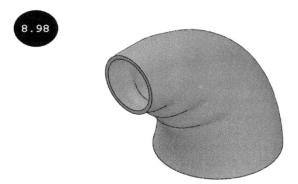

Display

The options available in the **Display** rollout are used to control the display style of the preview appears in the graphics area. These options are as follows.

Mesh preview

The **Mesh preview** check box is used to display the mesh preview in the graphics area. By default, this check box is selected. As a result, the preview of the boundary feature appears with mesh in the graphics area. You can control the number of lines in the mesh by increasing or decreasing the mesh density. To control the mesh density, you can use the **Mesh density** slider available below this check box.

Zebra stripes

The **Zebra stripes** check box is used to turn on the appearance of zebra stripes in the preview of boundary features. Select this check box to turn on the display of zebra stripes, see Figure 8.99. The zebra strips allows you to easy visible the small changes made in the feature that are hard to see with standard display style.

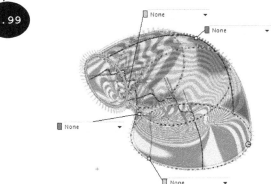

8.99

Curvature combs

The **Curvature combs** check box is used to turn on the appearance of curvature combs in the preview of boundary features. By default, this check box is selected. As a result, the preview of the feature appears with the curvature combs in the graphics area, see Figure 8.99. You can further control the scale and density of the displayed curvature combs by using the **Scale** thumbwheel and **Density** slider of the rollout, respectively.

Procedure to create boundary Feature

1. Create profiles/sections and curves for the boundary feature as an individual sketches.
2. Click on the **Boundary Boss/Base** tool, the **Boundary PropertyManager** appears.
3. Select all the profiles/sections one by one from the graphics area as the direction 1 guide.
4. Activate the **Curves** field of the **Direction 2** rollout and then select the curves, as direction 2 guides.
5. Click on the green tick mark ✅ of the PropertyManager, the boundary feature is created.

Creating Boundary Cut Feature

Creating boundary cut features are same as of creating boundary features with the 🗐 Boundary Cut only difference that the boundary cut features are created by removing material.
You can create boundary cut features by using the **Boundary Cut** tool available in the **Features CommandManager**.

Creating Curve Feature

In SOLIDWORKS, you can create different types of curves. These curves mainly used as path guide curves, and so on for creating sweep, loft, and boundary features. The tools for creating different type of curves are group together in **Curve** flyout, see Figure 8.100. Below are the methods for creating different types of curves.

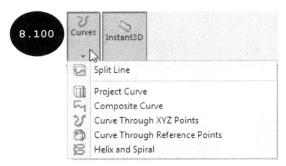

8.100

Creating Projected Curves

In SOLIDWORKS, you can create projected curves by using two methods: sketch on faces and sketch on sketch methods. In sketch on faces method, the projected curve is created by projecting a sketch on to an existing face of the model, see Figure 8.101. You can select any planar or curved face for projecting the sketch entities. In the sketch on sketch method, the projected curve is created by projecting one sketch on to another such that the resultant projected curve represents the intersection of sketches, see Figure 8.102.

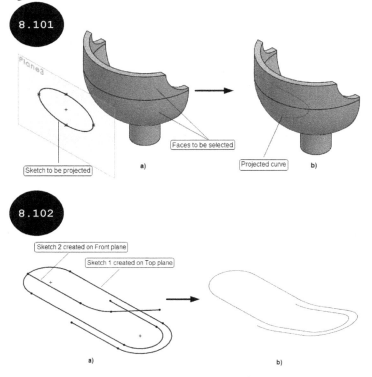

8.101

Sketch to be projected   Faces to be selected   a)   Projected curve   b)

8.102

Sketch 2 created on Front plane
Sketch 1 created on Top plane

a)   b)

To create projected curves, invoke the **Curve** flyout by clicking on the down arrow available in the **Curves** tool of the **Features CommandManager**, see Figure 8.100. Next, click on the **Project Curve** tool, the **Projected Curve PropertyManager** appears, see Figure 8.103. The options available in this PropertyManager are as follows.

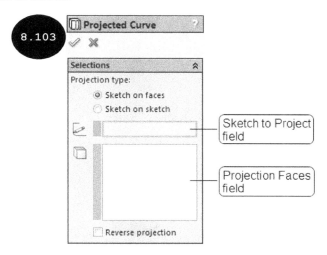

8.103

Selections
The options available in the **Selections** rollout of the PropertyManager allows you to select the projection method. Also, allows you to select reference objects to create projected curve depending upon the method of projection selected. These options are as follows.

Sketch on faces
The **Sketch on faces** radio button is used to create projected curves by projecting a sketch on to an existing face of the model. When this radio button is selected, the **Sketch to Project** and the **Projection Faces** fields appears in the rollout, see Figure 8.103. By default, the **Sketch to Project** field is activated. As a result, you can select a sketch to be projected from the graphics area. Select a sketch to be projected, see Figure 8.104. As soon as you select the sketch to be projected, the name of the sketch selected appears in the **Sketch to Project** field. Also, the **Projection Faces** field become activated, automatically. As a result, you are prompted to select projection faces. Select projection face or faces, see Figure 8.104. As soon as you select the projection faces, the preview of the projected curved appears in the graphics area, see Figure 8.105. Make sure that the direction of projection is towards the faces selected. You can reverse the direction of projection by using the **Reverse projection** check box. Once you are done, click on the green tick mark ✅ of the PropertyManager, the projected curve is created.

Sketch on sketch
The **Sketch on sketch** radio button is used to project one sketch on to another such that resultant projected curve represents the intersection of sketches. When this radio button is selected, the **Sketches to Project** field appears in the rollout. By default, this field is activated. As a result, you can select sketches to be projected. Select sketches to be projected from the graphics area, see Figure 106. As soon as you select sketches, the preview of the projected

curved appears in the graphics area. Once you are done, click on the green tick mark ✅ of the PropertyManager, the projected curve is created, , see Figure 8.107.

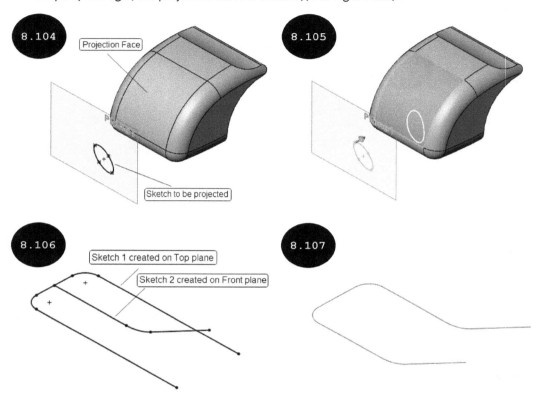

Procedure to Create Projected Curves using Sketch on faces Method

1. Invoke the **Curves** flyout and then click on the **Project Curve** tool, the **Projected Curve PropertyManager** appears.
2. Select the **Sketch on faces** radio button.
3. Select the sketch to be projected from the graphics area..
4. Select a face or faces of the model from the graphics area as projection faces.
5. Select the **Reverse projection** check box to reverse the direction of projection, if needed. Note that the direction of projection should be towards the selected projection faces.
6. Click on the green tick mark ✅ of the PropertyManager, the projected curve is created.

Procedure to Create Projected Curves using Sketch on sketch Method

1. Invoke the **Curves** flyout and then click on the **Project Curve** tool, the **Projected Curve PropertyManager** appears.
2. Select the **Sketch on sketch** radio button.
3. Select sketches to be projected from the graphics area one by one, a preview appears.
4. Click on the green tick mark ✅ of the PropertyManager, the projected curve is created.

Creating Helical and Spiral Curves

You can create helical and spiral curves by using the **Helix and Spiral** tool of the **Curves** flyout. As explained earlier, you can use curves as a path for creating a swept feature, as a guide curve for creating a lofted feature, and so on. Figure 8.108 shows a helical curve and a profile, and the resultant sweep feature created by using them. Figure 8.109 shows a spiral curve and a profile, and the resultant sweep feature created by using them. In SOLIDWORKS, to create a helical or spiral curves, you first need to create a circle whose diameter defines the starting diameter of the helical and spiral curve.

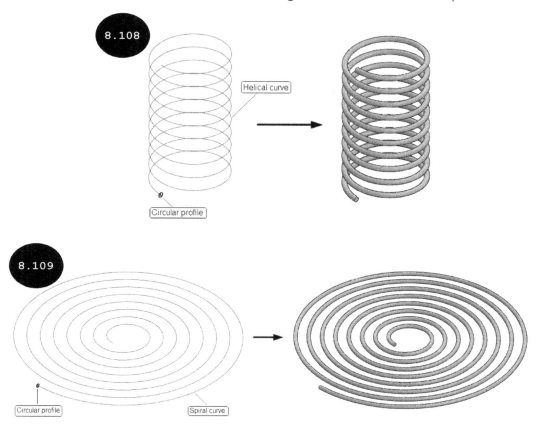

After creating a circle sketch for defining the starting diameter of the helical/spiral curve, invoke the **Curves** flyout and then click on the **Helix and Spiral** tool, the **Helix/Spiral PropertyManager** appears, see Figure 8.110. Also, you are prompted to select a sketching plane for creating a circle, if not created already or select a circle from the graphics area, if you have already created. Select the circle from the graphics area, the **Helix/Spiral PropertyManager** modified, see Figure 8.111. Also, a preview of curve appears in the graphics area depending upon the default parameters specified in the PropertyManager.

Note: You can also select circle sketch before invoking the **Helix and Spiral** tool. If you select circle sketch before invoking the tool, the modified **Helix/Spiral PropertyManager** appears directly. Also, a preview of curve appears in the graphics area.

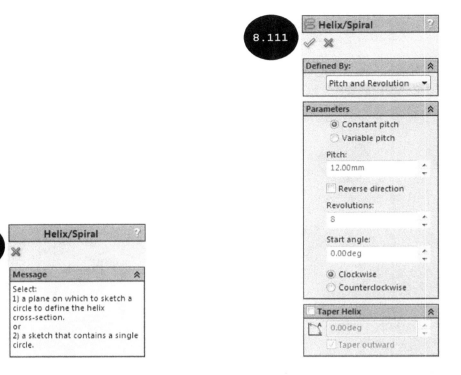

By using the options available in the **Helix/Spiral PropertyManager**, you can create constant pitch helical curves, variable pitch helical curves, and spiral curves. All these options are as follows.

Defined By

The **Defined By** rollout is used to define the type of curve (helical or spiral) to be created and the method of creating it. The options of this rollout are available in a drop-down list, see Figure 8.112. All these options are as follows.

Pitch and Revolution

On selecting the **Pitch and Revolution** option, you can create an helical curve by defining its pitch and number of revolutions. Note that when this option is selected, the options to create helical curve by defining its pitch and revolutions become available in the **Parameters** rollout of the PropertyManager, see Figure 8.111.

Height and Revolution

On selecting the **Height and Revolution** option, you can create an helical curve by defining its total height and number of revolutions. Note that when this option is selected, the options to create helical curve by defining its height and revolutions become available in the **Parameters** rollout of the PropertyManager.

Height and Pitch

On selecting the **Height and Pitch** option, you can create an helical curves by defining its total height and pitch. Note that when this option is selected, the options to create helical curve by defining its height and pitch become available in the **Parameters** rollout.

Spiral

On selecting the **Spiral** option, you can create a spiral curve by defining its pitch and number of revolutions. Note that when this option is selected, the options to create spiral curve by defining its pitch and revolutions become available in the **Parameters** rollout.

Parameters

The **Parameters** rollout is used to specify the parameters for creating the curve. Most of the options available in this rollout are depends upon the option selected in the **Defined By** rollout. The options of this rollout are as follows.

Constant pitch

The **Constant pitch** radio button of the **Parameters** rollout is used to create helical curve with constant pitch through out the helix height, see Figure 8.113.

Pitch/Revolutions/Height/Start angle

The **Pitch**, **Revolutions**, **Height**, and **Start angle** fields are used to specify pitch, revolutions, height, and start angle, respectively for the curve being created.

Reverse direction

The **Reverse direction** check box is used to reverse the direction of curve creation.

Clockwise/Counterclockwise

The **Clockwise** and **Counterclockwise** radio buttons are used to specify the direction of revolution to clockwise or counterclockwise, respectively.

Variable pitch

The **Variable pitch** radio button is used to create helical curve with variable pitch, see Figure 8.114. On selecting this radio button, the **Region parameters** table appears in the rollout which allow you to enter variable pitch for the helical curve being created as well as the variable diameter of the curve in their respective fields of the table, see Figure 8.115.

8.113

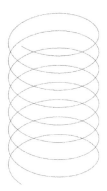

8.114

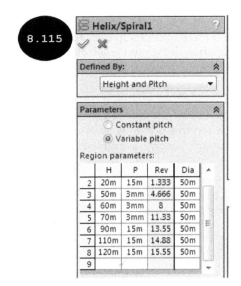

8.115

Note: In the **Region parameters** table which is shown in the above figure, you can specify variable pitch at different height as well as variable diameter at different height. Figure 8.116 shows a variable pitch and diameter helical curve created. This is because the **Height and Pitch** option is selected in the **Defined By** rollout. If you create variable pitch curve on selecting the **Height and Revolution** option then the **Region parameters** table allow you to specify revolutions and variable diameter at different height. In this case, the variable pitch of the curve is automatically calculated based on the number of revolutions at different height.

To enter a value in a field of this table, double click on the respective field of this table

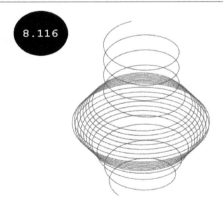

8.116

Taper Helix

The **Taper Helix** rollout is used to create tapered helical curves, see Figure 8.117. By default, the options of this rollout are not activated. Select the check box available in the title bar of this rollout to activate its options, see Figure 8.118. By using the **Taper Angle** field of this rollout, you can specify the taper angle for the helical curve being created. Note that if the **Taper outward** check box is cleared in this rollout, the helical curve being created tapered inwards to the sketch. If you select this check box, helical curve being created tapers outwards to the sketch.

8.117

8.118

Procedure to Create Constant Pitch Helical Curve

1. Create a circle whose diameter defines the diameter of the helical curve.
2. Select the created circle from the graphics area.
3. Invoke the **Curves** flyout and then click on the **Helix and Spiral** tool, the **Helix/Spiral PropertyManager** appears. Also, the preview of the curve appears in the graphics area.
4. Select a required option (**Pitch and Revolution, Height and Revolution,** or **Height and Pitch**) for creating helical curve from the drop-down list of the **Defined B**y rollout.
5. Make sure that the **Constant pitch** radio button is selected in the **Parameters** rollout.
6. Specify the parameters such as pitch, revolutions, and so on of the helical curve being created in their respective fields of the **Parameters** rollout.
7. Click on the green tick mark of the PropertyManager, the helical curve is created.

Procedure to Create Variable Pitch Helical Curve

1. Create a circle whose diameter defines the starting diameter of the variable helical curve.
2. Select the created circle from the graphics area.
3. Invoke the **Helix/Spiral PropertyManager**.
4. Select a required option (**Pitch and Revolution, Height and Revolution,** or **Height and Pitch**) for creating helical curve from the drop-down list of the **Defined B**y rollout.
5. Select the **Variable pitch** radio button from the **Parameters** rollout.
6. Specify the variable parameters such as pitch, revolution, and diameter in the fields of the **Region parameters** table of the **Parameters** rollout. You can double click on the fields of this table to enter values. Note that the edit able fields available in this table depends upon the option selected in the **Defined By** rollout.
7. Click on the green tick mark of the PropertyManager, the variable helical curve is created.

Procedure to Create Taper Helical Curve

1. Create a circle whose diameter defines the diameter of the helical curve and then select it.
2. Invoke the **Helix/Spiral PropertyManager**.
3. Select a required option (**Pitch and Revolution, Height and Revolution,** or **Height and Pitch**) for creating helical curve from the drop-down list of the **Defined By** rollout.
4. Select the **Constant pitch** radio button of the **Parameters** rollout.
5. Specify the parameters such as pitch, revolutions, and so on of the helical curve being created in their respective fields of the **Parameters** rollout.
6. Expand the **Taper Helix** rollout by selecting the check box available on its title bar.
7. Enter the taper angle in the **Taper Angle** field of the **Taper Helix** rollout.
8. Select or clear the **Taper outward** check box of the **Taper Helix** rollout, as required.
9. Click on the green tick mark ✅ of the PropertyManager, the helical curve is created.

Procedure to Create Spiral Curve

1. Create a circle whose diameter defines the starting diameter of the spiral curve.
2. Select the created circle from the graphics area.
3. Invoke the **Helix/Spiral PropertyManager**.
4. Select the Spiral option from the drop-down list of the **Defined By** rollout.
5. Specify the parameters such as pitch and revolutions in their respective fields of the **Parameters** rollout.
6. Click on the green tick mark ✅ of the PropertyManager, the spiral curve is created.

Creating Curves by Specifying XYZ Points

You can create curves by specifying coordinates of the curve points. You can define multiple points by specifying their coordinates in order to create a desired shape curves. To create curves by using this method, invoke the **Curves** flyout and then click on the **Curve Through XYZ Points** tool, the **Curve File** dialog box appears, see Figure 8.119.

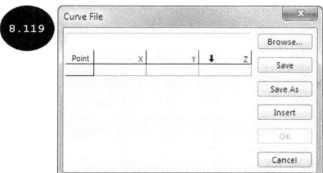

In the **Curve File** dialog box, you can specify coordinates of multiple points for creating a curve. In addition to specifying coordinate points in this dialog box, you can also import *.sldcrv* or *.txt* (notepad) files containing the coordinate points of a curve.

To specify the coordinates points in the dialog box, double click on the field corresponding to first row and **X** column to activate it. Once this field is activated, you can enter the X coordinate for point 1. Similarly, you can activate the Y and Z fields and enter Y and Z coordinates of point 1. Note that by default only one row is available in this dialog box. However, the moment you activate a field of first row, the second/next row added automatically in the dialog box. Specify the coordinates of point 2 in the second row. In this way, you can specify coordinates of other points. Note that as you specifying the coordinate points in the dialog box, the preview of the curve appears in the graphics area. Figure 8.120 shows the **Curve File** dialog box with multiple coordinate points specified and Figure 8.121 shows a preview of the resultant curve.

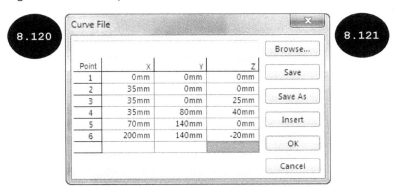

You can also save all the coordinate points specified in the dialog box as an *.sldcrv* file into your local drive. To save the coordinate points as *.sldcrv* file, click on the **Save** button of the dialog box, the **Save As** dialog box appears. Using this dialog box, browse to the location where you want to save the file and then specify the name of the file in the **File name** edit box. Next, click on the **Save** button, the file is save as *.sldcrv* file. Once you are done with specifying coordinate points in this dialog box, click on the **OK** button, the curve is created.

If you have *.sldcrv* or *.txt* (notepad) files containing the coordinate points information for creating a curve, click on the **Browse** button of the dialog box, the **Open** dialog box appears. Browse to the location where the *.sldcrv* or *.txt* (notepad) files is saved. Note that by default, the **Curves (*.sldcrv)** options is selected in the **File Type** drop-down list of the dialog box. As a result, you can only import *.sldcrv* file. To import a *.txt* (notepad) file, you need to select the **Text Files (*.txt)** option from this drop-down list. After selecting the required file type to be opened, select the file and click the **Open** button, the coordinates of all the points available in the selected file are filled in the dialog box. Also, the preview of the curve appears in the graphics area.

Tip: In *.txt* (notepad) file, the coordinates of all the points should be written in separate line. Also, the coordinates of a point should be separated by a comma and a space like X, Y, Z.

Procedure to Create Curve by Specifying XYZ Points

1. Invoke the **Curves** flyout.
2. Click on the **Curve Through XYZ Points** tool, the **Curve File** dialog box appears.
3. Specify coordinates of multiple points for creating curve in the dialog box.
4. Once you are done with specifying coordinates (X, Y, Z) of all the points, click on the **OK** button, the curve is created in the graphics area.

Procedure to Create Curves by Importing XYZ Points

1. Invoke the **Curves** flyout.
2. Click on the **Curve Through XYZ Points** tool, the **Curve File** dialog box appears.
3. Click on the **Browse** button, the **Open** dialog box appears.
4. Select the required file type either **Curves (*.sldcrv)** or **Text Files (*.txt)** from the **File Type** drop-down list.
5. Select the file to be imported and then click on the **Open** button, all coordinate points available in the selected file are filled in the **Curve File** dialog box and preview of the respective curve appears in the graphics area.
6. Click on the **OK** button, the curve is created in the graphics area.

Creating Curves by Selecting Reference Points

In SOLIDWORKS, you can also create 3D curve by selecting reference points from the graphics area. These reference points can be located on one or more than one planes. You can also select existing vertices of the model, and sketch points as the reference points. To create curves by selecting reference points, invoke the **Curves** flyout and then click on the **Curve Through Reference Points** tool, the **Curve Through Reference Points PropertyManager** appears, see Figure 8.122. Select the points or vertices from the graphics area, the preview of the respective curve appears, see Figure 8.123. Also, the name of the selected points/vertices listed in the **Thought Points** field of the PropertyManager.

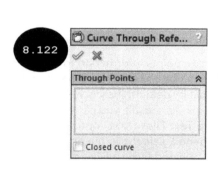

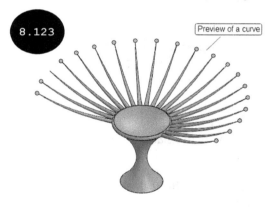

Note: On selecting the **Closed curve** check box of the PropertyManager, a closed curve is created by connecting the start and end specified point.

Procedure to Create Curve by Selecting Reference Points

1. Click on the **Curve Through XYZ Points** tool of the **Curves** flyout.
2. Select reference points (points and vertices) one by one from the graphics area.
3. Click on the green tick mark of the PropertyManager, the curve is created.

Creating Composite Curve

The composite curve is a curve which is created by joining two or more than two curves together. You can join curves together and form a composite curve by using the **Composite curve** tool of the **Curves** flyout.

After creating all the curves to be joined together, click on the **Composite curve** tool of the **Curves** flyout, the Composite Curve PropertyManager appears, see Figure 8.124. Next, select curves from the graphics area one by one and then click on the green tick mark ✓ of the PropertyManager, the composite curve is created. Figure 8.125 shows multiple curves created and Figure 8.126 shows resultant composite curve created. Figure 8.127 shows a sweep feature created by sweeping a profile (circle) along the composite curve shown in Figure 8.126 as a path.

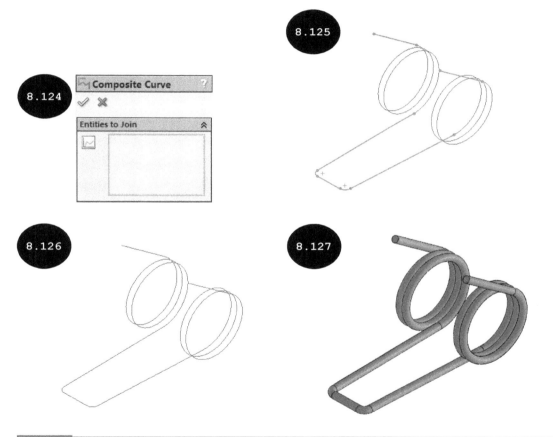

Note: The curves to be joint must be end to end connected with each other and should have Pierce relation with each other.

Tip: You can select sketch entities, curves, edges, and so on as the curves to be joint for creating composite curves.

Procedure to Create Composite Curve
1.   Invoke the **Curves** flyout.
2.   Click on the **Composite Curve** tool, the **Composite Curve PropertyManager** appears.
3.   Select the curves from the graphics area to be joint one by one.
4.   Click on the green tick mark ✓ of the PropertyManager, the composite curve is created.

Splitting Faces of a Model

You can split faces of a model by creating split lines. In SOLIDWORKS, you can create split lines by using the **Split Line** tool of the **Curve** flyout. To create split lines, click on the **Split Line** tool of the **Curves** flyout, the **Split Line PropertyManager** appears, see Figure 8.128. The options available in this PropertyManager are as follows.

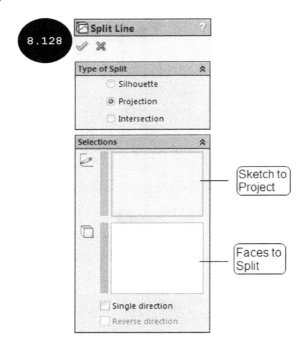

Type of Split
The options available in the **Type of Split** rollout are used to select the type of splitting to be used. These options are as follows.

Projection
The **Projection** radio button is used to create split line by projecting a sketch on to a face of the model. Figure 8.129 shows the sketch to be projected and Figure 8.130 shows the split line created on to a face. Note that the split lines divides the selected face of the model into multiple faces with respect to the projected sketch. After splitting a face into multiple faces, you can then apply different texture or appearance to each split face.

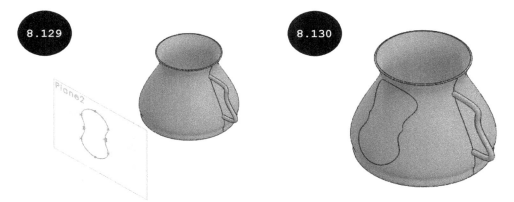

When the **Projection** radio button is selected, the **Sketch to Project** and **Faces to Split** fields are available in the **Selections** rollout of the PropertyManager, see Figure 8.128. By default, the **Sketch to Project** field is activated. As a result, you can select sketch to be projected from the graphics area. Select the sketch to be projected, the **Faces to Split** field become activated automatically in the PropertyManager. Now, select faces to split. You can select curved or planar faces as the faces to be split. To project the split line in one direction only, select the **Single direction** check box and to reverse the direction of projection, select the **Reverse direction** check box of the PropertyManager. Next, click on the green tick mark ✅ of the PropertyManager, the selected face is split, see Figure 8.130.

Intersection

The **Intersection** radio button is used to create split line at the intersection of two objects. The objects can be solid bodies, surfaces, faces of a model, or planes. Figure 8.131 shows an object and a plane. Figure 8.132 shows the split line created at the intersection of the object and the plane shown in Figure 8.131.

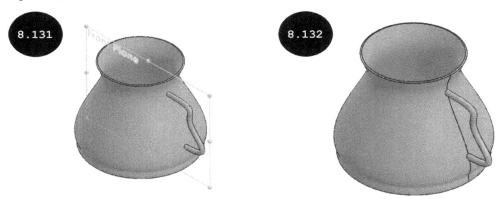

When the **Intersection** radio button is selected, the **Splitting Bodies/Faces/Planes** and **Faces/Bodies to Split** files area available in the **Selections** rollout of the PropertyManager. By default, the **Splitting Bodies/Faces/Planes** field is activated. As a result, you can select bodies, faces, or planes from the graphics area as the splitting object. Select the splitting object. As soon as you specify the splitting object, the **Faces/Bodies to Split** field become activated automatically in the PropertyManager. Now, you can select faces or bodies to split. As soon as you select faces or bodies, the preview of split lines appears in the graphics area. Figure 8.133 shows objects and Figure 8.134 shows the preview of split lines. Next, click on the green tick mark ✅ of the PropertyManager. Figure 8.135 shows the object with split lines are created and the visibility of object 1 is turn off.

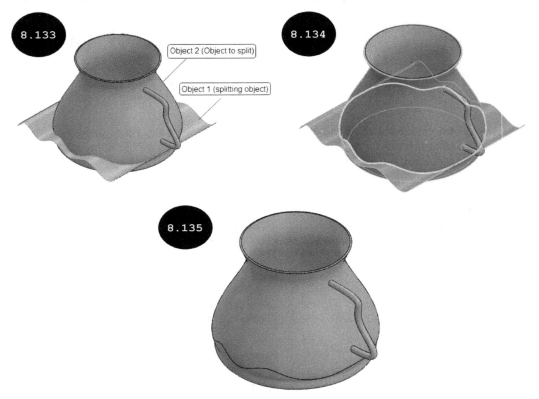

8.133

Object 2 (Object to split)

Object 1 (splitting object)

8.134

8.135

Note: The object 1 (splitting object) shown in Figure 8.133 is a extruded surface. The extruded surface is created by using the **Extruded Surface** tool of the **Surfaces CommandManager**. The options to created extruded surface are same as of creating extruded solid with the only difference that extruded surface is a surface model having zero thickness.

In Figure 8.135, the visibility of object 1 is turn off. To hide (turn off the visibility) of an object, select it from the **FeatureManager Design Tree**, a Pop up toolbar appears. Select the **Hide** tool from the Pop-up toolbar to hide the selected object.

Silhouette

The **Silhouette** radio button is used to create split line at the intersection of the direction of projection and the curved face. Figure 8.136 shows the direction of projection and the curved face to be split. Figure 8.137 shows the split line created at the intersection of the direction of projection and the curved face selected.

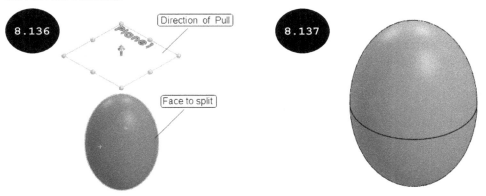

When the **Silhouette** radio button is selected, the **Direction of Pull** and **Faces to Split** fields are available in the **Selections** rollout of the PropertyManager. By default, the **Direction of Pull** field is activated. As a result, you can select a plane or planar face from the graphics area as the direction of projection. Select a plane or planar face, see Figure 8.136, the **Faces to Split** field become activated. Now, you can select the curved faces to split. Note that in case of creating silhouette split line, you can only select curved faces as the faces to split. After selecting the curve faces to be split, you can specify the draft angle in the **Angle** field of the PropertyManager. Next, click on the green tick mark ✅ of the PropertyManager, the split line is created. Figure 8.137 shows the split line created when the draft angle is set to 0 degree in the **Angle** field. Figure 8.138 shows the split line created when the draft angle is set to 40 degree.

Procedure to Split faces by using Projection Method

1.   Invoke the **Curves** flyout.
2.   Click on the **Split Line** tool, the **Split Line PropertyManager** appears.
3.   Make sure that the **Projection** radio button is selected in the **Type of Split** rollout.
4.   Select a sketch to be projected and then select faces to split from the graphics area.
5.   Click on the green tick mark ✅ of the PropertyManager, the selected faces are split.

Procedure to Split faces by using Intersection Method

1.   Invoke the **Curves** flyout.
2.   Click on the **Split Line** tool, the **Split Line PropertyManager** appears.
3.   Make sure that the **Intersection** radio button is selected in the **Type of Split** rollout.
4.   Select a splitting object (object 1) from the graphics area.
5.   Select object or faces to be split of an object (object 2) from the graphics area.
6.   Click on the green tick mark ✅ of the PropertyManager, the selected faces of the object 2 are split.

Procedure to create silhouette split lines

1.   Invoke the **Split Line PropertyManager**.
2.   Select the **Silhouette** radio button from the **Type of Split** rollout.
3.   Select a plane or planar face as the direction of projection.
4.   Select faces of the object to be split from the graphics area.
5.   Set the draft angle in the **Angle** field of the PropertyManager as required.
6.   Click on the green tick mark ✅ of the PropertyManager, the selected faces are split.

Creating 3D Sketches

In addition to creating 2D sketches and 3D curves, in SOLIDWORKS, you can create 3D sketches on to working planes or by specifying arbitrary points in 3D sketching environment. Most of the time, the 3D sketches are used for creating 3D path and guide curve for the sweep, loft, and boundary features. To create 3D sketches, you need to invoke the 3D sketching environment of SOLIDWORKS.

To invoke the 3D sketching environment, click on the down arrow available below the **Sketch** tool of the **Sketch CommandManager**, a flyout appears, see Figure 8.139. Next, click on the **3D Sketch** tool from this flyout, the 3D sketching environment is invoked, see Figure 8.140. Now, you can create 3D sketches by using the tools available in the **Sketch CommandManager**. Note that in 3D sketching environment, only the tools used for creating lines, arcs, circles, rectangles, points, and splines are activated. Its means that 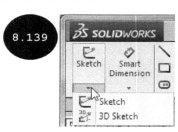 you can create 3D sketches only by using these tools. In addition to these tools, you can also use the **Convert Entities** and **Intersection Curve** tools to create 3D sketches. The procedure to work with some of the tools of 3D sketching environment are as follows.

Procedure to Work with Line tool in 3D Sketching Environment

1. Click on the **Sketch** tab of the **CommandManager** to invoke the **Sketch CommandManager**.

2. Click on the down arrow available below the **Sketch** tool of the **Sketch CommandManager**, a flyout appears, see Figure 8.139. Next, click on the **3D Sketch** tool, the 3D sketching environment is invoked, see Figure 8.140.

3. Click on the **Line** tool of the **Sketch CommandManager**, the cursor changes to pencil cursor with **XY** appears at its bottom side, see Figure 8.141. The display of XY indicate that the XY (Front) plane is the current sketching plane. You can press the **TAB** key to activate any other sketching plane to create 3D sketch.

4. Press the **TAB** key until the required sketching plane is activated.

5. Specify the start point of the line by clicking the left mouse button in the graphics area.

6. Move the cursor to a distance from the start point, a rubber band line appears whose one end is fixed with the specified start point and the other end is attached with the cursor, see Figure 8.142.

> **Tip:** You can also toggle the sketching plane even after specifying the start point of the line by using the **TAB** key.

7. Move the cursor to the required location and click to specify the end point of the line when the length of the line appears above the cursor closer to the required one. Next, move the cursor to a distance, the preview of another rubber band line appears, see Figure 8.143.

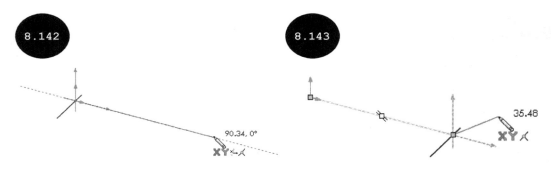

8. Toggle the sketching plane, if required, by pressing the **TAB** key. Next, move the cursor to the required location and specify the end point of the line, see Figure 8.144.

Tip: In Figure 8.144, the sketching plane XY is changed to YZ.

9. Similarly, continue creating all the sketch entities of a 3D sketch in different planes, see Figure 8.145.

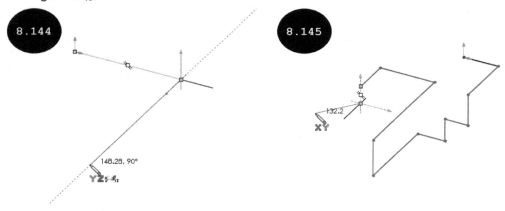

10. After creating all the sketch entities of a 3D sketch, right click in the graphics area and select the **Select** option from the shortcut menu to exit from the **Line** tool.
11. Exit from the 3D sketching environment.

   Figure 8.146 shows a 3D Sketch created and Figure 8.147 shows a sweep feature created by sweeping a profile along the 3D sketch created as the path.

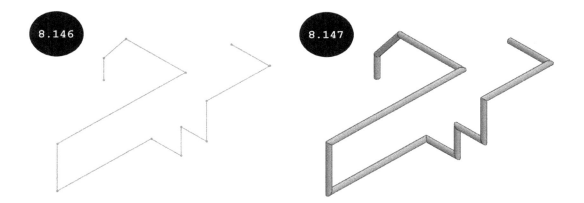

Procedure to Work with Spline tool in 3D Sketching Environment

1. Invoke the 3D sketching environment by clicking on the **3D Sketch** tool, see Figure 8.139.
2. Change the current orientation to isometric.
3. Click on the **Spline** tool of the **Sketch CommandManager**, the cursor changes to spline cursor and displays the name of the default active sketching plane at its bottom, see Figure 8.148.

4. Press the **TAB** key until the required sketching plane is activated and its name appears below the cursor.
5. Specify the start point of the spline by clicking on the left mouse button in the graphics area. Next, move the cursor to a distance from the start point, a rubber band spline appears whose one end is fixed with the specified start point and the other end is attached with the cursor, see Figure 8.149.
6. Toggle the sketching plane, if required, by pressing the **TAB** key. Next, move the cursor to the required location and specify the second point of the spline, see Figure 8.150. Next, move a cursor to a small distance, a preview of another rubber band spline appears, see Figure 8.150.

Tip: In Figure 8.150, the sketching plane XY is changed to YZ.

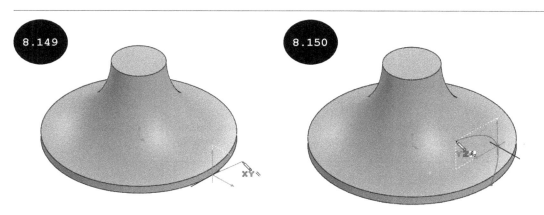

7. Toggle the sketching plane, as required, by pressing the **TAB** key. Next, move the cursor to the required location, see Figure 8.151 and then and specify the second point of the spline.

Tip: In Figure 8.150, the sketching plane YZ is changed to ZX.

8. Similarly, continue specifying the points of the spline in different planes. Once you are done with specifying all the points of the spline, press the **ESC** key to exit from the **Spline** tool. Figure 8.152 shows a spline created by specifying points on different planes in the graphics area.

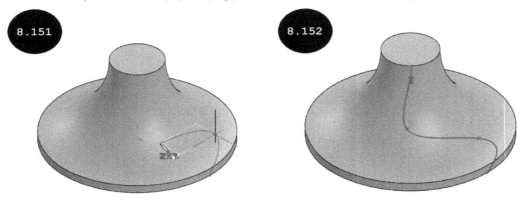

8.151   8.152

Tip: After creating 3D spline, you can further control the shape of the spline created by dragging its control points. Figure 8.153 shows a modified 3D spline and Figure 8.154 shows a sweep feature created by sweeping a rectangular profile along the 3d spline as the path.

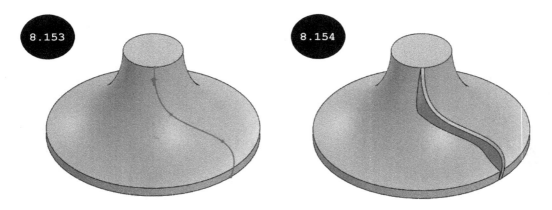

8.153   8.154

The procedure to work with rectangle, arc, circle, point, and centerline tools in the 3D sketching environment are same as discussed earlier while creating 2D sketches.

Tutorial 1

Create the model shown in Figure 8.155. Different views and dimensions are given in the same figure

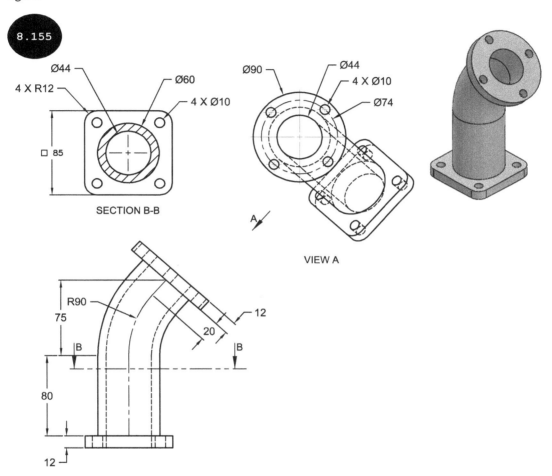

8.155

SECTION B-B

VIEW A

Section 1: Starting SOLIDWORKS

1. Double click on the **SOLIDWORKS** icon on your desktop to start SOLIDWORKS.

Section 2: Invoking Part Modeling Environment

1. Click on the **New** tool in the **Standard** toolbar, the **New SOLIDWORKS Document** dialog box appears.

2. In this dialog box, the **Part** button is activated by default. Click on the **OK** button.

    Once the Part modeling environment is invoked, you can set the unit system and create the base/first feature of the model.

Section 3: Specifying Unit Settings

1.   Move the cursor towards the lower right corner of the screen over the Status Bar and then click on the **Unit System** area of the Status Bar, the **Unit System** flyout appears, see Figure 8.156.

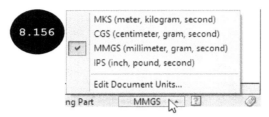

2.   Make sure that the **MMGS (millimeter, gram, second)** option is ticked marked in this flyout, see Figure 8.156.

Section 4: Creating Base/First Feature - Sweep Feature

1.   Invoke the Sketching environment by selecting the Front Plane as the sketching plane and then create the path of the sweep feature, see Figure 8.157.

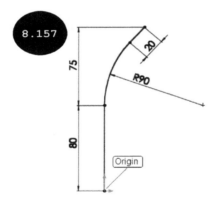

2.   Exit from the Sketching environment by clicking on the **Exit Sketch** button of the **Sketch CommandManager**.

     After creating the path of the sweep feature, you need to create profile for the sweep feature.

3.   Invoke the Sketching environment by selecting the Top Plane as the sketching plane and then change the orientation normal to the viewing direction by using the **Normal To** tool of the **View Orientation** flyout.

4.   Create a circle of the diameter 60 as the profile of the sweep feature, see Figure 8.158.

5.   Exit from the Sketching environment by clicking on the **Exit Sketch** button of the **Sketch CommandManager**.

6.   Change the orientation to isometric, see Figure 8.159.

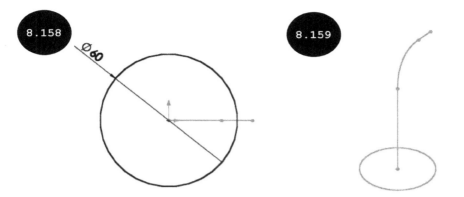

After creating the path and profile, you can create the sweep feature.

7. Click on the **Swept Boss/Base** tool, the **Sweep PropertyManager** appears and the **Profile** field of this PropertyManager is activated.

8. Click to select the circle as the profile of the sweep feature from the graphics area, the **Path** field of the **Sweep PropertyManager** become activated automatically.

9. Click to select the path of the sweep feature from the graphics area, the preview of the sweep feature appears in the graphics area, see Figure 8.160.

10. Expand the **Thin Feature** rollout of the PropertyManager by selecting the check box available in the title bar of the rollout, see Figure 8.161.

11. Enter **8** in the **Thickness** field of the **Thin Feature** rollout.

12. Click on the **Reverse Direction** button of the **Thin Feature** rollout to reverse the material addition direction such that material adds inwards direction of the profile, see Figure 8.162.

13. Click on the green tick mark ✅ of the PropertyManager, the thin sweep feature is created, see Figure 8.163.

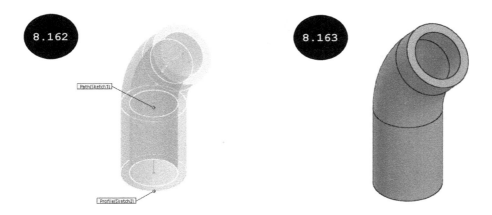

Section 5: Creating Second Feature - Extrude Feature

1. Rotate the model by dragging the cursor after pressing and holding the middle mouse button such that you can view the bottom face of the base feature (sweep), see Figure 8.164.

2. Invoke the Sketching environment by select the bottom face of the base feature as the sketching plane.

3. Change the orientation of the model normal to the viewing direction by using the **Normal To** tool of the **View Orientation** flyout.

4. Create the sketch of the second feature, see Figure 8.165.

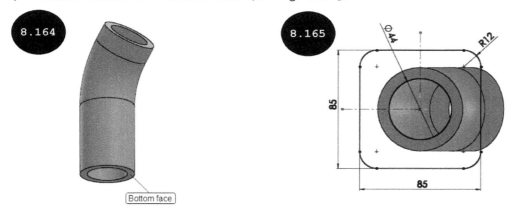

Tip:	The sketch created in Figure 8.165 is symmetric about the vertical and horizontal centerline. Also, the arcs of the sketch are of same radius and are created by using the fillet tool.

5. Click on the **Features** tab of the **CommandManager** to displays the tools of the **Features** CommandManager.

6. Click on the **Extruded Boss/Base** tool of the **Features CommandManager**, the **Boss-Extrude PropertyManager** and the preview of the extruded feature appears in the graphics area. Next, change the orientation of the model to isometric by using the **View Orientation** flyout, see Figure 8.166.

7. Enter **12** in the **Distance** field of the **Direction 1** rollout.

8. Click on the green tick mark ✅ of the PropertyManager, the extruded feature is created, see Figure 8.167.

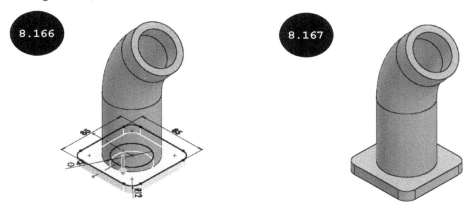

Section 6: Creating Third Feature - Extrude Cut Feature

1. Invoke the Sketching environment by selecting the top planar face of the second feature as the sketching plane.

2. Change the orientation of the model normal to the viewing direction by using the **Normal To** tool of the **View Orientation** flyout.

3. Create the sketch (four circles of same diameter) of the third feature, see Figure 8.168.

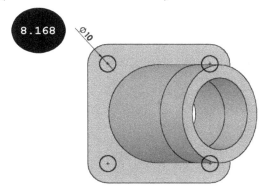

Tip: The sketch created in Figure 8.168 has four circles of same diameter therefore the equal relation is applied between all circles. Also, the center point of the circles is concentric with the semi-circular edge of the second feature.

4. Click on the **Features** tab of the **CommandManager** to displays the tools of the **Features CommandManager**.

5. Click on the **Extruded Cut** tool, the **Cut-Extrude PropertyManager** and the preview of the cut feature appears. Change the orientation of the model to isometric, see Figure 8.169.

6. Invoke the **End Condition** flyout of the **Direction 1** rollout and then click to select the **Through All** option from it.

7. Click on the green tick mark ✓ of the PropertyManager, the extruded cut feature is created, see Figure 8.170.

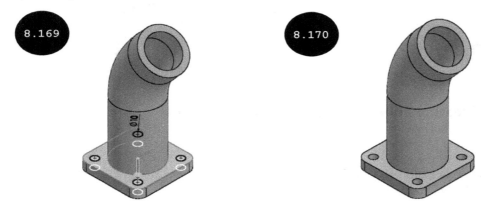

Section 7: Creating Forth Feature - Extrude Feature

1. Invoke the Sketching environment by select the top planar face of the sweep feature as the sketching plane, see Figure 8.171.

2. Change the orientation of the model normal to the viewing direction by using the **Normal To** tool of the **View Orientation** flyout.

3. Create the sketch of the forth feature, see Figure 8.172.

Tip: The sketch created in Figure 8.172 have two circles and are concentric to the circular edge of the sweep feature. You can take the reference of the circular edges of the sweep feature which creating circles.

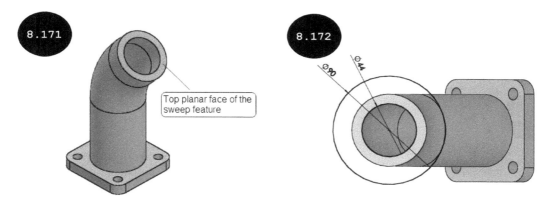

4. Click on the **Features** tab of the **CommandManager** to displays the tools of the **Features CommandManager**.

5. Click on the **Extruded Boss/Base** tool of the **Features CommandManager**, the preview of the extruded feature appears in the graphics area. Next, change the orientation of the model to isometric, see Figure 8.173.

6. Enter **12** in the **Distance** field of the **Direction 1** rollout.

7. Click on the green tick mark ✅ of the PropertyManager, the extruded feature is created, see Figure 8.174.

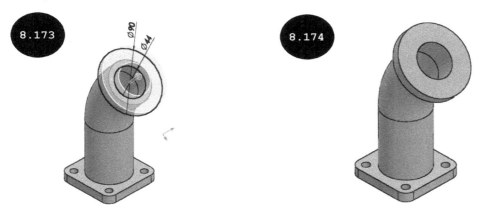

Section 8: Creating Fifth Feature - Extrude Cut Feature

1. Invoke the Sketching environment by selecting the top planar face of the forth feature as the sketching plane.

2. Change the orientation of the model normal to the viewing direction.

3. Create a circle of diameter 10, see Figure 8.175. Next, create circular pattern of it to create remaining circles of same diameter and same PCD by using the **Circular Sketch Pattern** tool, see Figure 8.176. Note that you need to change the position of the pattern center point to the center point of the circular edge of the forth feature by dragging the dot appears at the tip of the arrow in the pattern preview.

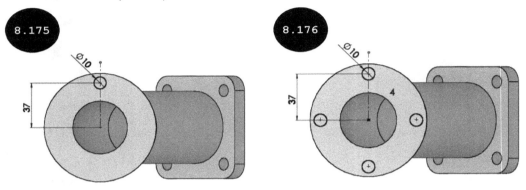

Tip: In Figure 8.175, the center point of the circle is coincident with the vertical centerline. Also, the start point of the vertical centerline is coincident with the circular edge of the forth feature.

While specifying the start point of the vertical centerline, move the cursor over the outer circular edge of the forth feature, the center point of the circular edge highlights. Next, move the cursor towards the highlighted center point and click to specify the start point of the vertical centerline when cursor snaps to the highlighted center point of the forth feature, the coincident relation is automatically applied between the start point of the vertical centerline and the center point of the circular edge of the forth feature.

Note: Similar to pattern sketch entity and create its multiple instances, you can also pattern a feature and create its multiple instances. Creating pattern of features is discussed in later chapters.

4. Click on the **Extruded Cut** tool of the **Features CommandManager**, the **Cut-Extrude PropertyManager** and the preview of the extruded cut feature appears. Change the orientation of the model to isometric, see Figure 8.177.

5. Invoke the **End Condition** flyout of the **Direction 1** rollout and click to select the **Up to Next** option.

6. Click on the green tick mark ✅ of the PropertyManager, the extruded cut feature is created, see Figure 8.178.

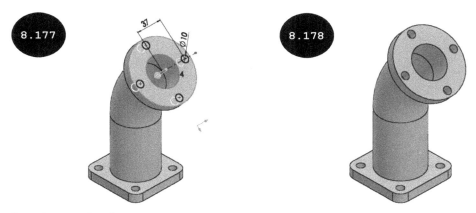

Section 9: Saving the Model

1. Click on the **Save** tool of the **Standard** toolbar, the **Save As** window appears.

2. Browse to the *SOLIDWORKS* folder and then create a folder named as *Chapter 8*. Next, create another folder named as *Tutorial* inside the *Chapter 8* folder.

3. Enter **Tutorial 1** in the **File name** field of the dialog box as the name of the file and then click on the **Save** button, the model is saved as Tutorial 1 in the *Tutorial* folder of *Chapter 8*.

Tutorial 2

Create the model shown in Figure 8.179. Different views and dimensions are given in the same figure.

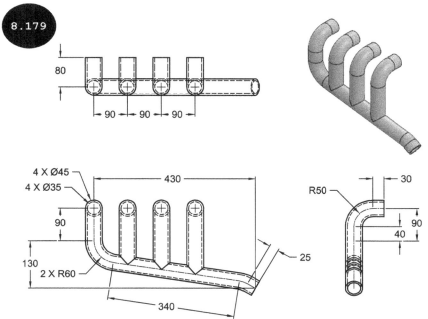

Section 1: Starting SOLIDWORKS

1. Double click on the SOLIDWORKS icon on your desktop to start SOLIDWORKS.

Section 2: Invoking Part Modeling Environment

1. Click on the **New** tool in the **Standard** toolbar, the **New SOLIDWORKS Document** dialog box appears.

2. In this dialog box, the **Part** button is activated by default. Click on the **OK** button.

   Once the Part modeling environment is invoked, you can set the unit system and create the base/first feature of the model.

Section 3: Specifying Unit Settings

1. Move the cursor towards the lower right corner of the screen over the Status Bar and then click on the **Unit System** area of the Status Bar, the **Unit System** flyout appears, see Figure 8.180.

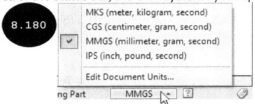

2. Make sure that the **MMGS (millimeter, gram, second)** option is ticked marked in this flyout, see Figure 8.180.

Section 4: Creating Base/First Feature - Sweep Feature

1. Invoke the Sketching environment by selecting the Right Plane as the sketching plane and then create the path of the sweep feature, see Figure 8.181.

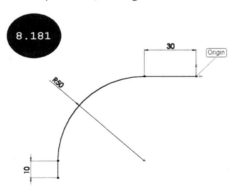

2. Exit from the Sketching environment by clicking on the **Exit Sketch** button of the **Sketch CommandManager**.

   After creating the path of the sweep feature, you need to create profile for the sweep feature.

3. Invoke the Sketching environment by selecting the Front Plane as the sketching plane and then change the orientation normal to the viewing direction by using the **Normal To** tool of the **View Orientation** flyout.

4. Create circles of the diameters 45 and 35 as the profile of the sweep feature, see Figure 8.182.

5. Exit from the Sketching environment by clicking on the **Exit Sketch** button of the **Sketch CommandManager**.

6. Change the orientation to isometric, see Figure 8.183.

After creating the path and profile, you can create the sweep feature.

7. Click on the **Swept Boss/Base** tool, the **Sweep PropertyManager** appears and the **Profile** field of this PropertyManager is activated.

8. Click to select the sketch created as profile (two circles) of the sweep feature from the graphics area, the **Path** field of the **Sweep PropertyManager** become activated automatically.

9. Click to select the path of the sweep feature from the graphics area, the preview of the sweep feature appears in the graphics area, see Figure 8.184.

10. Click on the green tick mark ✅ of the PropertyManager, the sweep feature is created, see Figure 8.185.

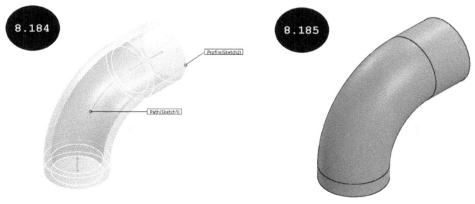

Section 5: Creating Second Feature - Sweep Feature

To create the second feature of the model, you will first create a reference plane at an office distance of 80 mm from the Front Plane.

1. Invoke the **Reference Geometry** flyout of the **Features CommandManager**, see Figure 8.186.

2. Click on the **Plane** tool of this flyout, the **Plane PropertyManager** appears.

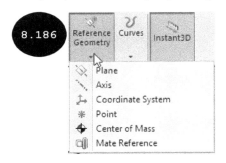

8.186

3. Expand the FeatureManager design tree available on the top left corner of the graphics area by clicking on its +sign.

4. Click to select the Front Plane of the FeatureManager Design Tree as the first reference, the preview of an offset reference plane appears in the graphics area.

5. Enter *80* in the **Distance** field of the **First Reference** rollout of the **Plane PropertyManager**. If needed, you can flip the direction of plane creation.

6. Click on the green tick mark ✓ of the PropertyManager, the offset reference plane is created, see Figure 8.187.

7. Invoke the Sketching environment by select the newly created reference plane as the sketching plane. Next, change the orientation of the model normal to the viewing direction.

8. Create the path of the second sweep feature, see Figure 8.188.

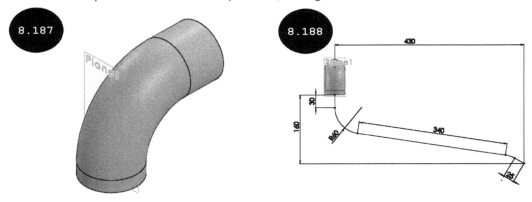

8.187

8.188

9. Exit from the Sketching environment by clicking on the **Exit Sketch** button of the **Sketch CommandManager**.

    After creating the path of the sweep feature, you need to create profile for the sweep feature.

10. Invoke the Sketching environment by selecting the bottom planar face of the base/first sweep feature as the sketching plane, see Figure 8.189.

11. Change the orientation normal to the viewing direction by using the **Normal To** tool of the **View Orientation** flyout.

12. Create circles of the diameters 45 and 35 as the profile of the sweep feature, see Figure 8.190.

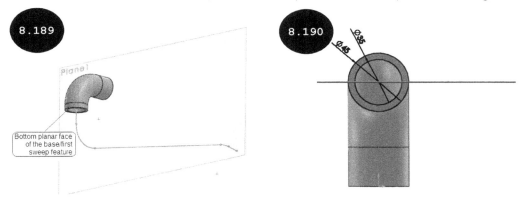

Note: While specifying the center point of the circles, move the cursor over the outer circular edge of the base feature, the center point of the circular edge highlights. Next, move the cursor towards the highlighted center point and then click to specify the center point of the circle when cursor snaps to the highlighted center point of the circular edge of the base feature.

---

13. Exit from the Sketching environment by clicking on the **Exit Sketch** button of the **Sketch CommandManager**.

14. Change the orientation to isometric, see Figure 8.191.

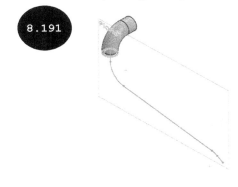

After creating the path and profile, you can create the sweep feature.

15. Click on the **Swept Boss/Base** tool, the **Sweep PropertyManager** appears and the **Profile** field of this PropertyManager is activated.

16. Click to select the sketch created as profile (two circles) of the sweep feature from the graphics area, the **Path** field of the **Sweep PropertyManager** become activated automatically.

17. Click to select the path of the sweep feature from the graphics area, the preview of the sweep feature appears in the graphics area, see Figure 8.192.

18. Click on the green tick mark ✅ of the PropertyManager, the sweep feature is created, see Figure 8.193.

19. Hide the reference plane by selecting the **Hide** option from the Pop-up toolbar which appears as soon as you select the plane to hide.

Note: In Figure 8.193, the reference plane is hidden.

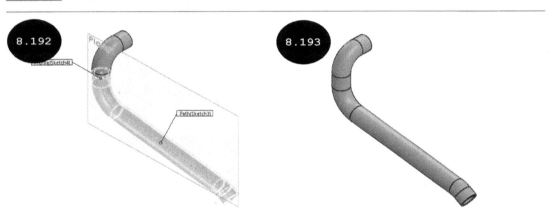

Section 6: Creating Third Feature - Extrude Feature

To create the second feature of the model, you will first create a reference plane at an office distance of 60 mm from the Top Plane.

1. Invoke the **Reference Geometry** flyout of the **Features CommandManager** and then click on the **Plane** tool to invoke the **Plane PropertyManager**.

2. Expand the FeatureManager design tree available on the top left corner of the graphics area by clicking on its +sign.

3. Click to select the Top Plane of the FeatureManager design tree as the first reference, the preview of an offset reference plane appears in the graphics area.

4. Enter **60** in the **Distance** field of the **First Reference** rollout of the **Plane PropertyManager**.

5. Click to select the **Flip** check box in order to reverse the direction of plane creation to downwards.

6. Click on the green tick mark ✅ of the PropertyManager, the offset reference plane is created, see Figure 8.194.

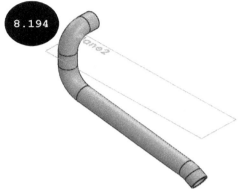

7. Invoke the Sketching environment by selecting the newly created reference plane as the sketching plane.

8. Change the orientation of the model normal to the viewing direction by using the **Normal To** tool of the **View Orientation** flyout.

9. Create the sketch of the third feature, see Figure 8.195.

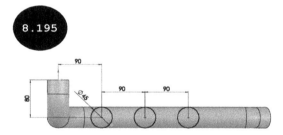

10. Click on the **Features** tab of the **CommandManager** to displays the tools of the **Features CommandManager**.

11. Click on the **Extruded Boss/Base** tool of the **Features CommandManager**, the **Boss-Extrude PropertyManager** and the preview of the extruded feature appears in the graphics area. Next, change the orientation of the model to isometric, see Figure 8.196.

12. Click on the **Reverse Direction** button of the **Direction 1** rollout to reverse the direction of extrusion to downwards.

13. Invoke the **End Condition** flyout of the **Direction 1** rollout and then select the **Up To Next** option from the flyout, the preview of the feature appears in the graphics area such that it terminated at its next intersection.

14. Click on the green tick mark ✓ of the PropertyManager, the extruded feature is created, see Figure 8.197.

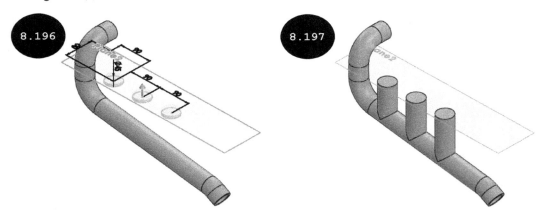

15. Hide the reference plane by selecting the **Hide** option from the Pop-up toolbar which appears as soon as you select the plane to hide.

Section 7: Creating Forth Feature - Extrude Cut Feature

1. Invoke the Sketching environment by selecting the top planar face of the third feature as the sketching plane.

2. Change the orientation of the model normal to the viewing direction by using the **Normal To** tool of the **View Orientation** flyout.

3. Create three circles of diameter 35 mm, see Figure 8.198.

4. Click on the **Extruded Cut** tool of the **Features CommandManager**, the **Cut-Extrude PropertyManager** and the preview of the extruded cut feature appears. Change the orientation of the model to isometric.

5. Invoke the **End Condition** flyout of the **Direction 1** rollout.

6. Click to select the **Up To Next** option of the **End Condition** flyout, the preview of the feature appears in the graphics area such that it terminated at its next intersection.

7. Click on the green tick mark ✓ of the PropertyManager, the extruded cut feature is created, see Figure 8.199.

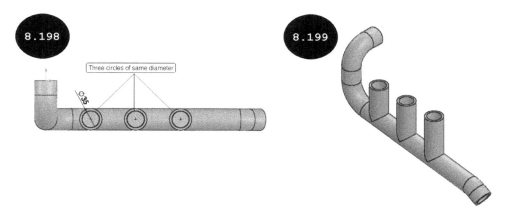

Section 8: Creating Fifth Feature - Sweep Feature

To create the fifth feature of the model, you will first create a reference plane at an office distance of 90 mm from the Right Plane.

1. Invoke the **Reference Geometry** flyout of the **Features CommandManager**, see Figure 8.200.

2. Click on the **Plane** tool of this flyout, the **Plane PropertyManager** appears.

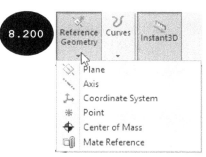

3. Expand the FeatureManager design tree available on the top left corner of the graphics area by clicking on its +sign.

4. Click to select the Right Plane of the FeatureManager design tree as the first reference, the preview of an offset reference plane appears in the graphics area.

5. Enter **90** in the **Distance** field of the **First Reference** rollout of the **Plane PropertyManager**.

6. Click on the green tick mark ✅ of the PropertyManager, the offset reference plane is created, see Figure 8.201.

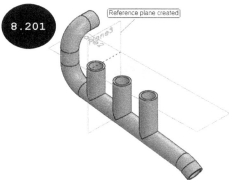

7. Invoke the Sketching environment by selecting the newly created reference plane as the sketching plane and then create the path of the sweep feature, see Figure 8.202.

8. Exit from the Sketching environment by clicking on the **Exit Sketch** button of the **Sketch CommandManager**.

9. Change the current orientation of the model to isometric. Next, hide the reference planes from the graphics area.

    After creating the path of the sweep feature, you need to create profile for the sweep feature.

10. Invoke the Sketching environment by selecting the top planar face of the extruded feature as the sketching plane, see Figure 8.203.

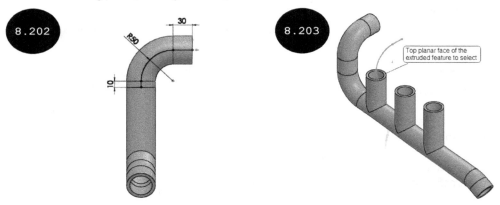

11. Change the orientation of the model normal to the viewing direction by using the **Normal To** tool of the **View Orientation** flyout.

12. Create three set of circles of diameters 45 and 35 as the profile of the sweep feature, see Figure 8.204.

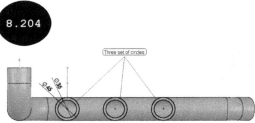

Note: While specifying the center point of the circles, move the cursor over the outer circular edge of the extrude feature, the center point of the circular edge highlights. Next, move the cursor towards the highlighted center point and then click to specify the center point of the circle when cursor snaps to the highlighted center point of the circular edge of the extruded feature. You can apply equal relation between the circles have equal diameter.

13. Exit from the Sketching environment by clicking on the **Exit Sketch** button of the **Sketch CommandManager**.

14. Change the orientation to isometric.

    After creating the path and profile, you can create the sweep feature.

15. Click on the **Swept Boss/Base** tool, the **Sweep PropertyManager** appears and the **Profile** field of this PropertyManager is activated.

16. Click to select the sketch (set of circles) created as profile of the sweep feature from the graphics area, the **Path** field of the **Sweep PropertyManager** become activated automatically.

17. Click to select the path of the sweep feature from the graphics area, the preview of the sweep feature appears in the graphics area, see Figure 8.205.

18. Click on the green tick mark ✅ of the PropertyManager, the sweep feature is created, see Figure 8.206.

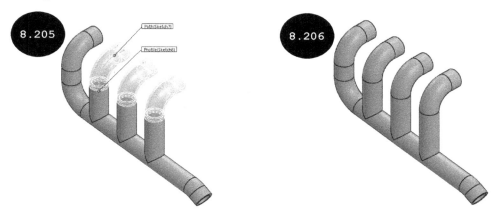

Section 9: Saving the Model

1. Click on the **Save** tool of the **Standard** toolbar, the **Save As** window appears.

2. Browse to the *Tutorial* folder of *Chapter 8* and then save the model as Tutorial 2.

Tutorial 3

Create the model shown in Figure 8.207.

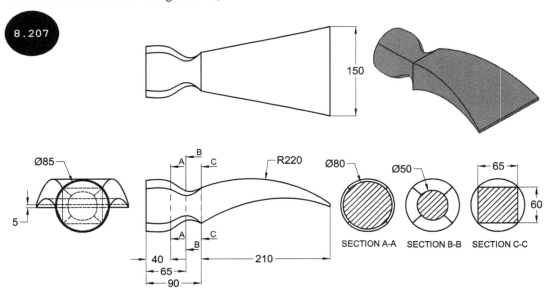

8.207

Section 1: Starting SOLIDWORKS

1. Double click on the **SOLIDWORKS** icon on your desktop to start SOLIDWORKS.

Section 2: Invoking Part Modeling Environment

1. Click on the **New** tool in the **Standard** toolbar, the **New SOLIDWORKS Document** dialog box appears.

2. In this dialog box, the **Part** button is activated by default. Click on the **OK** button.

   Once the Part modeling environment is invoked, you can set the unit system and create the base/first feature of the model.

Section 3: Specifying Unit Settings

1. Make sure that the **MMGS (millimeter, gram, second)** unit system is set for the current opened part document.

Section 4: Creating Base/First Feature - Loft Feature

To create the base/first feature (loft feature) of the model, you need to first create all sections (profiles) of the loft feature on reference planes.

1. Invoke the Sketching environment by selecting the Right Plane as the sketching plane.

2. Create first section (profile) of the loft feature (first/base feature), see Figure 8.208.

3. Exit from the Sketching environment by clicking on the **Exit Sketch** button of the **Sketch CommandManager** and then change the current orientation to isometric.

   After creating the first section (profile) of the loft feature, you need to create the second section at an offset distance of 40 mm from the Right Plane.

4. Invoke the **Reference Geometry** flyout of the **Features CommandManager** and create a reference plane at an offset distance of 40 mm from the Right Plane, see Figure 8.209.

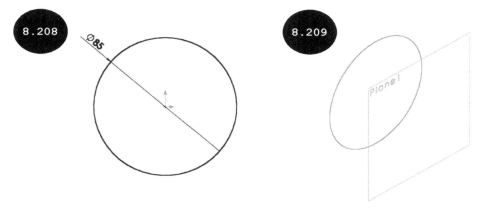

5. Invoke the Sketching environment by selecting the newly created reference plane as the sketching plane.

6. Change the orientation of the model normal to the viewing direction by using the **Normal To** tool of the **View Orientation** flyout.

7. Create the second section (a circle of diameter 80 mm) of the loft feature, see Figure 8.210.

8. Exit from the Sketching environment by clicking on the **Exit Sketch** button of the **Sketch CommandManager** and then change the current orientation to isometric.

   After creating the second section (profile) of the loft feature, you need to create the third section at an offset distance of 65 mm from the Right Plane.

9. Invoke the **Plane** tool of the **Reference Geometry** flyout available in the **Features CommandManager** and create a reference plane at an offset distance of 65 mm from the Right Plane, see Figure 8.211.

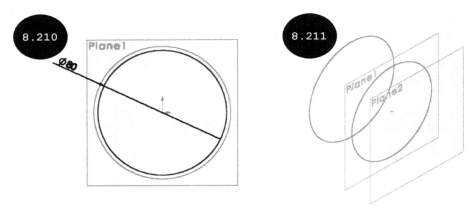

10. Invoke the Sketching environment by selecting the newly created reference plane as the sketching plane.

11. Change the orientation of the model normal to the viewing direction by using the **Normal To** tool of the **View Orientation** flyout.

12. Create the third section (a circle of diameter 50 mm) of the loft feature, see Figure 8.212.

13. Exit from the Sketching environment by clicking on the **Exit Sketch** button of the **Sketch CommandManager** and then change the current orientation to isometric.

    After creating the third section (profile) of the loft feature, you need to create the forth section at an offset distance of 90 mm from the Right Plane.

14. Invoke the **Plane** tool of the **Reference Geometry** flyout and create a reference plane at an offset distance of 90 mm from the Right Plane, see Figure 8.213.

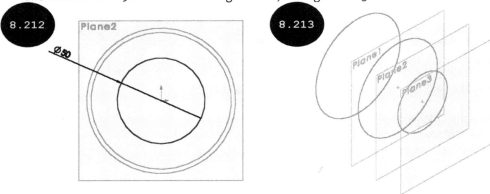

15. Invoke the Sketching environment by selecting the newly created reference plane as the sketching plane.

16. Change the orientation of the model normal to the viewing direction by using the **Normal To** tool of the **View Orientation** flyout.

17. Create the forth section (a rectangle of 65X60) of the loft feature, see Figure 8.214.

18. Exit from the Sketching environment and then change the current orientation to isometric, see Figure 8.215.

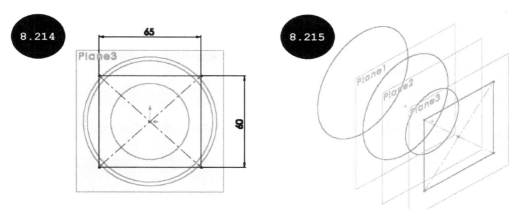

After creating all sections of the loft feature (base feature), you can create loft feature.

19. Click on the **Lofted Boss/Base** tool of the **Features CommandManager**, the **Loft PropertyManager** appears and the **Profile** field of this PropertyManager is activated.

20. Click to select all sections (profiles) of the loft feature from the graphics area one by one, the preview of the loft feature appears in the graphics area, see Figure 8.216.

21. Click on the green tick mark ✓ of the PropertyManager, the loft feature is created, see Figure 8.217. In Figure 8.217, the reference plane have been hidden.

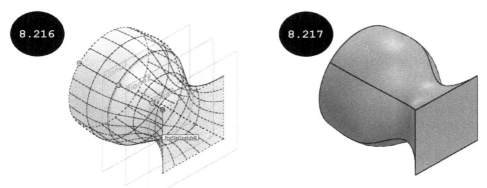

22. Hide the reference planes by selecting the **Hide** option from the Pop-up toolbar which appears as soon as you select a plane to hide.

Section 5: Creating Second Feature - Loft Feature

To create the second feature (loft feature) of the model, you need to first create all sections (profiles) of the loft feature on reference planes.

1. Invoke the Sketching environment by selecting the right planar face of the base feature (loft) as the sketching plane, see Figure 8.218.

2. Change the orientation of the model normal to the viewing direction by using the **Normal To** tool of the **View Orientation** flyout.

3. Create first section (profile) of the loft feature (second feature), see Figure 8.219.

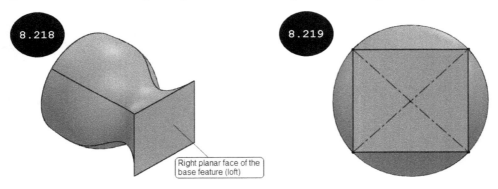

8.218

8.219

Right planar face of the base feature (loft)

Note: The first section (profile) of the loft feature is a rectangle of 65X50 and is created by taking the reference from the edges/vertex of the existing loft feature.

---

4. Exit from the Sketching environment by clicking on the **Exit Sketch** button of the **Sketch CommandManager** and then change the current orientation to isometric.

   After creating the first section (profile) of the loft feature, you need to create the second section at an offset distance of 210 mm from the right planar face of the base feature (loft).

5. Invoke the **Plane** tool of the **Reference Geometry** flyout and create a reference plane at an offset distance of 210 mm from the right planar face of the base feature (loft), see Figure 8.220.

6. Invoke the Sketching environment by selecting the newly created reference plane as the sketching plane.

7. Change the orientation of the model normal to the viewing direction by using the **Normal To** tool of the **View Orientation** flyout.

8. Create the second section (a rectangle of 150X5 mm) of the loft feature, see Figure 8.221.

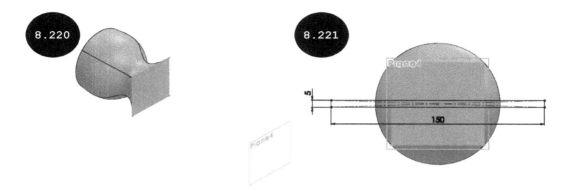

9. Exit from the Sketching environment by clicking on the **Exit Sketch** button of the **Sketch CommandManager** and then change the current orientation to isometric.

   After creating sections (profiles) of the loft feature, you need to create a guide curve on the Front Plane.

10. Invoke the Sketching environment by selecting the Front Plane as the sketching plane to create guide curve.

11. Change the orientation of the model normal to the viewing direction by using the **Normal To** tool of the **View Orientation** flyout.

12. Create the guide curve (a arc of radius 220 mm) of the loft feature, see Figure 8.222.

Note: The end points of the guide curve (arc) have Pierce relation with the respective sections (rectangles 65X60 and 150X5) of the loft feature. To apply the pierce relation, select a end point of the guide curve (arc) and then select a section (rectangles 65X60 or 150X5), the Pop-up toolbar appears, see Figure 8.223. Click on the **Pierce** tool to apply the Pierce relation.

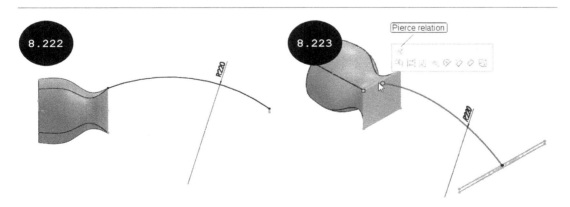

13. Exit from the Sketching environment by clicking on the **Exit Sketch** button of the **Sketch CommandManager** and then change the current orientation to isometric.

    After creating sections (profile) and guide curve of the loft feature (second feature), you can create the loft feature.

14. Click on the **Lofted Boss/Base** tool of the **Features CommandManager**, the **Loft PropertyManager** appears and the **Profile** field of this PropertyManager is activated.

15. Click to select both sections (rectangles 65X60 and 150X5) of the loft feature from the graphics area one by one, the preview of the loft feature appears in the graphics area, see Figure 8.224.

16. Click on the **Guide Curves** field of the **Guide Curves** rollout of the PropertyManager to activate it.

17. Click to select the guide curve (arc of radius 220 mm) from the graphics area, the preview of the loft feature is guided by the guide curve, see Figure 8.225.

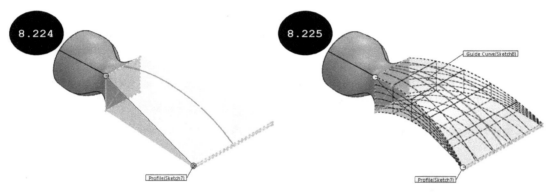

18. Click on the green tick mark ✔ of the PropertyManager, the loft feature is created, see Figure 8.226.

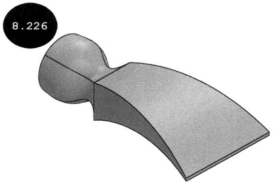

Section 6: Saving the Model

1. Click on the **Save** tool of the **Standard** toolbar, the **Save As** window appears.

2. Browse to the *Tutorial* folder of *Chapter 8* and then save the model as Tutorial 3.

Tutorial 4

Create the model shown in Figure 8.227.

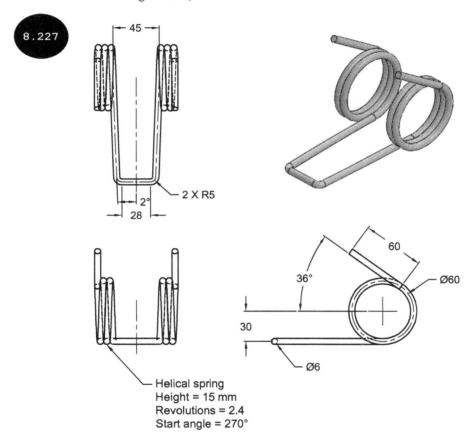

8.227

45

2 X R5

2°

28

30

36°

60

Ø60

Ø6

Helical spring
Height = 15 mm
Revolutions = 2.4
Start angle = 270°

Section 1: Starting SOLIDWORKS

1. Double click on the **SOLIDWORKS** icon on your desktop to start SOLIDWORKS.

Section 2: Invoking Part Modeling Environment

1. Click on the **New** tool in the **Standard** toolbar, the **New SOLIDWORKS Document** dialog box appears.

2. In this dialog box, the **Part** button is activated by default. Click on the **OK** button.

Once the Part modeling environment is invoked, you can set the unit system and create the base/first feature of the model.

Section 3: Specifying Unit Settings

1. Make sure that the MMGS (millimeter, gram, second) unit system is set for the current opened part document.

Section 4: Creating First Curve - Helical Curve

1. Invoke the Sketching environment by selecting the Right Plane as the sketching plane and then create a circle of diameter 60 mm which defines the diameter of helical curve, see Figure 8.228.

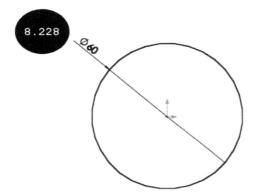

2. Exit from the Sketching environment by clicking on the **Exit Sketch** button.

3. Invoke the **Curves** flyout of the **Features CommandManager** and then click on the **Helix and Spiral** tool, the Helix/Spiral PropertyManager appears.

Note: If the circle created is selected before invoking the **Helix and Spiral** tool, the preview of the helical curve appears automatically in the graphics area along with the **Helix/Spiral PropertyManager**. You can select circle defines the diameter of helical curve before or after invoking the **Helix and Spiral** tool.

4. Select the circle from the graphics area, the preview of the helical curve appears in the graphics area, see Figure 8.229.

5. Invoke the **Type** drop-down list of the **Defined By** rollout of the PropertyManager, see Figure 8.230.

6. Click to select the **Height and Revolution** option from this drop-down list.

7. Enter **15** in the **Height** field, **2.4** in the **Revolutions** field, and **270** in the **Start angle** field of the **Parameters** rollout of the PropertyManager.

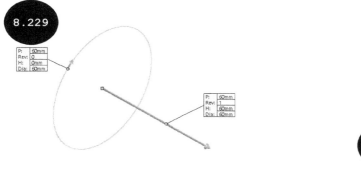

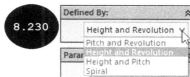

8. Click to select the **Reverse direction** check box of the **Parameters** rollout to reverse the direction of curve creation, see Figure 8.231.

9. Make sure that the **Counterclockwise** radio button is selected in the rollout.

10. Click on the green tick mark ✅ of the PropertyManager, the helical curve is created, see Figure 8.232.

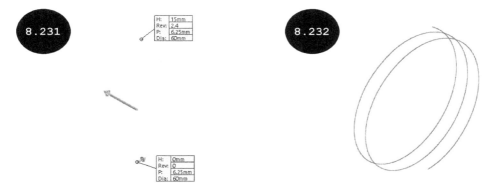

Section 5: Creating Second Curve - Helical Curve

After creating the first helical curve, you need to create the second helical curve at an offset distance of 45 mm from the Right Plane.

1. Invoke the **Plane** tool of the **Reference Geometry** flyout and create a reference plane at an offset distance of 45 mm from the Right Plane, see Figure 8.233.

2. Invoke the Sketching environment by selecting the newly created reference plane as the sketching plane.

3. Change the orientation of the model normal to the viewing direction by using the **Normal To** tool of the **View Orientation** flyout.

4. Create a circle of diameter 60 as the diameter of second helical curve, see Figure 8.234.

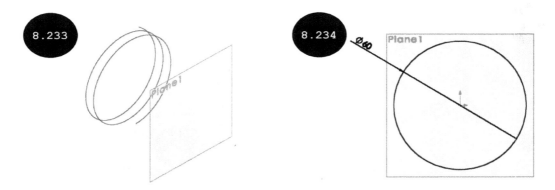

5. Invoke the **Curves** flyout of the **Features CommandManager** and then click on the **Helix and Spiral** tool, the preview of the helical curve and the **Helix/Spiral PropertyManager** appears.

6. Change the current orientation of the model to isometric.

7. Click to select the **Height and Revolution** option from the **Type** drop-down list of the **Defined By** rollout.

8. Enter **15** in the **Height** field, **2.4** in the **Revolutions** field, and **270** in the **Start angle** field of the **Parameters** rollout of the PropertyManager. The preview of the helical curve appears similar to one shown in Figure 8.235.

9. Make sure that the **Counterclockwise** radio button is selected in the rollout.

10. Click on the green tick mark ✔ of the PropertyManager, the helical curve is created, see Figure 8.236.

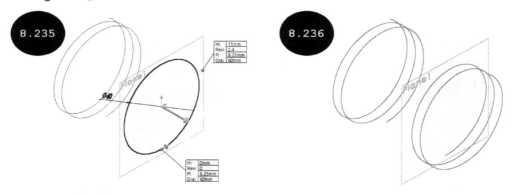

11. Hide the reference plane by selecting the **Hide** option from the Pop-up toolbar which appears as soon as you select the plane to hide.

Section 6: Creating third Curve - Sketch

After creating the helical curves, you need to create the sketch on the reference plane which is parallel to Top Plane and passing through the start point of the first helical curve.

1. Invoke the **Plane** tool of the **Reference Geometry** flyout and create a reference plane parallel to Top Plane and passing through the start point of the first helical curve, see Figures 8.237 and 8.238. Figure 8.237 shows the preview of the reference plane.

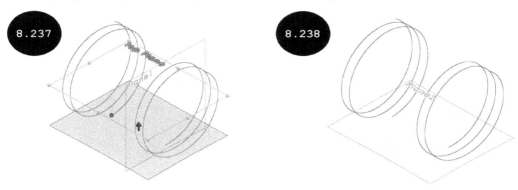

Note: To create a reference plane parallel to Top Plane and passing through the start point of the first helical curve, you need to select the Top Plane as the first reference and the start point of the first helical curve as the second reference to create plane.

2. Invoke the Sketching environment by selecting the newly created reference plane as the sketching plane.

3. Change the orientation of the model normal to the viewing direction by using the **Normal To** tool of the **View Orientation** flyout.

4. Create a sketch, see Figure 8.239.

Note: The end points of the sketch shown in Figure 8.239 have Pierce relation with helical curves. To apply the pierce relation, select a end point of the sketch and then select a respective helical curve, the Pop-up toolbar appears, see Figure 8.240. Click on the **Pierce** tool to apply the Pierce relation. .

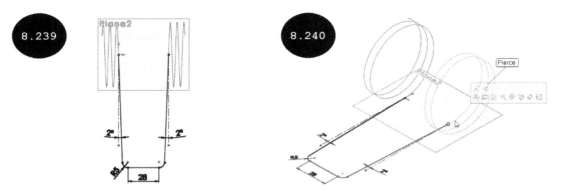

5. Exit from the Sketching environment by clicking on the **Exit Sketch** button.

6. Change the current orientation to isometric, see Figure 8.241.

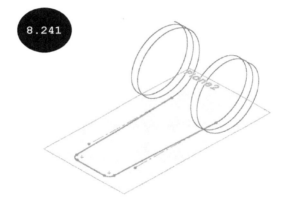

Section 7: Creating Forth Curve - Sketch

You need to create the forth sketch on the reference plane which is parallel to Right Plane and passing through the end point of the first helical curve.

1. Invoke the **Plane** tool of the **Reference Geometry** flyout and create a reference plane parallel to Right Plane and passing through the end point of the first helical curve, see Figures 8.242 and 8.243. Figure 8.242 shows the preview of the reference plane.

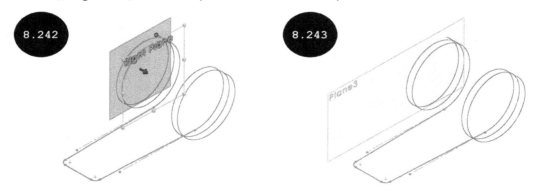

Note: To create a reference plane parallel to Right Plane and passing through the end point of the first helical curve, you need to select the Right Plane as the first reference and the end point of the first helical curve as the second reference to create plane.

2. Invoke the Sketching environment by selecting the newly created reference plane as the sketching plane.

3. Change the orientation of the model normal to the viewing direction by using the **Normal To** tool of the **View Orientation** flyout.

4. Create the forth sketch (a inclined line of length 60 mm), see Figure 8.244.

Note: The start point of the line shown in Figure 8.244 have Pierce relation with the first helical curves. To apply the pierce relation, select the start point of the line and then select the first helical curve, the Pop-up toolbar appears, see Figure 8.245. Click on the **Pierce** tool to apply the Pierce relation.

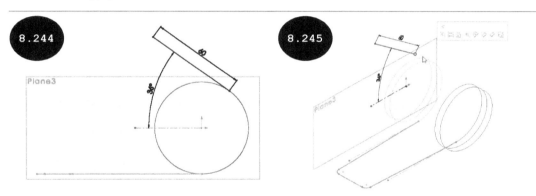

5. Exit from the Sketching environment by clicking on the **Exit Sketch** button and then hide the reference plane.

6. Change the current orientation to isometric, see Figure 8.246.

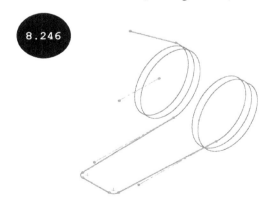

Section 8: Creating Fifth Curve - Sketch

You need to create the fifth sketch on the reference plane which is parallel to Right Plane and passing through the end point of the second helical curve.

1. Invoke the **Plane** tool of the **Reference Geometry** flyout and create a reference plane parallel to Right Plane and passing through the end point of the second helical curve, see Figures 8.247 and 8.248. Figure 8.247 shows the preview of the reference plane.

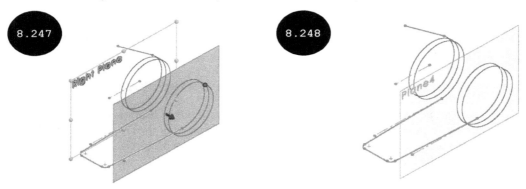

2. Invoke the Sketching environment by selecting the newly created reference plane as the sketching plane.

3. Change the orientation of the model normal to the viewing direction by using the **Normal To** tool of the **View Orientation** flyout.

4. Create the fifth sketch (a inclined line of length 60 mm), see Figure 8.249.

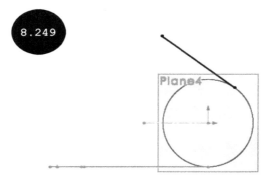

Note: The line shown in Figure 8.249 has been created by specifying its start and end points on the start and end points of the existing inclined line.

---

5. Exit from the Sketching environment by clicking on the **Exit Sketch** button and then hide the reference plane.

6. Change the current orientation to isometric, see Figure 8.250.

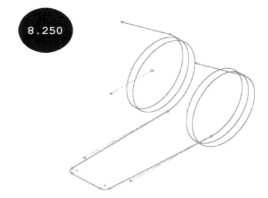

8.250

Section 9: Creating Composite Curve - Sweep Path

After creating all curves (helical and sketch), you need to create composite curve as the path of the sweep feature by combining all these curves together.

1. Invoke the **Curves** flyout of the **Features CommandManager**, see Figure 8.251. Next, click on the **Composite Curve** tool, the **Composite Curve PropertyManager** appears.

2. Click to select all the curves (helical and sketch) from the graphics area, one by one.

3. Click on the green tick mark ✅ of the PropertyManager, the composite curve is created, see Figure 8.251.

8.251

Section 10: Creating Profile - Sweep Profile

After creating the composite curve as the path of the sweep feature, you need to create the profile of the sweep feature. The profile of the sweep feature is a circle of diameter 6 mm and is created on the reference plane normal to the curve and passing through a end point of the curve.

1.   Click on the **Plane** tool of the **Reference Geometry** flyout, the **Plane PropertyManager** appears.

2.   Click to select the composite curve from the graphics area as the first reference.

3.   Click to select a end point of the composite curve from the graphics area as the second reference, the preview of the reference plane appears, see Figure 8.252.

4.   Click on the green tick mark ✓ of the PropertyManager, the reference plane is created, see Figure 8.253.

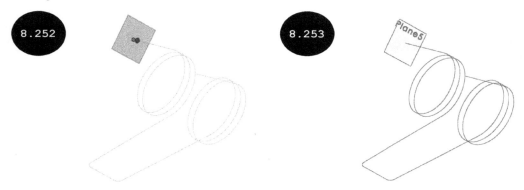

5.   Invoke the Sketching environment by selecting the newly created reference plane as the sketching plane.

6.   Change the orientation of the model normal to the viewing direction by using the **Normal To** tool of the **View Orientation** flyout.

7.   Create the sketch (a circle of diameter 6 mm) as the profile of the sweep feature, see Figure 8.254.

Note: The center point of the circle shown in Figure 8.254 has Pierce relation with the composite curve. To apply the pierce relation, select the center point of the circle and then select the composite curve, the Pop-up toolbar appears. Click on the **Pierce** tool from the Pop-up toolbar.

8.   Exit from the Sketching environment by clicking on the **Exit Sketch** button and then hide the reference plane.

9.   Change the current orientation to isometric, see Figure 8.255.

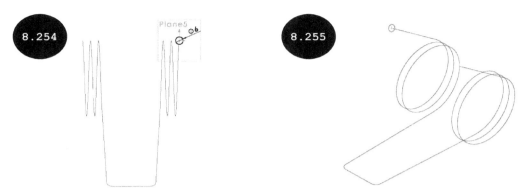

Section 11: Creating Sweep Feature

1. Click on the **Swept Boss/Base** tool, the **Sweep PropertyManager** appears and the **Profile** field of this PropertyManager is activated.

2. Click to select the circle created as profile of the sweep feature from the graphics area, the **Path** field of the **Sweep PropertyManager** become activated automatically.

3. Click to select the path (composite curve) of the sweep feature from the graphics area, the preview of the sweep feature appears in the graphics area, see Figure 8.256.

4. Click on the green tick mark ✓ of the PropertyManager, the sweep feature is created, see Figure 8.257.

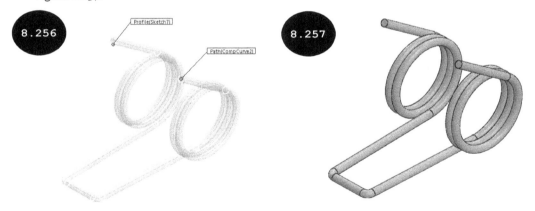

Section 12: Saving the Model

1. Click on the **Save** tool of the **Standard** toolbar, the **Save As** window appears.

2. Browse to the *Tutorial* folder of *Chapter 8* and then save the model as Tutorial 4.

Hands-on Test Drive 1

Create the model shown in Figure 8.258, apply the Cast Alloy Steel material, and calculate mass properties of the model.

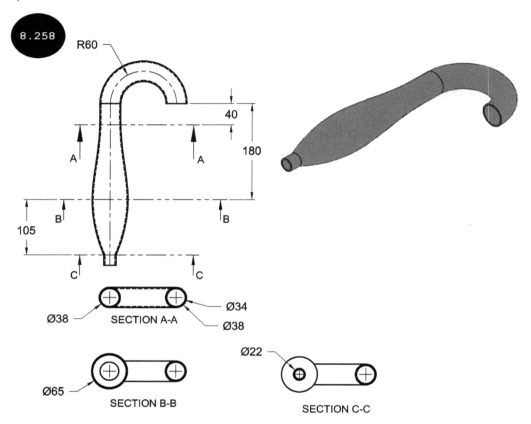

8.258

R60

40

180

105

Ø38
SECTION A-A
Ø34
Ø38

Ø65
SECTION B-B

Ø22
SECTION C-C

Hands-on Test Drive 2

Create the model shown in Figure 8.259, apply the Alloy Steel material, and calculate mass properties of the model.

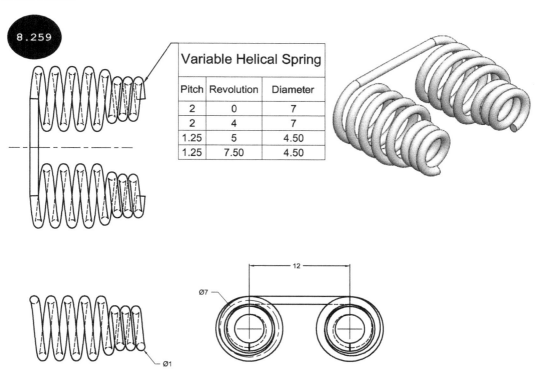

Variable Helical Spring		
Pitch	Revolution	Diameter
2	0	7
2	4	7
1.25	5	4.50
1.25	7.50	4.50

8.259

Summary

In this chapter, you have learnt how to create sweep features, sweep cut features, loft features, loft cut features, boundary features, boundary cut features, curves, split faces, and 3D Sketches.

A sweep feature is a feature which is created by adding material by sweeping a profile along a path. A profile of the sweep feature can be a closed sketch whereas a path can be a open or closed sketch. You can also use guide curves to guide the profile (section) of the sweep feature. Additionally, you can twist a profile along a path. You can also create thin sweep feature. You have also learnt that while creating sweep cut feature, you can use close sketch and a solid body as the profile to sweep along the path.

A loft feature is a feature created by lofting two or more than two profiles (sections) such that its cross-sectional shape transitions from one profile to another. You can also use guide curves to control the cross-sectional shape of loft feature. You can create open and close loft feature. Similar to create loft feature, you can create boundary features with high quality and complex shape.

You have also learnt about creating projected curves, helical and spiral curves, curves by specifying XYZ points, curves by selecting reference points, and composite curve. In addition to this, you have also learnt how to split faces of the model and create 3D sketches.

Questions

*   The _____ tool is used to create sweep features.

*   While creating a sweep feature, the _____ option is selected, by default. As a result, the profile follows the path.

*   On selecting the _____ option, the sweep feature is created such that profile twists along a path.

.
*   On selecting the _____ option, you can select a tool body which follows the path in order to create sweep cut feature.

*   You can create projected curves by using two methods: _____ and _____.

*   The _____ radio button is used to create helical curve with variable pitch.

*   On selecting _____ option you can create an helical curve by defining its pitch and number of revolutions.

*   The _____ tool is used to create curve by specifying coordinate points.

*   The profiles/sections of the loft feature must be closed (True/False).

*   In SOLIDWORKS, you can not create tapered helical curves. (True/False).

*   For creating sweep feature, the start point of the path must be laying on the plane of the profile created. (True/False).

Patterning and Mirroring

In this chapter:

- Patterning Features/Faces/Bodies
- Creating Linear Pattern
- Creating Circular Pattern
- Creating Curve Driven Pattern
- Creating Sketch Driven Pattern
- Creating Table Driven Pattern
- Creating Fill Pattern
- Creating Variable Pattern
- Mirroring Feature

Patterning and mirroring tools are very powerful tools which allow designers to speedup the creation of a design, increase the efficiency, and save time. For example, if a plate has 1000 holes, instead of creating all the holes one by one, you can create one of the hole and then pattern it to create all its remaining instances. Similarly, if the geometry is symmetric, you can create its one side and mirror it to create its other side of the geometry. The various methods for patterning and mirroring features, faces, or bodies are as follows.

Patterning Features/Faces/Bodies

In SOLIDWORKS, you can created different type of patterns such as linear pattern and circular pattern. The tools to create different type patterns are grouped together in the **Pattern** flyout of the **Features CommandManager**, see Figure 9.1.

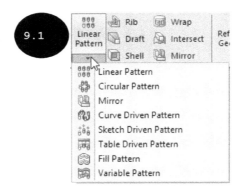

The different type of patterns that can be created by using the pattern tools are as follow:

1.   Linear Pattern
2.   Circular pattern
3.   Curve Driven Pattern
4.   Sketch Driven Pattern
5.   Table Driven Pattern
6.   Fill Pattern
7.   Variable Pattern

Creating Linear Pattern

The linear pattern is created by creating multiple instances of features, faces, or bodies, linearly in one or two linear directions, see Figure 9.2.

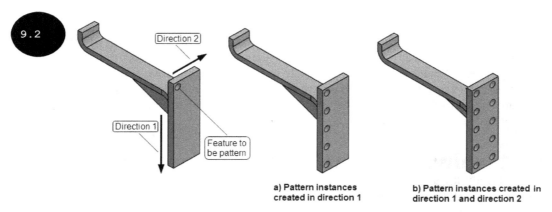

a) Pattern instances
created in direction 1

b) Pattern instances created in
direction 1 and direction 2

To create linear pattern, click on the **Linear Pattern** tool in the **Features CommandManager**, the **Linear Pattern PropertyManager** appears, see Figure 9.3. The options available in this PropertyManager are as follows.

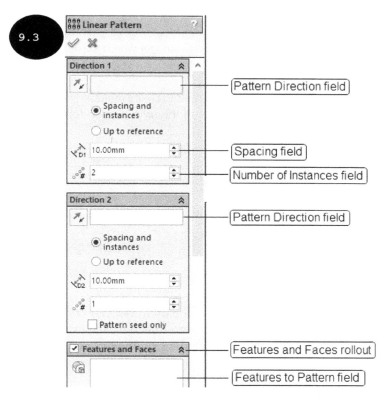

Features and Faces

The **Features and Faces** rollout of the PropertyManager allows you to select features and faces to pattern, see Figure 9.4. To select features to pattern, click on the **Features to Pattern** field of this rollout to activate its selection mode and then select features to pattern from the graphics area or from the FeatureManager design tree. Note that as soon as you select features to pattern, the name of the selected features appears in the of the **Features to Pattern** field. Note that the feature selected for patterning is also known as seed/parent feature.

To select faces to pattern, click on the **Faces to Pattern** field and then select faces to pattern from the graphics area. Note that faces to pattern should forms a closed volume and make up a feature.

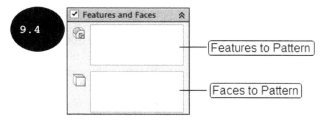

Tip: You can select features/faces to pattern before and after invoking the **Linear Pattern PropertyManager.**

After selecting features/faces to pattern, you need to defined pattern directions by using the **Direction 1** and **Direction 2** rollouts of the PropertyManager which are as follows.

Direction 1

The options available in the **Direction 1** rollout are used to create multiple instances/copies of selected features in direction 1, see Figure 9.5. The options of this rollout are as follows.

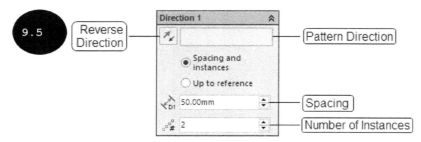

Pattern Direction

The **Pattern Direction** field is used to specify the pattern direction. You can select linear edge, linear sketch entity, axis, or dimension as the pattern direction from the graphics area. To specify the pattern direction, click on the **Pattern Direction** field to activate it and then select the pattern direction. As soon as you specify the pattern direction, the preview of the linear pattern appears in graphics area with a callout attached with the pattern direction and an arrow appears pointing towards the pattern direction, see Figure 9.6.

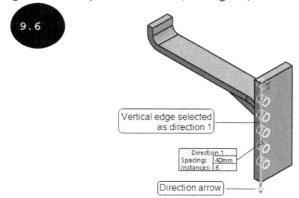

Spacing and instances

The **Spacing and instances** radio button is selected by default in the rollout. As a result, the **Spacing** and **Number of Instances** fields are available in the rollout which allows you to create pattern by specifying spacing between two pattern instances and number of instances to pattern in their respective fields. These options are explained below.

Spacing. The **Spacing** field allows you to specify the spacing between two instances of the pattern. You can also specify the spacing between two instances by using the callout appears in the graphics area. For doing so, click on the **Spacing** field of the callout and then enter the spacing in it.

Number of Instances. The **Number of Instances** field allows you to specify number of instances to be created in pattern direction. Figure 9.6 shows a preview of a linear pattern with 6 instances in direction 1. Note that the number of instances specified in the **Number of Instances** field also includes the parent or original feature selected for patterning. You can also specify number of instances in the callout appears in the graphics area.

Reverse Direction
The **Reverse Direction** button is used to reverse the pattern direction.

Up to reference
On selecting the **Up to reference** radio button, the options of the **Direction 1** rollout appears as shown in Figure 9.7. These options allows you to create pattern by specifying a reference geometry up to which pattern is to create based on the number of instances or spacing between instances specified in their respective fields. These options are explained below.

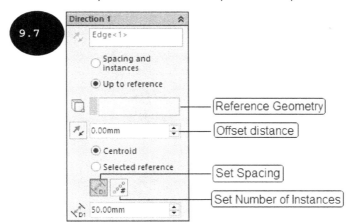

Reference Geometry. The **Reference Geometry** field allows you to select a reference geometry that control the pattern based on the number of pattern instances or spacing between instances specified. Note that on modifying the reference geometry, the respective pattern will also be modified automatically by adjusting the number of instances or spacing between the instances. Figure 9.8 shows the preview and the resultant patterns with a vertex is selected as the reference geometry and spacing between pattern instances is defined.

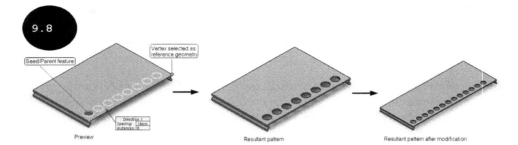

Offset distance. The **Offset distance** field allows you to specify the offset distance between the last pattern instance and reference geometry.

Centroid. On selecting the **Centroid** radio button, the offset distance specified in the **Offset distance** field measures between the center of last pattern instance and the reference geometry.

Selected reference. On selecting the **Selected reference** radio button, the **Seed Reference** field become available in the rollout. By using this field, you can select a reference geometry of the seed/parent feature to measure the offset distance.

Set Spacing / Set Number of Instances. The **Set Spacing** and **Set Number of Instances** buttons allow you to specify spacing between the pattern instances or the number of pattern instances in their respective field appears below these buttons, respectively.

Direction 2

The options available in the **Direction 2** rollout are used to create multiple instances of selected feature in direction 2. Figure 9.9 shows a preview of a linear pattern with 2 instances in direction 2.

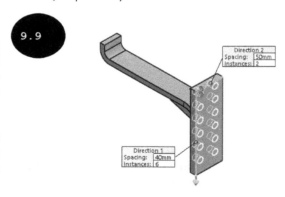

The options available in the **Direction 2** rollout are same as of the **Direction 1** rollout except the **Pattern seed only** check box which is as follows.

Pattern seed only

On selecting the **Pattern seed only** check box, the pattern is created only by using the seed/parent/original feature in the direction 2. Figure 9.10 shows a preview of a pattern feature when the **Pattern seed only** check box is cleared whereas Figure 9.11 shows a preview when the **Pattern seed only** check box is selected.

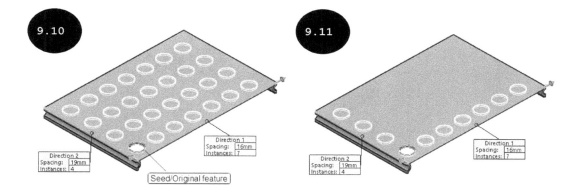

In addition to patterning features and faces, you can also pattern bodies by using the **Bodies** rollout of the PropertyManager which is explained below.

Bodies

The **Bodies** rollout allow you to select bodies to pattern. To select bodies, you need to expand this rollout by clicking on its title bar and then select the bodies to pattern from the graphics area or from the FeatureManager design tree.

Instances to Skip

The **Instances to Skip** rollout is used to skip some of the instances of the pattern being created. To skip the instances, expand this rollout by clicking on its title bar, pink dots displays at the center of all instances in the graphics area, see Figure 9.12. Next, move the cursor over the pink dot of the instance to be skipped and then click the left mouse button when the appearance of the cursor changes to hand cursor, see Figure 9.13. As soon as you click on the instance to skip, the appears of the selected instance disappear and pink dot changes to orange dot, see Figure 9.14. Also, the coordinate of the skipped pattern instance appears in the field of the **Instances to Skip** rollout. Similarly, you can skip multiple instances of the pattern, as required. You can also restore the skipped instances by clicking on the orange dot of the instance to be restore in the graphics area.

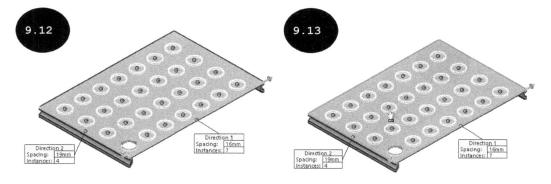

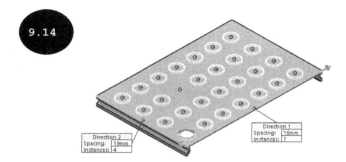

Options

The options available in the **Options** rollout are described next.

Vary sketch

The **Vary sketch** check box is used to vary the pattern instances with respect to a path. Figure 9.15 shows a feature to pattern and Figure 9.16 shows a variable linear pattern created by selecting the **Vary sketch** check box. By default this check box is not enabled and become enabled only on selecting a dimension as the patterning direction, see Figure 9.15.

Note: The sketch of the feature to be vary must contain reference sketch curve that can be used as the path to follow, see Figure 9.17. Also, the varying length of the sketch must not be restricted by dimension, see Figure 9.17.

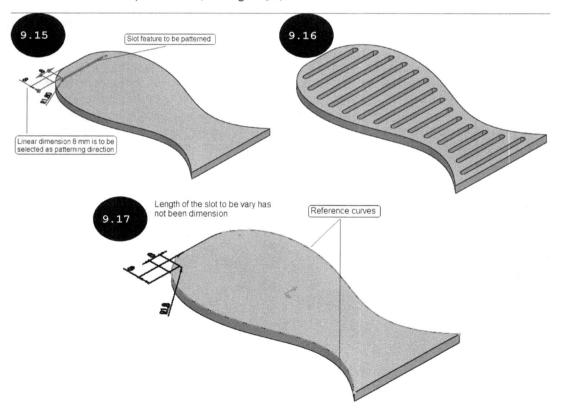

Geometry pattern

When the **Geometry pattern** check box is cleared, all the instances of the pattern being created maintain the same geometrical relations as that of the original or parent feature. By default this check box is cleared. Figure 9.18 shows the front view of a model have cut feature (the default **Shaded With Edges** display state of the model has been changed to **Hidden Lines Visible**). This cut feature is created by defining its end conditions as 4 mm offset from the bottom surface of the model by using the **Offset from Surface** option. Figure 9.19 shows the resultant pattern feature created by clearing the **Geometry pattern** check box and Figure 9.20 shows the resultant pattern with the check box is selected.

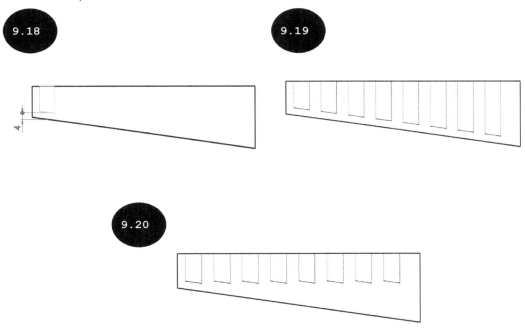

Propagate visual properties

By default, this check box is selected. As a result, all the visual properties such as colors, textures, and cosmetic thread, of the feature being pattern is propagates to all the instances of the pattern.

Full preview and Partial preview

The **Full preview** and **Partial preview** radio buttons are used to display full and partial preview of the pattern being created in the graphics area, respectively.

Instances to Vary

The **Instances to Vary** rollout is used to create a pattern with incremental spacing between pattern instances in directions 1 and 2. In addition to creating a pattern with incremental spacing between the instances, you can also vary the geometry of instances. Note that this rollout enables only after selecting a feature to be pattern and a pattering direction. Once this rollout enables, you can expand it by selecting the check box available on its title bar. Figure 9.21 shows the expanded view of the **Instances to Vary** rollout. The options of this rollout are described next.

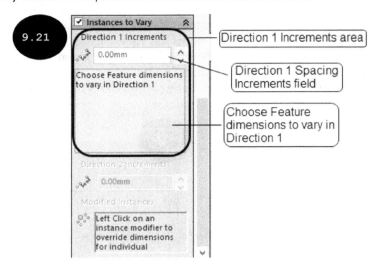

Direction 1 Increments

The **Direction 1 Increments** area of this rollout is used to specify the incremental spacing between pattern instances and the incremental dimensions such as diameter and height of a feature in direction 1. The options of this area are as follows.

Direction 1 Spacing Increments: The **Direction 1 Spacing Increments** field is used to specify the incremental spacing between the pattern instances. Figure 9.22 shows a preview of a pattern with increment spacing of 5 mm is specified in this field.

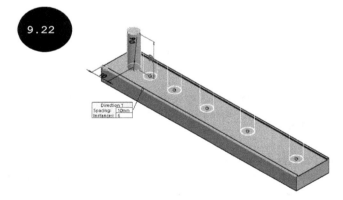

Choose Feature dimensions to vary in Direction 1: This field is used to select feature dimensions such as diameter and height to be vary in the pattern instances by specifying the incremental value, respectively. Select dimensions from the graphics area to be vary in the pattern instances, a table with dimension name, dimension value, and increment value columns appears in this field, see Figure 9.23. Now, you can click on the field corresponding to the increment value column to activate its editing mode and then enter the increment value for the selected dimension. Figure 9.24 shows a preview of a pattern instances with the incremental spacing of 5 mm and incremental diameter of 2 mm.

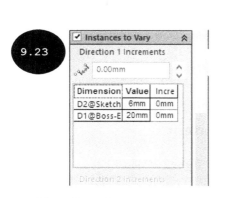

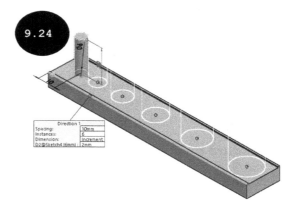

Direction 2 Increments

The Direction 2 Increments area of this rollout is used to specify the incremental spacing between pattern instances and incremental feature dimensions in direction 2. The options of this area works same as discussed earlier. Note that the options of this area enabled when you pattern features in direction 2.

Procedure to Create Linear Pattern in Direction 1 and Direction 2

1. Select a feature to pattern.
2. Click on the Linear Pattern tool, the Linear Pattern PropertyManager appears.
3. Specify the pattern direction by selecting a linear edge, linear sketch entity, axis, or dimension.
4. If required, flip the pattern direction by clicking on the Reverse Direction button.
5. Make sure that the Spacing and instances radio button is selected.
6. Specify the spacing between pattern instances in the Spacing field.
7. Specify pattern instances in the Number of Instances field.
8. Select a linear edge, linear sketch entity, axis, or dimension as the pattern direction 2.
9. Make sure that the Spacing and instances radio button is selected in the Direction 2 rollout.
10. Specify pattern instances in the Number of Instances field of the Direction 2 rollout.
11. Specify the spacing between pattern instances in the Spacing field of the Direction 2 rollout.
12. Flip the pattern direction 2, if required, by clicking on the Reverse Direction button.
13. Click on the green tick mark ✅ of the PropertyManager, a linear pattern in direction 1 and 2 is created.

Procedure to Create Linear Pattern using Reference Geometry

1. Select a feature to pattern.
2. Click on the Linear Pattern tool, the Linear Pattern PropertyManager appears.
3. Specify the pattern direction by selecting a linear edge, linear sketch entity, axis, or dimension.
4. If required, flip the pattern direction by clicking on the Reverse Direction button.
5. Select the Up to reference radio button.
6. Select a reference geometry to control the pattern. You can select vertex, face, and edge.

7. To define the offset distance between the last pattern instance and the reference geometry, make sure the **Centroid** radio button is selected.
8. Specify the offset distance in the **Offset distance** field.
9. Click to select the **Set Spacing** or **Set Number of Instances** button, respectively, to define the spacing between instances or number of pattern instances for creating pattern.
10. Define the spacing between instances or number of pattern instances for creating pattern in their respective fields.
11. Similarly, you can define parameters for creating pattern in direction 2.
12. Click on the green tick mark ✅ of the PropertyManager, a linear pattern using reference geometry is created.

Procedure to Skip Pattern Instances of Linear Pattern

1. Select feature to be pattern.
2. Click on the **Linear Pattern** tool, the **Linear Pattern PropertyManager** appears.
3. Specify parameters for creating linear pattern in direction 1 and 2, as discussed above.
4. Expand the **Instances to Skip** rollout of the PropertyManager, a pink dots appears at the center of all instances in the graphics area.
5. Click on the pink dot of the instances to be skipped.
6. Click on the green tick mark ✅ of the PropertyManager, a linear pattern after skipped some of the pattern instances is created.

Procedure to Create Vary Sketch Linear Pattern

1. Select a feature to pattern whose instances is to be varies.

Note: The sketch of the feature to be vary must contain reference sketch curve that can be used as the path to follow, see Figure 9.17. Also, the varying length of the sketch must not be restricted by dimension, see Figure 9.17.

2. Invoke the **Linear Pattern PropertyManager**.
3. Select a linear dimension as the pattern direction.
4. Select the **Vary sketch** check box of the **Option** rollout of the PropertyManager.
5. Specify other parameters such as spacing between the instances and number of instances in their respective fields of the PropertyManager.
6. Click on the green tick mark ✅ of the PropertyManager, a linear pattern with variable instances is created.

Procedure to Create Pattern with Spacing and Geometry Increment

1. Select feature to be pattern.
2. Invoke the **Linear Pattern PropertyManager**.
3. Specify parameters for creating linear pattern in direction 1 and 2.
4. Expand the **Instance to Vary** rollout of the PropertyManager.
5. For spacing increment, specify the incremental spacing between pattern instances in the **Direction 1 Spacing Increments** and **Direction 2 Spacing Increments** fields, respectively.
6. For geometry increment, select dimensions of the feature to be vary in the pattern instances.
7. Double click on the field corresponding to the **Increment value** column of the table to be edited available in the **Instance to Vary** rollout.

8. Specify the increment value for the selected dimension.
9. Click on the green tick mark ✓ of the PropertyManager, a linear pattern with specified incremental spacing and dimension is created.

Creating Circular Pattern

The circular pattern is created by creating multiple instances of features, faces, or bodies in circular manner about an axis, see Figure 9.25. To create circular pattern, click on the down arrow available at the bottom of **Linear Pattern** tool, the **Pattern** flyout appears, see Figure 9.26. In this flyout, click on the **Circular Pattern** tool, the **Circular Pattern PropertyManager** appears, see Figure 9.27.

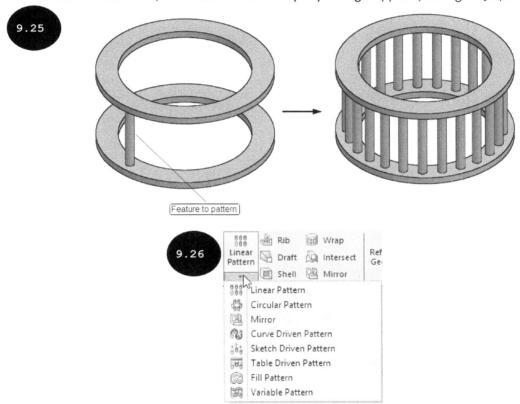

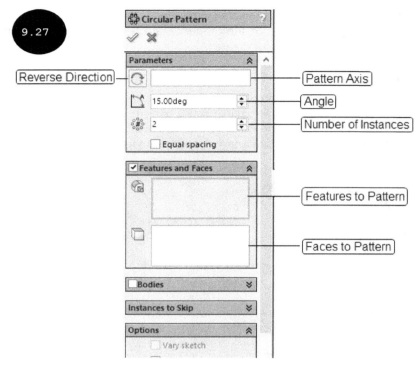

The options available in this **Circular Pattern PropertyManager** are as follows.

Features and Faces

The **Features and Faces** rollout is used to select features or faces to pattern in a circular manner. To select features, activate the **Features to Pattern** field of this rollout by clicking on it and then select features to pattern from the graphics area or from the FeatureManager design tree. Note that as soon as you select a feature, the name of the selected feature list in this field. You can select the features to pattern before and after invoking the PropertyManager.

To select faces to pattern, click on the **Faces to Pattern** field of the rollout and then select faces to pattern from the graphics area. Note that faces to pattern should forms a closed volume and make up a feature.

Parameters

The options available in the **Parameters** rollout are used to specify the parameters for patterning and are described next.

Pattern Axis

The **Pattern Axis** field allows you to select an axis around which you want to pattern. You can select an axis, circular face, circular edge, linear edge, linear sketch or angular dimension to define the axis of pattern, refer to Figures 9.28 through 9.31. Note that in case of selecting circular face and circular edge, their center axis will automatically be determined and used as the axis of circular pattern. To select pattern axis, click on the **Pattern Axis** field to activate it and then select an axis from the graphics area. As soon as you select pattern axis, the preview of the circular feature appears in the graphics area with a callout attached, see Figures 9.28 through 31.

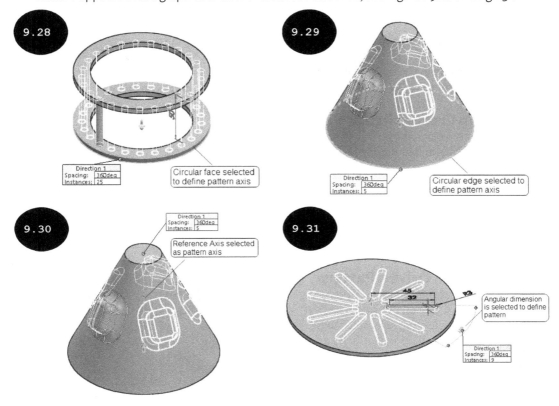

On selecting the circular face, circular edge, or angular dimension the axis of revolution for pattern instances will automatically be defined.

Angle

The **Angle** field is used to specify angle between pattern instances. By default, the angle 360 degrees is specified in this field. Also the **Equal spacing** check box is selected in the rollout. As a result, all the pattern instances is arranged with in the total angle specified with the equal angular spacing between all the instances. You can modify the total angle by entering new angle value in this field or by entering angle value in the callout appear in the graphics area.

On clearing the **Equal spacing** check box, you can specify the angle between instances in the **Angle** field instead of specifying the total angle.

Number of Instances

The **Number of Instances** field is used to specify number of instances to create. Figure 9.31 shows a preview of a circular pattern with 9 pattern instances. Note that the number of instances specified in this field also includes the parent or original feature selected for patterning. You can also specify number of instances in the callout appears in the graphics area.

Reverse Direction
The **Reverse Direction** button is used to reverse the angle of rotation.

The options available in the remaining rollouts of the PropertyManager: **Bodies, Instances to Skip, Options,** and **Instances to Vary** are same as of the **Linear Pattern PropertyManager.**

Procedure to Create Circular Pattern
1.   Select a feature to pattern.
2.   Invoke the **Pattern** flyout and then click on the **Circular Pattern** tool.
3.   Select an axis, circular face, circular edge, linear edge, linear sketch, or angular dimension as the axis of pattern.
4.   Specify the angle between pattern instances in the **Angle** field.
5.   Specify pattern instances in the **Number of Instances** field.
6.   Select or clear the **Equal spacing** check box, as required.
7.   Click on the green tick mark ✔ of the PropertyManager, a circular pattern is created.

Creating Curve Driven Pattern
The curve driven pattern is created by creating multiple instances of features, faces, or bodies along a curve, see Figure 9.32. You can select a 2D/3D sketch/curve or an edge as the curve to drive pattern instances. The curve/sketch selected can be an open or closed.

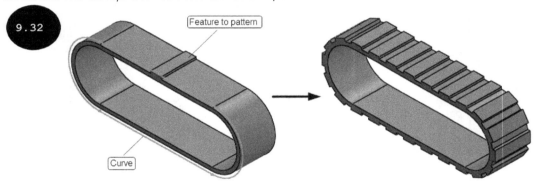

9.32   Feature to pattern   Curve

To create curve driven pattern, click on the down arrow available at the bottom of **Linear Pattern** tool, the **Pattern** flyout appears, see Figure 9.33. In this flyout, click on the **Curve Driven Pattern** tool, the **Curve Driven Pattern PropertyManager** appears, see Figure 9.34. The options available in this PropertyManager are as follows.

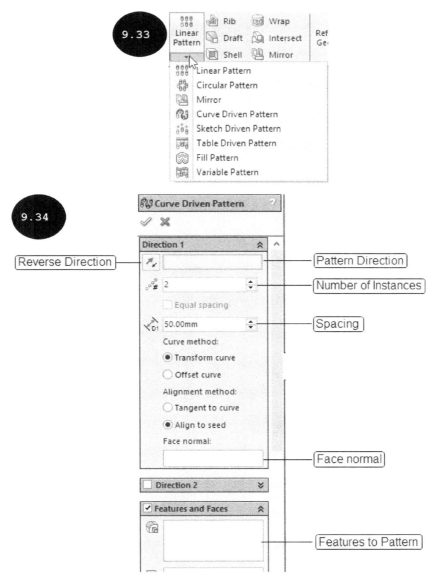

Features and Faces

The **Features and Faces** rollout of the PropertyManager is used to select features or faces to pattern. To select features to pattern, click on the **Features to Pattern** field of this rollout to activate it and then select the features to pattern from the graphics area or from the FeatureManager design tree. You can also select the features to pattern before and after invoking the PropertyManager.

To select faces to pattern, click on the **Faces to Pattern** field of the rollout and then select faces to pattern from the graphics area. Note that faces to pattern should forms a closed volume and make up a feature.

Direction 1

The options available in this rollout are used to select a driving curve and the parameters for patterning features in the direction 1. All the options of this rollout are as follows.

Pattern Direction

The **Pattern Direction** field is used to select a curve as the path for driving pattern instances. You can select a 3D curve, edge, sketch entity, or a sketch as the path for driving pattern instances. To select a curve, click on this field to activate it and then select a curve from the graphics area. As soon as you select a curve, the preview of the curve driven pattern appears in the graphics area with default parameters, see Figure 9.35.

> **Note:** If a sketch have multiple entities/segments is to be selected as a curve to drive pattern instances, you need to select it from the FeatureManager design tree. Also, a sketch can be an open or closed sketch. Figure 9.36 shows a preview of a curve driven pattern with an open curve selected.

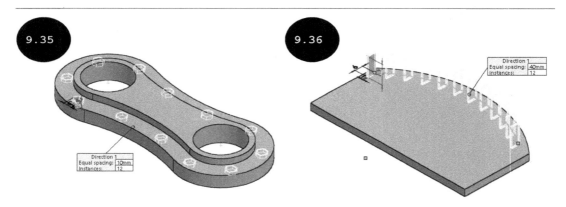

Number of Instances

The **Number of Instances** field is used to specify the number of instances in the pattern.

Equal spacing

When the **Equal spacing** check box is selected, the spacing between all pattern instances is equally arranged in accordance with the total length of the curve selected. If you clear this check box, the **Spacing** field enabled which allow you can specify the spacing between pattern instances.

Reverse Direction

This button is used to reverse the direction of pattern.

Curve method

The **Curve method** area is used to select the method for transforming the pattern instances along the curve. The options of this area are as follows.

Transform curve: When the **Transform curve** radio button is selected, the delta X and delta Y distances between the parent/original feature and the origin of the curve selected is maintained for pattern instances, see Figure 9.37.

Offset curve: When the **Offset curve** radio button is selected, the normal distance between the parent/original feature and the origin curve selected is maintained for pattern instances, see Figure 9.38.

Alignment method

The **Alignment method** area of the rollout is used to specify the method of alignment between the pattern instances and the curve selected. The options of this area are as follows.

Tangent to curve: When the **Tangent to curve** radio button is selected, each instance of the pattern is aligned tangent to the curve selected.

Figure 9.37 shows a preview of a curve driven pattern when the **Transform** curve method and the **Tangent to curve** alignment method is selected. Figure 9.38 shows a preview of the curve driven pattern when the **Offset** curve method and the **Tangent to curve** alignment method is selected.

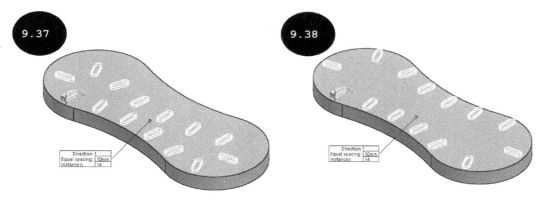

Align to seed: On selecting the **Align to seed** radio button, each instance of the pattern is aligned to match the parent/original feature.

Figure 9.39 shows a preview of a curve driven pattern when the **Transform** curve method and the **Align to seed** alignment method is selected. Figure 9.40 shows a preview of the curve driven pattern when the **Offset** curve method and the **Align to seed** alignment method is selected.

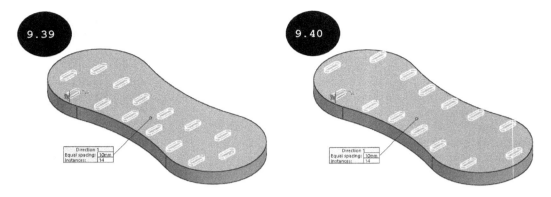

Face normal

The **Face normal** field is used to select a face to which pattern instances is to be created normal, see 9.41. It is used for creating curve driven pattern when the 3D curve is selected as the path to drive the pattern instances. Figure 9.41 shows a preview of a curve driven pattern with 3D curve (helix curve) is selected as the curve to drive pattern instances.

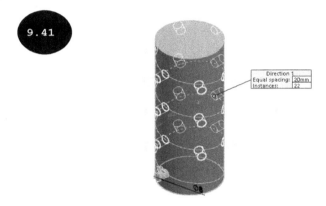

Direction 2

The options available in the **Direction 2** rollout are used to create pattern instances in the second direction. The options available in the rollout are same as of the **Direction 1** rollout. Figure 9.42 shows a preview of a curve driven pattern in two directions.

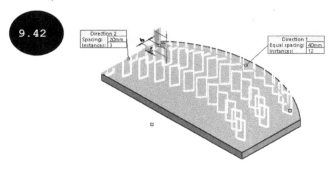

The options available in the remaining rollouts: **Bodies**, **Instances to Skip**, and **Options** of the PropertyManager are same as discussed earlier.

Procedure to Curve Driven Pattern

1. Select a feature to pattern.
2. Invoke the **Pattern** flyout and then click on the **Curve Driven Pattern** tool.
3. Select a curve from the FeatureManager design tree or from the graphics area.
4. Specify the number of pattern instances in the **Number of Instances** field.
5. Select the **Equal spacing** check box or specify the spacing between pattern instances in the **Spacing** field.
6. Select the curve method (**Transform curve** or **Offset curve**) from the **Curve method** area.
7. Select the alignment method (**Tangent to curve** or **Align to seed**) from the **Alignment method** area.
8. Click on the green tick mark ✅ of the PropertyManager, a curve driven pattern is created.

Creating Sketch Driven Pattern

The sketch driven pattern is created by driving the location of the pattern instances using the sketch points of a sketch. Figure 9.43 shows a sketch with multiple sketch points and a feature to be patterned and a resultant sketch driven pattern created.

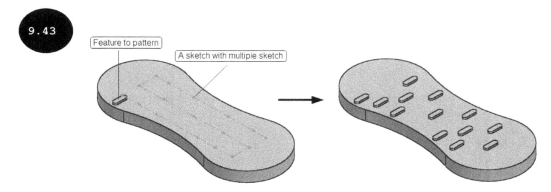

9.43

Feature to pattern

A sketch with multiple sketch

To create sketch driven pattern, invoke the **Pattern** flyout and then click on the **Sketch Driven Pattern** tool, the **Sketch Driven Pattern PropertyManager** appears, see Figure 9.44. The options available in this PropertyManager are as follows.

Features and Faces

The **Features and Faces** rollout of the PropertyManager is used to select features or faces to pattern. To select features to pattern, click on the **Features to Pattern** field of this rollout and then select features to pattern from the graphics area or from the FeatureManager design tree. You can select features to patterned before and after invoking the PropertyManager.

To select faces to pattern, click on the **Faces to Pattern** field of the rollout and then select faces to pattern from the graphics area. Note that faces to pattern should forms a closed volume and make up a feature.

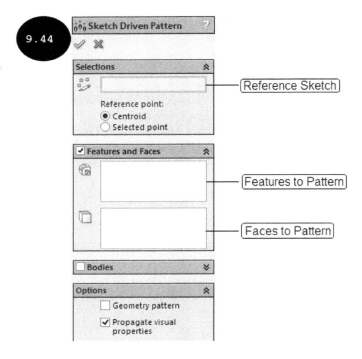

9.44

Selections

The options available in the **Selections** rollout are as follows.

Reference Sketch

The **Reference Sketch** field is used to select a sketch having multiple points for driving pattern instances. Click on this field to activate it and then select the sketch.

Centroid

By default, the **Centroid** radio button is selected in the **Reference point** area. As a result, the centroid of the parent feature is used as the base point for creating the pattern instances and the center point of each pattern instance is coincident with the sketch point, see Figure 9.45.

Selected point

On selecting the **Selected point** radio button, the **Reference Vertex** field appears in the rollout which allow you to select a reference point as the base point for the pattern, see Figure 9.46.

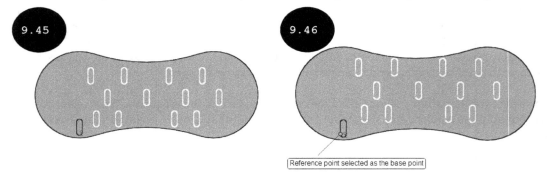

9.45

9.46

Reference point selected as the base point

The options available in the remaining rollouts: **Bodies** and **Options** of the PropertyManager are same as discussed earlier.

Procedure to Sketch Driven Pattern
1. Select a feature to pattern.
2. Invoke the **Pattern** flyout and then click on the **Sketch Driven Pattern** tool.
3. Select a sketch as the reference sketch having multiple sketch points.
4. Select the **Centroid** or **Selected point** radio button, as required.
5. Click on the green tick mark ✓ of the PropertyManager, a curve driven pattern is created.

Creating Table Driven Pattern
The table driven pattern is created by specifying coordinate points for each pattern instances with respect to a coordinate system. To create table driven pattern, you need to have a coordinate system created in the graphics area. After creating a coordinate system by using the **Coordinate System** tool that is available in the **Reference Geometry** flyout, click on the **Table Driven Pattern** tool of the **Pattern** flyout, the **Table Driven Pattern** dialog box appears, see Figure 9.47. Most of the options available in this dialog box are same as discussed earlier and the remaining options are as follows.

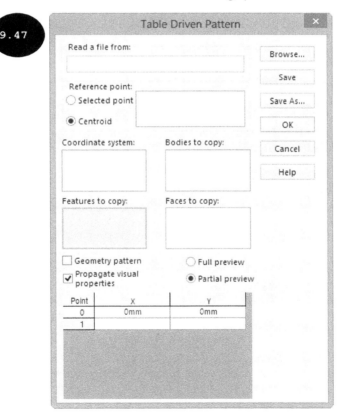

Figure 9.47

Features to copy

The **Features to copy** field of the dialog box is used to select features to pattern. To select features to pattern, click on this field to activate it, if not activated by default and then select the feature from the graphics area or from the FeatureManager design tree. Figure 9.44 shows a feature to pattern.

Coordinate system

The **Coordinate system** field is used to select a coordinate system from the graphics area. Note that the origin of the selected coordinate system is used as the origin for the table driven pattern. Figure 9.48 shows a coordinate system created.

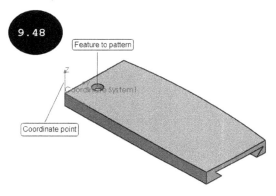

9.48

Feature to pattern

Coordinate System1

Coordinate point

Note: You can create coordinate system, as required, by using the **Coordinate System** tool available in the **Reference Geometry** flyout of the **Features CommandManager**. The procedure for creating coordinate system has been discussed in Chapter 6.

Coordinate table

The **Coordinate table** is available at the bottom of the dialog box and is used to specify the X and Y coordinates for each pattern instances. You can specify X and Y coordinates with respect to the selected coordinate system by double clicking on the **X** and **Y** fields of the table. Note that each row of this table represents a pattern instance and its X and Y fields represents X and Y coordinates of the pattern instance. You can add multiple rows in the table to specify coordinates for the multiple instances. Note that the new row is added automatically in the table as soon as you double click on a field of the last row of the table. Figure 9.49 shows the **Table Driven Pattern** dialog box with the coordinates of 5 pattern instances (including the coordinates of the original/parent feature) is specified in the table.

Note: To delete a row of the table, select the row to delete and then press the DELETE key.

Save/Save As

The **Save/Save As** button is used to save the defined pattern table or coordinate points of the table as an external *Pattern Table (*.sldptab)* file for later use.

Read a file from

The **Read a file from** field is used to read an existing *Pattern Table (*.sldptab)* or *.txt (notepad)* file containing the coordinate points for creating the pattern. To create pattern by using the existing *Pattern Table (*.sldptab)* or .txt (notepad) file, click on the **Browse** button and then select the required file to be imported. As soon as you import the file, the coordinate points specified in the file is filled automatically in the **Coordinate table** of the dialog box.

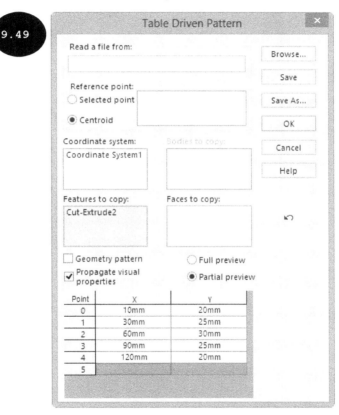

OK

Once you are done with specifying feature to pattern, coordinate system, reference point (**Selected point** or **Centroid**), and coordinates, click on the **OK** button to create table driven pattern. Figure 9.50 shows a table driven pattern created by specifying coordinates shown in Figure 9.49.

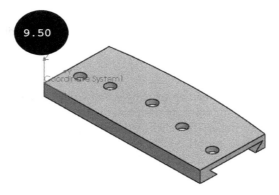

Procedure to Create Table Driven Pattern

1. Create a coordinate system in the graphics area with respect to which coordinates of the pattern instances is measured.
2. Invoke the **Pattern** flyout and then click on the **Table Driven Pattern** tool.
3. Select the feature to pattern from the graphics area.
4. Click on the **Coordinate system** field to activate it and then select the coordinate system.
5. In the **Coordinate table** of the dialog box, double click on the field corresponding to the **Point 1** row and **X** column to activate its edit mode. Next, enter the **X** coordinate of the point 1.
6. Similarly, specify the **Y** coordinate of the point 1.
7. Similarly, specify the **X** and **Y** coordinates for the remaining points (each point represents pattern instances) in the table.
8. Click on the **OK** button, the table driven pattern is created.

Creating Fill Pattern

A fill Pattern is created by filling an area by pattern instances. In fill pattern, you can select features, faces, bodies, or predefined cut shape to fill a particular area of a model. You can select a face as the area to be filled and a closed sketch to fill the area inside the closed sketch. Figure 9.51 shows a feature to pattern, face to fill, and the resultant fill pattern created. Figure 9.52 shows a feature to pattern, closed sketch to fill, and the resultant fill pattern created.

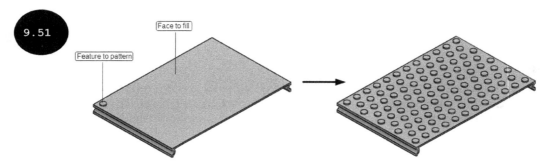

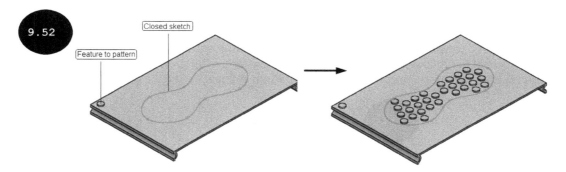

To create fill pattern, invoke the **Pattern** flyout and then click on the **Fill Pattern** tool, the **Fill Pattern PropertyManager** appears, see Figure 9.53. The options of this PropertyManager are as follows.

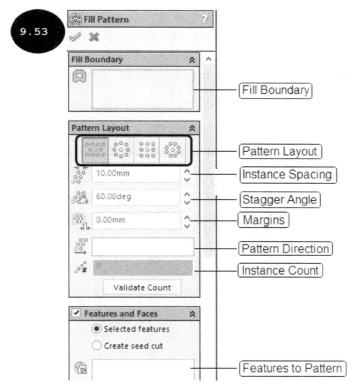

Fill Boundary
By default, the **Fill Boundary** field is activated in the **Fill Boundary** rollout. As a result, you are prompted to select a boundary/area to fill. You can select a face or a close sketch as the area to fill. Select a face/closed sketch from the graphics area, see Figures 9.51 and 9.52.

Features and Faces

By default, the **Selected features** radio button is selected in the **Features and Faces** rollout. As a result, you are allowed to select features to pattern. To select features to pattern, click on the **Features to Pattern** field of this rollout and then select feature to pattern. After specifying the boundary/area to fill and feature to pattern, the preview of the fill pattern appears, see Figure 9.54.

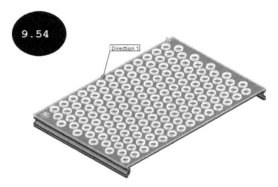

To select faces to pattern, click on the **Faces to Pattern** field of the rollout and then select faces to pattern from the graphics area. Note that faces to pattern should forms a closed volume and make up a feature.

On selecting the **Create seed cut** radio button of the **Features and Faces** rollout, the different type of predefined cut shapes appears in the rollout, see Figure 9.55. By default, the **Circle** button is selected. As a result, the selected boundary fills with predefined circular cut features, see Figure 9.56. You can specify the diameter for the circular cut feature, as required, by using the **Diameter** field available in this rollout. The **Vertex or Sketch Point** field is used to define the start point for pattern. You can select a vertex or a sketch point as the starting point. Note that if you do not specify the start point, by default, the pattern created in the centered of the boundary face selected.

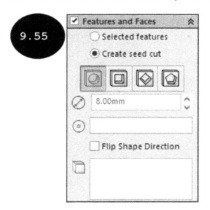

In addition to the predefined circular cut feature, you can also select predefined square, diamond, and polygon cut feature to pattern. Figures 9.57 through 9.59 shows the fill pattern with square, diamond, ellipse and polygon predefined cut shapes.

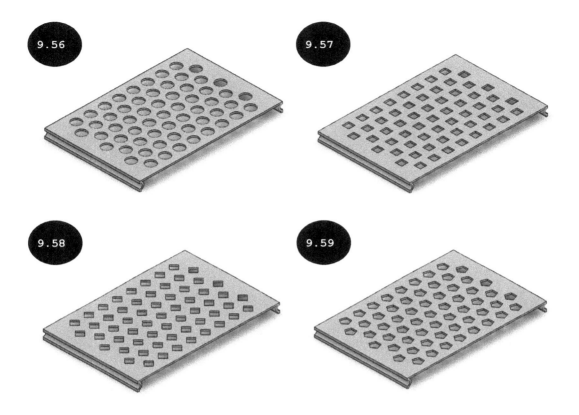

Pattern Layout

The **Pattern Layout** area of the **Pattern Layout** rollout is used to select type of pattern layout for the fill pattern. You can select the **Perforation**, **Circular**, **Square**, or **Polygon** button for defining the type of pattern layout to use for fill pattern, see Figures 9.60 through 9.63.

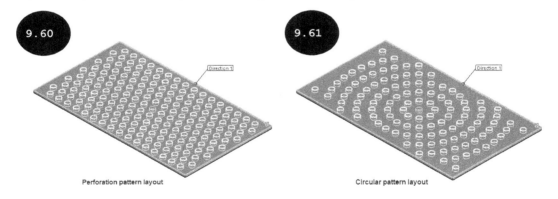

Perforation pattern layout

Circular pattern layout

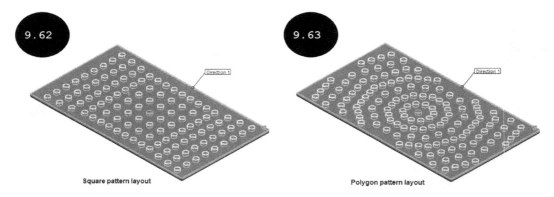

Square pattern layout   Polygon pattern layout

The remaining options available in the **Pattern Layout** rollout allows you to control the parameters of the pattern layout such as spacing between the pattern instances and margin between the fill boundary and the outermost instance. The remaining options of this PropertyManager are same as discussed earlier.

Procedure to Create Fill Pattern from Features
1. Select a feature to be pattern.
2. Invoke the **Pattern** flyout and then click on the **Fill Pattern** tool.
3. Select a face or closed sketch as the boundary to fill by pattern instances.
4. Select the type of pattern layout: **Perforation, Circular, Square,** or **Polygon.**
5. Specify the parameters for the pattern layout in the fields of the **Pattern Layout** rollout.
6. Click on the green tick mark ✅ of the PropertyManager, a curve driven pattern is created.

Procedure to Create Fill Pattern from Predefined Cut Feature
1. Invoke the **Pattern** flyout and then click on the **Fill Pattern** tool.
2. Select the **Create seed cut** radio button from the **Features to Pattern** rollout.
3. Select the predefined cut shapes: **Circle, Square, Diamond,** or **Polygon,** as required.
4. Specify the parameters for the predefined cut shape feature, as required, in the fields of the **Features to Pattern** rollout.
5. Select the type of pattern layout: **Perforation, Circular, Square,** or **Polygon.**
6. Specify the parameters for the pattern layout in the fields of the **Pattern Layout** rollout.
7. Click on the green tick mark ✅ of the PropertyManager, a fill pattern is created.

Creating Variable Pattern
In SOLIDWORKS, you can create variable pattern by using the **Variable Pattern** tool of the **Pattern** flyout. This tool allows you to create variable pattern such that you can vary dimensions and references of pattern instances, see Figure 9.64. The variable pattern shown in this figure has been created by varying the slot length and angle of the parent slot.

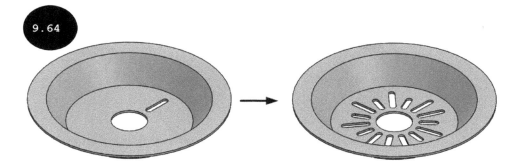

To create variable pattern, invoke the **Pattern** flyout and then click on the **Variable Pattern** tool, the **Variable Pattern PropertyManager** appears, see Figure 9.65. The options of this PropertyManager are described next.

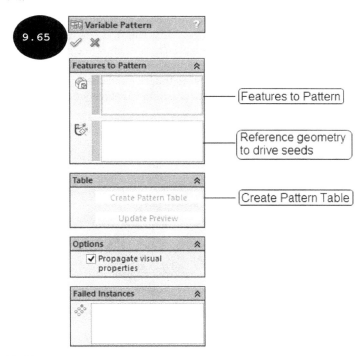

Features to Pattern

The **Features to Pattern** field allows you to select feature to pattern. You can select extruded, cut extruded, revolved, cut revolved, sweep, cut sweep, loft, cut loft, fillet, chamfer, dome, and draft features as the seed/parent features to pattern for creating the variable pattern. As soon as you select feature to pattern, their respective dimensions appears in the graphics area in order to select them as the dimensions to vary, see Figure 9.66.

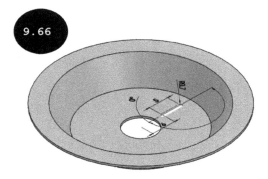

Reference Geometry to drive seeds

The **Reference Geometry to drive seeds** field allows you to select reference geometries on which the seed/parent feature is depended. On selecting reference geometries, their respective dimensions become available in the graphics area in order to select them as the dimensions to vary. You can select axis, plane, point, curve, 2D sketch, or 3D sketch as the reference geometry. Figure 9.67 shows a extruded feature selected along with their respective reference geometry (a plane and a 3D point) on which the extruded feature is depended on. Note that the extruded feature shown in the figure is created on the non planar face of the model with the help of reference plane and a 3D point.

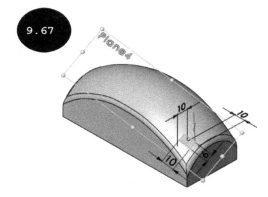

Create Pattern Table

The **Create Pattern Table** button is used to invoke the **Pattern Table** window which allows you to select dimensions of the features and reference geometries to be varied. Figure 9.68 shows the Pattern Table window invoked on clicking on the **Create Pattern Table** button.

Once the **Pattern Table** window is invoked, you can select the dimensions to vary from the graphics area, see Figure 9.69. In Figure 9.69, the slot angle and length of the model shown in Figure 9.66 is selected as the dimensions to vary.

9.68

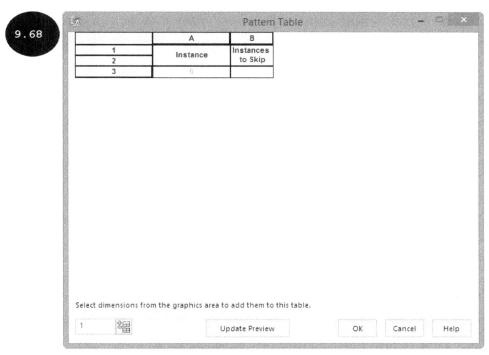

9.69

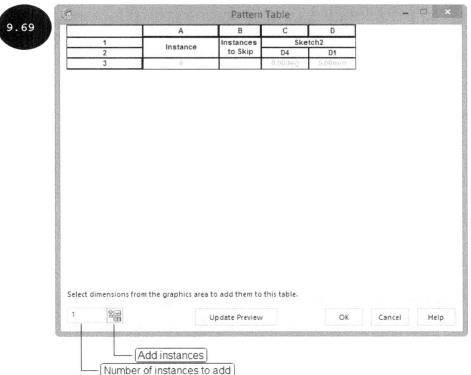

The **Number of instances to add** field of the **Pattern Table** window allows you to enter the number of instances to be created. After specifying number of instances in this field, click on the **Add instances** button of the window. As soon as you click on this button, multiple rows equivalent to the number of instances specified is added in the **Pattern Table** window, see Figure 9.70. Note that each row of this table represent a pattern instance and you can modify/control the dimensions for each pattern instance by entering the required dimension values, see Figure 9.70. This table works in the same manner as of *Microsoft Office Excel* works.

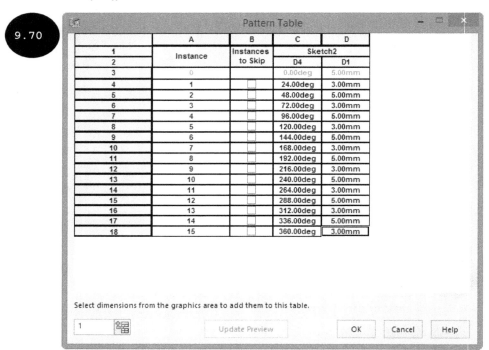

9.70

The **Update Preview** button of the window allows you to view the updated preview of the pattern instances. Once you are down, click on the **OK** button, the variable pattern is created, see Figure 9.71.

9.71

Procedure to Create Variable Pattern

1. Invoke the **Pattern** flyout and then click on the **Variable Pattern** tool.
2. Select features to pattern from the graphics area or from the FeatureManager design tree.
3. If the creation of feature being patterned depends on any reference geometry, click on the **Reference geometry to drive seeds** field and then select the reference geometries.
4. Click on the **Create Pattern Table** button, the **Pattern Table** window appears.
5. Click to select dimensions to vary from the graphics area.
6. Enter number of pattern instances to be created in the **Number of instances to add** field.
7. Click on the **Add instances** button of the window, the rows equivalent to the number of instances specified is added in the window.
8. Modify the dimensions for each pattern instance, as required, in their respective fields.
9. Click on the **OK** button of the **Pattern Table** window, the variable pattern is created.

Mirroring Feature

Mirror features are created by mirroring features, faces, or bodies about an mirroring plane. Figure 9.72 shows features to mirror, mirroring plane, and the resultant mirroring feature created.

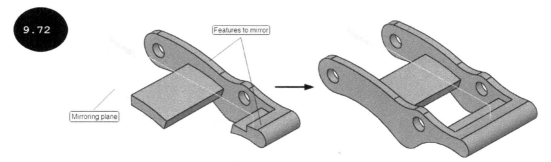

To create mirror feature, click on the **Mirror** tool available in the **Features CommandManager**, the **Mirror PropertyManager** appears, see Figure 9.73. You can also invoke this tool from the **Pattern** flyout. The options available in this PropertyManager are as follows.

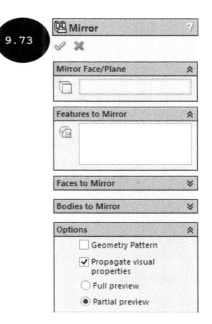

Mirror Face/Plane

The **Mirror Face/Plane** field of the **Mirror Face/Plane** rollout is activated, by default. As a result, you are prompted to select mirroring plane. You can select a reference plane or a planar face of the model as the mirroring plane from the graphics area or from the FeatureManager design tree, see Figure 9.72.

Features to Mirror

The **Features to Mirror** field of the **Features to Mirror** rollout is used to select features to mirror about the selected mirroring plane. To select features, activate this field by clicking on it. Next, select the features to mirror. After selecting the mirroring plane and features to mirror, the preview of the mirror features appears in the graphics area.

Faces to Mirror/Bodies to Mirror

The **Faces to Mirror** and **Bodies to Mirror** rollouts of the PropertyManager allow you to select faces that comprise a feature and bodies to mirror.

Options

The options available in this rollout are same as discussed while creating patterns. If the **Geometry Pattern** check box is cleared, the mirror image being created maintain the same geometrical relations as that of the original or parent feature. Figure 9.74 shows the front view of a model have cut feature (the default **Shaded With Edges** display state of the model has been changed to **Hidden Lines Visible**). This cut feature is created by defining its end conditions as 4 mm offset from the bottom surface of the model by using the **Offset from Surface** option. Figure 9.75 shows the resultant pattern feature created by clearing the **Geometry pattern** check box and Figure 9.76 shows the resultant pattern with the **Geometry Pattern** check box is selected.

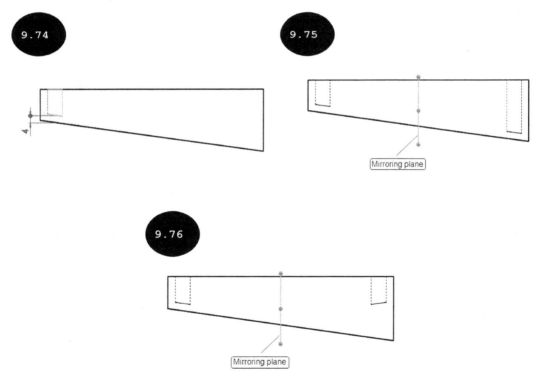

By default, the **Propagate visual properties** check box is selected. As a result, all the visual properties such as colors, textures, and cosmetic thread of the feature being mirror is propagates to the mirror feature.

Procedure to Create Mirror Feature

1. Click on the **Mirror** tool, the **Mirror PropertyManager** appears.
2. Select a reference plane or planar face as the mirroring plane.
3. Select the feature to mirror by using the **Features to Mirror** rollout.
4. Click on the green tick mark ✅ of the PropertyManager, a mirror feature is created.

Tutorial 1

Create the model shown in Figure 9.77.

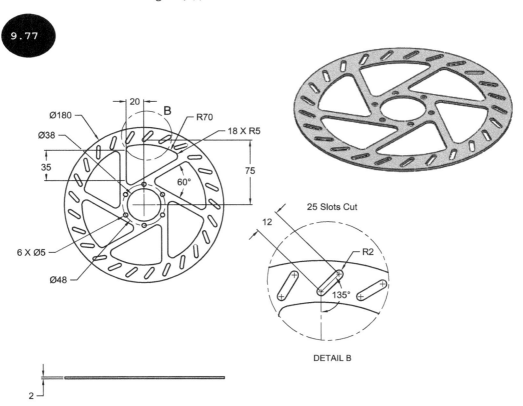

Section 1: Starting SOLIDWORKS

1. Double click on the **SOLIDWORKS** icon on your desktop to start SOLIDWORKS.

Section 2: Invoking Part Modeling Environment

1. Click on the **New** tool in the **Standard** toolbar, the **New SOLIDWORKS Document** dialog box appears.

2.   In this dialog box, the **Part** button is activated by default. Click on the **OK** button.

Once the Part modeling environment is invoked, you can set the unit system and create the base/first feature of the model.

Section 3: Specifying Unit Settings

1.   Move the cursor towards the lower right corner of the screen over the Status Bar and then click on the **Unit System** area of the Status Bar, the **Unit System** flyout appears, see Figure 9.78.

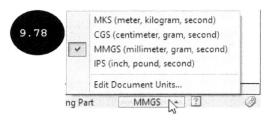

2.   Make sure that the **MMGS (millimeter, gram, second)** option is ticked marked in this flyout, see Figure 9.78.

Section 4: Creating First/Base Feature - Extrude Feature

1.   Invoke the Sketching environment by selecting the Top Planar as the sketching plane.

2.   Create the sketch of the base feature of the model, see Figure 9.79.

3.   Click on the **Features** tab of the **CommandManager** to displays the tools of the **Features CommandManager**.

4.   Click on the **Extruded Boss/Base** tool, the **Boss-Extrude PropertyManager** and the preview of the extruded feature appears.

5.   Enter **2** in the **Depth** field of the **Direction 1** rollout and then press ENTER key.

6.   Click on the green tick mark ✅ of the PropertyManager, the extruded feature is created, see Figure 9.80.

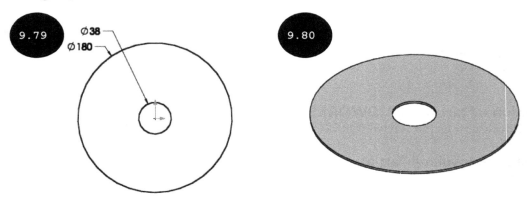

Section 5: Creating Second Feature - Extrude Cut Feature

1. Invoke the Sketching environment by selecting the top planar face of the base feature as the sketching plane.

2. Change the orientation of the model normal to the viewing direction by using the **Normal To** tool of the **View Orientation** flyout.

3. Create the sketch of the second feature, see Figure 9.81.

4. Click on the **Extruded Cut** tool of the **Features CommandManager**, the **Cut-Extrude PropertyManager** and the preview of the extruded cut feature appears. Change the orientation of the model to isometric.

5. Invoke the **End Condition** flyout of the **Direction 1** rollout and then select the **Through All** option from it.

6. Click on the green tick mark ✅ of the PropertyManager, the extruded cut feature is created, see Figure 9.82.

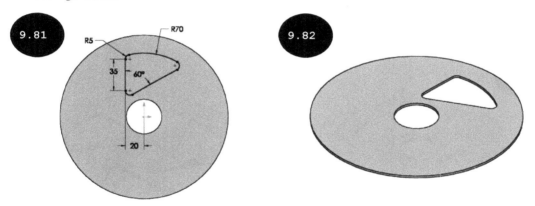

9.81

9.82

Section 6: Creating Third Feature - Circular Pattern

1. Click on the down arrow available at the bottom of **Linear Pattern** tool, the **Pattern** flyout appears, see Figure 9.83.

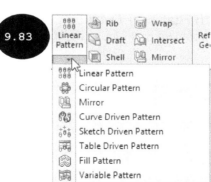

9.83

2. Click on the **Circular Pattern** tool of the **Pattern** flyout, the **Circular Pattern PropertyManager** appears.

3. Expand the FeatureManager design tree which is now available at the top left corner of the graphics area by clicking on its +sign.

4. Click to select the second feature (extrude cut) from the FeatureManager design tree as the feature to pattern.

5. Click on the **Pattern Axis** field of the **Parameters** rollout of the PropertyManager to activate it.

6. Click to select the circular edge of the base feature from the graphics area to define the pattern axis, see Figure 9.84, the preview of the circular pattern appears.

7. Make sure that the **Equal spacing** check box is selected in the **Parameters** rollout of the PropertyManager.

8. Enter **6** in the **Number of Instances** field of the **Parameters** rollout.

9. Click on the green tick mark ✅ of the PropertyManager, the circular pattern is created, see Figure 9.85.

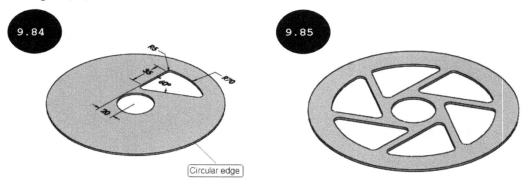

Circular edge

Section 7: Creating Forth Feature - Extrude Cut Feature

1. Invoke the Sketching environment by selecting the top planar face of the base feature as the sketching plane.

2. Change the orientation of the model normal to the viewing direction by using the **Normal To** tool of the **View Orientation** flyout.

3. Create the sketch of the forth feature, see Figure 9.86.

4. Click on the **Extruded Cut** tool of the **Features CommandManager**, the **Cut-Extrude PropertyManager** and the preview of the extruded cut feature appears. Change the orientation of the model to isometric.

5.   Invoke the **End Condition** flyout of the **Direction 1** rollout and then select the **Through All** option from it.

6.   Click on the green tick mark ✓ of the PropertyManager, the extruded cut feature is created, see Figure 9.87.

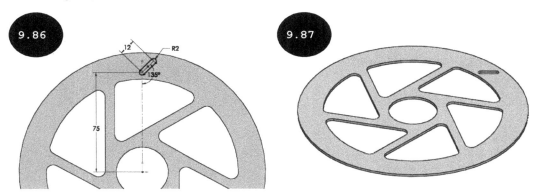

Section 8: Creating Fifth Feature - Circular Pattern

1.   Click on the down arrow available at the bottom of **Linear Pattern** tool, the **Pattern** flyout appears, see Figure 9.88.

2.   Click on the **Circular Pattern** tool of the **Pattern** flyout, the **Circular Pattern** PropertyManager appears.

3.   Expand the FeatureManager design tree which is now available at the top left corner of the graphics area by clicking on its +sign.

4.   Click to select the forth feature (extrude cut) from the FeatureManager design tree as the feature to pattern.

5.   Click on the **Pattern Axis** field of the **Parameters** rollout of the PropertyManager to activate it.

6.   Click to select the circular edge of the base feature from the graphics area to define the pattern axis, see Figure 9.89, the preview of the circular pattern appears.

7.   Make sure that the **Equal spacing** check box is selected in the **Parameters** rollout of the PropertyManager.

8.   Enter **25** in the **Number of Instances** field of the **Parameters** rollout.

9.   Click on the green tick mark ✓ of the PropertyManager, the circular pattern is created, see Figure 9.90.

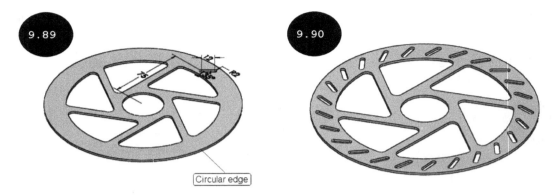

Circular edge

Section 9: Creating Sixth Feature - Extrude Cut Feature

1. Invoke the Sketching environment by selecting the top planar face of the base feature as the sketching plane.

2. Change the orientation of the model normal to the viewing direction.

3. Create the sketch of the Sixth feature (circle of diameter 5 mm), see Figure 9.91.

4. Click on the **Extruded Cut** tool of the **Features CommandManager** and then change the orientation of the model to isometric.

5. Select the **Through All** option from the **End Condition** flyout of the **Direction 1** rollout of the PropertyManager.

6. Click on the green tick mark ✔ of the PropertyManager, the extruded cut feature is created, see Figure 9.92.

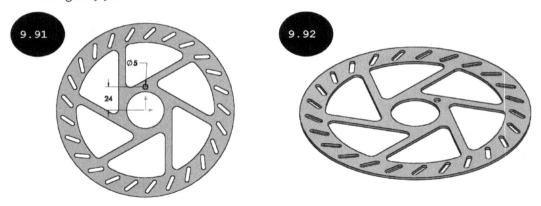

Section 10: Creating Seventh Feature - Circular Pattern

1. Invoke the **Pattern** flyout appears, see Figure 9.93 and then click on the **Circular Pattern** tool of this flyout, the **Circular Pattern PropertyManager** appears.

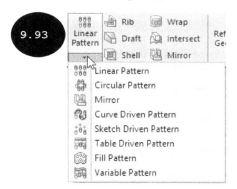

2. Expand the FeatureManager design tree which is now available at the top left corner of the graphics area by clicking on its +sign.

3. Click to select the six feature (extrude cut) from the FeatureManager design tree as the feature to pattern.

4. Click on the **Pattern Axis** field of the **Parameters** rollout of the PropertyManager to activate it.

5. Click to select the circular edge of the base feature from the graphics area to define the pattern axis, see Figure 9.94, the preview of the circular pattern appears.

6. Make sure that the **Equal spacing** check box is selected in the **Parameters** rollout of the PropertyManager.

7. Enter **6** in the **Number of Instances** field of the **Parameters** rollout.

8. Click on the green tick mark ✅ of the PropertyManager, the circular pattern is created, see Figure 9.95.

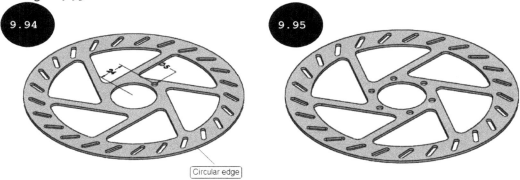

Circular edge

Section 11: Saving the Model

1. Click on the **Save** tool of the **Standard** toolbar, the **Save As** window appears.

2. Browse to the *SOLIDWORKS* folder and then create a folder named as *Chapter 9*. Next, create another folder named as *Tutorial* inside the *Chapter 9* folder.

3. Type **Tutorial 1** in the **File name** field of the dialog box as the name of the file and then click on the **Save** button, the model is saved as Tutorial 1 in the *Tutorial* folder of *Chapter 9*.

Tutorial 2

Create the model shown in Figure 9.96.

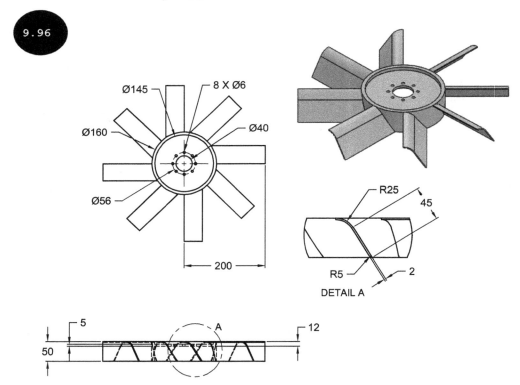

9.96

Section 1: Starting SOLIDWORKS

1. Double click on the **SOLIDWORKS** icon on your desktop to start SOLIDWORKS.

Section 2: Invoking Part Modeling Environment

1. Click on the **New** tool in the **Standard** toolbar, the **New SOLIDWORKS Document** dialog box appears.

2. In this dialog box, the **Part** button is activated by default. Click on the **OK** button.

Once the Part modeling environment is invoked, you can set the unit system and create the base/first feature of the model.

Section 3: Specifying Unit Settings

1. Make sure that the MMGS (millimeter, gram, second) unit system is set for the current opened part document.

Section 4: Creating First/Base Feature - Extrude Feature

1. Invoke the Sketching environment by selecting the Top plane as the sketching plane.

2. Create the sketch of the base feature of the model, see Figure 9.97.

3. Click on the **Features** tab of the **CommandManager** to displays the tools of the **Features CommandManager**.

4. Click on the **Extruded Boss/Base** tool, the **Boss-Extrude PropertyManager** and the preview of the extruded feature appears.

5. Invoke the **End Condition** drop-down list of the **Direction 1** rollout of the PropertyManager.

6. Click to select the **Mid Plane** option from the **End Condition** drop-down list.

7. Enter **50** in the **Depth** field of the **Direction 1** rollout and then press ENTER key.

8. Click on the green tick mark ✅ of the PropertyManager, the extruded feature is created, see Figure 9.98.

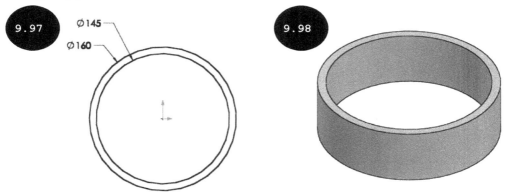

Section 5: Creating Second Feature - Extrude Feature

1. Invoke the Sketching environment by selecting the top planar face of the base feature as the sketching plane.

2. Change the orientation of the model normal to the viewing direction by using the **Normal To** tool of the **View Orientation** flyout.

3. Create the sketch (two circles of diameter 145 and 40 degrees) of the second feature, see Figure 9.99.

4. Click on the **Extruded Boss/Base** tool, the **Boss-Extrude PropertyManager** and the preview of the extruded feature appears. Change the orientation of the model to isometric.

5. Invoke the **Start Condition** drop-down list of the **From** rollout in the PropertyManager, see Figure 9.100.

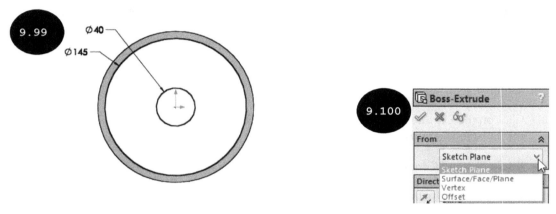

6. Select the **Offset** option from the **Start Condition** drop-down list of the **From** rollout.

7. Enter **12** in the **Enter Offset Value** field of the **From** rollout of the PropertyManager.

8. Click on the **Reverse Direction** button of the **From** rollout of the PropertyManager to reverse the direction of material creation.

9. Enter **5** in the **Depth** field of the **Direction 1** rollout of the PropertyManager.

10. Click on the green tick mark ✓ of the PropertyManager, the extruded feature is created, see Figure 9.101.

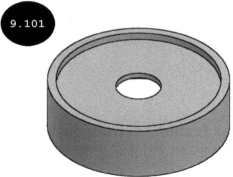

Section 6: Creating Third Feature - Extrude Cut Feature

1. Invoke the Sketching environment by selecting the top planar face of the second feature as the sketching plane.

2. Change the orientation of the model normal to the viewing direction by using the **Normal To** tool of the **View Orientation** flyout.

3. Create a circle of diameter 6 mm as the sketch of the third feature, see Figure 9.102.

4. Click on the **Extruded Cut** tool of the **Features CommandManager**, the **Cut-Extrude PropertyManager** and the preview of the extruded cut feature appears. Change the orientation of the model to isometric.

5. Invoke the **End Condition** flyout of the **Direction 1** rollout and then select the **Through All** option from it.

6. Click on the green tick mark ✅ of the PropertyManager, the extruded cut feature is created, see Figure 9.103.

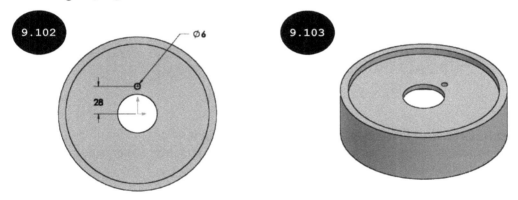

Section 7: Creating Forth Feature - Circular Pattern

1. Invoke the **Pattern** flyout by clicking on the down arrow available at the bottom of **Linear Pattern** tool.

2. Click on the **Circular Pattern** tool of the **Pattern** flyout, the **Circular Pattern PropertyManager** appears.

3. Expand the FeatureManager design tree which is now available at the top left corner of the graphics area by clicking on its +sign.

4. Click to select the third feature (extrude cut) from the FeatureManager design tree as the feature to pattern.

5. Click on the **Pattern Axis** field of the **Parameters** rollout of the PropertyManager to activate it.

6. Click to select the outer circular face of the base feature from the graphics area to define the pattern axis, see Figure 9.104, the preview of the circular pattern appears.

7. Make sure that the **Equal spacing** check box is selected in the **Parameters** rollout of the PropertyManager.

8. Enter **8** in the **Number of Instances** field of the **Parameters** rollout.

9. Click on the green tick mark ✅ of the PropertyManager, the circular pattern is created, see Figure 9.105.

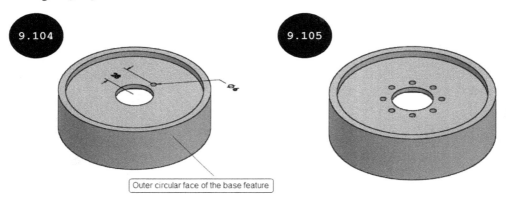

Outer circular face of the base feature

Section 8: Creating Fifth Feature - Extrude Feature

The third feature of the model is an extruded feature and its sketch is to be created on reference plane at an offset distance of 200 mm from the Right Plane.

1. Invoke the **Plane** tool of the **Reference Geometry** flyout and create a reference plane at an offset distance of 200 mm from the Right Plane, see Figure 9.106.

2. Invoke the Sketching environment by selecting the newly created reference plane as the sketching plane.

3. Change the orientation of the model normal to the viewing direction by using the **Normal To** tool of the **View Orientation** flyout.

4. Create the sketch of the third extruded feature, see Figure 9.107.

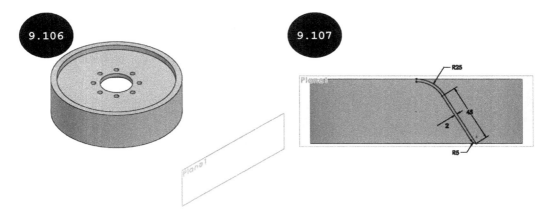

Note: In the sketch shown in Figure 9.107, the tangent relation is applied between the connecting arcs and lines of the sketch. Also, the center point of the arc having radius 25 mm is coincident with the origin.

5. Click on the **Features** tab of the **CommandManager** to displays the tools of the **Features CommandManager**.

6. Click on the **Extruded Boss/Base** tool, the **Boss-Extrude PropertyManager** and the preview of the extruded feature appears. Change the orientation of the model to isometric.

7. Invoke the **End Condition** drop-down list of the **Direction 1** rollout of the PropertyManager.

8. Click to select the **Up To Surface** option of the **End Condition** flyout, the **Face/Plane** field become available in the **Direction 1** rollout and is activated by default.

9. Click to select the outer circular face of the base feature as the surface up to which you want to extrude feature, the preview of the extrude feature appears in the graphics area, see Figure 9.108.

10. Click on the green tick mark ✅ of the PropertyManager, the extruded feature is created, see Figure 9.109.

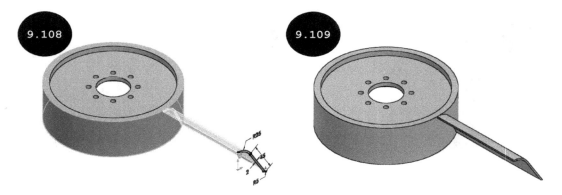

Section 9: Creating Six Feature - Circular Pattern

1. Invoke the **Pattern** flyout by clicking on the down arrow available at the bottom of **Linear Pattern** tool.

2. Click on the **Circular Pattern** tool of the **Pattern** flyout, the **Circular Pattern PropertyManager** appears.

3. Select the fifth feature (last created extruded feature) as the feature to pattern from the graphics area.

4. Click on the **Pattern Axis** field of the **Parameters** rollout of the PropertyManager to activate it.

5. Click to select the outer circular face of the base feature from the graphics area to define the pattern axis, the preview of the circular pattern appears.

6. Make sure that the **Equal spacing** check box is selected in the **Parameters** rollout of the PropertyManager.

7. Enter **8** in the **Number of Instances** field of the **Parameters** rollout.

8. Click on the green tick mark ✓ of the PropertyManager, the circular pattern is created, see Figure 9.110.

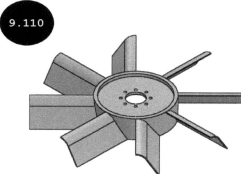

Section 10: Saving the Model

1. Click on the **Save** tool of the **Standard** toolbar, the **Save As** window appears.

2. Browse to the *Tutorial* folder of *Chapter 9* and then save the model as Tutorial 2.

Tutorial 3

Create the model shown in Figure 9.111. Different views and dimensions are given in the same figure.

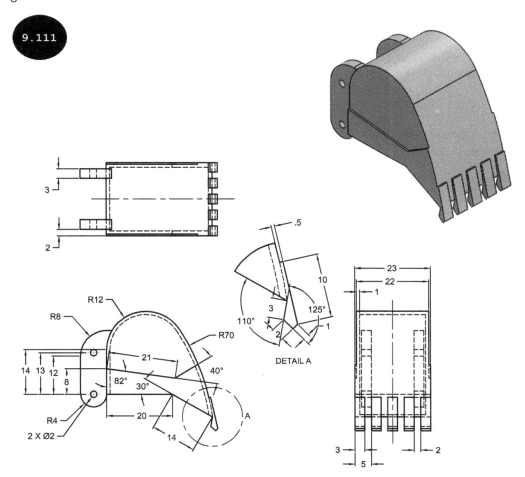

Section 1: Starting SOLIDWORKS

1. Double click on the **SOLIDWORKS** icon on your desktop to start SOLIDWORKS.

Section 2: Invoking Part Modeling Environment

1. Invoke the Part modeling environment by using the **New SOLIDWORKS Document** dialog box which appears on clicking the **New** tool in the **Standard** toolbar.

Section 3: Specifying Unit Settings

1.   Make sure that the MMGS (millimeter, gram, second) unit system is set for the current opened part document.

Section 4: Creating First/Base Feature - Extrude Feature

1.   Invoke the Sketching environment by selecting the Front plane as the sketching plane.

2.   Create the sketch of the base feature of the model, see Figure 9.112.

3.   Click on the **Features** tab of the **CommandManager** to displays the tools of the **Features CommandManager**.

4.   Click on the **Extruded Boss/Base** tool, the **Boss-Extrude PropertyManager** and the preview of the extruded feature appears.

5.   Enter *1* in the **Depth** field of the **Direction 1** rollout and then press ENTER key.

6.   Click on the green tick mark ✅ of the PropertyManager, the extruded feature is created, see Figure 9.113.

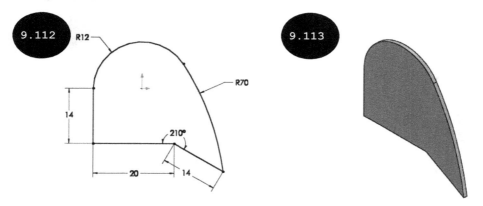

Section 5: Creating Second Feature - Extrude Feature

1.   Invoke the Sketching environment by selecting the front planar face of the base feature as the sketching plane.

2.   Change the orientation of the model normal to the viewing direction by using the **Normal To** tool of the **View Orientation** flyout.

3.   Click to select the outer edges (three edges) of the base feature, see Figure 9.114.

4.   Click on the **Convert Entities** tool of the **Sketch CommandManager**, the selected edges has been projected onto the current sketching plane and converted into sketch entities, see Figure 9.115.

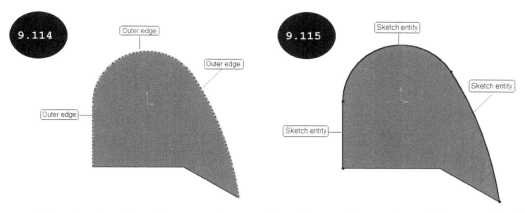

5. Offset the sketch entities created at an offset distance of 1 mm inwards by using the **Offset Entities** tool of the **Sketch CommandManager**, see Figure 9.116.

6. Click to select the horizontal and the inclined edge of the base feature, see Figure 9.117.

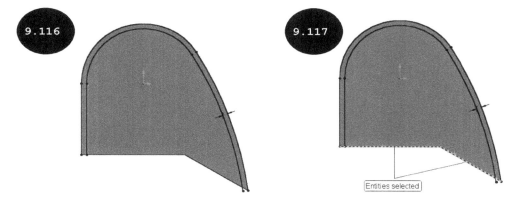

7. Click on the **Convert Entities** tool of the **Sketch CommandManager**, the selected edges has been projected onto the current sketching plane and converted into sketch entities, see Figure 9.118.

8. Trim the unwanted entities of the sketch by using the **Trim Entities** tool, see Figure 9.118. The sketch after trimming the unwanted entities is shown in Figure 9.119.

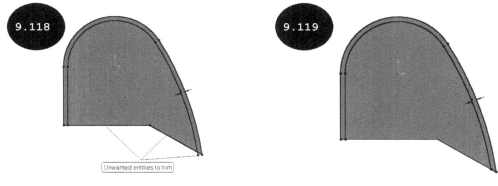

9. Click on the **Extruded Boss/Base** tool, the **Boss-Extrude PropertyManager** and the preview of the extruded feature appears. Change the orientation of the model to isometric.

10. Enter **20** in the **Depth** field of the **Direction 1** rollout of the PropertyManager.

11. Click on the green tick mark ✅ of the PropertyManager, the extruded feature is created, see Figure 9.120.

9.120

Section 6: Creating Third Feature - Extrude Feature

1. Invoke the Sketching environment by selecting the front planar face of the second feature as the sketching plane, see Figure 9.121.

2. Change the orientation of the model normal to the viewing direction by using the **Normal To** tool of the **View Orientation** flyout.

3. Click to select the outer edges (seven edges) of the model such that it forms a closed loop, see Figure 9.122.

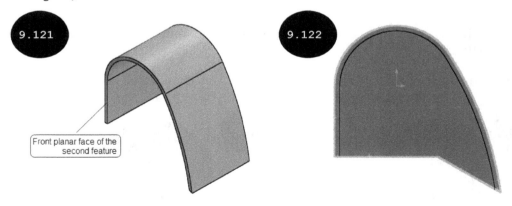

9.121

Front planar face of the second feature

9.122

4. Click on the **Convert Entities** tool of the **Sketch CommandManager**, the selected edges has been projected onto the current sketching plane and converted into sketch entities. Change the current orientation to isometric, see Figure 9.123.

5. Click on the **Extruded Boss/Base** tool, the **Boss-Extrude PropertyManager** and the preview of the extruded feature appears.

6. Enter 1 in the **Depth** field of the **Direction 1** rollout of the PropertyManager.

7. Click on the green tick mark ✅ of the PropertyManager, the extruded feature is created, see Figure 9.124.

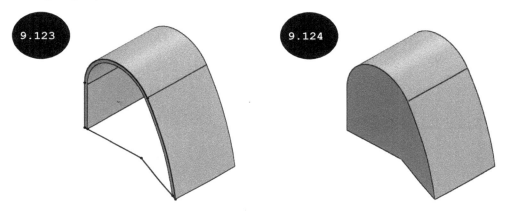

Section 7: Creating Forth Feature - Extrude Feature

1. Invoke the Sketching environment by selecting the front planar face of the third feature as the sketching plane.

2. Change the orientation of the model normal to the viewing direction by using the **Normal To** tool of the **View Orientation** flyout.

3. Click to select the edges (4 edges) of the model, see Figure 9.125.

4. Click on the **Convert Entities** tool of the **Sketch CommandManager**, the selected edges has been projected onto the current sketching plane and converted into sketch entities, see Figure 9.126.

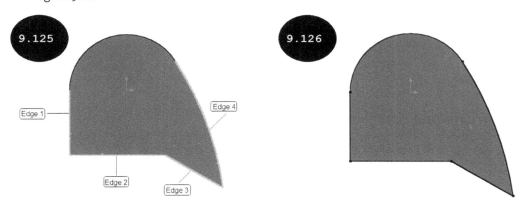

5. Draw two inclined line entities by using the **Line** tool and then apply dimensions, see Figure 9.127.

6. Trim the unwanted entities of the sketch by using the **Trim Entities** tool, see Figure 9.128. The sketch after trimming the unwanted entities is shown in Figure 9.129.

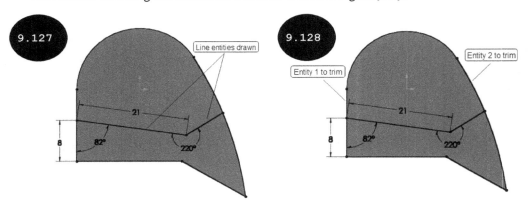

7. Click on the **Extruded Boss/Base** tool, the **Boss–Extrude PropertyManager** and the preview of the extruded feature appears. Next, change the orientation of the model to isometric.

8. Enter **0.5** in the **Depth** field of the **Direction 1** rollout of the PropertyManager.

9. Click on the green tick mark ✅ of the PropertyManager, the extruded feature is created, see Figure 9.130.

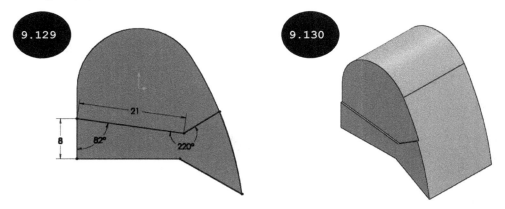

Section 8: Creating Fifth Feature - Mirror Feature

The fifth feature of the model can be created by mirroring the forth feature about a reference plane passing at the middle of front and back planar faces of the model.

1. Invoke the **Plane** tool of the **Reference Geometry** flyout and then create a reference plane at the middle of front and back planar faces of the model, see Figure 9.131.

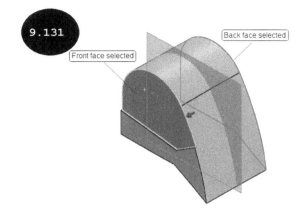

9.131

Front face selected

Back face selected

Note: To create plane at the middle of two planar faces, invoke the **Plane PropertyManager** and then select both the planar faces as the first and second references. As soon as you select two planar faces, the preview of the plane passing at the middle of selected faces appear.

2. Click on the **Features** tab of the **CommandManager** to displays the tools of the **Features CommandManager**.

3. Click on the **Mirror** tool, the **Mirror PropertyManager** appears.

4. Click to select the newly created reference plane as the mirroring plane from the graphics area.

5. Click to select the forth feature (last created extruded feature) as the feature to mirror from the graphics area or from the FeatureManager design tree, the preview of the mirror feature appears in the graphics area.

6. Click on the green tick mark ✓ of the PropertyManager, the mirror feature is created, see Figure 9.132.

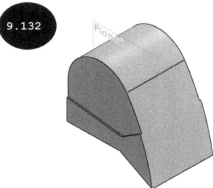

9.132

Section 9: Creating Sixth Feature - Extrude Feature

1. Invoke the Sketching environment by selecting the front planar face of the model as the sketching plane, see Figure 9.133.

2. Change the orientation of the model normal to the viewing direction by using the **Normal To** tool of the **View Orientation** flyout.

3. Create the sketch of the sixth feature of the model, see Figure 9.134.

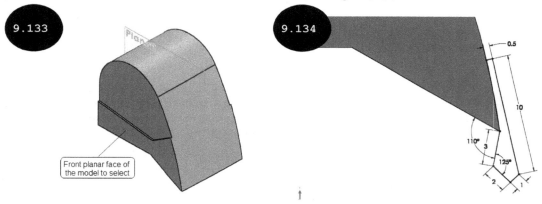

4. Click on the **Features** tab of the **CommandManager** to displays the tools of the **Features CommandManager**.

5. Click on the **Extruded Boss/Base** tool, the **Boss-Extrude PropertyManager** and the preview of the extruded feature appears. Change the orientation of the model to isometric.

6. Click on the **Reverse Direction** button of the **Direction 1** rollout to reverse the direction of extrusion.

7. Enter *3* in the **Depth** field of the **Direction 1** rollout and then press ENTER key.

8. Click on the green tick mark ✅ of the PropertyManager, the extruded feature is created, see Figure 9.135.

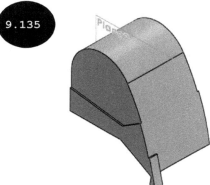

Section 10: Creating Seventh Feature - Linear Pattern

1. Click on the **Linear Pattern** tool of the **Features CommandManager**, the **Linear Pattern PropertyManager** appears.

2. Expand the FeatureManager design tree which is now available at the top left corner of the graphics area by clicking on its +sign.

3. Click to select the sixth feature (last created extruded feature) from the FeatureManager design tree as the feature to pattern.

4. Click to select a linear edge of the model to define the pattern direction, see Figure 9.136.

5. Enter **5** in the **Spacing** field of the **Direction 1** rollout of the PropertyManager.

6. Enter **5** in the **Number of Instances** field of the **Direction 1** rollout of the PropertyManager.

7. Enter **Reverse Direction** button of the **Direction 1** rollout to reverse the pattern direction.

8. Click on the green tick mark ✅ of the PropertyManager, the linear pattern is created, see Figure 9.137.

Linear edge to define pattern direction

Section 11: Creating Eight Feature - Extrude Feature

1. Invoke the Sketching environment by selecting the front planar face of the model as the sketching plane, see Figure 9.138.

2. Change the orientation of the model normal to the viewing direction by using the **Normal To** tool of the **View Orientation** flyout.

3. Create the sketch of the eight feature of the model, see Figure 9.139.

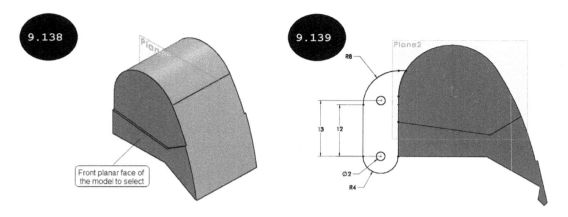

4. Click on the **Features** tab of the **CommandManager** to displays the tools of the **Features CommandManager**.

5. Click on the **Extruded Boss/Base** tool, the **Boss-Extrude PropertyManager** and the preview of the extruded feature appears. Change the orientation of the model to isometric.

6. Click on the **Reverse Direction** button of the **Direction 1** rollout to reverse the direction of extrusion.

7. Invoke the **Start Condition** drop-down list of the **From** rollout in the PropertyManager, see Figure 9.40.

8. Select the **Offset** option from the **Start Condition** drop-down list of the **From** rollout.

9. Enter **2** in the **Enter Offset Value** field of the **From** rollout of the PropertyManager.

10. Click on the **Reverse Direction** button of the **From** rollout of the PropertyManager to reverse the direction of material creation.

11. Enter **3** in the **Depth** field of the **Direction 1** rollout of the PropertyManager.

12. Click on the green tick mark ✅ of the PropertyManager, the extruded feature is created, see Figure 9.141.

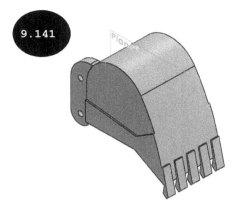

Section 12: Creating Ninth Feature - Mirror Feature

The fifth feature of the model can be created by mirroring the eight feature about the reference plane which is passing at the middle of front and back planar faces of the model.

1. Click on the **Mirror** tool of the **Features CommandManager**, the **Mirror PropertyManager** appears.

2. Click to select the reference plane (created at the middle of front and back planar faces of the model) as the mirroring plane from the graphics area.

3. Click to select the eight feature (last created extruded feature) as the feature to mirror from the graphics area or from the FeatureManager design tree, the preview of the mirror feature appears in the graphics area.

4. Click on the green tick mark ✔ of the PropertyManager, the mirror feature is created, see Figure 9.142. Hide the reference plane.

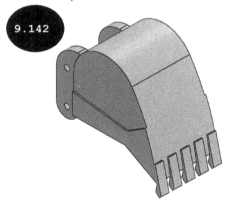

Section 13: Saving the Model

1.   Click on the **Save** tool of the **Standard** toolbar, the **Save As** window appears.

2.   Browse to the *Tutorial* folder of *Chapter 9* and then save the model as Tutorial 3.

Hands-on Test Drive 1

Create the model shown in Figure 9.143.

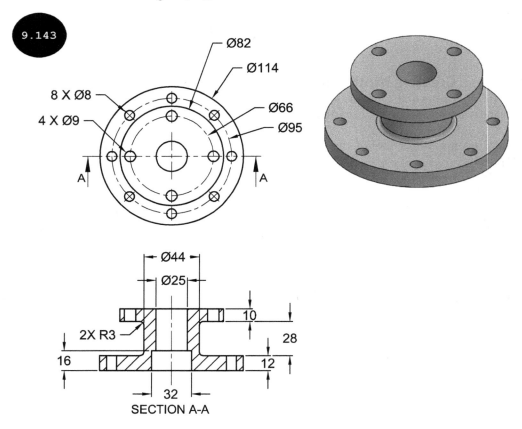

9.143

Ø82
Ø114
8 X Ø8
4 X Ø9
Ø66
Ø95
A
A

Ø44
Ø25
10
2X R3
28
16
12
32
SECTION A-A

Hands-on Test Drive 2

Create the model shown in Figure 9.144.

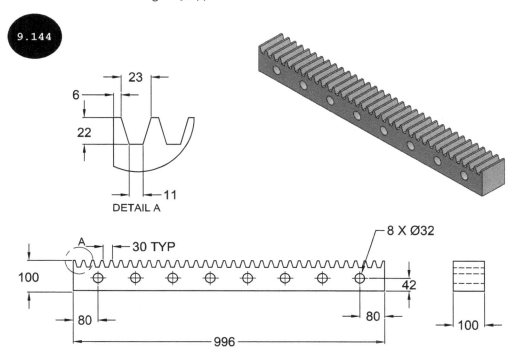

9.144

23

6

22

11

DETAIL A

A

30 TYP

8 X Ø32

100

42

80

80

100

996

Summary

In this chapter, you have learnt about various patterning and mirroring tools. After the successfully completion of this chapter, you can create different type of patterns such as linear pattern, circular pattern, Curve Driven Pattern, and Sketch Driven Pattern.

The linear pattern is created by creating multiple instances of features, faces, or bodies, linearly in one or two linear directions. You can also skip pattern instances those are not required to create in the pattern. The circular pattern is created by creating multiple instances of features, faces, or bodies in circular manner about an axis. You can select an axis, circular face, circular edge, linear edge, linear sketch or angular dimension to define the axis of circular pattern. The curve driven pattern is created by creating multiple instances of features, faces, or bodies along a curve. You can select a 2D/3D sketch/curve or an edge as the curve to drive pattern instances. Also, the curve/sketch selected as the curve to drive pattern instances can be an open or closed curve.

The sketch driven pattern is created by driving the location of the pattern instances using the sketch points of a sketch. The table driven pattern is created by specifying coordinate points for each pattern instances with respect to a coordinate system. The fill Pattern is created by filling an area by pattern instances of the selected feature. You can also used the predefined cut shapes to fill the define area or boundary. The variable pattern is created by varying dimensions and references of the features to pattern. At last in this chapter, you have learnt how to create mirror features, faces, or bodies about an mirroring plane.

Questions

- The _____ tool is used to create multiple instances of features, faces, or bodies, linearly in one or two linear directions.

- The _____ tool is used to create multiple instances of features, faces, or bodies along a curve.

- You can create variable pattern by using the _____ tool.

- In variable pattern, you can vary _____ and _____ of the features to pattern.

- When the _____ check box is cleared, all the instances of the linear pattern maintain the same geometrical relations as that of the original or parent feature.

- The _____ pattern is created by specifying coordinate points for each pattern instances with respect to a coordinate system.

- While creating a linear pattern, you can not vary the pattern instances with respect to a path. (True/False).

- In SOLIDWORKS, in addition to mirroring features, you can mirror faces. (True/False).

Advanced Modeling III

In this chapter you will:

- Working with Hole Wizard
- Adding Cosmetic threads
- Creating Fillets
- Creating Chamfer
- Creating Rib Features
- Creating Shell Features

In the earlier chapters, you learnt about creating circular cut/hole features by using **Extruded Cut** tool and in this chapter, you will learn about creating standard or customized holes such as counterbore, countersink, straight tap, and tapered tap as per the standard specifications by using the **Hole Wizard** tool.

Working with Hole Wizard

To created standard holes by using the **Hole Wizard** tool, click on the **Hole Wizard** tool available in the **Features CommandManager**, the **Hole Specification PropertyManager** appears, see Figure 10.1. The options available in this PropertyManager are as follows.

Type Tab

The PropertyManager is provided with two tabs at its top: **Type** and **Positions**. By default, the **Type** tab is activated and is used to specify the type of hole to be created and their specifications. The options available in the **Type** tab are as follows.

Hole Type

The **Hole Type** rollout is used to select the type of hole to be created. You can select the **Counterbore, Countersink, Hole, Straight Tap, Tapered Tap,** or **Legacy** button available in this rollout to create corresponding type of standard hole. Figure 10.2 shows counterbore holes and Figure 10.3 shows countersink holes created on the top face of a model.

In addition to selecting type of standard holes to be created by using this rollout, you can select the **Counterbore Slot, Countersink Slot,** or **Slot** button to create slot holes. Figure 10.4 shows counterbore slots and Figure 10.5 shows countersink slots created on the top face of a model. The remaining options of this rollout are as follows.

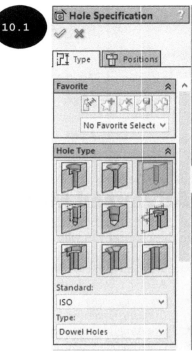

10.1

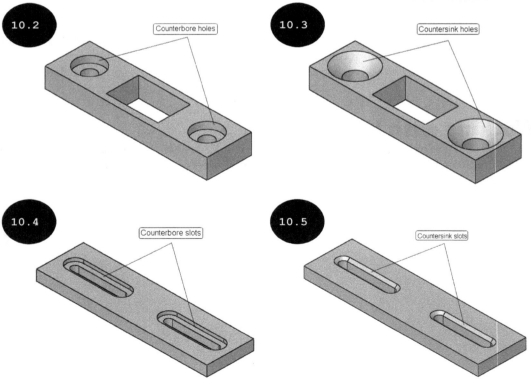

10.2 — Counterbore holes

10.3 — Countersink holes

10.4 — Counterbore slots

10.5 — Countersink slots

Standard

After selecting the type of hole to be created, you need to specify the type of standard to follow such as ANSI Metric, ANSI Inch, JIS, and ISO for the hole being created from the **Standard** drop-down list, see Figure 10.6.

Type

The **Type** drop-down list is used to specify the type of fastener to be inserted in the hole. The options available in this drop-down list depends upon the type of hole and standard selected. Figure 10.7 shows the **Type** drop-down list when the **Counterbore** hole type and **ANSI Metric** standard is selected.

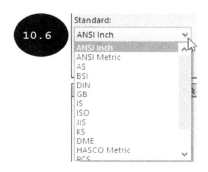
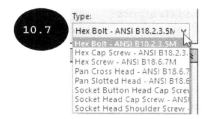

Hole Specifications

The **Hole Specifications** rollout of the PropertyManager is used to specify specifications for the fastener to be inserted into the hole. The options of this rollout are as follows.

Size

The **Size** drop-down list is used to specify the size of the fastener to be inserted. The options available in this drop-down list depends upon the type of hole and standard.

Fit

The **Fit** drop-down list is used to specify the type of fit between the fastener and hole. You can specify close, normal, or loose fastener fit.

Note: The size of the hole depends upon the size of fastener and the type of fit. In SOLIDWORKS, the hole size automatically adjust depending upon the fastener specification and type of fit defined.

Show custom sizing

The **Show custom sizing** check box is used to display the standard size of the hole being created accordingly to the specified specifications. Also, it allows you to customize the standard size of the hole, as required. Click on the **Show custom sizing** check box to select it, the standard size of the hole such as diameter and depth appears in their respective fields of the rollout, see Figure 10.8.

You can also modify the standard parameters of the hole by entering the required values in their respective fields. Note that the background color of the fields whose value is edited or customized is changed to yellow color. After editing the parameters, if you want to restore the default standard parameters, click on the **Restore Default Values** button of this rollout.

End Condition

The options available in the **End Condition** rollout are used to define the end condition or termination method for the hole. The options for defining the end condition are same as discussed earlier.

Options

The options available in this rollout depends upon the type of hole selected. These options are as follows.

Head clearance

On selecting the **Head clearance** check box, the **Head Clearance** field appears below the check box. By using this field, you can specify the head clearance value for counterbore and countersink holes. In other words, the value entered in the **Head Clearance** field defines the clearance between the top faces of the fastener head and the hole.

Near side countersink

The **Near side countersink** check box is used to create countersink shape at the near side of the placement face of the hole, see Figure 10.9. On selecting the **Near side countersink** check box, the **Near Side Countersink Diameter** and the **Near Side Countersink Angle** fields appears in the rollout. These fields are used to specify the diameter and angle for the countersink shape to be created on the near side of the placement face of the hole. Figure 10.9 shows a counterbore hole with countersink shape is created at its near side of the placement face.

Far side countersink

The **Far side countersink** check box is used to create countersink shape at the far side of the placement face of the hole, see Figure 10.10. On selecting the **Far side countersink** check box, the **Far Side Countersink Diameter** and the **Far Side Countersink Angle** fields appears in the rollout. These fields are used to specify the countersink diameter and angle for the countersink shape to be created on the far side of the placement face of the hole. Figure 10.10 shows a counterbore hole with countersink shape is created at its far side of the placement face.

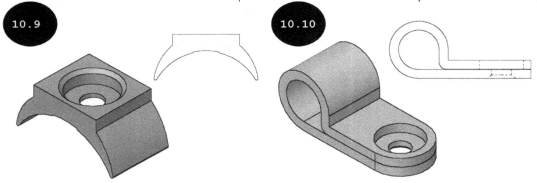

10.9   10.10

Under head countersink

The **Under head countersink** check box is used to create countersink shape at the under side of the hole head diameter, see Figure 10.11. On selecting the **Under head countersink** check box, the **Under Head Side Countersink Diameter** and the **Under Head Side Countersink Angle** fields appears. These fields are used to specify the countersink diameter and angle for the countersink shape to be created on the under side of the head diameter of the hole. Figure 10.11 shows a counterbore hole with countersink shape is created at its under side of the head diameter.

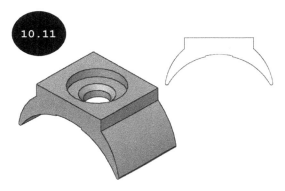

In case of Straight tap hole type, the options available in the **Options** rollout are appears as shown in Figure 10.12 and are as follows.

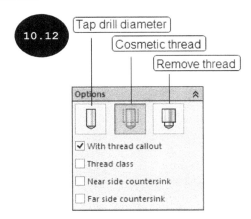

Tap drill diameter/Cosmetic thread/Remove thread

On activating the **Tap drill diameter** button, the Straight tab hole created will have the same diameter as that of the tapped diameter with no threads representation, see Figure 10.13. On activating the **Cosmetic thread** button, the Straight tab hole created will have the same diameter as of the tapped hole with the cosmetic representation of its threads, see 10.14. If you activate the **Remove thread** button, the Straight tab hole created will have the diameter equal to the thread diameter of the taped hole, see 10.15.

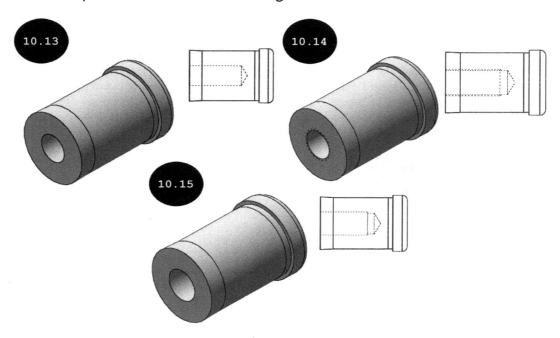

By default the Shaded display style of cosmetic threads is turned Off. To turn On the Shaded display style, select the **Annotations** node available in the FeatureManager design tree and then right click, a shortcut menu appears, see Figure 10.16. Next, click on the **Details** option, the **Annotation Properties** dialog box appears. Select the **Shaded cosmetic threads** check box to turn On the Shaded display style of cosmetic threads. Figure 10.17 shows a tapped hole with the Shaded display style of cosmetic threads is turned On.

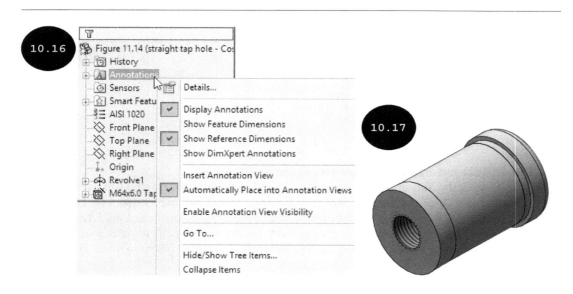

Thread class

On selecting the **Thread class** check box, the **Thread class** drop-down list appears next to it in the **Options** rollout. By using this drop-down list, you can select a class for the threaded/tapped hole.

After specifying all the specifications for creating hole in the **Type** tab of the PropertyManager, you need to now define the placement point for the hole being created in the model by using the **Position** tab of the PropertyManager.

Positions Tab

The **Positions** tab of the PropertyManager is used to define the position of the hole. After specifying all the specifications of the hole to be created in the **Type** tab, click on the **Positions** tab, the PropertyManager appears as shown in Figure 10.18 and you are promoted to specify the placement face. You can select a planar face, a plane, or a curved face as the placement face for the hole.

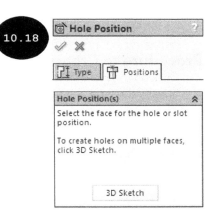

Select a face of the model as the placement face. As soon as you specify the placement face, the preview of the hole appears and follows the cursor as you move it over the placement face, see Figure 10.19. Now, you need to define the placement point for the hole. Click the left mouse button arbitrary to specify the placement point for the hole, the center point of the hole is placed at the defined placement point. Similarly, you can specify multiple placement points for creating multiple holes of similar parameters. After specifying the arbitrary placement points, you can use the dimension tools of the **Sketch CommandManager** to position the placement points of the hole, as required, see Figure 10.20. You can also apply relations such as horizontal and vertical to position the hole placement point. Once the position of the hole has been defined by applying dimensions, click on the green tick mark ✓ of the PropertyManager.

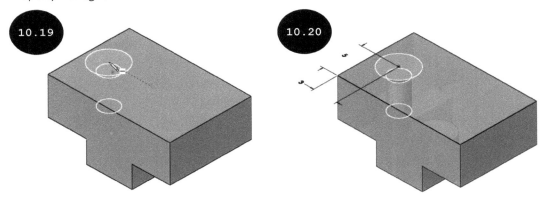

Note: In SOLIDWORKS, you can create similar type of multiple holes on a single planar placement face in the 2D sketch environment or on the multiple planar and curved placement faces in the 3D sketch environment. As soon as you select a planar placement face, the 2D sketch environment invokes which allows you to create multiple holes on the selected planar placement face only. However, on selecting a curved face as the placement face, the 3D sketch environment invokes which allows you to create multiple holes on multiple placement faces. You can also invoke the 3D sketch environment for creating multiple holes on multiple faces by clicking on the **3D Sketch** button of the PropertyManager.

Procedure to Create Hole using Hole Wizard

1. Click on the **Hole Wizard** tool, the **Hole Specification PropertyManager** appears.
2. Specify the type of hole and other hole specifications, as required using the PropertyManager.
3. After specifying the hole specifications, click on the **Position** tab of the PropertyManager.
4. Click on a planar face/plane/curved face as the placement face of the hole.
5. Click to specify the placement point of the hole on the placement face.
6. Apply dimensions and relations to position the placement point of the hole, as required.
7. Click on the green tick mark ✓ of the PropertyManager, a hole is created.

Adding Cosmetic threads

The cosmetic threads represent the real threads of the features such as holes. It is recommended to add cosmetic threads to the holes, fasteners, or cylindrical features of a 3D model. This is because, adding cosmetic threads helps in avoiding increase in the complexity of the model and improve overall performance of the system. Figure 10.21 shows cosmetic threads added to an cylindrical feature and Figure 10.22 shows cosmetic threads added to the hole feature.

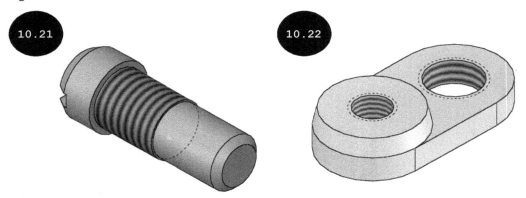

To add cosmetic threads, click on the **Insert > Annotations > Cosmetic Thread** in the SOLIDWORKS menus, the **Cosmetic Thread PropertyManager** appears, see Figure 10.23. The options of this PropertyManager are as follows.

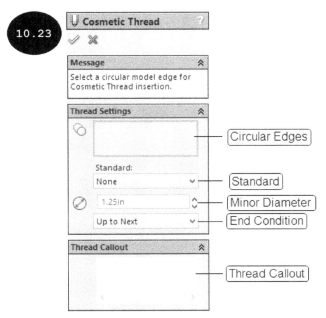

Message Rollout

This rollout prompt you to select circular edge of the model for adding cosmetic thread.

Thread Settings

The **Circular Edges** field of the **Thread Settings** rollout is activated by default and allows you to select circular edge for adding cosmetic thread. Select a circular edge, a dotted circle appears in the graphics area which represents the minor (inner) or major (outer) diameter of the thread, see Figures 10.24 and 10.25. Also, the name of the selected circular edge appears in this field. The remaining options of the **Thread Settings** rollout are as follows.

Note: On selecting the circular edge of a cylindrical feature, a dotted circle represents the minor (inner) diameter of the thread and for hole feature, dotted circle represents the major (outer) diameter of the thread, see Figures 10.24 and 10.25.

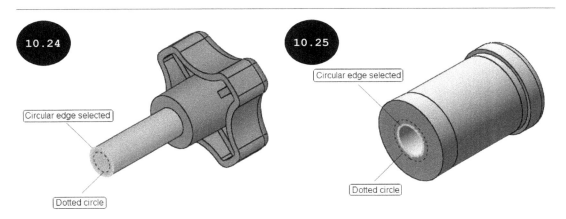

Standard

The **Standard** drop-down list is used to specify the type of standard to be follow such as ANSI Inch and ANSI Metric for creating cosmetic threads.

Type

The **Type** drop-down list is used to select the type of threads to be added. Note that this drop-down list will not be available if the **None** option is selected in the **Standard** drop-down list.

Size

The **Size** drop-down list is used to select standard size of the thread. Note that this drop-down list will not be available if the **None** option is selected in the **Standard** drop-down list.

Minor/Major Diameter

The **Minor Diameter** or **Major Diameter** field is used to specify the minor or major diameter of the thread. Note that this field is activated only if the **None** option is selected in the **Standard** drop-down list. Also, the name of the field (**Minor Diameter** or **Major Diameter**) appears depending upon the circular edge selected for applying threads. If the circular edge of a cylindrical feature selected, the **Minor Diameter** field appears and if the circular edge of a hole feature selected, the **Major Diameter** field appears.

End Condition

The **End Condition** drop-down list is used to specify the end condition or termination for the cosmetic thread. Note that the circular edge selected for adding the cosmetic thread is the start condition of the cosmetic thread.

Thread Callout

The **Thread Callout** field of this rollout allows you to enter text/comment for the thread to appears in the thread callout which appears in the drawing views. You can generate drawing views in the Drawing environment of SOLIDWORKS. You will learn about generating drawing views in later chapters.

Note: The **Thread Callout** field of the **Thread Callout** rollout is activated only if the **None** option is selected in the **Standard** drop-down list. On specifying the standard such as ANSI Inch and ANSI Metric, this field will not be activated. However, the default text appears automatically in this field depending upon the type of standards and thread type selected.

After specifying all the parameters for adding the cosmetic thread, click on the green tick mark of the PropertyManager, the respective cosmetic thread is added and appears in the graphics area, see Figure 10.26. Also a cosmetic thread feature added under the node of the feature on which the cosmetic thread has added in the FeatureManager design tree, see Figure 10.27.

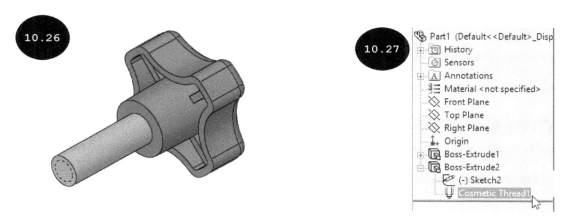

Note: In the Figure 10.26, the Shaded display style of Cosmetic threads is turned off. As a result, the only the dotted circle representing the thread diameter appears in the graphics area. To turn On the Shaded display style, select the **Annotations** node available in the FeatureManager design tree and then right click, a shortcut menu appears, see Figure 10.28. Next, click on the **Details** option, the **Annotation Properties** dialog box appears. Select the **Shaded cosmetic threads** check box to turn On the Shaded display style of the cosmetic thread. Figure 10.29 shows a cosmetic threads with Shaded display style turn On.

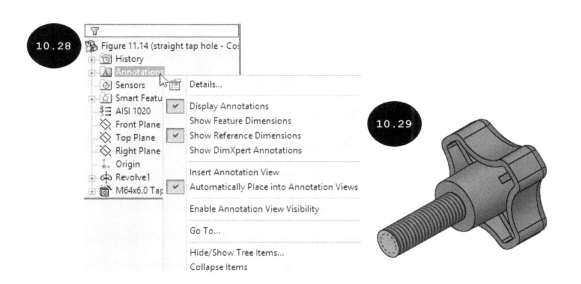

Procedure to Add Cosmetic Thread

1. Click on the **Insert > Annotations > Cosmetic Thread** in the SOLIDWORKS menus.
2. Select the circular edge to add cosmetic thread.
3. Specify other parameters such as standard, size, and end condition for the cosmetic thread.
4. Click on the green tick mark ✓ of the PropertyManager, cosmetic thread is added.

Creating Fillets

A fillet is a curved face of a constant or variable radius and is used to remove or eliminate sharp edges of the model that can cause injury while handling. Also, fillet distributes the stress over the broader of the fillet and the model becomes more durable and capable of withstanding under larger loads. Figure 10.30 shows a model before and after applying constant radius fillets.

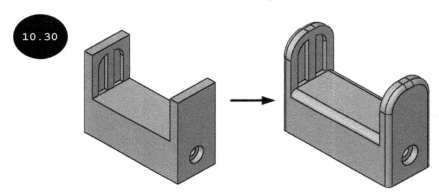

10.30

In SOLIDWORKS, you can create fillets by using two methods: Manual and FilletXpert. The Manual method allow you to create fillets manually. By using this method, you can create four type of fillets: constant radius fillet, variable radius fillet, face fillet, and full round fillet. On the other hand, the FilletXpert method create fillets automatically. Also, by using this method, you can only create constant radius fillets in a part that have multiple configurations. The methods of creating different type of fillets manually are as follows.

To create fillets using the Manual method, click on the **Fillet** tool of the **Features CommandManager**, the **Fillet PropertyManager** appears, see Figure 10.31. By using the options of this PropertyManager, you can create constant radius fillet, variable radius fillet, face fillet, and full round fillet. The methods of creating different type of fillets are as follows.

10.31

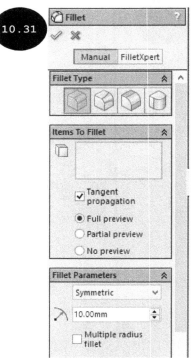

Note: If the FilletXpert PropertyManager appears on clicking the Fillet tool, click on the Manual tab to invoke the Fillet PropertyManager for controlling the creation of fillets manually.

Creating Constant Radius Fillet

A constant radius fillet is a fillet having constant radius throughout the selected edge, see Figure 10.32. You can create constant radius fillet by selecting the **Constant size** button of the **Fillet Type** rollout of the PropertyManager. When this button is selected, the options available in different rollouts of the PropertyManager are as follows.

Items To Fillet

The **Items To Fillet** rollout appears as shown in Figure 10.33. The options available in this rollout are as follows.

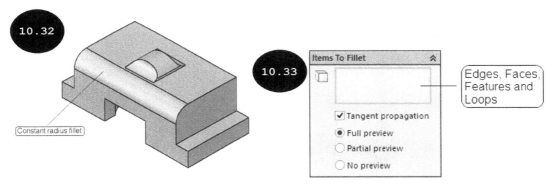

Edges, Faces, Features and Loops

The **Edges, Faces, Features and Loops** field of this rollout is activated by default and allow you to select edges, faces, features, and loops for creating constant radius fillet. Select edges, faces, features, or loops to create constant radius fillet, the preview of the constant fillet appear in the graphics area.

Note: In case of selecting a face to create fillet, all the edges of the selected face is filleted, see Figure 10.34 and on selecting a feature, all the edges of the selected feature is filleted, see Figure 10.35.

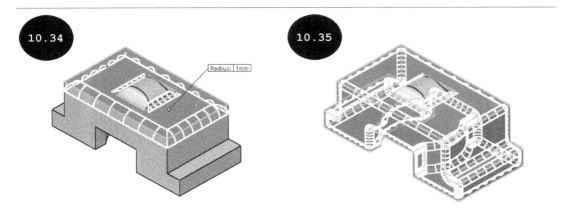

Tangent propagation

When the **Tangent propagation** check box is selected, fillet applies to all the edges that are tangent to the selected edge. Figure 10.36 shows the edge selected for applying fillet. Figures 10.37 and 10.38 shows a preview of the resultant fillet when the **Tangent propagation** check box is cleared and selected, respectively.

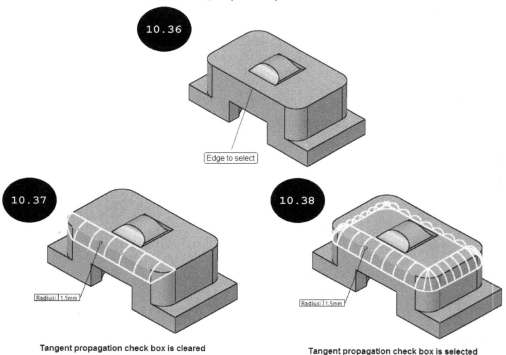

Tangent propagation check box is cleared   Tangent propagation check box is selected

Full preview/Partial preview/No preview

The **Full preview** radio button is used to displays full preview of the fillet being created which includes the preview of all the fillet edges. On selecting the **Partial preview** radio button, the partial view of the fillet appears. Note that in case of partial preview, the preview of only one fillet edge appears. On selecting the **No preview** radio button, the display of fillet preview is turns Off. It helps to improve the rebuilding time while working with complex models.

Fillet Parameters

The **Fillet Parameters** rollout appears as shown in Figure 10.39. The options available in this rollout are as follows.

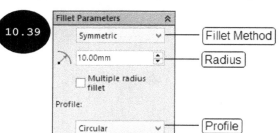

Fillet Method

The **Fillet Method** drop-down list allows you to select the type of method for creating fillet. On selecting the **Symmetric** option, you can create symmetric fillet having same radius on both sides of the edge selected for creating fillet, see Figure 10.40. When this option selected, the **Radius** field is available in the rollout which allows you to specify the symmetric radius for the fillet. On selecting the **Asymmetric** option, the **Distance 1** and **Distance 2** fields become available in the rollout which allows you to specify two different radii for both sides of the edge selected for creating fillet, respectively, see Figure 10.41.

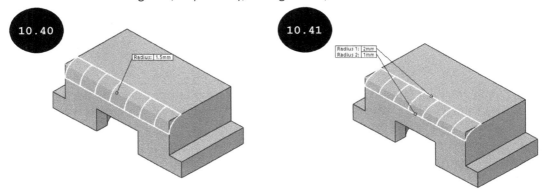

Multiple radius fillet

On selecting the **Multiple radius fillet** check box, you can assign different radius values for the selected multiple edges. For example, if you have selected two edges for applying fillet then on selecting this check box, you can assign different radius value or control the radius of both the edges, individually. By default, this check box is cleared. As a results, all the edges selected for fillet will have the same radius value of fillet.

Profile

The **Profile** drop-down list is used to select the type of fillet profile. Note that the fillet profile defines the cross sectional shape of the fillet. You can select the **Circular**, **Conic Rho**, or **Conic Radius** options from this drop-down list to define the fillet profile. On selecting the **Circular** option, the circular shape fillet is created, see Figure 10.42. On selecting the **Conic Rho** option, you need to specify the rho value in the **Rho** field which appears below this drop-down list. Note that the rho value can be in between 0 to 1, see Figures 10.43 through 10.45.

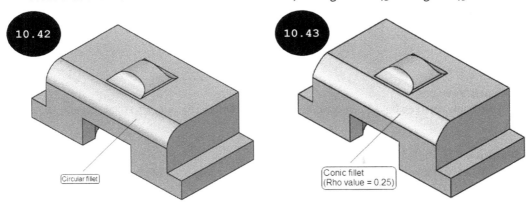

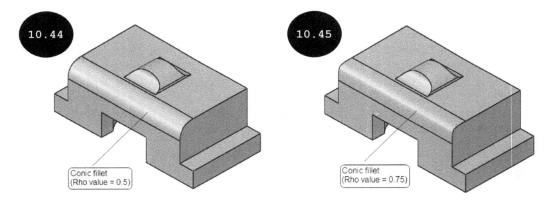

Tip: If the rho value is less than 0.5 then the fillet profile is of elliptical shape. If the rho value is 0.5 then the fillet profile is of parabola shape, and if the rho value is greater than 0.5 then the fillet profile is of hyperbola shape.

On selecting the **Conic Radius** option from the **Profile** drop-down list, you can specify the radius of curvature at the corner of the fillet in the **Conic radius** field appears below this drop-down list.

Setback Parameters

The options available in the **Setback Parameters** rollout are used to defined the parameters for creating setback fillet. A setback fillet is a fillet having smooth transition from the fillet edges to their common intersecting vertex. You can create setback fillet on three or more than three edges that are intersecting at a common vertex, see Figure 10.46. Figure 10.47 shows the expanded **Setback Parameters** rollout. The options of this rollout are as follows.

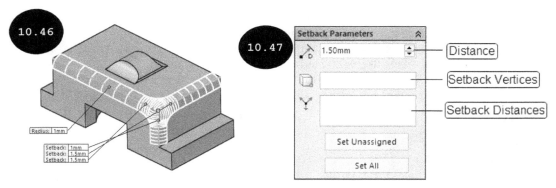

Setback Vertices

The **Setback Vertices** field is used to select a vertex where the edges to fillet intersection each other.

Distance

The **Distance** filed is used to specify the fillet setback distance measures from the selected setback vertex.

Setback Distances

The **Setback Distances** field allows you to specify the setback distance for individual edges from the setback vertex. Note that as soon as you select a setback vertex, a list of corresponding edges appears in this field. To assign setback distance to an edge, select the edge from this field and then enter the setback distance in the **Distance** filed. Next press ENTER. Figure 10.46 shows the preview of a setback fillet with different set back distance assigned with respect to the setback vertex.

Set Unassigned

The **Set Unassigned** button is used to assign the current setback distance to all the edges whose setback distance is not assigned.

Set All

The **Set All** button is used to assign the current setback distance to all the edges listed under the **Setback Distance** field.

Fillet Options

The **Fillet Options** rollout appears as shown in Figure 10.48. The options available in this rollout are as follows.

Select through faces

On selecting the **Select through faces** check box, you can select invisible edges of the models for applying fillets, see Figure 10.49. In this Figure, three edges are visible. However, the fourth edge is not visible. You can select the invisible edges of the model when the **Select through faces** check box is selected.

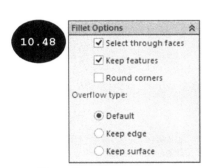

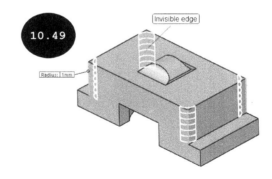

Keep features

On selecting the **Keep features** check box, if you apply a fillet of large radius which cover other feature (boss or cut) of the model then the fillet created such that the covered feature will be kept or remain available in the model. However, if you clear this check box then the fillet created such that it also covers the feature and the feature will no longer available in the model. Figure 10.50 shows a preview of the fillet with large radius and covers the cylindrical feature. Figures 10.51 and 10.52 shows the resultant model after creating the fillet if the **Keep feature**s check box is selected and cleared, respectively.

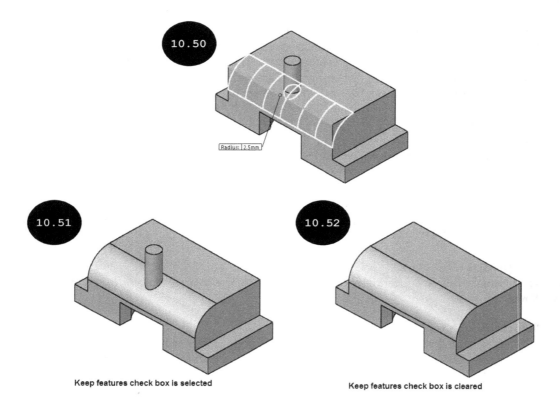

Keep features check box is selected

Keep features check box is cleared

Procedure to Create Constant Radius Fillet

1. Click on the **Fillet** tool, the **Fillet PropertyManager** appears.
2. Make sure that the **Constant size** button is selected in the **Fillet Type** rollout.
3. Select edges, faces, features, or loops to create constant radius fillet.
4. Specify the radius value of the fillet in the **Radius** field of the **Fillet Parameters** rollout.
5. Click on the green tick mark ✅ of the PropertyManager, the constant radius fillet is created.

Creating Variable Radius Fillet

A variable radius fillet is a fillet having variable radius, see Figure 10.53. You can create variable radius fillet by using the **Variable radius** button of the **Fillet Type** rollout. When this button is selected, the PropertyManager appears as shown in Figure 10.54.

The options available in the PropertyManager when the **Variable radius** button is selected are as follows.

Items To Fillet

The **Edges, Faces, Features and Loops** field of the **Item To Fillet** rollout is activated by default and allows you to select edges, faces, features, and loops for creating variable radius fillet. Similar to this option, the other options available in this rollout are same as discussed earlier.

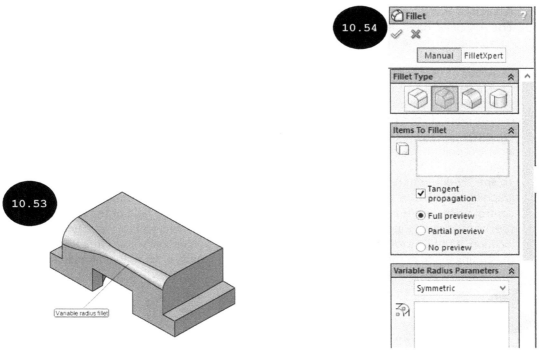

Variable Radius Parameters

The options available in the **Variable Radius Parameters** rollout are used to define the variable fillet radius. The options available in this rollout are shown in Figure 10.55 and are as follows.

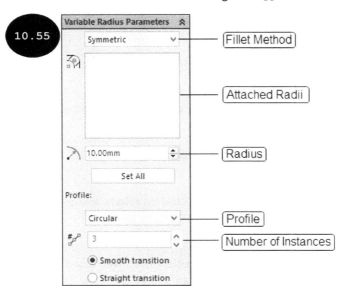

Attached Radii

The **Attached Radii** field displays the list of vertices of the selected edges and the specified control points for defining the variable radius.

Number of Instances

The **Number of Instances** field allows you to specify the number of control points on the selected edges for defining variable radius. Note that as soon as you define the number of control points in this field, the same number of pink dots appears along with the edge selected for applying variable radius fillet in the graphics area, see Figure 10.56. Each pink dot represent a control point and at each control point you can specify different radius value.

To specify different radius value at a control point, click on the control point appears in the graphics area whose radius value needs to be specified, a callout appears attached to the control point with R and P fields, see Figure 10.57. By using the R field of the callout, you can specify radius value at that control point and by using the P field, you can specify the accurate location of the control point along the edge in terms of percentage value. Note that by default the editing mode of the callout fields (R and P) are not enabled. To enabled the editing mode, you need to click on these fields once.

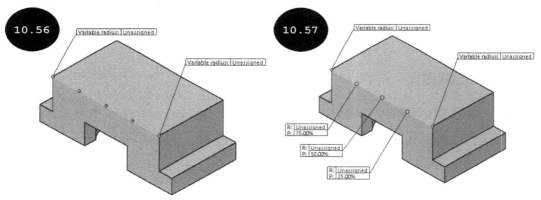

In addition to the display of callout in the graphics area, the name of the selected control point appears in the **Attached Radii** field of the PropertyManager. You can also specify the radius value for the control point by selecting their name in the **Attached Radii** field and then entering a radius value in the **Radius** field of the PropertyManager.

Smooth transition

The **Smooth transition** radio button is selected by default and creates smooth transition from one radius value to another radius value, see Figure 10.58.

Straight transition

On selecting the **Straight transition** radio button, the linear/straight transition creates from one radius value to another radius value, see Figure 10.59.

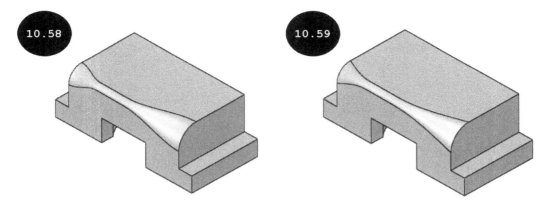

The other options of this rollout and the options of the other rollouts of the PropertyManager are same as discussed earlier.

Procedure to Create Variable Radius Fillet

1. Click on the **Fillet** tool, the **Fillet PropertyManager** appears.
2. Select the **Variable size** button in the **Fillet Type** rollout of the PropertyManager.
3. Select edges, faces, features, or loops to create variable radius fillet.
4. Specify the number of control points in the **Number of Instances** field of the **Variable Radius Parameters** rollout.
5. Click on the control points appears in the graphics area whose radius value is to be specified.
6. Specify radius value and location for each control point by using their respective callout.
7. Click on the green tick mark ✓ of the PropertyManager, the variable radius fillet is created.

Creating Face Fillets

A face fillet is a filet created between two non-adjacent or non-continuous faces of a model, see Figure 10.60.

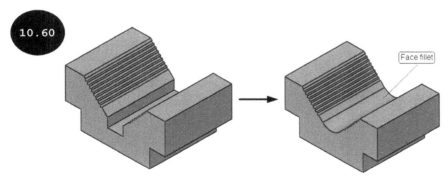

To create face fillets, select the **Face fillet** button from the **Fillet Type** rollout of the PropertyManager. When this button is selected, the PropertyManager appears as shown in Figure 10.61.

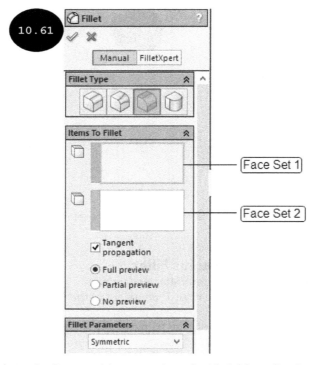

The options available in the PropertyManager when the **Variable radius** button is selected are as follows.

Items To Fillet
The options available in this rollout are as follows.

Face Set 1
The **Face Set 1** field is used to select the first face or first set of non-adjacent or non-continuous faces from the graphics area, see Figure 10.62.

Face Set 2
The **Face Set 2** field is used to select the second face or second set of non-adjacent or non-continuous faces from the graphics area, see Figure 10.62.

As soon as you select two non-adjacent or non-continuous set of faces, the preview of the face fillet appears in the graphics, see Figure 10.63. In case the preview of the face fillet does not appears, you need to adjust the radius value of the fillet in the **Radius** field of the **Fillet Parameters** rollout of the PropertyManager.

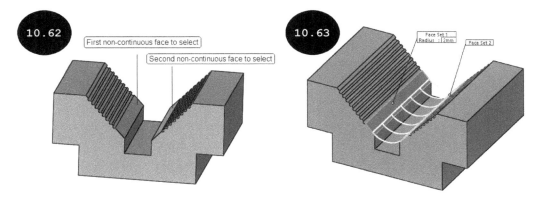

The other options available in the PropertyManager are same as discussed earlier. Once you done with specifying all the parameters for creating face fillet, click on the green tick mark ✓ of the PropertyManager, the face fillet is created.

Procedure to Create Face Fillet

1. Click on the **Fillet** tool, the **Fillet PropertyManager** appears.
2. Select the **Face fillet** button in the **Fillet Type** rollout of the PropertyManager.
3. Select first non-adjacent or non-continuous face from the graphics area.
4. Click on the **Face Set 2** field of the **Items To Fillet** rollout to active it.
5. Select second non-adjacent or non-continuous face from the graphics area.
6. Specify the fillet radius value in the **Radius** field of the **Fillet Parameters** rollout.
7. Click on the green tick mark ✓ of the PropertyManager, the face fillet is created.

Creating Full Round Fillet

A full round fillet is a fillet created between three adjacent face of a model, see Figures 10.64.

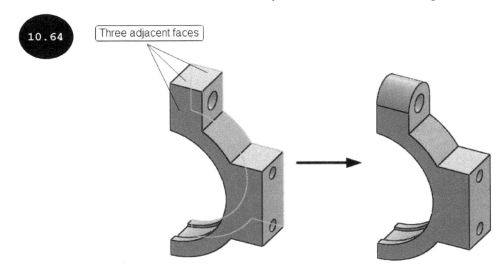

To create full round fillet, select the **Full round fillet** button from the **Fillet Type** rollout of the PropertyManager. When this button is selected, the PropertyManager appears as shown in Figure 10.65.

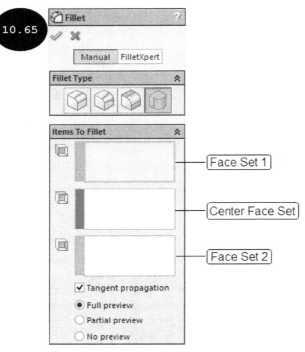

The options available in the PropertyManager when the **Full Round Fillet** button is selected are as follows.

Items To Fillet
The options available in this rollout are as follows.

Side Face Set 1
The **Side Face Set** 1 field is used to select the start adjacent face of the model from the graphics area, refer to Figure 10.66.

Center Face Set
The **Center Face Set** field is used to select the center adjacent face of the model, refer to Figure 10.66.

Side Face Set 2
The **Side Face Set** 2 field is used to select the end adjacent face of the model, refer to Figure 10.66.

As soon as you select three adjacent faces of a model, the preview of the full round fillet appears in the graphics, see Figure 10.67.

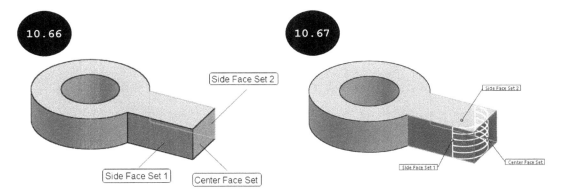

The other options available in the PropertyManager are same as discussed earlier. Once you done with specifying all the parameters for creating full round fillet, click on the green tick mark ✓ of the PropertyManager, the full round fillet is created.

Procedure to Create Full Round Fillet

1. Click on the **Fillet** tool, the **Fillet PropertyManager** appears.
2. Select the **Full round fillet** button in the **Fillet Type** rollout of the PropertyManager.
3. Select the first adjacent face as the Side Face Set 1 face from the graphics area.
4. Click on the **Center Face Set** field of the **Items To Fillet** rollout to active it.
5. Select the center adjacent face from the graphics area.
6. Click on the **Side Face Set 2** field of the **Items To Fillet** rollout to active it.
7. Select the end adjacent face from the graphics area.
8. Click on the green tick mark ✓ of the PropertyManager, the full round fillet is created.

Creating Chamfer

A chamfer is a bevel face that is non perpendicular to its adjacent faces, see Figure 10.68.

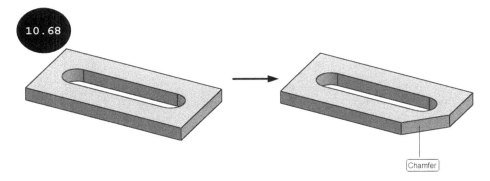

To create chamfer, click on the down arrow available below the **Fillet** tool of the CommandManager, a flyout appears, see Figure 10.69. Next, click on the **Chamfer** tool, the **Chamfer PropertyManager** appears, see Figure 10.70. The options available in this PropertyManager are as follows.

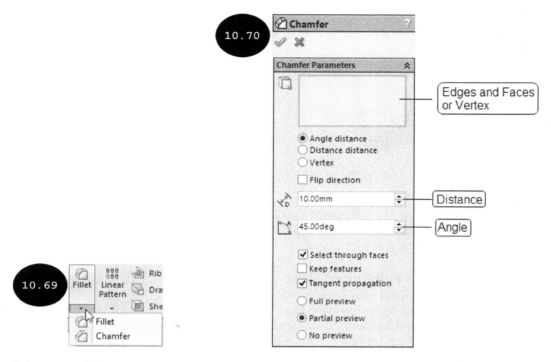

Edges and Faces or Vertex

The **Edges and Faces or Vertex** field of the PropertyManager allows you to select edges, faces, or vertex for creating chamfer. As soon as, you select edges, faces, or vertex, the preview of the chamfer appears in the graphics area.

Angle distance

The **Angle distance** radio button is used to create chamfer by specifying its angle and distance values. When this radio button is selected, the **Distance** and **Angle** fields appears in the PropertyManager which allows you to specify the distance and angle value of the chamfer, respectively. You can also specify the distance and angle value of the chamfer by using the callout which appears in the graphics area attached with the preview of the chamfer, see Figure 10.71.

Note that in the preview of the chamfer, a arrow appears that points in the direction in which the distance value of the chamfer is measured.

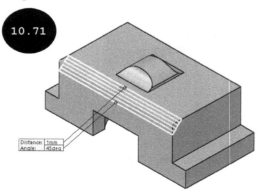

Distance distance

The **Distance distance** radio button is used to create chamfer by specifying its distance values on both side of the chamfer edge. When you select this radio button, the **Distance 1** and **Distance 2** fields appears in the PropertyManager which allows you to specify the distance values on both sides of the chamfer edge. Also, a callout with **Distance 1** and **Distance 2** fields appears attached with the preview of the chamfer in the graphics area, see Figure 10.72. You can also edit the distance values of the chamfer by using this callout.

> **Note:** If the **Equal distance** check box of this PropertyManager is selected, only the **Distance 1** field appears and the distance value specified in this field is equal in both sides of the chamfer edge.

Vertex

On selecting the **Vertex** radio button, you are allowed to select vertex for creating chamfer. Select a vertex to create chamfer, the preview of the chamfer appears, see Figure 10.73. Also, the **Distance 1**, **Distance 2**, and **Distance 3** fields appears in the PropertyManager. These fields allow you to specify distance values for all sides of the selected vertex. You can also specify the equal distance value for all chamfer sides by selecting the **Equal distance** check box.

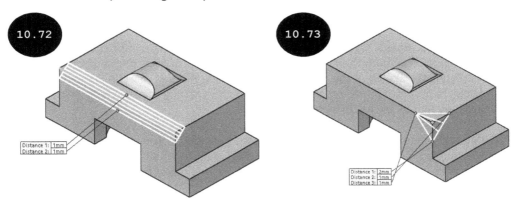

The remaining options of this PropertyManager are same as discussed while creating fillets.

Procedure to Create Chamfer on Edges

1. Click on the **Chamfer** tool, the **Chamfer PropertyManager** appears.
2. Select edges or faces for creating chamfer.
3. Specify a method for creating chamfer by either selecting the **Angle - distance** or **Distance - distance** radio button.
4. Specify the angle and distance or distance and distance for the chamfer, respectively, depending upon the radio button selected in Step 2.
5. Click on the green tick mark ✓ of the PropertyManager, the chamfer is created.

Procedure to Create Chamfer on Vertex

1. Click on the **Chamfer** tool, the **Chamfer PropertyManager** appears.
2. Specify the **Vertex** radio button for creating chamfer on vertex.
3. Select a vertex from the graphics area.
4. Specify the distance values in **Distance 1**, **Distance 2**, and **Distance 3** fields, respectively.
5. Click on the green tick mark ✓ of the PropertyManager, the chamfer is created on the vertex.

Creating Rib Features

Rib features are generally used to increase the strength of the model and act as supporting features. You can create rib features from open or closed sketch by adding thickness in a specified direction. Figure 10.74 shows a model with an open sketch and the resultant rib feature created.

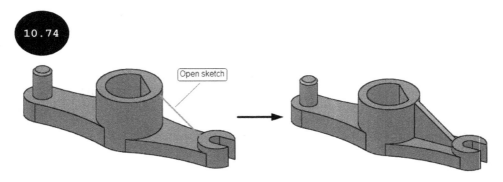

To create a rib feature, create an open sketch on a plane that intersects the model, see Figure 10.75. Note that the projection of both the ends of the open sketch should lies on the geometry of the model. After creating the sketch of the rib feature, click on the **Rib** tool, the **Rib PropertyManager** appears and you are promoted to select a sketching plane for creating the sketch of the rib feature or select an existing sketch for the rib feature.

If you have already created a sketch for the rib feature, select it from the graphics area, the **Rib PropertyManager** modified and appears as shown in Figure 10.76. Also, the preview of the rib feature appears in the graphics area, see Figure 10.77. The options available in this PropertyManager are as follows.

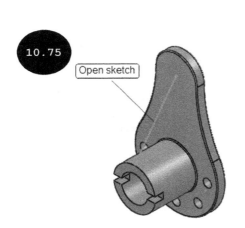

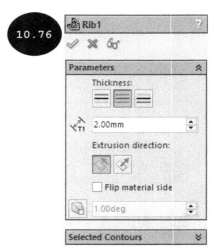

Note: If the sketch of the rib feature is selected before invoking the **Rib** tool then the modified **Rib PropertyManager** appears directly as shown in Figure 10.76 and preview of the rib feature appears in the graphics area.

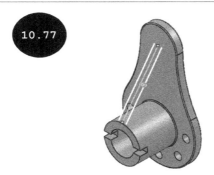

10.77

Parameters

The options available in the **Parameters** rollout of the PropertyManager are used to specify the parameters of the rib feature and are as follows.

Thickness

The **Thickness** area contains three buttons: **First Side**, **Both Sides**, and **Second Side**. On selecting the **First Side** button, the thickness adds to one side of the rib sketch. If you select the **Both Sides** button, the thickness adds to both side of the rib sketch equally. On selecting the **Second Side** button, the thickness adds to the second or other side of the sketch.

Rib Thickness

The **Rib Thickness** field is used to specify thickness value for the rib feature.

Extrusion direction

The **Extrusion direction** area contains two buttons: **Parallel to Sketch** and **Normal to Sketch**. On selecting the **Parallel to Sketch** button, the rib created by adding material parallel to the sketch. If you select the **Normal to Sketch** button, the rib created by adding material normal to the sketch. Figure 10.78 shows the sketch of the rib feature. Figures 10.79 and 10.80 shows the resultant rib feature created on selecting the **Normal to Sketch** and **Parallel to Sketch** buttons, respectively.

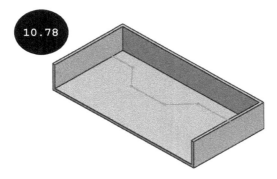

10.78

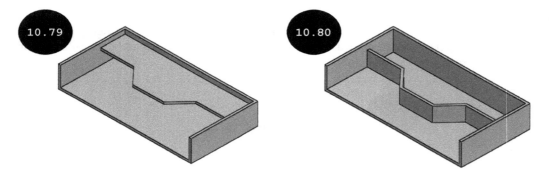

Flip material side

The **Flip material side** check box is used to flip the direction of extrusion for the rib feature.

Draft On/Off

The **Draft On/Off** button is used to add draft to the rib. On activating this button, the **Draft Angle** field enabled and the **Draft outward** check box appears in the PropertyManager. By using the **Draft Angle** field, you can specify the draft angle for the rib feature. To add draft outward side of the sketch, select the **Draft outward** check box. If the **Draft outward** check box is cleared, an inward draft is created.

Selected Contours

The **Selected Contours** rollout is used to select the required contour of the sketch to be used as the contour for creating the rib feature.

Procedure to Create Rib Feature

1. Create an open sketch for the rib feature.
2. Invoke the **Rib** tool and then select the open sketch for creating rib feature.
3. Specify the rib thickness in the **Rib Thickness** field.
4. Specify the extrusion direction for the rib feature (**Parallel to Sketch** and **Normal to Sketch**).
5. Flip the material side by selecting the **Flip material side** check box, if required.
6. Click on the green tick mark ✅ of the PropertyManager, the rib feature is created.

Creating Shell Features

A Shell Feature is a thin walled feature created by making the model hollow from inside, see Figure 10.81.

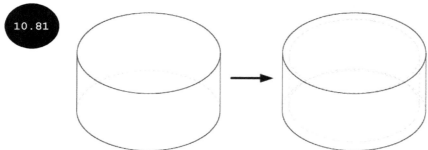

To create a shell feature, click on the **Shell** tool of the CommandManager, the **Shell PropertyManager** appears, see Figure 10.82. The options available in this PropertyManager are as follows.

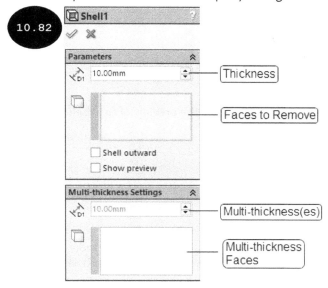

Parameters
The options available in the **Parameters** rollout are used to specified the required parameters for creating the shell feature and are as follows.

Thickness
The **Thickness** field is used to specify the wall thickness for the shell feature. Note that the thickness specified in this field applies to all the walls of the shell model and creates a uniform thicken shell feature, see Figure 10.81.

Faces to Remove
The **Faces to Remove** field is used to select faces of the model to be removed. Figure 10.83 shows a model and a face to remove. Figure 10.84 shows the resultant model after creating the shell feature.

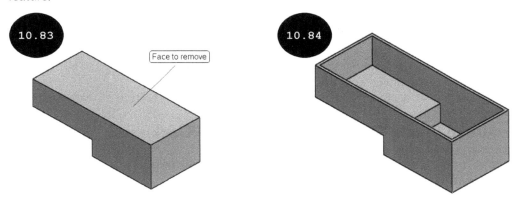

Note: If you do not select any face to remove, a closed hollow model is created.

Shell outward
On selecting the **Shell outward** check box, the thickness adds outward side of the model.

Show preview
On selecting the **Show preview** check box, the preview of the shell feature appears in the graphics area.

Multi-thickness Settings
The options available in this rollout are used to create multi-thickness shell feature and are as follows.

Multi-thickness Faces
The **Multi-thickness Faces** field is used to select faces of the model on which you want to apply the thickness other than the one specified in the **Thickness** field of the **Parameters** rollout. As soon as you select a face to apply different thickness by using this field, the **Multi-thickness(es)** field get enabled, which allows you to specify the thickness for the selected face of the model. Figure 10.84 shows a shell model with uniform thickness on all its faces and Figure 10.85 shows a shell model with multi-thickness wall faces.

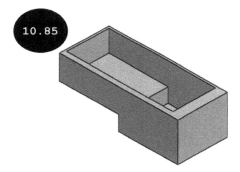
10.85

Procedure to Create Shell Feature with Uniform Thickness
1. Click on the **Shell** tool.
2. Specify the wall thickness for the shell feature in the **Thickness** field.
3. Select the faces to removed from the shell model, if required.
4. Click on the green tick mark ✅ of the PropertyManager, the shell feature is created.

Procedure to Create Shell Feature with Multi-Thickness
1. Click on the **Shell** tool.
2. Specify the wall thickness for the shell feature in the **Thickness** field.
3. Select the faces to removed from the shell model, if required.

4. Click on the **Multi-thickness Faces** field to activate it.
5. Select faces to apply different thickness value from the graphics area.
6. Specify different thickness value for the faces in the **Multi-thickness(es)** field one by one.
7. Click on the green tick mark ✅ of the PropertyManager, the shell feature with multi-thickness is created.

Tutorial 1

Create the model shown in Figure 10.86.

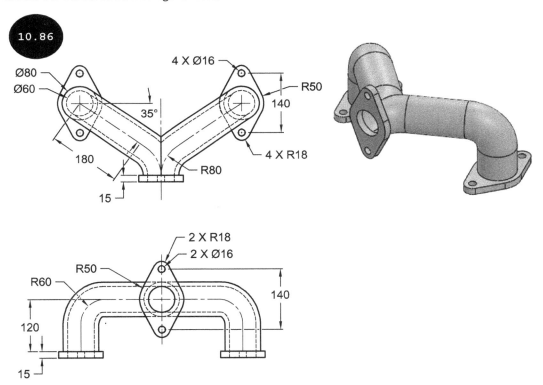

10.86

Section 1: Starting SOLIDWORKS

1. Double click on the **SOLIDWORKS** icon on your desktop to start SOLIDWORKS.

Section 2: Invoking Part Modeling Environment

1. Invoke the Part modeling environment by using the **New SOLIDWORKS Document** dialog box which appears on clicking the **New** tool in the **Standard** toolbar.

Section 3: Specifying Unit Settings

1. Make sure that the MMGS (millimeter, gram, second) unit system is set for the current opened part document.

Section 4: Creating 3D Path - Sweep Feature

The base feature of the model is a sweep feature. The path of the sweep feature is created as a 3D sketch.

1. Click on the **Sketch** tab of the **CommandManager** to invoke the tools of the **Sketch CommandManager**.

2. Click on the down arrow available below the **Sketch** button of the **Sketch CommandManager**, **Sketch** flyout appears, see Figure 10.87.

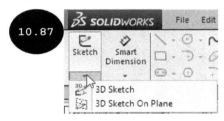

3. Click on the **3D Sketch** tool of the **Sketch** flyout, the 3D Sketching environment is invoked.

4. Click on the **Line** tool of the **Sketch CommandManager**, the line tool is invoked and the display of **XY** appears at the bottom of cursor, see Figure 10.88.

Note: The display of XY below the cursor indicates that the XY (Front) plane is the current sketching plane. You can press the **TAB** key to activate any other sketching plane to create 3D sketch.

---

5. Move the cursor towards the origin and click to specify the start point of the line when cursor snaps to the origin.

6. Move the cursor vertically upwards and click to specify the end point of the line when the length of the line appears close to 120 near the cursor tip, see Figure 10.89.

7. Press the **TAB** key twice to activate the ZX (Top) plane as the sketching plane, see Figure 10.90.

8. Click to specify the end point of the second line when the length of the line appears close to 180 near the cursor tip, see Figure 10.91.

9. Move the cursor away from the last specified point and than move it back to the last specified point, a dot appears in the graphics area, see Figure 10.92.

10. Move the cursor to a small distance, the arc mode is activated and the preview of a tangent arc appears in the graphics area, see Figure 10.93.

11. Click to specify the end point of the arc when the radius of the arc appears close to 80 near the cursor tip, see Figure 10.93.

12. Press the ESC key to exit from the tool.

13. Invoke the **Centerline** tool and then create a horizontal centerline by specifying the start point of the centerline at the end point of the first created line entity, see Figure 10.94.

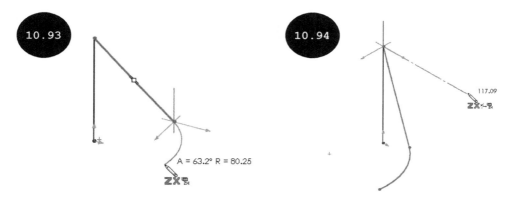

14. Press the ESC key to exit from the tool.

Section 5: Apply Dimensions

1. Click on the **Smart Dimension** tool and then click to select the vertical line entity from the graphics area, the vertical linear dimension attached with the cursor.

2. Click in the graphics area to specify the placement point for the attached dimension, the **Modify** dialog box appears.

3. Enter **120** in this dialog box and then click on its green tick mark ✓ , the length of the line changes to 120 and dimension applied, see Figure 10.95.

4. Click to select the inclined line entity from the graphics area to apply dimension, the dimension attached with the cursor.

5. Click in the graphics area to specify the placement point for the attached dimension, the **Modify** dialog box appears.

6. Enter **180** in this dialog box and then click on its green tick mark ✓ , the length of the line changes to 180 and dimension applied, see Figure 10.96.

7. Click to select the inclined line entity and then the horizontal centerline, the angular dimension attached with the cursor.

8. Click in the graphics area to specify the placement point for the attached dimension, the **Modify** dialog box appears.

9. Enter **35** in this dialog box and then click on its green tick mark ✅ , the angular dimension is applied, see Figure 10.97.

10. Click to select the arc, the radius dimension attached with the cursor.

11. Click in the graphics area to specify the placement point for the attached dimension, the **Modify** dialog box appears.

12. Enter **80** in this dialog box and then click on its green tick mark ✅ , the radius of the arc changes to 80 and dimension applied, see Figure 10.98.

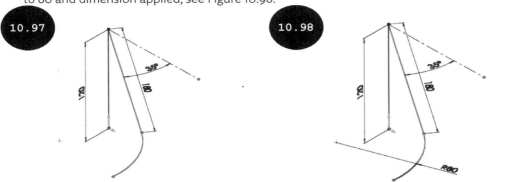

13. Change the current orientation of the sketch to Front by using the **Front** button of the **View Orientation** flyout, see Figure 10.99.

14. Click to select the vertical line and then horizontal line entities from the graphics area, the angular dimension appears attached with the cursor.

15. Click to specify the placement point in the graphics area, the **Modify** dialog box appears.

16. Enter 90 in the dialog box and then click on its green tick mark ✅ , the angular dimension is applied, see Figure 10.100.

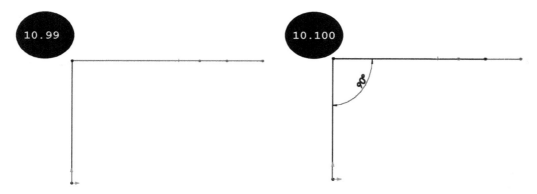

17. Press the ESC key to exit from the tool.

Section 6: Apply Relation

1. Change the current orientation of the sketch to Top by using the **Top** button of the **View Orientation** flyout, see Figure 10.101.

2. Press the CTRL key and then select center point of arc and the end point of arc from the graphics area. Next, release the CTRL key, the Pop-up toolbar appears, see Figure 10.102.

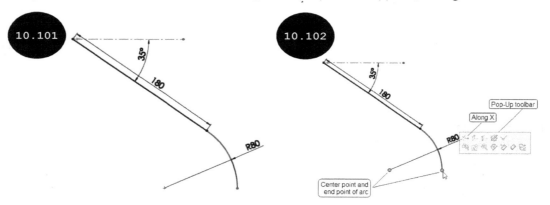

3. Click on the **Along X** button of the Pop-up toolbar.

4. Make sure that the Along X relation is also applied to the horizontal centerline.

5. Change the current orientation of the sketch to isometric, see Figure 10.103.

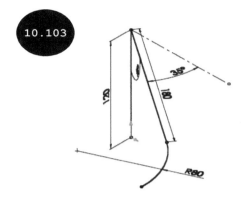

Section 7: Creating Fillet

1.   Click on the **Fillet** tool of the **Sketch CommandManager**, the **Fillet PropertyManager** appears.

2.   Enter **60** in the **Fillet Radius** field of the **Fillet Parameter** rollout of the PropertyManager.

3.   Click to select the vertex of the sketch, see Figure 10.102, the preview of the fillet appears, see Figure 10.104.

4.   Click on the green tick mark ✅ of the PropertyManager, the fillet of radius 60 is created, see Figure 10.105.

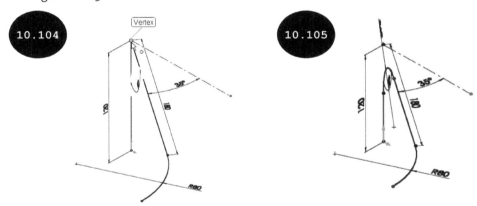

5.   Exit from the Sketching environment.

Section 8: Creating Profile - Sweep Feature

1.   Invoke the Sketching environment by selecting the Top plane as the sketching environment.

2.   Change the orientation of the model normal to the viewing direction by using the **Normal To** tool of the **View Orientation** flyout.

3.   Create a circle of diameter 80 whose center point is at the origin, see Figure 10.106.

4.   Exit from the Sketching environment and change the orientation of the model to isometric, see Figure 10.107.

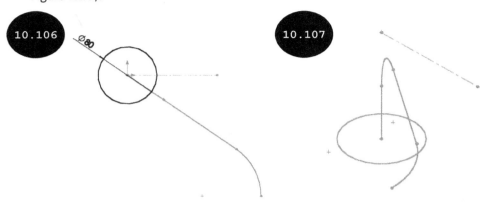

Section 9: Creating First/Base Feature - Sweep Feature

After creating the path and profile of the sweep feature, you can create the sweep feature.

1.   Click on the **Swept Boss/Base** tool, the **Sweep PropertyManager** appears and the **Profile** field of this PropertyManager is activated.

2.   Click to select the circle created as profile of the sweep feature from the graphics area, the **Path** field of the **Sweep PropertyManager** become activated automatically.

3.   Click to select the path (3D sketch) of the sweep feature from the graphics area, the preview of the sweep feature appears in the graphics area, see Figure 10.108.

4.   Click on the green tick mark ✅ of the PropertyManager, the sweep feature is created, see Figure 10.109.

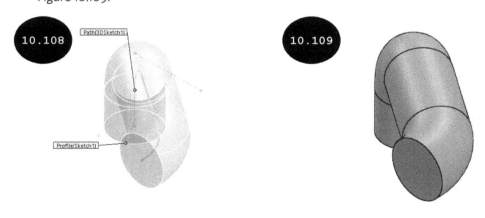

Section 10: Creating Second Feature - Mirror Feature

The second feature of the model can be created by mirroring the first feature about a reference plane which is passing through the center of end circular face of the first feature and parallel to the Right plane. To create this reference plane, you need to first create a reference point at the center of end circular face of the first feature.

1. Invoke **Reference Geometry** flyout and then click on the **Point** tool, the **Point PropertyManager** appears.

2. Click to select the end circular face of the first feature (sweep), see Figure 10.110, the preview of the reference point appears at the center of the circular face selected, see Figure 10.110.

3. Click on the green tick mark ✅ of the PropertyManager, the reference point is created, see Figure 10.111.

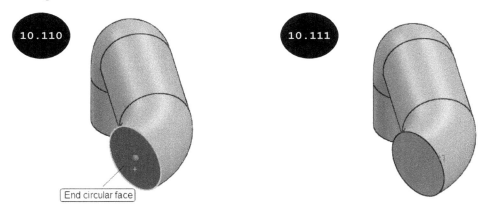

4. Invoke the **Reference Geometry** flyout and then click on the **Plane** tool, the **Plane PropertyManager**.

5. Expand the FeatureManager design tree which is now available at the top left corner of the graphics area by clicking on its +sign.

6. Click to select the Right plane from the FeatureManager design tree as the first reference, preview of the offset reference plane appears in the graphics area.

7. Click on select the newly created reference point from the graphics area as the second reference plane, the preview of the reference plane which is parallel to the Right plane and passing through the reference point is appears in the graphics area, see Figure 10.112.

8. Click on the green tick mark ✅ of the PropertyManager, the reference plane is created, see Figure 10.113.

After creating the reference plane, you can mirror the first feature.

9.   Click on the **Mirror** tool, the **Mirror PropertyManager** appears.

10. Click to select the newly created reference plane as the mirroring plane from the graphics area.

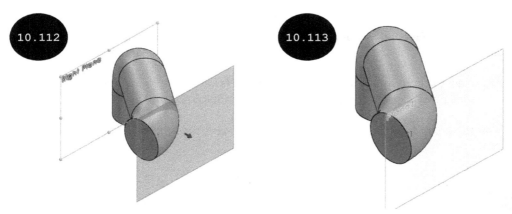

11. Click to select the first/base feature (sweep feature) as the feature to mirror from the graphics area or from the FeatureManager design tree, the preview of the mirror feature appears in the graphics area.

12. Click on the green tick mark ✅ of the PropertyManager, the mirror feature is created, see Figure 10.114.

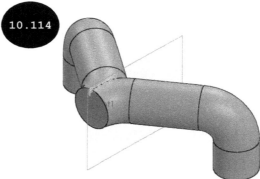

Section 11: Creating Third Feature - Shell Feature

1.   Click on the **Shell** tool of the **Features CommandManager**, the **Shell PropertyManager** appears.

2.   Enter **10** in the **Thickness** field of the **Parameters** rollout of the PropertyManager.

3.   Click to select three planar circular faces from the graphics area as the faces to removed, see Figure 10.115.

4. Click on the green tick mark ✓ of the PropertyManager, the shell feature is created, see Figure 10.116. The display of reference point and plane have been turned Off.

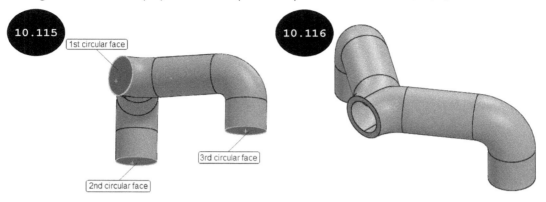

Section 12: Creating Forth Feature - Extrude Feature

1. Invoke the Sketching environment by selecting the Top plane as the sketching plane.

2. Change the view orientation of the model normal to the viewing direction.

3. Create the sketch of the forth feature (extrude), see Figure 10.117.

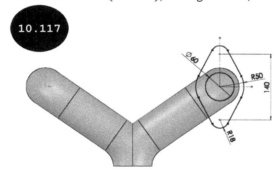

Note: While creating the sketch shown in Figure 10.117, you can take reference of the center point of the circular edge of the sweep feature such that the concentric relation applies between the circle of diameter 60 and the circular edge of the sweep feature.

---

4. Click on the **Features** tab of the **CommandManager** to displays the tools of the **Features CommandManager**.

5. Click on the **Extruded Boss/Base** tool of the **Features CommandManager**, the **Boss-Extrude PropertyManager** and the preview of the extruded feature appears in the graphics area. Next, change the orientation of the model to isometric by using the **View Orientation** flyout.

6.   Click on the **Reverse Direction** button of the **Direction 1** rollout of the PropertyManager to change the direction of extrusion.

7.   Enter **15** in the **Depth** field of the **Direction 1** rollout.

8.   Click on the green tick mark ✅ of the PropertyManager, the extruded feature is created, see Figure 10.118.

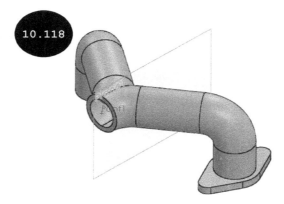

Section 13: Creating Fifth Feature - Mirror Feature

1.   Click on the **Mirror** tool, the **Mirror PropertyManager** appears.

2.   Click to select the reference plane (parallel to the Right plane and passing through the reference point) as the mirroring plane from the graphics area.

3.   Click to select the forth feature (last created extruded feature) as the feature to mirror from the graphics area, the preview of the mirror feature appears in the graphics area, see Figure 10.119.

4.   Click on the green tick mark ✅ of the PropertyManager, the mirror feature is created, see Figure 10.120. Hide the reference plane and point from the graphics area.

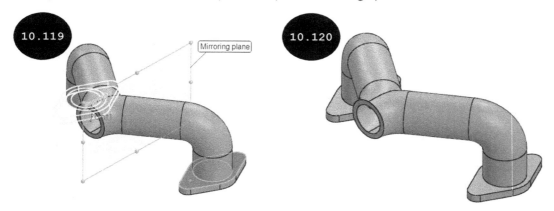

Section 14: Creating Sixth Feature - Extrude Feature

1. Invoke the Sketching environment by selecting the front planar face of the model as the sketching plane, see Figure 10.121.

2. Change the view orientation of the model normal to the viewing direction.

3. Create the sketch of the sixth feature (extrude), see Figure 10.122.

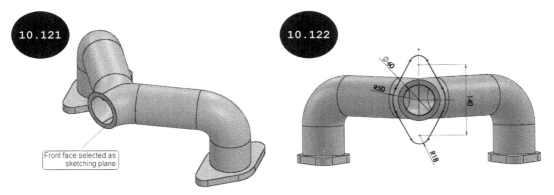

4. Click on the **Features** tab of the **CommandManager** to displays the tools of the **Features CommandManager**.

5. Click on the **Extruded Boss/Base** tool of the **Features CommandManager**, the **Boss-Extrude PropertyManager** and the preview of the extruded feature appears in the graphics area. Next, change the orientation of the model to isometric by using the **View Orientation** flyout.

6. Enter **15** in the **Depth** field of the **Direction 1** rollout.

7. Click on the green tick mark ✓ of the PropertyManager, the extruded feature is created, see Figure 10.123.

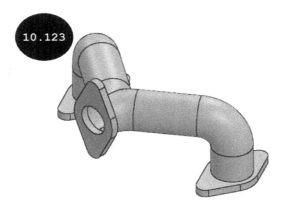

Section 15: Creating Seventh Feature - Hole Feature

In this section, you will create holes using the **Hole Wizard** tool.

1. Click on the **Hole Wizard** tool of the **Features CommandManager**, the **Hole Specification PropertyManager** appears, see Figure 10.124.

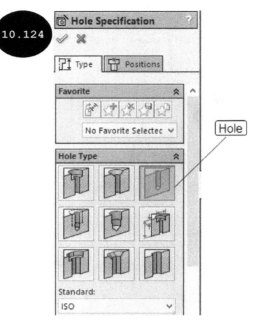

2. Click on the **Hole** tool of the **Hole Type** rollout of the PropertyManager.

3. Select the **ANSI Metric** option from the **Standard** drop-down list of the **Hole Type** rollout.

4. Select the **Drill sizes** option from the **Type** drop-down list of the **Hole Type** rollout.

5. Select the **ø16** from the **Size** drop-down list of the **Hole Specifications** rollout.

6. Select the **Up To Next** option from the **End Condition** rollout.

After specifying the hole type and specification, you need to define its placement.

7. Click on the **Positions** tab of the **Hole Specification PropertyManager**, the name of the PropertyManager changes to **Hole Position PropertyManager**, see Figure 10.125.

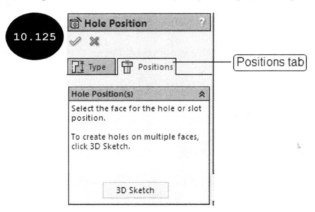

8. Move the cursor over the top planar face of the right side extruded feature, see Figure 10.126. Next, click to select it as the placement face.

9. Move the cursor over a semi-circular edge of the extruded feature,, see Figure 10.127, the center point of the semi-circular edge highlights, see Figure 10.127. Also, the preview of the hole appears.

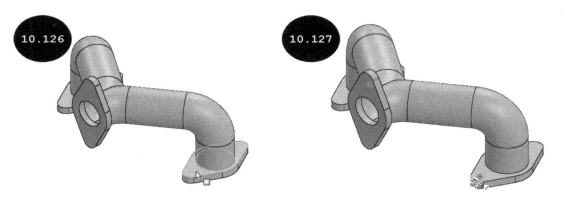

10. Move the cursor over the highlighted center point of the semi-circular edge of the extruded feature and then click to specify the center point of the hole when cursor snaps to it.

11. Similarly, move the cursor over the another side semi-circular edge of the extruded feature, see Figure 10.128, the center point of the semi-circular edge highlights, see Figure 10.128.

12. Move the cursor over the highlighted center point of this semi-circular edge and then click to specify the center point of the hole when cursor snaps to it.

13. Similarly, move the cursor over the semi-circular edges of the left side extruded feature and specify center point of remaining holes, see Figure 10.129.

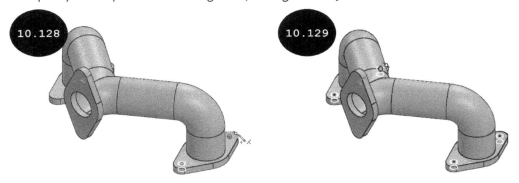

14. Click on the green tick mark ✅ of the PropertyManager, the holes are created, see Figure 10.130.

15. Similarly, invoke the **Hole Wizard** tool again and then create holes on the front planar face of the middle extruded feature, see Figure 10.131.

Section 16: Saving the Model

1. Click on the **Save** tool of the **Standard** toolbar, the **Save As** window appears.

2. Browse to the *SOLIDWORKS* folder and then create a folder named as *Chapter 10*. Next, create another folder named as *Tutorial* inside the *Chapter 10* folder.

3. Type **Tutorial 1** in the **File name** field of the dialog box as the name of the file and then click on the **Save** button, the model is saved as Tutorial 1 in the *Tutorial* folder of *Chapter 10*.

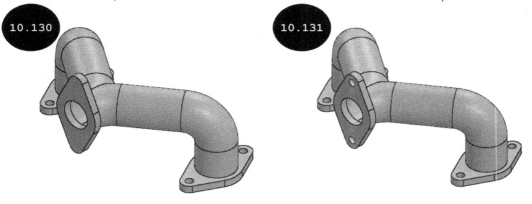

Tutorial 2

Create the model shown in Figure 10.132.

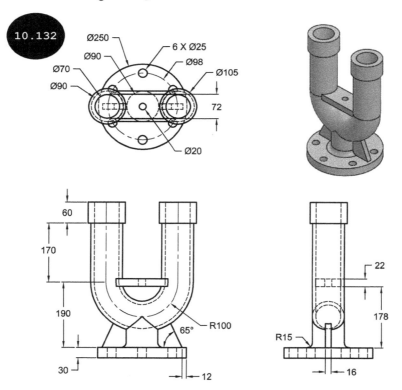

Section 1: Starting SOLIDWORKS
1.   Double click on the **SOLIDWORKS** icon on your desktop to start SOLIDWORKS.

Section 2: Invoking Part Modeling Environment
1.   Invoke the Part modeling environment by using the **New SOLIDWORKS Document** dialog box which appears on clicking the **New** tool in the **Standard** toolbar.

Section 3: Specifying Unit Settings
1.   Make sure that the **MMGS (millimeter, gram, second)** unit system is set for the current opened part document.

Section 4: Creating Path - Sweep Feature
The base feature of the model is a sweep feature. To create the sweep feature, you need to create path of the sweep feature first.

1.   Invoke the Sketching environment by selecting the Front plane as the sketching plane.

2.   Create the sketch of the path for the sweep feature, see Figure 10.133.

Note: In Figure 10.133, the center point of the arc is at the origin. Also, the line and arc entities have tangent relation with each other.

3.   Exit from the Sketching environment and change the orientation of the sketch to isometric.

Section 5: Creating Profile - Sweep Feature
After creating the path of the sweep feature, you need to create profile of the sweep feature at a plane which is normal to the path and passing through the end point of the path.

1.   Invoke the **Plane PropertyManager** by clicking on the **Plane** tool of the **Reference Geometry** flyout.

2.   Click to select the path as the first reference from the graphics area, see Figure 10.134.

3.   Click to select the end point of a vertical line entity of the path as the second reference from the graphics area, see Figure 10.134, the preview of the reference plane appears, see Figure 10.134.

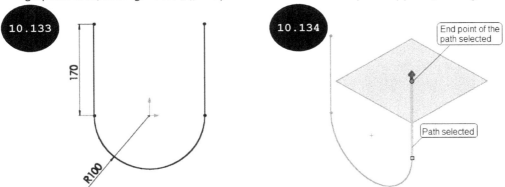

4. Click on the green tick mark ✔ of the PropertyManager, the reference plane is created.

5. Invoke the Sketching environment by selecting the newly created reference plane as the sketching plane.

6. Change the orientation normal to the viewing direction and create the sketch of the profile (circle of diameter 90) for the sweep feature, see Figure 10.135.

> **Note:** In Figure 10..135, the center point of the circle has Pierce relation with the path.

7. Exit from the Sketching environment and then change the orientation of the model to isometric, see Figure 10.136.

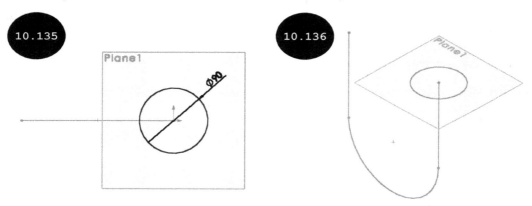

10.135

10.136

Section 6: Creating First/Base Feature - Sweep Feature

After creating the path and profile of the sweep feature, you can create the sweep feature.

1. Click on the **Swept Boss/Base** tool, the **Sweep PropertyManager** appears and the **Profile** field of this PropertyManager is activated.

2. Click to select the circle created as the profile of the sweep feature from the graphics area, the **Path** field of the **Sweep PropertyManager** become activated automatically.

3. Click to select the path of the sweep feature from the graphics area, the preview of the sweep feature appears in the graphics area.

4. Click on the green tick mark ✔ of the PropertyManager, the sweep feature is created, see Figure 10.137.

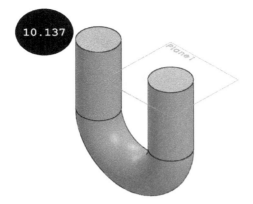

Section 7: Creating Second Feature - Shell Feature

1. Click on the **Shell** tool of the **Features CommandManager**, the **Shell PropertyManager** appears.

2. Enter **10** in the **Thickness** field of the **Parameters** rollout of the PropertyManager.

3. Click to select the planar faces of the model from the graphics area as the faces to removed, see Figure 10.138.

4. Click on the green tick mark ✅ of the PropertyManager, the shell feature is created, see Figure 10.139. Hide the display of reference plane from the graphics area.

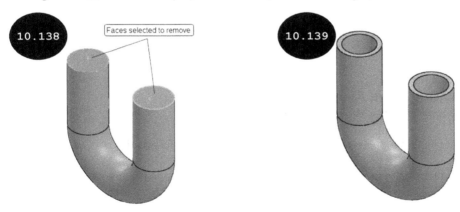

Section 8: Creating Third Feature - Extrude Feature

1. Invoke the Sketching environment by selecting the top planar face of the base feature (sweep) as the sketching plane, see Figure 10.140.

2. Change the view orientation of the model normal to the viewing direction.

3. Create the sketch of the third feature (two circles), see Figure 10.141.

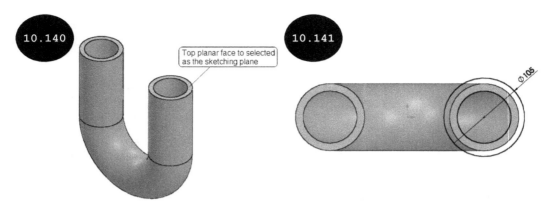

Note: The sketch of the third feature contain two circles: outer circle is of diameter 105 and inner circle has Coradial relation with the inner circular edge of the sweep feature. This is because the inner circle of the sketch has same diameter as that of the inner circular edge of the sweep feature.

4. Click on the **Features** tab of the **CommandManager** to displays the tools of the **Features CommandManager**.

5. Click on the **Extruded Boss/Base** tool of the **Features CommandManager**, the **Boss-Extrude PropertyManager** and the preview of the extruded feature appears in the graphics area. Next, change the orientation of the model to isometric by using the **View Orientation** flyout.

6. Enter **60** in the **Depth** field of the **Direction 1** rollout.

7. Click on the green tick mark ✅ of the PropertyManager, the extruded feature is created, see Figure 10.142.

Section 9: Creating Forth Feature - Mirror Feature

1. Click on the **Mirror** tool, the **Mirror PropertyManager** appears.

2. Click to select the Right plane from the FeatureManager design tree as the mirroring plane.

3. Click to select the third feature (last created extruded feature) as the feature to mirror from the graphics area, the preview of the mirror feature appears in the graphics area.

4. Click on the green tick mark ✅ of the PropertyManager, the mirror feature is created, see Figure 10.143.

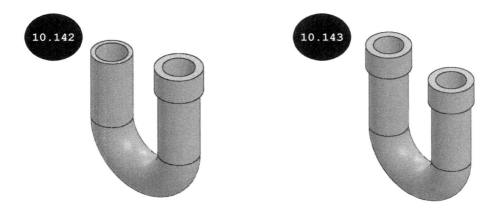

Section 10: Creating Fifth Feature - Extrude Feature

The sketch of this extruded feature is to be created on a reference plane.

1. Invoke the **Plane PropertyManager** by clicking on the **Plane** tool of the **Reference Geometry** flyout.

2. Click to select the Top plane from the FeatureManager design tree as the first reference, the preview of the offset reference plane appears.

3. Enter **190** in the **Distance** field of the **First Reference** rollout of the PropertyManager.

4. Click to select the **Flip** check box available below the **Distance** field to reverse the direction of plane creation.

5. Click on the green tick mark ✅ of the PropertyManager, the reference plane is created, see Figure 10.144.

6. Invoke the Sketching environment by selecting the newly created reference plane as the sketching plane.

7. Change the view orientation of the model normal to the viewing direction.

8. Create the sketch of the fifth feature (circle of diameter 90), see Figure 10.145.

9. Click on the **Features** tab of the **CommandManager** to displays the tools of the **Features CommandManager**.

10. Click on the **Extruded Boss/Base** tool of the **Features CommandManager**, the **Boss-Extrude PropertyManager** and the preview of the extruded feature appears in the graphics area. Next, change the orientation of the model to isometric by using the **View Orientation** flyout.

11. Invoke the **End Condition** drop-down list of the **Direction 1** rollout of the PropertyManager.

12. Click to select the **Up To Surface** option of the **End Condition** flyout, the **Face/Plane** field become available in the **Direction 1** rollout and is activated by default.

13. Click to select the outer circular face of the sweep feature as the surface up to which you want to extrude feature, the preview of the extrude feature appears in the graphics area, see Figure 10.146.

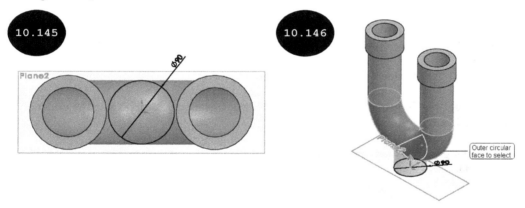

14. Click on the green tick mark ✅ of the PropertyManager, the extruded feature is created, see Figure 10.147.

Section 11: Creating Sixth Feature - Extrude Feature

1. Click on the **Extruded Boss/Base** tool of the **Features CommandManager**, the **Extrude PropertyManager** appears.

2. Rotate the model such that you can view the bottom planar face of the last created extruded feature.

3. Invoke the Sketching environment by selecting the bottom planar face of the last created extruded feature. Next, change the orientation of the model normal to the viewing direction.

4. Create the sketch of the sixth feature (circle of diameter 250), see Figure 10.148.

5. Exit from the Sketching environment, the **Boss-Extrude PropertyManager** and the preview of the extruded feature appears in the graphics area. Next, change the orientation of the model to isometric.

6. Enter **30** in the **Depth** field of the **Direction 1** rollout of the PropertyManager.

7. Click on the green tick mark ✅ of the PropertyManager, the extruded feature is created, see Figure 10.149. Hide the reference plane.

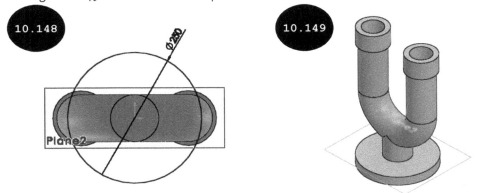

Section 12: Creating Seventh Feature - Extrude Cut Feature

1. Click on the Extruded Cut tool of the Features CommandManager, the Extrude PropertyManager appears.

2. Click to select the top planar face of the sixth feature (last created extruded feature) as the sketching plane.

3. Change the orientation of the model normal to the viewing direction.

4. Create the sketch of the feature (circle of diameter 25), see Figure 10.150.

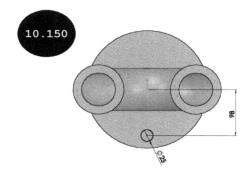

Note: In Figure 10.150, the vertical relation has been applied between the center point of the circle and the origin to make the sketch fully defined.

5. Exit from the Sketching environment, the **Cut-Extrude PropertyManager** appears. Next, change the orientation of the model to isometric.

6. Invoke the **End Condition** drop-down list of the **Direction 1** rollout and select the **Through All** option.

7. Click on the green tick mark ✅ of the PropertyManager, the extruded cut feature is created, see Figure 10.151.

Section 13: Creating Eight Feature - Circular Pattern

1. Invoke the **Pattern** flyout by clicking on the down arrow available at the bottom of **Linear Pattern** tool, see Figure 10.152.

2. Click on the **Circular Pattern** tool of the **Pattern** flyout, the **Circular Pattern PropertyManager** appears.

3. Select the seventh feature (last created extruded cut feature) as the feature to pattern from the graphics area.

4. Click on the **Pattern Axis** field of the **Parameters** rollout of the PropertyManager to activate it.

5. Click to select the outer circular face of the sixth feature from the graphics area to define the pattern axis, see Figure 10.153, the preview of the circular pattern appears.

6. Make sure that the **Equal spacing** check box is selected in the **Parameters** rollout of the PropertyManager.

7. Enter **6** in the **Number of Instances** field of the **Parameters** rollout.

8. Click on the green tick mark ✅ of the PropertyManager, the circular pattern is created, see Figure 10.154.

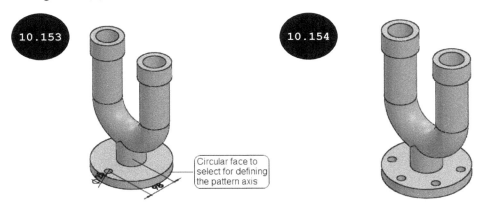

Circular face to select for defining the pattern axis

Section 14: Creating Ninth Feature - Fillet

1. Click on the **Fillet** tool of the **Features** CommandManager, the **Fillet PropertyManager** appears.

2. Make sure that the **Constant size** button is selected in the **Fillet Type** rollout of the PropertyManager.

3. Click to select the circular edge of the model to apply fillet, see Figure 10.155, the preview of the fillet appears in the graphics area.

4. Enter **15** in the **Radius** field of the **Fillet Parameters** rollout of the PropertyManager.

5. Click on the green tick mark ✅ of the PropertyManager, the fillet of radius 15 is created, see Figure 10.156.

Section 15: Creating Tenth Feature - Rib

1.   Click on the **Rib** tool of the **Features CommandManager**, the **Rib PropertyManager** appears.

2.   Expand the FeatureManager design tree which is now available at the top left corner of the graphics area and then select the Front Plane as the sketching plane.

3.   Change the orientation of the model normal to the viewing direction.

4.   Create the sketch of the rib feature (a inclined line entity), see Figure 10.157.

5.   Exit from the Sketching environment, the **Rib PropertyManager** appears. Next, change the orientation of the model to isometric.

6.   Make sure that the **Both Sides** button is activated in the **Thickness** area of the **Parameters** rollout of the PropertyManager.

7.   Enter **16** in the **Rib Thickness** field of the **Parameters** rollout of the PropertyManager.

8.   Make sure that the **Parallel to Sketch** button is activated in the **Extrusion direction** area of the **Parameters** rollout.

9.   Make sure that the **Flip material side** check box of the **Parameters** rollout is cleared.

10. Click on the green tick mark ✅ of the PropertyManager, the rib feature is created, see Figure 10.158.

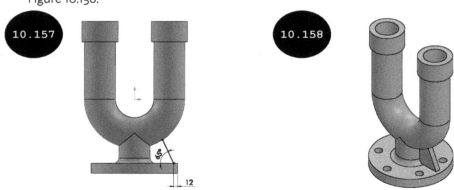

Section 16: Creating Eleventh Feature - Mirror Feature

1. Click on the **Mirror** tool, the **Mirror PropertyManager** appears.

2. Expand the FeatureManager design tree and then click to select the Right plane as the mirroring plane.

3. Click to select the rib feature as the feature to mirror from the graphics area, the preview of the mirror feature appears in the graphics area.

4. Click on the green tick mark ✅ of the PropertyManager, the mirror feature is created, see Figure 10.159.

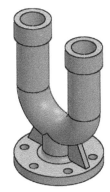

10.159

Section 17: Creating Twelfth Feature - Extrude Feature

1. Click on the **Extruded Boss/Base** tool of the **Features CommandManager**, the **Extrude PropertyManager** appears.

2. Expand the FeatureManager design tree and then click to select the Right plane as the sketching plane. Next, change the orientation of the model normal to the viewing direction.

3. Create the sketch of the twelfth feature (a rectangle), see Figure 10.160.

4. Exit from the Sketching environment, the **Boss-Extrude PropertyManager** appears in the graphics area. Next, change the orientation of the model to isometric.

5. Invoke the **End Condition** drop-down list of the **Direction 1** rollout of the PropertyManager and click to select the **Up To Next** option.

6. Expand the **Direction 2** rollout of the PropertyManager. Next, invoke the **End Condition** drop-down list of the **Direction 2** rollout and click to select the **Up To Next** option from it.

7. Click on the green tick mark ✅ of the PropertyManager, the extruded feature is created, see Figure 10.161.

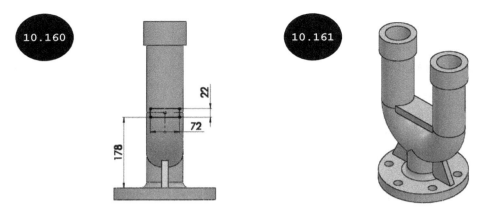

Section 18: Creating Thirteenth Feature - Extrude Cut Feature

1.   Click on the **Extruded Cut** tool of the **Features Command Manager**, the **Extrude Property Manager** appears.

2.   Click to select the top planar face of the twelfth feature (last created extruded feature) as the sketching plane.

3.   Change the orientation of the model normal to the viewing direction.

4.   Create the sketch of the feature (circle of diameter 20), see Figure 10.162.

5.   Exit from the Sketching environment, the **Cut-Extrude PropertyManager** appears. Next, change the orientation of the model to isometric.

6.   Invoke the **End Condition** drop-down list of the **Direction 1** rollout and select the **Up To Next** option.

7.   Click on the green tick mark ✅ of the PropertyManager, the extruded cut feature is created, see Figure 10.163.

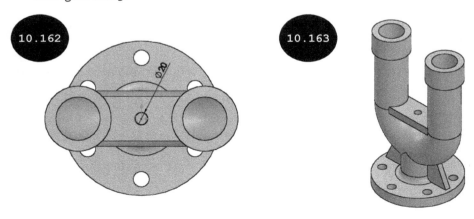

Section 19: Saving the Model

1. Click on the **Save** tool of the **Standard** toolbar, the **Save As** window appears.

2. Browse to the *Tutorial* folder of *Chapter 10* and then save the model as Tutorial 2.

Tutorial 3

Create the model shown in Figure 10.164.

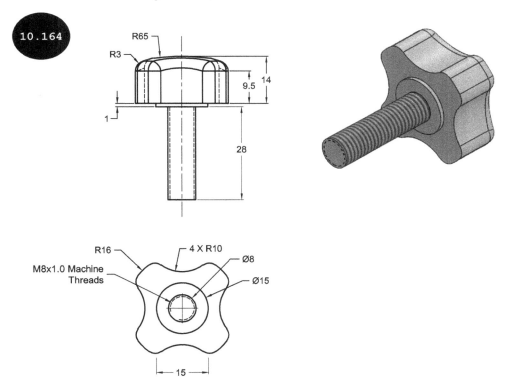

Section 1: Starting SOLIDWORKS

1. Double click on the **SOLIDWORKS** icon on your desktop to start SOLIDWORKS.

Section 2: Invoking Part Modeling Environment

1. Invoke the Part modeling environment by using the **New SOLIDWORKS Document** dialog box which appears on clicking the **New** tool in the **Standard** toolbar.

Section 3: Specifying Unit Settings

1. Make sure that the **MMGS (millimeter, gram, second)** unit system is set for the current opened part document.

Section 4: Creating First/Base Feature - Revolve Feature

1. Click on the **Revolved Boss/Base** tool of the **Features CommandManager**, the **Revolve PropertyManager** appears.

2. Click to select the Top Plane as the sketching plane and then create the sketch of the base feature (revolve), see Figure 10.165.

3. Exit from the Sketching environment, the preview of the revolve feature appears in the graphics area, see Figure 10.166. Also, the **Revolve PropertyManager** appears.

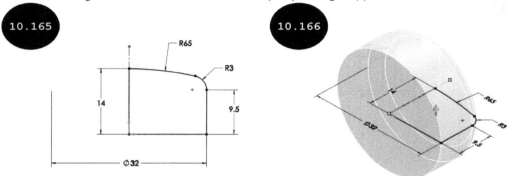

Note: If the sketch to revolve has one centerline, the preview of the revolve feature appears automatically in the graphics area as soon as you exit from the Sketching environment. However, if the sketch has more than one centerline, you need to select a centerline as the axis of revolution.

4. Click on the green tick mark ✅ of the PropertyManager, the revolve feature is created, see Figure 10.167.

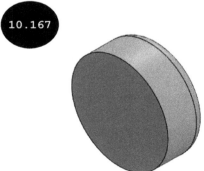

Section 5: Creating Second Feature - Extrude Cut Feature

1. Click on the Extruded Cut tool of the Features CommandManager, the Extrude PropertyManager appears.

2. Click to select the front planar face of the base feature as the sketching plane.

3. Change the orientation of the model normal to the viewing direction.

4. Create the sketch of the cut feature (arc of radius 10), see Figure 10.168.

Note: The end points of the arc shown in Figure 10.168 has symmetric relation applied with the vertical centerline. You can apply symmetric relation by selecting the end points of the arc and the vertical centerline by pressing the CTRL key and then click to select the **Symmetric** tool from the Pop-up toolbar.

5. Exit from the Sketching environment, the **Cut-Extrude PropertyManager** appears. Next, change the orientation of the model to isometric.

6. Click on the green tick mark ✓ of the PropertyManager, the extruded cut feature is created, see Figure 10.169.

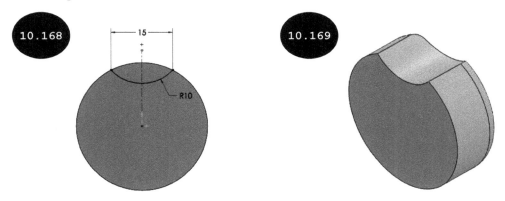

Section 6: Creating Third Feature - Circular Pattern

1. Invoke the **Pattern** flyout by clicking on the down arrow available at the bottom of **Linear Pattern** tool, see Figure 10.170.

2. Click on the **Circular Pattern** tool of the **Pattern** flyout, the **Circular Pattern PropertyManager** appears.

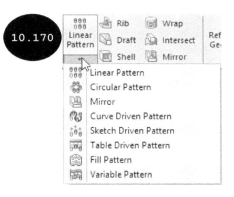

3. Select the second feature (extruded cut) as the feature to pattern from the graphics area.

4. Click on the **Pattern Axis** field of the **Parameters** rollout of the PropertyManager to activate it.

5. Click to select the outer circular face of the base feature to define the pattern axis, the preview of the circular pattern appears.

6. Make sure that the **Equal spacing** check box is selected in the **Parameters** rollout of the PropertyManager.

7. Enter **4** in the **Number of Instances** field of the **Parameters** rollout.

8. Click on the green tick mark ✅ of the PropertyManager, the circular pattern is created, see Figure 10.171.

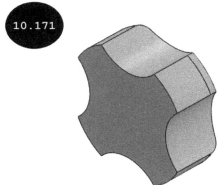

10.171

Section 7: Creating Forth Feature - Fillet

1. Click on the **Fillet** tool of the **Features CommandManager**, the **Fillet PropertyManager** appears.

2. Make sure that the **Constant size** button is selected in the **Fillet Type** rollout of the PropertyManager.

3. Rotate the model such that you can view the back face of the base feature, see Figure 10.172.

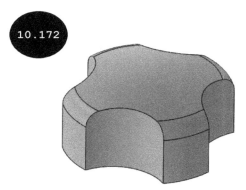

10.172

4. Enter **3** in the **Radius** field of the **Fillet Parameters** rollout of the PropertyManager.

5. Make sure that the **Tangent propagation** check box is selected in the **Items To Fillets** rollout.

6. Click to select the curved face of the base feature to apply fillet, see Figure 10.173. As soon as

you select the face to apply fillet, the preview of the fillet appears in all edges of the selected face, see Figure 10.173.

7. Click on the green tick mark ✓ of the PropertyManager, the fillet of radius 3 is created, see Figure 10.174.

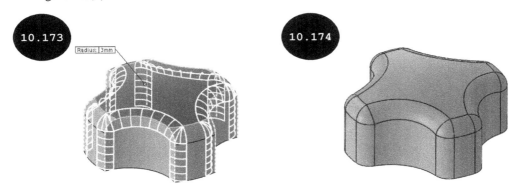

8. Change the orientation of the model to isometric.

Section 8: Creating Fifth Feature - Extrude Feature

1. Click on the **Extruded Boss/Base** tool of the **Features CommandManager**, the **Extrude PropertyManager** appears.

2. Click to select the front face of the model as the Sketching plane. Next, change the orientation of the model normal to the viewing direction.

3. Create the sketch of the fifth feature (circle of diameter 14), see Figure 10.175.

4. Exit from the Sketching environment, the **Boss-Extrude PropertyManager** and the preview of the extruded feature appears in the graphics area. Next, change the orientation of the model to isometric.

5. Enter 1 in the **Depth** field of the **Direction 1** rollout of the PropertyManager.

6. Click on the green tick mark ✓ of the PropertyManager, the extruded feature is created, see Figure 10.176.

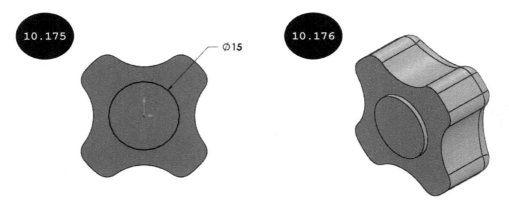

Section 9: Creating Sixth Feature - Extrude Feature

1. Click on the **Extruded Boss/Base** tool of the **Features CommandManager**, the **Extrude PropertyManager** appears.

2. Click to select the front face of the fifth feature (last created extruded feature) as the Sketching plane. Next, change the orientation of the model normal to the viewing direction.

3. Create the sketch of the sixth feature (circle of diameter 8), see Figure 10.177.

4. Exit from the Sketching environment, the **Boss-Extrude PropertyManager** and the preview of the extruded feature appears in the graphics area. Next, change the orientation of the model to isometric.

5. Enter **28** in the **Depth** field of the **Direction 1** rollout of the PropertyManager.

6. Click on the green tick mark ✅ of the PropertyManager, the extruded feature is created, see Figure 10.178.

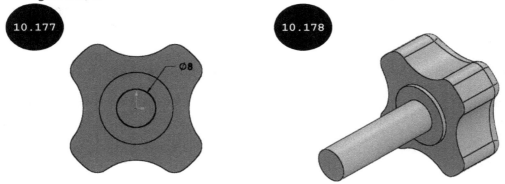

Section 10: Creating Seventh Feature - Cosmetic Thread

1. Click on the **Insert > Annotations > Cosmetic Thread** from the SOLIDWORKS menus, the **Cosmetic Thread PropertyManager** appears.

2. Click to select the front circular edge of the sixth feature (last created extruded feature) as the edge to start cosmetic thread, see Figure 10.179.

3. Select the **ANSI Metric** option from the **Standard** drop-down list of the **Thread Settings** rollout of the PropertyManager.

4. Select the **M8x1.0** option from the **Size** drop-down list of the **Thread Settings** rollout.

5. Select the **Up to Next** option from the **End Condition** drop-down list.

6. Click on the green tick mark ✅ of the PropertyManager, the cosmetic thread is created and represented as a doted circle in the graphics area, see Figure 10.180.

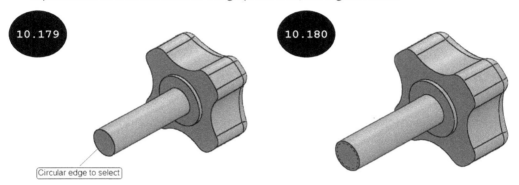

After applying the cosmetic thread, you can turn On the shaded display style of cosmetic thread.

7. Click to select the **Annotations** node of the FeatureManager design tree and then right click to display a shortcut menu, see Figure 10.181.

8. Click to select the **Details** option from the shortcut menu, the **Annotation Properties** dialog box.

9. Click to select the **Shaded cosmetic threads** check box of the dialog box and then click on the OK button, the shaded display style of cosmetic thread is turn On, see Figure 10.182.

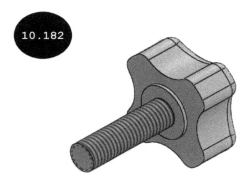

10.182

Section 11: Saving the Model

1. Click on the **Save** tool of the **Standard** toolbar, the **Save As** window appears.

2. Browse to the *Tutorial* folder of *Chapter 10* and then save the model as Tutorial 3.

Hands-on Test Drive 1

Create the model shown in Figure 10.183.

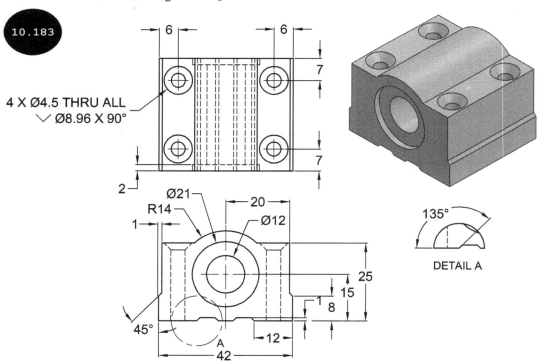

10.183

Hands-on Test Drive 2

Create the model shown in Figure 10.184.

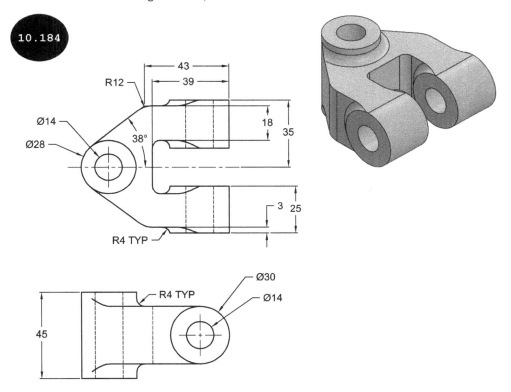

Summary

In this chapter, you have learnt how to create standard or customized holes such as counterbore, countersink, straight tap, and tapered tap as per the standard specifications. You have also learnt that cosmetic threads can be used to represent the real threads on holes, fasteners, and cylindrical features to avoid increase in the complexity of the model and improve overall performance of the system. You can add constant and variable radius fillets to remove sharp edges of the model. You have also learnt about various method of adding chamfer on the edges of the model. You can create rib features from open or closed sketch by adding thickness in a specified direction. At last you have learnt about creating shell feature which is a thin walled feature created by making the model hollow from inside. You can create a shell feature having uniform or variable wall thickness.

Questions

- The _____ tool is used to create standard holes such as counterbore and countersink.

- The _____ tool is used to add cosmetic threads on holes, fasteners, and cylindrical features. .

- By using the **Fillet** tool you can create _____, _____, _____, and _____ fillets.

- If the rho value is less than _____ then the fillet profile have elliptical shape.

- The _____ fillet is created between three adjacent face of a model.

- The _____ fillet is created between two non-adjacent or non-continuous faces of a model.

- You can create rib features by using the open or closed sketch. (True/False).

- You can not create rib features with a draft angle. (True/False).

- While creating a hole using the **Hole Wizard** tool, you can not customize the hole sizes. (True/False).

- By using the **Hole Wizard** tool, you can counterbore slot, countersink slot, or slot holes. (True/False).

CHAPTER

11

Working with Assemblies I

In this chapter:

- Understanding Bottom-up Assembly Approach
- Understanding Top-down Assembly Approach
- Creating Assembly using Bottom-up Approach
- Understanding Degree of Freedoms
- Applying Relations or Mates
- Moving and Rotating Individual Components
- Working with SmartMates

In the earlier chapters, you have learnt basic and advance technics of creating real world mechanical components. Now, in this chapters, you will learn different technics of creating mechanical assemblies. Note that an assembly is made-up of assembling two or more than two components together by applying proper relations. You will learn about applying relations later in this chapter. Figure 11.1 show an assembly.

11.1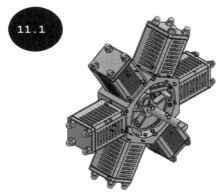

In SOLIDWORKS, you can create assemblies in the Assembly environment by using two approaches: **Bottom-up Assembly** and **Top-Down Assembly**. You can also use the combination of both these approaches to create an assembly. Both these approaches are as follows.

Understanding Bottom-up Assembly Approach

The Bottom-up Assembly Approach is most widely used approach for assembling the components. In this approach, you first create all the components of the assembly in the Part modeling environment one by one and save them in a common location. Later, you insert all the created components one by one in the Assembly environment and assemble them with respect to each other by applying required relations.

Tip: Because of the Bidirectional associative property of SOLIDWORKS, if you make any change in any of the part or component in the Part modeling environment, the same change will automatically reflect in the assembly environment as well and vice-versa.

Understanding Top-down Assembly Approach

The Top-down Assembly Approach is mainly used for creating concept based design where the individual component design or dimensions are not finalized and depends upon the other components shape and size.

In Top-down Assembly Approach, you create all the components of the assembly in the Assembly environment itself. Creating all the components in the Assembly environment helps you in creating a component by taking the reference from the existing components. This approach builds the entire assembly by creating all its components top of each other.

Creating Assembly using Bottom-up Approach

After creating all the components of an assembly in the Part modeling environment and saving them in a common location, you need to invoke the Assembly environment of SOLIDWORKS to assemble them. To invoke the Assembly environment, click **File > New** from the SOLIDWORKS menus or click the **New** tool available in the **Standard** toolbar, the **New SOLIDWORKS Document** dialog box appears, see Figure 11.2. In this dialog box, click on the **Assembly** button to activate it and then click on the **OK** button, the Assembly environment invoked with the display of **Begin Assembly PropertyManager** on its left, see Figure 11.3.

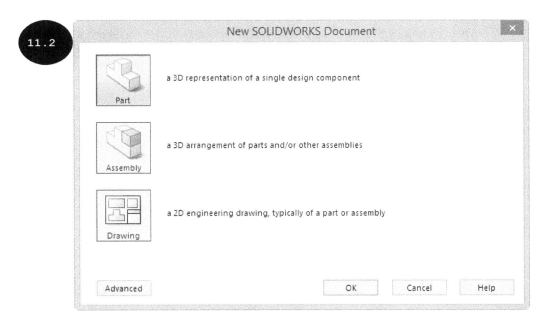

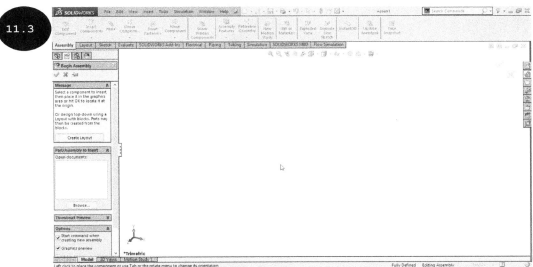

The **Begin Assembly PropertyManager** appears automatically on invoking the Assembly environment and is used to insert the existing created components in the Assembly environment.

Note: In the **Options** rollout of the **Begin Assembly PropertyManager**, the **Start command when creating new assembly** check box is selected, by default. As a result, this PropertyManager appears automatically on invoking the Assembly environment. If you clear this check box, next time on invoking the Assembly environment, the **Begin Assembly PropertyManager** will not appears. In that case, to insert the components in the Assembly environment, you can use the **Insert Component PropertyManager** which invokes on clicking the **Insert Components** tool available in the **Assembly CommandManager**, see Figure 11.4. To again turn on the display of **Begin Assembly PropertyManager** on invoking the Assembly environment, select the **Start command when creating new assembly** check box available in the **Options** rollout of the **Insert Component PropertyManager**.

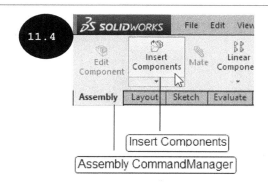

Inserting Components using Begin Assembly PropertyManager

To insert components in the Assembly environment, click on the **Browse** button of the **Part/Assembly to Insert** rollout of the **Begin Assembly PropertyManager**, the **Open** dialog box appears. In this dialog box, browse to the location where all components of the assembly are saved and then select a component to insert. Next, click on the **Open** button of the dialog box, the selected component is attached with the cursor, see Figure 11.5. Also, the **Rotate Context** toolbar appears automatically in the graphics area, see Figure 11.5. If needed, you can change the orientation of the component as required by using this toolbar before defining its placement point.

Note: The **Rotate Context** toolbar is used to change the orientation of the component as required before defining its placement point in the graphics area. By default, 90 degree is entered in the **Angle** field of this toolbar. As a result, on clicking the **X, Y,** or **Z** button of this toolbar, the component rotates 90 degree about X, Y, or Z axis, respectively. You can enter the angle of rotation as required in the **Angle** field of this toolbar.

By default the **Rotate Context** toolbar appears automatically while inserting the component in the Assembly environment. This is because, the **Show Rotate context toolbar** check box is selected in the **Options** rollout of the **Begin Assembly PropertyManager**.

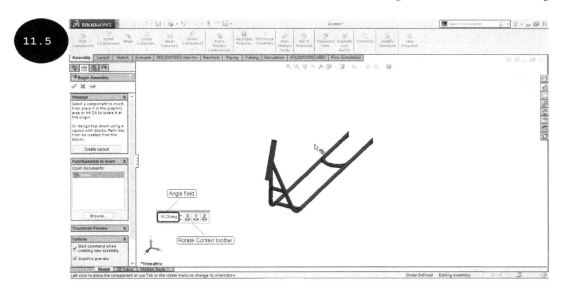

Once the orientation of the component is changed as required by using the **Rotate Context** toolbar. Click anywhere in the graphics area, the component move towards the origin of the assembly and coincident with the assembly origin such that it become fixed component. Also, the name of the inserted component is added in the **Assembly Manager design tree** with (f) sign in front of its name, see Figure 11.6. This (f) sign indicate that all the degrees of freedom of the first inserted components are fixed and component can not move or rotate in any direction. Also, as soon as the first component is inserted in the Assembly environment, the **Begin Assembly PropertyManager** is closed. Now, you can insert the remaining components of the assembly using the **Insert Component PropertyManager** which is as follows.

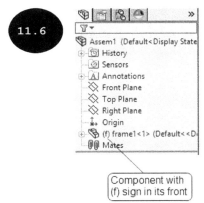

Tip: If you pin the **Begin Assembly PropertyManager** by clicking on the **Keep Visible** 📌 icon available at its upper right corner, the display of PropertyManager will not be closed after inserting the first component and you can continue insert the other components of the assembly using the **Begin Assembly PropertyManager**.

Note: The **Open documents** field of the **Part/Assembly to Insert** rollout of the **Begin Assembly PropertyManager** displays the list of components that are opened in the current session of SOLIDWORKS, see Figure 11.7. You can also select a component to insert in the Assembly environment by using this field.

Inserting Components using the Insert Component PropertyManager

As discussed earlier, as soon as you insert the first component in the Assembly environment, the **Begin Assembly PropertyManager** will close, automatically. To insert the second or remaining components of the assembly, click on the **Insert Components** tool available in the **Assembly CommandManager**, see Figure 11.4, the **Insert Component PropertyManager** appears, see Figure 11.8.

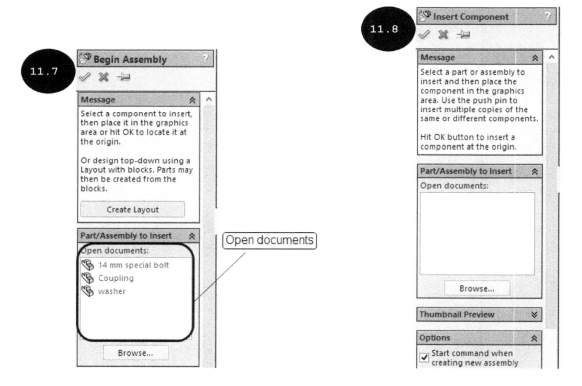

Click on the **Browse** button of the **Part/Assembly to Insert** rollout of the PropertyManager, the **Open** dialog box appears. In this dialog box, browse to the location where all components of the assembly are saved and then select the component to insert. Next, click on the **Open** button of the dialog box, the selected component is attached with the cursor. Also, the **Rotate Context** toolbar appears automatically in the graphics area, see Figure 11.9.

Change the current orientation of the component as required by using the **Rotate Context** toolbar. Once the orientation of the component is changed as required. You need to define the placement point for the attached component in the graphics area. Click the left mouse button anywhere in the graphics area, the attached component is placed on the defined location and the PropertyManager is closed. Also, the name of the inserted component is added in the FeatureManager design tree with (-) sign in front of its name, see Figure 11.10. This (-) sign indicate that all the degree of freedom of the component are not defined or fixed. Means the component is free to move or rotate in the graphics area. Now, you need to assemble the inserted free component with the already inserted component or components of the assembly by apply the required relations or mates. By applying required relations or mates, the respective degree of freedom of the free component can be fixed. You will learn more about the concept of degree of freedom and applying relations or mates later in this chapter.

11.10

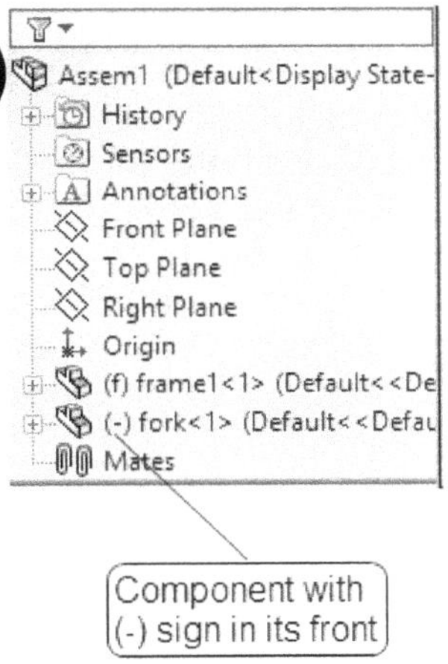

> Assem1 (Default<Display State-
> History
> Sensors
> Annotations
> Front Plane
> Top Plane
> Right Plane
> Origin
> (f) frame1<1> (Default<<De
> (-) fork<1> (Default<<Defau
> Mates

Component with
(-) sign in its front

Tip: While defining the placement point for the component in the graphics area make sure that the component being inserted should not intersect with the existing components of the assembly.

As mentioned above, as soon as you insert the component in the Assembly environment, the PropertyManager disabled, by default, therefore to insert the remaining components of the assembly, you again need to click on the **Insert Components** tool to invoke the PropertyManager for inserting the components in the Assembly environment.

Tip: If you pin the **Insert Component PropertyManager** by clicking on the **Keep Visible** icon available at its upper right corner, the display of PropertyManager will not be closed after inserting the component and you can continue insert the other components of the assembly using it.

After inserting the second component, it is recommended that before you insert the third or next component in the Assembly environment, you first assemble the second inserted component with the first component by applying required relations or mates. However, before you learn about applying relations or mates between the assembly components, it is important to first understand the concept of degree of freedom that is as follows.

Understanding Degree of Freedoms

A free component within the Assembly environment has six degrees of freedom: three translational and three rotational. Means a free component in the Assembly environment can move along X, Y, and Z axes and rotate about X, Y, and Z axes. As discussed earlier, the first component you insert in the Assembly environment become fixed component automatically and will not allow any translational and rotational movement. Means its all degree of freedoms are fixed. However, the second or further components you insert in the Assembly environment of SOLIDWORKS are free for all movement, initially. Means their all degree of freedoms are free. Now, this is a job of a designer to fix the degree of freedom of a free component to prevent their movements by applying proper relations or mates with other components. It is not about fixing movement, you need to maintain actual relationship between components of an assembly as exactly it is in the real world assembly or model. Also, you can allow movable components of an assembly to move freely in their respective movable direction by retaining the respective degree to freedom free. For example, the working of shaft in an assembly is to rotation about its axis therefore you can retain its rotation degree of freedom free to rotate.

Note: To check the degree of freedom of a component, you can move/rotate it in an assembly along/about their free degree of freedom by using the **Move Component/Rotate Component** tool. These tools are available in the **Assembly CommandManager**. Alternatively, you can move/rotate a component along their free degree of freedom by dragging it. Note that for moving, you need to press and hold the left mouse button on to the component to move and then drag the cursor. For rotating, press and hold the CTRL key, and then press and hold the right mouse button on to the component to rotate. Next, drag the cursor. You will learn more about moving or rotating individual component of an assembly later in this chapter.

Applying Relations or Mates

In SOLIDWORKS, you can assemble the components together by using three type of mates/relations: Standard, Advanced, and Mechanical. All these type of mates can be applied by using the **Mate PropertyManager** which appears on clicking the **Mate** tool available in the **Assembly CommandManager**.

To apply mates/relations between the components, click on the **Mate** tool of the **Assembly CommandManager**, the **Mate PropertyManager** appears, see Figure 11.11. Note that by default, the **Entities to Mate** field of the **Mate Selections** rollout of the PropertyManager is activated. As a result, you can select entities to mate. Select the required entities of two different components between which a mate needs to apply, a **Mate** Pop-up toolbar appears, see Figure 11.12. In this pop-up toolbar, the best suitable relation/mate that can apply between the selected entities is selected, by default. To accept the default selected mate, click on the green click mark ✅ of the

Pop-up toolbar, the selected mate applies between the entities. You can also select a relation/mate other than the default selected mate from the Pop-up toolbar. In addition to selecting required mate from the Pop-up toolbar, you can also select the required mate from the **Standard Mates** rollout of the **Mate PropertyManager**. The application of different type of **Standard** mates available in SOLIDWORKS are as follows.

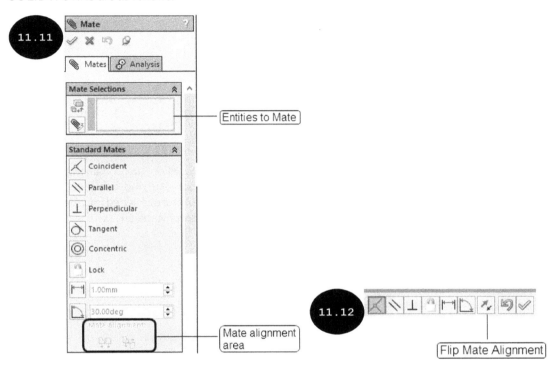

Note: The **Flip Mate Alignment** button of the **Mate** Pop-up toolbar allows you to flip the alignment of the selected entities. You can also flip the alignment of the selected entities by using the buttons: **Aligned** and **Anti-Aligned** available in the **Mate alignment** area of the **Standard Mates** rollout of the **Mate PropertyManager**. This area enabled only after selecting the entities to mate.

Working with Standard Mates

Below are the application of standard mates.

Coincident ⬚

Coincident mate is used to make selected entities of two different components coincident to each other, see Figure 11.13. You can select faces, edges, planes, or the combination of face, edge, plane, and vertex as the entities to mate. On applying coincident mate, the selected entities align in a single plane and will remain align through out the design process. Figure 11.13 shows two planar faces for applying coincident mate and the resultant model after applying the mate.

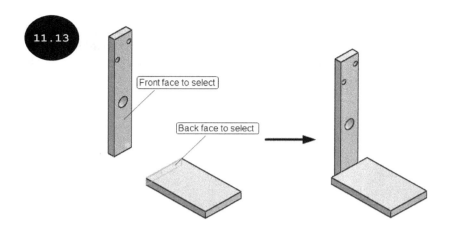

11.13

Front face to select

Back face to select

Note: If you click on the **Flip Mate Alignment** button of the **Mate** Pop-up toolbar, the alignment of the selected entities changes from Aligned to Anti-Aligned and vice versa, see Figure 11.14. You can also flip the alignment by using the buttons: **Aligned** and **Anti-Aligned** available in the **Mate alignment** area of the **Mate PropertyManager**.

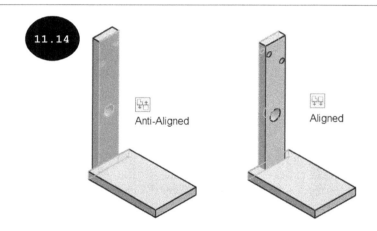

11.14

Anti-Aligned

Aligned

Parallel

The Parallel mate is used to make selected entities parallel to each other, see Figure 11.15. You can select planar faces, edges, planes, or the combination of face, edge, and plane as the entities to mate. On applying parallel mate, the selected entities become parallel to each other and will remain parallel throughout the design process. Figure 11.15 shows two planar faces for applying parallel mate and the resultant model after applying the mate.

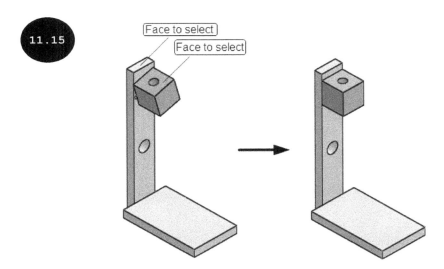

Perpendicular ⊥

The Perpendicular mate is used to make selected entities perpendicular to each other, see Figure 11.16. You can select planar faces, edges, planes, or the combination of face, edge, and plane as the entities to mate. Figure 11.16 shows two planar faces to select for applying perpendicular mate and the resultant model.

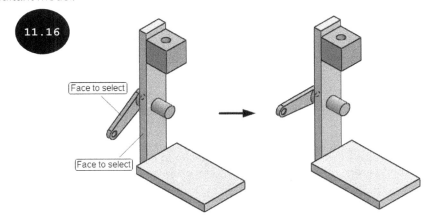

Concentric ◎

The Concentric mate is used to make selected entities concentric to each other. You can apply concentric mate between two circular faces, circular edges, or semi-circular faces/edges. On applying concentric mate, axis of two selected circular faces will share a common axis. Figure 11.17 shows a set of faces to select for applying concentric mate and the resultant model.

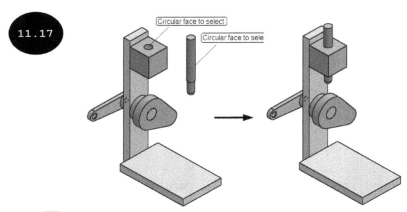

Tangent

The Tangent mate is used to make selected entities tangent to each other. You can select a planar face, curved face, edge, or plane as an first selection entity and a cylindrical, conical, or spherical face as an second selection entities. Figure 11.18 shows a set of faces to select for applying tangent mate and the resultant model.

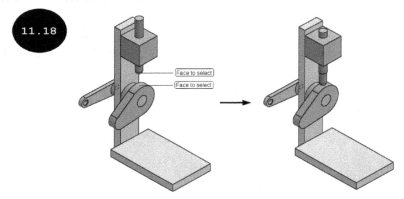

Distance

The Distance mate is used to keep distance between two selected entities. Figure 11.19 shows a set of faces to select for applying distance mate and the resultant model.

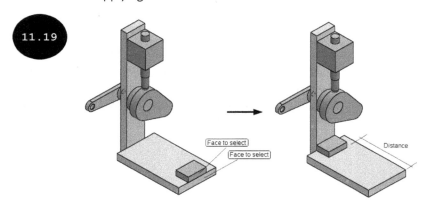

Angle

The Angle mate is used to maintain angle between two selected entities. Figure 11.20 shows a set of faces to select for applying angle mate and the resultant model.

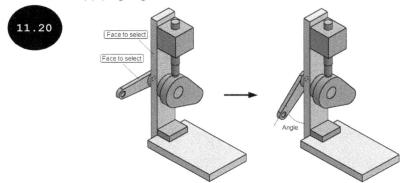

11.20

Face to select
Face to select
Angle

Note: In case of the Coincident, Parallel, Distance, and Angle mates, you can flip the alignment between the selected entities from Aligned to Anti-Aligned and vice versa.

Lock

The Lock mate is used to lock the selected entities at the desired position in the graphics area. On applying lock mate all degrees of freedom of selected entities get fixed.

Working with Advanced Mates

Advanced mates are special types of mates and work as one step forward in top of standard mates for reduced degree of freedom of components. By using advanced mates you can assign minimum and maximum distance/angle limit so that the component can move/rotate within the assigned limit, path motion so that component can move along the defined path, symmetry relation between two components, and so on.

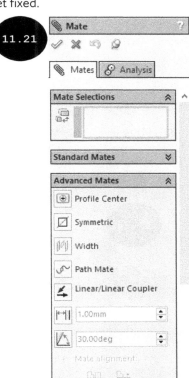

11.21

To apply advanced mates, click on the **Mate** tool of the **Assembly CommandManager**, the **Mate PropertyManager** appears. Note that the **Standard Mates** rollout of the PropertyManager is expanded by default. To apply advanced mates, expand the **Advanced Mates** rollout of the PropertyManager, see Figure 11.21. You can apply symmetric, width, path, linear/linear coupler, distance, and angle mates by using their respective buttons available in the **Advanced Mates** rollout. The application of different type of Advanced Mates are as follows.

Profile Center Mate ⊞

A Profile Center mate is used to center align two rectangular profiles, two circular profiles, or a rectangular and a circular profiles of two different components with each other, see Figures 11.22, 11.23, 11.24.

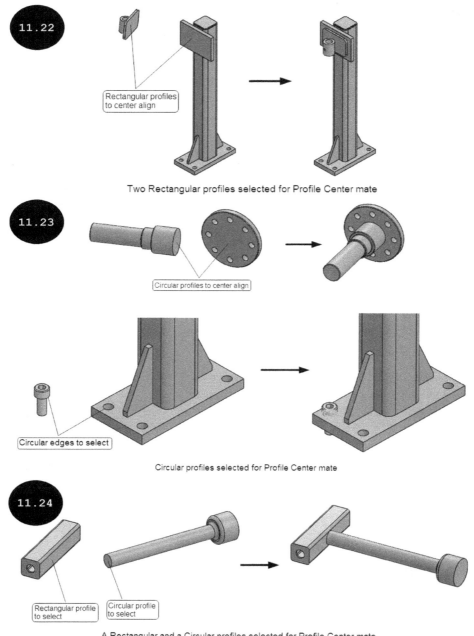

11.22

Rectangular profiles to center align

Two Rectangular profiles selected for Profile Center mate

11.23

Circular profiles to center align

Circular edges to select

Circular profiles selected for Profile Center mate

11.24

Rectangular profile to select

Circular profile to select

A Rectangular and a Circular profiles selected for Profile Center mate

To apply Profile Center mate, click on the **Profile Center** button of the **Advanced Mates** rollout, the **Entities to Mate** field enabled in the **Mate Selections** rollout of the PropertyManager. Also, the **Offset distance** field, **Flip dimension** check box, and **Lock rotation** check box enabled in the **Advanced Mates** rollout, see Figure 11.25.

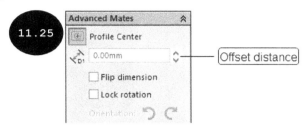

By default, the **Entities to Mate** field activated. Select two entities as the entities to center align. You can select two rectangular profiles, two circular profiles (circular faces/circular edges), or a rectangular and a circular profiles of two different components. As soon as you select entities, the preview appears. Next, click on the green click mark ✅ of the PropertyManager, the profile center mate is applied, see Figures 11.22, 11.23, and 11.24. Note that you can specify the offset distance between two selected profiles by using the **Offset distance** field. By default, 0 (zero) is entered in this field. You can also flip the offset dimension specified by using the **Flip dimension** check box and restrict the rotation movement of the selected entities by selecting the **Lock rotation** check box.

Symmetric Mate ▣

A symmetry mate is used to make a component symmetric about an symmetric plane or planar face. You can select two entities of different components to be symmetric with respect to each other about an symmetric plane or a planar face. You can select two vertices, sketch points, edges, axes, sketch lines, planes, planar faces, curved face of same radii and so on as the entities to be symmetric.

To apply symmetric mate, click on the **Symmetric** button of the **Advanced Mates** rollout, the **Entities to Mate** and **Symmetry Plane** fields enabled in the **Mate Selections** rollout of the PropertyManager. By default, the **Symmetry plane** field activated. Select the symmetric plane. As soon as you define symmetric plane, the **Entities to Mate** field become activated automatically. Select two entities as the entities to be symmetric about the symmetric plane. Once you are done with selections, click on the green click mark ✅ of the PropertyManager, the symmetric mate is applied. Figure 11.26 shows two planar faces to be symmetric about an symmetric plane and the resultant model after applying symmetric mate. Note that after applying the symmetric mate, both the components will remain symmetric to each other about the symmetric plane.

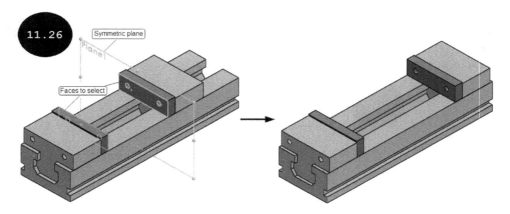

Width Mate

A Width mate is used to make two planar faces (parallel or non parallel), a cylindrical face, or an axis of a component at the center of two parallel or non parallel faces of another component, see Figures 11.27 and 11.28. The width mate requires two pairs of selections. One pair of selection is know as width selection and other pair of selection is know as tab selection. After applying the width mate, the tab selection set become centered to the width selection set, by default. You can select two parallel or non parallel faces as the width selection. For tab selection, you can select two planar faces (parallel or non parallel), a cylindrical face, or an axis. Figure 11.27 shows faces selected as width and tab selection set. Figure 11.28 shows the resultant model after applying width mate where tab selection set became centered to the width selection set.

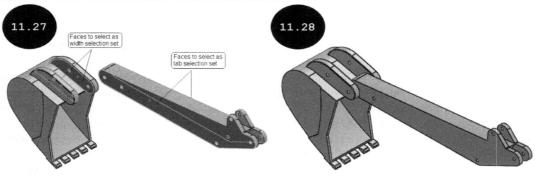

To apply the Width mate, click on the **Width** button, the **Width selections** and **Tab selections** fields enabled in the **Mate Selections** rollout. Also, the **Constraint** drop-down list become available in the **Advanced Mates** rollout, see Figure 11.29. By default, the **Centered** option is selected in this drop-down list. As a result, the tab selection set become centered to the width selection set, by default.

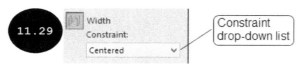

In the **Mate Selections** rollout, the **Width selections** field is activated, by default which allows you to select width selection set. Select two entities as the width selection set, see Figure 11.27. As soon as you select width selection set, the **Tab selections** field become activated. Select two planar faces or a cylindrical face as the tab selection, see Figure 11.27. Next, click on the green click mark ✔ of the PropertyManager, the width mate is applied, see Figure 11.28. Figure 11.30 shows two planar faces selected as the width selection, a cylindrical face selected as the tab selection, and the preview of the resultant width mate.

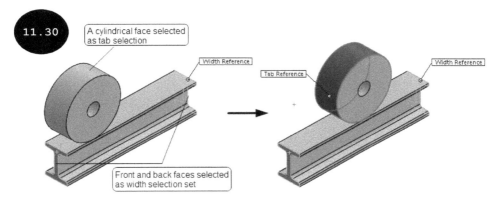

As discussed earlier, by default, the **Centered** option is selected in the **Constraint** drop-down list, see Figure 11.29. As a result, the tab selection set become centered to the width selection set. You can also select **Free**, **Dimension**, or **Percent** option from the **Constraint** drop-down list.

On selecting the **Free** option, the tab selection set can move freely within the limits of the width selection set. On selecting the **Dimension** option, you can control the position of the tab selection by specifying the distance in the **Distance from the End** field of the rollout. If you select the **Percent** option, you can control the position of the tab selection by specifying the percentage in the **Percentage of Distance from the End** field of the rollout.

Path Mate

The Path mate allows a component to move along the defined path. This mate constrain a point or vertex of a component such that it move along a path, see Figures 11.31 and 11.32.

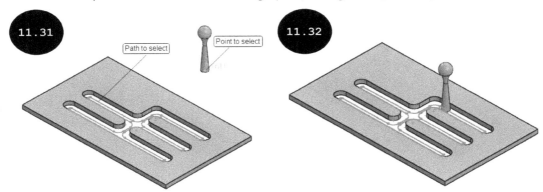

To apply the Path mate, click on the **Path** button, the **Component Vertex** and **Path Selection** fields enabled in the **Mate Selections** rollout. By default, the **Component Vertex** field is activated. Select a point or a vertex of the component to be moved, see Figure 11.31. As soon as you select a point or vertex, the **Path Selection** field become activated. Next, select a path from the graphics area. Note that you can also use the **SelectionManager** button of the **Mate Selections** rollout for selecting a path having multiple entities. On clicking this button, the **Selection** Pop-up toolbar appears, see Figure 11.33. By using the **Select Closed Loop** and **Select Open Loop** buttons of this Pop-up toolbar, you can select an closed and open loop as the path, respectively. Next, click on the tick mark of the Pop-up toolbar and then click on the green tick mark ✅ of the PropertyManager, the path mate is applied.

11.33

Select Open Loop

Select Closed Loop

Note: To achieve a specific type of motion such as path motion, you need to define degree of freedoms of the component to be moved such that the component can only move in its moveable direction.

Tip: To review the path motion, select the moveable component and then drag it such that it travel along the defined path.

Linear/Linear Coupler Mate

The Linear/Linear Coupler mate allows components to translate motion with respect to each other. After applying this mate between two components, when you move a component, the other component will also move respectively, see Figures 11.34. You can specify the translation ratio between two components by using the **Ratio** fields of the PropertyManager, see Figure 11.35. If the translation ratio is 1: 2 in mm units, on translating one component to a distance of 1 mm in an direction, the second component translate automatically to the distance of 2 mm, respectively. You can also reverse the direction of translation of components by using the **Reverse** check box.

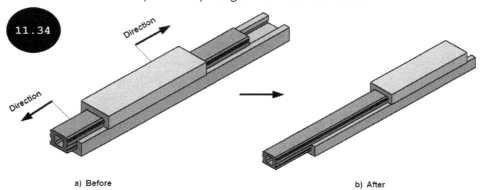

11.34

Direction

Direction

a) Before

b) After

To apply the Linear/Linear Coupler mate, click on the **Linear/Linear Coupler** button. Next, select linear edges of two components one by one as the direction to move components with respect to each other. Specify the translation ratio between two components in the **Ratio** fields of the PropertyManager. Next, click on the green tick mark ✅ of the PropertyManager, the linear/linear coupler mate is applied.

> **Tip:** To review the translation motion between components, you can select a component to translate and then drag it.

Distance Mate ⊢⋈

The Distance mate of the **Advance Mates** rollout is used to specify minimum and maximum distance limit which allows respective component to move or translate within the specified distance limit, see Figure 11.36.

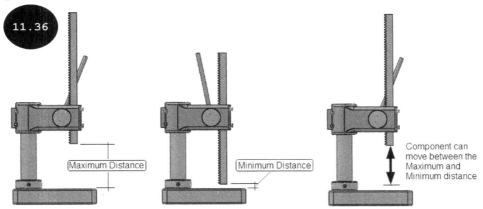

To apply the advanced Distance mate, click on the **Distance** button, the **Distance, Maximum Distance**, and **Minimum Distance** fields enabled in the PropertyManager, see Figure 11.37. Specify the maximum distance value in the **Distance** field, the same distance value will automatically be specified in the **Maximum Distance** field. Next, specify the minimum distance value in the **Minimum Distance** field. After specifying the maximum and minimum distance, select two entities (faces, planes, edges, points, and vertex) of two different components and then click on the green tick mark ✅ of the PropertyManager, the advanced Distance mate is applied between the selected entities such that the components can only move between the maximum and minimum distance limit, see Figure 11.36.

Tip: To review the distance motion between the components, select the component and then drag it.

Angle mate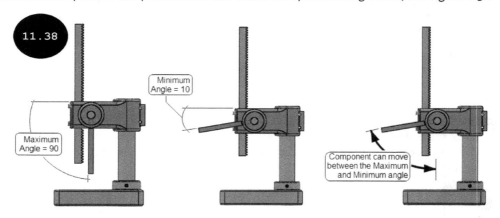

The Angle mate of the **Advance Mates** rollout is used to specify minimum and maximum angle limit which allows respective component to rotate within the specified angle limit, see Figure 11.38.

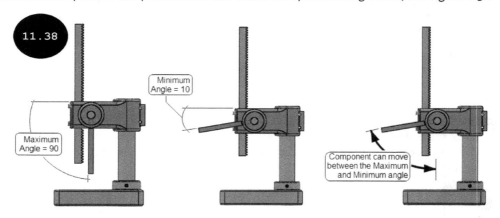

To apply the advanced Angle mate, click on the **Angle** button, the **Angle, Maximum Value,** and **Minimum Value** fields enabled in the PropertyManager, see Figure 11.39. Specify the maximum angle value in the **Angle** field, the same distance value will automatically be specified in the **Maximum Value** field. Next, specify the minimum distance value in the **Minimum Value** field. After specifying the maximum and minimum angle, select two faces of two different components and then click on the green tick mark ✓ of the PropertyManager, the advanced Angle mate is applied between the selected face such that the components can only move between the maximum and minimum angle limit, see Figure 11.38.

Tip: To review the angle motion between the components, select the component and then drag it.

Working with Mechanical Mates

Mechanical mates are used to create mechanical mechanism between two components of an assembly and allow mechanical motion between them. You can create cam and follower, gear, hinge, rack and pinion, screw, and universal joint relationships/ mechanisms between the components by using the mechanical mates. The different type of mechanical mates are available in the **Mechanical Mates** rollout of the **Mates PropertyManager**.

To apply mechanical mates, expand the **Mechanical Mates** rollout of the **Mate PropertyManager**, see Figure 11.40. By using this rollout, you can apply cam, slot, hinge, gear, rack and pinion, screw, and universal joint mates. The application of different type of Mechanical mates are as follows.

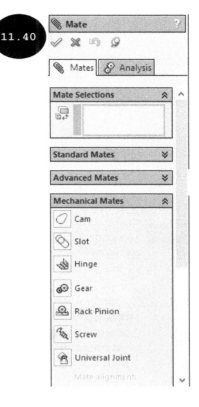

Cam Mate

A Cam mate is used to create cam and follower mechanism between two components. You can mate a cylindrical, semi-cylindrical, or planar face of a follower component to the series of continuous closed tangent faces of a cam component. After applying the cam mate, the follower component moves up and down in according to the cam profile.

To apply the Cam mate, click on the **Cam** button of the **Mechanical Mates** rollout, the **Entities to Mate** and **Cam Follower** fields appears in the **Mate Selections** rollout. By default, the **Entities to Mate** field is activated which allows you to select series of continuous closed tangent faces of a cam component. Select all the continuous closed tangent faces of the cam component, see Figure 11.41. Next, click on the **Cam Follower** field to activate it and then select a cylindrical/semi-cylindrical, or a planar face of the follower component, see Figure 11.42, the select face of follower component placed over the cam component, see Figure 11.43. Next, click on the green tick mark ✓ of the PropertyManager, the Cam mate is applied. Now, on rotating the cam component, the follower component moves up and down with respect to the cam profile such that it follows the cam and follower mechanism.

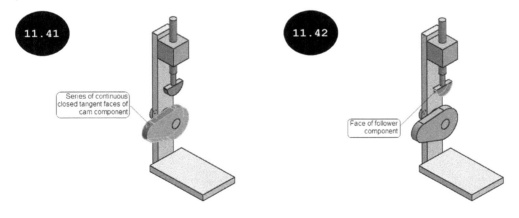

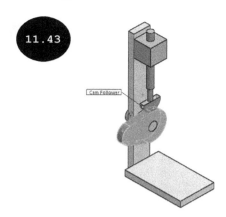

11.43

Tip: To review the cam and follower mechanism between the components, select the cam component and then drag it such that it rotate around its axis of rotation.

Note: In order to select faces of the components for applying mates, you may need to move or rotate the entire assembly and the individual components of the assembly. To rotate the assembly, drag the cursor by pressing the middle mouse button and to move/pan the assembly, drag the cursor by pressing the CTRL key and middle mouse button. The methods for moving or rotating individual components are discussed later in this chapter.

Slot Mate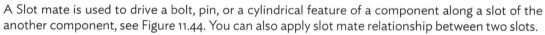

A Slot mate is used to drive a bolt, pin, or a cylindrical feature of a component along a slot of the another component, see Figure 11.44. You can also apply slot mate relationship between two slots.

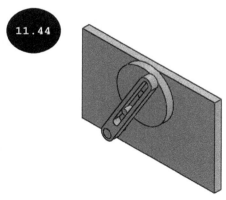

11.44

To apply the Slot mate, click on the **Slot** button of the **Mechanical Mates** rollout. Next, select a face of the slot. On selecting a face of the slot, all the remaining tangent faces of the slots is selected automatically, see Figure 11.45. Next, select a bolt, pin, or a cylindrical face of another component, see Figure 11.45, the cylindrical face placed in between the slot, see Figure 11.46. Next, click on the green tick mark ✓ of the PropertyManager, the Slot mate is applied and you can review the slot mechanism by dragging the components.

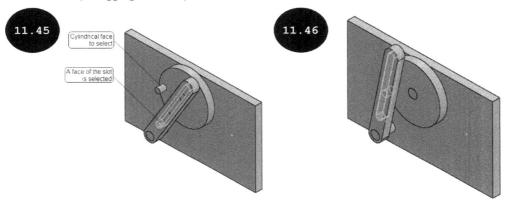

Note: As soon as you click on the **Slot** button, the **Constraint** drop-down list appears in the rollout, see Figure 11.47. By default, the **Free** option is selected in this drop-down list. As a result, a component having bolt, pin, or cylindrical feature can move freely within the slot of the another component. You can also constraint the movement of components by using the **Center in Slot**, **Distance Along Slot**, and **Percentage Along Slot** options of this drop-down list.

Hinge Mate

A Hinge mate is used to form a hinge mechanism between two components by fixing all the degree of freedom except the one rotational degree of freedom. You can also limit the angle of rotation while applying the hinge mate, as required by specifying minimum and maximum angle of rotation, see Figure 11.48.

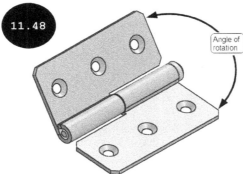

To apply the Hinge mate, click on the **Hinge** button, the **Concentric Selections** and **Coincident Selections** fields enabled in the **Mate Selections** rollout of the PropertyManager. As the **Concentric Selections** field is activated by default, select faces or edges of components to concentric with respect to each other, see Figure 11.49. Next, click on the **Coincident Selections** field to activate it and then select faces or edges of components to coincident with respect to each other, see Figure 11.50. As soon as you are done with selecting faces for concentric and coincident relations, the respective relations applied between the selected faces, see Figure 11.51. Now, click on the green tick mark ✅ of the PropertyManager, the Hinge mate is applied and you can review the hinge mechanism by dragging the components.

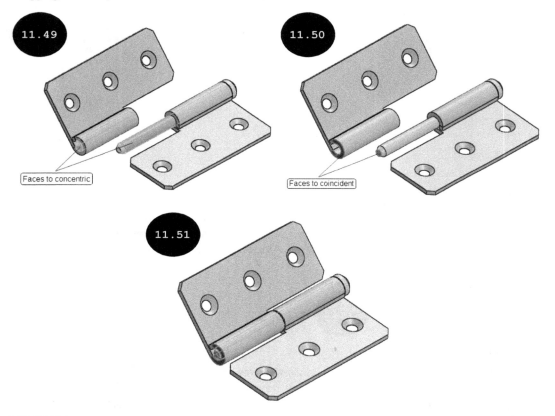

Note:	To limit the angle of rotation between the hinge components, select the **Specify angle limits** check box of the **Mate Selections** rollout. As soon as you select this check box, the **Angle**, **Maximum Value**, and **Minimum Value** fields enabled. By using these fields, you can specify the maximum and minimum angle limit of rotation.

Gear Mate 🔗
A Gear mate is allows two components to rotate relative to each other and form a gear mechanism, see Figure 11.52. To apply gear relationship, you need to define the axis of rotation of both components by selecting cylindrical faces, conical faces, axes, or linear edges of the components.

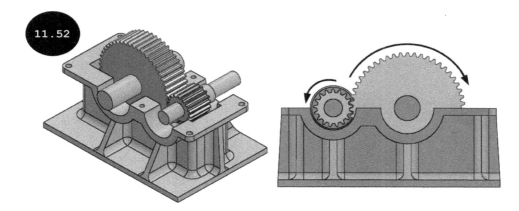

11.52

To apply the Gear mate, click on the **Gear** button of the **Mechanical Mates** rollout. Next, select cylindrical faces of the gear teeth of both the gears one by one, see Figure 11.53. On selecting cylindrical faces of the gears, the axis of rotation of the gears define automatically. You can select cylindrical faces, conical faces, axes, or linear edges of the gears to define their axis of rotation. Next, specify the gear ratios in the **Ratio** fields available in the **Mechanical Mates** rollout. Note that by default based on the relative size of the cylindrical/conical faces selected for defining the axis of rotation of gears, the gear ratios will automatically be defined and entered in the **Ratio** fields. After defining the gear ratios, click on the green tick mark ✅ of the PropertyManager, the Gear mate is applied and you can review the gear mechanism by dragging the gears.

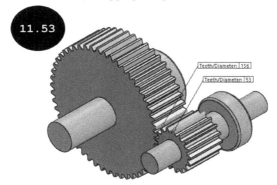

11.53

Teeth/Diameter: 156

Teeth/Diameter: 53

Tip: In assembly, you can hide components. To hide assembly components, select a component to hide from the FeatureManager design tree or from the graphics area, a Pop-up toolbar appear. In this Pop-up toolbar, select the **Hide Components** tool. To show the hidden component, select the component to show from the FeatureManager design tree and then select the **Show Components** button from the Pop-up toolbar.

Rack Pinion Mate

A Rack Pinion mate is used to translate linear motion to rotational motion from one component to another and vice versa. This mate create rack and pinion mechanism, see Figure 11.54, where linear motion of rack component creates rotary motion in pinion component and vice versa.

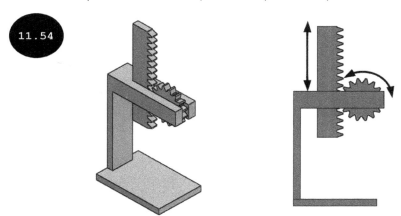

11.54

To apply the Rack Pinion mate, click on the **Rack Pinion** button, the **Rack** and **Pinion/Gear** fields enabled in the **Mate Selections** rollout of the PropertyManager. By default, the **Rack** field is activated. Select the linear edge of the rack component which defines the direction of movement of the rack component, see Figure 11.55. As soon as you select linear edge of the rack component, the **Pinion/Gear** field become activated. Select the circular face of the pinion/gear component which defines the axis of rotation of the pinion component, see Figure 11.55. Next, click on the green tick mark ✓ of the PropertyManager, the Rack Pinion mate is applied and you can review the rack and pinion mechanism by dragging the components.

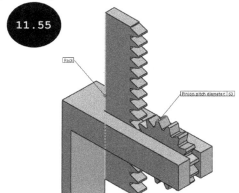

11.55

Screw Mate

A Screw mate applies pitch relationship between the rotation of one component and the translation of the other component such that it forms a screw mechanism, see Figure 11.56. On applying Screw mate, the translation motion of one component causes rotational motion in other component based on the pitch specified. You can specify pitch relationship between components by defining number of revolutions of one component per millimeter translation of other component or by defining distance travel by one component per revolution of other component.

To apply the Screw mate, click on the **Screw** button of the **Mechanical Mates** rollout. Next, select cylindrical faces of the revolving and translating components from the graphics area one by one, see Figure 11.57. On selecting cylindrical faces of both the components, the direction of revolution arrow appears in the graphics area, see Figure 11.57. You can reverse the direction of revolution by selecting or clearing the **Reverse** check box, respectively, see Figure 11.58. By default the **Revolutions/mm** radio button is selected, see Figure 11.58. As a result, you can specify the number of revolutions per millimeter translation of a component in the **Revolutions/Distance** field. If you select the **Distance/revolution** radio button, you can specify the translation value per revolution of a component in the **Revolutions/ Distance** field. Next, click on the green tick mark ✅ of the PropertyManager, the Screw mate is applied and you can review the screw mechanism by dragging the components.

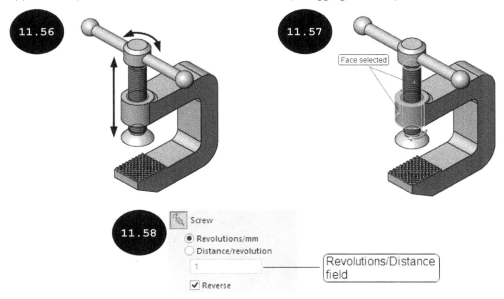

Universal Joint 🔧

A Universal Joint mate is used to translate rotational movement of one component about its axis to the rotational movement of another component about their axis of rotation, see Figure 11.59.

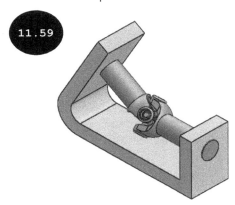

To apply the Universal Joint mate, click on the **Universal Joint** button of the **Mechanical Mates** rollout. Next, select cylindrical faces of the components from the graphics area one by one, see Figure 11.60. After selecting cylindrical faces, click on the green tick mark ✅ of the PropertyManager, the Universal Joint mate is applied and you can review the Universal Joint mechanism by dragging the components.

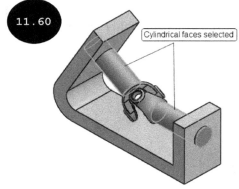

Moving and Rotating Individual Components

In SOLIDWORKS, you can move and rotate individual components of an assembly about their free degree of freedom by using the **Move Component** and **Rotate Component** tools, respectively. Both these tools are available in the **Assemble CommandManager**, see Figure 11.61, and are as follows.

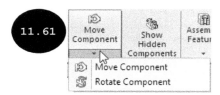

Moving Component using Move Component tool

In SOLIDWORKS, you can move individual components of an assembly along its free degree of freedom by using the **Move Component** tool. To move individual component along its free degree of freedom, click on the **Move Component** tool available in the **Assembly CommandManager**, the **Move Component PropertyManager** appears, see Figure 11.62. By default, the **Free Drag** option is selected in the **Move** drop-down list of the **Move** rollout in the PropertyManager. As a result, you can move the selected components freely by dragging the cursor. Select a component to move and then drag the cursor in the free degree of freedom by pressing and holding the left mouse button, the selected component start moving towards the moving direction of cursor. You can release the left mouse button for stopping the movement of the component. The other options available in the **Move** drop-down list are **Along Assembly XYZ**, **Along Entity**, **By Delta XYZ**, and **To XYZ Position**, see Figure 11.63. All these options are as follows.

Note: A component can not move along its fixed degree of freedom. For example, if the translation along X axis of the component is fixed by applying mates or relations, you can not move the component along X axis.

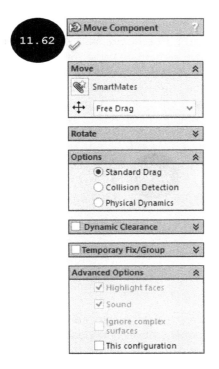

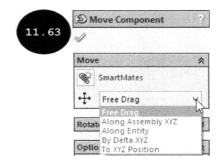

Along Assembly XYZ

On selecting the **Along Assembly XYZ** option, you can move the selected component along the X, Y, or Z axis of the assembly coordinate system by dragging the cursor.

Along Entity

On selecting the **Along Entity** option, the **Selected item** field appears in the **Move** rollout, see Figure 11.64. This field allows you to select an entity along which you want to move the selected component. You can select an liner edge, sketch line, or an axis as the entity to define the direction along which you want to move the component. After selecting the entity, select the component to move and then drag the cursor, the selected component starts moving along the direction of entity selected.

By Delta XYZ

On selecting the **By Delta XYZ** option, the **Delta X**, **Delta Y**, and **Delta Z** fields appear, see Figure 11.65. These field allows you to specify X, Y, and Z distance values for moving the component with respect to the current location of the selected component. After specifying the X, Y, and Z distance value in their respective fields, select a component to move and then click on the **Apply** button, the selected component moves with respect to the distance value specified.

To XYZ Position

On selecting the **To XYZ Position** option, the **X Coordinate**, **Y Coordinate**, and **Z Coordinate** fields appear, see Figure 11.66. These fields allow you to specify coordinate values of the location where you want to move the selected component. Note that if you select a vertex or a point of the component to be moved then after clicking on the **Apply** button, the selected vertex or point of the component, moves to the specified coordinates. However, if you select anything other than vertex or point of the component to be moved than the origin of the component will moves to the specified coordinates.

Note that by default moving component is not prevented for any interference or collisions occurs with other components of the assembly. As a result, the component moves continually even if any other component come across its way. This is because the **Standard Drag** radio button is selected in the **Options** rollout of the **Move Component PropertyManager**, see Figure 11.67. On selecting the **Collision Detection** and **Physical Dynamics** radio buttons, you can detect collisions and analyze motion between the components of the assembly with respect to the component being moved by using the **Move Component** tool.

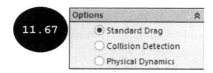

The options used to detect collisions and to specify their related settings appears in the **Options** rollout as soon as you select the **Collision Detection** or **Physical Dynamics** radio button. The method of detecting collision between components by using these radio buttons are as follows.

Detecting Collision using Collision Detection Radio Button

The **Collision Detection** radio button is used to detect collisions with the other components of the assembly while moving a component. To activate the collision detection mode, select the **Collision Detection** radio button. As soon as you select this radio button, the two radio buttons: **All components** and **These components**, and two check boxes: **Stop at collision** and **Dragged part only** appears in the **Options** rollout, see Figure 11.68.

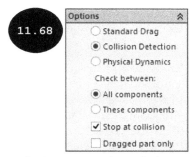

By default, the **All components** radio button is selected. As a result, collision detects when the component being moved touches any other component of the assembly. Note that as soon as the collision detected between the components, the components get highlighted in the graphics area, see Figure 11.69. Also, if the **Stop at collision** check box is selected, the component being moved is stopped its movement as soon as the collision gets detected.

On selecting the **These components** radio button, the **Components for Collision Check** field appears in the PropertyManager, see Figure 11.70. This field allows you to select components for collision detection. After selecting the components for collision detection, click on the **Resume Drag** button. Next, drag the component to move, the collision detects when the component you move touches any of the selected component of the assembly. Note that components that are not listed in the **Components for Collision Check** field are ignored while detecting collision with the components being moved.

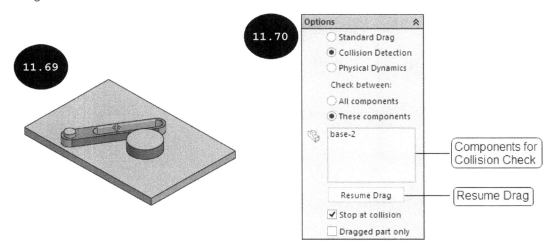

When the **Dragged part only** check box is selected, the collision with the component being moved will only be detected.

Detecting Collision and Analyzing Motion using Physical Dynamics

Similar to detecting collision by using the **Collision Detection** radio button, the **Physical Dynamics** radio button is also used to detect collisions with the only difference that it force the components that comes in contact or touches with the moving component to move along its moving direction. In other words, on selecting the **Physical Dynamics** radio button, you can analyze the motion between the contacted components of the assembly. Note that the components can only move or rotate within their free degrees of freedom.

Note: In addition to moving individual components, detecting collision, analyzing motion between components, you can also switch to the **Rotate Component PropertyManager** and the **SmartMates PropertyManager** by using the **Move Component PropertyManager**. For switching to the **Rotate Component PropertyManager**, expand the **Rotate** rollout of the **Move Component PropertyManager** and for switching to the **SmartMates PropertyManager**, click on the **SmartMates** button available in the **Move** rollout of the **Move Component PropertyManager**. Both these PropertyManager are as follows.

Rotating Component using Rotate Component tool

Similar to moving individual components, you can also rotate components of an assembly about its free degree of freedom by using the **Rotate Component** tool. To rotate components, click on the **Rotate Component** tool, see Figure 11.71, the **Rotate Component PropertyManager** appears, see Figure 11.72.

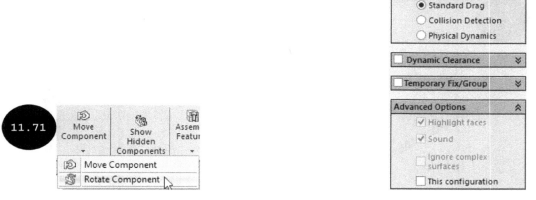

By default, the **Free Drag** option is selected in the **Rotate** drop-down list of the **Rotate** rollout in the PropertyManager. As a result, you can rotate the selected component freely by dragging the cursor. Select the component to rotate and then drag the cursor about its free degree of freedom by pressing and holding the left mouse button, the selected component start rotating. Once you are done with rotating component, release the left mouse button. All the options available in the **Rotate Component PropertyManager** are same as discussed earlier while moving the components using the **Move Component PropertyManager**.

Note: You can also invoke the **Rotate Component PropertyManager** by expanding the **Rotate** rollout of the **Move PropertyManager**.

Working with SmartMates

SmartMates is a method of applying standard mates such as coincident, parallel, and perpendicular between the components of an assembly. By using this method of applying mates, you can save time and speed up the designing process. You can invoke the SmartMates mode for applying mates by invoking the **SmartMates PropertyManager**, see Figure 11.73. To invoke this PropertyManager, first invoke the **Move PropertyManager** and then click on the **SmartMates** button available in its **Move** rollout. Once this PropertyManager is invoked, double click on an the entity of the component for applying mate, the selected entity is highlighted and the component appears transparent, see Figure 11.74. Next, drag the component by pressing the left mouse button towards the entity of the other component in the assembly between which you want to apply mate. Next, release the left button when the components snaps with each other and mate symbol appears in the graphics area, see Figure 11.75. As soon as you release the left mouse button, a Pop-up toolbar appears with the default suitable mate button activated. Select the required mate to apply from the Pop-up toolbar. Next, click on the green tick mark of the toolbar, the selected mate is applied.

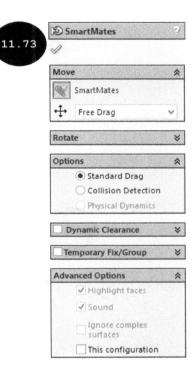

11.73

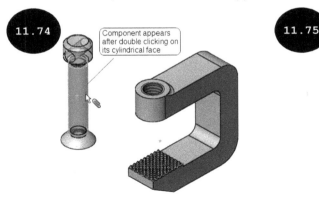

11.74

Component appears after double clicking on its cylindrical face

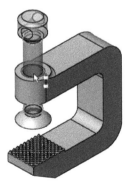

11.75

Note: You can also press the ALT key and then drag one component towards the another component for applying SmartMates in an assembly without invoking the **SmartMates PropertyManager**.

Tutorial 1

Create the model shown in Figure 11.76. For different views and dimensions of individual components of the assembly refer to Figure 11.77 through 11.79.

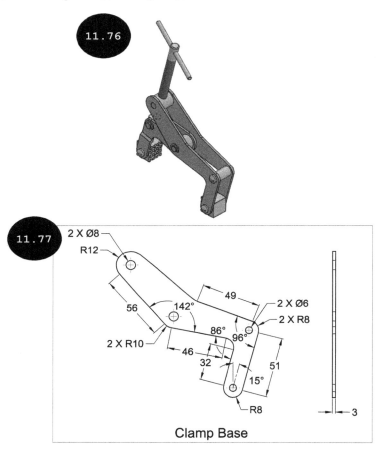

11.76

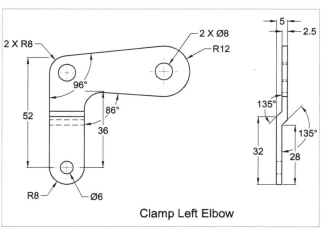

11.77

Clamp Base

Clamp Left Elbow

11.78

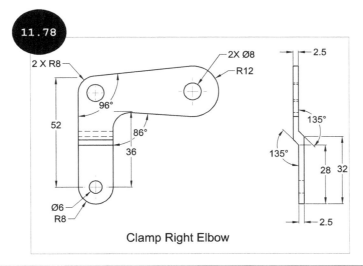

Clamp Right Elbow

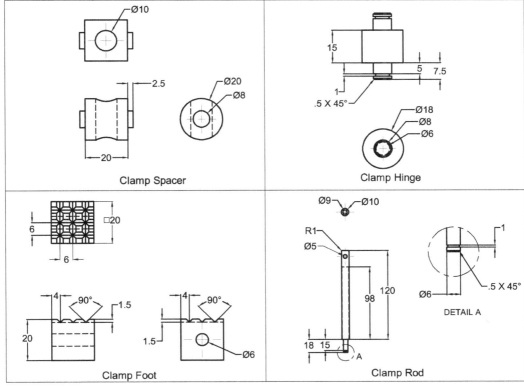

Clamp Spacer

Clamp Hinge

Clamp Foot

Clamp Rod

DETAIL A

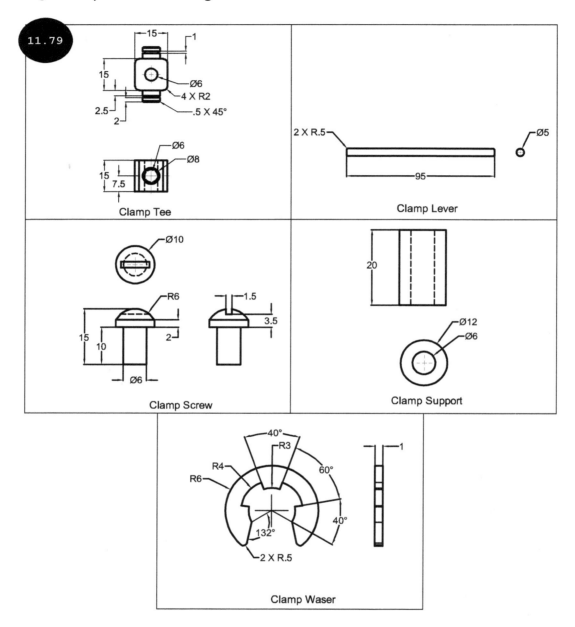

11.79

Clamp Tee

Clamp Lever

Clamp Screw

Clamp Support

Clamp Waser

Section 1: Creating Assembly Components

In this section, you will create all the components of assembly.

1. Create all components of the assembly one by one. See Figure 11.77 to 79 for dimensions. After creating the components save them in *Tutorial 1* folder of the *Chapter 11* folder. You need to create these folder inside the *SOLIDWORKS* folder.

Section 2: Invoking Assembly Environment

1. Click on the **New** tool in the **Standard** toolbar, the **New SOLIDWORKS Document** dialog box appears.

2. In this dialog box, click on the **Assembly** button to activated it. Next, click on the **OK** button, the assembly environment is invoked with the display of **Begin Assembly PropertyManager** at the left.

Section 3: Inserting First Component in Assembly Environment

1. Click on the **Browse** button of the **Part/Assembly to Insert** rollout of the **Begin Assembly PropertyManager**, the **Open** dialog box appears.

2. Browse to the location where all components of the assembly are saved.

3. Select the *Clamp Base* component and then click on the **Open** button of the dialog, the selected component is attached with the cursor tip, see Figure 11.80. Also, the **Rotate Context** toolbar appears in the graphics area, see Figure 11.80.

4. As the orientation of the attached model is correct, click anywhere in the graphics area, the attached component move towards the origin of the assembly and become fix component automatically.

Section 4: Inserting Second Component

1. Click on the **Insert Components** tool of the **Assembly CommandManager**, the **Insert Component PropertyManager** appears.

2. Click on the **Browse** button, the **Open** dialog box appears.

3.   Click to select the second component (*Clamp Spacer*) to insert in the Assembly environment. Next, click on the **Open** button, the second component (*Clamp Spacer*) is attached with the cursor, see Figure 11.81. Also, the **Rotate Context** toolbar appears in the graphics area.

4.   Click on the Y button of the **Rotate Context** toolbar to rotate the component about Y axis and to change the orientation of the component as shown in Figure 11.82.

5.   Click anywhere in the graphics area to specify the placement point, the second component (*Clamp Spacer*) is placed in the specified location, see Figure 11.82. Make sure that you specify the placement point such that the inserted component should not intersect with the other component of the assembly.

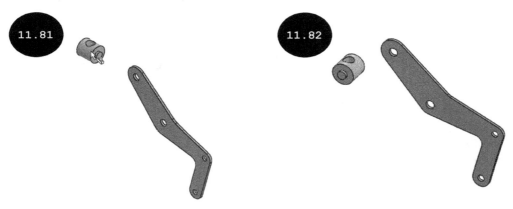

Note: All the degree of freedom of the second inserted component in the assembly environment is free. It means that the second inserted component is free to translate and rotate along and about its three axis. You need to apply required mates (relations) to fix it required degree of freedom to assembly it with respect to the other components of the assembly.

Section 5: Assembling Second Component

1.   Click on the **Mate** tool of the **Assembly CommandManager**, the **Mate PropertyManager** appears.

2.   Select the circular face of the upper hole of the first component (Clamp Base), see Figure 11.83, and the circular face of the second component (Clamp *Spacer*) to apply concentric mate one by one, see Figure 11.82. As soon as you select the circular faces to apply mate, the Pop-up toolbar appears with the **Concentric** tool is activated by default, see Figure 11.84.

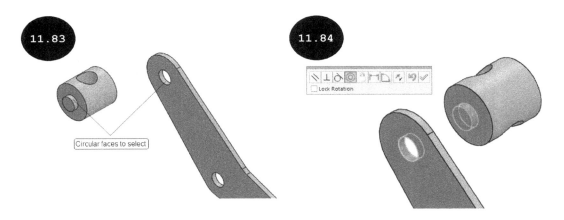

Note: If needed, you can flip the mate alignment by using the **Flip Mate Alignment** tool of the Pop-up toolbar.

3. Click on the green tick mark ✓ of the Pop-up tool bar, the concentric relation is applied between the selected faces.

Tip: You can move the component along its free degree of freedom by selecting and dragging it to the required location.

4. Select the back planar face of the first component (*Clamp Base*), see Figure 11.85, and the front planar face of the second component (*Clamp Spacer*) to apply coincident mate, see Figure 11.85. As soon as you select the planar faces to apply mate, the Pop-up toolbar appears with the **Coincident** tool is activated by default, see Figure 11.86.

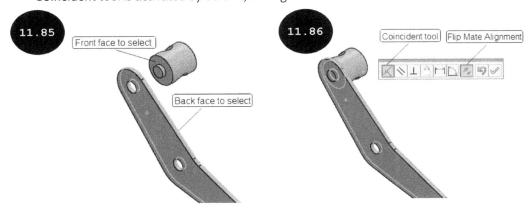

Note: To select the back planar face of the first component to apply coincident mate, you need to rotate the assembly by using the middle mouse button such that you can view the back planar face of the component easily.

If needed, you can flip the mate alignment by using the **Flip Mate Alignment** tool of the Pop-up toolbar.

5.   Click on the green tick mark ✅ of the Pop-up tool bar, the coincident relation is applied between the selected faces. Next, exit from the PropertyManager.

Section 6: Inserting Third Component

1.   Click on the **Insert Components** tool of the **Assembly CommandManager**, the **Insert Component PropertyManager** appears.

2.   Click on the **Browse** button of the **Part/Assembly to Insert** rollout of the PropertyManager, the **Open** dialog box appears.

3.   Click to select the third component (*Clamp Base*) to insert in the Assembly environment. Next, click on the **Open** button, the third component (*Clamp Base*) is attached with the cursor, see Figure 11.87.

Note: The *Clamp Base* component has been already inserted in the Assembly environment as the first component. You can insert a component in the Assembly environment multiple times.

4.   Click anywhere in the graphics area to specify the placement point, the third component (*Clamp Base*) is placed in the specified location, see Figure 11.88. Make sure that you specify the placement point such that the inserted component should not intersect with the other component of the assembly.

Section 7: Assembling Third Component

1. Click on the **Mate** tool of the **Assembly CommandManager**, the **Mate PropertyManager** appears.

2. Select the back planar face of the second component (*Clamp Spacer*), see Figure 11.89, and the front planar face of the third component (*Clamp Base*) to apply coincident mate, see Figure 11.89. As soon as you select the planar faces to apply mate, the Pop-up toolbar appears with the **Coincident** tool is activated by default, see Figure 11.90.

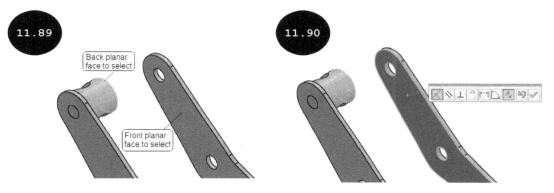

3. Click on the green tick mark ✅ of the Pop-up toolbar, the coincident mate is applied between the selected faces.

4. Select the circular face of the upper hole of the third component (*Clamp Base*), see Figure 11.91, and the circular face of the second component (*Clamp Spacer*) to apply concentric mate, see Figure 11.91. As soon as you select the circular faces to apply mate, the Pop-up toolbar appears with the **Concentric** tool is activated by default, see Figure 11.92.

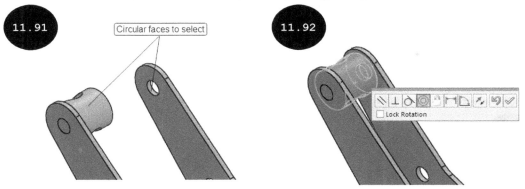

5. Click on the green tick mark ✅ of the Pop-up toolbar, the concentric relation is applied between the selected faces. Next, exit from the PropertyManager.

Section 8: Inserting Forth Component

1. Click on the **Insert Components** tool of the **Assembly CommandManager**, the **Insert Component PropertyManager** appears.

2. Click on the **Browse** button of the **Part/Assembly to Insert** rollout of the PropertyManager, the **Open** dialog box appears.

3. Click to select the forth component (*Clamp foot*) to insert in the Assembly environment. Next, click on the **Open** button, the forth component (*Clamp foot*) is attached with the cursor, see Figure 11.93.

4. Change the current orientation of the forth component (*Clamp foot*) similar to one shown in Figure 11.94 by using the **Rotate Context** toolbar.

5. Click anywhere in the graphics area to specify the placement point, the forth component (*Clamp foot*) is placed in the specified location, see Figure 11.94.

11.93

11.94

Section 9: Assembling Forth Component

1. Click on the **Mate** tool of the **Assembly CommandManager**, the **Mate PropertyManager** appears.

2. Select the circular face of the lower hole of the first component (Clamp Base), see Figure 11.95, and the circular face of the hole of the forth component (*Clamp foot*) to apply concentric mate, see Figure 11.95. As soon as you select the faces, the Pop-up toolbar appears with the **Concentric** tool is activated by default, see Figure 11.96.

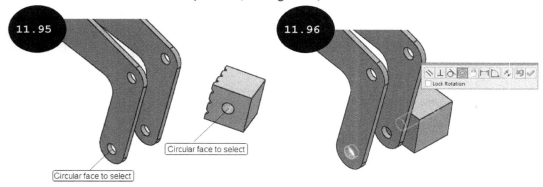

11.95

11.96

Circular face to select

Circular face to select

3. Click on the green tick mark ✓ of the Pop-up toolbar, the concentric mate is applied between the selected faces.

4. Select the back planar face of the first component (*Clamp Base*), see Figure 11.97, and the front planar face of the forth component (*Clamp foot*), see Figure 11.97. As soon as you select the faces, the Pop-up toolbar appears with the **Coincident** tool is activated by default, see Figure 11.98.

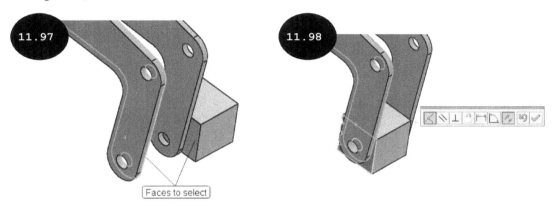

5. Click on the green tick mark ✓ of the Pop-up tool bar, the coincident relation is applied between the selected faces.

6. Click to select the third component (*Clamp Base*). Next, press and hold the left mouse button and drag the cursor to change the position of the third component similar to one shown in Figure 11.99.

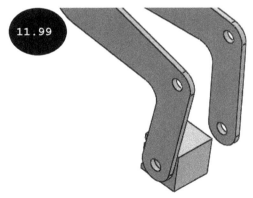

7. Select the circular face of the lower hole of the third component (Clamp Base), see Figure 11.100, and the circular face of the hole of the forth component (*Clamp foot*), see Figure 11.100. As soon as you select the faces, the Pop-up toolbar appears with the **Concentric** tool is activated by default, see Figure 11.101.

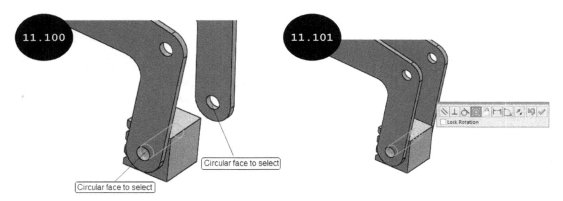

Section 10: Inserting Fifth Component

1. Click on the **Insert Components** tool of the **Assembly CommandManager**, the **Insert Component PropertyManager** appears.

2. Click on the **Browse** button of the **Part/Assembly to Insert** rollout of the PropertyManager, the **Open** dialog box appears.

3. Click to select the fifth component (*Clamp Left Elbow*) to insert in the Assembly environment. Next, click on the **Open** button, the fifth component (*Clamp Left Elbow*) is attached with the cursor, see Figure 11.102.

4. Click anywhere in the graphics area to specify the placement point, the fifth component (*Clamp Left Elbow*) is placed in the specified location, see Figure 11.103.

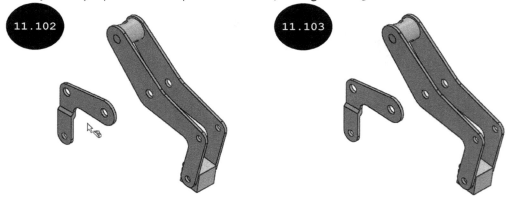

Section 11: Assembling Fifth Component

1. Click on the **Mate** tool of the **Assembly CommandManager**, the **Mate PropertyManager** appears.

2. Select the circular face of the hole of the fifth component (*Clamp Left Elbow*), see Figure 11.104, and the circular face of the hole of the first component (*Clamp Base*), see Figure 11.104. As soon as you select the faces, the Pop-up toolbar appears with the **Concentric** tool is activated by default, see Figure 11.105.

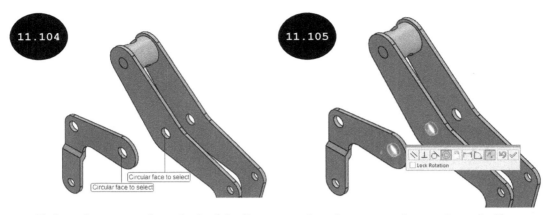

3. Click on the green tick mark ✅ of the Pop-up toolbar, the concentric mate is applied between the selected faces.

4. Select the back planar face of the first component (*Clamp Base*), see Figure 11.106, and the front planar face of the fifth component (*Clamp Left Elbow*), see Figure 11.106. As soon as you select the faces, the Pop-up toolbar appears with the **Coincident** tool is activated by default, see Figure 11.107.

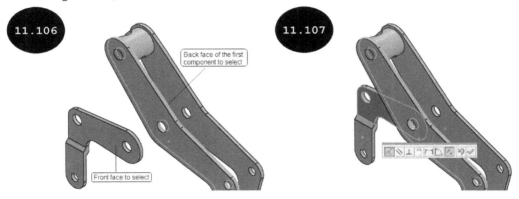

5. Click on the green tick mark ✅ of the Pop-up tool bar, the coincident relation is applied between the selected faces.

Note: The fifth component (*Clamp Left Elbow*) is assembled with the first component (*Clamp Base*). However, a rotational degree of freedom of the fifth component is still free. You need to keep this rotational degree of freedom of the component free.

Section 12: Inserting Sixth Component

1. Click on the **Insert Components** tool of the **Assembly CommandManager**, the **Insert Component PropertyManager** appears.

2. Click on the **Browse** button of the **Part/Assembly to Insert** rollout of the PropertyManager, the **Open** dialog box appears.

3. Click to select the sixth component
    (*Clamp Right Elbow*) and then click on
    the **Open** button of the dialog box, the
    sixth component (*Clamp Right Elbow*) is
    attached with the cursor.

4. Click anywhere in the graphics area to
    specify the placement point, the sixth
    component (*Clamp Right Elbow*) is placed
    in the specified location, see Figure 11.108.

Section 13: Assembling Sixth Component

1. Click on the **Mate** tool of the **Assembly CommandManager**, the **Mate PropertyManager**
    appears.

2. Select the circular face of the hole of the sixth component (*Clamp Right Elbow*), see Figure 11.109,
    and the circular face of the hole of the third component (*Clamp Base*), see Figure 11.109. As
    soon as you select the faces, the Pop-up toolbar appears with the **Concentric** tool is activated
    by default, see Figure 11.110.

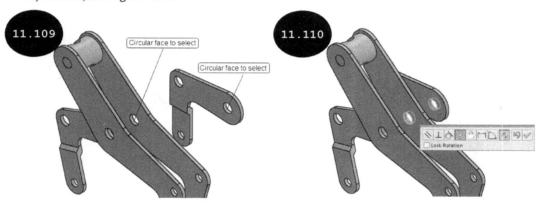

3. Click on the green tick mark ✅ of the Pop-up toolbar, the concentric mate is applied between
    the selected faces.

4. Select the back planar face of the sixth component (*Clamp Right Elbow*), see Figure 11.111, and
    the front planar face of the third component (*Clamp Base*), see Figure 11.111. As soon as you
    select the faces, the Pop-up toolbar appears with the **Coincident** tool is activated by default,
    see Figure 11.112.

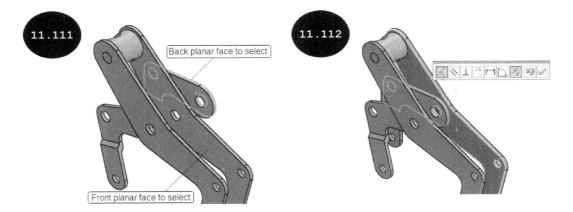

5. Click on the green tick mark ✅ of the Pop-up tool bar, the coincident relation is applied between the selected faces.

Section 14: Inserting Seventh Component

1. Click on the **Insert Components** tool of the **Assembly CommandManager**, the **Insert Component PropertyManager** appears.

2. Click on the **Browse** button of the **Part/Assembly to Insert** rollout of the PropertyManager, the **Open** dialog box appears.

3. Click to select the seventh component (*Clamp foot*) and then click on the **Open** button, the seventh component (*Clamp foot*) is attached with the cursor.

4. Change the current orientation of the component similar to one shown in Figure 11.114 by using the **Rotate Context** toolbar.

5. Click anywhere in the graphics area to specify the placement point, the seventh component (*Clamp foot*) is placed in the specified location, see Figure 11.114.

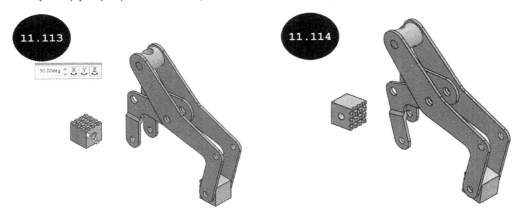

Section 15: Assembling Seventh Component

1. Click on the **Mate** tool of the **Assembly CommandManager**, the **Mate PropertyManager** appears.

2. Select the circular face of the lower hole of the fifth component (*Clamp Left Elbow*), see Figure 11.115 and the circular face of the hole of the seventh component (*Clamp foot*), see Figure 11.115. As soon as you select faces, the Pop-up toolbar appears with the **Concentric** tool is activated by default, see Figure 11.116.

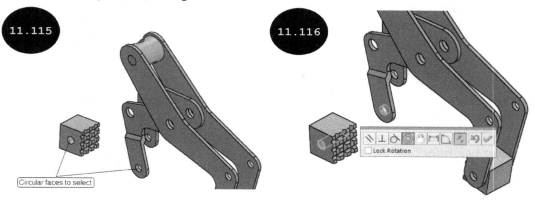

3. Click on the green tick mark ✅ of the Pop-up toolbar, the concentric mate is applied between the selected faces.

4. Select the back planar face of the fifth component (*Clamp Left Elbow*), see Figure 11.117, and the front planar face of the seventh component (*Clamp foot*), see Figure 11.117. As soon as you select faces, the Pop-up toolbar appears with the **Coincident** tool is activated by default, see Figure 11.118.

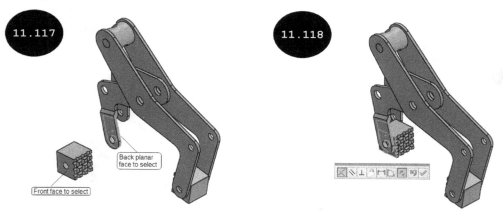

5. Click on the green tick mark ✅ of the Pop-up tool bar, the coincident relation is applied between the selected faces.

6. Click to select the fifth component (*Clamp Left Elbow*). Next, press and hold the left mouse button and drag the cursor to change the position of the fifth component similar to one shown in Figure 11.119.

7. Select the circular face of the lower hole of the fifth component (*Clamp Left Elbow*), see Figure 11.120, and the circular face of the hole of the sixth component (*Clamp Right Elbow*), see Figure 11.120. As soon as you select the faces, the Pop-up toolbar appears with the **Concentric** tool is activated by default, see Figure 11.121.

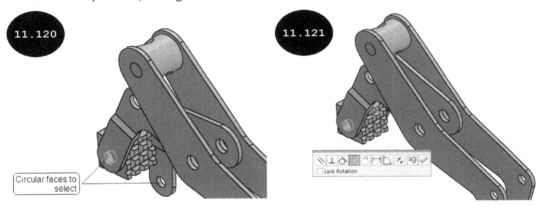

8. Click on the green tick mark ✅ of the Pop-up toolbar, the concentric relation is applied between the selected faces.

9. Select the right planar face of the seventh component (*Clamp foot*), see Figure 11.122, and the left planar face of the forth component (*Clamp foot*), see Figure 11.122. As soon as you select the faces, the Pop-up toolbar appears with the **Coincident** tool is activated by default, see Figure 11.123.

10. Click on the **Parallel** tool of the Pop-up toolbar to apply parallel relation between the planar faces of the seventh and forth components (*Clamp foot*) instead of applying coincident relation between them, see Figure 11.124. The model appears after applying the relations similar to one shown in Figure 11.125.

11. Click on the green tick mark ✅ of the Pop-up toolbar, the parallel relation is applied between the selected faces. Next, exit from the PropertyManager.

Section 16: Inserting Eight Component

1. Click on the **Insert Components** tool of the **Assembly CommandManager**, the **Insert Component PropertyManager** appears.

2. Click on the **Browse** button of the **Part/Assembly to Insert** rollout of the PropertyManager, the **Open** dialog box appears.

3. Click to select the eight component (*Clamp Tee*) and then click on the **Open** button, the eight component (*Clamp Tee*) is attached with the cursor.

4. Click anywhere in the graphics area to specify the placement point, the eight component (*Clamp Tee*) is placed in the specified location, see Figure 11.126.

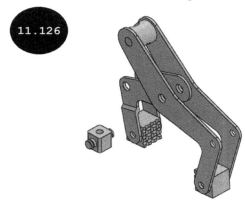

Section 17: Assembling Eight Component

1. Click on the **Mate** tool of the **Assembly CommandManager**, the **Mate PropertyManager** appears.

2. Select the circular face of the eight component (*Clamp Tee*), see Figure 11.127, and the circular face of the hole of the fifth component (*Clamp Left Elbow*), see Figure 11.127. As soon as you select the faces, the Pop-up toolbar appears with the **Concentric** tool is activated by default, see Figure 11.128.

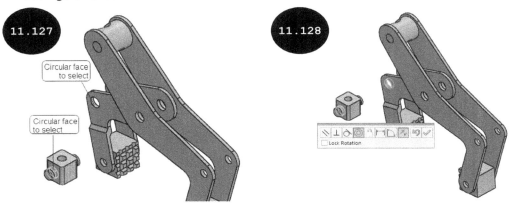

3. Click on the green tick mark ✅ of the Pop-up toolbar, the concentric mate is applied between the selected faces.

4. Select the planar face of the eight component (*Clamp Tee*), see Figure 11.129, and the back planar face of the fifth component (*Clamp Left Elbow*), see Figure 11.129. As soon as you select the faces, the Pop-up toolbar appears with the **Coincident** tool is activated by default, see Figure 11.130.

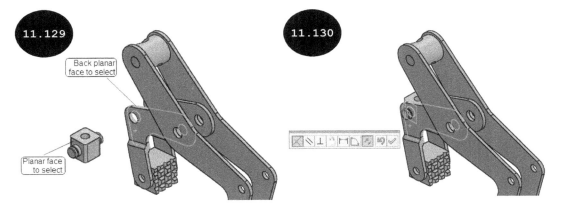

5. Click on the green tick mark ✅ of the Pop-up tool bar, the coincident relation is applied between the selected faces. Next, exit from the PropertyManager.

Section 18: Inserting Ninth Component

1. Click on the **Insert Components** tool of the **Assembly CommandManager**, the **Insert Component PropertyManager** appears.

2. Click on the **Browse** button of the **Part/Assembly to Insert** rollout of the PropertyManager, the **Open** dialog box appears.

3. Click to select the ninth component (*Clamp Rod*) and then click on the **Open** button, the ninth component (*Clamp Rod*) is attached with the cursor.

4. Click anywhere in the graphics area to specify the placement point, the ninth component (*Clamp Rod*) is placed in the specified location, see Figure 11.131.

11.131

Section 19: Assembling Ninth Component

1. Click on the **Mate** tool of the **Assembly CommandManager**, the **Mate PropertyManager** appears.

2. Select the circular face of the ninth component (*Clamp Rod*), see Figure 11.132, and the circular face of the hole of the eight component (*Clamp Tee*), see Figure 11.132. As soon as you select the faces, the Pop-up toolbar appears with the **Concentric** tool is activated by default, see Figure 11.133.

11.132 11.133

3. Click on the green tick mark ✅ of the Pop-up toolbar, the concentric mate is applied between the selected faces.

4. Select the circular face of the ninth component (*Clamp Rod*), see Figure 11.134, and the circular face of the hole of the second component (*Clamp Spacer*), see Figure 11.134. As soon as you select the faces, the Pop-up toolbar appears with the **Concentric** tool is activated by default, see Figure 11.135.

Note: You may need to rotate the second component (*Clamp Spacer*) by dragging it so that you can view its hole feature in order to select its circular face.

5. Click on the green tick mark ✅ of the Pop-up toolbar, the concentric mate is applied between the selected faces.

6. Rotate the assembly such that you can view it from the left side, see Figure 11.136. To rotate the assembly, press and hold the middle mouse button and drag the cursor such that assembly appears similar to one shown in Figure 11.136.

7. Select the planar face of the ninth component (*Clamp Rod*), see Figure 11.137, and the bottom planar face of the eight component (*Clamp Tee*), see Figure 11.137. As soon as you select the faces, the Pop-up toolbar appears with the **Coincident** tool is activated by default, see Figure 11.138.

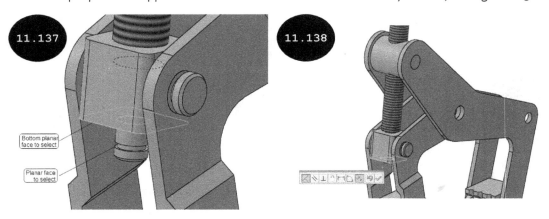

11.137   11.138

Bottom planar face to select

Planar face to select

Note: You may need to zoom in or out the display area of the assembly by scrolling the middle mouse button. You can also using the **Zoom In/Out** tool of the shortcut menu that displays on right clicking in the graphics area.

8. Click on the green tick mark ✅ of the Pop-up toolbar, the coincident relation is applied between the selected faces. Next, exit from the PropertyManager.

9. Change the orientation of the model to isometric.

Section 20: Inserting Tenth Component

1. Click on the **Insert Components** tool of the **Assembly CommandManager**, the **Insert Component PropertyManager** appears.

2. Click on the **Browse** button of the **Part/Assembly to Insert** rollout of the PropertyManager, the **Open** dialog box appears.

3. Click to select the tenth component (*Clamp Hinge*) and then click on the **Open** button, the tenth component (*Clamp Hinge*) is attached with the cursor.

4. Click anywhere in the graphics area to specify the placement point, the tenth component (*Clamp Hinge*) is placed in the specified location, see Figure 11.139.

11.139

Section 21: Assembling Tenth Component

1. Click on the **Mate** tool of the **Assembly CommandManager**, the **Mate PropertyManager** appears.

2. Select the circular face of the tenth component (*Clamp Hinge*), see Figure 11.140, and the circular face of the hole of the first component (*Clamp Base*), see Figure 11.140. As soon as you select the faces, the Pop-up toolbar appears with the **Concentric** tool is activated by default, see Figure 11.141.

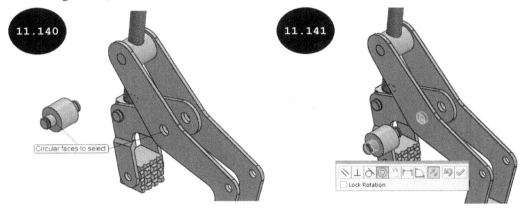

11.140   Circular faces to select   11.141   Lock Rotation

3. Click on the green tick mark ✅ of the Pop-up toolbar, the concentric mate is applied between the selected faces.

4. Select the back side planar face of the tenth component (*Clamp Hinge*), see Figure 11.142, and the front planar face of the sixth component (*Clamp Right Elbow*), see Figure 11.142. As soon as you select the faces, the Pop-up toolbar appears with the **Coincident** tool is activated by default, see Figure 11.143.

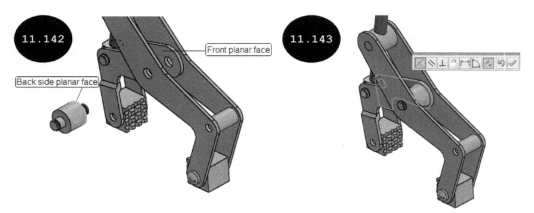

5.   Click on the green tick mark ✅ of the Pop-up tool bar, the coincident relation is applied between the selected faces. Next, exit from the PropertyManager.

Section 22: Inserting Eleventh Component

1.   Insert the eleventh component (*Clamp Support*) in the Assembly environment by using the **Insert Components** tool, see Figure 11.144.

Section 23: Assembling Eleventh Component

1.   Invoke the **Mate PropertyManager**.

2.   Select the circular face of the hole of the eleventh component (*Clamp Support*), see Figure 11.145 and the circular face of the hole of the first component (*Clamp Base*), see Figure 11.145. As soon as you select the faces, the Pop-up toolbar appears with the **Concentric** tool is activated by default, see Figure 11.146.

3.   Click on the green tick mark ✅ of the Pop-up toolbar, the concentric mate is applied between the selected faces.

4.   Select the front planar face of the eleventh component (*Clamp Support*), see Figure 11.147, and the back planar face of the first component (*Clamp Base*), see Figure 11.147. As soon as you select the faces, the Pop-up toolbar appears with the **Coincident** tool is activated, see Figure 11.148.

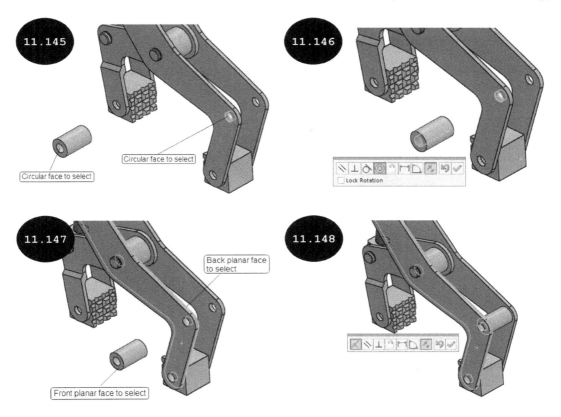

5. Click on the green tick mark ✅ of the Pop-up tool bar, the coincident relation is applied between the selected faces. Next, exit from the PropertyManager.

Section 24: Inserting Twelfth Component

1. Insert the twelfth component (*Clamp Lever*) in the Assembly environment by using the **Insert Components** tool, see Figure 11.149.

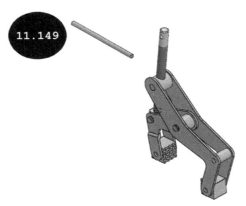

Section 25: Assembling Twelfth Component

1. Invoke the **Mate PropertyManager**.

2. Select the circular face of the twelfth component (*Clamp Lever*), see Figure 11.150, and the circular face of the hole of the ninth component (*Clamp Rod*), see Figure 11.150. As soon as you select the faces, the Pop-up toolbar appears with the **Concentric** tool is activated, see Figure 11.151.

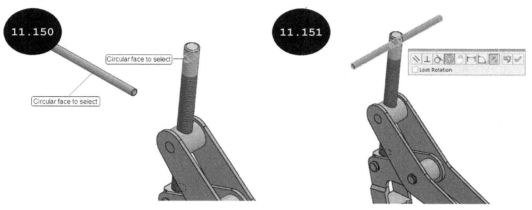

3. Click on the green tick mark ✅ of the Pop-up toolbar, the concentric mate is applied between the selected faces.

4. Expand the **Advanced Mates** rollout of the **Mate PropertyManager** to displays the advances mates.

5. Click to select the **Width** button of the **Advanced Mates** rollout, the **Width selections** and **Tab selections** fields enabled in the **Mate Selections** rollout of the PropertyManager. The **Width selections** field is achieved, by default.

6. Select the front and back planar face of the twelfth component (*Clamp Lever*) as the width selection, see Figure 11.152. Next, select the circular face of the ninth component (*Clamp Rod*) as the tab selection, see Figure 11.152. As soon as you select the width and tab selection faces, the model appears similar to one shown in Figure 11.153.

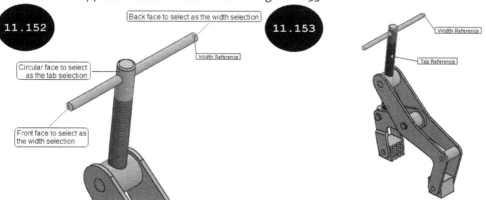

7. Click on the green tick mark ✅ of the PropertyManager, the width mate (relation) is applied between the selected faces. Next, exit from the PropertyManager.

Section 26: Inserting Thirtieth Component

1. Insert the thirtieth component (*Clamp Screw*) in the Assembly environment by using the **Insert Components** tool, see Figure 11.154.

11.154

Section 27: Assembling Thirtieth Component

1. Invoke the **Mate PropertyManager**.

2. Select the circular face of the thirtieth component (*Clamp Screw*), see Figure 11.155, and the circular face of the hole of the first component (*Clamp Base*), see Figure 11.155. As soon as you select the faces, the Pop-up toolbar appears with the **Concentric** tool is activated, see Figure 11.156.

3. Click on the green tick mark ✅ of the Pop-up toolbar, the concentric mate is applied between the selected faces.

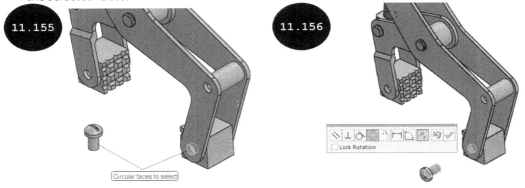

11.155

Circular faces to select

11.156

Lock Rotation

4. Select the back planar face of the head of the thirtieth component (*Clamp Screw*), see Figure 11.157 and the front planar face of the first component (*Clamp Base*), see Figure 11.157. As soon as you select the faces, the Pop-up toolbar appears with the **Coincident** tool is activated, see Figure 11.158.

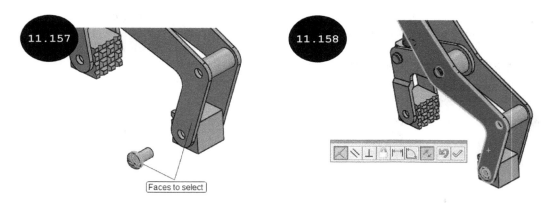

Faces to select

5. Click on the green tick mark ✅ of the Pop-up tool bar, the coincident relation is applied between the selected faces. Next, exit from the PropertyManager.

Section 28: Inserting Fortieth Component

1. Insert the fortieth component (*Clamp Washer*) in the Assembly environment by using the **Insert Components** tool, see Figure 11.159.

Section 29: Assembling Fortieth Component

1. Invoke the **Mate PropertyManager**.

2. Select the inner circular face of the fortieth component (*Clamp Washer*), see Figure 11.160, and the circular face of the tenth component (*Clamp Hinge*), see Figure 11.160. As soon as you select the faces, the Pop-up toolbar appears with the **Concentric** tool is activated, see Figure 11.161.

3. Click on the green tick mark ✅ of the Pop-up toolbar, the concentric mate is applied between the selected faces.

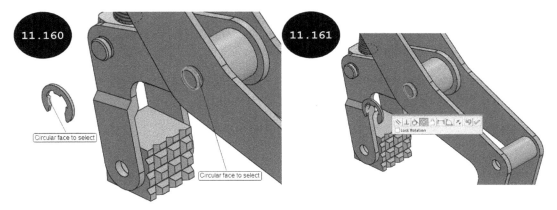

4. Select the back planar face of the fortieth component (*Clamp Washer*), see Figure 11.162 and the front planar face of the first component (*Clamp Base*), see Figure 11.162, the Pop-up toolbar appears with the **Coincident** tool is activated, see Figure 11.163.

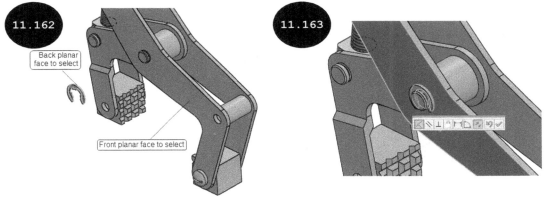

5. Click on the green tick mark ✅ of the Pop-up tool bar, the coincident relation is applied between the selected faces. Next, exit from the PropertyManager.

Section 30: Inserting and Assembling Remaining Components

1. Insert and assemble the remaining components (*Five instances of the Clamp Screw and three instances of the Lock Washer*). Assembly after inserting and assembling all the components appears similar to one shown in Figure 11.164.

Section 31: Applying Screw Mate Relationship

You will need to apply the screw mate relationship between the ninth component (*Clamp Rod*) and the second component (*Clamp Spacer*).

1. Invoke the **Mate PropertyManager** and then expand the **Mechanical Mates** rollout to display the mechanical mates.

2. Click to select the **Screw** button of the **Mechanical Mates** rollout.

3. Click to select the circular face of the ninth component (*Clamp Rod*) as the first entity, see Figure 11.165.

    Now, you need to select the circular face of the hole of the second component (*Clamp Spacer*) which is not visible.

4. Move the cursor over the outer circular face of the second component (*Clamp Spacer*) and right click to display a shortcut menu, see Figure 11.166.

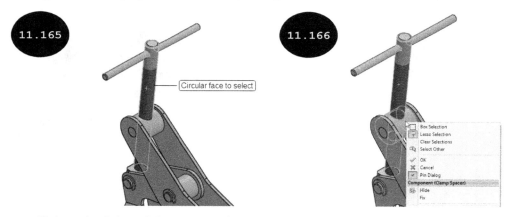

5. Click on the **Select Other** option of the shortcut menu, the **Select Other** window appears, see Figure 11.167.

6. Move the cursor over the faces listed in the window. As you move the cursor, the respective faces highlight in the graphics area.

7. Click on the face of the **Select Other** window when the circular face of the hole of the second component (*Clamp Spacer*) is highlighted in the graphics area, see Figure 11.167. As soon as you select the faces to apply screw mate, a arrow appears in the graphics area which represent the revolving direction of the screw (*Clamp Rod*), see Figure 11.168.

Note: You can reverse the revolving direction by selecting or clearing the **Reverse** check box of the **Mechanical Mates** rollout of the PropertyManager.

8. Click to select the **Distance/revolution** radio button of the **Mechanical Mates** rollout and then enter **5** mm in the **Distance** field as the distance to travel per revolution of the screw (*Clamp Rod*).

9. Click on the green tick mark ✓ of PropertyManager, the screw mate relationship is applied. The final assembly after assembling all components is shown in Figure 11.169. Now, you can rotate the *Clamp Rod* component to view its motion and relationship with other component.

Section 32: Saving the Model

1. Click on the **Save** tool of the **Standard** toolbar, the **Save As** window appears.

2. Browse to the *Tutorial 1* folder of *Chapter 11* folder and then save the assembly as Tutorial 1.

Tutorial 2

Create the assembly shown in Figure 11.170. Different views and dimensions of individual components of the assembly are shown in Figures 11.171 through 11.174.

11.170

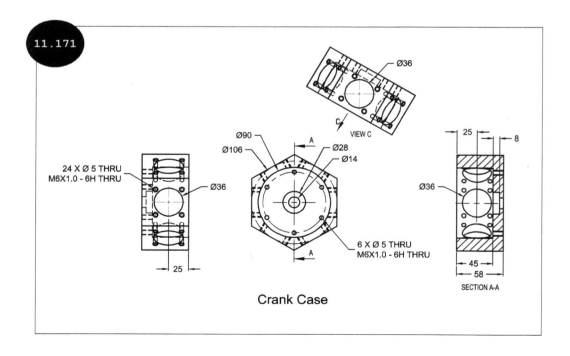

11.171

24 X Ø 5 THRU
M6X1.0 - 6H THRU

Ø36

25

Ø90
Ø106

VIEW C

Ø36

A

Ø28
Ø14

Ø36

25

8

6 X Ø 5 THRU
M6X1.0 - 6H THRU

A

45

58

SECTION A-A

Crank Case

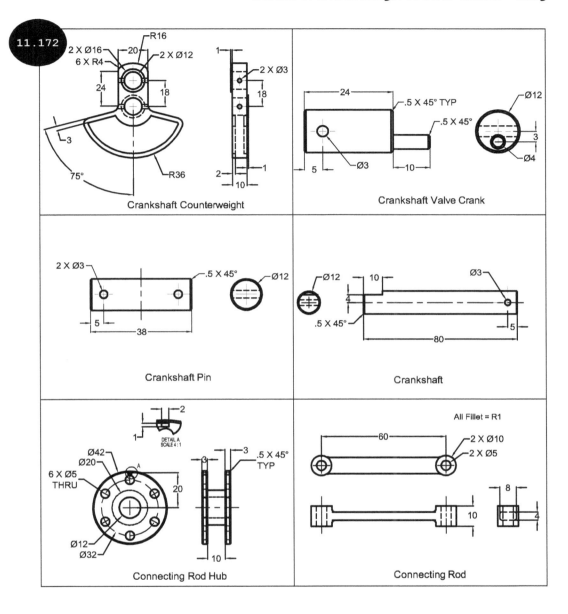

11.172

Crankshaft Counterweight

Crankshaft Valve Crank

Crankshaft Pin

Crankshaft

Connecting Rod Hub

Connecting Rod

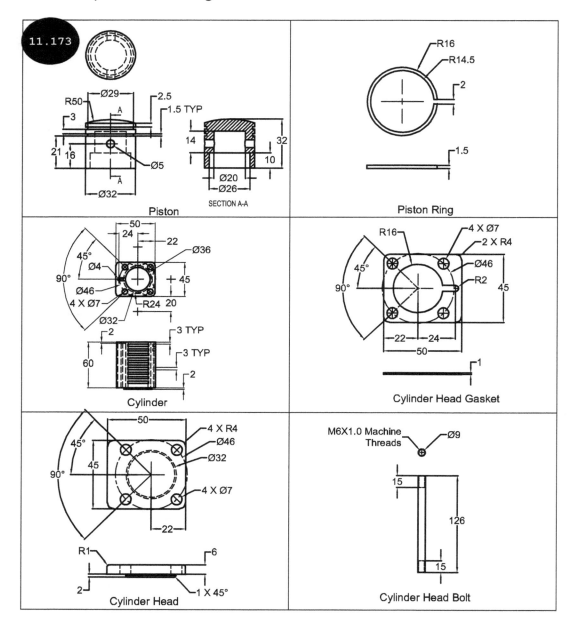

11.173

Piston

SECTION A-A

Piston Ring

Cylinder

Cylinder Head Gasket

Cylinder Head

Cylinder Head Bolt

M6X1.0 Machine Threads

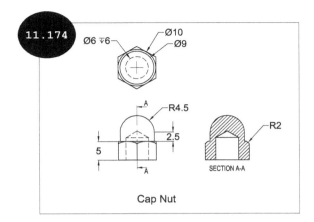

Cap Nut

Section 1: Creating Assembly Components

In this section, you will create all the components of assembly.

1. Create all components of the assembly one by one. See Figure 11.171 through 11.174 for dimensions of individual components. After creating all the components of the assembly, save them in *Tutorial 2* folder of the *Chapter 11* folder. You need to create *Tutorial 2* folder inside the *Chapter 11* folder.

Note: You can also download all the components of the assembly from *www.cadartifex.com*.

Section 2: Invoking Assembly Environment

1. Click on the **New** tool in the **Standard** toolbar, the **New SOLIDWORKS Document** dialog box appears.

2. In this dialog box, click on the **Assembly** button to activated it. Next, click on the **OK** button, the assembly environment is invoked with the display of the **Begin Assembly PropertyManager** at the left.

Section 3: Creating Piston Sub-Assembly

In this section, you will create Piston sub-assembly.

1. Click on the **Browse** button of the **Part/Assembly to Insert** rollout of the **Begin Assembly PropertyManager**, the **Open** dialog box appears.

2. Browse to the *Tutorial 2* folder of *Chapter 11* where all components of the assembly are saved.

3. Select the first component (*Piston*) and then click on the **Open** button, the first component (*Piston*) is attached with the cursor.

4. Click anywhere in the graphics area, the first component (*Piston*) move towards the origin of the assembly and become fix component automatically, see Figure 11.175.

Now, you need to insert the second component of the Piston sub-assembly.

5. Click on the **Insert Components** tool of the **Assembly CommandManager**, the **Insert Component PropertyManager** appears.

6. Click on the **Browse** button, the **Open** dialog box appears.

7. Click to select the second component (*Piston Ring*) and then click on the **Open** button, the second component (*Piston Ring*) is attached with the cursor.

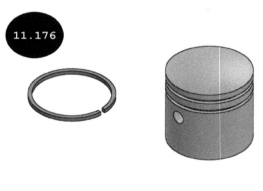

8. Click anywhere in the graphics area to specify the placement point, the second component (*Piston Ring*) is placed in the graphics area, see Figure 11.176. Make sure that you specify the placement point such that the inserted component should not intersect with the other component of the assembly.

Note: All the degree of freedom of the second inserted component (*Piston Ring*) in the assembly environment are free. It means that the second inserted component (*Piston Ring*) is free to translate and rotate along and about its three axis. You need to apply required mates (relations) to fix its degree of freedom.

Now, you will assemble the second component (*Piston Ring*) with the first component (*Piston*).

9. Click on the **Mate** tool of the **Assembly CommandManager**, the **Mate PropertyManager** appears.

10. Select the bottom planar face of the second component (*Piston Ring*), see Figure 11.177 and the planar face of the first component (*Piston*), see Figure 11.177. As soon as you select the faces, the Pop-up toolbar appears with the **Coincident** tool is activated by default, see Figure 11.178.

Planar face to select

Bottom planar face to select

Note: To select faces that are not visible, you can rotate the component by using the **Rotate Components** tool such that you can view them.

11. Click on the green tick mark ✓ of the Pop-up toolbar, the coincident relation is applied between the selected faces.

12. Select the circular face of the second component (*Piston Ring*), see Figure 11.179 and the circular face of the first component (*Piston*), see Figure 11.179. As soon as you select the circular faces to apply mate, the Pop-up toolbar appears with the **Concentric** tool is activated by default, see Figure 11.180.

Inner circular face to select

Outer circular face to select

13. Click on the green tick mark ✓ of the Pop-up toolbar, the concentric relation is applied between the selected faces.

14. Similarly, insert one more instance of the second component (Piston Ring) in the assembly environment and then assemble it with the first component (Piston Ring). Figure 11.181 shows the **Piston** sub-assembly created after assembling the components.

11.181

Section 4: Saving the Piston Sub-Assembly

1. Click on the **Save** tool of the **Standard** toolbar, the **Save As** window appears.

2. Browse to the *Tutorial 2* folder of *Chapter 11* and then save the assembly as Piston Sub Assembly. Next, close the assembly.

Section 5: Creating Cylinder Sub-Assembly

In this section, you will create Cylinder sub-assembly.

1. Invoke the Assembly environment. As soon as you invoke the Assembly environment, the **Begin Assembly PropertyManager** appears.

2. Click on the **Browse** button of the **Part/Assembly to Insert** rollout of the **Begin Assembly PropertyManager**, the **Open** dialog box appears.

3. Browse to the *Tutorial 2* folder of *Chapter 11* where all components of the assembly are saved.

4. Select the first component (*Cylinder*) of the Cylinder sub-assembly and then click on the **Open** button, the first component (*Cylinder*) is attached with the cursor.

5. Click anywhere in the graphics area, the first component (*Cylinder*) move towards the origin of the assembly and become fix automatically, see Figure 11.182.

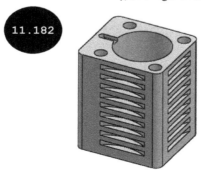

11.182

Now, you need to insert the second component (*Cylinder Head Gasket*).

6. Click on the **Insert Components** tool of the **Assembly CommandManager**, the **Insert Component PropertyManager** appears.

7. Click on the **Browse** button, the **Open** dialog box appears.

8. Click to select the second component (*Cylinder Head Gasket*) to insert in the Assembly environment. Next, click on the **Open** button, the second component (*Cylinder Head Gasket*) is attached with the cursor, see Figure 11.183.

9. Enter **180** in the **Angle** field of the **Rotate Context** toolbar and then click on the **Y** button of this toolbar to change its current orientation of the model similar to the one shown in Figure 11.184.

10. Click anywhere in the graphics area to specify the placement point, the second component (*Cylinder Head Gasket*) is placed in the specified location, see Figure 11.184.

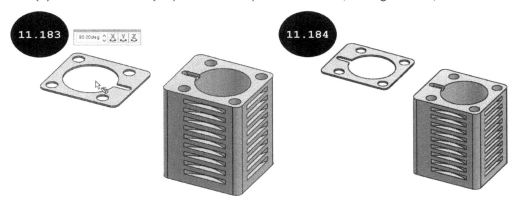

Now, you will assemble the second component (*Cylinder Head Gasket*) with the first component (*Cylinder*).

11. Click on the **Mate** tool of the **Assembly CommandManager**, the **Mate PropertyManager** appears.

12. Select the bottom planar face of the second component (*Cylinder Head Gasket*), see Figure 11.185 and the top planar face of the first component (*Cylinder*), see Figure 11.185. As soon as you select faces, the Pop-up toolbar appears with the **Coincident** tool is activated, see Figure 11.186.

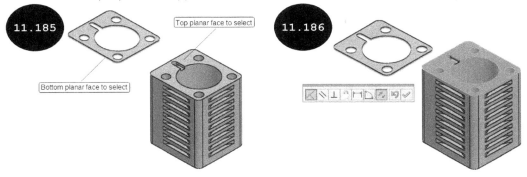

13. Click on the green tick mark ✅ of the Pop-up toolbar, the coincident relation is applied between the selected faces.

14. Select the inner circular face of the hole of the second component (*Cylinder Head Gasket*), see Figure 11.187 and the inner circular face of the hole of the first component (*Cylinder*), see Figure 11.187. As soon as you select circular faces, the Pop-up toolbar appears with the **Concentric** tool is activated, see Figure 11.188.

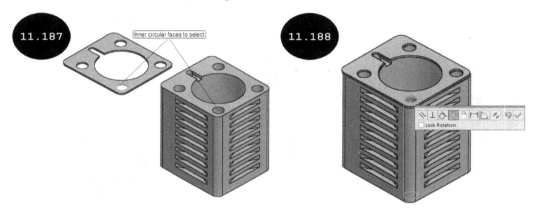

15. Click on the green tick mark ✅ of the Pop-up toolbar, the concentric relation is applied between the selected faces.

16. Select the inner circular face of the hole of the second component (*Cylinder Head Gasket*), see Figure 11.189 and the inner circular face of the hole of the first component (*Cylinder*), see Figure 11.189. As soon as you select circular faces, the Pop-up toolbar appears with the **Coincident** tool is activated, see Figure 11.190.

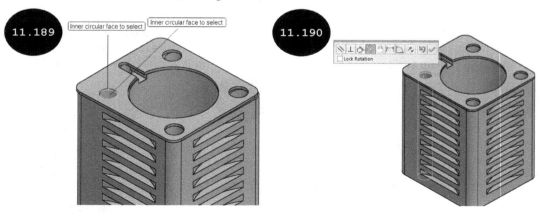

17. Click on the green tick mark ✅ of the Pop-up toolbar, the concentric relation is applied between the selected faces.

    Now, you need to insert the third component (*Cylinder Head*) of the Cylinder sub-assembly.

18. Click on the **Insert Components** tool to invoke the **Insert Component PropertyManager.**

19. Click on the **Browse** button, the **Open** dialog box appears.

20. Click to select the third component (*Cylinder Head*) and then click on the **Open** button, the third component (*Cylinder Head*) is attached with the cursor.

21. Click anywhere in the graphics area to specify the placement point for the third component (*Cylinder Head*), see Figure 11.191.

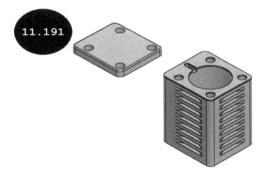

    Now, you will assemble the third component (*Cylinder Head*).

22. Click on the **Mate** tool of the **Assembly CommandManager**, the **Mate PropertyManager** appears.

23. Select the bottom planar face of the third component (*Cylinder Head*), see Figure 11.192 and the top planar face of the second component (*Cylinder Head Gasket*), see Figure 11.192. As soon as you select planar faces, the Pop-up toolbar appears with the **Coincident** tool is activated, see Figure 11.193.

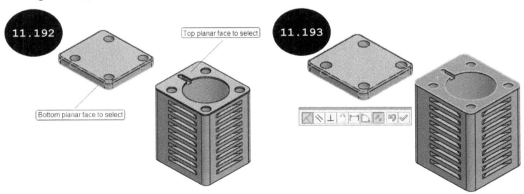

Note: To select the faces that are not visible such as bottom and back faces, you can rotate the component by using the **Rotate Components** tool such that you can view these faces.

---

24. Click on the green tick mark ✅ of the Pop-up toolbar, the coincident relation is applied between the selected faces.

25. Select the inner circular face of the hole of the second component (*Cylinder Head Gasket*), see Figure 11.194 and the inner circular face of the hole of the third component (*Cylinder Head*), see Figure 11.194. As soon as you select the faces, the Pop-up toolbar appears with the **Concentric** tool is activated, see Figure 11.195.

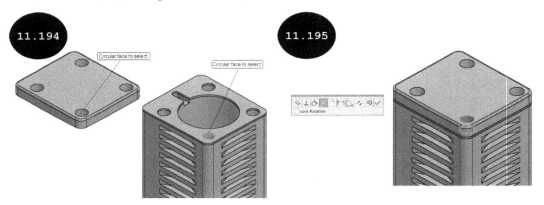

26. Click on the green tick mark ✅ of the Pop-up toolbar, the concentric relation is applied between the selected faces.

27. Press and hold the left mouse button on the third component (*Cylinder Head*) and then drag the cursor to change the position of the component such that it appears similar to one shown in Figure 11.196.

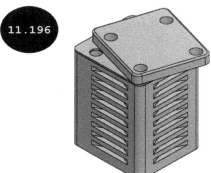

28. Select the inner circular face of the hole of the second component (*Cylinder Head Gasket*), see Figure 11.197 and the inner circular face of the hole of the third component (*Cylinder Head*), see Figure 11.197. As soon as you select the faces, the Pop-up toolbar appears with the **Concentric** tool is activated, see Figure 11.198.

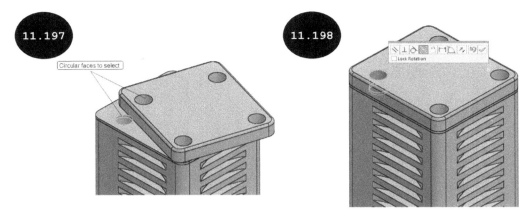

29. Click on the green tick mark ✅ of the Pop-up toolbar, the concentric relation is applied between the selected faces. Next, exit from the PropertyManager.

   Now, you need to insert the forth component (*Cylinder Head Bolt*) of the Cylinder sub assembly.

30. Insert the forth component (*Cylinder Head Bolt*) in the Assembly environment by using the **Insert Components** tool, see Figure 11.199.

   Now, you will assemble the forth component (*Cylinder Head Bolt*).

31. Invoke the **Mate PropertyManager**.

32. Apply the concentric relation/mate between the circular face of the forth component (*Cylinder Head Bolt*) and the circular face of a hole of the third component (*Cylinder Head*), see Figure 11.200.

33. Apply the distance mate of 6 mm between the top planar face of the forth component (*Cylinder Head Bolt*) and the top planar face of the third component (*Cylinder Head*), see Figure 11.201. Note that as soon as you select two planar faces, the **Coincident** tool become activated by default in the Pop-up toolbar.

34. Click on the **Distance** tool of the Pop-up toolbar and then enter **6** in the **Distance** field of Pop-up toolbar, see Figure 11.202.

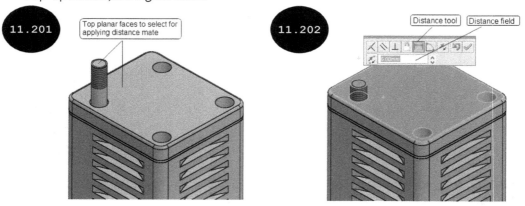

Now, you need to insert the fifth component (*Cylinder Head Nut*) of the Cylinder sub assembly.

35. Insert the fifth component (*Cylinder Head Nut*) in the Assembly environment by using the **Insert Components** tool, see Figure 11.203.

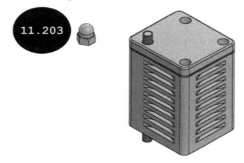

Now, you will assemble the fifth component (*Cylinder Head Nut*).

36. Invoke the **Mate PropertyManager**.

37. Apply the concentric relation between the hole of the fifth component (*Cylinder Head Nut*) and the circular face of the forth component (*Cylinder Head Bolt*), see Figure 11.204.

38. Apply the coincident relation between the bottom planar face of the fifth component (*Cylinder Head Nut*) and the top planar face of the forth component (*Cylinder Head Bolt*), see Figure 11.205.

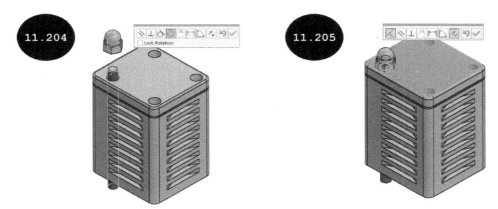

Now, you will insert and assembly the remaining components.

39. Similarly, insert and assemble the remaining components (*three instances of the Cylinder Head Bolt and three instances of the Cylinder Head Bolt*). The Cylinder sub-assembly after assembling all its components appears similar to one shown in Figure 11.206.

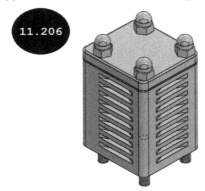

Section 6: Saving the Cylinder Sub-Assembly

1. Click on the **Save** tool of the **Standard** toolbar, the **Save As** window appears.

2. Browse to the *Tutorial 2* folder of *Chapter 11* and then save the assembly as Cylinder Sub Assembly. Next, close the assembly.

Section 7: Creating Main Assembly - Radial Engine

In this section, you will create the main assembly (*Radial Engine*).

1. Invoke the Assembly environment. As soon as you invoke the Assembly environment, the **Begin Assembly PropertyManager** appears.

2. Click on the **Browse** button of the **Part/Assembly to Insert** rollout of the **Begin Assembly PropertyManager**, the **Open** dialog box appears.

3. Browse to the *Tutorial 2* folder of *Chapter 11* where all components of the assembly are saved.

4. Select the first component (*Crank Case*) of the Main assembly (*Radial Engine*) and then click on the **Open** button, the first component (*Crank Case*) is attached with the cursor.

5. Click anywhere in the graphics area, the first component (*Crank Case*) move towards the origin of the assembly and become fixed automatically, see Figure 11.207.

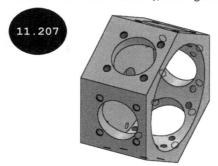

11.207

Section 8: Inserting and Assembling the Second Component

Now, you need to insert the second component (*Crankshaft Valve Crank*) of the Main assembly (*Radial Engine*).

1. Click on the **Insert Components** tool of the **Assembly CommandManager**, the **Insert Component PropertyManager** appears.

2. Click on the **Browse** button, the **Open** dialog box appears.

3. Click to select the second component (*Crankshaft Valve Crank*) to insert in the Assembly environment. Next, click on the **Open** button, the second component (*Crankshaft Valve Crank*) is attached with the cursor, see Figure 11.208.

4. Enter **180** in the **Angle** field of the **Rotate Context** toolbar and then click on the **Y** button of this toolbar to change the current orientation of the model similar to the one shown in Figure 11.209.

5. Click anywhere in the graphics area to specify the placement point, the second component (*Crankshaft Valve Crank*) is placed in the specified location, see Figure 11.209.

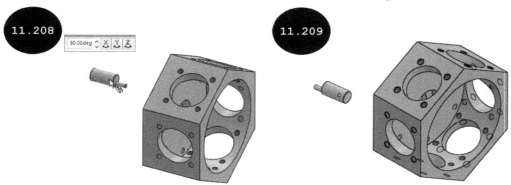

11.208

11.209

Now, you will assemble the second component (*Crankshaft Valve Crank*).

6. Invoke the **Mate PropertyManager** and then apply concentric mate between the circular face of the second component (*Crankshaft Valve Crank*) and the circular face of the hole of the first component (*Crank Case*), see Figure 11.210.

> **Note:** To select the faces easily for applying mates, you can rotate the assembly by pressing and dragging the middle mouse button.

7. Apply the coincident mate between the planar face of the second component (*Crankshaft Valve Crank*) and the planar face the first component (*Crank Case*), see Figure 11.211.

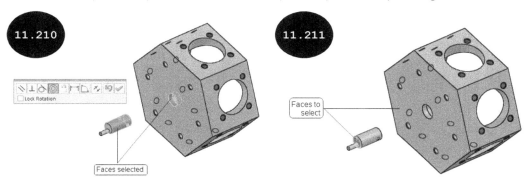

8. Change the current orientation of the assembly to isometric.

Section 9: Inserting and Assembling the Third Component

1. Insert the third component (*Crankshaft Counterweight*) in the Assembly environment by using the **Insert Components** tool, see Figure 11.212.

2. Hide the first component (*Crank Case*) so that you can easily select faces to apply mates, see Figure 11.213. To hide the component, click to select the component to hide from the graphics area and then click on the **Hide Components** tool from the Pop-up toolbar.

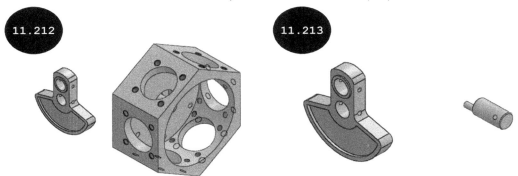

Now, you will assemble the third component (*Crankshaft Counterweight*).

3. Apply concentric mate between the bottom hole of the third component (*Crankshaft Counterweight*) and the circular face of the second component (*Crankshaft Valve Crank*), see Figure 11.214.

Note: If the mate alignment does not appears similar to one shown in Figure 11.214 then you need to click on the **Flip Mate Alignment** tool of the Pop-up toolbar to flip the mate alignment between the faces.

4. Apply concentric mate between the circular face of the hole of the third component (*Crankshaft Counterweight*) and the circular face of the hole of the second component (*Crankshaft Valve Crank*), see Figure 11.215.

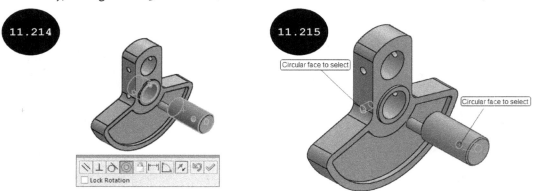

Circular face to select

Circular face to select

Lock Rotation

Section 10: Inserting and Assembling the Forth Component

1. Insert the forth component (*Crankshaft Pin*) in the Assembly environment by using the **Insert Components** tool, see Figure 11.216.

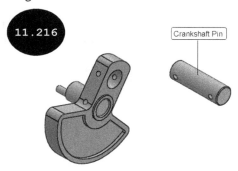

Crankshaft Pin

2. Apply concentric mate between the upper hole of the third component (*Crankshaft Counterweight*) and the circular face of the forth component (*Crankshaft Pin*), see Figure 11.217.

3. Apply concentric mate between the circular face of the hole of the third component (*Crankshaft Counterweight*) and the circular face of the hole of the forth component (*Crankshaft Pin*), see Figure 11.218.

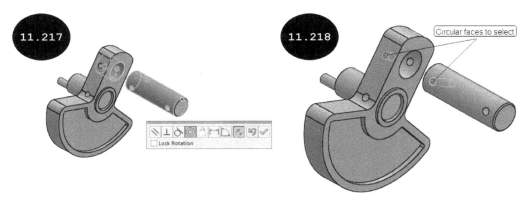

Section 11: Inserting and Assembling the Fifth Component

1. Insert the fifth component (*Crankshaft Counterweight*) in the Assembly environment by using the **Insert Components** tool, see Figure 11.219.

2. Similar to assembling the third component (*Crankshaft Counterweight*), assemble the fifth component (*Crankshaft Counterweight*) with the forth component (*Crankshaft Pin*) by applying two concentric relations, see Figure 11.220.

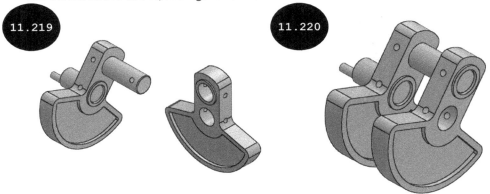

Section 12: Inserting and Assembling the Sixth Component

1. Insert the sixth component (*Crankshaft*) in the Assembly environment, see Figure 11.221. Note that you need to change the orientation of the model similar to one shown in Figure 11.221 by using the **Rotate Context** toolbar.

2. Apply concentric mate between the bottom hole of the fifth component (*Crankshaft Counterweight*) and the circular face of the sixth component (*Crankshaft*), see Figure 11.222.

3. Apply concentric mate between the circular face of the hole of the fifth component (*Crankshaft Counterweight*) and the circular face of the hole of the sixth component (*Crankshaft*), see Figure 11.223.

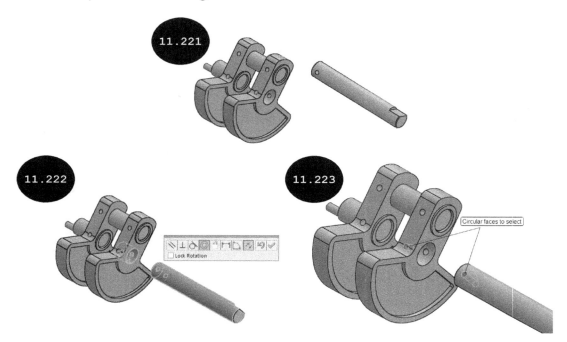

Section 13: Inserting and Assembling the Seventh Component

1. Insert the seventh component (*Connecting Rod Hub*) in the Assembly environment, see Figure 11.224.

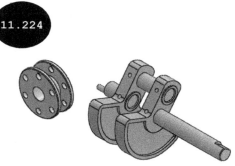

2. Apply concentric mate between the circular face of the seventh component (*Connecting Rod Hub*) and the circular face of the forth component (*Crankshaft Pin*), see Figure 11.225.

3. Apply coincident mate between the back planar face of the seventh component (*Connecting Rod Hub*) and the front planar face of the third component (*Crankshaft Counterweight*), see Figure 11.226.

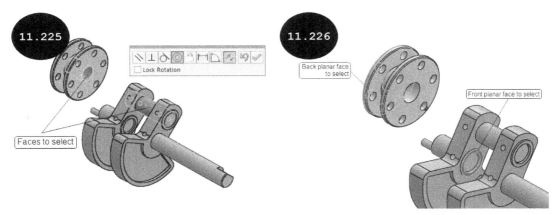

Section 14: Inserting and Assembling the Eight Component

1. Insert the eight component (*Connecting Rod*) in the Assembly environment, see Figure 11.227. Note that you need to change the orientation of the eight component (*Connecting Rod*) similar to one shown in Figure 11.227 by using the **Rotate Context** toolbar.

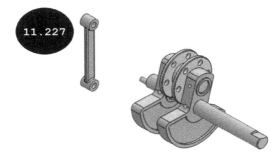

2. Apply concentric mate between the circular face of the bottom hole of the eight component (*Connecting Rod*) and the circular face of a hole of the seventh component (*Connecting Rod Hub*), see Figure 11.228.

3. Apply coincident mate between the back planar face of the eight component (*Connecting Rod*) and the front planar face of the seventh component (*Connecting Rod Hub*), see Figure 11.229.

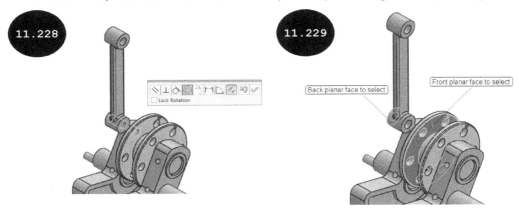

Section 15: Inserting and Assembling the Remaining Connecting Rods

1.   Similarly, insert and assembly the five more instances of the *Connecting Rod* component with the remaining holes of the seventh component (*Connecting Rod Hub*), see Figure 11.230.

Section 16: Inserting and Assembling the Piston Sub-Assembly

1.   Insert the *Piston Sub-Assembly* in the Assembly environment, see Figure 11.231.

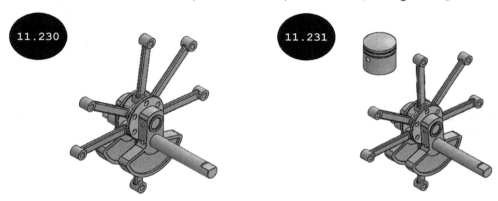

2.   Apply concentric mate between the hole of the *Piston Sub-Assembly* and the upper hole of a *Connecting Rod* component, see Figure 11.232.

3.   Apply width mate between the *Piston Sub-Assembly* and the *Connecting Rod* components, see Figure 11.233. To apply width mate, expand the **Advanced Mates** rollout of the **Mate PropertyManager** and then click on the **Width** button to activate it. Next, select the upper front and back planar face of the *Connecting Rod* as the width selection set and the outer circular face of the *Piston Sub-Assembly* as the tab selection, see Figure 11.233.

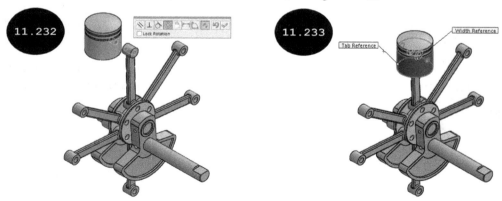

Section 17: Inserting and Assembling Remaining Piston Sub-Assembly

1.   Similarly, insert and assembly the five more instances of the *Piston Sub-Assembly* with the remaining *Connecting Rod* components, see Figure 11.234.

2. Turn On the visibility of first component (*Crank Case*), see Figure 11.235. To show the first component (*Crank Case*) in the graphics area, click to select its name (*Crank Case*) from the FeatureManager design tree, a Pop-up toolbar appear. Next, click to select the **Show Components** option from the Pop-up toolbar.

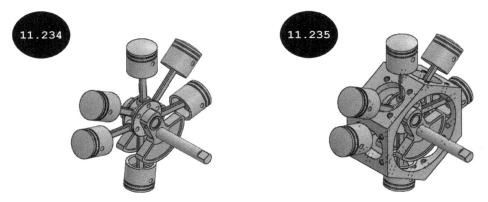

Now, you will apply the concentric relation between the *Piston Sub Assembly* and the first component (*Crank Case*).

3. Apply the concentric relation between the circular face of a *Piston Sub Assembly* and the respective hole of the first component (*Crank Case*), see Figure 11.236.

4. Similarly, apply concentric relation between the remaining *Piston Sub Assembly* and the respective hole of the first component (*Crank Case*), see Figure 11.237.

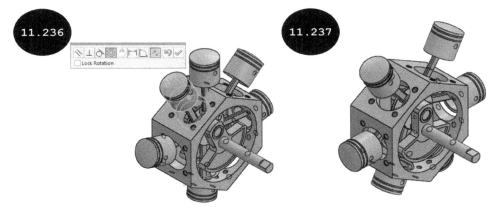

Now, you will apply the parallel relation between the slot cut face of the *Connecting Rod Hub* and the inclined face the *Crank Case* component.

5. Apply the parallel relation between the slot cut planar face of the seventh component (*Connecting Rod Hub*), see Figure 11.238 and the inclined face of the first component (*Crank Case*), see Figure 11.239.

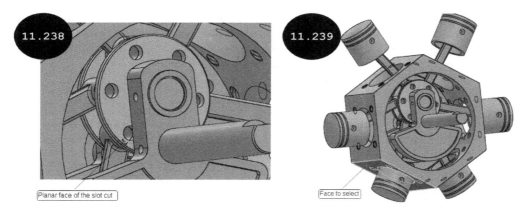

Planar face of the slot cut

Face to select

Section 18: Inserting and Assembling Cylinder Sub-Assembly

1.   Insert the *Cylinder Sub-Assembly* in the Assembly environment, see Figure 11.240.

2.   Apply concentric mate between the inner circular face of the *Cylinder Sub-Assembly* and the outer circular face of the respective *Piston Sub-Assembly*, see Figure 11.241.

3.   Apply coincident mate between the bottom planar face of the *Cylinder Sub-Assembly* and the respective top planar face of the first component (*Crank Case*), see Figure 11.242.

4.   Apply parallel mate between the right planar faces of the *Cylinder Sub-Assembly* and the first component (*Crank Case*), see Figure 11.243.

Faces to select

Section 19: Inserting and Assembling Remaining Cylinder Sub-Assembly

1. Similarly, insert and assembly the five more instances of the *Cylinder Sub-Assembly*, see Figure 11.244.

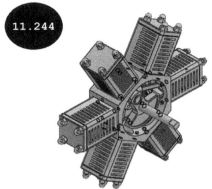

Section 20: Saving the Model

1. Click on the **Save** tool of the **Standard** toolbar, the **Save As** window appears.

2. Browse to the *Tutorial 2* folder of *Chapter 11* and then save the assembly as Tutorial 2.

Hands-on Test Drive 1

Create the assembly shown in Figure 11.245. Different views and dimensions of individual components of the assembly are shown in Figures 11.246 through 11.247.

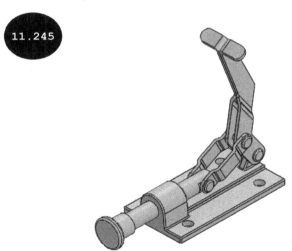

11.246

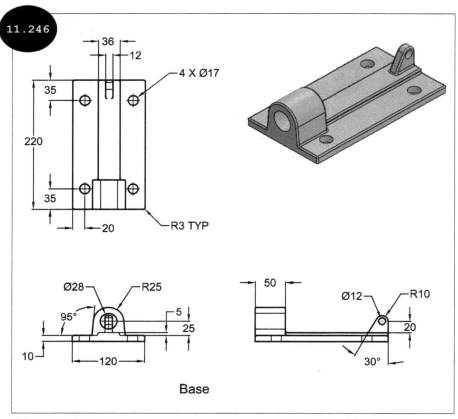

Base

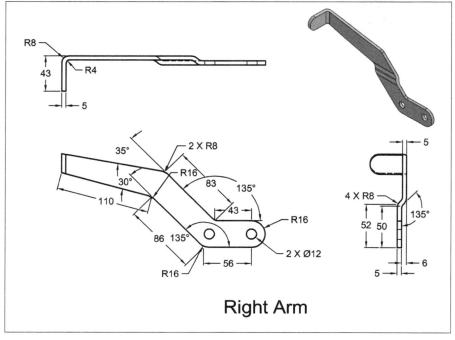

Right Arm

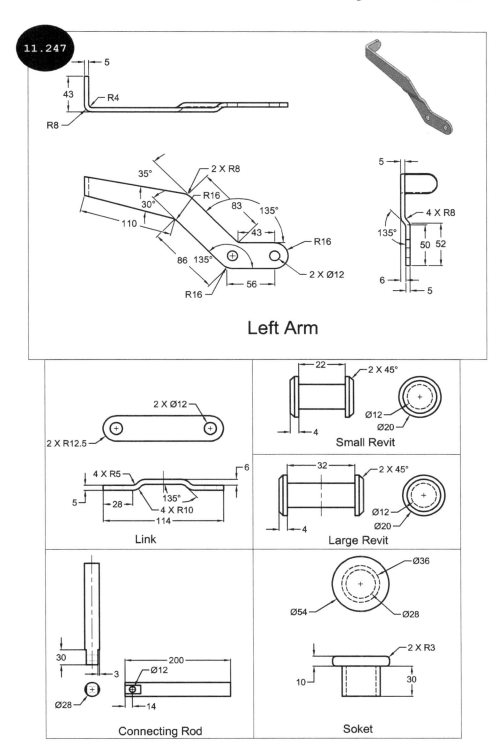

11.247

Left Arm

Link

Small Revit

Large Revit

Connecting Rod

Soket

Summary

In this chapter, you have learnt about creating assemblies by using bottom-up assembly approach. In the bottom-up assembly approach, you first create all the components in the Part modeling environment one by one and then assemble them with respect to each other by applying mates/relations in the Assembly environment. In SOLIDWORKS, you can apply Standard, Advanced, and Mechanical mates to assembly the components with respect to each other. Note that a free component within the Assembly environment has six degrees of freedom: three translational and three rotational. Therefore to assemble a component, you need to fix its free degrees of freedom by using required mates. You have also learnt how to move and rotate individual component within the Assembly environment. At last in this chapter, you have learnt about detecting collisions between components of the assembly and working with SmartMates for applying Standard mates.

Questions

• In SOLIDWORKS, you can create assemblies by using the _____ and _____ approaches.

• Because of the _____ property of SOLIDWORKS, if you make any change in a component in the Part modeling environment, the same change automatically reflects in the assembly environment and vice-versa.

• The _____ toolbar allows you to change the orientation of the component before defining its placement point in the Assembly environment.

• A free component within the Assembly environment has _____ degrees of freedom.

• The _____ mate is used to center align two rectangular profiles, two circular profiles, or a rectangular and a circular profiles with each other.

• The _____ mate allows two components to rotate relative to each other and form a gear mechanism.

• The _____ mate is used to translate linear motion to rotational motion from one component to another and vice versa.

• The _____ mate allows a component to move along the defined path.

• You can move individual components of an assembly along its free degree of freedom. (True/False).

• You can apply mechanical mates by using the SmartMates method. (True/False).

• In SOLIDWORKS, you can detect collisions between components of the assembly. (True/False).

Working with Assemblies II

In this chapter:

In the previous chapter, you learn about creating assemblies using bottom up assembly approach, applying mates, and moving/rotating components. In this chapter, you will learn about creating assemblies using top down assembly approach, editing assembly components, patterning and mirroring assembly components, creating assemblies features, exploded assemblies, and so on.

Creating Assembly using Top-down Approach

In Top-down Assembly Approach, you creates all components of an assembly in the Assembly environment itself. Creating components in the Assembly environment helps in taking the reference from the existing created components. This approach builds the entire assembly by creating all its components top of each other in the Assembly environment. This approach is mainly used for creating concept based design where the individual components design or dimensions are not finalized and depends upon the other components shape and size. The procedure to create assembly by using Top-down Assembly Approach is as follows.

Procedure to Create Assembly using Top-down Approach

1.   Invoke the Assembly environment, see Figure 12.1.

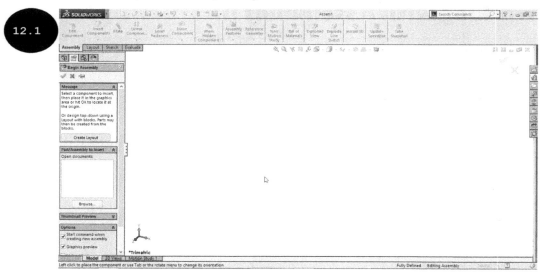

2.   Close the **Begin Assembly PropertyManager** by clicking on the red cross mark ✖ available at its top. This is because you need to create all components of the assembly in the Assembly environment itself instead of importing them.
3.   Click on the arrow available at the bottom of the **Insert Components** tool, a flyout appears, see Figure 12.2.
4.   In this flyout, click on the **New Part** tool, a new part is added in the Assembly environment and appears in the FeatureManager design tree with its default name, see Figure 12.3. Also, a green color tick mark appears attached with the cursor ⬚✓ in the graphics area. As a result, you are prompted to select a face or plane as the placement plane to position the newly added component.

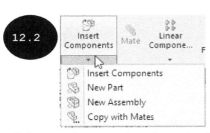

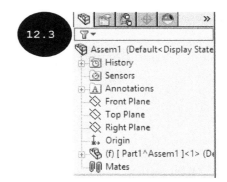

5. Select a reference plane from the FeatureManager design tree, the sketching environment is invoked within the Assembly environment such that the selected reference plane become the sketching plane for creating the base feature of the part, see Figure 12.4.

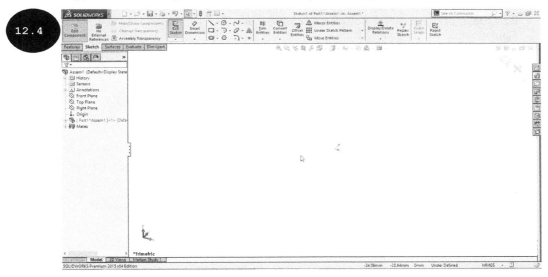

Note: You can also click anywhere in the graphics area to define the position of the part instead of selecting a reference plane or a face. In this case, the origin of the part being created will coincident with the origin of the assembly. However, the sketching environment for creating the base feature will not be invoked. To invoke the sketching environment, select the name of the part from the FeatureManager design tree and then click on the **Edit Component** tool from the **Assembly CommandManager**, the **Sketch CommandManager** is invoked. Next, click on the **Sketch** tool and select a reference plane or a planar face as the sketching plane for creating the base feature of the part.

6. Change the current orientation normal to the viewing direction by using the **Normal To** tool of the **View Orientation** flyout, see Figure 12.5.

7. Draw the sketch of the base feature by using the sketching tools available in the **Sketch CommandManager**, see Figure 12.6.

After creating the sketch, you need to covert it into a solid feature by using the solid modeling tools.

8. Click on the **Features** tab of the **CommandManager**, solid modeling tools available in the **Features CommandManager** appears. Now, by using the solid modeling tools such as **Extruded Boss/Base** and **Revolved Boss/Base**, convert the sketch created into a solid feature, see Figure 12.7.

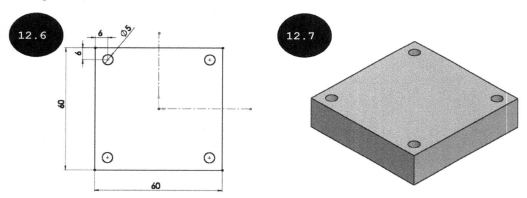

Similar to creating the base feature of a part, you can create its remaining features one after another.

9. Invoke the sketching environment again by clicking on the **Sketch** tool and select a planar face of the base feature or a plane as the sketching plane to create the second feature of the part.

10. Create the sketch of the second feature, see Figure 12.8 and then convert it into the feature by using the solid modeling tools, as discussed earlier, see Figure 12.9. Similarly you can create all the remaining features of the part one after another.

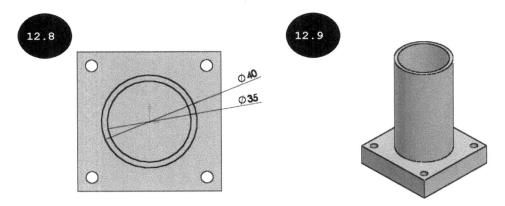

11. Once the part is created, click on the **Edit Component** tool of the **Features CommandManager**, the Assembly environment is invoked.

Note: By default, components created in the Assembly environment are fixed components and their degree of freedoms are restricted. This is because of the Inplace mate applies automatically between the plane of part and the assembly plane that is selected to position the part in the Assembly environment. You can convert a fixed part into a floating part whose all degree of freedom is free by deleting the Inplace mate. To delete a mate, expand the **Mates** node of the FeatureManager design tree and then delete the required mate from it. Also, the components fixed automatically without Inplace mate, select them and right click to display a shortcut menu. Next, select the **Float** option.

After creating the first component, you can create the second component of the assembly.

12. Click on the arrow available at the bottom of the **Insert Components** tool and then select the **New Part** tool from the flyout appears, see Figure 12.10. As soon as you click on this tool, a new empty part is added in the Assembly environment and its default name appears in the FeatureManager design tree.

13. Click anywhere in the graphics area to define the placement of the second added component.

14. Select the default name of the newly added component from the FeatureManager design tree, a Pop-up toolbar appears, see Figure 12.11.

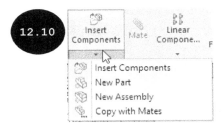

15. Click on the **Edit Part** tool from the Pop-up toolbar, the edit mode for creating the geometry of the second component is invoked. Also, the first component appears transparent so that you can take its references for creating the component features, see Figure 12.12.

16. Invoke the sketching environment by selecting a plane or a planar face of the first component and then create the sketch of the second component by taking the reference of the first component, see Figure 12.13.

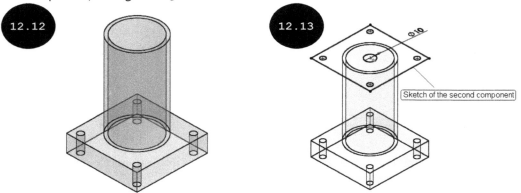

17. Convert the sketch in feature, see Figure 12.14. Similarly you can create the remaining features of the component.
18. Once all the features of the component is created, click on the **Edit Component** tool of the **Features CommandManager**, the Assembly environment is invoked and the entire assembly appears in shaded display style, see Figure 12.15.

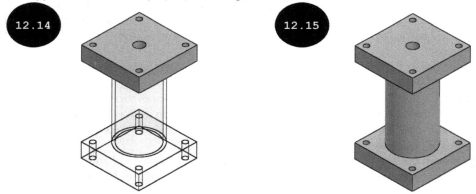

19. Similarly create the remaining components of the assembly one after another, see Figure 12.16.

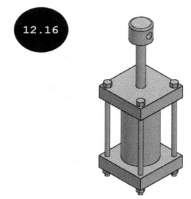

Note: By default, the components of the assembly are fixed. You can make these component floating components by deleting their respective Inplace mate applied or by selecting the **Float** option from the shortcut menu which appears on right clicking on a component. Also, a floated component can be mate as required. The method to apply mates or relations between the floating components created using the Top-Down assembly approach is same as Bottom up assembly approach.

After creating all the components of the assembly, you can save the assembly file and its individual components internally or externally in the assembly file.

20. Click on the **Save** button, the **Save Modified Documents** dialog box appears, see Figure 12.17.

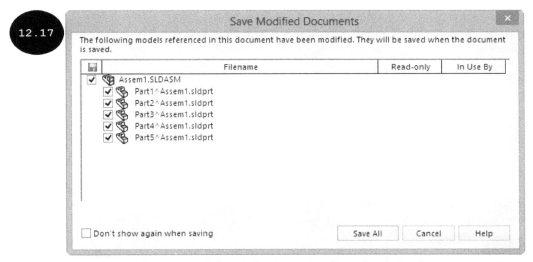

21. Click on the **Save All** button of the dialog box, the **Save As** dialog box appears, browse to the location where you want to save the assembly file and then click on the **Save** button of the dialog box. As soon as you click on the **Save** button, another **Save As** dialog box appears, see Figure 12.18.

By default, the **Save internally (inside the assembly)** radio button is selected in this dialog box. As a result, all the components of the assembly will be saved internally in the assembly file on clicking the **OK** button of the dialog box. On selecting the **Save externally (specify paths)** radio button, all components of the assembly will be saved externally as an individual component in the same folder where the assembly file is saved.

22. Select the **Save externally (specify paths)** radio button and then click on the **OK** button, all the components and the assembly file are save in the specified folder, individually.

Editing Assembly Components

In the process of creating an assembly, you may need to edit its components several time depending upon the design changes or to validate your design. Keeping this in mind, SOLIDWORKS allow you to edit the components of an assembly within the assembly environment or by opening them in the separate part modeling environment. The different method of editing assembly components are as follows.

Editing Assembly Components within the Assembly Environment

To edit the components of an assembly within the Assembly environment, select the component to edit from the graphics area or from the FeatureManager design tree, a Pop-up toolbar appears, see Figure 12.19.

In this Pop-up toolbar, click on the **Edit Part** button, the editing mode to edit the selected component is invoked, see Figure 12.20. Also, the other components of the assembly become transparent and the name of the component selected to edit appears blue in the FeatureManager design tree, see Figure 12.20.

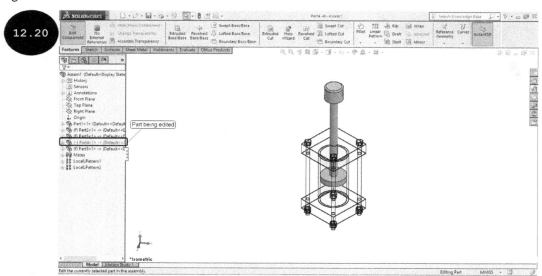

Expand the node of the component being edited in the FeatureManager design tree to list all its features, see Figure 12.21, if not expanded already. Next, select the feature to edit from the expanded node, a Pop-up toolbar appears, see Figure 12.21. Next, click on the **Edit Feature** button from the Pop-up toolbar for editing the parameters such as extrusion depth of the selected feature. If you want to edit the sketch of the selected feature, click on the **Edit Sketch** button of the Pop-up toolbar. Depending upon the option you select, you are allowed to edit the selected feature of the component. In addition to edit the existing feature of a component, you can also add features to the component in its editing mode by using the tools

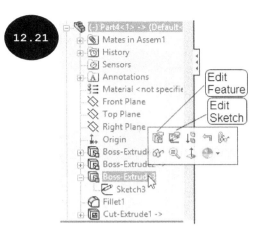

available in the **Features CommandManager**. Once all the required editing operation has been done in the component, click on the **Edit Component** tool available in the **Features CommandManager** or in the confirmation corner to exit from the editing mode and switching back to the Assembly environment.

Editing Assembly Components in Part Modeling environment

In addition to editing components of an assembly in the Assembly environment, you can also open an component to edit in the separate Part modeling environment and then perform the editing operations. To edit the component in the separate Part modeling environment, select the component to edit from the FeatureManager design tree, a Pop-up toolbar appears, see Figure 12.22. Next, select the **Open Part** button from the Pop-up toolbar, the select part opened separately the Part modeling environment. Now, you can edit the part by editing their feature parameters and the sketch of the features by using the **Edit Feature** and **Edit Sketch** buttons of the Pop-up toolbar, respectively, which appears on selecting a feature to edit. You can also add additional features to the part by using the tools available in the **Features CommandManager**.

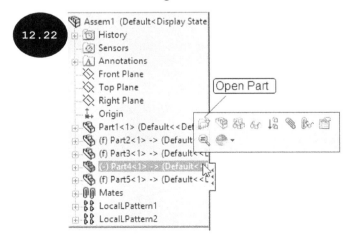

Once the editing operation has been done in a part in the Part modeling environment, save the part. Next, you need to switch to the Assembly environment. Click on the **Window >** *name of the assembly* from the SOLIDWORKS menus, the SOLIDWORKS message window appears. Click on the **Yes** button, the process of updating the assembly starts and once its done, the updated assembly appears in the Assembly environment. Note that the modification made in the part will also be reflected in the assembly.

> **Note:** In SOLIDWORKS, because of its Bi-directional associative properties, modifications made in a part in any of the environment, the same modification reflects in the other environments of SOLIDWORKS, as well.

Editing Mates

In SOLIDWORKS, you can edit the existing mates applied between the components of an assembly. To edit an existing mates, expand the **Mates** node available at the bottom of FeatureManager design tree, see Figure 12.23. The **Mates** node contain the list of all the mates applied between the components.

Select the mate to edit from the expanded **Mates** node. As soon as you select a mate, a Pop-up toolbar appears, see Figure 12.24. Also, the geometries between which the selected mate is applied are highlighted in the graphics area. Select the **Edit Feature** tool from the Pop-up toolbar, a PropertyManager appears depending upon the type of mate being edited. By using options of this PropertyManager, you can replace the existing selected geometry between the mate is applied with the new geometries. You can also change the type of mate, type of alignment, or so on by using the options of the PropertyManager. Once the editing is done, click on the green tick mark of the PropertyManager to accept the change.

12.23

Assem1 (Default<Display State-1>)
- History
- Sensors
- Annotations
- Front Plane
- Top Plane
- Right Plane
- Origin
- Part1<1> (Default<<Default>_Display
- Part2<1> -> (Default<<Default>_Displ
- (-) Part3<1> -> (Default<<Default>_Di
- (-) Part4<1> -> (Default<<Default>_Di
- (-) Part5<1> -> (Default<<Default>_Di
- (-) Part3<5> -> (Default<<Default>_Di
- (-) Part3<6> -> (Default<<Default>_Di
- (-) Part3<7> -> (Default<<Default>_Di
- (-) Part5<5> -> (Default<<Default>_Di
- (-) Part5<6> -> (Default<<Default>_Di
- (-) Part5<7> -> (Default<<Default>_Di
- Mates
  - InPlace1 (Part1<1>,Top Plane)
  - Concentric1 (Part2<1>,Part4<1>)
  - Concentric2 (Part2<1>,Part3<1>)
  - Coincident1 (Part2<1>,Part3<1>)
  - Concentric3 (Part3<1>,Part5<1>)
  - Coincident2 (Part1<1>,Part5<1>)
  - Concentric4 (Part1<1>,Part2<1>)

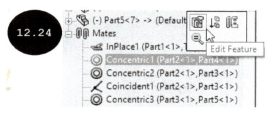

12.24

- (-) Part5<7> -> (Default
- Mates
  - InPlace1 (Part1<1>,
  - Concentric1 (Part2<1>,Part4<1>)   Edit Feature
  - Concentric2 (Part2<1>,Part3<1>)
  - Coincident1 (Part2<1>,Part3<1>)
  - Concentric3 (Part3<1>,Part5<1>)

Patterning Assembly Components

Similar to pattern features of a part in the Part modeling environment and create its multiple instances, you can pattern components of an assembly in Assembly environment, see Figure 12.25.

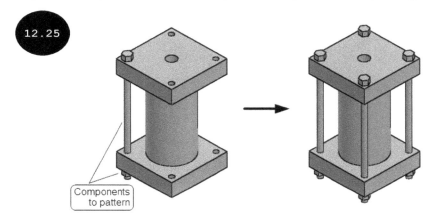

12.25

Components to pattern

In Assembly environment, you can create different type of patterns by using the **Linear Component Pattern**, **Circular Component Pattern**, **Sketch Driven Component Pattern**, **Curve Driven Component Pattern**, and **Pattern Driven Component Pattern** tools available in the **Pattern** flyout of the **Assembly CommandManager**, see Figure 12.26. The method of created linear pattern, circular pattern, sketch driven pattern, and curve driven pattern by using their respective tool is same as discussed while creating patterns in the Part modeling environment with the only difference that in Part modeling environment, you pattern features to create its multiple instances however in Assembly environment, you pattern components or parts to create its multiple instances. The method of creating remaining patterns are as follows.

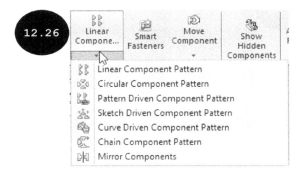

12.26

Creating Pattern Driven Pattern

The **Pattern Driven Component Pattern** is very effective tool of patterning a component in an assembly with respect to the pattern feature of other component. In this type of pattern, the component to pattern in the assembly drives by the pattern feature of the other component of the assembly. Figure 12.27 shows an assembly with three components: Component 1, Component 2, and Component 3. The Component 3 is the component to pattern with respect to the pattern feature of Component 2. Figure 12.28 shows the resultant assembly after patterning the component by using the **Pattern Driven Component Pattern** tool available in the **Pattern** flyout.

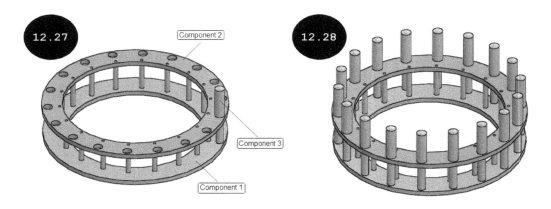

In Figures 12.28, the pattern created is driven by the pattern feature of the Component 2. As a result, on modifying the pattern instances of the Component 2, the number of instances of the pattern component will also be modified automatically.

Note: The pattern driven pattern can only be created, if the driving feature is a pattern feature. On modifying the instances of the driving feature, the driven pattern instances will also be modified in the assembly environment.

To create to pattern driven pattern, invoke the Pattern flyout, see Figure 12.26 and then click on the **Pattern Driven Component Pattern** tool, the **Pattern Driven PropertyManager** appears, see Figure 12.29. The options of this PropertyManager are as follows.

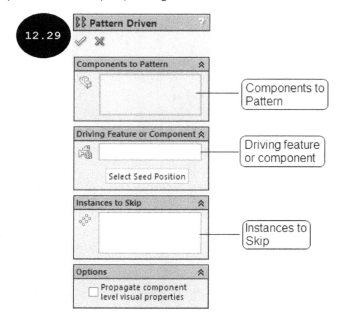

Components to Pattern

The Components to Pattern field is used to select component to pattern. By default, this field is activated.

Driving feature or component

The Driving feature or component field is used to select a pattern instance of a component as the driving feature, see Figure 12.30. To select a pattern instance, click on this field to activate it and then select the pattern instance. After selecting the component to pattern and a pattern instance, the preview of the driving feature appears in the graphics area, see Figure 12.31.

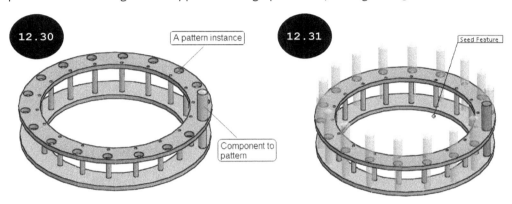

12.30   A pattern instance   Component to pattern

12.31   Seed Feature

Note: By default, the position of the parent component is taken as the position of the seed pattern instance of the pattern being created. You can change the position of the seed pattern instance other than the default position. To change the position of the seed pattern instance, click on the **Select Seed Position** button of the **Driving Feature or Component** rollout, blue dots appears in the preview of the pattern instances. You can click on a blue dot of an pattern instance to select it as the position of the seed pattern instance of the pattern being created, as required.

Instances to Skip

The Instances to Skip field is used to select pattern instances to skip. To select instances to skip, click on this field to activate it. As soon as you activate this field, pink dots appears on each pattern instances, see Figure 12.32. Move the cursor on the instance to skip and then click to skip it.

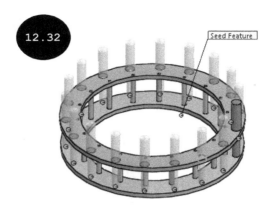

Procedure to Create Pattern Driven Pattern

1. Invoke the Pattern flyout.
2. Click on the **Pattern Driven Component Pattern** tool.
3. Select the component to pattern.
4. Click on the **Driving feature or component** field to activate it and then select a pattern instance of a component as the driving feature.
5. If required, you can skip the pattern instances by activating the **Instances to Skip** field.
6. Click on the green tick mark ✅ button of the PropertyManager, the driven pattern is created.

Creating Chain Component Pattern

The **Chain Component Pattern** is very effective and powerful tool of patterning a component along an open or closed path to dynamically simulate a chain drive or cable carrier in an assembly, see Figure 12.33.

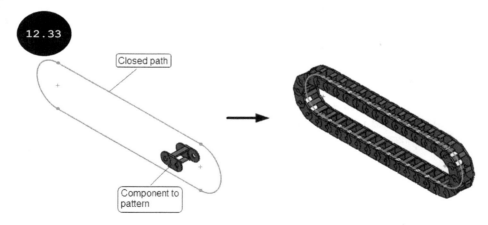

In this type of pattern, the component drives along an open or closed path such that you can dynamically simulate its motion by dragging the pattern instances created. To create to chain driven pattern, invoke the **Pattern** flyout, see Figure 12.34 and then click on the **Chain Driven Component Pattern** tool, the **Chain Pattern PropertyManager** appears, see Figure 12.35.

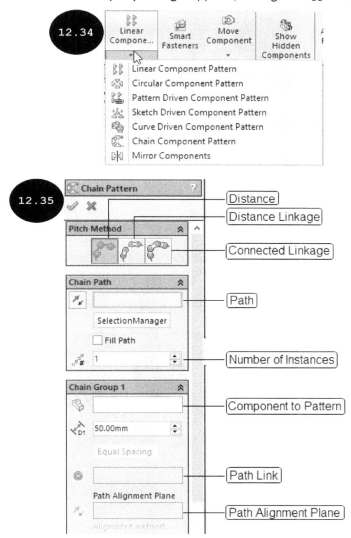

The **Chain Pattern PropertyManager** allows you to create three types of chain patterns: Distance, Distance Linkage, and Connected Linkage. The Distance chain pattern is used to patterns a component with a single link along a chain path. The Distance Linkage chain pattern is used to pattern a component with two unconnected links along a chain path. The Connected Linkage chain pattern is used to pattern component with connected links along a chain path. The procedure to create these chain patterns are as follows.

Procedure to Create Distance Chain Pattern

1.   Invoke the **Chain Pattern PropertyManager** flyout.
2.   Make sure the **Distance** button is selected in the **Pitch Method** rollout.
3.   Click on the **SelectionManager** button of the **Chain Path** rollout, the **Selection** toolbar appears, see Figure 12.36.

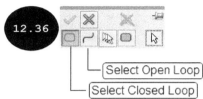

4.   Depending upon the type of path (open or close), select the **Select Open Loop** or **Select Closed Loop** button from the **Selection** toolbar.
5.   Click to select the path from the graphics area, see Figure 12.37. Next, click on the green tick mark ☑ of the **Selection** toolbar, the path is selected.
6.   Select the **Fill Path** check box from the **Chain Path** rollout to fill the path with pattern instances or specify the number of instances to create along the path in the **Number of Instances** filed.
7.   Click on the **Component to Pattern** field of the **Chain Group 1** rollout to active it.
8.   Select the component from the graphics area as the component to pattern, see Figure 12.37.
9.   Click on the **Path Link** field of the **Chain Group 1** rollout to active it, if not activated.
10.   Select an cylindrical face, circular edge, linear edge, or reference axis as the path link from the graphics area, see Figure 12.37.
11.   Select a plane or planar face as the path alignment plane, the preview appears, see Figure 12.38.
12.   Specify the spacing between the pattern instances in the **Spacing** field.

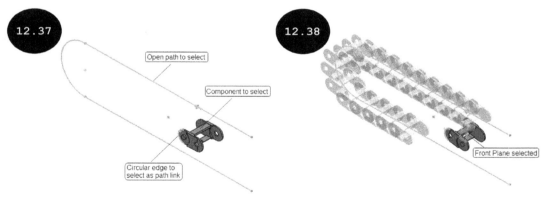

13.   Click on the green tick mark ☑ button of the PropertyManager, the chain driven pattern is created, see Figure 12.39.

Note: In Figure 12.39, the chain driven pattern is created by specifying 18 number of pattern instances.

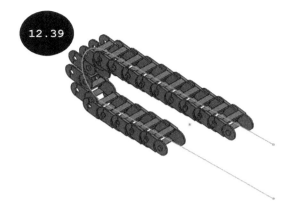

Procedure to Create Distance Linkage Chain Pattern

1. Invoke the **Chain Pattern PropertyManager** flyout.
2. Click to select the **Distance Linkage** button of the **Pitch Method** rollout.
3. Select the open or close path from the graphics area with the help of **SelectionManager** button of the **Chain Path** rollout, see Figure 12.40.
4. Specify the number of pattern instances to create along the path in the **Number of Instances** filed or select the **Fill Path** check box to fill the path with pattern instances.
5. Click on the **Component to Pattern** field of the **Chain Group** 1 rollout to active it.
6. Select the component from the graphics area as the component to pattern.
7. Click on the **Path Link** 1 field of the **Chain Group** 1 rollout to active it, if not activated.
8. Select an cylindrical face, circular edge, linear edge, or reference axis as the path link 1 from the graphics area, see Figure 12.40.
9. Select an cylindrical face, circular edge, linear edge, or reference axis as the path link 2 from the graphics area, see Figure 12.40.
10. Select a plane or planar face as the path alignment plane, see Figure 12.40, the preview appears, see Figure 12.41.

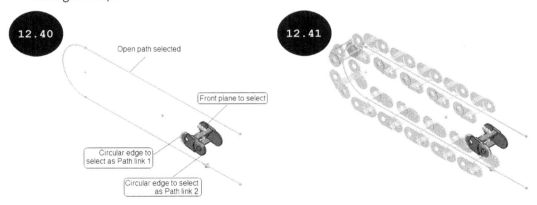

11. Specify the spacing between the pattern instances in the **Spacing** field.
12. Click on the green tick mark button of the PropertyManager, the distance linkage chain pattern is created, see Figure 12.42.

Note: In the **Options** rollout of the **Chain Pattern PropertyManager**, the **Dynamic** radio button is selected by default, see Figure 12.43. As a result, you can drag any pattern instance to move the chain. On selecting the **Static** radio button, you can move the chain only by dragging the parent/seed component. Selecting the **Static** radio button improves performance in large assemblies.

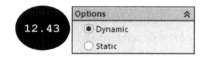

Procedure to Create Connected Linkage Chain Pattern

1. Invoke the **Chain Pattern PropertyManager** flyout. Connected linkage chain pattern
2. Click to select the **Connected Linkage** button of the **Pitch Method** rollout.
3. Select the open or close path from the graphics area with the help of **SelectionManager** button of the **Chain Path** rollout, see Figure 12.44.
4. Specify the number of pattern instances to create along the path in the **Number of Instances** filed or select the **Fill Path** check box to fill the path with pattern instances.
5. Click on the **Component to Pattern** field of the **Chain Group 1** rollout to active it.
6. Select the component from the graphics area as the component to pattern.
7. Click on the **Path Link 1** field of the **Chain Group 1** rollout to active it, if not activated.
8. Select an cylindrical face, circular edge, linear edge, or reference axis as the path link 1 from the graphics area, see Figure 12.44.
9. Select an cylindrical face, circular edge, linear edge, or reference axis as the path link 2 from the graphics area, see Figure 12.44.
10. Select a plane or planar face as the path alignment plane, see Figure 12.44, the preview appears, see Figure 12.45. If the pattern preview does not appears in the graphics area, you need to reverse the direction of pattern creation by clicking on the arrow appears along the path in the graphics area.

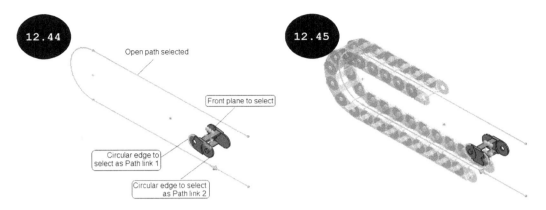

11. Click on the green tick mark ✅ button of the PropertyManager, the connected linkage chain pattern is created, see Figure 12.46.

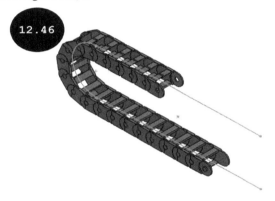

Note: In the **Options** rollout of the **Chain Pattern PropertyManager**, the **Dynamic** radio button is selected by default. As a result, you can drag any pattern instance to move the chain. On selecting the **Static** radio button, you can move the chain only by dragging the parent/seed component. Selecting the **Static** radio button improves performance in large assemblies.

Mirroring Components

Similar to mirroring features in Part modeling environment, you can also mirror components in the Assembly environment by using the **Mirror Components** tool of the **Pattern** flyout, see Figure 12.47.

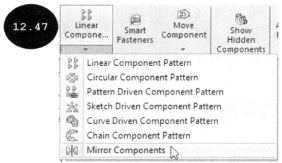

To mirror components of an assembly, invoke the **Pattern** flyout and then click on the **Mirror Components** tool, the **Mirror Components PropertyManager** appears, see Figure 12.48. The options of this PropertyManager are as follows.

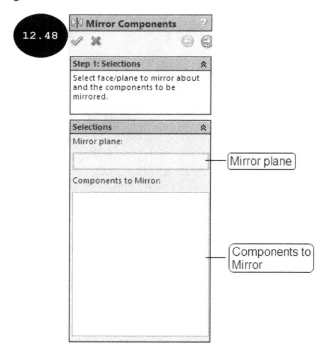

Mirror plane

The **Mirror plane** field is used to select a mirroring plane about which you want to mirror selected components of an assembly. By default, this field is activated. As a result, you can select a planar face or a reference plane as the mirroring plane, see Figure 12.49.

Components to Mirror

The **Components to Mirror** field is used to select components to mirror about the mirroring plane. This field activates as soon as you select the mirroring plane. You can also activate this field by clicking on it and then select components to mirror from the graphics area or from the FeatureManager design tree, see Figure 12.49.

After selecting the mirroring plane and component to mirror, click on the green tick mark ✅ of the PropertyManager, the selected component is mirrored, see Figure 12.50.

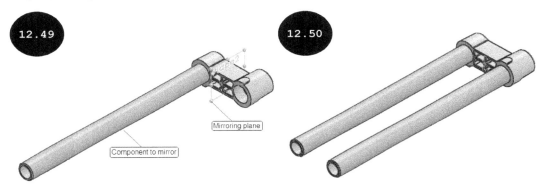

Procedure to Mirror Components

1. Invoke the Pattern flyout.
2. Click on the **Mirror Components** tool, the **Mirror Components PropertyManager** appears.
3. Select a plane or planar face as the mirroring plane.
4. Select components to mirror about the selected mirroring plane.
5. Click on the green tick mark ✅ button of the PropertyManager, the mirror image of the selected components is created.

Creating Assembly Features

In manufacturing, several cut operations may take place after assembling all the components together in order to give final touchup and to align components perfectly with respect to each other. By keeping this in mind, SOLIDWORKS also provides you tools for creating cut feature in the Assembly environment. These cut features are known as assembly features. Note that the assembly features created in the Assembly environment will not actually affect the original geometry of any component. For example, if you create an assembly feature on a component of the assembly in the Assembly environment, the created assembly feature exists only in the assembly and if you open the same component in the Part modeling environment, you will not find the existence of the assembly feature. It indicate It means that the assembly features exists in the assembly only and will not affects the original geometry of any component.

In SOLIDWORKS, you can create assembly features such as holes, extruded cut, revolved cut, swept cut, and fillets. The tools to create assembly features are provided in the **Assembly Features** flyout, see Figure 12.51. This flyout can be invoked on clicking the arrow available at the bottom of the **Assembly Features** tool of the **Assembly CommandManager**. The procedure to create assembly features are same as creating the features in the Part modeling environment. For your ready reference, to create extruded cut feature, click on the **Extruded Cut** tool of the **Assembly Features** flyout, the **Extrude PropertyManager** appears. Select a plane or planar face as the sketching plane, the Sketching environment is invoked. Create the sketch of the extruded cut feature and then exit from the Sketching environment. As soon as you exit from the Sketching environment, the preview of the cut feature appears in the graphics area. Specify the required parameters of extrusion in the PropertyManager and then click on the green tick mark, the extruded cut feature is created in the Assembly environment.

Suppressing or Unsuppressing Components

In SOLIDWORKS, you can suppress or unsuppress components of an assembly. A suppressed component removed from the assembly and will not appears in the graphics area. Also, the name of the suppressed component appears in gray color in the FeatureManager design tree. Note that the suppressed component is not deleted, it only removes from the assembly display and RAM (random access memory) which helps you in speedup the performance of the system when you are working with large assemblies.

To suppress a component of an assembly, select the component to suppress from the graphics area or from the FeatureManager design tree, a Pop-up toolbar appears, see Figure 12.52. Click on the **Suppress** tool available in this Pop-up toolbar, see Figure 12.52, the selected component is suppressed.

To unsuppressed the suppressed component, select the suppressed component from the FeatureManager design tree, a Pop-up toolbar appears. Click on the **Unsuppress** tool, the component is now unsuppressed and appears in the assembly.

Inserting Parts having Multiple Configurations

In SOLIDWORKS, you can insert parts/components in the Assembly environment having multiple configurations. To insert components having multiple configurations in the Assembly environment, click on the **Insert Components** tool, the **Insert Component PropertyManager** appears. Click on the **Browse** button available in the **Part/Assembly to Insert** rollout of the PropertyManager, the **Open** dialog box appears. Browse to the location where the component to insert is saved. Next, select the component having multiple configuration to insert in the Assembly environment and then invoke the **Configurations** drop-down list of the **Open** dialog box, see Figure 12.53. Now, select the required configuration of the component to insert from this drop-down list. Next, click on the **Open** button of the dialog box, the selected configuration of the component is attached with the cursor. Now, click in the graphics area to specify the position of the component, the selection configuration of the component is inserted in the Assembly environment.

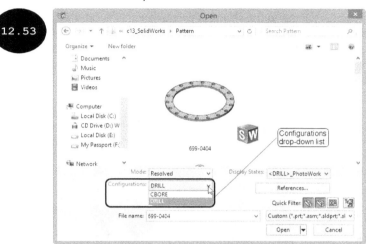

Note: In SOLIDWORKS, you can create multiple configuration of a component in the Part modeling environment. For example, if a bolt of same geometry has to be used in an assembly several time with minor change in its diameter, you can create a single bolt with multiple configuration of different diameters instead of creating multiple bolts with different diameters.

You can also change the configuration of a component even after inserting it in the Assembly environment. To change the configuration of an already inserted component, select the component from the assembly environment whose configuration has to change, a Pop-up toolbar appears with **Configuration** drop-down list, see Figure 12.54. Invoke the **Configuration** drop-down list by clicking on its down arrow. Next, select the required configuration of the component and then click on the green tick mark to confirm the selection, the configuration of the component changed to the selected configuration.

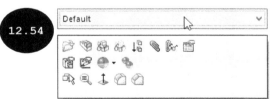

Creating and Dissolve Sub-Assemblies

SOLIDWORKS allows you to create sub-assemblies from the components of the assembly within the Assembly environment. To create sub-assemblies, select components to be included in the sub-assembly from the FeatureManager design tree by pressing the CTRL key and then right click, a shortcut menu appears. Expand the shortcut menu by clicking on the down arrows available at its bottom. Next, click on the **Form New Subassembly** option from the expanded shortcut menu, see Figure 12.55. As soon as you select this option, a sub-assembly is created with default name and the selected components become the part of the sub-assembly. You can rename the default name of the sub-assembly by selecting the sub-assembly from the FeatureManager design tree and then press the F2 key.

You can also dissolved the created sub-assembly. To dissolved sub-assembly, select the sub-assembly to dissolved from the FeatureManager design tree and then right click to display a shortcut menu, see Figure 12.56. Next, click the **Dissolve Subassembly** option the shortcut menu, the selected sub-assembly is dissolved and its components become individual components of the main assembly.

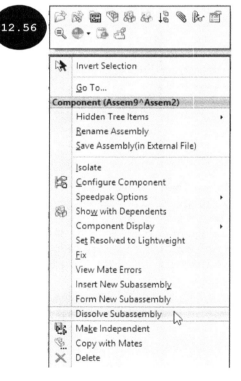

Creating Exploded View

Creating exploded view of an assembly is important from the presentation point of view. By creating exploded view of an assembly, you can easily identify the position of each component of an assembly with respect to other components. Also, it helps you to make technical documentation, technical and non technical clients understand easily about various components of the assembly, components positions, and way components have been assembled with each other. Figure 12.57 shows an assembly and Figure 12.58 shows the exploded view of the assembly.

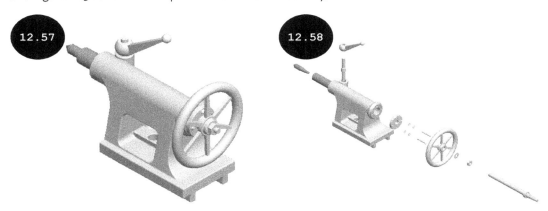

In SOLIDWORKS, you can create an exploded view of an assembly by using the **Exploded View** tool of the **Assembly CommandManager**. To create exploded view of an assembly, click on the **Exploded View** tool, see Figure 12.59, the **Explode PropertyManager** appears, see Figure 12.60. The options of this PropertyManager are as follows.

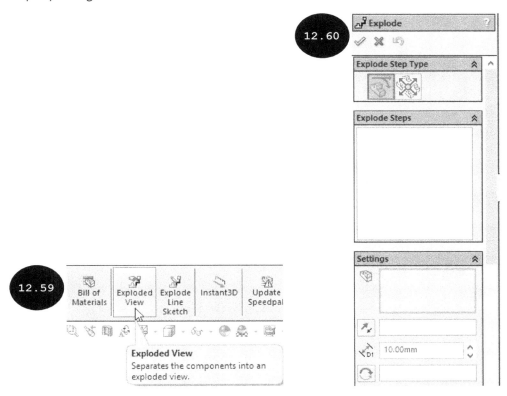

Explode Step Type

The **Explode Step Type** rollout of the PropertyManager allows you to choose the type of exploded step: Regular and Radial to be created by clicking on their respective button. The buttons available in this rollout are as follows.

Regular Step

On activating the **Regular Step** button of the **Explode Step Type** rollout, you can explode components of the assembly by translating and rotating them along and about an axis, see Figure 12.61.

Radial Step

On activating the **Radial Step** button, you can explode components of the assembly by aligning them radially or cylindrically about an axis, see Figure 12.62.

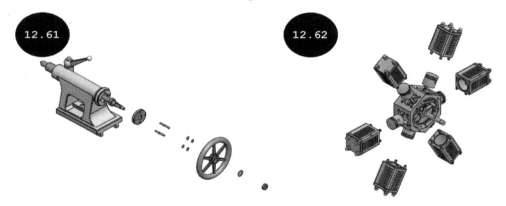

Explode Steps

The **Explode Steps** rollout displays the list of all the exploded steps created for creating an exploded assembly, see Figure 12.63. Note that to create an exploded assembly, you may need to create multiple exploded steps (regular and radial steps). In each exploded step, one or more then one component can explode. You can create exploded steps by using the options of the **Settings** rollout of the PropertyManager and are as follows.

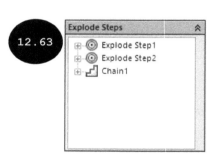

Settings

The options available in the **Settings** rollout are used to create exploded steps. Note that the options of this rollouts depends upon the button (**Regular step** or **Radial step**) selected in the **Explode Step Type** rollout. Figures 12.64 shows the **Settings** rollout when the **Regular step** button is selected. The options of the **Settings** rollout are as follows.

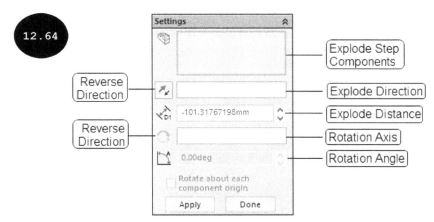

Explode Step Components

The **Explode Step Components** field is used to select components of an assembly to explode in a exploded step. You can select one or more than one components at a time from the graphics area. By default, this field is activated. Note that as soon as you select components to explode, the three rotation and three translation handles appears in the graphics area, see Figure 12.65. Note that these handles (three rotation and three translation) appears in case of creating regular exploded view. If you are creating radial exploded view, on selecting the set of components to explode, a rotation and a translation handle appears in the graphics area, see Figure 12.66.

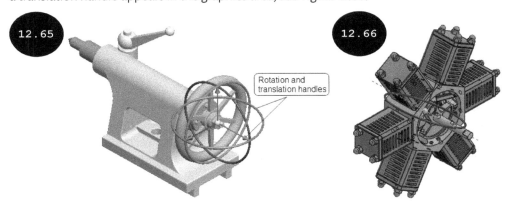

You can drag a required rotation or translation handle for create the first exploded step. The translation handles are used for translating selected components along the direction of respective translation handle. By using the rotation handles, you can rotate selected components about the axis of respective rotation handle. Note that the rotation handles appears while creating the regular exploded view only when the **Auto-spac components on drag** check box is cleared and the **Show rotation rings** check is selected in the **Options** rollout of the PropertyManager.

Note: The regular exploded view is created by translating and rotating components along and about an axis and the radial exploded view is created by aligning components radially or cylindrically about an axis.

> **Tip:** For translation movement, move the cursor over a translation handle, as required and then drag it, the selected component start translating along the direction of translation handle. Once the desired location has been achieved, stop dragging the handle. As soon as you stop dragging the handle, the first explode step is created and is appears in the **Explode Steps** rollout.
>
> For rotational movement, move the cursor over a rotation handle and then drag it, the selected component start rotating about the axis of rotational handle. On achieving the desired location, stop dragging the handle, a exploded step is created.

Explode Direction

The **Explode Direction** field displays the translational direction along which selected components translates. The display of exploded direction in this field depends upon the translation handle selected.

Explode Distance

The **Explode Distance** field displays the translation distance on translating selected components using the translation handle. You can also enter the translation distance for translating selected components in this field instead of dragging the translation handle. Note that after entering the translation distance in this field, you need to click on the **Apply** button and then **Done** button of the **Settings** rollout.

Rotation Axis

The **Rotation Axis** field displays the rotational axis about which selected components are to be rotated. The display of rotational axis in this field depends upon the rotation handle selected.

Rotation Angle

The **Rotation Angle** field displays the rotational angle on rotating selected components using the rotation handle. You can also enter the rotational angle for rotating selected components in this field instead of dragging the rotation handle. Note that after entering the rotational angle in this field, you need to click on the **Apply** button and then **Done** button.

Rotate about each component origin

On selecting the **Rotate about each component origin** check box, the selected components rotate about the component origin. This check box is available only when the **Regular Step** button is activated in the **Explode Step Type** rollout of the PropertyManager.

Diverge from axis

On selecting the **Diverge from axis** check box, the selected components exploded away from the axis. This check box is available only when the **Radial Step** button is activated in the **Explode Step Type** rollout of the PropertyManager.

Apply

The **Apply** button is used to display the preview of the exploded step.

Done

The **Done** button is used to accept the preview of the exploded step and create an exploded step.

Options

The options available in the **Options** rollout are shown in Figure 12.67 and are as follows. Note that the options of this rollouts depends upon the button (**Regular step** or **Radial step**) selected in the **Explode Step Type** rollout. Figures 12.67 shows the **Settings** rollout when the **Regular step** button is selected.

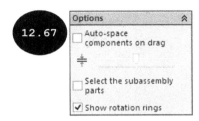

Auto-space components on drag

The **Auto-space components on drag** check box is used to translate or rotate group of selected components in equal spacing automatically on exploding along or about selected handle direction. Note that the equal spacing for exploding group of selected components, automatically, can be adjusted by using the **Adjust the spacing between chain components** slider.

Adjust the spacing between chain components

The **Adjust the spacing between chain components** slider is used to adjust auto spacing between the group of selected components for exploding automatically in a chain.

Show rotation rings

By default, the **Show rotation rings** check box is selected. As a result, the rotation rings appears in the graphics area on selecting components to explode. If you clear this check box, the display of rotation rings disabled.

Select the subassembly's parts

On selecting the **Select the subassembly's parts** check box, you can select individual components of an subassembly to explode. If this check box is cleared, you can select entire subassembly to explode. This check box is available only when the **Radial Step** button is activated in the **Explode Step Type** rollout of the PropertyManager.

Reuse Subassembly Explode

The **Reuse Subassembly Explode** button allows you to use the existing exploded steps created in the selected subassembly.

Note: By default, selected components can only explode along the X, Y, and Z axis by using the handles appears in the graphics area. To translate component other than X, Y, and Z axis, move the cursor over a translation handle appears in the graphics area and then right click, a shortcut menu appears, see Figure 12.68. Click on the **Align with selection** option. Next, select a linear edge of an component to align the selected handle along its. As soon as you select an edge for alignment, the selected handle aligns with respect to the selected linear edge. Now, drag the aligned handle to translate components along the direction of aligned handle.

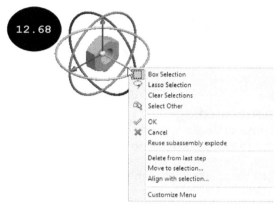

Procedure to Create Regular Exploded View

1. Click on the **Exploded View** tool, the **Explode PropertyManager** appears.
2. Make sure that **Regular step** button is selected in the **Explode Step Type** rollout.
3. Select a set of components to explode as the first regular exploded step.
4. Select a set of components to explode as the first regular exploded step.
5. Select the **Auto-space components on drag** check box from the **Options** rollout, if you want to translate or rotate selected set of components in equal spacing automatically with respect to each other. Make sure this check box is cleared if you want to translate or rotate selected set of components as a single unit.
6. Select a translation or a rotation handle and then drag the cursor to a distance in order to create first exploded step. You can also enter the translation distance or rotational angle to explode the selected components in their respective fields of the **Settings** rollout instead of dragging the handle.
7. Similarly, select the other sets of components and then create other exploded steps.
8. Click on the green tick mark ✅ button of the PropertyManager, the exploded view of the assembly is created.

Procedure to Create Radial Exploded View

1. Click on the **Exploded View** tool, the **Explode PropertyManager** appears.
2. Make sure that **Radial step** button is selected in the **Explode Step Type** rollout.
3. Select a set of components to explode as a first exploded step, see Figure 12.69.
4. Click to activate the **Explode Direction** field of the **Settings** rollout and then click to select a cylindrical face, linear edge, or axis to define the exploded direction, see Figure 12.69.

5. Select the translation or the rotation handle appears in the graphics area and then drag the cursor to a distance for creating first radial exploded step, see Figure 12.70. You can also enter the translation distance or rotational angle to explode the selected components in their respective fields of the **Settings** rollout instead of dragging the handle.
6. Similarly, select the other sets of components and then create other exploded steps.
7. Click on the green tick mark ✅ button of the PropertyManager, the exploded view of the assembly is created.

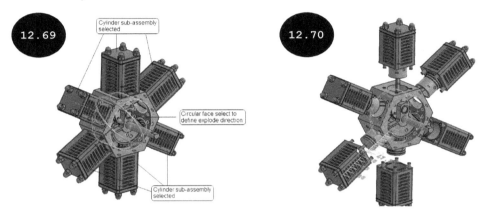

Note: You can also create exploded view by creating combination of regular and radial exploded steps.

Collapsing Exploded View

After creating the exploded view of an assembly, you can restore assembly components back to their original positions by collapsing the exploded view. To collapse the exploded view, select the name of the assembly from the FeatureManager design tree and then right click, a shortcut menu appears, see Figure 12.71. Select the **Collapse** option, the exploded view of the assembly is collapsed.

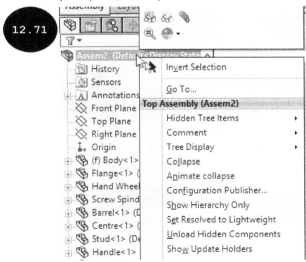

After displaying the collapse view, you can again display the exploded view. To display the exploded view of an assembly, again select the name of the assembly from the FeatureManager design tree and then right click to display a shortcut menu. Next, select the **Explode** option from the shortcut menu.

Animating Exploded View

In SOLIDWORKS, after creating the exploded view, you can animate the components of the assembly to display its collapsed and exploded views, respectively. To animate the collapsed or exploded view of an assembly, select the name of the assembly in the FeatureManager design tree and right click to display the shortcut menu, see Figure 12.71. Next, select the **Animate collapse** or **Animate explode** option from the shortcut menu, the components start animating and the **Animation Controller** toolbar appears, see Figure 12.72. By using the tools available in this toolbar, you can control the animation. You can also record the animation and save it as an *.avi, .bmp*, and *.tga* file.

Note: The display of the **Animate collapse** or **Animate explode** option in the shortcut menu depends upon the current display state of the assembly. If the assembly appears in its exploded view in the graphics area then the **Animate collapse** option display in the shortcut menu. If the assembly appears in its collapsed view then the **Animate explode** option displays in the shortcut menu.

Editing Exploded View

You can edit the existing created exploded view of an assembly and make the necessary modifications by editing the existing exploded steps and creating new exploded steps. To edit the existing exploded view, invoke the **ConfigurationManager** by clicking on the **ConfigurationManager** tab, see Figure 12.73. The **ConfigurationManager** displays the list of assembly configuration's created. Figure 12.73 shows the default configuration (**Default [Assem2]**) of the assembly. Expand the configuration of the assembly by clicking on the +sign appears on its left, see Figure 12.74.

Figure 12.74 shows two exploded views created (**ExplView1** and **ExplView2**) and the **ExplView1** is activated. You can activate the required exploded view by double clicking on its name. To edit the exploded view, select the exploded view to exit and then right click to display a shortcut menu, see Figure 12.75. Next, select the **Edit Feature** option from the shortcut menu, the **Explode**

PropertyManager appears. Now, by using the options of the PropertyManager, you can edit the exploded view as required.

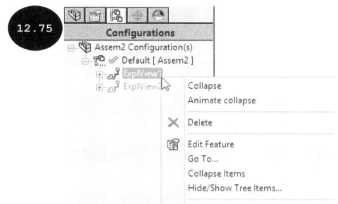

Adding Explode Lines in an Exploded View

After creating the exploded view of an assembly, you can add exploded lines. Figure 12.76 shows an assembly and Figure 12.77 shows a exploded view of the assembly with explode lines.

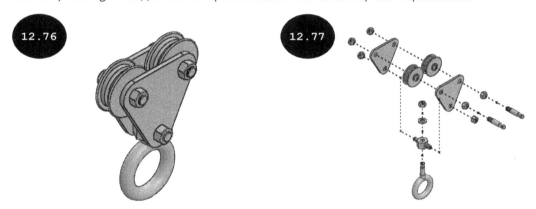

The exploded lines are used to show relationships between components in the exploded view. You can create exploded lines in an exploded view by using the **Explode Line Sketch** tool of the **Assembly CommandManager**. The procedure to created exploded lines to an exploded view of an assembly is as follows.

Procedure to Create Exploded Lines

1. Click on the **Explode Line Sketch** tool, the **Route Line PropertyManager** appears, see Figure 12.78.
2. Select faces, circular edges, straight edges, or planar faces of the components have same assembly line one after another to connect them with a single route line.
3. Select the **Reverse** check box to reverse the direction of route line, if required. Also, you can select the **Alternate Path** check box to see the alternate route between the selection set.
4. Click on the green tick mark ✅ button of the PropertyManager, a sketched route line is created which represent their assembly line.

5. Similarly, create route lines for remaining set of components having same assembly line.
6. Once you are done with creating all exploded sketch lines, exit from the PropertyManager.

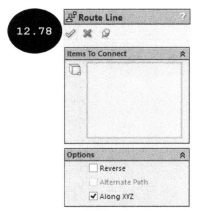

Creating Bill of Material (BOM) in an Assembly

A BOM is one of the important feature of any drawing which contains the information related to number of components, material, quantity, and so on. In addition to creating BOM in drawings, SOLIDWORKS also allow you to create BOM in the Assembly environment. You will learn about creating BOM in drawings in the later chapter. To create BOM in Assembly environment, click on the **Bill of Materials** tool available in the **Assembly CommandManager**, the **Bill of Materials PropertyManager** appears, see Figure 12.79. Accept the default parameters specified in the PropertyManager for creating BOM by clicking on the green tick mark of the PropertyManager. As soon as you click on the green tick mark of the PropertyManager, the BOM is attached with the cursor. Note that as you move the cursor, the BOM moves accordingly in the graphics area. Now you need to specify the location for the BOM in the Assembly environment. Click in the graphics area, the BOM is placed on the specified location, see Figure 12.80.

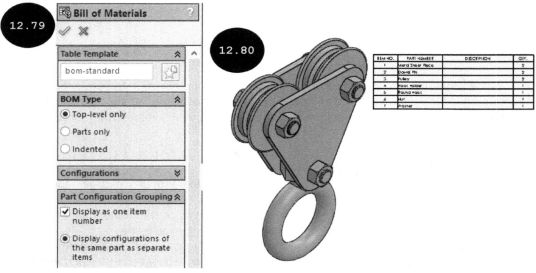

Tutorial 1

Create the assembly shown in Figure 12.81 by using the Top-down approach. Different views and dimensions of individual components of the assembly are shown in Figure 12.82.

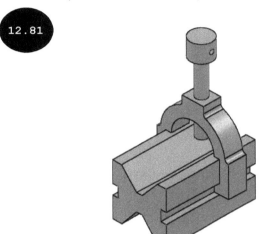

12.81

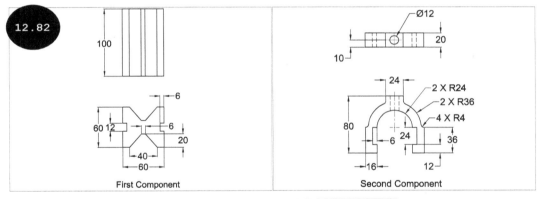

12.82

First Component

Second Component

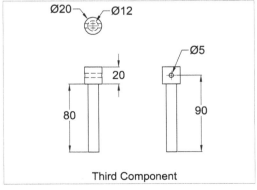

Third Component

Section 1: Starting SOLIDWORKS

1. Double click on the **SOLIDWORKS** icon on your desktop to start SOLIDWORKS.

Section 2: Invoking Assembly Environment

1. Click on the **New** tool in the **Standard** toolbar, the **New SOLIDWORKS Document** dialog box appears.

2. In this dialog box, click on the **Assembly** button to activated it. Next, click on the **OK** button, the assembly environment is invoked with the display of **Begin Assembly PropertyManager**.

Section 3: Creating First Component of the Assembly

1. Close the **Begin Assembly PropertyManager** by clicking on the red cross mark available at its top.

2. Click on the arrow available at the bottom of the **Insert Components** tool, a flyout appears, see Figure 12.83.

3. In this flyout, click on the **New Part** tool, a new part is added in the Assembly environment and appears in the FeatureManager design tree with its default name, see Figure 12.84. Also, a green color tick mark appears attached with the cursor in the graphics area. As a result, you are prompted to select a face or plane as the placement plane to position the newly added component.

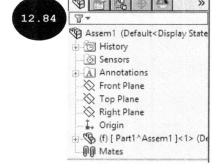

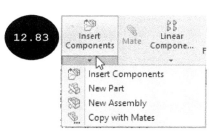

4. Click anywhere in the graphics area to define the position of the first component with respect to the origin of the assembly.

5. Click to select the newly added component from the FeatureManager design tree, a Pop-up toolbar appears, see Figure 12.85.

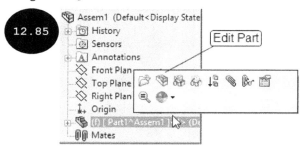

6. Click on the **Edit Part** tool of the Pop-up toolbar, the Part modeling environment invoked.

7. Click on the **Extruded Boss/Base** tool of the **Features CommandManager**, the **Extrude PropertyManager** appears.

8. Expand the FeatureManager design tree available at the top left corner of the graphics area and then expand the **Part 1** node of the FeatureManager design tree which appears in blue color, see Figure 12.86.

9. Click to select the Front Plane as the sketching plane from the FeatureManager design tree, the sketching environment invoked.

10. Change the orientation of the model normal to the viewing direction.

11. Click on the **Sketch** tab of the CommandManager to display the tools of the **Sketch CommandManager**.

12. Create the sketch of the first/base component of the assembly, see Figure 12.87.

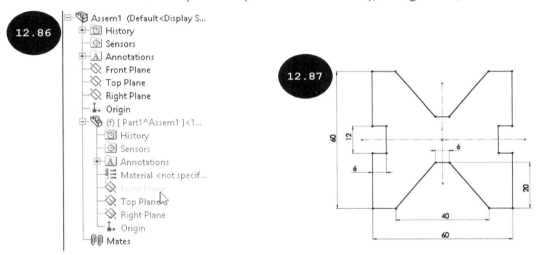

13. Exit from the Sketching environment by clicking on the **Exit Sketch** tool of the **Sketch CommandManager**, the preview of the extruded feature appears in the graphics area.

14. Change the orientation of the model to isometric.

15. Invoke the **End Condition** drop-down list of the **Direction 1** rollout of the **Boss-Extrude PropertyManager** and then click to select the **Mid Plane** option from it.

16. Enter **100** in the **Depth** field of the **Direction 1** rollout.

17. Click on the green tick mark ✓ of the PropertyManager, the base component is created, see Figure 12.88.

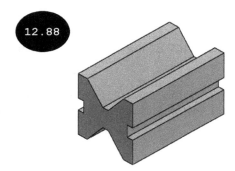

18. Click on the **Edit Component** tool of the CommandManager to exit from the Part modeling environment and to invoke the Assembly environment again.

Section 4: Creating Second Component

1. Click on the arrow available at the bottom of the **Insert Components** tool, a flyout appears, see Figure 12.89.

2. In this flyout, click on the **New Part** tool, a new part is added in the Assembly environment and appears in the FeatureManager design tree with its default name.

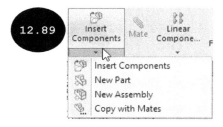

3. Click anywhere in the graphics area to define the position of the second component with respect to the origin of the assembly.

4. Click to select the newly added component from the FeatureManager design tree, a Pop-up toolbar appears, see Figure 12.90.

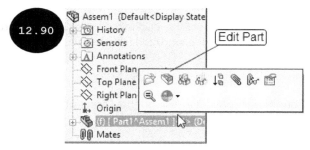

5. Click on the **Edit Part** tool of the Pop-up toolbar, the Part modeling environment invoked and the base component become transparent in the graphics area.

6. Click on the **Extruded Boss/Base** tool of the **Features CommandManager**, the **Extrude PropertyManager** appears.

7. Expand the FeatureManager design tree available at the top left corner of the graphics area and then expand the **Part 2** node of the FeatureManager design tree which appears in blue color.

8. Click to select the Front Plane of the second component as the sketching plane from the FeatureManager design tree, the sketching environment invoked.

9. Click on the **Sketch** tab of the CommandManager to display the tools of the **Sketch CommandManager**.

10. Change the orientation of the model normal to viewing direction.

11. Create the sketch of the first feature of the second component of the assembly, see Figure 12.91.

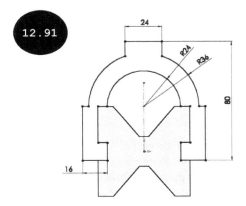

12.91

Note: You can take reference of existing edges of the first component for creating the sketch of the second component.

---

12. Exit from the Sketching environment by clicking on the **Exit Sketch** tool of the **Sketch CommandManager**, the preview of the extruded feature appears in the graphics area.

13. Change the orientation of the model to isometric.

14. Invoke the **End Condition** drop-down list of the **Direction 1** rollout of the **Boss-Extrude PropertyManager** and then click to select the **Mid Plane** option from it.

15. Enter **20** in the **Depth** field of the **Direction 1** rollout.

16. Click on the green tick mark ✅ of the PropertyManager, the base feature of the second component is created, see Figure 12.92.

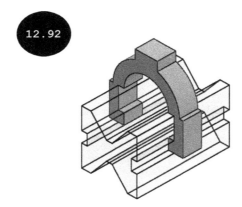

12.92

Now, you will create second feature of the second component.

17. Click on the **Extruded Cut** tool of the **Features CommandManager** and then click to select the top planar face of the base feature of the second component as the sketching plane.

18. Change the orientation of the model normal to the viewing direction.

19. Create a circle of diameter 12 as the sketch of the second feature, see Figure 12.93.

20. Exit from the Sketching environment by clicking on the **Exit Sketch** tool of the **Sketch CommandManager**, the preview of the cut feature appears in the graphics area.

21. Change the orientation of the model to isometric.

22. Invoke the **End Condition** drop-down list of the **Direction 1** rollout of the PropertyManager and then click to select the **Up To Next** option from it.

23. Click on the green tick mark ✅ of the PropertyManager, the second feature of the second component is created, see Figure 12.94.

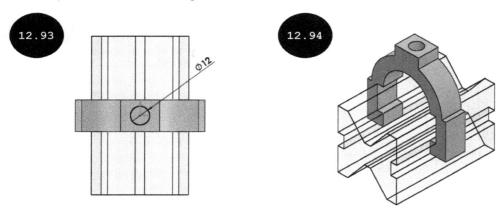

12.93   12.94

Now, you will create third feature of the second component.

24. Click on the **Fillet** tool of the Features CommandManager and then make sure that the **Constant size** radio button is selected in the **Fillet Type** rollout of the PropertyManager.

25. Enter **4** in the **Radius** field of the **Fillet Parameters** rollout of the PropertyManager.

26. Click to select required edges of the second component as the edges to create fillet of radius 4 mm, the preview of the fillet appears, see Figure 12.95.

27. Click on the green tick mark ✅ of the PropertyManager, the third feature of the second component is created.

28. Click on the **Edit Component** tool of the CommandManager to exit from the Part modeling environment and to invoke the Assembly environment again. Figure 12.96 shows the assembly after creating two components.

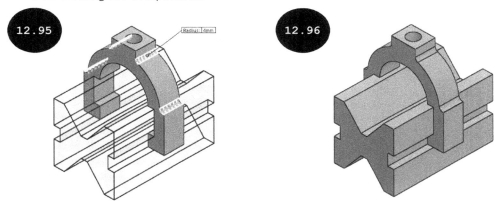

Section 5: Creating Third Component

1. Click on the arrow available at the bottom of the **Insert Components** tool, a flyout appears.

2. In this flyout, click on the **New Part** tool, a new part is added in the Assembly environment and appears in the FeatureManager design tree with its default name.

3. Click to select the top planar face of the second component as the sketching plane for creating the base feature of the third component, the sketching environment invoked.

4. Change the orientation of the model normal to viewing direction.

5. Create the sketch (circle of diameter 12) of the base feature of the third component, see Figure 12.97.

Note: You can take reference of circular edge of the second component for creating the sketch of the third component.

6. Click on the **Extruded Boss/Base** tool of the **Features CommandManager**, the **Boss-Extrude PropertyManager** appears.

7. Change the orientation of the model to isometric.

8. Invoke the **End Condition** drop-down list of the **Direction 1** rollout of the PropertyManager and then click to select the **Mid Plane** option from it.

9. Enter **80** in the **Depth** field of the **Direction 1** rollout.

10. Click on the green tick mark ✅ of the PropertyManager, the base feature of the third component is created, see Figure 12.98.

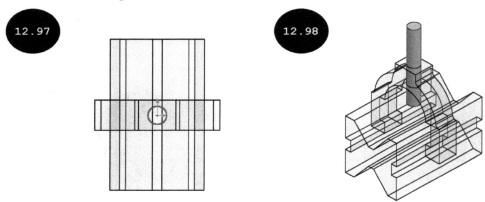

12.97   **12.98**

Now, you will create second feature of the third component.

11. Click on the **Extruded Boss/Base** tool of the **Features CommandManager** and then click to select the top planar face of the base feature of the third component as the sketching plane.

12. Change the orientation of the model normal to the viewing direction.

13. Create a circle of diameter 20 as the sketch of the second feature, see Figure 12.99.

14. Exit from the Sketching environment by clicking on the **Exit Sketch** tool of the **Sketch CommandManager**, the preview of the extruded feature appears in the graphics area.

15. Change the orientation of the model to isometric.

16. Enter **20** in the **Depth** field of the **Direction 1** rollout.

17. Click on the green tick mark ✅ of the PropertyManager, the second feature of the third component is created, see Figure 12.100.

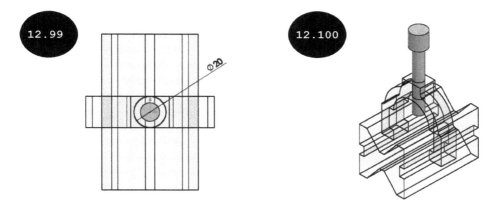

Now, you will create third feature of the third component.

18. Click on the **Extruded Cut** tool of the **Features CommandManager.**

19. Expand the FeatureManager design tree available at the top left corner of the graphics area and then expand its **Part 3** node which appears in blue color.

20. Click to select the Right Plane as the sketching plane and then change the orientation of the model normal to the viewing direction.

21. Create a circle of diameter 5 as the sketch of the third feature, see Figure 12.101.

22. Exit from the Sketching environment by clicking on the **Exit Sketch** tool of the **Sketch CommandManager**, the preview of the cut feature appears in the graphics area.

23. Change the orientation of the model to isometric.

24. Invoke the **End Condition** drop-down list of the **Direction 1** rollout of the PropertyManager and then click to select the **Through All - Both** option from it.

25. Click on the green tick mark ✅ of the PropertyManager, the third feature of the third component is created, see Figure 12.102.

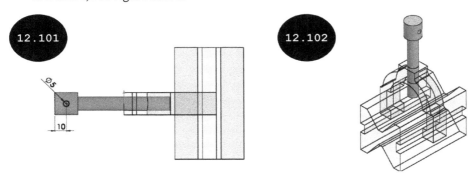

26. Click on the **Edit Component** tool of the **CommandManager** to exit from the Part modeling environment and to invoke the Assembly environment again. Figure 12.103 shows the final assembly after creating all components.

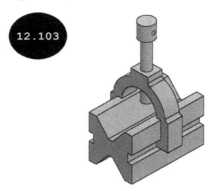

12.103

Section 6: Saving Assembly and its Component

1. Click on the **Save** button, the **Save Modified Documents** dialog box appears.

2. Click on the **Save All** button of the dialog box, the **Save As** dialog box appears, browse to the location where you want to save the assembly file.

3. Enter **Tutorial 1** in the **File name** field of the dialog box as the name of the assembly and then click on the **Save** button of the dialog box. As soon as you click on the **Save** button, the another **Save As** dialog box appears, see Figure 12.104.

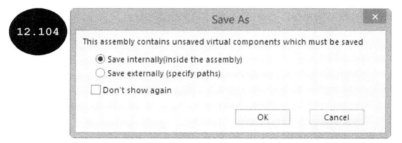

12.104

4. Select the **Save externally (specify paths)** radio button and then click on the **OK** button, all components and the assembly file are save in the specified folder, individually.

Hands-on Test Drive 1

Create the assembly shown in Figure 12.105 by using the Top-down approach. Different views and dimensions of individual components of the assembly are shown in Figure 12.106 through 12.108.

12.105

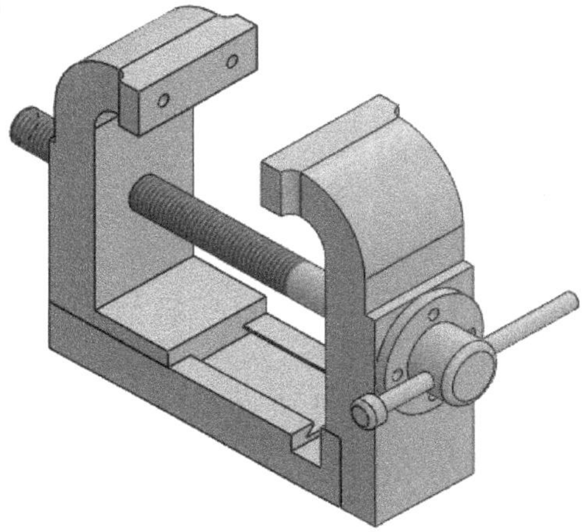

12.106

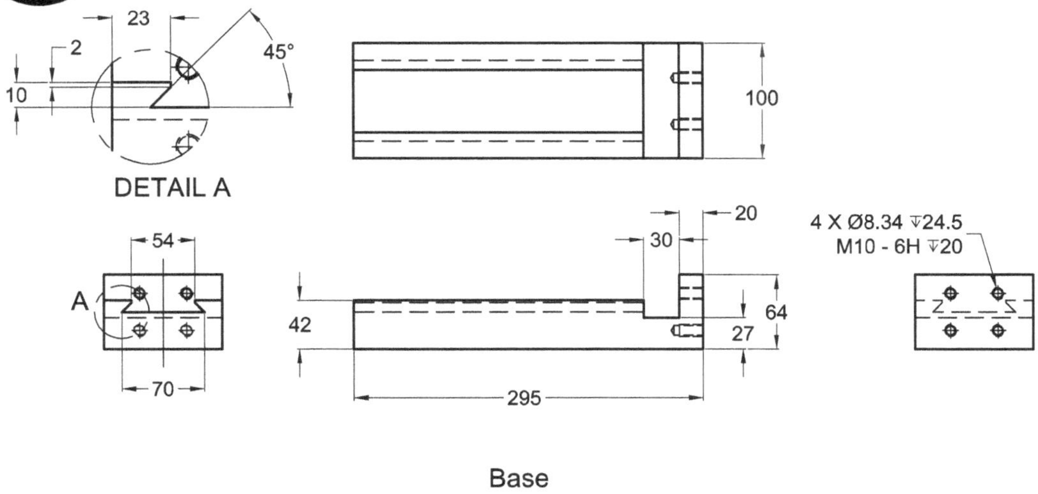
23
2
10
45°
DETAIL A
100
54
A
70
42
30
20
64
27
295
4 X Ø8.34 ⧩24.5
M10 - 6H ⧩20
Base

12.107

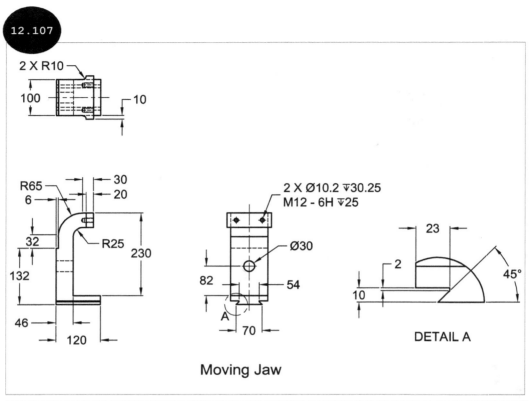

Moving Jaw

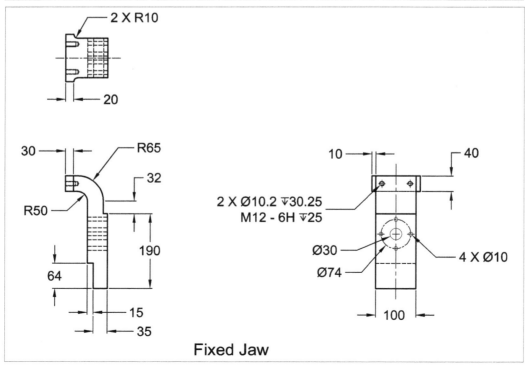

Fixed Jaw

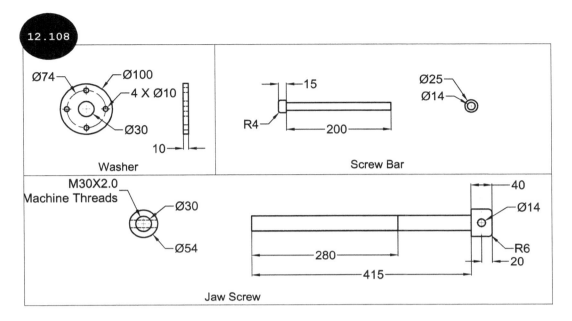

Summary

In this chapter, you have learnt about creating assemblies using the Top-down Assembly approach. In Top-down Assembly approach, you creates all components of an assembly in the Assembly environment itself. Once an assembly is created, you can edit its components depending upon the design requirement within the Assembly environment or by opening the component in the Part modeling environment. You can also edit the existing mates applied between the components of an assembly. In this chapter, you have also learnt how to create different type of patterns such as Linear Component Pattern, Pattern Driven Component Pattern, and Chain Component Pattern in Assembly environment. Also, similar to mirroring features in Part modeling environment, you can mirror components in the Assembly environment by using the **Mirror Components** tool. You have also learnt about creating assembly features, suppressing or unsuppressing components of an assembly, and inserting components in the Assembly environment having multiple configurations.

In addition to this, you can create sub-assemblies from the components of the assembly within the Assembly environment. You can also dissolve the already created sub-assemblies into individual components of the assembly. You have also learnt how to create, edit, or collapse the exploded view of an assembly. You can also animate the exploded/collapse view of an assembly. At last you have learnt how to add exploded lines in an exploded view and create bill of material (BOM) of an assembly.

Questions

- In _____ approach, you creates all components of an assembly in the Assembly environment itself.

- In the _____ pattern, the component to pattern drives by the pattern feature of the other component of the assembly.

- The _____ pattern allows you to dynamically simulate a chain drive or cable carrier in an assembly.

- In SOLIDWORKS, you can create three types of chain patterns _____, _____, and _____ .

- The _____ tool is used to create an exploded view of the assembly.

- In SOLIDWORKS, you can create _____ and _____ type of exploded views.

- The _____ tool is used to create exploded lines in an exploded view.

- You can edit components of an assembly within the Assembly environment. (True/False).

- In SOLIDWORKS, you can create cut features in the Assembly environment. (True/False).

- In SOLIDWORKS, you can not create sub-assemblies from components of the assembly. (True/False).

Working with Drawing

In this chapter:

- Invoking Drawing Environment using New tool
- Creating Model or Base View of a Model
- Invoking Drawing Environment from an Part/Assembly Environment
- Creating Model View
- Creating Projected View
- Creating 3 Standard View
- General Concept for Angle of Projection
- Defining Angle of Projection for a Drawing
- Editing Sheet Format
- Creating Section View
- Creating Auxiliary View
- Creating Detail View
- Creating Broken-out Section View
- Creating Break view
- Creating Crop View
- Creating Alternate Position View
- Applying Dimensions
- Adding Notes
- Adding Surface Finish symbol
- Adding Weld Symbol
- Adding Hole Callout
- Adding Center Mark
- Adding Centerlines
- Creating Bill of Material (BOM)
- Adding Balloons

After creating parts and assemblies, you need to generate their 2D drawings. 2D drawings are the only source for manufacturing components. You can also says, 2D drawings are not only drawings its a language of engineers to communicated with each other. By using 2D drawings, a designer communicate the information about the components to be manufacture with the engineers available in the shop floor. Looking at the importance of 2D drawings from the designers and engineers point of view, the role of designers become very important to generate correct or error free drawings for production. Any incorrect or missing information in drawings about an component can lead to the wrong production. Keeping this in mind, SOLIDWORKS provides you an environment which allows you to generate error free 2D drawings. This environment is known as Drawing environment.

You can invoke the Drawing environment for generating 2D drawings by using the **New** tool available in the **Standard** toolbar and in the **File** menu of the SOLIDWORKS menus. You can also invoke the Drawing environment by using the **Make Drawing from Part/Assembly** tool which is available within the Part and Assembly environments. Different methods of invoking the Drawing environment are discussed next.

Invoking Drawing Environment using New tool

To invoke the Drawing environment by using the **New** tool, click on the **New** tool available in the **Standard** toolbar, the **New SOLIDWORKS Document** dialog box appears, see Figure 13.1. Click on the **Drawing** button of this dialog box and then click on the **OK** button, the **Sheet Format/Size** dialog box appears, see Figure 13.2. The options available in this dialog box are used to specify sheet size/format to be used for creating drawings. These options are discussed next.

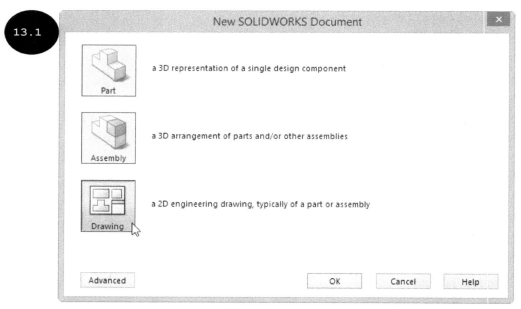

13.1

New SOLIDWORKS Document

Part
a 3D representation of a single design component

Assembly
a 3D arrangement of parts and/or other assemblies

Drawing
a 2D engineering drawing, typically of a part or assembly

Advanced   OK   Cancel   Help

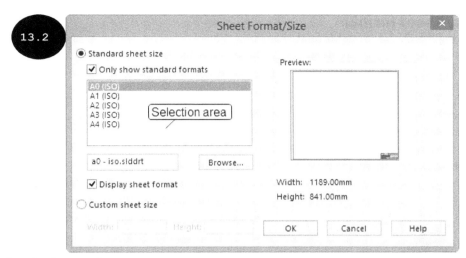

Standard sheet size

By default, the **Standard sheet size** radio button is selected. As a result, a list of standard sheet sizes enabled in the **Selection** area of dialog box, see Figure 13.2. You can select the required standard drawing sheet for creating drawing views from this area. Note that if the **Only show standard formats** check box of the dialog box is selected, the standard drawing sheets of the current drawing standard is appears in the **Selection** area of the dialog box, see Figure 13.2. If this check is cleared, all the standard sheet sizes will be listed in this area, see Figure 13.3.

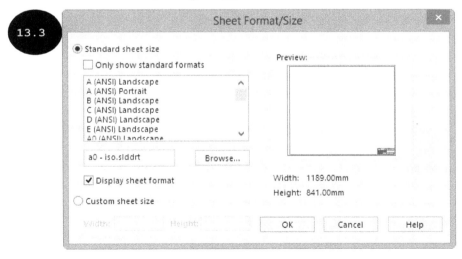

Display sheet format

On clearing the **Display sheet format** check box, a blank drawing sheet appears. If this check box is selected, the drawing sheet appears with the default standard sheet format. You can also select the sheet format other than the default. For doing so, click on the **Browse** button, the **Open** dialog box appears, select the required sheet format from the **Open** dialog box and then click on the **Open** button, the preview of the sheet format appears in the **Preview** area of the dialog box. Note that the **Display sheet format** check box enabled only if the **Standard sheet size** radio button is selected in the dialog box.

Custom sheet size

On selecting the **Custom sheet size** radio button, the **Width** and **Height** fields of the dialog box enabled and all other remaining options of the dialog box will be disabled, see Figure 13.4. In the **Width** and **Height** fields, you can specify custom width and height for the drawing sheet, as required.

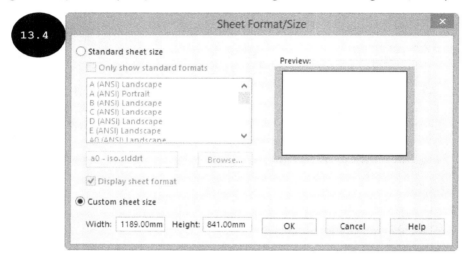

After selecting the required standard sheet size or specifying the custom sheet size by using the options available in the **Sheet Format/Size** dialog box, click on the **OK** button, a drawing sheet of specified size/format appears in the Drawing environment. Also, the **Model View PropertyManager** appears at the left of the drawing sheet, see Figure 13.5.

Note that the **Model View PropertyManager** appears automatically on invoking the Drawing environment and is used to create model or base drawing view of a part or assembly. The method of creating model/base view of a part/assembly using this PropertyManager is discussed next.

Note: In the **Options** rollout of the **Model View PropertyManager**, the **Start command when creating new drawing** check box is selected by default. As a result, every time when you invoke the Drawing environment, the **Model View PropertyManager** appears automatically and is used to create model/base view of the model. If you clear this check box, next time on invoking the Drawing environment, this PropertyManager will not appears. In that case, to create the model or base view of a model, you need to invoke this PropertyManager by clicking on the **Model View** tool available in the **View Layout CommandManager**.

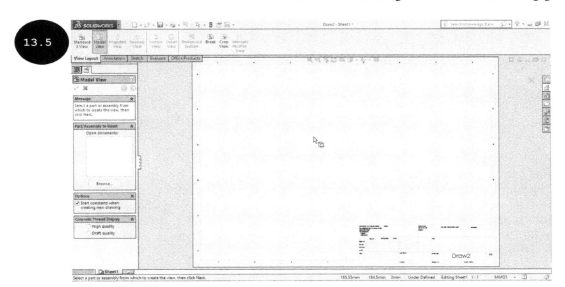

Creating Model or Base View of a Model

To create model or base view of a model in the Drawing environment, click on the **Browse** button of the **Part/Assembly to Insert** rollout of the **Model View PropertyManager**, the **Open** dialog box appears. In this dialog box, browse to the location where the model whose drawing views is to be created is saved and then click to select the model. Next, click on the **Open** button of the dialog box, a rectangular box representing the model/base view of the selected model is attached with the cursor, see Figure 13.6. Also, the options of the PropertyManager modified and are discussed next.

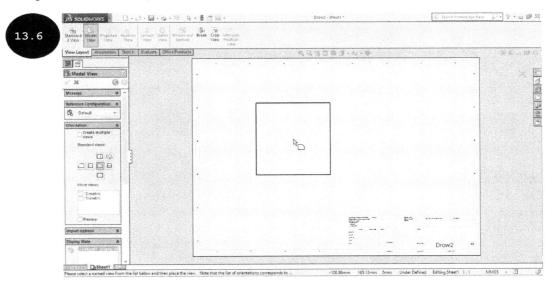

Tip: You can also select a part or assembly whose drawing views is to be created from the **Open documents** field of the **Part/Assembly to Insert** rollout of the **Model View PropertyManager**. However, this field only displays the list of models which are opened in the current session of SOLIDWORKS. If the model whose drawing views is to be created appear in this field, double click on it and then move the cursor towards the graphics area, a rectangular box representing the model/base view of the selected model is attached with the cursor.

Reference Configuration

The drop-down list of the **Reference Configuration** rollout contains the list of all the configurations of the selected model whose drawing views is being created. You can select the required configuration for creating their respective drawing views. Note that if the selected model does not have any configuration other than the default, only the **Default** option is available in this drop-down list and is selected by default, see Figure 13.7.

Orientation

The options available in the **Standard views** area of the **Orientation** rollout are used to select the standard view. By default, the **Front** button is activated in the **Standard views** area, see Figure 13.7. As a result, the front view will be created as the model/base view of the model. You can create Front, Top, Right Side, Left, Back, Bottom, and Isometric views by activating their respective button available in this area of rollout.

You can also create Dimetric and Trimetric views by using the **More views** field of this rollout, see Figure 13.7. To create Dimetric or Trimetric view, select their respective check box available in the **More views** field of the rollout.

By default, the **Preview** check box of this rollout is cleared, see Figure 13.7. As a result, a empty rectangular box is attached with the cursor representing the standard view. On selecting this check box, the preview of the standard view appears inside the rectangular box which is attached with the cursor.

You can also create multiple views of the select part/assembly by selecting the **Create multiple views** check box of this rollout, see Figure 13.7.

Import Options

The options available in this rollout are used to import annotation of the part/assemble to the drawing view, see Figure 13.8. On selecting the **Import annotations** check box, the **Design annotations**, **DimXpert annotations**, and **Include items from hidden features** check boxes enabled. Depending upon the check boxes selected in this rollout, the respective annotations of the part/assembly will be imported to the drawing view.

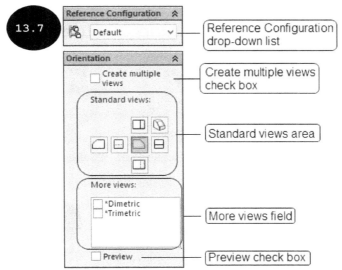

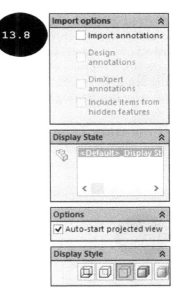

Options

By default, the **Auto-start projected view** check box is selected, see Figure 13.8. As a result, as soon as you are done with creating model/base view, the **Projected View PropertyManager** appears automatically and the projected view of the model attached with the cursor and you can start creating the projected views of the model.

Display Style

The option available in this rollout are used to select the type of display for the drawing view, see Figure 13.8. On selecting the **Wireframe** button, all the visible and hidden edges of the model will be represented as continues line in the drawing view, see Figure 13.9. If you select the **Hidden Lines Visible** button, the visible edges will be represented as continues lines and the hidden edges will be represented as doted lines in the drawing view, see Figure 13.9. On selecting the **Hidden Lines Removed** button, only the visible edges of the model displays in the drawing view and are represented as continues lines, see Figure 13.9. On selecting the **Shaded With Edges** button, the drawing view displays in the shaded display style with the display of visible edges only, see Figure 13.9. If you select the **Shaded** button, the drawing view displays in shaded model with the display of visible and hidden edges turned Off, see Figure 13.9.

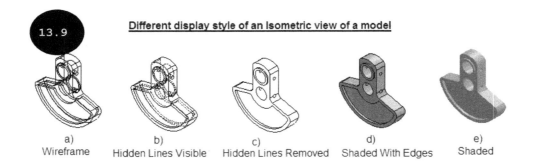

13.9

Different display style of an Isometric view of a model

a)
Wireframe

b)
Hidden Lines Visible

c)
Hidden Lines Removed

d)
Shaded With Edges

e)
Shaded

Scale

By default, the **Use sheet scale** radio button is selected in this rollout, see Figure 13.10. As a result, the scale of the drawing view will be same as of the scale of the drawing sheet. On selecting the **Use custom scale** radio button, the **Scale** drop-down list enabled. By using this drop-down list, you can set scale for the drawing view other than the scale of the drawing sheet. You can select pre-defined scale values from this drop-down list. Also, on selecting the **User defined** option from the **Scale** drop-down list, the **Scale** field enabled. In this field, you can specify user defined scale for the drawing view.

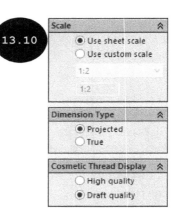

13.10

Dimension Type

This rollout is used to specify the type of dimension for the drawing view either true or projected. The projected dimensions are appears as 2D dimensions and are applied on orthogonal/projected views such as Front, Top, and Right views, see Figure 13.11. The true dimensions are accurate model values and are applied on isometric, dimetric, and trimetric views, see Figure 13.12.

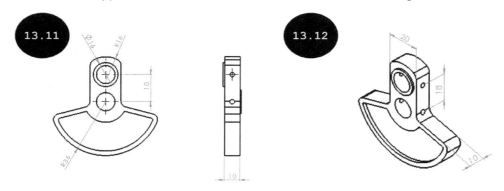

13.11

13.12

Cosmetic Thread Display

The **High quality** and **Draft quality** radio buttons available in this rollout are used to control the display of cosmetic threads. On selecting the **High quality** radio button, cosmetic threads appears in precise line fonts. On selecting the **Draft quality** radio button, cosmetic threads displays with less details.

After specifying the required settings such as selecting standard view, display style, and scale factor for creating the model/base view, click anywhere in the drawing sheet to position the drawing view, the drawing view is created and placed in the specified position in the drawing sheet. Also, the **Projected View PropertyManager** appears and on moving the cursor, a projected view is attached with the cursor. You can continue with the creation of projection views by specifying their placement point in the drawing sheet. The most of the options of the **Projected View PropertyManager** are same as discussed earlier and are used for specifying the settings of the projected views. Figure 13.13 shows different projected views that can be created from a model/base view. Once you are done with the creations of required projected views, press the ESC key.

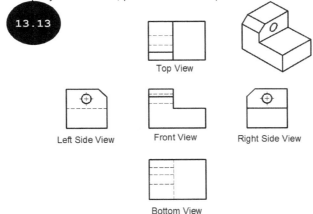

13.13

Top View

Left Side View   Front View   Right Side View

Bottom View

Note: The **Projected View PropertyManager** appears automatically as soon as you specify the placement point for the model/base view. This is because the **Auto-start projection view** check box is selected in the **Options** rollout of the **Model View PropertyManager**. If this check box is cleared, the **Projected View PropertyManager** will not be invoked automatically. In this case, you need to invoke this PropertyManager by clicking on the **Projected View** tool of the **View Layout CommandManager** to creates projected views. You will learn more about the **Projected View** tool later in this chapter.

Note: You can also control/modify the settings such as display style and scale factor for a drawing view which has been placed in the drawing sheet. To control the settings of a drawing view which is already placed in the drawing sheet, click on the drawing view whose settings has to be modified, the **Drawing View PropertyManager** appears. By using the options of this PropertyManager you can control the settings of the selected drawing view. All the options of this PropertyManager are same as discussed earlier.

Invoking Drawing Environment from an Part/ Assembly Environment

Similar to invoking drawing environment by using the **New** tool and creates different drawing views of a model, you can also invoke the Drawing environment from an opened Part or Assembly and creates different drawing views.

To invoke the Drawing environment from an Part or Assembly environment, click on the down arrow available next to the **New** tool of the **Standard** toolbar, a flyout appears, see Figure 13.14.

13.14

Note: The options of this flyout appears only if you are in a Part or an Assembly environment.

Click on the **Make Drawing from Part/Assembly** tool from this flyout, the **Sheet Format/Size** dialog box appears. The options of this dialog box are same as discussed earlier. By using this dialog box, you can specify required format/size for the drawing sheet. After defining the sheet format/size, click on the **OK** button, the Drawing environment is invoked with the display of **View Palette Task Pane** at its right, see Figure 13.15.

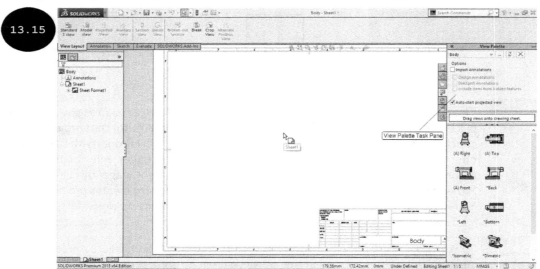

13.15

Note that the bottom half area of the **View Palette Task Pane** displays different drawing views of the model that was opened in the Part or Assembly environment. By using this task pane, you can drag and drop the required drawing view onto the drawing sheet at the required location. The first placed view in the drawing sheet is known as the model, base, or parent view. Also note that the **Auto-start projected view** check box is selected in the upper half of the **View Palette Task Pane**, see Figure 13.15. As a result, as soon as you placed the model/base view in the drawing sheet by dragging and dropping from the **View Palette Task Pane**, the **Projected View PropertyManager** appears at the left of the drawing sheet. Also, on moving the cursor, you will notice that a projected view is attached automatically with the cursor. You can click anywhere in the drawing sheet to specify the position of the projected view attached with the cursor. If the **View Palette Task Pane** closed automatically after placing the model view, click on the **View Palette** tab of the **Task Pane** available on the right side of the screen to display it back. You can also pin it to stay available all time during the process of creating drawing views by clicking on the **Auto Show** pin icon 📌 available at the top right corner of the **View Palette Task Pane**.

Creating Model View

A model view is an independent view or a first, base, or parent view of all other drawing views. You can create model view by using the **Model View PropertyManager** and **View Palette Task Pane**, as discussed earlier.

In addition to this, you can also create model/base view by using the **Model View** tool of the **View Layout CommandManager**. Note that as soon as you click on the **Model View** tool, the **Model View PropertyManager** appears and the options available in this PropertyManager are same as discussed earlier.

Procedure to Create Model/Base View

1. Invoke the **Model View PropertyManager**, if not invoked by default.
2. Click on the **Browse** button of the **Part/Assembly to Insert** rollout of the PropertyManager.

Note: If the part or assembly whose drawing views is to be created appears in the **Open documents** field of the **Part/Assembly to Insert** rollout then you can directly select it from this field instead of choosing the **Browse** button.

---

3. Select a part or assembly whose drawing view is to be created and then click on the **Open** button of the dialog box, a rectangular view representing the model view of the selected part/assembly appears attached with the cursor.
4. Specify the required settings such as standard view, display style, and scale factor for the drawing view by using the options of the PropertyManager.
5. Specify the placement position for the model/base view in the drawing sheet by clicking the left mouse button.
6. After creating the required drawing views, press the ESC key to exit from the creation of drawing views.

Creating Projected View

Projected views are different views of an object visualizing from different sides such as top, front, and side. You can create projected views of a drawing view which act as the model/base view. Figure 13.16 shows the model/base view (Front view) and its respective projected views. Note that the model/base view and their respective projected views are the orthogonal views of an object. Figure 13.17 shows different orthogonal views of an object.

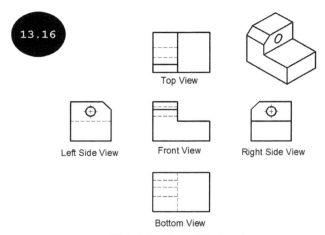

Third Angle of Projection

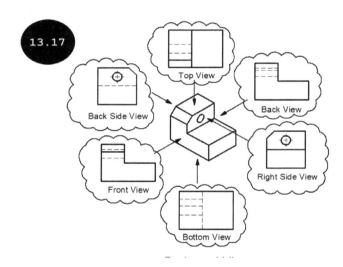

As discussed earlier, the **Projected View PropertyManager** invokes automatically as soon as you are done with created model/base view using the **Model View PropertyManager**. You can also invoke this PropertyManager, if not invoked automatically, by clicking on the **Projected View** tool available in the **View Layout CommandManager**. The options available in the **Projected View PropertyManager** are same as discussed earlier and are used to create projected views of the selected model/base view.

Procedure to Create Projected Views
1. Invoke the **Projected View PropertyManager** by clicking on the **Projected View** tool.
2. Select a view as the model/base view whose projected views are to be created.

Note: If only one drawing view is available in the drawing sheet, it will automatically be selected for creating its projected views. Also, the preview of a projected view is attached with the cursor. However, if two or more than two views are available in the drawing sheet then you need to select a view whose projected views are to be created.

3. Move the cursor to the required location in the drawing sheet and then click to specify the placement point for the attached projected view. You can continue with the creation of other projected views by specifying their placement location in the drawing sheet, as required.
4. Once you are done with the creation of projected views, press the ESC key.

Creating 3 Standard View

In addition to creating orthogonal views such as Front and Top by using the **Model View PropertyManager** and **Projected View PropertyManager**, you can also created three standard orthogonal views: Front, Top, and Side by using the **Standard 3 View** tool. On clicking this tool, the **Standard 3 View PropertyManager** appears. If the part/assembly whose drawing views is to be created is displayed in the **Open documents** field of the PropertyManager then double-click on it, three standard views are created in the drawing sheet, automatically, see Figure 13.18. If the part/assembly file is not displayed in the **Open documents** field, click on the **Browse** button and browse to the location where the required part/assembly is saved.

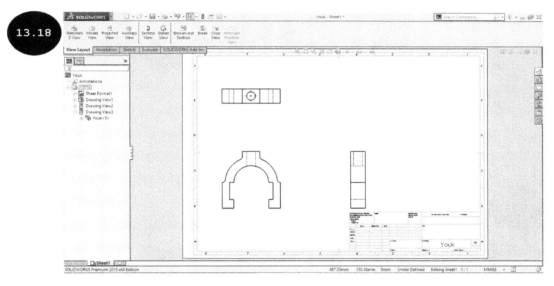

Note: The creation of standard views depends upon the current angle of projection defined for the drawing sheet. You can define first angle of projection or third angle of projection for creating standard drawing views. The concept of angle of projection and procedure to define angle of projection are discussed next.

General Concept for Angle of Projection

Engineering drawings follows two type of angle of projection: First angle of projection and Third angle of projection. In first angle of projection, object is assumed to be kept in the first quadrant, see Figure 13.19 and viewer viewing the object from the direction shown in Figure 13.19. As the object is kept in the first quadrant, its views projections are on the planes as shown in Figure 13.19. Now, on unfolding the planes of projections, the front view appears at the upper side and the top views appears at the bottom side in a drawing. Also, the right side view appears at the left and left side view appears at right side of the front view, see Figure 13.20. Similarly, in third angle of projection, object is assumed to be kept in the third quadrant, see Figure 13.19 and the front view projection appears at the bottom and top view projection appears at the top side in the drawing. Also, the right side view appears at the right and left side view appears at the left of the front view, see Figure 13.21.

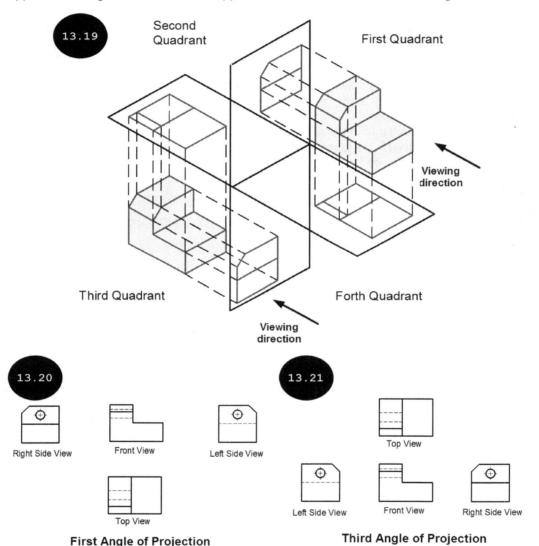

First Angle of Projection

Third Angle of Projection

Defining Angle of Projection for a Drawing

In SOLIDWORKS, to define required angle of projection for creating drawing views, select the **Sheet** node from the FeatureManager design tree and right-click, a shortcut menu appears, see Figure 13.22. Next, click on the **Properties** option of the shortcut menu, the **Sheet Properties** dialog box appears, see Figure 13.23. In this dialog box, you can select the required type of projection to be followed for creating drawing views by selecting their respective radio button from the **Type of projection** area of the dialog box. Next, click on the **OK** button to accept the change and exit from the dialog box.

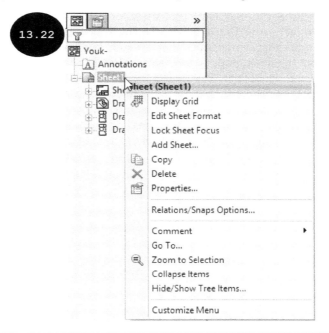

Editing Sheet Format

While invoking the Drawing environment, you can select the required sheet template by specifying required sheet size and sheet format. Note that sheet formats contain title blocks which contain information such as Project name, Drawn by, checked by, approved by, date, sheet number, and so on. You can create or edit sheet formats such that it match your company standard format. To edit the sheet format, select the **Sheet** node of the FeatureManager design tree and then right click to invoke shortcut menu, see Figure 13.22. Next, select the **Edit Sheet Format** option, the editing mode for editing sheet format is invoked, see Figure 13.24. Now you can delete or edit the existing text and lines of the title block. Also, you can add the new lines and text by using the sketch tools available in the **Sketch CommandManager**. To delete existing lines and text, select them and press the DELETE key. To edit the existing text, double click on the text to be edited, the editing mode invokes and allows you to edit the text or write the new text. You can add new lines in the title block by using the **Line** tool available in the **Sketch CommandManager**. Once you are done with editing, click on the confirmation corner available at the upper right corner of the drawing area to exit from the editing mode.

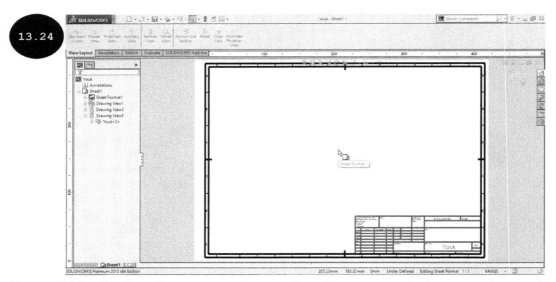

After modifying the sheet format or creating new sheet format, as required, you can also save it for future use for other drawings. For doing so, click on the **Files > Save Sheet Format** from the SOLIDWORKS menus, the **Save Sheet Format** dialog box appears. In this dialog box, specify name and location for the sheet format, as required and then click on the **Save** button.

Creating Other View Types

In SOLIDWORKS, in addition to creating orthogonal views such as Front, Top, and Right, and isometric and trimetric views of an object, you can also create following type of drawing views. Note that these drawing views are driven from an existing orthogonal view.

- Section View
- Aligned Section View

- Auxiliary View
- Detail View
- Broken View
- Crop View
- Alternate Position View
- Broken-out Section View

Creating Section View

A section view is a view created by cutting an object using an imaginary cutting plane or a section line and then viewing the object from the direction normal to the cutting plane. Figure 13.25 show an object, a cutting plane, and the resultant section view. A section view is used to illustrate internal features clearly, reduce the number of hidden-detail lines, facilitate the dimensioning of internal features, shows cross-section at section line position, and so on. In SOLIDWORKS, you can create full section view and half section view by using the **Section View** tool available in the **View Layout** CommandManager.

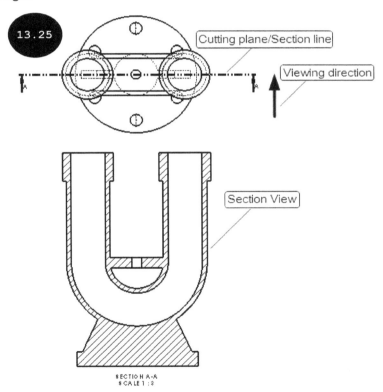

Creating Full Section View

The full section views are most widely used section views in engineering drawings. In full section view, a object is assumed to be cut through all its length by an imaginary cutting plane or a section line, see Figure 13.25. In SOLIDWORKS, you can create four type of full section views: Horizontal, Vertical, Auxiliary, and Aligned section views by using the **Section View** tool.

To create full section view, click on the **Section View** tool, the **Section View Assist PropertyManager** appears, see Figure 13.26.

> **Note:** In the **Section View Assist PropertyManager**, two tabs are available at its top: **Section** and **Half Section**. Out of which the **Section** tab is activated, by default. As a result, options to creating full section view are appears in the PropertyManager. On activating the **Half Section** tab, the options to creating half section view appears. You learn more about creating half section views later in this chapter.

The **Cutting Line** rollout of this PropertyManager allows you to select the type of cutting line for creating respective section view. You can create vertical section view, horizontal section view, auxiliary section view, and aligned section view by activating their respective button from the **Cutting Line** rollout.

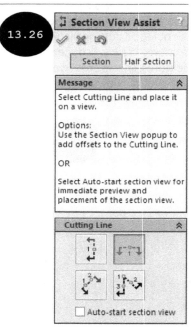

13.26

Creating Horizontal/Vertical section View

To create horizontal section view, activate the **Horizontal** button, a horizontal cutting line attached with the cursor. Next, select the **Auto-start section view** check box available in the **Cutting Line** rollout. Once you are done, move the cursor towards an existing drawing view and then click to specify the placement point at the location on the existing view from where you wanted to cut the object, the preview of the horizontal section view appears attached with the cursor. Note that the direction of arrows in the cutting section line representing the viewing direction. You can reverse the viewing direction by clicking on the **Flip Direction** button of the PropertyManager. Next, click to specify the placement point for the attached horizontal section view at the required location of the sheet, the horizontal section view is created, see Figure 13.25.

> **Note:** If the **Auto-start section view** check box of the **Cutting Line** rollout is cleared, the **Section View** Pop-up toolbar appears as soon as you define the placement point for the section line in the drawing sheet, see Figure 13.27. By using the options of this Pop-up toolbar, you can further control/edit the section line, if needed. Once you are done with editing or modifying the section line, click on the green tick mark of the Pop-up toolbar, the preview of the section view appears according to the modified section line attached with the cursor. Now, you can specify the placement point for the section view in the drawing sheet.

Similar to creating horizontal section view, you can create vertical section view by activating the **Vertical** button of the **Cutting Line** rollout. Figure 13.28 shows a vertical section view created.

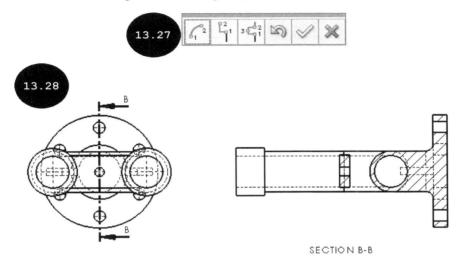

If you create an section view of an assembly then on specifying the placement point for the section line, the **Section View** dialog box appears, see Figure 13.29. The **Excluded components/rib features** field of this dialog box allows you to select the components or features such as fasteners and ribs as the components/features to be excluded from the section cut. Once you are done with selecting components, click on the **OK** button of the dialog box, the preview of the section view without cutting the selected components is attached with the cursor. Next, specify the placement point to place the section view in the drawing sheet.

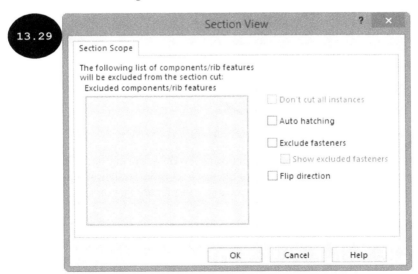

Creating Auxiliary Section View

An auxiliary section view is created by cutting an object using an sight line which is not parallel to any of the principal projection planes: frontal, horizontal, or profile and then viewing the object from the direction normal to the sight line, see Figure 13.30

To create an auxiliary section view, invoke the **Section View Assist PropertyManager** and then activate the **Auxiliary** button of the **Cutting Line** rollout, a sight line is attached with the cursor. Move the cursor to an existing drawing view which will act as the parent view for the auxiliary section view being created. Next, click to specify the placement point at the location on the existing view from where you wanted to cut the object, the preview of the auxiliary section view attached with the cursor and the cutting section line appears on the specified location in the parent view. Note that if the **Section View** Pop-up toolbar appears on the specified the placement point, click on its green tick mark. You can also reverse the default viewing direction by clicking on the **Flip Direction** button of the PropertyManager. Next, click to specify the placement point for the auxiliary section view at the required location in the sheet, the auxiliary section view is created, see Figure 13.30.

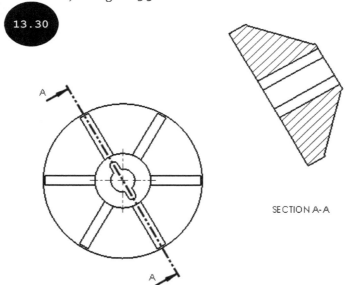

13.30

SECTION A-A

Creating Aligned section view

An aligned section view is created by cutting the object using the cutting section line which is comprises of two non parallel lines/planes and then straighten the cross section that is generated through selection line by revolving it, see Figure 13.31.

Procedure to Create Aligned Section View

1. Invoke the **Section View Assist PropertyManager** by clicking on the **Section View** tool.
2. Activate the **Aligned** button of the **Cutting Line** rollout, a cutting section line comprises of two non parallel lines attached with the cursor.
3. Move the cursor to an existing drawing view.

4. Click to specify the center point for the section line, see Figure 13.31.
5. Move the cursor and then click to specify position for the first cutting line, see Figure 13.31.
6. Similarly, move the cursor and click to specify the position for the second cutting line, see Figure 13.31, the preview of the aligned section view is attached with the cursor.
7. Move the cursor to the required location and then click to specify the placement point for the aligned section view, see Figure 13.31.
8. Press ESC to exit.

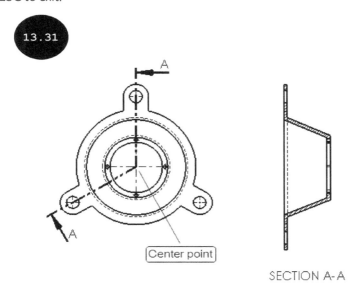

SECTION A-A

Creating Half Section View

An half section view is created by cutting the object by using an imaginary cutting plane which passes halfway through the object and one quarter of it is removed, see Figure 13.32. In SOLIDWORKS, you can also created half section view by using the **Section View** tool.

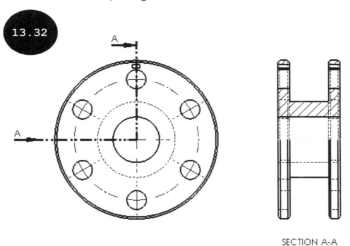

SECTION A-A

Procedure to Create Half Section View

1. Click on the **Section View** tool, the **Section View Assist** **PropertyManager** appears.
2. Click on the **Half Section** tab available at the top of the PropertyManager, see Figure 13.33. By using the buttons of the **Half Section** rollout of the PropertyManager, you can create pre-defined shape of half section views.
3. Activate the required button available in the **Half Section** rollout by clicking on it for creating their respective half section view, the respective half section cutting line is attached with the cursor.
4. Move the cursor over an existing view and then click to specify the placement point for the half section cutting line on to the required position in the existing view, the preview of the half section view is attached with the cursor.
5. If you want to flip the viewing direction, click on the **Flip Direction** button available in the **Section Line** rollout of the PropertyManager else skip this step.
6. Click to specify the position for the half section view in the required location of the drawing sheet, see Figure 13.32.
7. Press ESC key.

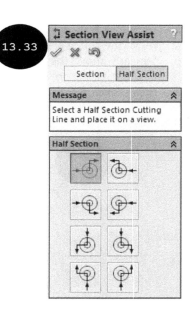

Creating Auxiliary View

An auxiliary view is a projected view created by projecting edges of the object normal to an selected edge of the existing drawing view, see Figure 13.34. You can create an auxiliary view by using the **Auxiliary View** tool available in the **View Layout CommandManager**.

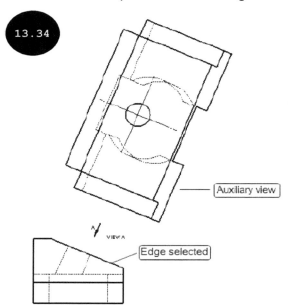

Procedure to Create Auxiliary View

1.   Click on the **Auxiliary View** tool available in the **View Layout CommandManager**.
2.   Select an edge of the existing drawing view, see Figure 13.34, the preview of the auxiliary view attached with the cursor.
3.   Click to specify the position for the auxiliary view in the drawing sheet, see Figure 13.34.
4.   Press ESC to exit.

Creating Detail View

In SOLIDWORKS, the detail view is created in order to show a portion of an existing view at an enlarged scale, see Figure 13.35. You can define a portion to be enlarge of an existing view by drawing a circle or other closed contour for creating its detail view. You can create detail view of a portion of an existing view by using the **Detail View** tool.

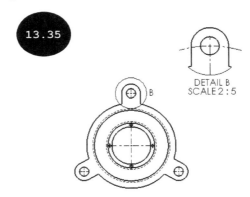

Procedure to Create Detail View

1.   Click on the **Detail View** tool, the **Detail View PropertyManager** appears and you are promoted to draw a circle to define the portion of an existing view to be enlarged.
2.   Draw a circle around the portion of an existing view to be enlarged. As soon as you draw a circle, the enlarged view of the portion enclosed inside the circle drawn attached with the cursor.
3.   If needed, you can increase or decrease the default scale factor for the attached detail view by using the **Scale** field available in the **Scale** rollout of the PropertyManager.
4.   Move the cursor to the required location in the drawing sheet and then click to specify the placement point for the attached detail view, the detail view is created, see Figure 13.35.
5.   Press ESC key to exit.

> **Note:** In addition to defining portion to be enlarged by drawing circle, you can also define a portion to enlarge by using the closed sketch profile. For doing so, before invoking the **Detail View** tool, first select an existing view and then draw a closed sketch profile of any shape by using the sketch tools available in the **Sketch CommandManager**. Once the close sketch profile is drawn, select it and then invoke the **Detail View** tool, see Figure 13.36.

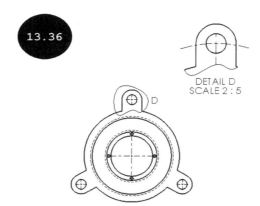

DETAIL D
SCALE 2 : 5

Creating Broken-out Section View

A broken-out section is created by removing portion of an existing view to a specified depth in order to expose inner details, see Figure 13.37. You can define portion of an existing view to be removed by drawing a closed sketch. Generally a closed sketch profile is drawn by using **Spline** tool.

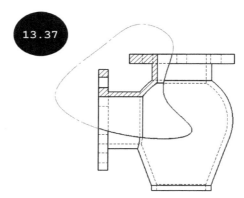

Procedure to Create Broken-out Section

1. Click on the **Broken-out Section** tool, the **Spline** tool is invoked automatically for drawing a closed profile that defines the portion to be removed.
2. Move the cursor over the existing view whose portion is to be removed to an specified depth.
3. Draw a closed profile around the portion to be removed. As soon as the closed profile is drawn, the **Broken-out Section PropertyManager** appears.
4. Enter the depth value in the **Depth** field of the PropertyManager upto which material needs to be removed. Alternatively, you can also select an edge or axis of the view to define the depth by using the **Depth Reference** field of the PropertyManager.
5. Select the **Preview** check box, to turn On the display of preview of the broken-out section in the drawing sheet.
6. Click on the green tick mark of the PropertyManager to accept the setting defined and to exit from the PropertyManager, the broken-out section is created, see Figure 13.37.

Creating Break View

The break view is used to display a large scale view on to a small scale sheet by removing some of the its portion having same cross-section, see Figure 13.38. It is created by breaking an existing view using a pair of break lines and removes the portion that exist between the breaking lines.

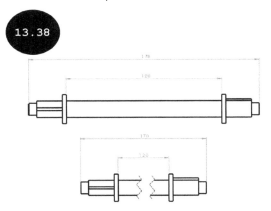

Note: The dimension applied to the break view, represents its actual dimension, see Figures 13.38. It is evident from Figures 13.38 that even on breaking the view, dimension value associated to it remains same. You will learn more about applying dimensions later in this chapter.

Procedure to Create Break View

1. Click on the **Break** tool, the **Broken View PropertyManager** appears.
2. Move the cursor over the view whose break view is to be created.
3. Click to select the view, the first vertical or horizontal break line is attached with the cursor.

Note: The display of break line (vertical or horizontal) depends upon whether the **Add vertical break line** or **Add horizontal break line** button is activated in the PropertyManager. If the **Add vertical break line** button is activated, vertical break line appears and if the **Add horizontal break line** button is activated, horizontal break line appears.

4. Make sure that the require button **Add vertical break line** or **Add horizontal break line** is selected in the PropertyManager.
5. Specify the placement point for the first break line by clicking the left mouse button in the required location of the drawing view, the second break line is attached with the cursor.
6. Specify the placement point for the second break line in the view, the view is braked and the portion inside the breaking lines is removed, see Figure 13.38.

Note: You can control the gap between the break lines in the view by using the **Gap size** field of the PropertyManager. You can also select the required type of breaking line by using the **Break line style** drop-down list of the PropertyManager.

7. Click on the green tick mark to confirm the creation of break view and to exit from the PropertyManager.

Creating Crop View

A crop view is created by cropping an existing view using a closed sketch in such a way that only the portion lies inside the closed sketch retain in the view, see Figure 13.39. You can create crop view by using the **Crop View** tool. Note that to create a crop view, you first need to create a closed sketch in the view to be cropped by using the sketching tools available in the **Sketch CommandManager**.

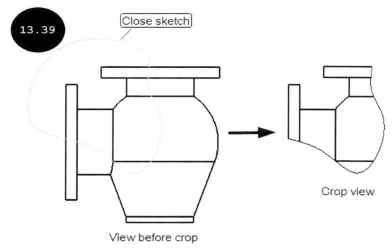

Close sketch

13.39

View before crop

Crop view

Procedure to Create Crop View

1. Select the view to be cropped.
2. Draw the closed sketch around the portion of the view to be cropped, see Figure 13.39.
3. Make sure that the sketch created is selected.
4. Click on the **Crop View** tool, the crop view is created by retaining only the portion that lies inside the closed sketch.
5. Press the ESC key.

Creating Alternate Position View

In SOLIDWORKS, you can show/create alternate position of an assembly component in an assembly view by using the **Alternate Position View** tool, see Figure 13.40. In other words, by using the **Alternate Position View** tool, in addition to the current positing of an assembly, you can also create its multiple positions.

Procedure to Create Alternative View

1. Click on the **Alternative Position View** tool, the **Alternate Position PropertyManager** appears.
2. Select an assembly view in which you want to create an alternative position of an component, the **Alternate Position PropertyManager** modified.

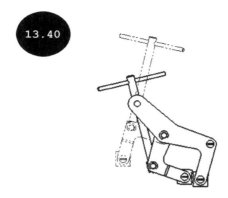

Note: In the **Configuration** rollout of the PropertyManager, the **New configuration** radio button is selected. As a result, you can create new alternative position for the assembly. Also, the default name for the alternate position appears in the **New Configuration Name** field. You can accept the default name or enter new name in this field, as required. The **Existing configuration** radio button allows you to select existing configuration created as an alternative view in the assembly.

3. Make sure that the **New configuration** radio button is selected in the **Configuration** rollout.
4. Accept the default settings and click on the green tick mark of the PropertyManager, the assembly environment is invoked with the display of the **Move Component PropertyManager** on its left.

Note: In the **Move Component PropertyManager**, the **Free Drag** option is selected. As a result, you can freely drag components of the assembly to the desired position.

5. Drag to rotate or move the assembly component whose alternate position has to be created to the desired position.
6. Once the desired position is achieved, click on the green tick mark of the **Move Component PropertyManager**, the Drawing environment invoked again and the alternative position of the assembly component is created, see Figure 13.40. Note that the alternative position of the component displays in doted lines.

Applying Dimensions

After creating various drawing views of a part or assembly, you need to apply dimensions to them. In SOLIDWORKS, two type of dimensions can be applied: reference dimensions and driving dimensions. The reference dimensions are the dimensions that are applied manually by using the dimension tools such as **Smart Dimension, Horizontal Dimension**, and **Vertical Dimension**. The driving dimensions are the dimensions that are generated automatically by retrieving dimensions that are applied while creating the model. You can apply driving dimensions by using the **Model Items** tool available in the **Annotation CommandManager**. The method of applying both these type of dimensioning are discussed next.

Applying Reference Dimensions

You can apply reference dimensions by using dimension tools such as **Smart Dimension,** **Horizontal Dimension,** and **Vertical Dimension** available in the **Annotation CommandManager,** see Figure 13.41.

Applying reference dimension is the manual method of applying dimensions to the drawing views and is same as discussed in Sketching environment while dimensioning sketch entities. For example, to apply dimension to an linear edge in a view, click on the **Smart Dimension** tool and then select the edge, the dimension value of the selected edge is attached with the cursor. Next, place the dimension to the required location.

Controlling Dimension and Arrow style

In SOLIDWORKS, you can also control the dimension and arrow styles such as dimension font, dimension height, and arrow height by using the options available in the **Document Properties - Dimensions** dialog box. To invoke this dialog box, click on the **Options** tool of the **Standard** toolbar, the **System Options - General** dialog box appears. Next, click on the **Document Properties** tab and then click on the **Dimensions** option, the **Document Properties - Dimensions** dialog box invoked, see Figure 13.42.

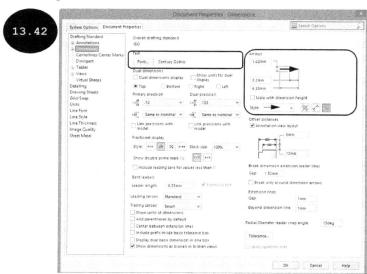

In this dialog box, click on the **Font** button available in the **Text** area, the **Choose Font** dialog box appears. By using this dialog box, you can specify the required font, style, and height for the dimensions. Once you are done, click on the **OK** button of the dialog box.

You can also control the dimension arrow height by using the options available in the **Arrows** area of the **Document Properties - Dimensions** dialog box, see Figure 13.42.

Applying Driving Dimensions

Driving dimensions are the dimensions that are applied automatically in the drawing view by retrieving the dimensions applied in sketches and features of the model while creating them. Also, on modifying the driving dimension applied in drawing view, the respective sketch or features dimension will also be modified in the model and vice-versa.

In SOLIDWORKS, you can apply driving dimensions by using the **Model Items** tool. To apply driving dimensions, click on the **Model Items** tool available in the **Annotation CommandManager**, the **Model Items PropertyManager** appears, see Figure 13.43. By using the options available in this PropertyManager, you can retrieve dimensions, symbols, annotations, and other elements that are used to create the model and apply them onto the drawing views. Some of the options of this PropertyManager are discussed next.

Source/Destination

The options available in the **Source/Destination** rollout are used to select the source for retrieving dimensions, symbols, annotations. By default, the **Selected feature** option is selected in the **Source** drop-down list of this rollout. As a result, you can select a feature of the model in the drawing view. As soon as, you select the feature in the drawing view, the dimensions applied while creating the selected feature are retrieved and applied in the drawing view. In the Figure 13.44, the hole feature has been selected as the source feature in the drawing view and the respective dimensions are applied in it.

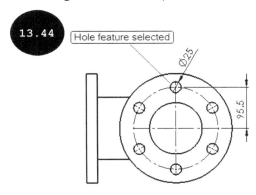

On selecting the **Entire model** option in the **Source** drop-down list of this rollout, all the dimensions, symbols, and annotations applied in the entire model and applied in the drawing views, respectively.

By default the **Import items into all views** check box is selected. As as result, the items such as dimensions and annotations applies to all the views present in the drawing sheet, respectively.

Dimensions

The buttons available in the **Dimensions** rollout are used to select the type of dimensions to be retrieve from the model and applies in the drawing view. On selecting the **Eliminate duplicates** check box of this rollout, applying duplicates dimensions in the drawing view will be eliminated.

Annotations

The buttons available in the **Annotations** rollout are used to select the type of annotations to be retrieved from the model and applies in the drawing view. You can select all the buttons by selecting the **Select all** check box for retrieving and applying all the annotations applied in the model in the drawing views.

Reference Geometry

The buttons available in the **Reference Geometry** rollout are used to select the type of reference geometry such as planes, axis, and origin to be retrieved from the model and applies in the drawing view.

After selecting the required options in the **Model Items PropertyManager**, click on the green tick mark of the PropertyManager, the respective dimensions, annotations, and reference geometry retrieves and applied in the drawing views, see Figure 13.45.

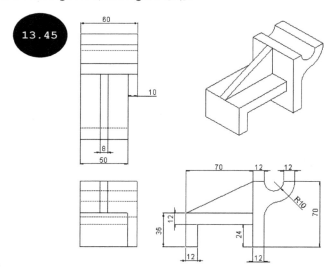

Note: The driving dimensions applied in the drawing view by using the **Model Item** tool are some time not appear in the required position and maintain uniform spacing in views. You can drag the dimensions and placing them in the required position by maintaining proper spacing between dimensions.

Modifying Driving Dimension

On modifying driving dimensions in the Drawing environment, the same modification reflects in the model as well. To modify driving dimension, double click on the dimension to be modified in the drawing view, the **Modify** dialog box appears, see Figure 13.46. Enter the new dominions value in the field of this dialog box and then click on its green tick mark, the respective dimension as well as the respective feature modified accordingly.

Adding Notes

In SOLIDWORKS, you can add notes in the drawing sheet by using the **Note** tool. Adding notes in drawings are generally used to convey/provide additional information which are not present in the drawing.

To add notes, click on the **Note** tool available in the **Annotation CommandManager**, the **Note PropertyManager** appears, see Figure 13.47. Also a rectangular box is attached with the cursor. Now, specify the required settings such as text style, text format, type of leader, leader style, so on for the note by using the options available in the PropertyManager, respectively. Once the required settings for the note has been specified, move the cursor over the required entity of the drawing view, the preview of the note with leader attached with the entity of the drawing view appears in the drawing sheet. Next, click to specify the entity for adding note on it, the leader pointer is attached with the selected entity. Now, move the cursor to the required location and click to place the note, a edit box and the **Formatting** toolbar appears. Write text as a note in the edit box. You can used the **Formatting** toolbar to control the formatting of the text such as font, style, height, and alignment. Once you are done, click anywhere in the drawing sheet, the note is added to the selected entity of the drawing view, see Figure 13.48. You can also add note anywhere in the drawing sheet without selecting any entity.

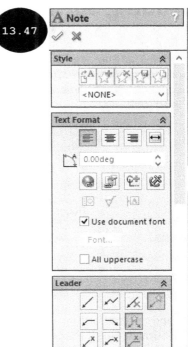

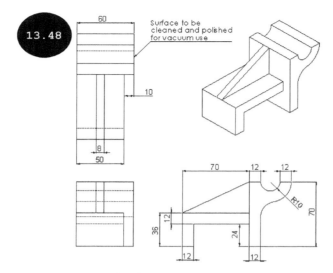

Adding Surface Finish Symbol

In SOLIDWORKS, you add surface finish symbol in order to specify the surface texture/finish for a face of the model. Note that a surface finish symbol has three components: surface roughness, waviness, and lay, see Figure 13.49. The specifications of surface finish given in a surface finish symbol are used to machined the respective surface of the object to the specified specifications. You can add surface finish symbol to an edge of the respective face in the drawing view by using the **Surface Finish** tool.

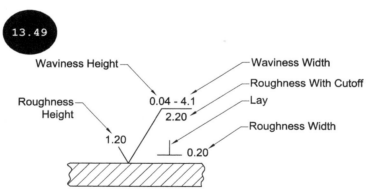

To add surface finish symbol, click on the **Surface Finish** tool of the **Annotation CommandManager**, the **Surface Finish PropertyManager** appears, see Figure 13.50. Also, the default selected surface finish symbol √ is attached with the cursor. Select the required type of surface finish symbol to be added from the **Symbol** rollout of the PropertyManager. Next, in the **Symbol Layout** rollout, specify the required surface finish specification (roughness, waviness, and lay) in their respective fields, see Figure 13.49.

If needed, you can rotate the symbol of surface finish to an angle by using the options available in the **Angle** rollout of the PropertyManager. Also, by using the options of the **Leader** rollout, you can select the type of leader to be attached with the surface finish symbol.

Once you are done with specifying the surface finish specification, move the cursor over the required edge in a view for applying surface finish symbol and then click on the edge when it highlights, the surface finish symbol is applied and attached with the specified edge, see Figure 13.51.

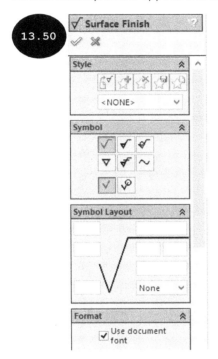

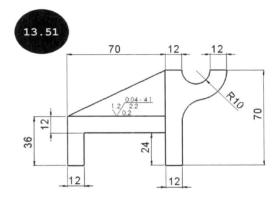

Adding Weld Symbol

A weld symbol is added in a drawing view in order to represent the welding specification used while welding two parts of the model. To add weld symbol, click on the **Weld Symbol** tool, the **Properties** dialog box appears, see Figure 13.52. Also, the **Weld Symbol PropertyManager** appears in the left of the drawing sheet. By using the **Properties** dialog box, you can specify the welding properties to be include in the weld symbol, see Figure 13.53. Note that welding properties depends upon the type of drafting standard is selected in the **Document Properties - Drafting Standard** dialog box.

Tip: To invoke the **Document Properties - Drafting Standard** dialog box, click on the **Options** button of the **Standard** toolbar, the **System Options - General** dialog box appears. Next, click on the **Document Properties** tab of the dialog box, the **Document Properties - Drafting Standard** dialog box appears. In this dialog box, you can select the required type of drafting standard to be followed in the drawings by using the **Overall drafting standard** drop-down list.

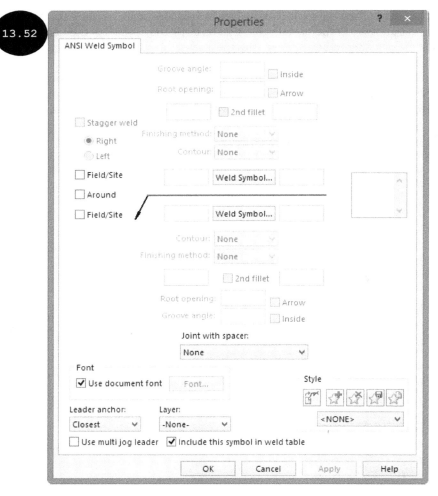

13.52

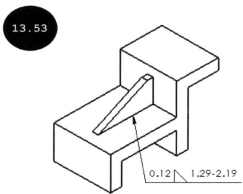

13.53

Adding Hole Callout

In SOLIDWORKS, you can add hole callout to an hole in a drawing view which contains hole specification such as diameter and type of hole, see Figure 13.54. The diameter of hole applied using hole callout is driven diameter dimension. As a result, on modifying the hole parameters of the model in the Part modeling environment, the callout updates accordingly, in the Drawing environment.

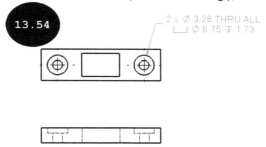

13.54

To add hole callout to an hole in a view, click on the **Hole Callout** tool, the symbol of hole callout attached and appears below the cursor. Move the cursor over the hole for adding hole callout and then click to select the hole when it highlight, the preview of the hole callout is attached with the cursor. Next, move the cursor to the required location and then click to specify the placement point for the hole callout to place it, see Figure 13.54.

Tip: You can add hole callouts to the holes and circular cut features created by using the **Hole Wizard** tool and the **Extruded Cut** tool.

Adding Center Mark

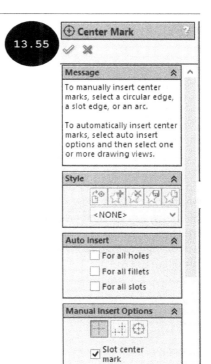

13.55

Center marks are used as references for dimensioning circular edges, slot edges, or circular sketch entities in drawing views. You can add center marks on circular edges, slot edges, or circular sketch entities by using the **Center Mark** tool. To add center marks, click on the **Center Mark** tool, the **Center Mark PropertyManager** appears, see Figure 13.55. By using this PropertyManager, you can add center marks automatically and manually in a drawing view.

To add center marks automatically to all holes, fillets, slots, or all of these, present in a drawing view, select the respective check box or check boxes such as **For all holes** and **For all fillets** from the **Auto Insert** rollout of the PropertyManager. Next, select the drawing view, the center marks are added automatically in the drawing view, depending upon the check box or boxes. In automatic method, you can further control the connection of center marks by using the check boxes available in the **Options** area of the **Auto Insert** rollout, see Figures 13.56 through 13.59. Note that the **Options** area appears as soon as you select a check box of the **Auto Insert** rollout, see Figure 13.60.

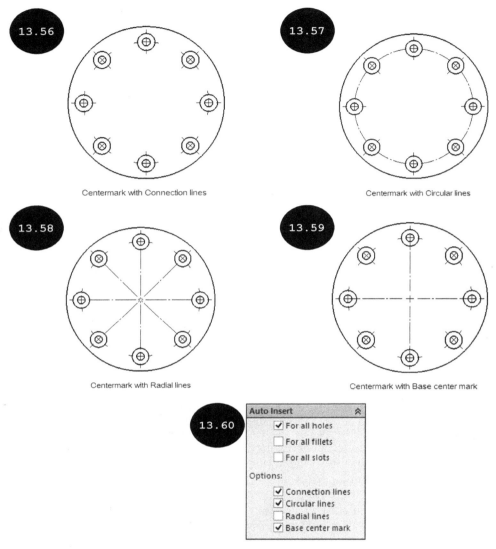

13.56

Centermark with Connection lines

13.57

Centermark with Circular lines

13.58

Centermark with Radial lines

13.59

Centermark with Base center mark

13.60

Auto Insert
- ☑ For all holes
- ☐ For all fillets
- ☐ For all slots

Options:
- ☑ Connection lines
- ☑ Circular lines
- ☐ Radial lines
- ☑ Base center mark

To add center marks manually, move the cursor over an circular edge, slot edge, or circular sketch entity in a drawing view and then click to select the entity when it highlights, the center mark added. Similarly, you can add center marks to other required entities of drawing views, manually. In manual method, you can also select the type of center marks to be added on selecting the entities by activating their respective button from the **Manual Insert Options** rollout of the PropertyManager, see Figure 13.61.

13.61

Manual Insert Options

- ☑ Slot center mark

Slot center marks:

Once you are done with adding center marks either by manually or automatically, click on the green tick mark of the PropertyManager.

Adding Centerlines

Similar to center mark, centerlines are used as references for dimensioning circular cut feature and hole features in the drawing views, see Figure 13.62. In SOLIDWORKS, you can add centerline between two linear edges that represents the edges of circular cut or hole feature in a drawing view by using the **Centerline** tool.

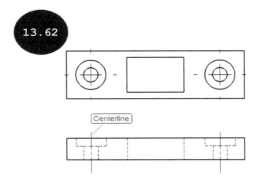

To add center lines, click on the **Centerline** tool, the **Centerline PropertyManager** appears. Select two linear edges one by one by clicking the left mouse button for adding centerline between them, the centerline is added at the center of two selected edges, see Figure 13.62. You can also select two sketch segments, or a single cylindrical, conical, toroidal, or swept feature for applying centerline.

Creating Bill of Material (BOM)

After crating all the required drawing views of an assembly, applied required dimensions, and other related information in the Drawing environment, you need to create Bill of Material. A bill of material (BOM) contain all the required information such as number of parts used in the assembly, part number, quantity of each part and so on that needed in order to build the assembly. Because of the information contain by an Bill of material, it serves as a primary source of communication between the manufacture to the vendors and suppliers.

To create Bill of Material (BOM), click on the down arrow available below the **Tables** tool in the **Annotation CommandManager**, a flyout appears, see Figure 13.63. Next, click on the **Bill of Material** tool, the **Bill of Materials PropertyManager** appears. Next, click to select the assembly view whose Bill of Materials has to be created, the **Bill of Materials PropertyManager** modified, see Figure 13.64. The options of this PropertyManager are used to set the parameters for the Bill of Material. Some of the options of this PropertyManager are discussed next.

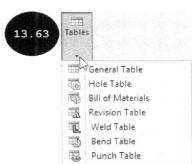

Tip: If an assembly view is selected before invoking the **Bill of Material** tool, the modified **Bill of Material PropertyManager** appears directly, see Figure 13.64.

Table Template

The **Table Template** rollout is used to specify template for BOM being created. By default, bom-standard template is selected is this rollout. You can also select template other than the default by clicking on the **Open table template for Bill of Materials** button of this rollout. As soon as you click on this button, the **Open** dialog box appears and redirected to the folder where the template files are saved. You can select the required template for the BOM and then click on the **Open** button.

Table Position

The **Table Position** rollout is used to specify the position for the BOM table being creating in the drawing sheet. By default, the **Attach to anchor point** check box is cleared is this rollout. As a result, on clicking the green tick mark of the PropertyManager, the BOM attach with the cursor and you can define its position in the drawing sheet by specifying the placement point in the required location of the drawing sheet. However, on selecting the **Attach to anchor point** check box, the BOM will be placed directly in the drawing sheet such that the top left corner of the BOM attach with the anchor point present in the drawing sheet.

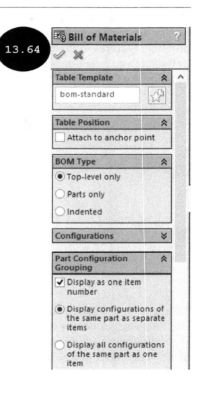

13.64

Note: You can define the position of the anchor point in the drawing sheet. Note that while defining the anchor point position, the PropertyManager should not be invoked. To define the anchor point position, select the **Sheet** node in the FeatureManager Design Tree and right click to display a shortcut menu. Next, click on the **Edit Sheet Format** option, the editing mode is invoked, see Figure 13.65. Now, you can click to select existing sketch vertex/point available in the drawing sheet, see Figure 13.65, and then right click to display a shortcut menu. Next, select the **Set as Anchor > Bill of Materials** from the shortcut menu, see Figure 13.66, the selected vertex/point defined as the anchor point for the BOM. In addition to the existing sketch vertex/point, you can create new sketch point using the **Point** tool available in the **Sketch CommandManager** and then define that point as the anchor point. Once you have defined the anchor point, exit from the exiting mode by clicking on the confirmation corner available at the upper right corner of the drawing sheet.

Item Number

The **Start at** field of the **Item Number** rollout of the PropertyManager is used to specify starting number for components count, see Figure 13.67. By default, the 1 is entered in this field. As a result, the counting of components start from number 1. In the **Increment** field, you can specify the incremental value after ever component count. Note that on selecting the **Do not change item numbers** button of this rollout, the components counts/numbers assigned will be locked and will not be updated.

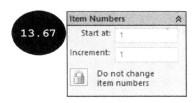

Border

The options of the Border rollout of the PropertyManager are used to define the thickness of the BOM border, see Figure 13.68.

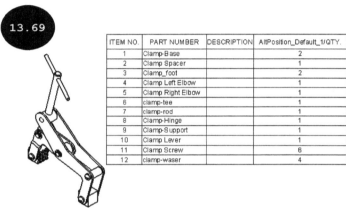

13.68

Item Numbers	⊗
Start at:	1
Increment:	1
🔒 Do not change item numbers	

Accept the default parameters specified in the PropertyManager and then click on the green tick mark of the PropertyManager, the BOM is attached with the cursor. Next, click on the drawing sheet to specify the position for the BOM, the BOM is placed at the specified position in the drawing sheet, see Figure 13.69.

13.69

ITEM NO.	PART NUMBER	DESCRIPTION	AltPosition_Default_1/QTY.
1	Clamp-Base		2
2	Clamp Spacer		1
3	Clamp_foot		2
4	Clamp Left Elbow		1
5	Clamp Right Elbow		1
6	clamp-tee		1
7	clamp-rod		1
8	Clamp-Hinge		1
9	Clamp-Support		1
10	Clamp Lever		1
11	Clamp Screw		6
12	clamp-waser		4

Procedure to Create Bill of Material (BOM)

1. Invoke the flyout by click on the down arrow available below the **Tables** tool of the **Annotation CommandManager**.
2. Click on the **Bill of Material** tool, the **Bill of Materials PropertyManager** appears.
3. Click to select the assembly drawing view from the drawing sheet.
4. Click on the green tick mark of the PropertyManager, the BOM is attached with cursor.
5. Click to specify the placement point for the BOM in the drawing sheet.

Adding Balloons

A Balloon is connected to a component with a leader line and displays their respective part numbers assigned in the Bill of Material (BOM), see Figure 13.70. In drawings, balloons are generally added to individual components of an assembly in order to identify them easily with respect to the part number assigned in the Bill of Materials (BOM).

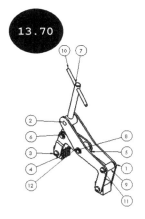

ITEM NO.	PART NUMBER	DESCRIPTION	AltPosition_Default_1/QTY.
1	Clamp-Base		2
2	Clamp Spacer		1
3	Clamp_foot		2
4	Clamp Left Elbow		1
5	Clamp Right Elbow		1
6	clamp-tee		1
7	clamp-rod		1
8	Clamp-Hinge		1
9	Clamp-Support		1
10	Clamp Lever		1
11	Clamp Screw		6
12	clamp-waser		4

In SOLIDWORKS, you can add balloons to components of an assembly by using two methods: Automatic and Manual. In Automatic method, balloons will be added automatically to all the components of the assembly with respect to the part number assigned in the BOM. However, in Manual method, you need to add balloons manually to the components of an assembly one by one.

Both these method of adding balloons are discussed next.

Adding Balloon Automatically

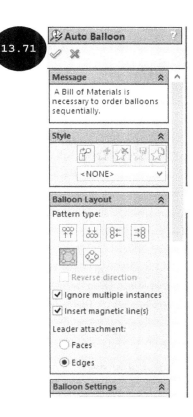

To add balloon automatically to components of an assembly, click on the **Auto Balloon** tool of the **Annotation CommandManager**, the **Auto Balloon PropertyManager** appears, see Figure 13.71. The options of this PropertyManager are used to set the parameters for the balloons. Some of these options are discussed next.

Balloon Layout

The options available in this rollout are discussed next.

Pattern type

The buttons available in the **Pattern type** area of the **Balloon Layout** rollout are used to select the required type of layout (Square, Circular, Top, Bottom, Left, and Right) to be followed for the balloons.

Ignore multiple instances

By default, the **Ignore multiple instances** check box is selected. As a result, the duplicacy of balloons addition is avoided by not adding balloons to all instances of a components.

Insert magnetic line(S)

By default, the **Insert magnetic line(S)** check box is selected. As a result, magnetic lines is inserted along with the balloons which aligns the balloons together. Note that this check box is not enabled in case the **Layout Balloons to Circular** button is selected in the **Pattern type** area.

Leader attachment

By default, the **Edges** radio button is selected in the **Leader attachment** area. As a result, leader lines of balloons is connected to the edges of the components. However, on selecting the **Faces** radio button, the balloons is connected to faces of the components through leader lines.

Balloon Settings

The options of this rollout are discuss next.

Style

The **Style** drop-down list of the **Balloon Settings** rollout is used to select the required type of style for balloons border. By default, the **Circular** option is selected in this drop-down list. As a result, balloons border appears as circle, see Figure 13.70. You can select any style such as triangle, hexagon, and diamond from this drop-down list, as required. Note that on selecting **None** option, the balloons appears without border, see Figure 13.72. Also, if you select the **Circular Split Line** option, the balloons border appears as circle split into two areas, see Figure 13.73. By default, its upper area displays part number information and the lower area displays the information about the quantity of the component.

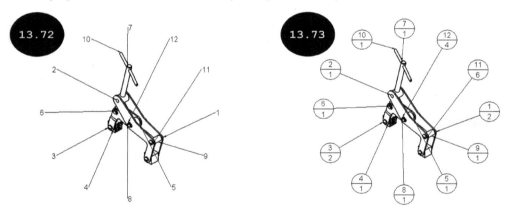

Size

The **Size** drop-down of the **Balloon Settings** rollout is used to select the required pre-defined size for balloons. Note that in addition to the predefined size, you can select the **User Defined** option from this drop-down list and specify the required size for balloons in the **User defined** field of the rollout.

Balloon text

The **Balloon text** drop-down list is used to select the required text to be displayed with balloons. By default, the **Item Number** option is selected. As a result, balloons appears with part numbers.

Lower text

The **Lower text** drop-down list is used to select the required text to be displayed at the lower area of the balloons. Note that this drop-down list will be available only if the **Circular Split Line** option is selected in the **Style** drop-down list. By default, the **Quantity** option is selected in this drop-down list. As a result, the lower area of balloons displays the quantity information, see Figure 13.73.

After specifying the required parameters for balloons, click on the green tick mark of the PropertyManager, balloons attachés with the components.

Procedure to Add Balloons Automatically

1. Click on the **Auto Balloon** tool of the **Annotation CommandManager**.
2. Click to select the assembly drawing view, if not selected automatically.
3. Click to select the required button available in the **Pattern type** area of the **Balloon Layout** rollout to defined the pattern layout (Square, Circular, Top, Bottom, Left, and Right).
4. Accept the other default settings in the PropertyManager.
5. Click on the green tick mark of the PropertyManager, the balloons applied automatically.

Adding Balloon Manually

To add balloon manually to components of an assembly, click on the **Balloon** tool of the **Annotation CommandManager**, the **Balloon PropertyManager** appears, see Figure 13.74. The options available in this PropertyManager are same as discussed earlier. By using this PropertyManager, you can add balloons to the components of an assembly one by one by selecting them from the drawing view. As soon as you select a component, a balloon is attached with cursor. Next, move the cursor to the required location and click to specify the location for the balloon. Similarly, you can apply balloons to all the remaining components of the assembly drawing view one by one. Once you are done, click on the green tick mark of the PropertyManager.

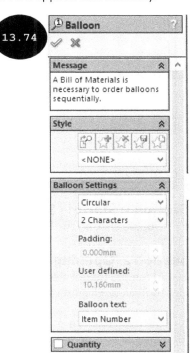

Procedure to Add Balloons Manually

1. Click on the **Balloon** tool of the **Annotation CommandManager**.
2. Click to select the component of the assembly.
3. Move the cursor to the required location and click to specify the placement point for the balloon.
4. Similarly, apply balloons to the remaining components of the assembly one by one.
5. Click on the green tick mark of the PropertyManager.

Tutorial 1

Open the model created in Tutorial 2 of Chapter 7 and then create different drawing views as shown in Figure 13.75. You also need to apply the driving dimensions to the Front, Top, and Right Side views of the model.

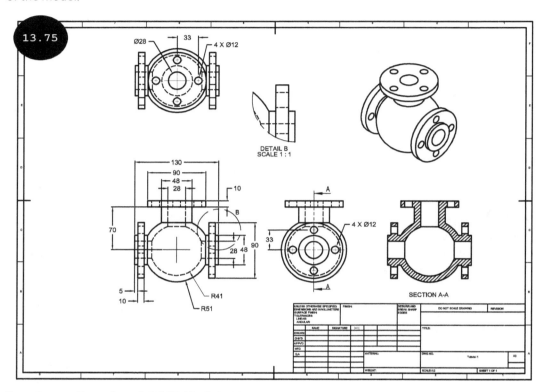

Section 1: Starting SOLIDWORKS

1.   Double click on the **SOLIDWORKS** icon on your desktop to start SOLIDWORKS.

Section 2: Opening and Saving Model Created in Tutorial 2 of Chapter 7

1.   Open the model created in Tutorial 2 of Chapter 7 by using the **Open** button of the **Standard** toolbar, see Figure 13.76.

2.   Click on the **File > Save As** from the SOLIDWORKS menus and then save the model as Tutorial 1 inside the *Tutorial* folder of *Chapter 13*. Note that you need to create *Chapter 13* and then *Tutorial* folder inside the *SOLIDWORKS* folder.

Section 3: Invoking Drawing Environment

1.   Click on the arrow available next of the **New** tool in the **Standard** toolbar, a flyout appears, see Figure 13.77.

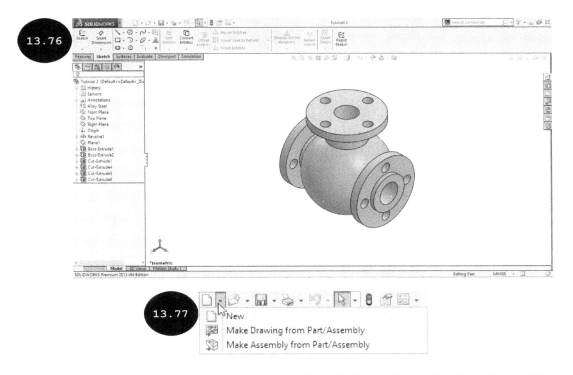

13.76

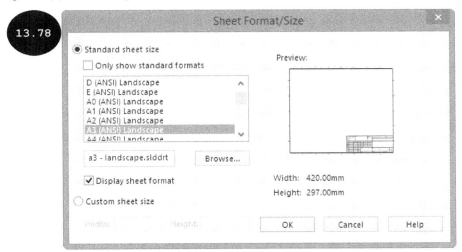

13.77

2. Click on the **Make Drawing from Part/Assembly** tool of this flyout, the **Sheet Format/Size** dialog box appears, see Figure 13.78.

13.78

3. Make sure that the **Standard sheet size** radio button is selected, see Figure 13.78.

4. Make sure that the **Only show standard formats** check box is cleared, see Figure 13.78.

5. Select the **A3 (ANSI) Landscape** sheet size from the **Selection** area of the dialog box, see Figure 13.78.

6. Make sure that the **Display sheet format** check box is selected, see Figure 13.78.

7. Click on the **OK** button of the dialog box, the Drawing environment is invoked with the display of **View Palette Task Pane** at its right, see Figure 13.79.

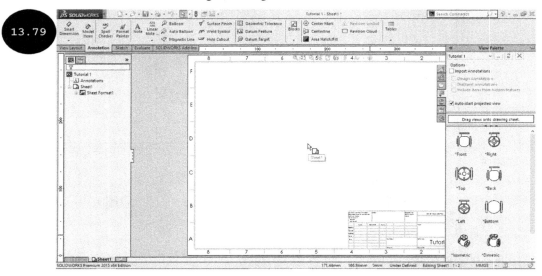

13.79

Section 4: Creating Front, Top, and Right Drawing Views

1. Press and hold the left mouse button over the **Front** view of the model appears in the **View Palette Task Pane**.

2. Drag and drop the front view of the model in the lower left corner of the sheet, see Figure 13.80.

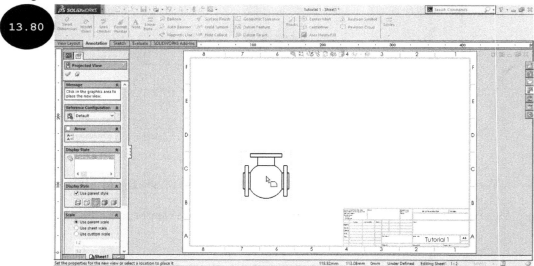

13.80

3. Move the cursor vertically upwards, the projected view (Top view) attached with the cursor.

4. Click to specify the location for the Top view of the model, see Figure 13.81.

5. Move the cursor horizontal towards the right, the projected view (Right Side view) of the model attached with the cursor.

6. Click to specify the location for the Right Side view of the model, see Figure 13.81. Next, click on the green tick mark of the PropertyManager to exit from the creation of drawing views.

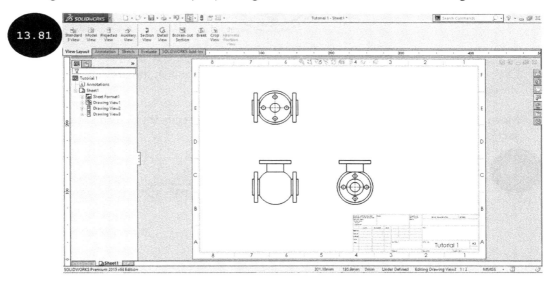

Section 5: Creating Vertical Section View

1. Click on the **Section View** tool of the **View Layout CommandManager**, the **Section View Assist PropertyManager** appears, see Figure 13.82.

2. Make sure that the **Vertical** button is selected in the **Cutting Line** rollout, see Figure 13.82. Note that on selecting the **Vertical** button, the vertical section line appears attached with the cursor in the drawing area.

3. Move the cursor over the Right Side view of the model in the drawing sheet.

4. Click to specify the placement point for the vertical section line when the cursor snap to center point of the Right Side view of the model, see Figure 13.83. As soon as you define the placement point for the section line, the **Section View** Pop-up toolbar appears.

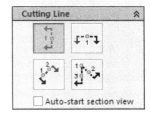

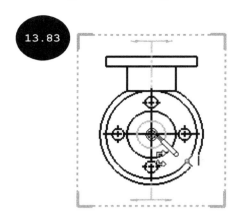

13.83

5. Click on the green tick mark of the **Section View** Pop-up toolbar, the preview of the section view appears attached with the cursor.

6. Move the cursor horizontal towards the right and click to specify the placement point for the section view in the drawing sheet, see Figure 13.84.

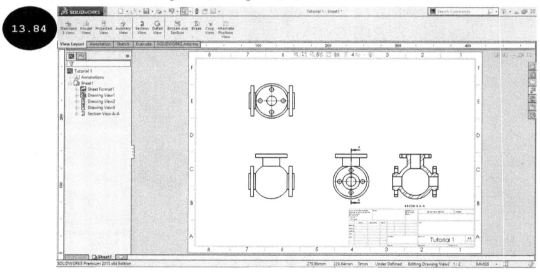

13.84

Section 6: Creating Detail View

1. Click on the **Detail View** tool of the **View Layout CommandManager**, the **Detail View PropertyManager** appears.

2. Move the cursor over the Front view of the drawing sheet, see Figure 13.85 and click to specify the center point of the circle which defines detail view area.

3. Move the cursor to a distance and then click to define the radius of the circle, see Figure 13.86. As soon as you define the radius of the circle, the preview of the detail view attached with the cursor.

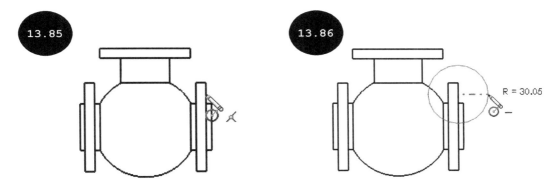

4. Click to define the placement point for the detail view in the drawing sheet, see Figure 13.87.

Section 7: Creating Isometric View

1. Click on the **Model View** tool of the **View Layout CommandManager**, the **Model View PropertyManager** appears.

2. Double-click on the **Tutorial 1** available in the **Open documents** area of the **Part/Assembly to Insert** rollout of the PropertyManager, a rectangular box representing the model view is attached with the cursor. Also, the options of the PropertyManager modified.

3. Click on the **Isometric** button of the **Standard views** area of the **Orientation** rollout of the PropertyManager to create isometric view of the model.

4. Move the cursor towards the upper right corner of the drawing sheet and then click to specify the placement point for the isometric view, see Figure 13.87. Next, click anywhere in the drawing sheet.

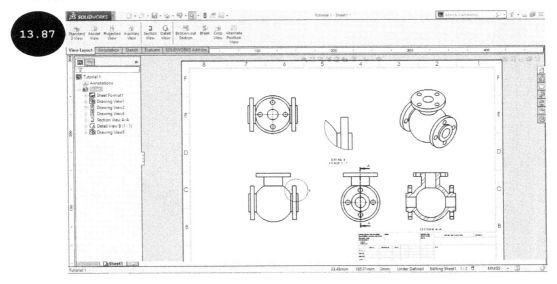

Section 8: Changing Display Styles

1. Click to select the Front view of the model from the drawing sheet, the **Drawing View PropertyManager** appears.

2. Click on the **Hidden Lines Visible** ⬚ button of the **Display State** rollout of the PropertyManager to display the hidden lines in the drawing views, see Figure 13.88.

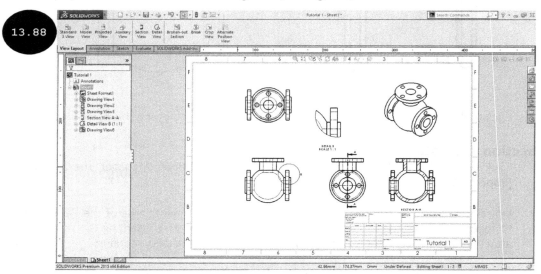

13.88

Section 9: Applying Driving Dimensions

1. Invoke the **Annotation CommandManager**.

2. Click on the **Model Items** tool of the **Annotation CommandManager**, the **Model Items PropertyManager** appears.

3. Make sure that the **Entire model** option is selected in the **Source** drop-down list of the **Source/Destination** rollout of the PropertyManager, see Figure 13.89.

13.89

4. Clear the **Import items into all views** check box of the **Source/Destination** rollout, the **Destination view(s)** field appears in the rollout.

5. Click to select the Front, Top, and Right Side views from the drawing sheet as the drawing views to import driving dimensions.

6. Click on the green tick mark of the PropertyManager, the driving dimensions are applied to the selected drawing views, see Figure 13.90. Note that the dimensions applied are not placed on the proper locations and are not maintaining uniform spacing.

Section 10: Arranging Driving Dimensions

1. Create a selection window by dragging the cursor over the Front, Top, and Right Side views, see Figure 13.90. As soon as these drawing views have been covered by the selection window, release the left mouse button, the **Dimension Palette Rollover** button appears in the drawing sheet.

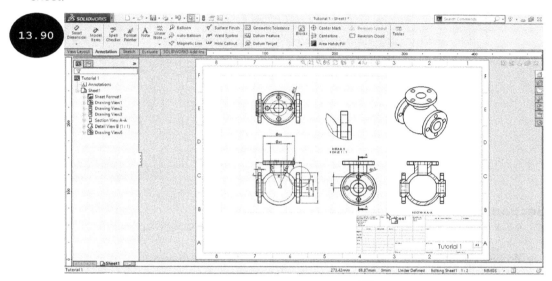

2. Move the cursor over the **Dimension Palette Rollover** button, the **Dimension Palette** appears, see Figure 13.91.

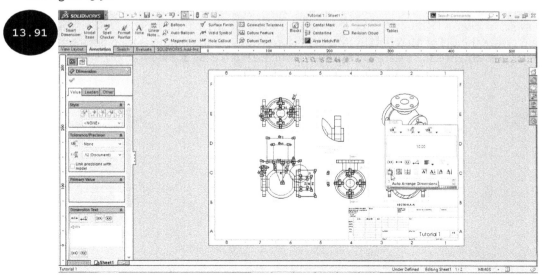

3.   Click on the **Auto Arrange Dimensions** button of the **Dimension Palette**, see Figure 13.91, all the dimensions are arranged automatically in the drawing sheet, see Figure 13.92. You can further drag individual dimensions and arrange them as required, see Figure 13.92.

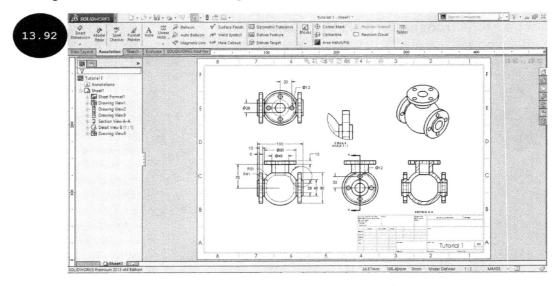

Section 11: Saving the Model

1.   Click on the **Save** tool of the **Standard** toolbar, the **Save As** window appears.

2.   Browse to the *Tutorial* folder of *Chapter 13* and then save the drawing as Tutorial 1.

Hands-on Test Drive 1

Open the assembly created in Hands-on Test Drive 1 of Chapter 11 and then create different drawing views as shown in Figure 13.93. You also need to add balloons in the isometric view of the assembly and create the Bill of Material (BOM), see Figure 13.93. In addition to creating different views and BOM, you also need to create alternative view in the Front view of the assembly, see Figure 13.93.

13.73

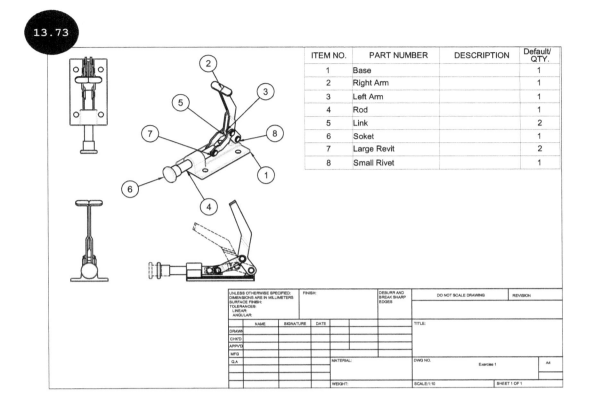

ITEM NO.	PART NUMBER	DESCRIPTION	Default/QTY.
1	Base		1
2	Right Arm		1
3	Left Arm		1
4	Rod		1
5	Link		2
6	Soket		1
7	Large Revit		2
8	Small Rivet		1

UNLESS OTHERWISE SPECIFIED: DIMENSIONS ARE IN MILLIMETERS SURFACE FINISH: TOLERANCES: LINEAR: ANGULAR:			FINISH:			DEBURR AND BREAK SHARP EDGES		DO NOT SCALE DRAWING		REVISION	
	NAME	SIGNATURE	DATE				TITLE:				
DRAWN											
CHK'D											
APPV'D											
MFG											
Q.A						MATERIAL:		DWG NO.	Exercise 1		A4
				WEIGHT:				SCALE:1:10		SHEET 1 OF 1	

Summary

In this chapter, you have learnt about creating 2D drawings from parts and assemblies. 2D drawings are act as very important source for manufacturing components. In SOLIDWORKS, you can create 2D drawings in the Drawing environment. You can create various drawing views such as model/base views, projected views, section views, auxiliary views, and detail views of an component or assembly by using their respective tools. You have also learnt about the concept of angle of projections, defining angle of projection for a drawing, and edit sheet format. After creating required drawing views of an component or assembly, you can apply reference and driving dimensions. Note that on modifying driving dimensions in the Drawing environment, the same modification reflects in the model as well.

In addition to this, you have learnt about adding notes in the drawing sheet in order to convey additional informations which are not present in the drawing. You can also add surface finish symbol for specifying the surface texture/finish for a face of the model, weld symbols for represent the welding specification, hole callout to an hole, center mark, and centerlines. At last in this chapter, you have learnt about adding bill of material (BOM) and balloons. In SOLIDWORKS, you can add balloons on different components of an assembly by using the automatic and manual methods.

Questions

*   By using the _____ environment of SOLIDWORKS, you can generate error free 2D drawings of an component or assembly.

*   The _____ PropertyManager invokes automatically on invoking the Drawing environment.

*   A _____ view is an independent first drawing view.

*   The **Standard 3 View** tool is used to create three standard orthogonal views: _____, _____, and _____.

*   Engineering drawings follows the _____ and the _____ angle of projections.

*   A _____ view is created by cutting an object using an imaginary cutting plane and viewing the object from the direction normal to the cutting plane.

*   A _____ view is created in order to show the portion of an existing view at an enlarged scale.

*   The _____ view is created by removing portion of an existing view to a specified depth in order to expose its inner details.

*   In SOLIDWORKS, you can show/create alternate position of an assembly component by using the _____ tool.

*   In SOLIDWORKS, you can apply _____ and _____ dimensions in drawing views.

*   A surface finish symbol has three components: _____, _____, and _____.

*   In SOLIDWORKS, you can add balloons by using the automatic and manual methods. (True/False).

*   On modifying reference dimensions in a drawing view, the respective modifications also reflect in the model. (True/False).

*   In SOLIDWORKS, you can select standard or custom sheet size for creating drawing views. (True/False).

INDEX

INDEX

4 INDEX

www.ingramcontent.com/pod-product-compliance
Lightning Source LLC
Chambersburg PA
CBHW080128060326
40689CB00018B/3713